Experiencing the World's Religions

SIXTH EDITION

Experiencing the World's Religions

TRADITION, CHALLENGE, AND CHANGE

Michael Molloy

Mc
Graw
Hill

Connect
Learn
Succeed™

The McGraw·Hill Companies

Mc Graw Hill

Connect
Learn
Succeed™

EXPERIENCING THE WORLD'S RELIGIONS: TRADITION, CHALLENGE, AND CHANGE, SIXTH EDITION

7 8 9 10 LCR 21 20 19 18 17

ISBN   978-0-07-803827-3
MHID   0-07-803827-8

Senior Vice President, Products & Markets: *Kurt L. Strand*
Vice President, General Manager, Products
  & Markets: *Michael Ryan*
Vice President, Content Production & Technology
  Services: *Kimberly Meriwether David*
Managing Director: *William Glass*
Director: *Chris Freitag*
Brand Manager: *Laura Wilk*
Director of Development: *Dawn Groundwater*
Development Manager: *Barbara A. Heinssen*
Development Editor: *Betty Slack*
Editorial Coordinator: *Jessica Holmes*

Marketing Manager: *Kelly Odom*
Content Project Manager: *Jodi K. Banowetz*
Buyer: *Susan K. Culbertson*
Designer: *Colleen P. Havens*
Interior Designer: *Maureen McCutcheon Design*
Cover Image: *Design Pics/Natural Selection John Reddy/RF*
Content Licensing Specialist: *Ann Marie Jannette*
Photo Research: *Jerry Marshall*
Compositor: *Aptara®, inc.*
Typeface: *10/12 Adobe Caslon*
Printer: *LSC Communications*

All credits appearing on this page or at the end of the book are considered to be an extension of the copyright page.

Library of Congress Cataloging-in-Publication Data

Molloy, Michael, 1942-
  Experiencing the world's religions: tradition, challenge, and change / Michael Molloy.—6th ed.
    p. cm.
  Includes index.
  ISBN 978-0-07-803827-3—ISBN 0-07-803827-8 (alk. paper) 1. Religions–Textbooks. I. Title.
  BL80.3.M65 2013
  200—dc23

                                                2012028490

www.mhhe.com

To honor the founders of the
Manoa Chinese Cemetery and to thank
all those who care for it.

Contents

3 Hinduism   *72*

4 Buddhism *122*

5 Jainism and Sikhism   *180*

6 Daoism and Confucianism   *204*

8 Judaism   *280*

9 Christianity   *332*

10 Islam   *406*

11 Alternative Paths   *470*

12 The Modern Search   *506*

Preface

I've been asked why this book is named as it is—*Experiencing the World's Religions: Tradition, Challenge, and Change.* I've also been asked why each chapter describes experiences both possible and real. These are challenging questions. I think that the answers go back to my experiences of religion when I was young. Entering religious buildings involved some mystery—I never knew what would be inside. Sometimes the ceilings were immensely high. There might be paintings or statues or gold candlesticks. Even unadorned religious buildings could have interiors that were memorable for their very simplicity. The services were sometimes exotic—featuring antique robes, bells, and books with ribbons and gold edges; candles being lit; old languages being spoken. Often the experience felt like entering a time machine. These buildings were places, too, where babies were named, couples were married, and deceased family members were mourned. Sensing the emotions that had been felt in these spaces was very moving.

As I traveled to new countries and new encounters, my wonder grew. I could climb bell towers and I could stand in prayer on bright rugs. I could chant ancient words. I could talk with people inside an old religious building about their deepest experiences.

I learned quickly that religions begin to show their richness when you experience them firsthand. You have to approach each one with an open heart, talk to people, and try out things you have never seen or done before. Reading about doctrine and history is interesting, but it is not enough. Such topics become really meaningful through experience. The experiences described in this book will suggest possibilities for each reader.

Aims and Approach

This book is written for beginners. With each new edition, I have tried to remain true to those readers who are just starting their study of religions. Five aims have guided me:

1. *Offering the essentials.* What would a person seeking to be an informed world citizen want to know about the major religions? This book presents that essential content, but it also encourages further discovery by pointing to additional places, texts, and people of interest.

2. *Providing clarity.* Some years ago I heard this ironic axiom: When you see the spark of ambition, water it! I have learned that students come to a course in world religions eager to learn. But waves of details presented in overly academic language can easily drown their initial enthusiasm. I aim to present the essentials of each religion in the

clearest language possible. Maps, photos, definitions, and timelines are incorporated into the text to provide additional clarity.

3. *Showing the multidimensional nature of religions.* A religion is not just a system of beliefs. It is also a combination of ways in which beliefs are expressed—in ceremony, food, clothing, art, architecture, pilgrimage, scripture, and music. This book tries to make the multifaceted expressions of religion clear, with photographs that have been carefully chosen to help achieve this goal.

4. *Encouraging direct experience.* Religions are better understood through firsthand experience. I hope to encourage students to imagine and seek out direct experience of religions both at home and abroad.

5. *Blending scholarship and respect.* This book necessarily presents religions from a somewhat academic point of view. At the same time, it tries to show its empathy for the thoughts and emotions of people who live within each religious tradition.

The theme of the cover remains flowing water. It symbolizes the purification, new life, and hope that religions promise. It also symbolizes the constant change that is an essential part of religions, as it is of everything. The flowing water should remind us of the possibilities of religions to renew both their followers and themselves.

In the small space of this single volume, much should be said that cannot be; therefore simplification and generalization are unavoidable. Also, no one person can know the entire field of religion, which is as full of facts as a galaxy is full of stars. But these shortcomings should invite instructors and students to compensate for what is missing by adding their own insights and interpretation.

Boxed Features

Turn knowledge into meaning and understanding with *Experiencing the World's Religions* and *Connect® Religion*

Experiencing the World's Religions immerses students in the practices and beliefs of the world's major religions. The author's vivid narrative, coupled with integrated digital assessments in the new Connect Religion program, helps students understand the origins of the world's religions, explore common themes across religions, and think critically about religion as a framework for interpreting how the world's major religious traditions shape individuals and whole cultures.

The author introduces students to each new religion through his hallmark "First Encounter" essays. From there, students embark on an exploration through intimate photos, religious works of art, and scripture passages to develop a deeper appreciation for each faith. Instructors can assign the integrated assessments in Connect Religion to reinforce students' understanding and better prepare them for active class discussions, exams, and research assignments. The results are greater engagement and greater course success.

Critical Reading Skills

Interactive assessments reinforce students' comprehension of key learning objectives in each chapter and check their understanding of the cause-and-effect relationships between historic events that influenced the formation of each faith.

Primary Source Analysis

Scripture readings and works of art introduce students to religious doctrine, history, ceremonies, and everyday practices in each chapter. The accompanying assessment in Connect Religion guides students through the process of reading and interpreting these primary sources for symbolism and meaning and turning that knowledge into a deeper understanding of the world's religions.

Critical Thinking Skills

Critical analysis questions tied to each of the pedagogical boxes in each chapter challenge students to engage in interfaith dialogue by making connections across religions, and over time and continents, to understand the role religion plays in shaping our lives and our world.

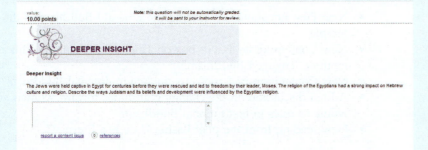

Changes in the Sixth Edition

Although the core of religions remains fairly constant, change is always happening. Followers of different religions split and form new branches, religious values change, new leaders arise. These transitions are reflected in the new edition. Special attention has also been given to adding significant information on the evolving leadership of women in each religion, as well as attitudes toward the natural environment. New reading selections have been added to each chapter.

NEW TO THE SIXTH EDITION

Chapter 1, Understanding Religion

- New discussion on the problem of defining religion
- New section on The Study of Religion
- New section on Recent Theories
- Revised and condensed discussion of Key Critical Issues
- New Conflict in Religion box, "Religious Blends"
- New reading from mythologist Joseph Campbell, "Finding What Brings Joy"

Chapter 2, Indigenous Religions

- New Deeper Insights box, "Australian Aboriginal Religion"
- New reading, the Hawaiian chant "The Kumulipo," provided in Hawaiian with an accompanying English translation

Chapter 3, Hinduism

- New table on major Hindu gods
- New Personal Experience section, "A Party"
- New Contemporary Issues box, "The Chipko Movement"
- Added discussion on the growing women's movement in India
- New reading, "Finding Union with the Divine," from the *Crest-Jewel of Discrimination*

Chapter 4, Buddhism

- New First Encounter on visiting the Emerald Buddha and the Wat Po temple
- New Contemporary Issues box on Thich Nhat Hanh and his movement of "engaged Buddhism"
- New Contemporary Issues box on "environmental Buddhism"
- Added discussion on the changing attitudes toward women and women's roles in institutional Buddhism
- New reading from the poet Basho, "Life Is a Journey"

Chapter 5, Jainism and Sikhism

- New reading from Satish Kumar, "A Prayer for Peace"

Chapter 6, Daoism and Confucianism

- New First Encounter on the visit to a Daoist temple
- New Deeper Insights box, "Daoism and Nature"
- Added discussion on female imagery and themes and the role of women in Daoism
- New reading, "Holding onto Harmony," from the Daoist classic, The Zhuangzi

Chapter 7, Shinto

- New First Encounter on visiting a Shinto shrine in the city of Naha in Okinawa
- New Deeper Insights box, "Shinto and Nature," on Shinto roots in the natural world
- New reading, "Shinto Prayer for Peace"

Chapter 8, Judaism

- Revised and condensed section on Jewish Holy Days
- Added material on differing views on women's roles in Judaism
- New reading, "Tending the Garden," from the biblical story of creation

Chapter 9, Christianity

- Added material on women among Jesus's friends and followers, women and women's roles in the early Church, and women in the Protestant missionary movement
- Revised and condensed section on The Christian Year, with a diagram depicting the Christian year
- Revised section on The Challenges of Science and Secularism, including a new paragraph on "Prosperity Christianity"
- Revised section on Contemporary Influences and Developments, including a discussion of views on female equality, biblical interpretation, fundamentalism, and the spread of Christianity in Africa and Asia
- New reading from Julian of Norwich, "Revelations of Divine Love"

Chapter 10, Islam

- New section, Islam and the Roles of Women
- New Contemporary Issues box, "Islamic Ecology"
- Added discussion on the conservatism of al-Qaida
- Added discussion on the Arab Spring, particularly events in Egypt and Libya
- New reading from the Turkish writer Fazil bin Tahir Enderuni, "Beauty Leads to God"

Chapter 11, Alternative Paths

- New Rituals and Celebrations box, "The Contemporary Pagan Year," with an accompanying diagram of the year
- Revised Deeper Insights box, "Major Orishas of Santería"
- New Contemporary Issues box, "Ecology and the New Religious Movements"
- New reading, "Baha'i Prayer"

Chapter 12, The Modern Search

- New First Encounter on a conference of religious leaders and a discussion of the role of women in religion
- New Personal Experience, "A Picnic," a discussion of the good and bad effects of religion
- New reading, "A Starry Night," from Audrey Sutherland's *Paddling My Own Canoe*

Teaching and Learning with *Experiencing the World's Religions*

Online Learning Center (www.mhhe.com/molloy6e)

- **Instructor's Manual,** including an outline for each chapter, learning objectives, lecture supplements, notes on the For Fuller Understanding feature, discussion starters, and video resources
- **Test Bank,** including over 750 multiple-choice and essay questions
- **PowerPoint slides** for each chapter, outlining key concepts and ideas

CourseSmart

This text is available as an eTextbook at www.CourseSmart.com. At CourseSmart, students can take advantage of significant savings off the cost of a print textbook, reduce their impact on the environment, and gain access to powerful Web tools for student learning. You can view CourseSmart eTextbooks online or download them to a computer. CourseSmart eTextbooks allow students to do full text searches, add highlighting and notes, and share notes with classmates. Visit www.CourseSmart.com to learn more and try a sample chapter.

McGraw-Hill Create (www.mcgrawhillcreate.com)

Design your own ideal course materials with McGraw-Hill Create™. Rearrange or omit chapters, combine material from other sources, upload your syllabus or any other content you have written to make the perfect resource for your students. Search thousands of leading McGraw-Hill textbooks to find the best content for your students; then arrange it to fit your teaching style. You can even personalize your book's appearance by selecting the cover and adding your name, school, and course information. When you order a Create book, you receive a complimentary review copy. Get a printed copy in three to five business days or an electronic copy via email in about an hour. Register today at www.mcgrawhillcreate.com.

Tegrity

Tegrity is a service that makes class time available around the clock. It automatically captures every lecture in a searchable format for students to review when they study and complete assignments. With a simple one-click start-and-stop process, you capture all computer screens and corresponding audio. Students can replay any part of any class with easy-to-use browser-based viewing on a PC or Mac. Students can also quickly recall key moments by using Tegrity Campus's unique search feature, which lets them efficiently find what they need, when they need it, across an entire semester of class recordings. To learn more about Tegrity, watch a two-minute Flash demo at **http://tegritycampus.mhhe.com**.

McGraw-Hill Campus

McGraw-Hill Campus is a new one-stop teaching and learning experience available to users of any learning-management system. This institutional service allows faculty and students to enjoy single sign-on (SSO) access to all McGraw-Hill Higher Education materials, including the award-winning McGraw-Hill Connect® platform, from directly within the institution's Web site. McGraw-Hill Campus provides faculty with instant access to all McGraw-Hill Higher Education teaching materials (for example, eTextbooks, test banks, PowerPoint slides, animations and learning objects), allowing them to browse, search, and use any instructor ancillaries content in our vast library at no additional cost. Students enjoy SSO access to a variety of free (for instance, quizzes, flash cards, narrated presentations) and subscription-base products (for example, McGraw-Hill Connect).

Acknowledgments

Many great teachers have shared their insights with me—I am simply passing on the torch. I will always be especially thankful to Arthur Daspit, Sobharani Basu, Abe Masao, Eliot Deutsch, Winfield Nagley, and David Kidd. It is a joy to recall the influence of their unique personalities. I remain grateful to the East-West Center in Honolulu for a grant that early on assisted my studies in Asia, and I encourage students and professors to apply for grants there and elsewhere. Several monasteries were kind in allowing me to share in their life: Songgwang-sa in South Korea, Engaku-zan in Japan, Saint John's Abbey in Minnesota, and Saint Andrew's Abbey in California. I am grateful to my editors Meredith Grant and Laura Wilk, to my developmental editor Betty Slack, to my copy editor Andrea McCarrick, and to those who assisted with the photos, design, index, and cover. Because so many people work on this project, and because we are spread from Honolulu to Boston, perfection is a difficult goal. Despite such challenges, it's wonderful to see how much turns out right. But the never-ending work of clearing typos and getting captions right is like trying to bathe your dog. I apologize if you find a flea.

Thanks also go to these teachers and scholars who offered their ideas for earlier editions: Richard Anderson, Oregon State University; Nikki Bado-Fralick, Iowa State University; Lee W. Bailey, Ithaca College; Lulrick Balzora, Broward College; Robert M. Baum, Iowa State University; Wendell Charles Beane, University of Wisconsin–Oshkosh; Ann Berliner, California State University–Fresno; Dan Breslauer, University of Kansas; Harold Bruen, Wake Technical Community College; Charlene Embrey Burns, Loyola University–New Orleans; Dexter Callender, University of Miami–Coral Gables; Lee Carter, Glendale Community College, Arizona; Ron Cooper, Central Florida Community College; Madhav M. Deshpande, University of Michigan; Michael Desmarais, University of Nebraska–Omaha; Jonathan Ebel, University of Illinois–Urbana-Champaign; D. Kerry Edwards, Red Rocks Community College; Tanya Erzen, Ohio State University–Columbus; Steven Fink, University of Wisconsin–Eau Claire; Brett Greider, University of Wisconsin–Eau Claire; Rita M. Gross, University of Wisconsin–Eau Claire; Mark Hanshaw, Richland College; George Alfred James, University of North Texas; Philip Jenkins, Pennsylvania State University; Ramdas Lamb, University of Hawaii–Manoa; Richard A. Layton, University of Illinois–Urbana-Champaign; Jared Ludlow, Brigham Young University–Hawaii; R. F. Lumpp, Regis University; Thomas F. MacMillan, Mendocino College; Mark MacWilliams, St. Lawrence University; Sarah McCombs, University of West Florida; Robert J. Miller, Midway College; G. David Panisnick, Honolulu Community College; Sarah Paulk, Okaloosa-Walton College; Lloyd Pflueger, Truman State University; Robert Platzner, California State University–Sacramento; Kenneth

Rose, Christopher Newport University; Lori Rowlett, University of Wisconsin–Eau Claire; Stephen Sapp, University of Miami; Gerald Michael Schnabel, Bemidji State University; Marla Selvidge, University of Central Missouri; John G. Spiro, Illinois Wesleyan University; Mark Stewart, San Joaquin Delta College; R. C. Trussell, Pikes Peak Community College; David D. Waara, Western Michigan University; Ralph Wedeking, Iowa Central Community College; Brannon M. Wheeler, University of Washington; and Daniel Wolne, University of New Mexico.

To the reviewers and pedagogical advisors of the sixth edition, I am also indebted:

REVIEWERS	SCHOOLS
Catherine Alvarez	University of South Florida
Vanda Bozicevic	Bergen Community College
Chris Brawley	Central Piedmont Community College
Charlene Burns	University of Wisconsin–Eau Claire
Dan Campbell	St. Petersburg College
Tim Cannon	Forsyth Technical Community College
Jeff Christ	Moraine Valley Community College
Brandon Cleworth	Glendale Community College
Jonathan Ebel	University of Illinois–Urbana-Champaign
Steven Fink	University of Wisconsin–Eau Claire
Stephen C. Finley	Louisiana State University
Steve Godby	Broward College
Amanda Hayden	Sinclair Community College
Karen L. Hornsby	North Carolina A&T State University
Fotini Katsanos	University of North Carolina–Charlotte
Carolyn M. Jones Medine	University of Georgia
Steven D. Meigs	University of South Florida
Micki Pulleyking	Missouri State University
Curtis Smith	Pennsylvania State University
Lori Stewart	San Diego State University
Debbie Thompson	Ozarks Technical Community College

The book is far better as a result of their reviews. Although it is a truism, this book has also been influenced by hundreds of other people who are also owed my sincere thanks. They planted in me seeds that I hope have come to flower.

ARC

EUROPE

ATLANTIC

OCEAN

PACIFIC

OCEAN

NORTH
AMERICA

SOUTH
AMERICA

CHRISTIANITY
ISLAM
(MUSLIM MINORITY
HINDUISM
✡ JUDAISM
CHRISTIANITY and NATIVE RELIGIONS
BUDDHISM
CHINESE RELIGIONS
SHINTO and BUDDHISM
NATIVE RELIGIONS

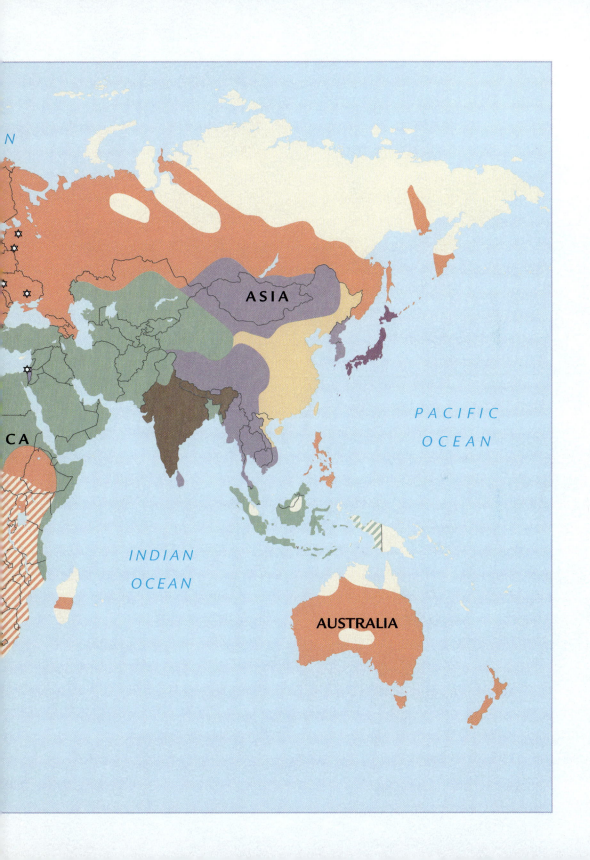

N

ASIA

PACIFIC

OCEAN

CA

INDIAN

OCEAN

AUSTRALIA

CHAPTER 1

Understanding Religion

FIRST ENCOUNTER

For months you have wanted to take a break from work and everyday life, and recently some friends invited you to vacation with them at their mountain cabin. At first you hesitate. This is not the kind of trip you had in mind. After reconsidering, you realize that a remote getaway with friends is just the change of pace you need.

Now, three weeks later, you have been traveling all day and have just arrived at the cabin. It is late afternoon, and the air is so cold you can see your breath. Your friends welcome you warmly, and there's a nice fire in the living room. Your hosts show you to your room and give you a short tour. Soon you are all fixing supper together—pasta, mushrooms, salad. During the meal you discuss your work, your zany relatives, and your mutual friends. Everyone is laughing and having a good time. It's confirmed: coming here was a great idea.

After supper, your friends won't let you help with the dishes. "I think I'll go out for a walk," you say, putting on your heavy, hooded jacket. As the front door closes behind you, you step into a world transformed by twilight.

What strikes you first is the smell in the air. There is nothing quite like the scent of burning wood—almost like incense. It fits perfectly with the chill. You walk farther, beyond the clearing that surrounds the house, and suddenly you are on a path beneath tall pine trees. As a strong breeze rises, the trees make an eerie, whispering sound. It is not exactly a rustle; it is more like a rush. You recall reading once that the sound of wind in pines is the sound of eternity.

Moving on, you find yourself walking along the mountain's ridge. To your left, you see the evening star against the blue-black sky. To your right, it's still light and you see why you are cold: you are literally above the clouds. You sit down on a flat rock, pull up your hood, and watch the pine tree silhouettes disappear as darkness spreads its thickening veil.

It's difficult to pull yourself away. All around you stars begin to pop out, and soon they are blooming thick as wildflowers. Overhead, the mass of stars resembles a river—it must be the Milky Way. You get up and slowly turn full circle to take it all in.

You had almost forgotten about stars. You don't see them much back home, let alone think of them. Where you live, stars appear in movies. Here, though, stars are mysterious points of light. You remember what you once learned: stars are so distant that their light can take millions of years to reach earth. You realize that some of the stars you see may no longer exist. Only their light remains.

At last you begin to walk back to the cabin. A cluster of clouds emerges on the horizon, lit from behind by the rising moon. You see your friends' wooden cabin in the distance. From here it looks so small. The stars seem like the permanent, real world, while the house appears little and temporary—more like a question mark in the great book of the universe. Questions flood your mind. Who are we human beings? Do we make any difference to the universe? Are we part of any cosmic plan? Is there any point to the universe at all? What is it all about?

WHAT IS RELIGION?

The Starry Night, one of the world's most loved paintings, depicts a sky full of luminous, spinning stars. Painted near the end of its creator's life, the work summarizes the vision of Vincent van Gogh (1853–1890). Van Gogh was an intensely religious man who had planned to be an ordained minister in the Dutch Reformed Church, as was his father. But he struggled with his studies and had a falling-out with Church authorities. For a time, he lived as a lay preacher, working with poor miners in Belgium. When he was 27, his brother Theo, an art dealer, encouraged him to take up painting.

Despite his new career, van Gogh continued to think of himself as a minister. If he could not preach in words, he would preach in pictures. His

Vincent van Gogh's *The Starry Night* provides a startling perspective. The familiar world that we know, with a steeple in the middle, is dwarfed by the vast, mysterious cosmos.

subjects were the simple things of life: trees, sunflowers, a wicker chair, a bridge, his postman, a farmer sowing seeds, peasants eating a meal, workers bringing in the harvest. His paintings express a quiet awe before the wonder that he sensed in everyday objects and ordinary people. It was his special sense of the sacredness he saw all around him that he wanted to share. Almost as a reminder, in *The Starry Night* van Gogh placed the little church tower below the night sky, pointing like a compass needle upward to the stars. The heavenly realm with its spinning fires illuminates van Gogh's vision of the sacred character of the entire universe.

Key Characteristics of Religion

When people begin their study of religions, they bring ideas from the religion in which they were raised or from the predominant religion of their society. They may assume, for example, that every religion has a sacred book or that it worships a divine being or that it has a set of commandments. Indeed, many religions do share all these characteristics, but some do not. Shinto, for example, does not have a set of commandments, nor does it preach a moral code; Zen Buddhism does not worship a divine being; and many tribal religions have no written sacred scripture. Nevertheless, we call them all religions. What, then—if not a common set of elements—must be present for something to be called a religion?

An obvious starting point for many scholars is to examine linguistic clues: What are the linguistic roots of the term *religion?* Intriguingly, the word's Latin roots are *re-,* meaning "again," and *lig-,* meaning "join" or "connect" (as in the word *ligament*).[1] Thus the common translation of *religion* is "to join again," "to reconnect." If this derivation is correct, then the word *religion* suggests the joining of our natural, human world to the sacred world. In classical Latin, the term *religio* meant awe for the gods and concern for proper ritual.[2] We must recognize, though, that the term *religion* arose in Western culture and may not be entirely appropriate when applied across cultures; *spiritual path,* for example, might be a more fitting designation to refer to other religious systems. We will keep these things in mind when we use the long-established term *religion.*

> Religion [is] a way of life founded upon the apprehension of sacredness in existence.
>
> —Julian Huxley, biologist[3]

People have constantly tried to define religion, and there are thus many notable attempts. These definitions may emphasize a sense of dependence on a higher power, awareness of the passing nature of life, the use of symbolism and ritual, the structuring of time, or the acceptance of moral rules. But reading these definitions makes one aware of their limitations. The definitions often seem inadequate and time-bound, the product of a particular culture or period or discipline. Perhaps, for the time being, it is better to simply be open to many possible definitions, without as yet embracing any single one. After studying the major world religions, we will undoubtedly come closer to our own definition of religion.

The problem of how to define religion continues to plague scholars, who love definition. A definition may apply well to some religions, but not to others. A definition may apply to religions of the past, but may not be suitable for a religion of the future.

Traditional dictionary definitions of *religion* read something like this: a system of belief that involves worship of a God or gods, prayer, ritual, and a moral code. But there are so many exceptions to that definition that it is neither comprehensive nor accurate. So instead of saying that a religion *must* have certain characteristics, it is more useful to list a series of characteristics that are found in what are commonly accepted as religions. Scholars note that what we ordinarily call religions manifest to some degree the following eight elements:[4]

Belief system Several beliefs fit together into a fairly complete and systematic interpretation of the universe and the human being's place in it; this is also called a *worldview.*

Community The belief system is shared, and its ideals are practiced by a group.

Central myths Stories that express the religious beliefs of a group are retold and often reenacted. Examples of central myths include the major events in the life of the Hindu god Krishna, the enlightenment experience of the Buddha, the exodus of the Israelites from oppression in Egypt, the death and resurrection of Jesus, or Muhammad's escape from Mecca to Medina. Scholars call such central stories *myths.* We should note that the term *myth,* as scholars use it, is a specialized term. It does not in itself mean that the stories are historically untrue (as in popular usage) but only that the stories are central to the religion.

Ritual Beliefs are enacted and made real through ceremonies.

Ethics Rules about human behavior are established. These are often viewed as having been revealed from a supernatural realm, but they can also be viewed as socially generated guidelines.

Characteristic emotional experiences Among the emotional experiences typically associated with religions are dread, guilt, awe, mystery, devotion, conversion, "rebirth," liberation, ecstasy, bliss, and inner peace.

Material expression Religions make use of an astonishing variety of physical elements—statues, paintings, musical compositions, musical instruments, ritual objects, flowers, incense, clothing, architecture, and specific locations.

Sacredness A distinction is made between the sacred and the ordinary; ceremonies often emphasize this distinction through the deliberate use of different language, clothing, and architecture. Certain objects, actions, people, and places may share in the sacredness or express it.

Each of the traditions that we will study in the pages ahead will exhibit most of these characteristics. But the religious traditions, like the people who practice them, will manifest the characteristics in different ways and at different times.

Religious rituals are often symbolic reenactments of a religion's key stories. The presentation of crowns to the bride and groom reminds them of the crowns that await them in heaven.

The Sacred

All religions are concerned with the deepest level of reality, and for most religions the core or origin of everything is sacred and mysterious. This sense of a mysterious, originating holiness is called by many names: Brahman, Dao, Great Mother, Divine Parent, Great Spirit, Ground of Being, Great Mysterious, the Ultimate, the Absolute, the Divine, the Holy. People, however, experience and explain sacred reality in different ways, as we shall see in the chapters that follow.

One familiar term for the sacred reality, particularly in the

Western world, is *God*, and **monotheism*** is the term that means a belief in one God. In some systems, the term *God* often carries with it the notion of a Cosmic Person—a divine being with will and intelligence who is just and compassionate and infinite in virtues. God is also called *omnipotent* ("having total power over the universe"). Although God may be said to have personal aspects, all monotheistic religions agree that the reality of God is beyond all categories: God is said to be pure spirit, not fully definable in words. This notion of a powerful God, distinct from the universe, describes a sacredness that is active in the world but also distinct from it. That is, God is **transcendent**—unlimited by the world and all ordinary reality.

In some religions, however, the sacred reality is not viewed as having personal attributes but is more like an energy or mysterious power. Frequently, the sacred is then spoken of as something **immanent** within the universe. In some religions, there is a tendency to speak of the universe not just as having been created but also as a manifestation of the sacred nature itself, in which nothing is separate from the sacred. This view, called **pantheism** (Greek: "all divine"), sees the sacred as being discoverable within the physical world and its processes. In other words, nature itself is holy.

Some religions worship the sacred reality in the form of many coexisting gods, a view called **polytheism.** The multiple gods may be fairly separate entities, each in charge of an aspect of reality (such as nature gods), or they may be multiple manifestations of the same basic sacred reality.

In recent centuries, we find a tendency to deny the existence of any God or gods (**atheism**), to argue that the existence of God cannot be proven (**agnosticism**), or simply to take no position (**nontheism**). (Such tendencies are not strictly modern; they can also be found in some ancient systems, such as Jainism; see Chapter 5.) However, if one sees religion broadly, as a "spiritual path," then even systems based on these three views—particularly if they show other typical characteristics of a religion—can also be called religions.

Religious Symbolism

Religions present views of reality, and most speak of the sacred. Nevertheless, because religions are so varied in their teachings and because the teachings of some religions, when taken at face value, conflict with those of others, it is common to assert that religions express truth *symbolically.* A symbol is something fairly concrete, ordinary, and universal that can represent—and help human beings intensely experience—something of greater complexity. For example, water can represent spiritual cleansing; the sun, health; a mountain, strength; and a circle, eternity. We frequently find symbolism, both deliberate and unconscious, in religious art and ritual.

Symbols and their interpretation have long played an important part in analyzing dreams. It was once common to think of dreams as messages from

---

**Note:* Words shown in boldface type are listed and defined in the "Key Terms" section at the end of each chapter.

a supernatural realm that provided a key to the future. Although this type of interpretation is less common nowadays, most people still think that dreams are significant. Sigmund Freud introduced his view of the dream as a door into subconscious levels of the mind; he argued that by understanding dreams symbolically we can understand our hidden needs and fears. For example, a dream of being lost in a forest might be interpreted as distress over losing one's sense of direction in life, or a dream of flying could be interpreted as a need to seek freedom.

Carl Gustav Jung extended the symbol-focused method of dream interpretation to the interpretation of religion. Some religious leaders have been cautious about this approach—popularized by the mythologist Joseph Campbell—lest everything be turned into a symbol and all literal meaning be lost. And specialists in religion oppose the view that two religions are basically the same simply because they share similar symbols.

Nevertheless, there are many scholars and religious leaders who recognize the importance of symbolic interpretation, because the use of religious symbols may point to some structure that underlies all religions. There is no doubt that many of the same symbolic images and actions appear repeatedly in religions throughout the world. Water, for instance, is used in all sorts of religious rituals: Hindus bathe in the Ganges River; Christians use water for

The mandala, according to Jung, illustrates "the path to the center, to individuation."

Before entering a mosque, men symbolically purify themselves with water. Ablution and purification rituals are found in most religions.

baptisms; Jews use water for ritual purification; and Muslims and followers of Shinto wash before prayer. Ashes also have widespread use among religious traditions to suggest death and the spirit world: ashes are used by tribal religions in dance ceremonies, by Hindu holy men to represent asceticism and detachment, and by some Christians, whose foreheads are marked by ashes in observance of Ash Wednesday. Likewise, religious buildings are placed on hills or are raised on mounds and reached by stairs—all suggesting the symbol of the holy mountain, where the sacred can be encountered.

We also see in various religions the recurrence of a symbolic story of transformation: a state of original purity degenerates into pollution or disorder, or a battle to fight disorder culminates in a sacrificial death that results in a renewed sense of purity and order. Scholars point out, too, that religions frequently use words in a symbolic way; for example, the divine is often described as existing "up above," insight can be "awakened," and a person can feel "reborn."

When viewed this way, religious symbols, myths, and terminology at times suggest a universal symbolic "language" that all religions speak. Those interested in religious symbolism hope that understanding the "language" of symbols will help uncover what is universally important in all religions.

Speculations on the Sources of Religion

Why does religion exist? The most evident answer is that it serves many human needs. One of our primary needs is having a means to deal with our mortality. Because we and our loved ones must die, we have to face the pain of death and the inevitable questions it brings about whether there is any soul, afterlife, or rebirth. People often look to religion for the answers. Religion can help us cope with death, and religious rituals can offer us comfort. Human beings also desire good health, a regular supply of food, and the conditions (such as suitable weather) necessary to ensure these things. Before the development of modern science, human beings looked to religion to bring about these practical benefits, and they often still do.

Human beings are also social by nature, and religion offers companionship and the fulfillment that can come from belonging to a group. Moreover, religion often provides a structure for caring for the needy.

Human beings have a need to seek out and create artistic forms of expression. Religion stimulates art, music, and dance, and it has been the inspirational source of some of the most imaginative buildings in the world. Religion not only makes use of multiple arts but also integrates them into a living, often beautiful whole.

Perhaps the most basic function of religion is to respond to our natural wonder about ourselves and the cosmos—our musings on a starry night. Religion helps us relate to the unknown universe around us by answering the basic questions of who we are, where we come from, and where we are going.

Issues relating to the origins of religion have engaged thinkers with new urgency ever since the dawn of the age of science. Many have suggested that religion is a human attempt to feel more secure in an unfeeling universe. The

A so-called Chac-Mool figure, used in sacrifice, sits in front of the ruins of the Pyramid of Kulkulkán in Chichén Itzá, Mexico.

English anthropologist E. B. Tylor (1832–1917), for example, believed religion was rooted in spirit worship. He noted how frequently religions see "spirits" as having some control over natural forces and how commonly religions see those who die—the ancestors—as passing into the spirit world. Fear of the power of all these spirits, he thought, made it necessary for people to find ways to please their ancestors. Religion offered such ways, thus allowing the living to avoid the spirits' dangerous power and to convert that power into a force that worked for the good of human beings. Similarly, the Scottish anthropologist James Frazer (1854–1941), author of *The Golden Bough*, saw the origins of religion in early attempts by human beings to influence nature, and he identified religion as an intermediate stage between magic and science.

Sigmund Freud (1856–1939) theorized that belief in a God or gods arises from the long-lasting impressions made on adults by their childhood experiences, in which their parents play a major part; these adults then project their sense of their parents into their image of their God or gods. According to Freud, these experiences—of fear as well as of security—are the basis for adults' attempts to deal with the anxieties of a complicated present and an unknown future. Freud argued that since a major function of religion is to help human beings feel secure in an unsafe universe, religion becomes less necessary as human beings gain greater physical and mental security. Freud's major works on religion include *Totem and Taboo, The Future of an Illusion,* and *Moses and Monotheism.*

Who are we, where do we come from, and where are we going? Each religion offers answers to these questions, and graveyards often hint at believers' visions of what happens after death.

Another psychologist, William James (1842–1910), came to his ideas on religion via an unusual course of study. Although he began his higher education as a student of art, he made a radical switch to the study of medicine. Finally, when he recognized the influence of the mind on the body, he was led to the study of psychology and then of religion, which he saw as growing out of psychological needs. James viewed religion as a positive way of fulfilling these needs and praised its positive influence on the lives of individuals. He wrote that religion brings "a new zest" to living, provides "an assurance of safety," and leads to a "harmonious relation with the universe."[5]

The German theologian Rudolf Otto (1869–1937) argued in his book *The Idea of the Holy* that religions emerge when people experience that aspect of reality which is essentially mysterious. He called it the "mystery that causes trembling and fascination" (*mysterium tremendum et fascinans*). In general, we take our existence for granted and live with little wonder, but occasionally something disturbs our ordinary view of reality. For example, a strong manifestation of nature—such as a violent thunderstorm—may startle us. It is an aspect of reality that is frightening, forcing us to tremble (*tremendum*) but also to feel fascination (*fascinans*). The emotional result is what Otto called *numinous awe*.[6] He pointed out how often religious art depicts that which is terrifying, such as the bloodthirsty Hindu goddess Durga.[7]

Carl Gustav Jung (1875–1961), an early disciple of Freud, broke with his mentor because of fundamental differences of interpretation, particularly about religion. In his books *Modern Man in Search of a Soul, Psychology and Alchemy,* and *Memories, Dreams, Reflections,* Jung described religion as something that grew out of the individual's need to arrive at personal fulfillment, which he called *individuation.* According to Jung, many religious insignia can be seen as symbols of personal integration and human wholeness: the circle, the cross (which is made of lines that join at the center), and the sacred diagram of the mandala (often a circle within or enclosing a square), which he called "the path to the center, to individuation."[8] He pointed out that as people age, they can make a healthy use of religion to understand their place in the universe and to prepare for death. For Jung, religion was a noble human response to the complexity and depth of reality.

The view of Karl Marx (1818–1883) about religion is often cited, but it may have been softer than that of the Russian and Chinese forms of Marxism that emerged from it. While many types of Marxism have been strongly atheistic, Marx himself was not so militant. He indeed called religion an opiate of the masses. But for him religion had both a bad and a good side. Religion, he thought, emerged naturally because people felt poor, powerless, and alienated from their work. On the other hand, Marx also thought that religion gave great consolation, for it spoke of a suffering-free life after death. For Marx, religion was a symptom of the sickness of society. The need for religion, he thought, would dissolve when society improved.

Some recent theories do not look specifically at religion, but their wide-ranging insights are applied in the study of the origin of religions, as well as in many other fields. Among these theoretical approaches are structuralism and post-structuralism, along with the technique of deconstruction. We will look at some of these ideas and applications later.

Various scholars have attempted to identify "stages" in the development of religions. Austrian ethnographer and philologist Wilhelm Schmidt (1868–1954) argued that all humankind once believed in a single High God and that to this simple monotheism later beliefs in lesser gods and spirits were added. The reverse has also been suggested—namely, that polytheism led to monotheism. Influenced by the notion of evolution, some have speculated that religions "evolve" naturally from **animism** (a worldview that sees all elements of nature as being filled with spirit or spirits) to polytheism and then to monotheism. Critics of this view feel it is biased in favor of monotheism, in part because it is a view originally suggested by Christian scholars, who presented their belief system as the most advanced.

Scholars today hesitate to speak of any "evolution" from one form of religion to another. To apply the biological notion of evolution to human belief systems seems biased, oversimple, and speculative. Even more important, such a point of view leads to subjective judgments that one religion is more "highly evolved" than another—a shortsightedness that has kept many people from appreciating the unique insights and contributions of every religion. Consequently, the focus of religious studies has moved from the study of religion to the study of religions, a field that assumes that all religions are equally worthy of study.

PATTERNS AMONG RELIGIONS

When we study religions in a comparative and historical sense, we are not looking to validate them or to disprove them or to enhance our own belief or practice—as we might if we were studying our personal religious tradition. Instead, we want to comprehend the particular religions as thoroughly as possible and to understand the experience of people within each religion. Part of that process of understanding leads us to see patterns of similarity and difference among religions.

Although we do look for patterns, we must recognize that these patterns are not conceptual straitjackets. Religions, especially those with long histories and extensive followings, are usually quite complex. Furthermore, religions

Religion is the substance of culture, and culture the form of religion.
—Paul Tillich, theologian[9]

are not permanent theoretical constructs but are constantly in a process of change—influenced by governments, thinkers, historical events, changing technology, and the shifting values of the cultures in which they exist.

First Pattern: Views of the World and Life

Religions must provide answers to the great questions that people ask. How did the universe come into existence, does it have a purpose, and will it end? What is time, and how should we make use of it? What should be our relationship to the world of nature? Why do human beings exist? How do we reach fulfillment, transformation, or salvation? Why is there suffering in the world, and how should we deal with it? What happens when we die? What should we hold as sacred? The questions do not vary, but the answers do.

Given the great variety in their worldviews, religions, not surprisingly, define differently the nature of sacred reality, the universe, the natural world, time, and human purpose. Religions also differ in their attitudes toward the role of words in expressing the sacred and in their relations to other religious traditions. By examining different views on these concepts, we will have further bases for comparison that will lead us to a more complete understanding of the world's religions.

The nature of sacred reality Some religions, as we have seen, speak of the sacred as transcendent, existing primarily in a realm beyond the everyday world. In other religions, though, sacred reality is spoken of as being immanent; that is, it is within nature and human beings and can be experienced as energy or holiness. Sometimes the sacred is viewed as having personal attributes, while elsewhere it is seen as an impersonal entity. And in certain religious traditions, particularly in some forms of Buddhism, it is hard to point to a sacred reality at all. Such facts raise the question as to whether "the sacred" exists outside ourselves or if it is better to speak of the sacred simply as what people "hold to be sacred."

The nature of the universe Some religions see the universe as having been begun by an intelligent, personal Creator who continues to guide the universe according to a cosmic plan. Other religions view the universe as being eternal; that is, having no beginning or end. The implications of these two positions are quite important to what is central in a religion and to how the human being acts in regard to this central belief. If the universe is created, especially by a transcendent deity, the center of sacredness is the Creator rather than the universe, but human beings imitate the Creator by changing and perfecting the world. If, however, the universe is eternal, the material universe itself is sacred and perfect and requires no change.

The human attitude toward nature At one end of the spectrum, some religions or religious schools see nature as the realm of evil forces that must be overcome. For them, nature is gross and contaminating, existing in opposition to the nonmaterial world of the spirit—a view, known as **dualism,** held by some forms of Christianity, Jainism, and Hinduism. At the other end of the spectrum, as in Daoism and Shinto, nature is considered to be sacred and needs no alteration. Other religions, such as Judaism and Islam, take a middle ground, holding that the natural world originated from a divine action but that human beings are called upon to continue to shape it.

Time Religions that emphasize a creation, such as Judaism, Christianity, and Islam, tend to see time as being linear, moving in a straight line from the beginning of the universe to its end. Being limited and unrepeatable, time is important. In some other religions, such as Buddhism, however, time is cyclical. The universe simply moves through endless changes, which repeat themselves over grand periods of time. In such a religion, time is not as crucial or "real" because, ultimately, the universe is not moving to some final point; consequently, appreciating the present may be more important than being oriented to the future.

Human purpose In some religions, human beings are part of a great divine plan, and although each person is unique, individual meaning comes also from the cosmic plan. The cosmic plan may be viewed as a struggle between forces of good and evil, with human beings at the center of the stage and the forces of good and evil at work within them. Because human actions are so important, they must be guided by a prescribed moral code that is meant to be internalized by the individual. This view is significant in Judaism, Christianity, and Islam. In contrast, other religions do not see human life in similarly dramatic terms, and the individual is only part of much larger realities. In Daoism and Shinto, a human being is a small part of the natural universe, and in Confucianism, an individual is part of the family and of society. Such religions place less emphasis on individual rights and more emphasis on how the individual can maintain harmony with the whole. Actions are not guided by an internalized moral system but by society, tradition, and a sense of mutual obligation.

Words and scriptures In some religions, the sacred is to be found in written and spoken words, and for those religions that use writing and create scriptures, reading, copying, and using sacred words in music or art are important. We see the importance of words in indigenous religions (which primarily pass on their traditions orally), in Judaism, in Christianity, in Islam, and in Hinduism. Other religions— such as Daoism and Zen Buddhism, which show a certain mistrust of words—value silence and wordless meditation. Although Zen and Daoism utilize language in their practices and have produced significant literature, each of these religions finds language limited in expressing the richness or totality of reality.

Exclusiveness and inclusiveness Some religions emphasize that the sacred is distinct from the world and that order must be imposed by

Vajrayana monks in Bhutan are making electronic copies of Buddhist scriptures to help make them available to a worldwide audience.

separating good from bad, true from false. In that view, to share in sacredness means separation—for example, withdrawal from certain foods, places, people, practices, or beliefs. Judaism, Christianity, and Islam are among the religions that have been generally exclusive, making it impossible to belong to more than one religion at the same time. In contrast, other religions have stressed inclusiveness. Frequently, such religions also have emphasized social harmony, the inadequacy of language, or the relativity of truth, and they have accepted belief in many deities. Their inclusiveness has led them to admit many types of beliefs and practices into their religions, to the point that it is possible for an individual to belong to several religions—such as Buddhism, Daoism, and Confucianism—simultaneously. Such inclusiveness has led to misunderstanding at times, as in the case of a Christian missionary having "converted" a Japanese follower only to find the new convert still visiting a Shinto shrine.

Second Pattern: Focus of Beliefs and Practices

Realizing the limitations of all generalizations, we nonetheless might gain some perspective by examining the orientations exhibited by individual religions. When we look at the world's dominant religions, we see three basic orientations in their conception and location of the sacred.[10]

Sacramental orientation The sacramental orientation emphasizes carrying out rituals and ceremonies regularly and correctly as the path to salvation; in some religions, correct ritual is believed to influence the processes of nature. All religions have some degree of ritual, but the ceremonial tendency is predominant, for example, in most indigenous religions, in Roman Catholic and Eastern Orthodox Christianity, in Vedic Hinduism, and in Tibetan Buddhism. Making the Catholic sign of the cross, for example, is done in a certain way: only with the right hand, beginning with a touch on the forehead, then on one's chest, and finally on each shoulder, left to right.[11]

Prophetic orientation The prophetic orientation stresses that contact with the sacred is ensured by proper belief and by adherence to moral rules. This orientation also implies that a human being may be an important intermediary between the believer and the sacred; for example, a prophet may speak to believers on behalf of the sacred. Prophetic orientation is a prominent aspect of Judaism, Protestant Christianity, and Islam, which all see the sacred as being transcendent but personal. The television crusades of evangelistic ministers are good examples of the prophetic orientation in action.

Mystical orientation The mystical orientation seeks union with a reality greater than oneself, such as with God, the process of nature, the universe, or reality as a whole. There are often techniques (such as seated meditation) for lessening the sense of one's individual identity to help the individual experience a greater unity. The mystical orientation is a prominent aspect of Upanishadic Hinduism, Daoism, and some schools of Buddhism. (Master Kusan [1909–1983], a Korean teacher of Zen Buddhism, described the disappearance of self in the enlightenment experience of unity with this memorable question: "Could a snowflake survive inside a burning flame?"[12]) Although the mystical orientation is more common in religions that stress the immanence of the sacred or that are nontheistic, it is an important but less prominent tendency in Judaism, Christianity, and Islam as well.

Any one of these three orientations may be dominant in a religion, yet the other two orientations might also be found in the same religion to a lesser extent and possibly be subsumed into a different purpose. For example, ceremony can be utilized to help induce mystical experience, as in Catholic and Orthodox Christianity, Japanese Shingon Buddhism, Tibetan Buddhism, Daoism, and even Zen Buddhism, which has a strongly ritualistic aspect of its own.

Third Pattern: Views of Male and Female

Because gender is such an intrinsic and important part of being human, religions have had much to say about the roles of men and women, both on earth and in the divine spheres. Because of differences in how religions view these differences, they may constitute another underlying pattern that we can investigate when studying religions. Thus, views of what is male and what is female provide another basis for comparing religions.

In many influential religions today, male imagery and control seem to dominate; the sacred is considered male, and the full-time religious specialists

Deeper Insights

MULTIPLE IMAGES OF THE FEMALE

Religions frequently have been criticized for the dominance of males, both in their religious leadership and in their images of the sacred. While there is truth to such criticism, scholarly attention helps us to note the multitude of female roles and images to be found among religions. Consider these examples:

- In India, the divine is worshiped in its female aspects as the Great Mother (also known as Kali and Durga) or as other female deities.
- In Catholic and Orthodox Christianity, Mary, the mother of Jesus, receives special veneration; she is held to possess superhuman powers and is a strong role model for women's behavior.
- In the Mahayana Buddhist pantheon, Guanyin (Kannon) is worshiped as a female ideal of mercy.
- In Japan, the premier Shinto divinity is the goddess Amaterasu, patroness of the imperial family. In contrast to many other religious systems, the goddess Amaterasu is associated with the sun, and a male god is associated with the moon.
- In Korea and Japan, shamans are frequently female.
- In Africa, India, and elsewhere, some tribal cultures remain matriarchal.
- In Wicca—a contemporary restoration of ancient, nature-based religion—devotees worship a female deity they refer to as the Goddess.
- Symbolic forms of the female divine are still prominent in the rites of several religions. Common symbols include the moon, the snake, spirals and

Easter, a springtime festival of fertility, is marked by these Easter eggs decorating a European shop window.

labyrinths, the egg, *yoni* (symbolic vagina), water, and earth. These symbolic representations of the female suggest generation, growth, nurturance, intuition, and wisdom.

are frequently male. But this may not always have been the case. Tantalizing evidence suggests that female divinities once played an important role in many cultures and religions. The most significant female deity was particularly associated with fertility and motherhood and has been known by many names, such as Astarte, Asherah, Aphrodite, and Freia (the origin of the word *Friday*). Statues of a Mother-Goddess—sometimes with many breasts to suggest the spiritual power of the nurturing female—have been found throughout Europe, as well as in Turkey, Israel, and the Middle East.

Is it possible that female images of the divine were once more common and that female religious leadership once played a more important role? It has been argued that male dominance in religion became more common as the result of the growth of city-states, which needed organized defense and so elevated the status of men because of their fighting ability. In Israel, worship of a female deity was stamped out by prophets who preached exclusive worship of the male god Yahweh and by kings who wanted loyalty paid to them and their offspring. We read passages like this in the Hebrew scriptures: "They abandoned the Lord and worshipped Baal and the Astartes. So the anger of the Lord was kindled against Israel" (Judg. 2:13–14).[13] The Christian New Testament contains words that sometimes have been interpreted to mean that women should not play a prominent role in public worship: "I do not allow them to teach or to have authority over men; they must keep quiet. For Adam was created first, and then Eve. And it was not Adam who was deceived; it was the woman who was deceived and broke God's law" (1 Tim. 2:12–14).[14] In Asia, Confucianism has been distrustful of women in general and has ordinarily refused them leadership roles. In Buddhism, despite recognition in scripture that women can be enlightened, in practice the great majority of leaders have been men.[15]

A century ago, great numbers of people across the world had little experience of the different beliefs and practices in other regions. But radio, television, the Internet, smartphones, and other technologies have changed this. Thus it is no surprise that long-established customs regarding gender should now be challenged and changed.

Such changes may not come easily. In some religious traditions, the possibility of changes can produce a rift. This is happening today, for example, in the Christian Anglican Communion and several other Christian denominations. We can expect similar disruptions in other religious traditions, as technological changes bring knowledge of different cultures.

In many religions, the gender associated with positions of power is no longer exclusively male. Here, female priests lead a communion service.

Knowledge of other cultures will continue to grow, and the study of other religions will contribute to this process. Such study will open people's eyes not only to the gender expectations in religions of the past, but also to today's evolving practices. This is nudging several religious traditions to accept women in areas where in earlier centuries they were not expected to have a role. Although there are many resultant tensions (those in Buddhism, Christianity, and Islam are currently receiving publicity), we can expect that women will be widely successful in receiving full acceptance in roles of leadership.

MULTIDISCIPLINARY APPROACHES TO THE STUDY OF RELIGION

Religion has influenced so many areas of human life that it is a subject not only of religious studies but of other disciplines, too. As we have seen, the social sciences, in particular, have long studied religion. More recently, linguistics, literary theory, and cultural studies have offered us new ways of seeing and interpreting religion.

There are other approaches, too. We can focus our study on a single religion or look at several religions at the same time. Believers may opt to explore their own religion "from the inside," while nonbelievers may want to concentrate on the answers that several religions have given to a single question, such as the purpose of human life. Following is a list of some common approaches to religion.

Psychology Psychology (Greek: "soul study") deals with human mental states, emotions, and behaviors. Despite being a fairly young discipline, psychology has taken a close look at religion because it offers such rich human "material" to explore. A few areas of study include religious influences on child rearing, human behavior, gender expectations, and self-identity; group dynamics in religion; trance states; and comparative mystical experiences.

Mythology The study of religious tales, texts, and art has uncovered some universal patterns. Mythology is full of the recurrent images and themes found in religions, such as the tree of knowledge, the ladder to heaven, the fountain of life, the labyrinth, the secret garden, the holy mountain, the newborn child, the suffering hero, initiation, rebirth, the cosmic battle, the female spirit guide, and the aged teacher of wisdom.

Philosophy Philosophy (Greek: "love of wisdom") in some ways originated from a struggle with religion; although both arenas pose many of the same questions, philosophy does not automatically accept the answers given by any religion to the great questions. Instead, philosophy seeks answers independently, following reason rather than religious authority, and it tries to fit its answers into a rational, systematic whole. Some questions philosophy asks are, Does human life have any purpose? Is there an afterlife? How should we live? Philosophy is essentially the work of individuals, while religion is a community experience; philosophy tries to avoid emotion, while religion often nurtures it; and philosophy is carried on without ritual, while religion naturally expresses itself in ceremony.

Theology Theology (Greek: "study of the divine") is the study of topics as they relate to one particular religious tradition. A theologian is an individual who usually studies his or her own belief system. For example, a person who is in training to become a Christian minister might study Christian theology.

The arts Comparing patterns in religious art makes an intriguing study. For example, religious architecture often uses symmetry, height, and archaic styles to suggest the sacred; religious music frequently employs a slow pace and repeated rhythms to induce tranquillity; and religious art often incorporates gold, haloes, equilateral designs, and circles to suggest otherworldliness and perfection.

Anthropology Anthropology (Greek: "study of human beings") has been interested in how religions influence the ways different cultures deal with issues such as family interaction, individual roles, property rights, marriage, child rearing, social hierarchies, and division of labor.

Archeology Archeology (Greek: "study of origins") explores the remains of earlier civilizations, often uncovering the artifacts and ruins of religious buildings from ancient cultures. When possible, archeologists translate writings left by these people, much of which can be religious in origin. Archeology occasionally sheds light on how one religion has influenced another. For example, the excavation of a cuneiform library at Nineveh 150 years ago revealed a story (in the *Epic of Gilgamesh*) that is similar

Volunteers assist with excavations in Caesarea Maritima, exploring the foundations of a 2,000-year-old seaside temple possibly built by King Herod.

to—and may have influenced—the biblical story of Noah and the flood. Archeology can also reveal religious material that enables scholars to decipher an entire writing system. For example, the discovery in the early nineteenth century of the Rosetta Stone (which contained the same inscription in three different scripts) led researchers to unlock the meaning of Egyptian hieroglyphics.

Linguistics and literary theory The study of linguistics has sometimes involved a search for patterns that may underlie all languages. But linguistics has occasionally also suggested general patterns and structures that may underlie something broader than language alone: human consciousness. This interest in underlying patterns has brought new attention to the possible structures behind religious tales, rituals, and other expressions of religious beliefs and attitudes. Linguistics has also examined religious language for its implications and often-hidden values. (Consider, for example, the various implications of the religious words *sin* and *sacred*.) Literary theory, on the other hand, has studied the written texts of religion as reflections of the cultural assumptions and values that produced the texts. Literary theory has thus pointed out some of the ways in which religions have reflected and promoted the treatment of women and minorities, for example, as different from or inferior to more dominant groups. Literary theory also has shown that nonwritten material—such as religious statues, paintings, songs, and even films—can be viewed as forms of discourse and can therefore be studied in the same ways that written texts are studied.

The use of theory for the study of religion is not limited to the fields of linguistics and literature. In fact, increasing numbers of academic disciplines are studying religions as part of the human search for understanding. Thus a scholar in the field of art may see and interpret religions as forms of art. Specialists in psychology may interpret religions primarily as expressions of individual human needs. Sociologists may see religions as ways of shaping groups and of promoting and maintaining group conformity. The viewpoints of these and other disciplines can also be adopted by scholars of religion as keys to understanding the complexities of religions.

The Study of Religion

Originally, religions were studied primarily within their own religious traditions. The goal of this approach was that faith and devotion would be illuminated by intellectual search. Although this approach continues in denominational schools, the study of religion began to take new form two centuries ago.

There were several causes for the change. First, the early scientific movement accepted belief in a creator-god, but it rejected belief in miracles and demanded scientific proof for beliefs. The emerging scientific movement thus forced people to revise some of their traditional religious beliefs. Second, because of the growth of historical studies, academic experts began to question the literal truth of some statements and stories presented in the scriptures. (For example, did the story of Noah and the Ark actually happen, or was it meant mainly to be a teaching parable whose real purpose was moral?) Third, because of the growth of trade and travel, even faraway cultures were becoming known. Their religions proved to be not only colorful but also wise. The morality taught by Buddhism, the sense of duty found in Confucianism, the love of nature taught in Shinto—all these seemed admirable. But what did this mean for other religions? In the nineteenth and twentieth centuries this question intensified, as more information became available through history, anthropology, and sociology. Scriptures and ritual texts were translated, and anthropologists began to have direct experience of even small and rare religions.

In the university world, the study of religions was at first fragmented. The great questions of religion were studied in philosophy departments. Other aspects of religion could be found in departments of history, psychology, anthropology, and art. But there was as yet no department of religious studies that unified these interests.

The fragmented academic approach changed in the twentieth century, as departments of religious studies were formed and became a regular part of academic life. At first it was uncertain if these departments of religion would survive. But the popularity of some courses in religion—particularly those in world religions, death and dying, and the psychology of religion—demonstrated the worth of having separate, permanent departments of religious studies.

The study of religion has further expanded, and in the twenty-first century we are able to examine religions from additional and sometimes unexpected points of view. For example, one of the most provocative new perspectives is neurology. Are religious beliefs and practices a part of our genetic makeup, or are they merely manufactured by cultures and learned by people? Is a religious experience the intrusion of a sacred being on individual consciousness, or is it the activity of a particular chemical in the brain? Similar questions may be asked about morality. Are moral demands a part of our physical constitution, or are they simply rules taught by society? As academic disciplines expand and additional disciplines emerge, new aspects of religion will be discovered.

Recent Theories

Recent thinking about religion has been influenced by the field studies of anthropologists and other behavioral scientists. Archeology has also contributed much to newer thinking.

At one time it was thought that religions were best traced to a "great founder," such as Moses, the Buddha, Jesus, or Muhammad. This is no longer the common approach. Rather, sociologists have pointed out how religions seem to emerge from whole tribes and peoples. One of the first thinkers to speak of this was the French sociologist Émile Durkheim (1858–1917).[16] He noted how religions reinforce the values of groups, and his approach was empirical, based on research. His approach has been continued by later French thinkers, such as Claude Levi-Strauss.

Claude Levi-Strauss (1908–2009) did fieldwork in Brazil, where he studied the mythology of tribal groups. There he began to see great similarities in the myths of indigenous peoples. This led him to see large structural similarities between kinship patterns, languages, and social relations. He theorized that structures in the human mind formed these similarities. His thought, called **structuralism,** has influenced the study of religion, particularly regarding taboos, marriage, and laws about food purity.

A countermovement, called **post-structuralism**, soon emerged. It emphasized the individuality of each experience and argued that belief in grand structures may keep investigators from appreciating that individuality. Michel Foucault (1926–1984) is thought of as its primary exponent. His work especially focused on those marginalized by society—prisoners, medical patients, and the insane.

Jacques Derrida (1930–2004) began with a structuralist approach, but he moved away from grand theories in order to focus on language, meaning, and interpretation. He is known for going behind the ordinary interpretation of texts to discover new cultural meanings. This method is known as **deconstruction**. In the area of religion, it can be quite effective. For example, traditional religious texts can be looked at from many new points of view; one can look at scriptural passages to investigate, say, underlying attitudes toward the treatment of women, slaves, indigenous people, children, and the old. Deconstructive principles can also be used to investigate religious art, architecture, and music.

Increasingly, religious investigation relies on anthropologists who have lived with native peoples and learned their languages. One researcher of this type was E. E. Evans-Pritchard (1902–1973), who lived among the Azande and Nuer people in Africa. Another esteemed anthropologist was Clifford Geertz (1926–2006), who lived in Indonesia and Morocco and wrote about practices there. Geertz championed what he called *thick description*—a description not only of rituals and religious objects, but also of their meaning for the practitioners.

The so-called phenomenological approach to religious studies has been very popular. This approach emphasizes direct experiential research to gather data. It seeks to understand religious acts and objects from the consciousness of the believers, and it tries to avoid projecting the researcher's beliefs and expectations into the data. Specialists of this type have sometimes focused on one religion. Contemporary examples are Wendy Doniger (O'Flaherty, b. 1940) and Diana Eck (b. 1945). Both of them have specialized in Hinduism, but their writings and other work have incorporated other world religions.

KEY CRITICAL ISSUES

The research-based approach to the study of religions, though valuable, brings problems and questions. Are we genuinely listening to the voices of the practitioners, or are we only paying attention to the experiences of the observer? Can an outsider be truly objective, or is the outsider merely imposing the

Conflict in Religion

RELIGIOUS BLENDS

A book like this has to treat religions as somewhat separate. While there is truth to that separateness, it is also true that religions are constantly borrowing from each other. One example that we know of occurs in the Catholic practice of Mexico. Our Lady of Guadalupe is not only one form of the Virgin Mary; she is also a continuation of the pre-Christian deity Tonantzin, who was once worshiped at the modern-day site of the main church of Our Lady of Guadalupe. Other native beliefs and practices continue in the Christianity of South America; for example, the veneration of earlier nature deities has influenced the current veneration of saints. In Zen Buddhism, there is influence from Daoism and Confucianism; the Daoist love of nature appears in Zen flower arrangement and garden design, and the Confucian respect for a teacher appears in the obedience given to a Zen master. The Shiite Islam of Iraq contains practices that can be traced back to Zoroastrianism. In recent times, Scientology seems to have elements very similar to those found in Hinduism and Buddhism, and the Vietnamese religion of Cao Dai unites beliefs of Asian religions with elements of Christianity and spiritism. As we study the religions of the world, we must remember this tendency to borrow and blend, which enriches them all.

theories of other cultures? Doesn't scientific observation contaminate the people and culture being observed? Could informants give deliberately false answers to questions that they think are inappropriate? (They do.)

Moral questions also arise. Does the research arise from respect for a different culture and religion, or is it just a more modern form of domination and colonialism? And doesn't research introduce new ideas and new objects, such as cell phones, cameras, and different clothing? Don't these objects alter cultures that have been unchanged for centuries?

In addition, research has revealed to investigators the enormous variety within major religions. Because some major religions have blended with earlier religions to produce unique hybrids, can we really speak of single great religions, such as "Buddhism" or "Christianity"? Do they really exist, or are they just useful fictions?

Some scholars also have pointed out that the religious experience of women within a religious tradition may be quite different from that of men. In Islam, for example, women's religious experience may be centered primarily in the home, while men's may be centered more on the mosque. And the religious experience will be quite different for a child, a teenager, or an adult. In addition, the varying meaning of being a Buddhist or a Christian or a Hindu will depend considerably on the culture and the period. Think, for example, of the difference of being a Christian in first-century Rome and

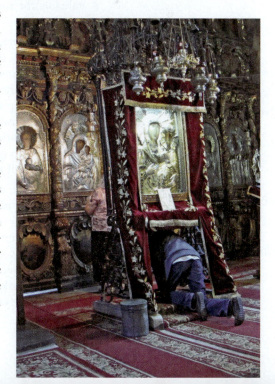

Whatever their religion, people tend to turn to it with hope. Here a supplicant in Romania crawls under an icon to secure greater attention from the Virgin Mary, who is portrayed.

twenty-first-century North America, or of being a Hindu in medieval India and modern-day New York City.

Although this book obviously has not abandoned the category of religions, it tries to show that religions are not separate and unchanging. It sees world religions as grand patterns, but it recognizes that we are true to these religions only when we see the great diversity within them.

WHY STUDY THE MAJOR RELIGIONS OF THE WORLD?

Science investigates; religion interprets. Science gives man knowledge which is power; religion gives man wisdom which is control.

—Martin Luther King Jr.[17]

Because religions are so wide-ranging and influential, their study helps round out a person's education, as well as enriches one's experience of many other related subjects. Let's now consider some additional pleasures and rewards of studying religions.

Insight into religious traditions Each religion is interesting in its own right as a complex system of values, relationships, personalities, and human creativity.

Insight into what religions share The study of religions requires sympathy and objectivity. While it is true that being a believer of a particular religion brings a special insight that an outsider cannot have, it is also true that an outsider can appreciate things that are not always obvious to the insider. This is particularly true of shared patterns of imagery, belief, and practice.

Insight into people Understanding a person's religious background tells us more about that person's attitudes and values. Such understanding is valuable for successful human relations—in both public life and private life.

Tolerance and appreciation of differences Because human beings are emotional creatures, their religions can sometimes allow inflamed feelings to override common decency. As we see daily, religions can be employed to justify immense cruelty. Examining the major religions of the world helps us develop tolerance toward people of varying religious traditions. In a multicultural world, tolerance of differences is valuable, but enjoyment of differences is even better. Variety is a fact of nature, and the person who can enjoy variety—in religion and elsewhere—is a person who will never be tired of life.

Intellectual questioning Religions make claims about truth, yet some of their views are not easy to reconcile. For example, doesn't the theory of reincarnation of the soul, as found in Hinduism, conflict with the teaching of several other religions that a soul has only one lifetime on earth? And how can the notion of an immortal soul be reconciled with the Buddhist teaching that nothing has a permanent soul or essence? We must also ask questions about tolerance itself. Must we be tolerant of intolerance, even if it is preached by a religion? Questions such as

Rituals and Celebrations

TRAVEL AND PILGRIMAGE

One of the most universal religious practices is pilgrimage—travel undertaken by believers to important religious sites. But you do not have to belong to a specific religion to benefit from this ancient practice. Travel to religious sites is a wonderful way to experience the varieties of human belief firsthand, particularly at times of religious celebration. Travel that is not specifically religious can also offer similar benefits, because it allows us to experience religious art and architecture in the places and contexts for which they were created.

Travel programs for young and old abound. Many colleges offer study-abroad programs, including summer courses that incorporate travel, as well as semester- and year-long study programs. Scholarships and other financial aid may be available for these programs. Large travel companies also offer summer tours for students, particularly to Europe and Asia; these companies are able to offer affordable tours by scheduling charter flights and inexpensive hotel accommodations. Programs such as these often make an excellent first trip abroad for students. Young travelers touring on their own can also join a youth hostel association, such as Hostelling International, and make use of a worldwide network of inexpensive youth hostels. Older adults can take advantage of programs in Road Scholar (formerly called Elderhostel). These programs encompass a wide variety of activities—educational courses, excursions, and service projects—all around the world.

Information on travel, youth hostels, and home exchanges can be found online and in the travel sections of libraries and bookstores. The Internet is also a good source for the dates of religious festivals in other countries.

these arise naturally when we study religions side by side. Such study sharpens our perception of the claims of religions and invites us to examine important intellectual questions more closely.

Insight into everyday life Religious influences can be found everywhere in modern culture, not just within religious buildings. Politicians make use of religious images, for example, when they speak of a "new covenant" with voters. Specific religions and religious denominations take public positions on moral issues, such as abortion and war. Our weekly routines are regulated by the originally Jewish practice of a six-day work week followed by a day of rest, and the European- American school calendar is divided in two by the originally Christian Christmas holidays. Even comic strips use religious imagery: animals crowded onto a wooden boat, a man holding two tablets, angels on clouds, a person meditating on a mountaintop. The study of religions is valuable for helping us recognize and appreciate the religious influences that are everywhere.

Appreciation for the arts Anyone attracted to painting, sculpture, music, or architecture will be drawn to the study of religions. Because numerous religious traditions have been among the most significant patrons of art, their study provides a gateway to discovering and appreciating these rich works.

Enriched experience of travel Study of religion allows us to see cultural forms in new ways. One of the great pleasures of our age is travel. Visiting the temple of Angkor Wat in Cambodia or a Mayan pyramid in Mexico is quite different from just reading about them. The study of world religions gives travelers the background necessary to fully enjoy the many wonderful places they can now experience directly.

Insight into family traditions Religions have influenced most earlier cultures so strongly that their effects are readily identifiable in the values of our parents and grandparents—even if they are not actively religious individuals. These values include attitudes toward education, individual rights, gender roles, sex, time, money, food, and leisure.

Help in one's own religious quest Not everyone is destined to become an artist or a musician or a poet, yet each one of us has some ability to appreciate visual arts, music, and poetry. In the same way, although some people may not be explicitly religious, they may have a sense of the sacred and a desire to seek ways to feel at home in the universe. Those who belong to a religion will have their beliefs and practices enriched by the study of the world's religions, because they will learn about their religion's history, major figures, scriptures, and influences from different points of view. Others who have little interest in traditional religions yet nonetheless have a strong interest in spirituality may view their lives as a spiritual quest. For any person involved in a spiritual search, it is extremely helpful to study a variety of religions. Stories of others' spiritual quests provide insights that we may draw on for our own spiritual journey.

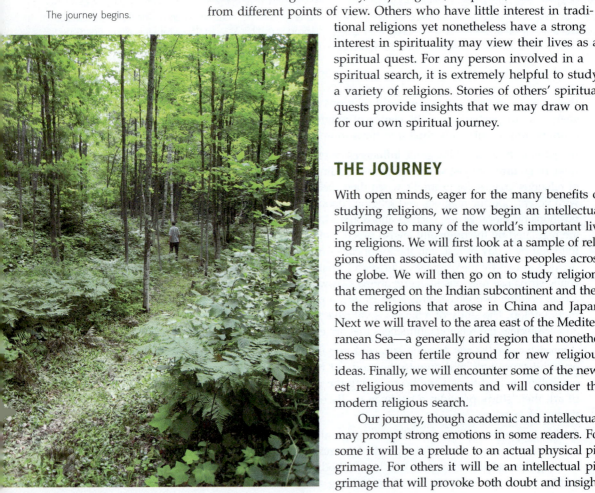

The journey begins.

THE JOURNEY

With open minds, eager for the many benefits of studying religions, we now begin an intellectual pilgrimage to many of the world's important living religions. We will first look at a sample of religions often associated with native peoples across the globe. We will then go on to study religions that emerged on the Indian subcontinent and then to the religions that arose in China and Japan. Next we will travel to the area east of the Mediterranean Sea—a generally arid region that nonetheless has been fertile ground for new religious ideas. Finally, we will encounter some of the newest religious movements and will consider the modern religious search.

Our journey, though academic and intellectual, may prompt strong emotions in some readers. For some it will be a prelude to an actual physical pilgrimage. For others it will be an intellectual pilgrimage that will provoke both doubt and insight.

We begin with the knowledge that at the end of every journey we are not quite the same as we were when we started. Ours is a journey of discovery, and through discovery, we hope to become more appreciative of the experience of being human in the universe.

Reading FINDING WHAT BRINGS JOY

The mythologist Joseph Campbell helped people become sensitive to symbol and myth, which he loved deeply. He followed his path only because it gave him so much joy. The study of mythology became his life's work. Here he describes why.

If you follow your bliss, you put yourself on a kind of track that has been there all the while, waiting for you, and the life that you ought to be living is the one you are living. Wherever you are—if you are following your bliss, you are enjoying that refreshment, that life within you, all the time. . . .

Now, I came to this idea of bliss because in Sanskrit, which is the great spiritual language of the world, there are three terms that represent the brink, the jumping-off place to the ocean of transcendence: sat-chit-ananda. The word "Sat" means being. "Chit" means consciousness. "Ananda" means bliss or rapture. I thought, "I don't know whether my consciousness is proper consciousness or not; I don't know whether what I know of my being is my proper being or not; but I do know where my rapture is. So let me hang on to rapture, and that will bring me both my consciousness and my being." I think it worked.[18]

TEST YOURSELF

1. Religions manifest eight possible elements: belief system, community, central myths, ritual, ethics, characteristic emotional experiences, material expression, and _____.
   a. science
   b. sacredness
   c. dualism
   d. deconstruction

2. The belief that all is divine is called _____.
   a. atheism
   b. monotheism
   c. pantheism
   d. agnosticism

3. _____ argues that the existence of God cannot be proven.
   a. Agnosticism
   b. Pantheism
   c. Monotheism
   d. Nontheism

4. Anthropologist _____ believed that religion was rooted in spirit worship.
   a. James Frazer
   b. E. B. Tylor
   c. Sigmund Freud
   d. Carl Gustav Jung

5. _____ theorized that belief in a God or gods arises from the long-lasting impressions made on adults by their childhood experiences.
   a. James Frazer
   b. E. B. Tylor
   c. Sigmund Freud
   d. Carl Gustav Jung

6. Rudolf Otto argued that religions emerge when people experience that aspect of reality which is essentially mysterious; while _____ believed that religion was a noble human response to the complexity and depth of reality.
   a. James Frazer
   b. E. B. Tylor
   c. Sigmund Freud
   d. Carl Gustav Jung

7. Religions express truth _____. For example, water can represent spiritual cleansing; the sun, health; a mountain, strength; and a circle, eternity.
   a. symbolically
   b. prophetically
   c. mystically
   d. structurally

8. In early religions, the most significant female deity was particularly associated with _____ and motherhood and has been known by many names, such as Asherah, Aphrodite, and Freia.
   a. strength
   b. wisdom
   c. the arts
   d. fertility

9. When we look at the world's dominant religions, we see three basic orientations in their conceptions and location of the sacred: sacramental, prophetic, and _____.
   a. mystical
   b. spiritual
   c. immanent
   d. animistic

10. As an academic discipline, the field of religious studies is now more than _____ years old.
    a. 10
    b. 25
    c. 200
    d. 2,000

11. Based on what you have read in this chapter, what are some benefits of finding patterns among different religions? What are some possible risks?

12. In this chapter we see attempts by numerous thinkers to answer the question, Why does religion exist? Whose idea do you think presents the most interesting insight into religious experience? Why?

RESOURCES

Books

Armstrong, Karen. *The Great Transformation: The Beginning of Our Religious Traditions.* New York: Knopf, 2006. An exploration of the evolution of the world's major religious traditions, written by a popular historian of comparative religion.

Campbell, Joseph, and Bill Moyers. *The Power of Myth.* New York: Doubleday, 1991. An investigation of myths, fairy tales, and religious symbols in readable style.

Dawkins, Richard. *The God Delusion.* New York: Houghton Mifflin, 2006. A book by an evolutionary biologist and atheist that argues the case against belief in God.

Feierman, Jay, ed. *The Biology of Religious Behavior.* Santa Barbara, CA: ABC-CLIO/Praeger, 2009. Explanations of religion that attempt to bridge the gap between religion and science.

Foucault, Michel. *Religion and Culture.* Ed. Jeremy Carette. New York: Routledge, 1999. Writings of Foucault that show his lifelong interest in religious topics.

Haught, John, ed. *Science and Religion in Search of Cosmic Purpose.* Washington, DC: Georgetown University Press, 2001. A search of major religions to see if they can concur with science.

Juschka, Darlene, ed. *Feminism in the Study of Religion: A Reader.* New York: Continuum, 2001. A discussion by feminist scholars of religion from a multicultural perspective.

Lewis-Williams, David. *Conceiving God.* London: Thames & Hudson, 2010. A study of the psychological origin of belief in God.

Pals, Daniel L. *Eight Theories of Religion.* New York: Oxford University Press, 2006. A very readable survey of major theories of the origin and purpose of religion, including theories of Freud, Marx, Eliade, and Evans-Pritchard, with good biographical sketches of the thinkers.

Wright, Robert. *The Evolution of God.* Boston: Little, Brown, 2009. A tracing of the evolution of the concept of gods and God.

Film/TV

Bill Moyers on Faith and Reason. (PBS.) A seven-part miniseries, first broadcast in 2006, that explores the tension between belief and disbelief in religion.

Freud. (Director John Huston; Universal International.) A classic film that sees the young Freud as a hero in a painful search for new understanding of unconscious motivations.

In Search of the Soul. (BBC.) An examination of Jung's vision of reality.

Joseph Campbell and the Power of Myth. (PBS.) A six-part presentation on mythology.

The Question of God: Sigmund Freud and C. S. Lewis. (PBS.) A four-part miniseries that examines belief in God through the context of the lives of Sigmund Freud and C. S. Lewis, two noted intellectuals with sharply divergent views on religious faith.

Internet
American Academy of Religion: http://www.aarweb.org/. Information about conferences, grants, and scholarships, presented by the primary organization of professors of religion in North America.

Internet Sacred Text Archive: http://www.sacred-texts.com/index.htm. An electronic archive of texts about religion, mythology, and folklore.

The Pluralism Project: http://www.pluralism.org/. An excellent resource for studying the many religions now present in the United States.

KEY TERMS

agnosticism: "Not know" (Greek); a position asserting that the existence of God cannot be proven.

animism: From the Latin *anima,* meaning "spirit," "soul," "life force"; a worldview common among oral religions (religions with no written scriptures) that sees all elements of nature as being filled with spirit or spirits.

atheism: "Not God" (Greek); a position asserting that there is no God or gods.

deconstruction: A technique, pioneered by Jacques Derrida, that sets aside ordinary categories of analysis and makes use, instead, of unexpected perspectives on cultural elements; it can be used for finding underlying values in a text, film, artwork, cultural practice, or religious phenomenon.

dualism: The belief that reality is made of two different principles (spirit and matter); the belief in two gods (good and evil) in conflict.

immanent: Existing and operating within nature.

monotheism: The belief in one God.

nontheism: A position that is unconcerned with the supernatural, not asserting or denying the existence of any deity.

pantheism: The belief that everything in the universe is divine.

polytheism: The belief in many gods.

post-structuralism: An analytical approach that does not seek to find universal structures that might underlie language, religion, art, or other such significant areas, but focuses instead on observing carefully the individual elements in cultural phenomena.

structuralism: An analytical approach that looks for universal structures that underlie language, mental processes, mythology, kinship, and religions; this approach sees human activity as largely determined by such underlying structures.

transcendent: "Climbing beyond" (Latin); beyond time and space.

RELIGION BEYOND THE CLASSROOM

Visit the Online Learning Center at www.mhhe.com/molloy6e for additional exercises and features, including "Religion beyond the Classroom" and "For Fuller Understanding."

CHAPTER 2

Indigenous Religions

FIRST ENCOUNTER

As it is for most visitors, your first stop in Hawai`i is crowded Waikiki, on the island of O`ahu.* After four days of swimming, sightseeing, and viewing the sunsets, you fly to Maui for a few days, and then on to the much less populated island of Hawai`i—called the Big Island by local residents. From the airport in Hilo, you begin to drive upcountry, toward the little town of Volcano. The area around Hilo, on the rainy side of the island, resembles the tropical paradise of fantasy: the leaves of the trees are bright lime-colored flames, and the yards of the houses are planted with vanda orchids and fragrant white-flowered plumeria trees.

As you drive inland and upward, lawns and homes yield to fields of beige grass and clusters of dark brown rock. Banyan trees give way to small, silver-leaved `ohi`a lehua bushes, as delicate as their red flowers. Now you are closer to the volcanoes that are still

---

*Note: The `okina (glottal stop mark) is used throughout this book in the spelling of certain Hawaiian words. It is indicated by a backward apostrophe.

producing the island. The land here is raw and relatively new. You check into the old lava-rock hotel near the volcanic crater and look forward to settling in for the night. After supper you listen to ukulele music in front of the big fireplace in the lobby and watch a man and two women perform a slow hula for the guests.

The next morning, after a good sleep, you walk out to the rim of the crater. You are a bit startled by the steam rising through cracks and holes in the rock. You hike down a trail that leads to a bed of old lava, passing yellow ginger and tiny wild purple orchids on the way. The lava in the crater at this spot is dry; it crunches underfoot. Here and there you see stones wrapped in the broad leaves of the *ti* plant and wonder why they're there.

On the way back up the trail, you fall in step with a woman who explains that she was raised on the Big Island but now lives on another island. She is here just for a few days, to visit the volcano area and to see old friends. She tells you about Pele, the goddess of fire, whose place of veneration is the volcano.

"When I was young I learned that Pele came from the island of Kaua`i to Maui, where she lived in Haleakala Crater before she moved to this island. Nowadays, people here are mostly Buddhist or Christian, but they still respect Pele. I know a man who says Pele once appeared to him. He told me she had long hair and was surrounded by fire. Other people have seen her on the road. Pele gets a lot of offerings—mostly ti leaves and food. But when the lava is flowing toward Hilo, people also bring out pork and gin," the woman says with a laugh, "and my friends tell me that the offerings work."

The lava, she explains, is active now at the other end of a series of craters, closer to the ocean. She suggests that you drive to the lava flow before dark and adds, "Be sure to have good walking shoes, as well as a flashlight in case it gets dark before you go back to your car. And don't take any lava rock away with you. They say it brings bad luck, you know."

In midafternoon, you drive down the curving black asphalt road, past old lava flows, to the highway near the ocean. You stop and park near the cars of other lava watchers and then begin hiking with a few people across the fresh lava, toward the ocean. About half a mile in, you encounter yellow caution strips and overhear an officer warning one man to stop. "Farther on it's just too dangerous. It looks solid on top, but you can slip through the crust." You and the others crowd up next to the barriers and see steam rising on the right up ahead. Through the rising steam you glimpse a bright orange band of molten lava underneath the dry crust as the lava falls into the ocean.

Sunset comes quickly, and even more people arrive, some with blankets around their shoulders. As darkness falls, the flowing lava becomes more visible, and the steam takes on a reddish glow. "Look over there," someone says. In the distance a bright stream of orange lava slides down a hill, a slow-motion waterfall of fire. You watch at least an hour as the sky becomes completely dark. Now the only light comes from the flowing lava and a few flashlights. It is, you think, like being present at the time of creation: this land is being born.

The next morning in the lobby you see the Hawaiian woman again. "Well, did you see Pele last night?" she asks, smiling. You smile back. For the rest of your stay you wonder about Pele, about what else might remain of native Hawaiian religion. Isn't hula, you ask as you think back over what you've read, an expression of Hawaiian beliefs? Why do people make offerings of ti leaves? How much of the ancient religion lives on?

DISCOVERING INDIGENOUS RELIGIONS

The practice of native religions takes place throughout the world. Among the Ainu of far northern Japan, the Inuit (Eskimo) of Canada, the aboriginal peoples of Australia, the Maori of New Zealand, and the many indigenous peoples of Africa and the Americas, religious teachings have been passed on primarily by word of mouth rather than through written texts. In some areas, the ancient religious ways of traditional peoples may not be easily apparent, but certain characteristics live on in local stories and customs.

There is no agreement on how to speak of these ancient religious ways. Various terms include *traditional, aboriginal, indigenous, tribal, nonliterate, primal, native, oral,* and *basic.* Each term is inadequate. For example, although the word *native* is used frequently in the Americas, that term in Africa—with memories of colonial offices of native affairs—can be offensive. The words *oral* and *nonliterate* describe correctly the fact that most indigenous religions were spread without written texts. But there have been exceptions: the Mayans and Aztecs, for example, had writing systems, and even many native religions without writing systems have had their sacred stories and beliefs written down by scholars at some point. The distinction between oral religions and others is also blurred by the fact that religions that have written texts are also, to a large degree, transmitted orally—for example, through preaching, teaching, and chanting. The term *traditional* would be suitable, except that all religions but the very newest have many traditional elements. Some terms, such as *primal* and *basic,* may be viewed as derogatory (like the older term *primitive religions*). The word *indigenous* has the advantage of being neutral in tone; however, it means the same thing as *native,* except that it comes from Greek rather than Latin. There is no easy solution. Although *indigenous* comes closest to capturing these ancient religions, we will use several of the preceding terms interchangeably throughout the text.

Indigenous religions are found in every climate, from the tropical rain forest to the arctic tundra, and some are far older than today's dominant religions. Because most of them developed in isolation from each other, there are major differences in their stories of creation and origin, in their beliefs about the afterlife, in their marriage and funeral customs, and so on. In fact, there is as much variation among indigenous religions as there is, for example, between Buddhism and Christianity. In North America, for instance, there are several hundred Native American nations and more than fifty Native American language groups. The variety among indigenous religious traditions is stunning, and each religion deserves in-depth study. But because of the limitations of space, this book must focus on shared elements; regrettably, we can barely touch on the many differences. (You can complement your study of basic patterns by making your own study of a native religion, especially one practiced now or in the past by the indigenous peoples of the area in which you live.)

Past Obstacles to the Appreciation of Indigenous Religions

Up until the early part of the twentieth century, scholars focused more on religions that had produced written texts than on those that expressed themselves through orally transmitted stories, histories, and rituals. This lack of attention to oral religions may have been due in part to the relative ease of studying religions with written records. Religions with written records don't necessarily require travel or physically arduous research. Moreover, when scholars have mastered reading the necessary languages, they can study, translate, and teach the original writings either at home or to students anywhere.

There has also been a bias toward text-based religions because of a misconception that they are complex and that oral religions are simple. Greater research into oral religions, however, has dispelled such notions of simplicity. Consider, for example, the sandpaintings of the Navajo people and the ceremonies of which the paintings are a part. "In these ceremonies, which are very complicated and intricate, sandpaintings are made and prayers recited. Sandpaintings are impermanent paintings made of dried pulverized materials that depict the Holy People [gods] and serve as a temporary altar. Over 800 forms of sandpaintings exist, each connected to a specific chant and ceremony."[1]

Indigenous religions have, of course, created much that is permanent, and sometimes even monumental. We have only to think of the Mayan pyramids in Yucatán and the great city of Teotihuacán, near Mexico City. But native religions often express themselves in ways that have less permanence: dance, masks, wood sculpture, paintings that utilize mineral and plant dyes, tattoo, body painting, and memorized story and chant. Perhaps we have to begin to see these transitory expressions of religious art as being equal in stature to more permanent sacred writings and artistic creations. In speaking of African art, one scholar has called it the "indigenous language of African belief and thought," even saying that African art "provides a kind of scripture of African religion."[2] We also have to see that indigenous religions have sometimes blended with more dominant religions. For example, elements of Mayan religion live on in the Catholicism of Mexico and Guatemala, and elements of belief in nature gods live on in the Buddhism of Myanmar (Burma). This blending has made the existence of indigenous religions less obvious, but sometimes it has also made their continued existence possible.

The Modern Recovery of Indigenous Religions

We know about native religious traditions through the efforts of scholars from a number of disciplines, particularly anthropology. One pioneer was Franz Boas (1858–1942), a professor at Columbia University and curator at the American Museum of Natural History in New York. Other notable contributors to this field include Bronislaw Malinowski (1884–1942), Raymond Firth (1901–2002), Mary Douglas (1921–2007), and E. E. Evans-Pritchard (mentioned in Chapter 1).

The ecological movement has also made our study of indigenous religions more pressing. Environmentalist David Suzuki argues that we must look to native peoples and religions for insightful lessons in the relationship between human beings and nature. In his introduction to the book *Wisdom of the Elders,* he writes that the earth is rapidly moving toward what he calls "ecocrisis." He quotes the ecologist Paul Ehrlich in saying that solutions will have to be "quasi-religious." Suzuki argues that "our problem is inherent in the way we perceive our relationship with the rest of Nature and our role in the grand scheme of things. Harvard biologist E. O. Wilson proposes that

These masked dancers in Papua New Guinea celebrate spirits of their ancestors.

we foster *biophilia,* a love of life. He once told me, 'We must rediscover our *kin,* the other animals and plants with whom we share this planet.'"[3]

Some of this interest derives, of course, from a sometimes romanticized view of native peoples and their relationship with nature. We should recognize that some native peoples, such as the Kwakiutl of the Pacific Northwest, have viewed nature as dangerously violent, and others have seriously damaged their natural environment. Despite such cases, one finds in many indigenous religions extraordinary sensitivity to the natural elements.

The development of photography and sound recording has helped the recovery of native religious traditions. Photography captures native styles of life and allows them to be seen with a certain immediacy. Ethnomusicology involves the recording of chants and the sounds of musical instruments that might otherwise be lost. Gladys Reichard, a specialist who pioneered the study of the ritual life of the Navajo (Diné), has written that chanters in the Navajo religion need to memorize an "incalculable" number—that is, thousands—of songs.[4] The fact that listeners can replay such recordings has no doubt added to the appreciation of this music.

In this old photo, we see women in Okinawa undergoing priestly initiation.

All our histories, traditions, codes were passed from one generation to another by word of mouth. Our memories must be kept clear and accurate, our observation must be keen, our self-control absolute.

—Thomas Wildcat Alford, Shawnee[7]

Artists in many cultures, trying to go beyond their own limited artistic traditions, have found inspiration in native wood sculpture, masks, drums, and textile design. Pablo Picasso (1881–1973), for example, often spoke of the strong influence that African religious masks had on his work. By the early 1900s, West African masks had found their way to Paris and the artists there. A scholar describes the effect of one African work on several artists who were close friends. "One piece . . . is a mask that had been given to Maurice Vlaminck in 1905. He records that [André] Derain was 'speechless' and 'stunned' when he saw it, bought it from Vlaminck and in turn showed it to Picasso and Matisse, who were also greatly affected by it."[5] French artist Paul Gauguin moved to Tahiti and the Marquesas to find and paint what he hoped was a fundamental form of religion there, and some of his paintings allude to native Tahitian religious belief.[6] Gauguin thereby hoped to go beyond the limited views of his European background. The work of such artists as Picasso and Gauguin helped to open eyes to the beauty produced by indigenous religions.

Of course, the religious art of native peoples needs no authentication from outsiders. And outsiders present a problem: they tend to treat native religious objects as purely secular works of art, while people within an indigenous religious tradition do not make such a distinction. Indigenous religions exist generally within **holistic** cultures, in which every object and act may have religious meaning. Art, music, religion, and social behavior within such cultures can be so inseparable that it is hard to say what is distinctly religious and what is not. Although we can find a similar attitude among very pious practitioners of the dominant world religions, for whom every act is religious, people in modern, industrial cultures commonly see the secular and religious realms as separate.

Fortunately, the bias that once judged native religions to be "primitive" manifestations of the religious spirit—as opposed to the literate, so-called higher religions—is disappearing. It is an inescapable fact that the span of written religions is relatively brief—barely five thousand years—yet scientists now hold that human beings have lived on earth for at least a million (and possibly two or three million) years. Although we do not know how long human beings have been manifesting religious behavior, we believe it goes back as long as human beings have been capable of abstract thought.

STUDYING INDIGENOUS RELIGIONS: LEARNING FROM PATTERNS

The study of indigenous religious traditions presents its own specific challenges. Happily, oral traditions are being written down, translated, and published. Yet our understanding of these religions depends not only on written records but also on field study by anthropologists, ethnomusicologists, and others.

It would be ideal if we could study and experience each native religion separately; barring that, however, one workable approach is to consider them collectively as "sacred paths" that share common elements. Thus, in this chapter we will concentrate on finding patterns in native religions—while keeping in mind that beyond the patterns there is enormous variety. The patterns we identify in indigenous religions will also enrich our encounter with other religions in later chapters. Three key patterns we will consider are the human relationship with nature, the framing of sacred time and space, and the respect for origins, gods, and ancestors.

Human Relationships with the Natural World

Most indigenous religions have sprung from tribal cultures of small numbers, whose survival has required a cautious and respectful relationship with nature. In the worldview of these religions, human beings are very much a part of nature. People look to nature itself (sometimes interpreted through traditional lore) for guidance and meaning.

Some native religions see everything in the universe as being alive, a concept known as *animism* (which we discussed briefly in Chapter 1). The life force (Latin: *anima*) is present in everything and is especially apparent in living things—trees, plants, birds, animals, and human beings—and in the motion of water, the sun, the moon, clouds, and wind. But life force can also be present in apparently static mountains, rocks, and soil. Other native religions, while more theistic, see powerful spirits in nature, which temporarily inhabit natural objects and manifest themselves there.

In an animistic worldview, everything can be seen as part of the same reality. There may be no clear boundaries between the natural and supernatural and between the human and nonhuman. Everything has both its visible ordinary reality and a deeper, invisible sacred reality. Four Oglala Sioux shamans, when asked about what was *wakan* ("holy," "mysterious"), said, "Every object in the world has a spirit and that spirit is *wakan*. Thus the spirit[s] of the tree or things of that kind, while not like the spirit of man, are also *wakan*."[8] To say that nature is full of spirits can be a way of affirming the presence of both a universal life force and an essential, underlying sacredness.

Among many peoples, particular objects—a specific rock, tree, or river—are thought of as being animated by an individual spirit that lives within. And in some native traditions, we find deities that care about and influence a whole category of reality, such as the earth, water, or air. Among the

Deeper Insights

AUSTRALIAN ABORIGINAL RELIGION

Aboriginal people came to Australia from Asia, probably via a land bridge, about forty thousand to sixty thousand years ago. From the north of the continent they spread throughout Australia, eventually evolving into many groups and languages. At the time of the first European contact, there were several hundred Aboriginal languages. Now there are fewer than a hundred, and some of these are close to extinction. Although Christianity is currently the majority religion of Australian Aboriginal people, indigenous religions are still alive and are becoming increasingly significant.

No single Aboriginal religion exists, but there are many similarities among them. Perhaps the best known is belief in the Dreamtime—an early creative period when legendary gods and ancestors created the mountains, rivers, and other features of the earth. Another is belief in the Rainbow Serpent, a divine figure of power that appears in the rainbow and in water and that shaped the rivers and mountains. (The Rainbow Serpent has many indigenous names.) The early creative figures have a prominent place in Aboriginal art and music, which tell their stories.

Because the Aboriginal peoples were nomadic, they did not create great temples. And because of the generally warm climate, the peoples did not need intricate clothing. But the Australian Aboriginal peoples told complex stories of their origins that linked elements of nature with the gods. As the people experienced everyday life, they recalled their stories of the gods and ancestors. Dreams also made it possible to be in contact with the gods and ancestors.

Aboriginal art presents many figures from the Dreamtime—particularly the Rainbow Serpent, the lizard, and the kangaroo. These are presented along with dots, geometric figures, circles, and swirls in strong, stylized forms. In the last fifty years, Aboriginal carving, painting, and music have grown in popularity both within and outside the Aboriginal communities. They appear in public places and are now also influencing other religions in Australia.

Aboriginal dot painting of an Emu.

Yoruba of Africa, storms are the work of the deity Shangó, a legendary king with great powers who climbed to heaven (see Chapter 11). The Igbo (Ibo) pray to Ala, an earth-mother deity, for fertility of the earth. Women also pray to her for children, and men pray to her to increase their crops. In the Ashanti religion, Ta Yao is the god of metal. The work of blacksmiths and mechanics is under his charge.[9]

In a world that is animated by spirits, human beings must treat all things with care. If a spirit is injured or insulted, it can retaliate. Human beings must therefore show that they respect nature, especially the animals and plants that they kill to eat. Human beings must understand the existence and ways of the spirit world so that they can avoid harm and incur blessings. (We will revisit this spirit world later, when we discuss trance states and the spiritual specialist, the shaman.)

Native American religions are noted for their reverential attitude toward the natural world; human beings and animals are often pictured as coming into existence together, and the sun, moon, trees, and animals are all considered kin. Hehaka Sapa, or Black Elk, an Oglala Sioux, although he had become a Christian, explained the sense of relationship to nature that he had experienced when he was growing up among his people in South Dakota. In his autobiography, which he dictated in 1930, he points out that his community, which traditionally lived in *tipis* (circular tents made of animal skins and poles), arranges itself in a circle—as does all nature, which is constantly making circles, just like the sun, the moon, and the whirlwind.

Native American religions often express the kinship bond between human beings and animals in ritual. (To a lesser extent, some other religions do this, as well.) Åke Hultkrantz, a Swedish scholar, clarifies with an example the meaning of many dances that imitate animals. "Plains Indian dances in which men imitate the movements of buffaloes . . . are not, as earlier research took for granted, magic rituals to multiply the animals. They are rather acts of supplication in which Indians, by imitating the wild, express their desires and expectations. Such a ritual tells us the Indian's veneration for the active powers of the universe: it is a prayer."[10]

In many Native American religious traditions, there is little distinction between the human and animal worlds; rather, there is a sense of kinship. To exploit nature mindlessly is even thought to be as sacrilegious as harming one's own mother. As Smohalla of the Nez Perce people said, "You ask me to plow the ground. Shall I take a knife and tear my mother's breast? Then when I die she will not take me to her bosom to rest."[12]

Native religions also frequently embrace an ethic of restraint and conservation concerning nature's resources. One is expected to take only what one needs and to use all the parts of an animal or plant. In traditional Hawai`i, for example, fishing in certain areas would be temporarily forbidden (*kapu,* or taboo) in order to allow the fish population to be replenished. Of course, the ideal is never universally maintained, and even native peoples

> Birds make their nests in circles, for theirs is the same religion as ours.
>
> —Black Elk, Oglala Sioux[11]

have sometimes been unaware of the destructive effects of their actions. Consider, for example, the devastation of the beaver by native peoples in North America who sold the pelts to European traders, or the cutting of most sandalwood trees by native Hawaiians for sale in China. Given examples like these, it is clear that native peoples who did not live in harmony with nature could not long survive.

It is difficult, perhaps, for urban human beings today to experience fully the intimate connection with the rest of nature that has been a common aspect of native religions. The predominant contemporary view sees human beings as fundamentally different from other animals. Perhaps this tendency is a result of our modern culture, which emphasizes the skills of writing and reading. We also have little connection with the origins of our food, and we live and work indoors. Electric light diminishes our awareness of day and night and obstructs the light of the moon and stars. Except for insects, rodents, and the most common birds, we seldom see wildlife firsthand. Traffic noise drowns out the sounds of wind, rain, and birdsong.

In contrast, consider the sense of kinship with animals found, for example, among the Haida people of the Pacific Northwest: "the Haida refer to whales and ravens as their 'brothers' and 'sisters' and to fish and trees as the finned and tree *people*."[13]

Another example of contrast is apparent in the way the BaMbuti, forest dwellers of central Africa, perceive their forest. Outsiders might find the darkness and thick foliage frightening. But, as one anthropologist has written, for the people who live within it and love it, the forest "is their world. . . . They know how to distinguish the innocent-looking *itaba* vine from the many others it resembles so closely, and they know how to follow it until it leads them to a cache of nutritious, sweet-tasting roots. They know the tiny sounds that tell where the bees have hidden their honey; they recognize the kind of weather that brings a multitude of different kinds of mushrooms springing to the surface. . . . They know the secret language that is denied all outsiders and without which life in the forest is an impossibility."[14]

Sacred Time and Sacred Space

Our everyday lives go on in ordinary time, which we see as moving forward into the future. Sacred time, however, is "the time of eternity." Among the Koyukon people of the Arctic it is called "distant time," and it is the holy ancient past in which the gods lived and worked.[15] Among Australian Aborigines it is often called Dreamtime, and it is the subject of much of their highly esteemed art.

Sacred time is cyclical, returning to its origins for renewal. By recalling and ritually reliving the deeds of the gods and ancestors, we enter into the sacred time in which they live. Indigenous religions even tend to structure daily lives in ways that conform to mythic events in sacred time; this creates a sense of holiness in everyday life.

A woman sits quietly in Ireland's Drombeg Stone Circle, where particular stones are aligned with the setting sun on the winter solstice.

Like ordinary time, ordinary space exists in the everyday. Sacred space, however, is the doorway through which the "other world" of gods and ancestors can contact us and we can contact them. Sacred space is associated with the center of the entire universe, where power and holiness are strongest and where we can go to renew our own strength.

In native religions, sacred space may encompass a great mountain, a volcano, a valley, a lake, a forest, a single large tree, or some other striking natural site. For Black Elk and his people, after the Lakota had moved west, it was Harney Peak in South Dakota. In Australian Aboriginal religion, Uluru (Ayers Rock) has served as this sacred center. In Africa, Mount Kilimanjaro and other high mountains have been considered sacred spaces.

Sacred space can also be constructed, often in a symbolic shape such as a circle or square, and defined by a special building or by a boundary made of rope or rocks, such as Stonehenge in England. It can even be an open area among trees or buildings, such as the great open space between the temples of Teotihuacán, near Mexico City.

Respect for Origins, Gods, and Ancestors

Origins Most indigenous religions have cosmic tales of their origins that are regularly recited or enacted through ritual and dance. Some tell how the world originated from a supernatural realm. According to other emergence stories, the earth rose out of previous earths or from earlier, more chaotic material forms. Often the land and creatures emerged from watery depths. In a Hopi creation story, the earth, before it took shape, was mist.

Deeper Insights

RELIGION OF THE PUEBLO PEOPLES

One of the great sights of the world is the group of multistoried buildings hidden high up in the cliffs at Mesa Verde, Colorado. Inhabited for more than seven hundred years, the now-empty buildings give an unparalleled view into the life of the Ancestral Pueblo peoples (also called Hisatsinom and Anasazi). Visitors can walk down from the top of the cliff, via narrow stone paths and stairs, to visit some of the houses and to experience the plazas that were once used for ceremonial dance. Visitors can then climb down a wooden ladder to enter a *kiva*, a dark and womb-like ritual chamber beneath the surface. There they can see the *sipapu*, the hole in the floor that is a symbol of the emergence of human beings into this world. The kiva and sipapu show how thoroughly oriented to the earth the religion practiced here was.

Similar cliff dwellings may be seen at Canyon de Chelly in Arizona and at Bandelier National Monument in New Mexico. In New Mexico one may also visit the great spiritual center of Chaco Canyon, once a flourishing city. Tens of thousands of pilgrims would come here

regularly, and as many as forty thousand would be present at the time of the twice-yearly solstices. This site is sacred to the Pueblo peoples even today.

The religious life of the Ancestral Pueblo peoples is not fully known, but some evidence comes from traces of ancient roads and from archeology, petroglyphs, and paintings. Some of their buildings were oriented to coincide with the solstices and equinoxes. The presence of kivas suggests that ceremony took place there, and in some of the kivas the remains of wall paintings have been found. Remaining petroglyphs show elements from nature, including stars and the moon, and in the period from about 1200 to 1250 CE there was a profuse growth of the cult and imagery of *kachinas*—benevolent guardian spirits who are believed to appear among the people on ceremonial occasions (and whom we will discuss in a moment).*

---

*Note: This text uses the time designations BCE ("before the Common Era") and CE ("of the Common Era") in place of the Christianity-centered abbreviations BC ("before Christ") and AD (*anno Domini*, "in the year of the Lord").

The kiva at Chaco is an important ancestral site for the Pueblo peoples.

When the large settlements, such as the one at Mesa Verde, were abandoned, their people moved to villages—primarily in modern-day northeastern Arizona and northwestern New Mexico—but they took with them their religious beliefs, images, and ritual, especially the cult of the kachinas. The traditional style of multistoried buildings continued, as well, suggesting to the Spanish colonizers the name by which the peoples are still commonly known: *pueblo* (Spanish: "village").

The Pueblo peoples share many features of their architecture, governance, and religious practice, but there are also great differences among them in all these areas. Each of the more than two dozen pueblos governs itself independently, and multiple languages are spoken: Keresan, Zunian, three Tanoan dialects (Tiwa, Tewa, and Towa), and Hopi. The independence of each pueblo may have actually been to its advantage, helping each unique culture to survive. Despite the pressures to change, the Pueblo peoples have kept their identities intact—particularly through fidelity to their religious beliefs and practices.

Each pueblo has its own religious traditions. Here we will touch on just a few. The stories of human origins

differ among the peoples and clans, but many tell of human emergence from a lower world, of assistance from supernatural beings in learning to live, of help from animals, and of wanderings before final settlement. Among the seven Keresan-speaking pueblos, for example, the story of origin tells of how people moved upward through four different-colored worlds. Standing in an eagle's nest on top of a tree, with the help of a woodpecker and a badger, they made a hole large enough to climb up into this world.

Religious symbolism is complex. Among the Zía, for example, four is a sacred number. It symbolizes the four seasons, four directions, and four stages of life (infancy, youth, adulthood, and old age). It is used in many designs found in Zía art. (The state flag of New Mexico, which shows a crosslike symbol made of four lines in each of the four directions, is based on a Zía design.)

Some of the Pueblo peoples, influenced by Christianity, are monotheists, but many retain a belief in the traditional deities, and they sense no disharmony. The Great Spirit, they believe, can take many forms. Among the Hopis, for example, more than thirty gods are recognized. Perhaps the most important are Tawa, the sun god,

(continued)

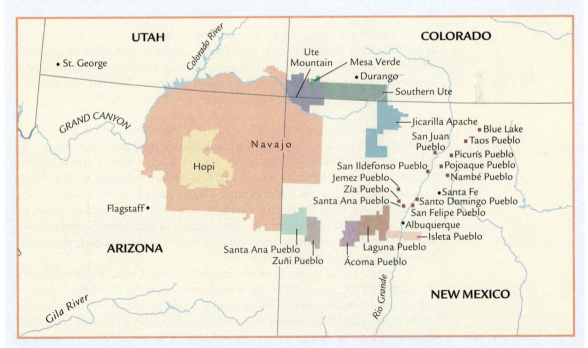

FIGURE 2.1 The Pueblo peoples and other Native American tribes of the American Southwest.

prayed to each morning; Mu-yao, the moon god, imagined as an old man; Sotuqnangu, god of the sky, who sends clouds and lightning; and Kokyang Wuuti, called Spider Woman in English, who is thought of as a loving grandmother.

Among all the Pueblo peoples there is a belief in guardian spirits, who play a role something like angels and patron saints. These are the kachinas. They are not gods but rather the spirits of ancestors, birds, animals, plants, and other beings. They are believed to have once lived among the people and then to have retreated to their own world; but they return yearly. Human beings represent them when dressed in specific masks and costumes.

One of the most complex systems of belief in guardian spirits is found among the Hopis, whose traditional religion has been least affected by other cultures. From February through the summer, dancers represent the spirits, and more than two hundred different masked figures appear in the dances. In the Hopi language they are called *katsinam* (singular: *katsina*). Bird and animal spirits are based on many birds and animals, including the deer, badger, sheep, cow, horse,

hummingbird, and eagle; and nature spirits express the rain cloud, rainbow, moon, and fertile earth. Some figures show human characteristics, such as warriors, corn-grinding maidens, guards, clowns, and children. There is also a wide variety of ogrelike figures. Each has a name, special costume, and specific mask. The Zuñi recognize similar guardian spirits, whom they call *koko*.

The Hopi and the Zuñi are also well known for their painted representations of these spirits, called *tithu* (singular: *tihu*). (Outsiders know the figurines as "kachina dolls.") They are re-creations in miniature of the masked kachina figures that dance in the villages. The tithu were originally created to be given as gifts from the masked dancers to girls in the villages—a form of religious teaching through images. But they have become collectors' items, cherished by outsiders.

Visitors who have the privilege of observing Pueblo ceremonies come away with a renewed appreciation for the variety of religious paths and a sense of amaze-ment at the persistence through the centuries of such beautiful, ancient ways.

Stories of the origin of a tribe may be connected with its story of the earth's creation. Among the Ácoma Pueblo, there is a story of two sisters who lived entirely underground. Eventually they climbed up the roots of a tree and into the sunlight through a hole in the ground, to become the first human beings on earth. One became mother of the Pueblo.[16]

Gods Native religions frequently speak of a High God who is superior to all other deities and is considered to be wise, ancient, and benevolent. The Inuit speak of a Great Spirit living in the sky who is female and to whom all human spirits eventually return. In a few African religions, too, the High God is female, neuter, or androgynous; and in some religions there are two complementary High Gods, characterized as male/female, brother/sister, or bad/good. The BaKuta of central Africa speak of the twins Nzambi-above and Nzambi-below, although in their myths the lower twin disappears and Nzambi-above becomes the High God.[17]

In some African religions, stories of the High God, who is almost always the creator of the world, offer some explanation for the ills of the world or the distance between human beings and the divine. Many African religions tell how the High God created the world and then left it—sometimes out of dismay at human beings or simply for lack of interest. "Many people of central and southern Africa say that God (Mulungu) lived on earth at first, but men began to kill his servants and set fire to the bush, and so God retired

As part of indigenous New Year's festivities in northern Thailand, elders in front of an ancestral altar receive homage from family members.

to heaven on one of those giant spiders' webs that seem to hang from the sky in morning mists. In Burundi, however, it is said that having made good children God created a cripple, and its parents were so angry that they tried to kill God and he went away."[18] The High God in African religions, however, is not always remote. The Diola, for example, believe in direct, prophetic revelation from the High God, and the Igbo and Shona have oracles from the supreme being. While monotheism is common in African religions, it can express itself in many ways.

Although indigenous religions often revere a High God, altars and imagery dedicated to a High God are not common. Large temples, temple ritual, and priesthoods have been found in a few cultures, such as in Mexico and western Africa, but these elements are rare. Instead, in their prayer, ritual, and art many native religions tend to focus on lesser deities, especially those associated with the forces of nature. More commonly, ceremonies in indigenous religions are performed at small-scale shrines or meeting places. Sometimes the religious ceremonies occur indoors, such as in a

These kachina figures represent the spirits of ancestors.

sweat lodge or *kiva* (a submerged meeting hall). At other times they occur outdoors, at a riverbank, beside a rock formation, or in a grove of trees.

Ancestors   Many indigenous religions make little distinction between a god and an ancestor. Both are important, because living people must work with both for success in life. Spirits of ancestors must be treated well out of love for them, but also out of respect for their power. Some native religions, such as that of the Navajo, distance themselves from the spirits of the dead, fearing them. But more commonly the dead are venerated. In African religions, ancestor spirits are commonly thought to bring health, wealth, and children if they are pleased, and disease and childlessness if they are not. The way to appease angry ancestors is through ritual, sometimes including sacrifice. The ancestors often are thought to live in an afterlife that is a state of existence much like earthly life. Belief in reincarnation is found sometimes, as in native Tahitian religion and in many African religions, from the Diola of Senegal to the BaKongo of the Congo region. In traditional Hawaiian religion, it was believed that the spirits of the dead went to an underworld, while the spirits of cultural heroes ascended into the sky.

SACRED PRACTICES IN INDIGENOUS RELIGIONS

In native societies, everyday religious activity and practice are significant because their primary purpose is often to place individuals, families, and groups in "right relationships" with gods, ancestors, other human beings, and nature. Rituals are the basic way in which human beings ensure they are living in harmony with each other and with nature. Rituals are frequently devoted to major aspects of human life: key events in the life cycle, rules concerning certain kinds of behavior, sacrifice, and access to the spirit world. In addition, artifacts such as masks and statues are an essential part of specific rituals.

Life-Cycle Ceremonies

In indigenous societies, the human journey through life is aided and marked by rites of passage. In addition to being important to the individual, these rites also help hold the society together by renewing bonds and admitting new members to the community.

Rites of passage mark an important life event, such as the birth of a child. In some native religions, a woman about to give birth goes off by herself to bear her child at a sacred site or in a house built for that purpose.

Read myths. They teach you that you can turn inward, and you begin to get the message of the symbols. Read other people's myths, not those of your own religion, because you tend to interpret your own religion in terms of facts—but if you read the other ones, you begin to get the message.

—Joseph Campbell[19]

Birth is considered a powerful time for the mother and child, and the blood associated with it is believed to have dangerous power.

After the birth, the newborn is often celebrated with a public event that may occur immediately or anytime from a week to a year after the actual birth. In some parts of Africa, babies do not become members of the community until they receive their names in a special public ceremony that is accompanied by song, dance, and a meal. A name is chosen carefully because of the influence it is thought to have on the child's future.

Special rituals also mark a person's entry into adulthood. They may include a period of instruction in sex, adult responsibilities, and tribal history and belief. They often involve an initiation ritual that may be experienced in seclusion or in the company of other initiates. Rites can include a symbolic death—painful and frightening—meant to turn a boy into a man. Across Africa, circumcision for boys in their early teens is a common rite for entering adulthood.

In western Africa, initiation societies oversee coming-of-age rituals. "The Poro [a secret initiation society] is for boys, controlled by a hierarchy of elders, different in each village, which meets in a sacred grove where the clan founder was buried. The purpose of the initiation is the rebirth of the youths, who are said to be swallowed by the Poro spirit at the beginning and returned to their parents as reborn at the end of the initiation."[20] A parallel initiation society exists for girls, who receive sexual instruction and training in the skills necessary for marriage.

A girl's first menstrual period may also be marked publicly. For example, among the Apache, a four-day ceremony marks a girl's *menarche* (first menstruation). During the ceremony, which is elaborate, the girl performs a dance, receives a massage from her female sponsor, kneels to receive the rays of the sun, and circles repeatedly around a ceremonial cane.

In Native American religions, a common ritual of early maturity is the "vision quest," or "dream quest," which may involve prolonged fasting and some kind of preliminary cleansing, such as washing or undergoing a sweat bath. Details of the construction of the sweat lodge and the attendant ritual can include cutting willow branches, during which tobacco might be offered; gathering sticks, rocks, moss, and sweet grass; making an altar and heating a stone; rubbing smoke over the body; marking the ground; and saying appropriate prayers at each stage.

Some indigenous peoples of western Canada erect totem poles, often in front of their houses, to honor ancestors. Images on the totem pole are related to the ancestor's life story.

An Ojibwe practitioner explains uses of the sweat lodge and fire pit to visitors during the summer.

There, when I was young, the spirits took me in my vision to the center of the earth and showed me all the good things in the sacred hoop of the world.

—Black Elk, speaking of his vision quest at age nine.[22]

For years before the vision quest, the young person may receive training to prepare for the experience. Commonly, a tribal religious specialist will create a sacred space by ritually marking the four directions of the compass and the center. The sacred space, set apart from the community, should be a place of natural beauty.

The seeker remains in the sacred space until a vision, or dream, comes. Although the vision quest is often a part of the coming-of-age ceremonies for males, among some peoples it is also employed for females. The vision quest may be used at other times, too—particularly when the individual or the group must make an important life decision.

In indigenous societies, as in many other cultures, marriage is a ritual that not only publicly affirms and stabilizes a union but also cements economic arrangements and, through the ceremony, ensures fertility. In both Africa and North America, however, marriage in tribal cultures often has been a practical arrangement. Among Native American peoples, marriage has frequently been celebrated simply as a social contract that is worked out by the families. Monogamy has been the norm, but divorce is acceptable when a marriage is not successful. In indigenous African religions, marriage is sometimes marked by rituals to unite the two lineages and transfer the power of fertility; but often its religious aspect "is not distinctive. It is regarded as the normal sequel to rites of adolescence, whose purpose was to prepare for this state."[21]

As the final passing from this life, death is accompanied by rituals that serve to comfort close relatives, assist the spirit of the dead person in moving on, and protect the living from bad influences that could come from an unhappy spirit. Because the spirit of the dead person may be sad to leave the family circle, it must be helped to make its trip to the spirit world. Relatives and friends assist by placing clothing, food, money, and favorite objects with the body. In the case of a chief or other notable person, the body may be embalmed or mummified for public display until a large funeral can be arranged. In the past, great African chiefs have had wives, children, and servants buried alongside them. Among Native American tribes, the sacrifice of relatives and attendants to accompany a dead leader has also occurred. For example, after the death of the Natchez leader Tattooed Serpent in 1725, two of his wives and six others, after preparation by fasting, were strangled as a part of the funeral ritual.[23] In Native American religions, bodies of the dead are usually buried, but sometimes they are placed on platforms or in trees.

Deeper Insights

THE IGBO: AN INDIGENOUS RELIGION IN TRANSITION

Today, at least six million Igbo (or Ibo, pronounced *ee ̄ -bo*) live in western Africa, mostly in the nation of Nigeria. While there are some variations among tribes, traditional Igbo people worship the goddess of the earth (Ala) and various spirits (*alusi*), such as the spirit of the river, the spirit of the yam, and the spirit of the hearth. Many Igbo worship a High God (Chukwu, or Chineke), conceived of as the creator. They also venerate the souls of ancestors, who are believed to have power over the lives of their descendants. The Igbo believe that each person has a unique spirit (*chi*), which plays a major role in determining the person's fate.

Within Igbo religion, special rituals mark significant life events. Daily ritual takes place in the home at a central shrine with wooden images of ancestors. These images receive regular offerings of food, drink, and sometimes the blood of sacrificial animals. Religious rites mark the naming of children, marriage, planting, and harvest. The most important and complex rituals occur at funerals, when the Igbo believe they must help the deceased enter the spirit world contentedly. For these ceremonies, the Igbo have developed elaborate masks for use in religious dances and masquerades.

Christian missionaries began to work among the Igbo in the mid-nineteenth century. Throughout the British colonization of Nigeria in the nineteenth and the twentieth centuries, the Church of England, also known as the Anglican Church, sent many missionaries to the region. Catholic missionaries, who arrived after 1880, were also successful with conversions. As a result, Christian belief and practice have strongly influenced Igbo religion. Sometimes Christianity has displaced traditional beliefs and practices. But more commonly, in varied forms of religious syncretism (blending), the two religions have mixed and sometimes even produced new independent religions.

Many parallels between traditional Igbo faith and Christianity assisted the mixing of the two religions. The High God of the Igbo resembles the Creator Father God of Christianity. Igbo spirits of nature resemble Christian angels, and souls of Igbo ancestors intercede on behalf of the living, as do Christian saints. Igbo belief in an individual's spirit resembles Christian belief in the soul.

Although Christianity prohibits traditional Igbo polygamy, other elements of older practice remain. Igbo who worship at Christian churches on Sunday may visit traditional priests and shrines during the week in order to seek the advice and help of the spirits. And the souls of ancestors continue to receive veneration. Masquerades are used even for celebrating Christmas, a major national holiday in Nigeria.

What has happened among the Igbo is quite typical of what has happened throughout sub-Saharan Africa. Christianity is becoming the dominant religion, but its flavor is African.

Dancers are chosen by their villages to perform in masks at the annual Ibo yam festival, called Onwa Asato.

Rituals and Celebrations

THE VISION QUEST

Among the Ojibwe, who live in the northern plains and Great Lakes area of North America, fasting was often expected of children as preparation for a great fast upon reaching puberty. Girls were expected to make a special fast at menarche, but boys were expected, in addition, to undertake a vision quest. Frequently, religious instruction and purification were an introduction. Then the Ojibwe boy "was led deep into the forest, where a lofty red pine tree was selected. In this tree, a platform of woven sticks covered with moss was placed upon a high branch as a bed upon which the youth was to conduct the fast. Perhaps a canopy of branches would be prepared to shelter him from the wind and rain. Left alone in this place, the youth was strictly warned not to take any kind of nourishment or drink. He was to lie quietly day and night on this platform in a patient vigil for his vision."[24] He might be checked secretly by elders and would be allowed to go home if he could not continue, but he would have to return the following year. "When visions rewarded the fast, they commonly took the form of a journey into the world of the spirits, a spiritual journey on a cosmic scale. During this journey the visionary was shown the path upon which his life should proceed. He was associated with one or more spirit beings who would serve as his guardians and protectors throughout his life."[25] The boy would also gather, or later be given, physical symbols of his guardian spirits, which he would keep for the rest of his life to remind him of his quest and the spirits' protection.

Taboo and Sacrifice

A **taboo** is a rule that forbids specific behavior with regard to certain objects, people, animals, days, or phases of life. Taboos represent a codification of the social and religious order. In our language, *taboo* means, often negatively, something that is prohibited. This is essentially the viewpoint of an outsider. From inside native religions, a taboo is often better seen as a way of protecting the individual and of safeguarding the natural order of things.

Taboos frequently relate to sex and birth. Blood, too, is always an element of mysterious power—both helpful and dangerous. For example, in some but not all groups, menstruating women are expected to remain separate from everyone else, because menstrual blood is considered powerful and dangerous. In contrast, a few cultures (such as the Apache) hail a girl's menarche as a time when she has power to heal illness.

Probably because of the blood involved during childbirth, a woman in some native cultures must remain alone or in the company of women only during the birth—not even the woman's husband may be present. In traditional Hawai`i, for example, women of high rank gave birth in isolation, at the site of special large stones used only for this purpose. Indigenous societies also frequently forbid a husband from resuming sexual relations with his wife for some time after childbirth—this period can even last until the child is weaned.

Like birth, death is also surrounded by taboos concerning the spirit of the dead person, who may seek to reward or take revenge on the living because of the way he or she was treated in life. The afterlife can be a shadowy, uncertain realm that the departing spirit is reluctant to enter, especially if the spirit is leaving a happy family circle. Proper rituals must be performed, accompanied by public mourning, to avoid angering the dead person's spirit.

A number of taboos regulate other social behavior. One common taboo relates to rank: people of high position, such as chiefs, nobility, priests, and shamans, must be treated with extraordinary care because of their special powers; taboos protect them from insult or inappropriate action. In traditional Hawaiian culture, for example, the shadow of a commoner could not fall on a member of the nobility. In a strongly hierarchical native culture, such as in many African groups, the health of the people and the fertility of the land are believed to depend on the health of the sacred king. To maintain his health, the king is protected by taboos—particularly regarding the people with whom he may associate. Because of these taboos and the fear his role inspires, the sacred king may live a life quite separate from his subjects.

Foods and food sources in many cultures are governed by taboos. Among some African peoples, commoners have been forbidden to touch or eat the food of a king. In traditional Hawai`i, women were forbidden to eat certain foods.

Antisocial actions may also be subject to taboo. In Native American religions, taboos and rules encourage a sense of harmony with other members of one's people. Strong taboos against adultery and stealing within the tribal unit, for example, are enforced by shame, warnings, shunning, and expulsion, often administered by a tribal council. Nevertheless, although harmony is important, warfare against another people has at times been considered justified.

The person or group must atone, often through sacrifice, when a taboo has been broken or a spirit must be placated. The usual offering is food and drink. A **libation** (the act of pouring a bit of drink on the ground as an offering) may be made or a portion of a meal set aside for a spirit. An animal may be sacrificed and its blood poured out on the ground or on an altar as an offering of the life force to the deity. Sacrificial animals ordinarily are food animals, such as chickens, pigs, and goats.[27] After the sacrifice, all the participants (including ancestral and nature spirits) may eat the cooked animal—thus pleasing the spirits by feeding them and including them in the meal.

Although it has been rare, human sacrifice (and sometimes cannibalism) has occurred in some native cultures. The sacrifice of human beings was practiced (at least for a time) for specific purposes in Aztec religion, Hawaiian religion, and among tribal peoples of New Guinea; it was much less common among native peoples of North America and Africa.

Before leaving the topic of taboos, it might be good to note that taboos exist plentifully in every society, including our own. Many are associated with sex, marriage, and parenthood. In modern societies, for example, taboos exist against polygamy, incest, and marriage between close relations. Such taboos may seem "natural" to the society that enforces them but "unusual" to outsiders. Taboos are not inherently valid across groups and societies; they are culturally determined.

Do not kill or injure your neighbor, for it is not him that you injure. Do not wrong or hate your neighbor, for it is not him that you wrong, you wrong yourself. Moneto, the Grandmother, the Supreme Being, loves him also as she loves you.

—Shawnee rules[26]

Deeper Insights

TRADITIONAL HAWAIIAN RELIGION

The essentials of traditional Polynesian culture and religion were brought to Hawai'i by settlers who came over the sea from islands in the southern Pacific Ocean. Because of the great navigational skills of the Polynesians, their culture spread widely.

Before contact with westerners, the Polynesian people of Hawai'i had a well-developed belief system, made of many strands. Their belief system spoke of a primeval darkness (*po*), in the midst of which a separation had occurred, forming the sky and the earth. In the space between the two, all the varied forms of life emerged. (This emergence is beautifully detailed in the *Kumulipo,* the most elaborate of the Hawaiian chants of creation.) The primal deities of sky and earth were Wakea and his female consort Papa. But the Hawaiian religion also spoke of thousands of other deities (*akua*) who were descendants of the earliest gods.

Of the thousands of deities that eventually were said to exist, several dozen were commonly invoked, and the greatest deities had priesthoods dedicated to their worship. Among the most important were Ku and Lono, gods who were in many ways complementary. Ku, with several manifestations, was a god of vigorous action. He was the patron, for example, of digging, bird catching, and fishing. In a darker aspect he was also patron of war.

The second god, Lono, was a god of peace, associated with rain, fertility, love, and the arts. Although a large part of the year was dedicated to Ku, the winter period was a time of truce, under the protection of Lono. During this time the temples dedicated to Ku were temporarily closed. The four-month period dedicated to Lono began when the Pleiades first appeared above the horizon in the night sky—something that happened between late October and late November. This period was called *Makahiki* (literally, "eye movement"), a term that referred to the appearance and movement of the stars. The time was given over to religious services, dance, sports contests, and leisure. During Makahiki, priests of Lono collected offerings in his name. To announce the presence of Lono, his priests bore around each island a white banner made of *kapa* (bark cloth). It was attached to a long pole that had at its top the face of Lono or his birdlike symbol.

Two other gods of importance were Kane and Kanaloa, traveling companions or brothers who came together from their homeland of Kahiki to the Hawaiian islands. The two were said to have introduced and planted all of the bananas in Hawai'i.[28] Kane was protector of the water but was seen in many other aspects of nature—particularly in thunder and the rainbow. Houses often had a shrine to Kane, the heart of which was a phallic stone at which Kane received daily prayer. Kanaloa was associated with the sky and the ocean—particularly with ocean fishponds, marine life, the tides, and sailing.

These major gods (with the possible exception of Kanaloa) had their own temples. In the lunar calendar followed by the Hawaiians, ten days in each lunar month were sacred to one of these four gods, and most work was forbidden on those days.[29] Fishing and the planting and harvesting of food plants were regulated by this calendar.

The goddess Pele was also a major subject of devotion. She was worshiped as a goddess of fire, active in volcanoes. Pele was so important that she also had her own priests and, later, priestesses. Other popular goddesses included Pele's younger sister Hi'iaka, of whom Pele was sometimes jealous; Hina, goddess associated with the moon; and Laka, the patron of hula.

Just as deities had many aspects, they could also manifest themselves in varied shapes (*kinolau,* "multiple selves"). Pele, for example, might show herself as a girl, a white dog, a volcano, fire, or an old woman with long hair. (The ethnobotanist Isabella Abbott recounted a characteristic tale told her by her father. He said that once he gave an old lady a ride in his truck and offered her a cigarette. Before he had a chance to light her cigarette, however, it had lit by itself, and the old lady was smoking it. Then suddenly she disappeared.)

Deceased ancestors were, and are, also thought of as having elements of divinity. Known as `*aumakua,* they

A traditional heiau usually had a wooden platform (lele) on which worshipers left offerings.

act as powerful family guardians. Like the gods, they might appear in varied forms—the best-known shapes being those of animals such as sharks, dogs, owls, turtles, and giant lizards (mo`o).

Places of worship varied in size—from enormous stone temples to small wayside shrines, temporary altars, and the site of sacred objects in the home. Many temples and shrines were used for specific purposes, such as treating the sick or requesting good fishing, rain, or an increase of crops. The design of temples, called heiau, was derived from that of temples in Tahiti and the Marquesas, and seems to have become more elaborate over time. The heiau generally were outdoor stone platforms, often enclosed by walls. In the heiau, images of the deities (ki`i) were set up, food offerings were placed on wooden platforms, and priests performed carefully memorized chants.

A complex system of classification came to exist in all traditional Hawaiian society, and religion provided the taboos (kapu). Underpinning the entire social system was a notion of spiritual power, called mana. Nobles, who were considered to be representatives of the gods,

were believed to have the greatest mana; but their mana had to be protected. Commoners, for example, had to crouch or prostrate themselves when close to nobles.

In 1819, King Kamehameha the Great, who had unified the islands, died. In the same year, his son King Kamehameha II ate with women, an act that represented a clear and public rejection of the old system of prohibitions. (This act was influenced by several decades of Western contact.) Many heiau were destroyed and allowed to fall into ruin, most images of the gods were burned, and the religious priesthoods officially ended. The following year, Protestant Christian missionaries arrived from Boston, and Christianity stepped into the vacuum.

Traditional religion, however, did not entirely die out. Elements of it remain alive even today. Among the clearest are widespread reverence for Pele, veneration of ancestors, and belief in guardian spirits. There have also been theoretical attempts at integrating the traditional native polytheism with monotheism, by saying that the many traditional deities are angels or are just aspects of the one God.[30]

(continued)

The revival in recent decades of hula, Hawaiian language, and traditional arts has brought about a new interest in ceremonies of the traditional religion. A good number of heiau have been repaired and even rebuilt, including several large ones on Maui and the Big Island of Hawaiʻi. Some traditional religious services have been conducted at the reconstructed heiau, and there may be further attempts to restore traditional religious practices.[31]

Although hula is often thought of as entertainment, much of it tells the stories of Hawaiian gods and goddesses.

I enter the earth. I go in at a place like a place where people drink water. I travel a long way, very far. When I emerge, I am already climbing threads [up into the sky]. I climb one and leave it, then I climb another one. . . . You come in small to God's place. You do what you have to do there. . . . [Then] you enter, enter the earth, and you return to enter the skin of your body.

—Bushman trance dancer[33]

Shamanism, Trance, and Spiritual Powers

As we have seen, native religions take for granted that a powerful and influential but invisible spirit world exists and that human beings can access it. A **shaman** acts as an intermediary between the visible, ordinary world and the spirit world. The shaman can contact this realm, receive visions of it, and transmit messages from it, often to help or heal others. As one commentator remarks, "The shaman lies at the very heart of some cultures, while living in the shadowy fringes of others. Nevertheless, a common thread seems to connect all shamans across the planet. An awakening to other orders of reality, the experience of ecstasy, and an opening up of visionary realms form the essence of the shamanic mission."[32] Sometimes the spirits speak through the shaman, who knows entry points to their world. The spirits may be reached in dreams or trances by climbing a sacred tree, descending through a cave into the underworld, flying through the air, or following a sacred map.

The shaman understands the primordial unity of things and experiences a shared identity with animals and the rest of nature. Thus the shaman can interpret the language of animals, charm them, and draw on their powers.

Deeper Insights

ISAAC TENS BECOMES A SHAMAN

Isaac Tens, a shaman of the Gitksan people of northwest Canada, spoke to an interviewer in 1920 about how he had become a shaman. On a snowy day at dusk, when he was gathering firewood, he heard a loud noise, and an owl appeared to him. "The owl took hold of me, caught my face, and tried to lift me up. I lost consciousness. As soon as I came back to my senses I realized that I had fallen into the snow. My head was coated with ice, and some blood was running out of my mouth."[34] Isaac went home, but he fell into a trance. He woke up to find medicine men working to heal him. One told him that it was now time for him, too, to become a *halaait* (medicine man). Isaac refused. Later, at a fishing hole, he had another fainting spell and fell into a trance again. He was carried home. When he woke up, he was trembling. "My body was quivering. While I remained in this state, I began to sing. A chant was coming out of me without my being able to do anything to stop it. Many things appeared to me presently: huge birds and other animals. They were calling me."[35] Soon Isaac began to treat others.

The shaman gains the powers of animals and the rest of nature by wearing items taken from important animals, such as deer antlers, lion skins, and eagle feathers.

Part of becoming a shaman involves having one or more encounters with the spirit realm in the form of a psychological death and rebirth. A person may have experienced some great loss—of sight, of a child, or of something equally precious. He or she may have had a mental breakdown, been terribly sick, or suffered a serious accident and come close to dying. Upon recovering from such an extreme experience, this person can have new powers of insight and healing, which can lead to becoming a shaman. Those who have experienced vivid dreams and visions that are thought to be manifestations of the spirit world are also sometimes trained as shamans.

The shaman often blends the roles of priest, oracle, psychologist, and doctor. A common English term for the shaman is *medicine man,* yet it stresses only the therapeutic role and obscures the fact that shamans are both female and male. In Korean and Japanese native religious paths, in fact, shamans are frequently female.

The shamanic trance state that brings visions, both to the shaman and to others, can be induced in several ways: weakening the visual boundaries (for example, by sitting in the darkness of a cave or hut for prolonged periods), fasting, experiencing sensory deprivation, making regular rhythmic sounds (such as drumming, rattling, bell ringing, and chanting), and dancing in a repetitive way, especially in circles. The ingestion of natural substances is also common; peyote cactus, datura, cannabis (marijuana), coca, opium, and the mushroom *Amanita muscaria* have all been used to induce trance states, both by the shaman alone and sometimes by participants in a ceremony.

Some Native American peoples have used a **calumet**—a long sacred pipe— for smoking a special kind of tobacco that is far stronger than commercial cigarette tobacco; it is so strong, in fact, that it can have a hallucinatory effect. The bowl of the pipe is usually made of clay but sometimes of bone, ivory, wood, or metal, and the stem is made of wood. Many pipes are also made of stone. (A red stone, popular among Plains Indians and Eastern Woodlands Indians for this purpose, was quarried in Pipestone, Minnesota.) The calumet is an object that gives protection to the person who carries it. The pipe is smoked as part of a shared ceremony that establishes strong bonds among all the participants, and oaths sworn at these ceremonies have the greatest solemnity.

Rituals involving the use of peyote have developed primarily within the past two centuries in some native North American tribes.[36] The practice seems to have moved north from Mexico, where peyote grows easily and has long been used for religious purposes. When the fruit of the peyote cactus is eaten, it elicits a psychedelic experience that lasts six or more hours and produces a forgetfulness of the self and a sense of oneness with all of nature. Ceremonies commonly begin in the early evening and last until dawn.

Among North American tribes, the rituals involving peyote are often mixed with Christian elements. For example, a member of the Native American Church described his preparation for the ceremony: "First we set up an altar—a Mexican rug and on it a Lakota Bible in our own language. We use only the revelations of St. John in our meetings. It's . . . full of visions, nature, earth, stars. . . . Across the Bible we put an eagle feather—it stands for the Great Spirit. . . . On the left is a rawhide bag with cedar dust to sprinkle on the fire. That's our incense."[37] The blending of elements, he says, is intentional, because it illustrates that, at their core, all religions are the same. It is interesting to note that although the ordinary use of peyote is illegal, its religious use by the Native American Church has been legally upheld.

In native African religions and their Caribbean offshoots, powerful but invisible spiritual forces are believed to be able to do either great good or tremendous evil. Diviners and healers direct these powers through incantations, figurines, and potions in what is sometimes called **sympathetic magic.** Magic in the hands of certain individuals can be used, as one commentator remarks, "for harmful ends, and then people experience it as bad or evil magic. Or they may use it for ends which are helpful to society, and then it is considered as good magic or 'medicine.' These mystical forces of the universe are neither evil nor good in themselves, they are just like other natural things at [our] disposal."[38]

Spiritual powers and trance states are believed to make it possible to look into the past and future, a process called **divination** (from the Latin *divus,* "god," and *divinare,* "to foretell"). Looking into the past is thought to help determine the causes of illness and other misfortune, while looking into the future can guide an individual to act wisely. It is a common belief in African religions that an individual has a predetermined future that can be discovered through divination.

The general worldview common to native religions allows for a number of specialized religious roles. A diviner looks for causes of sickness, depression, death, and other difficulties. A healer works with a person afflicted with physical or mental illness to find a cure. A rainmaker ends drought.

The powwow provides opportunities for Indian nations to share their dances and to pass age-old stories to new generations.

Malevolent sorcerers manipulate objects to cause damage; they may bury an object in the victim's path or take fingernails, hair, clothes, or other possessions of the victim and then burn or damage them in order to cause harm. Witches need only use their spiritual powers. "Another belief is that the spirit of the witches leaves them at night and goes to eat away the victim, thus causing him to weaken and eventually die. It is believed, too, that a witch can cause harm by looking at a person, wishing him harm or speaking to him words intended to inflict harm on him."[39] Of course, the powers of these sorcerers and witches are also employed for good ends as well.

Artifacts and Artistic Expression in Indigenous Religions

The masks, drums, statues, rattles, and other objects that are important in native religions were once seen as curiosities to be collected and housed in anthropological museums. Today, however, we view them differently; we realize that we must respect both their importance to the cultures that produced them and their inherent artistic value. The arts of native religions are not created by "artists" as "art" but as functional objects to be used in particular settings and special ways. Navajo sandpaintings, for example, are often photographed and reproduced in books as though they were permanent works of art. In fact, when used by a healer, they are temporary creations that are made and then destroyed as a part of the ritual. And unlike art in most industrialized cultures, sacred

This Aztec stone calendar shows how religious deities and beliefs were incorporated into complex artifacts.

objects and images in native religions are not separate endeavors but an essential part of the religious expression itself. Although modern secular culture does not usually think of dance or tattoo or body painting as religious expression, in many native religions these art forms all fulfill that role.

In religions that do not rely on the written word, artistic expressions take on unique significance because they are filled with meaning and remind practitioners of the specifics of the oral tradition. Statues and paintings, of course, are common in a great many religions, both oral and written. Dance, which takes on particular importance in native religions, incorporates religious objects such as carved and painted masks, headdresses, costumes, ornaments, and musical instruments. In native Hawaiian religion, *hula kahiko* (ancient hula) is danced in conjunction with chanting to honor the gods. Instruments for marking rhythm and *lei* (wreaths of flowers or other plants worn around the head, wrists, and ankles), when used in hula, are considered religious objects.

Chants, too, are essential, for they repeat the sacred words and re-create the stories of the religious traditions. To be used properly in religious ceremonies, they must be memorized carefully. Chanters must not only have prodigious memories and be able to recall thousands of chants; they must also be able to create special variations on traditional chants and oral texts for individual occasions.

Masks play a significant role in native religions, especially when used in dance. When a dancer is wearing a mask and any accompanying costume, the spirit is not merely represented by the masked dancer. The dancer actually becomes the spirit, embodied on earth, with the spirit's powers. Among the BaPunu in Africa, for example, dancers not only wear masks but also walk on stilts—the overall effect must be intense. Particularly complex masks have been produced in the Pacific Northwest by such tribes as the Haida, Tsimshian, and Kwakiutl (Kwakwaka`wakw).[40] Some of their masks, especially those depicting animal spirits, have movable parts that make them even more powerful for those who wear and see them.

Besides masks and statues, other forms of wood carving can manifest religious inspiration. Perhaps the most famous of all wood carvings is the carved pole, commonly called a *totem pole*, found in the Pacific Northwest. The totem pole usually depicts several totems, stacked one upon the other. A **totem** is an animal figure—such as the bear, beaver, thunderbird, owl, raven, and eagle—that is revered for both its symbolic meaning and its clan symbolism. The totem animals may be memorials to ancestors or may represent badges of kinship groups, with specialized meaning for the individual or the family responsible for the totem pole.[41] Some totem poles are a part of the structure of a traditional wooden house or lodge. Others—apparently a later development—are raised to stand alone, frequently to mark an important event.

Other important art forms that can have religious meaning are weaving, beading, and basketry. These creations may seem to have less obvious religious significance, but the imagery used is frequently of religious derivation, particularly figures from tribal myths, nature deities, and guardian birds and animals.

Feathers and featherwork also feature prominently in many native religions because of their powerful association with flight and contact with the world above and beyond our own. Richard W. Hill, in an essay on the religious meaning of feathers, remarks that "some cultures associate certain birds with spiritual or protective powers. Birds are believed to have delivered songs, dances, rituals, and sacred messages to humankind. Feathers worn in the hair blow in the wind and evoke birds in flight. For followers of the Ghost Dance religion of the late nineteenth century, birds became important symbols of rebirth."[42] Feathers are worn in the hair, made into headdresses, and attached to clothing. In Native American cultures, they are also attached to horse harnesses, dolls, pipes, and baskets.

The symbols that appear in myths and in dreams are the basic vocabulary of native religious art. Common symbols include a great mountain located at the center of the universe, the tree of life, the sun and moon, fire, rain, lightning, a bird or wings, death's head and skeleton, a cross, and a circle. These images, however, often appear in unusual forms; for example, lightning may be represented by a zigzag, the sun may appear like a swastika, and the tree of life may look like a ladder. Colors are universally used with symbolic meaning, although the exact meaning differs from culture to culture.

PERSONAL EXPERIENCE

Gods in Hawai`i

On the southernmost island of the Hawaiian Islands lies Pu`uhonua `o Honaunau ("place of refuge"). It was once a sanctuary for Hawaiians who had done something that was kapu (taboo, forbidden). They could be purified and escape punishment if they could reach this place, or one of its sister sanctuaries, by water or land.

Seeking refuge from the frenzy of life in Honolulu, I fly to the Kona airport and drive my rental car down the Big Island's southwest coast to Pu`uhonua `o Honaunau, now run by the United States National Park Service. After a short walk toward the shore, I see the tall, long stone wall of the sanctuary. Closer to the ocean are its heiau (temples), made of large, nearly black lava rock. Most dramatic to my outsider's eyes are the tall carved wooden images (in Hawaiian, called *ki`i*, and in English, commonly called *tikis*) that once no doubt beckoned to the refugee who sought out this place at the ocean's edge. The offering platform and thatched houses near the ki`i have been restored so that I can see what it might have been like when this was a sacred site within traditional Hawaiian religion. Because King Kamehameha II dissolved the official kapu system in 1819, it is no longer a place for seeking sanctuary—at least officially.

The ki`i at Pu`uhonua `o Honaunau mark this place of refuge as sacred ground.

Even on this sunny day, the stone wall, the tall images, and the stark landscape speak not of the "peace and comfort" we may typically associate with a refuge but rather of power, law, and awesome majesty. The ground is hard, black lava rock and white coral, and except for the coconut trees here and there amid the few structures, there is little green vegetation. Ocean waves lap at the shore, but an almost eerie quiet reigns.

Late afternoon: I'm the only person here. It is not hard for me to imagine being a native who has fled from home and now awaits a priestly blessing in order to be made safe for returning home. I sense that the Hawaiian religion drew its power from the land, from this very place. The rocks that make up the heiau are petrifications of fire, water, air, and earth. This is not the tour director's tropical fantasyland. Nor, I realize, is it a place of living religious practice. But that doesn't matter to me today. What I sense in the land is still alive.

As I drive back up the hill toward the main road, I see a small directional sign that says Painted Church. Ready for an experience of contrast, I follow its arrow and soon arrive at Saint Benedict's Catholic Church—a tiny, white wooden structure that has elements of Gothic style. A sign near the door says that its interior was painted a century ago by a Belgian missionary priest. The church sits on a grassy hillside, with a small cemetery spreading out below. I ascend the wooden stairs of the church and walk in.

The interior is "tropical Gothic." Ten small windows have pointed Gothic arches. The wooden pillars look like candy canes, painted with red and white swirls; their tops turn into palm trees, with fronds like painted feathers on the pastel sky of the ceiling. Behind the altar is a mural of Gothic arches, stretching back into an imaginary distance, creating the pretense of a European cathedral. On one side-wall, Saint Francis experiences a vision of Jesus on the cross. In another painting, Jesus is being tempted by Satan. The other wall shows a man on his deathbed, his face bathed in heavenly light. A cross of execution, the pains of death—these are not pleasant experiences, but they are softened by the way they are depicted here.

Back outside, from the top of the stairs, I see the shining ocean below and can even see, at the edge of the ocean, the Hawaiian place of refuge that I had visited not long before. This little church, charming as it appears, presents old familiar themes: a High God, a sacrificial victim, an offering of blood, a restoration of justice. The themes may not be obvious, but they are there. This, I reflect, is the religion that replaced the native Hawaiian religion; the cycle of replacement evident here is typical, I think, of what has happened to so many other native religious traditions. Does it make all that much difference how religions die and rise? I am deep in thought as I pass a stone grotto enclosing a statue of Mary and then walk past the resident priest's small house. From inside come the sounds of a baseball game and a roaring crowd. "Strike two!" a voice shouts. Passing a flowerbed of honeysuckle, and preparing to return to big-city life, I get in my car and drive away.

The walls of Saint Benedict's Catholic Church were painted by a missionary to suggest the grandeur (and perhaps superiority) of the missionary's religion.

INDIGENOUS RELIGIONS TODAY

Native religions show many signs of vitality. Some indigenous religions are spreading and even adapting themselves to urban life. For example, religions of the Yoruba tradition are practiced not only in western Africa, their place of origin, but also in Brazil and the Caribbean, and they are growing in cities of North America (see Chapter 11). Awareness of indigenous religions is also becoming widespread, and respect for them is taking many shapes. In some countries (such as Mexico, Ecuador, and Peru) we can see a growth in governmental protection of the rights of indigenous peoples. Native peoples themselves are often taking political action to preserve their cultures. In many places (such as Hawai`i, New Zealand, and North America) a renaissance of native cultures is under way. Sometimes this involves primarily cultural elements, but where the indigenous religions are still practiced, those religions are increasingly cherished and protected.

In some places, however, indigenous religions appear fragile. There are four principal threats to their existence: the global spread of popular culture, loss of natural environments, loss of traditional languages, and conversion to other religions.

Television, radio, films, airplanes, and the Internet are carrying modern urban culture to all corners of the earth. (American television reruns that are broadcast in Mali are just one example.) Change is also evident in the realm of clothing. Traditional regional clothing began to disappear a century ago, as western styles became the standard. Western business wear is now worn in all the world's cities, and informal clothing—baseball caps and T-shirts—is seen everywhere. Some cultures are trying to hold on to their traditional clothing, especially for formal occasions. (This is common in Korea, the Philippines, and Japan.) Architecture, too, is becoming standardized, as the "international style"—with its plate glass, aluminum, and concrete—takes the place of traditional styles. As modern urban culture spreads across the earth, it tends to dominate everyone's worldview. It would be hard to convince today's young people to undergo the deprivation of a vision quest, when all they need to visit other worlds is a television, a computer, or an airplane ticket. But everywhere we go, we find hamburgers, pizza, rap, rock, and jeans. (Some even believe that popular culture is becoming a religion of its own, displacing all others.)

Another great threat to indigenous religions is their loss of traditional lands and natural environment. Because so much personal and group meaning comes from the natural environment, its degradation or loss can be devastating to a native people's identity. Logging interests are a problem almost universally, but especially in Southeast Asia, Indonesia, Brazil, Alaska, and western Canada. Much of northern Thailand, where many native peoples live, has already been badly deforested, and the logging companies are now beginning the same process in Myanmar, another home of indigenous peoples. Fights are intense over conservation, land ownership, and governmental protection. Luckily, there have been gains (such as in New Zealand and Australia) where aboriginal rights to land have been recognized.

A third threat is the loss of native languages. It has been estimated that of the approximately six thousand languages that are spoken in the world today,

Contemporary Issues

HALLOWEEN: "JUST GOOD FUN" OR FOLK RELIGION?

Many of us think of native religions as having little connection to our everyday life. Yet elements of them persist in modern culture. Their oral nature is apparent when we see how the manner of practice is taught—not in books of instruction, but by word of mouth and by example. Halloween is an excellent example of this, but other festivals also invite examination.

- *Halloween* means the evening before All Hallows (All Saints) Day, which falls on November 1. Although Halloween gets its name from Christianity, the celebration is, in fact, a continuation of *Samhain* (pronounced *sa'-win*), the New Year's festival celebrated in pre-Christian England and Ireland. There is a strong theme of death and rebirth, as winter comes on and the old year disappears. It was believed that spirits of ancestors roamed free at this time and needed to be fed and placated. We see this underlying the practice of children going door to door, receiving food. We also see it in the many Halloween costumes that suggest death (skeletons) and communication with the spirit world (angels, devils, and religious figures).

- Although Christmas has a Christian name and purpose, the origins of this festival, too, are pre-Christian. It began as a festival of the winter solstice, when the days are the coldest and shortest in the northern hemisphere. People compensated by celebrating a holiday of extra light, warmth, and abundance. The lighted Christmas tree and the evergreen wreaths and decorations have nothing to do with the story of Jesus' birth; rather, they are clear symbols of fertility and life, which the celebrants hope will persist through a cold winter. The giving of presents is related to this idea of abundance, and the Christian Saint Nicholas has been transformed over the past two hundred years into the grandfatherly Santa Claus. Like a shaman or wizard, Santa Claus flies through the air, carried by

The costumes of these trick-or-treaters are not unlike those used in some ceremonies of indigenous religions.

his magical reindeer, dispensing presents from his overflowing bag to children all around the earth.

- Easter's Christian meaning is mixed with elements that derive from the Jewish Passover, but underlying this tradition are symbols of fertility and new life—eggs, flowers, and rabbits. (The name *Easter* comes from an Old English term for a spring festival in honor of Eastre, goddess of the dawn.) Easter has maintained a close tie to nature in that it is always celebrated at the time of a full moon.

We can see in these examples of contemporary folk religion the "universal language" of religious symbols. It is the same language, whether found in folk religion, native religions, or the other religions that we will take up in the chapters ahead.

in a hundred years only three thousand will remain. A comparison of Native American languages once spoken and still in use illustrates well how many languages and dialects have already been lost. In the United States and Canada, only about 500,000 indigenous people still speak their native languages. A single example of this phenomenon is the Kwakiutl (Kwakwaka`wakw) of

Contemporary Issues

THE GREEN MOVEMENT: A NEW GLOBAL INDIGENOUS RELIGION?

All indigenous religions honor nature in some way. These religions sometimes associate natural forces such as wind, rain, volcanoes, and earthquakes with invisible spirits living beyond the earth. Other traditions see these forces as residing more visibly in mountains, trees, rivers, the moon, and the sun. Whatever form it is conceived as, nature commands respect, and people are expected to show their respect by working harmoniously with their environment.

In contrast with indigenous religions, major religions have traditionally shown limited concern for nature. However, this is changing. Today, many major religions have begun to display a new sensitivity to the earth. The Tibetan religious leader, the Dalai Lama, speaks frequently of the need to show compassion and respect for all living things—not just for human beings. The first Catholic pope elected in this century, Benedict XVI, labeled acts that harm the environment as "sinful." The Orthodox Patriarch of Constantinople, Bartholomew I, is called "the Green Patriarch" for his interest in ecology. Increasingly, presidents and prime ministers, whatever their religions, as well as ordinary citizens, are making calls to protect the environment, participating in what has become a worldwide Green Movement.

The first phase of the Green Movement in the United States came more than a hundred years ago, when the federal government began to create national parks.

People had become aware that the treasures of the scenic natural world needed protection. The second phase began fifty years ago, with the publication of books like Rachel Carson's *Silent Spring*, which warned about the dangers of pesticides. Works like Carson's gave scientific underpinning to growing ecological concern. The third phase is now under way, as environmentalism gains popular support around the world. Individuals, schools, businesses, and governments deliberately "move from gray to green." Part of the world's energy now comes from sunshine, wind, ocean waves, and plants. Construction materials for buildings now include bamboo, reused brick, and recycled wood. A common watchword is *sustainability*, and a well-known mantra is "reduce, reuse, recycle." After decades of being considered a fringe movement of flaky "tree-huggers," environmentalism is entering the mainstream. Industries that were once opposed to environmental needs are beginning to realize the commercial benefits of "going green," and they are at last using their enormous power to make real change.

Indigenous peoples are now also becoming an explicit and vocal part of the Green Movement. For example, in Brazil the Yanomamö (Yanomami) have demonstrated in Brasilia to protect their native lands from roads and mining. In Kenya, Wangari Maathai (1940–2011) was called "Tree Mother of Africa" because

British Columbia. Although their population has been rising and is now as high as 5,000, only about 250 people speak the native language. Clearly, the loss of a native language endangers the continued transmission of a religion that expresses itself in that language.

A fourth threat is the spread of proselytizing religions, particularly Christianity and Islam. In the Pacific, native cultures are undergoing a revival, but few elements of the native religions of those cultures remain unchanged from their earlier forms. Christianity, brought since the nineteenth century by missionaries (particularly Methodist, Catholic, and, more recently, Mormon), has replaced some beliefs and reshaped others. Christianity has spread widely in sub-Saharan Africa over the past hundred years, creating both mainstream Western denominations and independent African churches. As a result, there are now more black members of the Anglican Church than there are white members. Islam has also gained many converts in Africa.

Kenyan Green-Movement activist Wangari Maathai won the Nobel Peace Prize in 2004 "for her contribution to sustainable development, democracy, and peace."

of her work as founder of the Green Belt Movement, which has planted more than 40 million trees. For her efforts, she was awarded the Nobel Peace Prize in 2004.

Those who espouse the Green Movement most likely don't see themselves as embracing a religion, but the movement has many hallmarks of religion. Its statements of political principles form a list of commandments and virtues, which include not only sustainability and biodiversity but also consensus, grass-roots democracy, and nonviolence. Its priests are the world's scientists and environmental experts, and its prophets are environmental activists. It promotes a way of life, and it holds promise of rewards and punishments for all inhabitants of this earth.

Whether or not the Green Movement comes to be seen as a world religion makes little difference. If the multinational Green Movement can change human behavior for the good of all, it will be accomplishing as much as many recognized religions. Somewhat ironically, the Green Movement, by leading the world's citizens back to a respect for nature, is also leading people to a new appreciation of the indigenous religions that are built on such respect.

Despite the threats to their existence, indigenous religions continue to thrive in several forms throughout the world. In their purest form, they live on in those pockets where modern influence has penetrated the least, such as in Borneo and the Amazon River basin. They may also coexist, sometimes in diluted form, alongside other religions. In Taiwan, Korea, and Japan, for example, shamanism exists side by side with Buddhism, Christianity, and other religions. (Because the shamans there are often female, their native religious practices allow them roles that are not open to them in the adopted religions.) Indigenous religions have also intermixed with mainstream religions. In the Caribbean, the gods of African religions have sometimes been combined with forms of French and Spanish Catholicism in the religions of Voodoo and Santería (see Chapter 11). In Central America, people who are otherwise practicing Catholics also worship deities of earlier native religions. We see similar types of synthesis in Mexico and the southwestern United States.

In North America, in the Pacific, and in Africa, people have continued or are attempting to restore the practices of their ancestral ways. In New Zealand, for example, Maori culture is experiencing a revival in canoe building, tattooing, dance, and wood sculpture. This attempt at revival is complicated by debates over such issues as land ownership and the introduction of Maori language into schools and public life. In Hawai`i, a renaissance of Hawaiian culture, language, and hula necessarily means retelling the stories of the gods and goddesses of Hawaiian mythology. Some schools now teach all their lessons in Hawaiian, and hula schools are flourishing. Citizens of many native nations in North America are instructing their young in traditional dance and other religious practices. Nevertheless, how to deal with a traditional belief in deities in the face of some dominant monotheistic religions presents intriguing questions. One result, as in the Native American Church, is that beliefs and practices now often incorporate both oral and text-based traditions.

Interest in indigenous religions is a potential restorative for cultures that have moved quickly from their traditional rural homes to homes in the city. In native traditions, we see religion before it was compartmentalized. These holistic traditions make us aware of the religious dimensions that can be found in our own everyday life, and they expand our sensitivity to nature. Their remembrance of the sacred past makes holy the present and the future.

Reading **THE KUMULIPO**

This is the most famous of Hawaiian chants. Combining both a genealogy and a description of the creation of nature, it was recited for Captain James Cook when he arrived in Hawai`i in 1789. It is in two parts—the first dedicated to the creative darkness and the second to the light. Here—given in both Hawaiian and a classic English translation—the chant begins.

Ka Wa Akahi

CHANT ONE

O ke au i kahuli wela ka honua
  At the time when the earth became hot
O ke au i kahuli lole ka lani
  At the time when the heavens turned about
O ke au i kuka`iaka ka la
  At the time when the sun was darkened
E ho`omalamalama i ka malama
  To cause the moon to shine
O ke au o Makali`i ka po
  The time of the rise of the Pleiades
O ka walewale ho`okumu honua ia
  The slime, this was the source of the earth
O ke kumu o ka lipo, i lipo ai
  The source of the darkness that made darkness

O ke kumu o ka Po, i po ai
  The source of the night that made night
O ka lipolipo, o ka lipolipo
  The intense darkness, the deep darkness
O ka lipo o ka la, o ka lipo o ka po
  Darkness of the sun, darkness of the night
Po wale ho—`i
  Nothing but night
Hanau ka po
  The night gave birth
Hanau Kumulipo i ka po, he kane
  Born was Kumulipo in the night, a male
Hanau Po`ele i ka po, he wahine
  Born was Po`ele in the night, a female[43]

TEST YOURSELF

1. Although there is no agreement on how to speak of ancient religious ways, they are often inadequately referred to as traditional, aboriginal, indigenous, tribal, _____, primal, native, oral, and basic.
   a. holistic
   b. shamanistic
   c. nonliterate
   d. wakan

2. Indigenous religions exist generally within _____ cultures, in which every object and act may have religious meaning.
   a. holistic
   b. sacred
   c. symbolic
   d. sacrificial

3. In many Native American religious traditions, there is little distinction between the human and animal worlds. These native religions see everything in the universe as being alive, a concept known as _____.
   a. taboo
   b. sacredness
   c. origins
   d. animism

4. Sacred time is "the time of _____." Among the Koyukon people of the Arctic, it is called "distant time," and it is the holy ancient past in which gods lived and worked. Among Australian Aborigines it is often called Dreamtime, and it is the subject of much of their highly esteemed art.
   a. eternity
   b. ceremonies
   c. life cycles
   d. gods

5. _____ is the doorway through which the "other world" of gods and ancestors can contact us and we can contact them. It is associated with the center of the universe and can be constructed, often in a symbolic shape such as a circle or square.
   a. Dualism
   b. Sacred space
   c. Ceremony
   d. Eternity

6. Most indigenous religions have cosmic tales of their _____. They frequently speak of a High God and make little distinction between a god and an ancestor.
   a. life cycle
   b. ceremonies
   c. taboos
   d. origins

7. In native societies, everyday religious activity and practice are significant, because their primary purpose is often to place individuals, families, and groups in "right _____" with gods, ancestors, other human beings, and nature.
   a. origins
   b. relationships
   c. ceremonies
   d. taboos

8. Special rituals mark a person's entry into adulthood. In Native American religions, a common ritual of early maturity is the "vision quest," or "_____."
   a. dream quest
   b. trance
   c. sacred time
   d. symbolic death

9. A _____ is a rule that forbids specific behavior with regard to certain objects, people, animals, days, or phases of life.
   a. sacrifice
   b. totem
   c. taboo
   d. divination

10. A(n) _____ acts as an intermediary between the visible, ordinary world and the spirit world.
    a. god
    c. artist
    c. totem
    d. shaman

11. Think of a major problem facing twenty-first century Western society. How might a holistic perspective typical of indigenous religions help in dealing with this problem?

12. Imagine you are assigned a research paper on one of the following topics in indigenous religions: life-cycle ceremonies, taboos, or shamanism. Based on what you have read in this chapter, which one would you most want to investigate and why? What challenges do you think you would encounter while researching this topic?

RESOURCES

Books

Abbott, Isabella Aiona. *La`au Hawai`i: Traditional Hawaiian Uses of Plants.* Honolulu: Bishop Museum Press, 1992. A demonstration by a Hawaiian botanist of the holistic nature of traditional religion. Abbott specifically discusses the use of plants in religious ceremony and hula.

Achebe, Chinua. *Arrow of God.* New York: Anchor, 1989. An exploration, through the framework of a personal struggle between father and son, of the breakdown of traditional Igbo beliefs under British colonial rule.

Cowan, James. *Aborigine Dreaming.* Wellingborough, UK: Thorsons, 2002. An exploration of the spiritual beliefs of the Australian Aborigines.

Fitzhugh, William, and Chisato Dubreuil, eds. *Ainu: Spirit of a Northern People.* Seattle: University of Washington Press, 2001. A well-illustrated collection of essays on Ainu history, religion, and culture.

Grim, John, ed. *Indigenous Traditions and Ecology.* Cambridge, MA: Center for the Study of World Religions, 2001. Essays on environmental elements in indigenous religions.

Harvey, Graham, ed. *Indigenous Religions: A Companion.* New York: Continuum, 2000. A collection of essays by many scholars regarding mana, taboo, sacrifice, and other beliefs and practices of indigenous religions.

——. *Shamanism: A Reader.* New York: Routledge, 2002. Articles and extracts that examine shamanism, exploring issues of gender, initiation, hallucinogenic consciousness, and political protest.

Johnston, Basil. *Ojibway Ceremonies.* Lincoln: University of Nebraska Press, 1990. An insider's description of the important traditional ceremonies of his people, including the naming ceremony, marriage ceremony, and funeral ritual.

Marcos, Sylvia, ed. *Women and Indigenous Religions.* Santa Barbara, CA: ABC-CLIO, 2010. Essays on the roles of indigenous women regarding ritual, kinship, and related topics.

Pijoan, Teresa. *Pueblo Indian Wisdom.* Santa Fe: Sunstone Press, 2000. A collection of the legends of the Pueblo peoples of New Mexico.

Ray, Benjamin. *African Religions.* 2nd ed. Englewood Cliffs, NJ: Prentice Hall, 1999. A presentation of the most important native African religions, with additional information on Christianity and Islam in Africa.

Silko, Leslie Marmon. *Ceremony.* New York: Penguin, 2006. A novel that shows how an emotionally and spiritually wounded Native American veteran, facing a grim future, is healed by a traditional ceremony arranged by the elders of his tribe.

Vitebsky, Piers. *The Shaman: Voyages of the Soul; Trance, Ecstasy and Healing from Siberia to the Amazon.* London: Duncan Baird, 2001. A colorfully illustrated exploration of the history and practice of shamanism around the world.

Film/TV

Dancing in Moccasins: Keeping Native American Traditions Alive. (Films Media Group.) An examination of how contemporary Native Americans keep their traditions alive.

Earl's Canoe: A Traditional Ojibwe Craft. (Smithsonian Institution Center for Folklife Programs and Cultural Heritage.) A documentary of Earl Nyholm, a member of the Ojibwe Nation, as he builds a canoe according to traditional Ojibwe methods and explains his tribe's beliefs concerning the construction and use of canoes.

Healers of Ghana. (Films Media Group.) An exploration of the traditional medical practices of the Bono people of central Ghana, which involve the use of herbs and spirit possession.

The Shaman's Apprentice. (Miranda Productions.) A documentary, filmed in the rain forests of Suriname, that shows efforts by Dr. Mark Plotkin to preserve the rain forest and the religious practices of its people.

Walkabout. (Director Nicholas Roeg; Films Inc.) A classic film about two British children abandoned in the Australian outback and rescued by a young Aborigine who is on a walkabout, a sacred initiation intended to convey a boy into manhood.

Whalerider. (Director Niki Caro; Columbia Tristar.) An exploration of the conflict between Maori tribal tradition and one girl's determination to prove herself as a tribal leader.

Music

The Baoule of the Ivory Coast. (Smithsonian Folkways.) Music from the Baoule tribe of Africa.

The Bora of the Pascoe River: Cape York Peninsula, Northeast Australia. (Smithsonian Folkways.) Stories and songs of the Bora Aborigines.

Dogon Music of the Masks and the Funeral Rituals. (Inedit.) A collection of traditional ritual music of the Dogon people of Mali.

The Rough Guide to Australian Aboriginal Music. (World Music Network.) An anthology of music by various Aboriginal musicians.

Sacred Spirit: Chants and Dances of the Native Americans. (Virgin Records.) A compilation of songs that spans the history and tradition of Native American ritual chant and music.

Uwolani. (Mountain Apple Company.) Twenty traditional Hawaiian chants, including creation chants (*ko`ihonua*), name chants (*mele inoa*), chants to honor gods, and chants to recognize the beauty of places, winds, and rains.

Yunupingu, Geoffrey. *Gurrumul.* (Skinnyfish/Dramatico.) Songs written and sung by a blind Aboriginal man.

Internet

Center for World Indigenous Studies (CWIS): http://www.cwis.org. A Web site devoted to challenges confronting indigenous peoples, research into indigenous topics, conflict resolution, and related conferences.

The Foundation for Shamanic Studies (FSS): http://www.shamanism.org/. Information about a foundation whose goal is to preserve and teach the religious beliefs of indigenous peoples.

Internet Sacred Text Archive: http://www.sacred-texts.com/index.htm. A large electronic archive that contains sections devoted to the tales and folklore of indigenous religions in Africa, Australia, the Americas, and the Pacific Islands.

United Nations Permanent Forum on Indigenous Issues (UNPFII): http://social.un.org/index/IndigenousPeoples.aspx. The official Web site of the U.N. advisory body that addresses indigenous issues, including economic and social development, culture, the environment, education, health, and human rights.

KEY TERMS

calumet: A long-stemmed sacred pipe used primarily by many native peoples of North America; it is smoked as a token of peace.

divination: A foretelling of the future or a look into the past; a discovery of the unknown by magical means.

holistic: Organic, integrated; indicating a complete system, greater than the sum of its parts; here, refers to a culture whose various elements (art, music, social behavior) may all have religious meaning.

libation: The act of pouring a liquid on the ground as an offering to a god.

shaman: A human being who contacts and attempts to manipulate the power of spirits for the tribe or group.

sympathetic magic: An attempt to influence the outcome of an event through an action that has an apparent similarity to the desired result—for example, throwing water into the air to produce rain or burning an enemy's fingernail clippings to bring sickness to that enemy.

taboo: A strong social prohibition (Tongan: *tabu;* Hawaiian: *kapu*).

totem: An animal (or image of an animal) that is considered to be related by blood to a family or clan and is its guardian or symbol.

RELIGION BEYOND THE CLASSROOM

Visit the Online Learning Center at www.mhhe.com/molloy6e for additional exercises and features, including "Religion beyond the Classroom" and "For Fuller Understanding."

CHAPTER 3

Hinduism

F I R S T   E N C O U N T E R

The plane that you have taken to Benares circles in preparation for landing at the Varanasi airport. Looking down from your window seat, you can see the blue-white Ganges River, quite wide here. Everything else is a thousand shades of brown. Beyond the coffee-colored city, the beige fields spread out, seemingly forever.

At the small airport, a dignified customs inspector with a turban and a white beard asks, "Why have you come to India?" Before you can think of an appropriate response, he answers his own question. "I know," he says with a smile and a wave of the hand. "You people who come to Benares are all the same." He shakes his head from side to side. "You have come for *spirituality*." After pausing briefly, he adds, "Haven't you!" It sounds more like a statement than a question. It takes you a second to understand his quick pronunciation of that unexpected word—*spirituality*. In a way, he is right. You *have* come for that. You nod in agreement. He smiles again, writes something down on his form, and lets you through.

As you take the small black taxi to your hotel, you realize that you have just accepted—willingly or not—the ancient role that the customs inspector has bestowed upon you. You are now just one more pilgrim who has come to Mother India for her most famous product: religious insight. You are now a Seeker.

After unpacking at your hotel, you walk out into the streets. It is dusk. Pedicab drivers ring their bells to ask if you want a ride, but you want to walk, to see the life of the streets. Little shops sell tea, and others sell vegetarian foods made of potatoes, wheat, beans, and curried vegetables. Children play in front of their parents' stores. Down the street you see a "gent's tailor" shop, as a thin cow wanders past, chewing on what looks like a paper bag. Another shop sells books and notepaper, and others sell saris and bolts of cloth. From somewhere comes a smell like jasmine. As night falls, the stores are lit by dim bulbs and fluorescent lights, and vendors illuminate their stalls with bright Coleman lanterns. Because you will be rising long before dawn the next day to go down to the Ganges, you soon return to your hotel. You fall asleep quickly.

The telephone rings, waking you out of a dream. The man at the front desk notifies you that it is four a.m. Being somewhat groggy, you have to remind yourself that you are in Benares. You get up and dress quickly.

At the front of the hotel you wake a driver sleeping in his pedicab. You negotiate the fare, climb onto the seat, and head off to the main crossing of town, near the river, as the sky begins to lighten. The pedicab drops you near the *ghats* (the stairs that descend to the river), which are already full of people, many going down to the river to bathe at dawn. Some are having sandalwood paste applied to their foreheads as a sign of devotion, and others are carrying brass jugs to collect Ganges water.

As you descend to the river, boat owners call to you. You decide to join the passengers in the boat of a man resembling a Victorian patriarch, with a white handlebar mustache. Off you go, moving slowly upstream. Laughing children jump up and down in the water as men and women wade waist-deep and face the rising sun to pray. Upstream, professional launderers beat clothes on the rocks and lay them out on the stones of the riverbank to dry.

The boat turns back downstream, passing the stairs where you first descended to the river. In the bright morning light you see large umbrellas, under which teachers sit cross-legged, some with disciples around them. Who, you wonder, are these teachers? The area near the shore is crammed with people and boats. On a nearby boat, people shout, *Ganga Ma ki Jai*—"Victory to Mother Ganges!"

The boat continues downstream. On the shore, smoke rises from small pyres, where bodies wrapped in red and white cloth are being cremated. The boatman warns, "No photos here, please." The boat pulls in to shore downstream of the pyres, and everyone gets off. Walking up the stairs, you see small groups of people quietly watching the cremations. At the pyres, a man tends the fires with a bamboo pole, and a dog wanders nearby.

Later, as you make your way back to the center of town, you notice a pedicab with a covered body tied onto the back. It cycles past women sitting beside the road, selling plastic bracelets and colored powders. The pedicab must be on its way to the pyres, you think. The blend of opposites fills your mind; on the banks of the very same river, laundry is washed and bodies are burned; in the streets, life and death appear side by side—yet no one seems to notice the contrasts. Here, the two are one.

THE ORIGINS OF HINDUISM

Looking at a map of India (Figure 3.1, p. 76) you can see that this subcontinent, shaped like a diamond, is isolated. Two sides face the sea, while the north is bounded by the steep Himalaya Mountains. There are few mountain passes, and the only easy land entry is via the narrow corridor in the northwest, in the vicinity of the Indus River, where Pakistan now lies. It is the relative isolation of India that has helped create a culture that is rare and fascinating.

India's climate, except in the mountain regions, is generally warm for most of the year, allowing people to live outdoors much of the time. Indeed, some people may even claim that the climate has helped promote religious values that, at least for some, minimize the importance of material goods such as clothing, housing, and wealth.

Although hot and dry in many parts, India has many rivers and streams. Most important is the Ganges, which flows out of the Himalayas and is enlarged by tributaries as it moves east toward the Bay of Bengal. By the time the Ganges has reached the town of Benares (also known as Varanasi and Kashi), the river is enormous; in fact, after the summer monsoons, the river becomes so wide that often one cannot see to the other side. Because the water of the Ganges is regular and dependable, it has enabled civilization to flourish across much of northern India. It has also given Indian culture a sense of security, protection, and even care, which has led to the popular name for the river, *Ganga Ma* ("Mother Ganges").

The religious life of India is something like the river Ganges. It has flowed along for thousands of years, swirling from its own power but also from the power of new streams that have added to its force. Hinduism, the major religion of India, has been an important part of this flowing energy. Many influences—early indigenous religion and influences from later immigrants—have added to its inherent momentum. It has no one identifiable founder, no strong organizational structure to defend it and spread its influence, nor any creed to define and stabilize its beliefs; and in a way that seems to defy reason, Hinduism unites the worship of many gods with a belief in a single divine reality. In fact, the name *Hinduism* can be misleading. Hinduism is not a single, unified religion; it is more like a family of beliefs.

But the limitations of Hinduism may also be its strengths. It is like a palace that began as a two-room cottage. Over the centuries, wings have

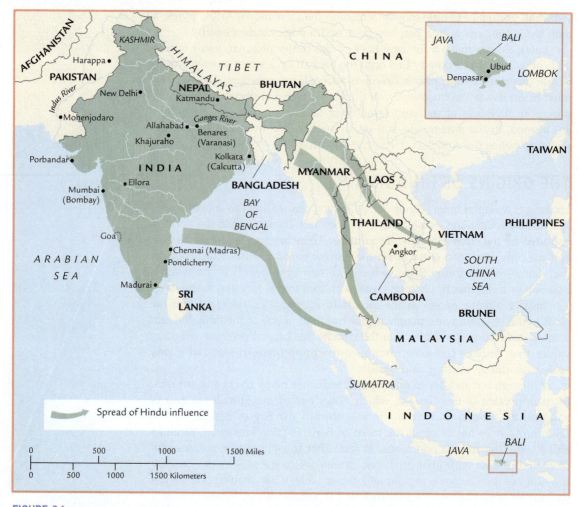

FIGURE 3.1

India, Bali, and the area of Hindu influence.

been built on to it, and now it has countless rooms, stairs, corridors, statues, fountains, and gardens. There is something here to please and astonish—and dismay—almost everyone. In fact, its beliefs are so rich and profound that Hinduism has greatly influenced the larger world, and its influence continues to grow. In this chapter we will explore the various elements of this religion's foundation and the stages in which additions were made to the sprawling house of Hinduism.

The Earliest Stage of Indian Religion

In the early twentieth century, engineers who were building a railroad discovered the ruins of an ancient culture in the Indus River valley. Today, most of the Indus River lies in Pakistan, but it traditionally formed the natural border of northwestern India—in fact, the words *India* and *Hindu* derive from *Indus.* The culture that archeological workers uncovered there flourished

TIMELINE 3.1

	before **2000** BCE	● Existence of Harappa culture in Indus River valley
Traditional period of early Vedic religion ●	**c. 2000–500** BCE	
	c. 1500 BCE	● Beginning of creation of the Vedas
Beginning of creation ● of Upanishads; Axis Age	**c. 800–500** BCE	
	c. 200 BCE–**200** CE	● Creation of the Bhagavad Gita
Life of philosopher Shankara ●	**c. 788–820** CE	
	c. 1200	● Muslim entry into northern India
Portuguese entry into India ●	**1498**	
	c. 1750–1947	● British domination of India
Life of political activist ● Mohandas (Mahatma) Gandhi	**1869–1948**	
	1947	● India achieves political independence
Periodic religion-related acts of violence involving India and ● Pakistan	**1965–present**	
	1998	● Victory of Hindu nationalist party (BJP) in Indian national elections

Timeline of significant events in the history of Hinduism.

before 2000 BCE and is named the Harappa culture, after one of its ancient cities (Timeline 3.1).

Archeologists were amazed by the type of civilization they found. The cities contained regular streets and solid brick houses. Pots and coins were discovered, as well as evidence that running water was used for toilets and baths. As one historian remarks, "no other ancient civilization until that of the Romans had so efficient a system of drains"[1]—a genuine sign of technical development. This complex culture had also invented a writing system, which scholars are still working to decipher.

Property owners marked their belongings with seals bearing the images of animals, such as the bull, tiger, and rhinoceros, as well as images of men and women. Three seals show a male, sitting in a yogic meditation posture, with horns on his head.[2] Small pillars that suggest male sexuality were also found. Because many of these same symbols still appear in contemporary Indian culture, we can assume that some current religious practices have survived from the distant past. For example, the male with the horns on his head may be a deity and an early form of the god Shiva, and the pillars resemble the low columns that some contemporary Indians worship in honor of Shiva. It is also quite possible that the present-day worship of the divine Great Mother and of tree spirits goes back to this early time.

The Religion of the Vedic Period

The ancient scriptures of India are called the **Vedas.** They give a great deal of information about gods and worship during what is often called the Vedic period, generally thought to cover about 2000 to 500 BCE. The origin of the Vedas and of the religion they describe, however, is uncertain.

In the late eighteenth century, Western scholars recognized that Sanskrit—the ancient language of India and the language of the Vedas—was related to Greek and Latin. They also realized that many of the gods mentioned in the Vedas were the same gods who had been worshiped in Greece and Rome; they discovered, as well, that gods of similar names were mentioned in Iranian sacred literature. Later scholars theorized that a single people, who called themselves Aryans, moved from present-day southern Russia about 2000 BCE in two directions—westward into Europe and eastward into Iran and India. Entering new lands, these people were thought to have carried their language and religion with them. Scholars initially believed that in India the outsiders imposed their social order quickly and violently on the older culture. According to this theory, called the "Aryan invasion theory," the Vedas were believed to be the religious writings of this invading people.

Next, a variant on the older theory arose: instead of speaking of a single invasion, the newer theory held that there were repeated waves of migrations into Pakistan and northern India, and that from these contacts between foreign and indigenous cultures the religion of the Vedas emerged. More recently, however, this second theory, called the "Aryan migration theory," has been questioned. The migration theory is still commonly held, but some scholars view any theory that assumes influence from outside India to be a continued relic of Western cultural imperialism. Archeological, linguistic, and genetic investigations continue to offer more clues, but their interpretation has not resolved the issue.

No matter what its origins, the religion described by the Vedas seems to have consisted of the worship of mostly male gods, who were believed to control the forces of nature. The father of the gods was Dyaüs Pitr, whose name means "shining father." (He is clearly the same god as the Roman god Jupiter and the Greek god Zeus Pater.) The god Indra, god of storm and war, received great attention because of the strength his worshipers hoped to receive from him. He was possibly the memory of a military ancestor, deified by later generations. The god of fire, Agni (whose name is related to the English word *ignite* and to the Latin word for fire, *ignis*), carried sacrifices up to the world of the gods. Dawn and renewal were the charge of the goddess Ushas, one of the few female deities. The god Rudra brought winds. Varuna was the god of the sky and justice; Vishnu was a god of cosmic order; and Surya was the major sun god. The god Soma was thought to cause altered states of mind and to expand consciousness. He worked through a ritual drink, possibly made from a psychedelic mushroom that had the same name (*soma*) and allowed contact with the realm of the gods. The god Yama ruled the afterlife.

Vishnu is mentioned in the Vedas, Hinduism's ancient scriptures, as a god of cosmic order. This sculpture, at Bangkok's very modern Suvarnabhumi Airport, illustrates the same god Vishnu in a tale that is still told today.

Worship of the gods took place at outdoor fire altars. Priestly specialists set apart a square or rectangular space, purified it with water, and constructed one to three low altars inside the space for sacrifice. The usual offerings were milk, clarified butter (called *ghee*), grains, and sometimes animals. A special horse sacrifice, believed to confer great power on a king, occurred on rare occasions.

Sacred chants, which the priests knew from memory, were an essential part of the ceremonies; and because they believed that the chants had power of their own, the priestly class protected them and handed them down orally from father to son. It is these chants, in written form, that make up the core of the earliest Hindu sacred literature, the Vedas. Although many of the Vedic gods are no longer worshiped, elements of the Aryan religion—such as the use of fire and some of the ancient chants by a priestly class—continue to be of great importance to Hindus today.

The Vedas

The Vedas, which originally were preserved only in oral form but eventually were written down, are the earliest sacred books of Hinduism. The name means "knowledge" or "sacred lore," and related words in English are *vision* and *wisdom*. Although scholars date the earliest versions of the Vedas to about 1500 BCE, Hindus consider them to be far more ancient. They say that the Vedas were revealed to *rishis* (holy men of the distant past), who did not create the Vedas but heard them and transmitted them to later generations.

There are four basic sacred text collections that constitute the Vedas. The Rig Veda[3] ("hymn knowledge") is a collection of more than a thousand chants to the Aryan gods; the Yajur Veda ("ceremonial knowledge") contains matter for recitation during sacrifice; the Sama Veda ("chant knowledge") is a handbook of musical elaborations of Vedic chants; and the Atharva Veda ("knowledge from [the teacher] Atharva") consists of practical prayers and charms, such as prayers to protect against snakes and sickness.

The Rig Veda, the most important of the Vedas, has an account of the origin of the universe. The universe is said to have emerged from a division and cosmic sacrifice of a primeval superperson, Purusha. But the account includes an admission of uncertainty: "Who knows it for certain; who can proclaim it here; namely, out of what it was born and wherefrom his creations issued? The gods appeared only later—after the creation of the world. Who knows, then, out of what it has evolved?"[4]

The term *Vedas* sometimes indicates only these four collections. In its more common use, it also refers to some later material as well. Detailed ceremonial rules, called Brahmanas and Aranyakas, were added by later generations to each of the four Vedic collections. The Brahmanas, named for the priests who would use them, give details about the proper time and place for ceremonies, the preparation of the ground, ritual objects, and purification rites. The Aranyakas ("forest books") allowed the rituals to be understood and practiced in nonliteral, symbolic ways by men who had left society and become ascetics in the forests. The four Vedas end with even later works, called the **Upanishads,** which express philosophical and religious ideas that arose in introspective and meditative traditions.

THE UPANISHADS AND THE AXIS AGE

Around 500 BCE, Indian civilization experienced such widespread and important changes that the period is known as the Axis Age, meaning that everything turned in a new direction at this time. Interestingly, great changes were taking place in other religions and cultures as well: it was the time of the Buddha, Confucius, major Hebrew prophets, and early Greek philosophers.

After many centuries, questioning of Vedic religious beliefs and practices began to emerge with strength. It is possible that earlier religious disciplines reasserted themselves, and there may have been resentment against the priestly class. Some critics questioned the value of the Vedic sacrifices, and we know from the Aranyakas that certain people abandoned social life to live alone in the forests, giving themselves much time for thought and religious experimentation. Thinkers questioned the ancient belief in many gods, seeking instead a single divine reality that might be the source of everything.[5] Some went even further and saw all things as being mystically united. And a few rejected religious ritual altogether.

During this period there seems to have been interest in all sorts of techniques for altering consciousness, such as sitting for long periods in meditation, breathing deeply, fasting, avoiding sexual activity, practicing long periods of silence, going without sleep, experimenting with psychedelic plants, and living in the darkness of caves. People of any social class—not just priests—could do all of these things. Evidence of this intellectual ferment and the practice of spiritual disciplines is recorded in the Upanishads.

The Origin of the Upanishads

The Upanishads comprise about a hundred written works that record insights into external and internal reality. Although several interpretations of the name *Upanishads* have been proposed, it is commonly thought to derive from words that mean "sitting near."[6] If the term's derivation is correct, it suggests disciples sitting near a master, learning techniques for achieving religious experience. In any case, primary to the Upanishads is the notion that with spiritual discipline and meditation, both priests and non-priests can experience the spiritual reality that underlies all seemingly separate realities. Unlike much of the earlier Vedic material, which dictates that only hereditary priests can be religious masters, the Upanishads tell us that a person who has the necessary experience can be a spiritual master. The Upanishads thus possibly continue the religious interest of the forest dwellers of the Aranyakas.

The Upanishads are written primarily in dialogue form, appearing both as prose and as poetry. Because they were produced over many hundreds of years, dating them is not easy. It is generally thought that those in prose form (such as the Chandogya, Brihadaranyaka, Taittiriya, and Kena Upanishads) may be earlier works than those in poetic form (such as the Katha and Mandukya Upanishads). About a dozen Upanishads are especially popular.

Important Concepts of the Upanishads

The most important notions in the Upanishads are *Brahman, Atman, maya, karma, samsara,* and *moksha.*[7] These primary concepts, which would become essential notions in much later Hindu spirituality, continue to be taught today.

Brahman and Atman   The term **Brahman** originally stood for the cosmic power present in the Vedic sacrifice and chants, over which the priest had control. (The Sanskrit word *Brahman* is neuter and comes from a stem meaning "to be great.") In the Upanishads the word *Brahman* was expanded to mean a divine reality at the heart of things. One of the most famous dialogues appears in the Chandogya Upanishad. It involves a priestly father and his son in discussion. The young man, Shvetaketu, has been away, studying with a specialist for many years. He has memorized chants and learned priestly rituals. The young man's father questions him about what he has learned, and the son proudly recites the formulas he knows. The father then asks him what he knows about Brahman, the Supreme Spirit; but

Many Hindu concepts are complex, and serious Hindus often seek guidance from a priest as they try to improve their practice and understanding.

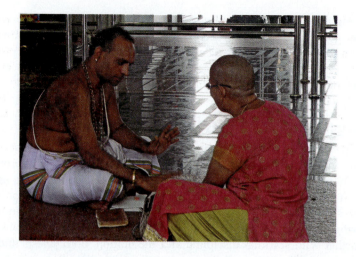

the young man knows nothing. Trying to assist the son's understanding, the father asks his son to fill a glass with water, put salt in it, and leave it overnight. The next day he asks his son to find the salt:

> "Bring me the salt you put into the water last night."
> Shvetaketu looked into the water, but could not find it, for it had dissolved.
> His father then said: "Taste the water from this side. How is it?"
> "It is salt [salty]."
> "Taste it from the middle. How is it?"
> "It is salt."
> "Taste it from that side. How is it?"
> "It is salt."
> "Look for the salt again and come again to me."
> The son did so, saying: "I cannot see the salt. I only see water."
> The father then said: "In the same way, O my son, you cannot see the Spirit. But in truth he is here.
> "An invisible and subtle essence is the Spirit of the whole universe. That is Reality. That is Truth. Thou art That."[8]

The Upanishads insist that Brahman is something that can be known—not simply believed in. The Shvetasvatara Upanishad, for example, says "I *know* that Spirit whose infinity is in all, who is ever one beyond time."[9] Brahman, the Divine Spirit, is so real that it may be known directly, and, as the boy Shvetaketu learned, knowledge of it can be as immediate as tasting the flavor of salt.

What is it to know Brahman? The Upanishads insist that it cannot be put fully into words, but they give hints. Brahman is the lived experience that all things are in some way holy because they come from the same sacred source. It is also the experience that all things are in some way ultimately one. This is an experience that seems to defy common sense, since the world appears to be divided into many objects and types of reality. Nevertheless, when we consider reality more deeply, we recognize many unities: a piece of wood can become a boat or a house or fire or ash; water can turn into a cloud or a plant. So, on closer inspection, all apparent separations and divisions blur. To experience Brahman is to know, firsthand, that every apparently individual reality in the world is actually a wave of the same sacred ocean of energy. Brahman, according to the Upanishads, "is the sun, the moon, and the stars. He is the fire, the waters, and the wind."[10] Brahman is "the God who appears in forms infinite."[11]

Brahman is also referred to by three words that help describe its nature as perceived by the knower: Brahman is *sat*, reality itself; *chit*, pure consciousness; and *ananda*, bliss. And although Brahman can be experienced within our everyday world of time and space, those who speak of their experience say that Brahman is ultimately beyond time and beyond space. Thus the Upanishads often add that experiencing the timelessness of Brahman can bring an end to everyday suffering and to the fear of death.

The notion of **Atman** is related to Brahman and is an equally important term in the Upanishads. Although Atman is sometimes translated as "self" or "soul," the notion of Atman in the Upanishads is different from the notion of an individual soul. Perhaps the term *Atman* would be better translated as "deepest self." In Hindu belief, each person has an individual soul (*jiva*), and the individual soul confers uniqueness and personality. But Hinduism asks this question: At the very deepest level, what really am I? I am clearly not just my body—my height and weight and hair color, all of which are subject to alteration. But am I then my tastes, thoughts, and memories? Or is there more? Is there not in me a reality more fundamental than those changing individual characteristics? According to the Upanishads, at the deepest level of what I am is a divine reality, a divine spirit that everything shares. The Upanishads teach that it is true to say that I am God, because, for the person who understands reality at the deepest level, everything is God. Atman, when experienced fully, is identical with Brahman. Atman, like Brahman, is divine, holy, and timeless. Often the term *Brahman* refers to the experience of the sacred within nature and the external universe, while *Atman* refers to the experience of the sacred within oneself. However, the same divine nature simply has two names, and both terms may be used interchangeably.

Maya   The Upanishads speak of the everyday world as **maya,** which is usually translated as "illusion."[12] This translation, though, needs explanation. Its root suggests illusion and mystery (as in "magic"), but it also has a more positive, objective connotation that suggests the original stuff of which something is made (as in "material"). The word *maya* thus contains both meanings: "magic" and "matter." To say that all reality is "maya" is not to say that the world does not exist or that the world is a totally false perception. The world is real, but not in quite the way most people assume. For one thing, human beings view the world as consisting of individual things and people, all separate. In reality, the world is one basic holy reality that takes on many different forms. The Shvetasvatara Upanishad advises us to "know therefore that nature is Maya, but that God is the ruler of Maya; and that all beings in our universe are parts of his infinite splendour."[13]

People also assume that the world is solid and permanent. In reality, the outside world is more like the inner world of thoughts and dreams—it shifts and changes, just as thoughts and dreams do. People assume that time is real, that it advances at a regular rate, and that past, present, and future are distinct divisions. In reality, time is relative.

The model of reality set forth by the Upanishads is less like a machine made of individual moving parts; it is more like a great consciousness. This view also produces a sense of amazement at the forms and shifts that the universe takes—it is all, ultimately, unexplainable magic.

As I look out at reality from my own individual standpoint, I may see the end of my life as the end of everything. The Upanishads see things differently. First, individuals are not as individual as they suppose. Rather, they are all manifestations of the Divine Spirit, which does not end when the individual dies. They are also the continuation of earlier forms of life that have simply taken new forms. Hinduism, from about 500 BCE, generally adopted the belief that everything living has its own life force and that every life force, when it loses one form, is reborn into another. This process is known as reincarnation.

Karma The general Hindu notion of rebirth assumes that human beings have at one or another time existed as a "lower" form, such as animal, insect, and possibly even plant. Hinduism also recognizes grades of human life, from limited and painful to exceptionally pleasant and free. Human beings are also capable of achieving "higher" forms of life, such as superhuman beings and demigods. Rebirth can move in either direction, and the human stage is a dangerous one because each human being must make dramatic choices about how to live. If a human being does not live properly, he or she may be reborn into a very poor or cruel human family—or possibly in a form of life that may be even more limited and difficult, such as a dog, a pig, or an ant. A human being can also make a spectacular leap upward beyond the human level to a superhuman existence or even beyond, to complete freedom.

What determines the direction of one's rebirth is **karma.** The word comes from a root that means "to do" and implies the notion of moral consequences that are carried along with every act. Karma is the moral law of cause and effect, and belief in karma is a belief that every action has an automatic moral consequence. One well-known saying expresses nicely the nature of karma: What goes around comes around. Karma does not work because it is the will of God or Brahman, but simply because karma is an essential part of the nature of things. It is the way things work. Good karma brings "higher" rebirth; bad karma brings rebirth in "lower," more painful forms. In a certain way, this belief allows for upward mobility, since human beings, by their actions, have influence over their future births. Ultimate freedom comes when karma ceases to operate; rebirth, whether upward or downward on the scale, has entirely ended.

Some teachers say that karma is intrinsically neither good nor bad but only seems so to the person who experiences it. In this conception, karma is like gravity—it works like a force of nature. It is like rain, which can cause a plant to grow just as it can bring a picnic to its end. Karma helps explain why some people are born with great gifts and others are born with no advantages at all.

Samsara   The term **samsara** refers to the wheel of life, the circle of constant rebirth, and it suggests strongly that the everyday world is full of change as well as struggle and suffering. The Hindu view of human life, because of its belief in reincarnation, is rather different from that commonly held in the West. Think of how often you hear someone say, You only live once. This view of life is not shared by Hindus, who believe an individual is constantly being reborn, having come from different earlier forms and going on to emerge in new forms in the future. Because our present human life is so short, we may think that we would like several lives in the future as well. But how many would each of us really like? Ten might sound reasonable, but a hundred? a thousand? ten thousand? a million? It's tiring just to think about all those lifetimes! And many of those forms would inevitably be unhappy ones. Sooner or later most of us would want to jump off the merry-go-round of life. We would want escape, release, liberation. This leads us to the next important concept of the Upanishads.

Moksha   The term **moksha** means "freedom" or "liberation" and comes from a root that means "to be released." In the Upanishads, moksha is the ultimate human goal. It has various connotations. Moksha certainly includes the notion of getting beyond egotistic responses, such as resentment and anger, which limit the individual. Furthermore, unlike the modern ideal of seeking complete freedom to satisfy one's individual desires, moksha implies liberation even from the limitations of being an individual—from being born a particular person at a specific time to a unique pair of parents—a person with distinct physical characteristics, emotions, desires, and memories. One can take action to overcome these restrictions (for example, by leaving home), which is sometimes a means of attaining moksha, but one can also accept the limitations even while living with them, thereby gaining inner peace and mental freedom.

As one becomes freer, one looks at life less from a selfish and egotistic point of view and more from a perspective that embraces the whole. The unity and sacredness that everything shares become a part of everyday experience. Kindness to all—to animals as well as to people—is one natural result of this insight, and kind actions also generate helpful karma. Detaching oneself from pleasure or pain is another practice that leads to freedom from egotism.

Ultimately, with enough insight and ascetic practice, the individual can go entirely beyond the limited self to know the sacred reality that everything shares. When insight and kindness are perfect, at last the pain of rebirth ends; the limitations of individuality are gone, and only Brahman remains. The Brihadaranyaka Upanishad explains complete freedom: "when all has become Spirit, one's own Self, how and whom could one see?"[14]

The Upanishads, though sometimes obscure, are devoted to promoting an insight into ultimate oneness. But the Upanishads do not give detailed instructions for achieving that kind of insight or for living spiritually in the everyday world. Such guidance would have to be developed by later Hindu commentators and practitioners.

LIVING SPIRITUALLY IN THE EVERYDAY WORLD

The Hinduism that guides people's lives today is a practical mixture of elements. Some of these came from the early stages of religious practice, which we've already discussed, and others developed later. For the ordinary layperson, Hindu practice usually involves devotion to at least one deity. It recommends finding one's proper work and then doing it unselfishly. Hindu practice may also include the study of religious texts, meditation, and other specifically religious disciplines. The following section will deal with the elements of this practical synthesis, much of which can be found in the short classic, the Bhagavad Gita.

The Bhagavad Gita

The **Bhagavad Gita** ("divine song" or "song of the Divine One") is part of a very long epic poem called the Mahabharata. The Mahabharata, written some time between 400 BCE and 400 CE, tells how the sons of Pandu (Pandavas) conquered their cousins, the Kauravas, with the help of the god Krishna. The Bhagavad Gita was inserted at some time into this poem but has its own identity and is often printed separately from the Mahabharata. The Bhagavad Gita, shaped by the priestly class between 200 BCE and 200 CE, has become a spiritual classic. It recalls themes from the Upanishads, but it also tries to strike a balance between mysticism and the practical needs of everyday life. Action and adherence to duty are approved and can even be thought of as a spiritual path. As the Bhagavad Gita says, "the wise see knowledge and action as one."[15]

The Bhagavad Gita, like the Upanishads, is written in dialogue form. It occurs almost entirely between two figures: a prince, Arjuna, and his charioteer and advisor, Krishna. Arjuna's royal power is threatened by his hundred cousins, called Kauravas, and he must decide whether to fight with his brothers against them to restore his throne or to accept their rule. He is torn. On the one hand, he knows that his rule is correct, but on the other, he wants to avoid violence. That his enemies are close family members makes the matter even harder. Depressed, Arjuna "[throws] aside his arrows and his bow in the midst of the battlefield. He [sits] down on the seat of the chariot, and his heart [is] overcome with sorrow."[16] In response, Krishna, who later reveals that he is a form of the god Vishnu, explains the need for action. "Now you shall hear how a man may become perfect, if he devotes himself to the work which is natural to him. A man shall reach perfection if he does his duty as an act of worship to the Lord."[17] This means that Arjuna must follow not merely his own desires—neither his fears nor his hope for reward—but he must simply do what is right.

Contrary to the teaching of nonviolence, which was at the time of this epic's creation growing strong in India in such religious traditions as Buddhism and Jainism, Krishna advises Arjuna to fight to protect his throne and the structure of society—to fight is his duty. At a moment of great revelation, Krishna shows Arjuna that a divine reality is at work within everything in the universe—in living and also in dying. Krishna even says that for the warrior "there is nothing nobler than a righteous war.[18]

The recommendation that Arjuna should fight has posed a moral problem for some followers of Hinduism. Mohandas Gandhi is typical of those who have solved this problem by saying that the Bhagavad Gita is religious allegory. Gandhi held that the call to arms is not about real war but rather a call to fight against dangerous moral and psychological forces, such as ignorance, selfishness, and anger. This interpretation, though it seems to go against the literal intent of the text, has been influential.

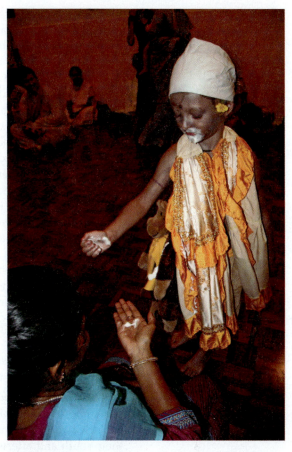

Krishna has long been one of Hinduism's most venerated divinities. Here, a temple's celebration of Krishna's birthday includes a child dressed as Krishna, sharing fresh butter that he has taken from milkmaids.

The Caste System

When Krishna urges Arjuna to do what his position as a warrior demands, he is reinforcing the **caste** system (a division of society into social classes that are created by birth or occupation). The caste system, the prevalent social system of Hinduism, had already been mentioned in the Rig Veda: "When they divided Purusha [the first person, a superbeing], in how many different portions did they arrange him? What became of his mouth, what of his two arms? What were his two thighs and his two feet called? His mouth became the brahman [priest]; his two arms were made into the rajanya [warrior-noble]; his two thighs the vaishyas [merchants]; from his two feet the shudra [peasant] was born."[19]

The caste system receives further religious approval in the Bhagavad Gita, which recognizes that there are different types of people and that their ways to perfection will differ, depending on their personality types and roles in society.[20] For example, active people will perfect themselves through the unselfishness of their work, and intellectual people will perfect themselves through teaching and study.

Traditionally, the caste system was based on more than one's type of work, and in modern times it does not always indicate the type of work a person does. Castes (as the term is commonly used) are really social classes (*varna*), which are subdivided into hundreds of subcastes.[21] The caste system dissuades members of different castes, and often subcastes, from intermarrying. It remains strongest in the countryside and in more conservative southern India, but it is weakening in the cities, where people regularly eat together in restaurants and travel together on buses and trains. Although an individual cannot change the caste into which she or he is born, it is believed that a good life in one's present caste will guarantee rebirth in a higher caste or better circumstances. Thus, from the perspective of Hinduism, upward social mobility is possible—even if it takes more than one lifetime to accomplish!

Members of society are divided into five main social classes:

1. The priest (**brahmin**)[22] traditionally performs Vedic rituals and acts as a counselor.

2. The warrior-noble (*kshatriya*) has the role of protecting society. This is the traditional caste of the aristocracy.

3. The merchant (*vaishya*) class includes landowners, moneylenders, and sometimes artisans. Males of the three upper castes (brahmin, kshatriya, and vaishya) receive a sacred cord during a ceremony in their youth and afterward are called "twice-born."

4. The peasant (*shudra*) does manual labor and is expected to serve the higher castes. The origin of this caste probably goes back to the Aryan subjection of native people, who were forced to do the work of servants. The peasant is called "once-born."

5. The untouchable (*dalit*) traditionally does the dirtiest work—cleaning toilets, sweeping streets, collecting animal carcasses, and tanning animal hides. This caste's low status prompted the Indian reformer Mohandas Gandhi to promote another name for the class—*Harijan* ("children of God")—and he urged their inclusion in regular society.[23] Present-day India has laws and rules to help overcome discrimination against untouchables.

The Stages of Life

Just as the individual's path to "correct action" is suggested by caste and subcaste, traditional Hinduism holds that each stage of life also has its proper way of being lived. Every culture recognizes specific life stages through which each individual passes. In modern secular life the stages seem to be childhood, adolescence, the career years, and retirement (these stages are strongly colored by employment—or the lack of it). But in India the notion of life stages is more religious. The conception was shaped by the ancient ideal of the development of the upper-caste male, particularly of the priestly caste:

1. Student (*brahmacharin*): This first stage is spent laying a religious foundation for life. The young person, between the ages of 8 and 20, studies religious works. Celibacy is a necessary part of the training.

2. Householder (*grihastha*): Marriage (traditionally, arranged by the parents) occurs at about age 20, and the person fulfills the demands of society by raising children.

3. Retiree (*vanaprastha*): When grandchildren arrive, the individual may retire somewhat from ordinary life to spend time once again on religious matters. The ancient ideal was to go into the forest to live, possibly with one's wife, away from society. In reality, retirees often continue to live with their children and with other relatives in an extended-family setting, but they may eat separately from the rest of the family and spend time on religious pursuits with friends.

Hindus see life in stages. Here a priest, as part of a wedding ceremony, blesses the groom to help him successfully enter a new stage: starting and sustaining a new family. A statue of Ganesha is in the foreground.

4. Renunciate **(sannyasin):** To enter this last stage is considered to be appropriate only after retirement. It is not expected of everyone but is simply an option. If one wishes to live entirely free from society, one is permitted to leave home. For such a person, the entire world is now his home. A man may leave his wife, although he must ensure that she will be supported. Celibacy is expected, and the sign of this devout, celibate state is an orange robe. The sannyasin, considered to be outside the caste system, is free to wander, begging his food along the way, and many temples have endowments to feed such pilgrims. The sannyasin may remain a constant traveler, making pilgrimage to the sacred sites of India, or he may settle in an **ashram** (religious community) or even live in a cave. The purpose of this kind of life is to hasten mystical insight, to free oneself of all attachments, to end rebirth, and to attain moksha.

The Goals of Life

Although the Hindu spiritual ideal—such as the lifestyle of the sannyasin—is generally world-denying, Hinduism also exhibits a respect for more worldly goals. In order of increasing value these goals are pleasure (*kama*), economic security and power (*artha*), and social and religious duty (*dharma*). These life goals, which may be pursued simultaneously, are acceptable and even virtuous, as long as they are tempered by moderation and social regulation. Considered highest of the goals, however, is moksha—complete freedom.

The Yogas

Although the Bhagavad Gita endorses quiet contemplation, it also recommends active spiritual paths. It endorses not only meditation but also the work demanded by one's caste and individual place in society. The various types of **yoga** are methods that can be used to help people live spiritually. The word *yoga* means "union" and is related to the English words *join* and *yoke.* A yoga is a way for people to perfect their union with the divine, and because the yogas suggest roads to perfection, they are also called *margas* ("paths"). There is a tolerant recognition in Hinduism that different sorts of people need different spiritual paths, and an individual's caste and personality type will help determine the appropriate yoga to practice.

Jnana Yoga ("Knowledge Yoga")   This type of yoga brings insight into one's divine nature by studying the Upanishads and the Bhagavad Gita and by learning from teachers who have attained insight. **Jnana yoga** is particularly appropriate for priests and intellectuals.

This yoga was highly refined by a school of philosophy that is still quite vital, the school of Vedanta ("Veda end").[24] The term refers to the

Upanishads—which come at the end of the Vedas—and to the fact that the Vedanta school has used the ideas of the Upanishads as its primary inspiration.

The greatest teacher of Vedanta, Shankara (c. 788–820), argued that everything is ultimately one—all is Brahman.[25] According to Shankara, although our ordinary experience leads us to see things as being separate and different, this perception is mistaken. To show that sense perception can be wrong, Shankara used the example of a person who at dusk is frightened by a coil of rope—the observer mistakenly perceives the rope to be a snake. In the same way, Shankara would say, a person who perceives things as being ultimately separate and different from Brahman is mistaken. In the *Crest-Jewel of Discrimination*, attributed to Shankara, the author likens Brahman to gold, which can take many shapes. Brahman "is that one Reality which appears to our ignorance as a manifold universe of names and forms and changes. Like the gold of which many orna-ments are made, it remains in itself unchanged. Such is Brahman, and 'That art Thou.' Meditate upon this truth."[26] Similarly, the waves of the ocean and the drops of water in the waves may be considered separate entities; but the larger truth is that they are all just the same ocean in varied, changing forms.

Shankara thought that spiritual liberation was achieved when the indi-vidual personally came to understand the unity of all things. Shankara so emphasized **monism**—the oneness of everything—that his branch of the Vedanta school is called *Advaita,* which, literally translated, means "not-two-ness" (*a-dvai-ta*). The significance of the term is very subtle. If I say that all reality is "one," some "other" reality could also exist—something in contrast to the one. But the term *not-two* makes clear that ultimately there is no other reality.

For Shankara, therefore, any devotion to a god or goddess who is thought to be different from the worshiper is also mistaken. This rejec-tion of devotion, however, posed a great problem for those types of Hin-duism that emphasized it. As a result, later thinkers of the Vedanta school, such as Ramanuja (d. 1137) and Madhva (active 1240), qualified or denied ultimate monism. They emphasized passages in the Upani-shads that seem to speak of Brahman as being separate in some way from the world. They could thereby create systems that made room for religious devotion.

Karma Yoga ("Action Yoga") This type of yoga proposes that all useful work, if done unselfishly, can be a way to perfection. (The word *karma* here is used in its basic sense of "activity.") Much of what we ordinarily do is motivated by money or pleasure or praise, but deeds performed without a desire for reward are the heart of **karma yoga.** As the Bhagavad Gita says, "Desire for the fruits of work must never be your motive in working."[27]

Rituals and Celebrations

HINDU MEDITATION: MORE THAN EMPTYING THE MIND

Over the past three decades, meditation has become popular in the Western world. From students in elementary schools to executives in corporate offices, all kinds of people take time out to sit quietly, empty the mind, and let stress float away.

Meditation in Eastern religious traditions, however, is more complex, at least theoretically. The Yoga Sutras, often attributed to the grammarian Patanjali,[28] list eight steps necessary for perfection of meditation:

- Self-control (*yama*) is the fundamental reorientation of the personality away from selfishness. It involves practicing **ahimsa** (not hurting living beings), exhibiting sexual restraint, shunning greed, refusing to steal, and embracing truthfulness.
- Observance (*niyama*) is the regular practice of the five preceding virtuous pursuits.

- Posture (*asana*) is an integral aspect of meditation, particularly the "lotus posture" (*padmasana*), in which the person meditating is seated with the legs crossed, each foot touching the opposite leg.
- Breath control (*pranayama*) involves deep, regular breathing, holding the breath, and breathing in various rhythms.
- Restraint (*pratyahara*) helps the meditator tune out external distractions.
- Steadying of the mind (*dharana*) teaches the meditator to focus on only one object in order to empty the mind of everything else.
- Meditation (**dhyana**) occurs when the mind is focused only on the object of concentration.
- **Samadhi** is the mental state achieved by deep meditation, in which the individual loses the sense of being separate from the rest of the universe.[29]

Bhakti Yoga ("Devotion Yoga") Most of us have at one time or another fallen in love, and we know that there is something purifying about the experience, because it forces us to look outward, beyond ourselves, to another object of affection. Religions utilize this purifying power when they promote devotion to a god or saint—who is often made visible in a painting or statue. Hinduism, because of its belief in multiple gods, offers rich possibilities for devotion. In the Bhagavad Gita, Krishna tells Arjuna, "Regard me as your dearest loved one. Know me to be your only refuge."[30]

Bhakti yoga can involve various expressions of devotion—most commonly chants, songs, food offerings, and the anointing of statues. Bhakti yoga can extend also to acts of devotion shown to one's **guru** (spiritual teacher), to one's parents, and to one's spouse. The gods worshiped in bhakti yoga will be described later.

Raja Yoga ("Royal Yoga") This type of yoga promotes meditation. The term **raja yoga** does not appear in the Bhagavad Gita but was introduced later to refer to the steps of meditation described in the box "Hindu Meditation: More Than Emptying the Mind." Nonetheless, chapter 6 of the Bhagavad Gita describes basic meditation—sitting quietly, turning inward, and calming the mind. Done for short periods of time on a regular basis, meditation lowers stress and brings a sense of peace; done for longer periods of time, it can induce new states of consciousness.

There are many types of meditation. Some involve emptying the mind of thought; others involve focusing on some physical or mental object.

Meditation can be done with one's eyes closed or open or focused on a point a short distance in front of the face. A word or brief phrase, called a **mantra,** is often recited with each breath to help clear the mind of thought. (The short mantra *Om*—which is sometimes called the sound of creation—is frequently used.) Meditation can be done in silence or to gentle music; it can also be done while gazing at a candle, at the moon, or at moving water. Some advanced types of meditation involve techniques taken from additional yogas. They may have the meditator create symbolic mental images (frequently of a deity), contemplate a sacred diagram (called a *yantra*), or repeat complicated sacred phrases. The many techniques of meditation are called *sadhanas* ("practices").

In recent years, hatha yoga has become a part of daily life for millions of people across the planet.

Hatha Yoga ("Force Yoga")   When most of us in the West think of yoga, we think of the physical exercises of **hatha yoga.** These exercises, which were originally developed to help make long periods of meditation easier, mostly involve stretching and balancing. Breathing exercises are usually considered a part of hatha yoga.

There are many schools of hatha yoga, often named after their founders. Several have gained great popularity. Among them, Iyengar yoga focuses on correct technique and sequence in doing a large number of traditional breathing exercises and yoga postures. Bikram yoga involves a series of twenty-six hatha yoga exercises and two breathing exercises in a heated room (the heat is meant to make the muscles limber and to assist circulation). Ashtanga yoga, named after teachings of the Yoga Sutras, is a demanding series of six sequences of highly athletic yogic postures.

Kundalini Yoga   Combining elements of both raja yoga and hatha yoga, **Kundalini yoga** teaches that there are seven psychic centers, called *chakras* ("wheels"), that exist along the spinal column, one above the other. Meditation and physical exercises (as described below) help the meditator lift spiritual energy—called *kundalini* and envisioned as a coiled serpent—from one center to the next. (Literally *kundalini* means "she who lies coiled.") Each chakra is like a gateway through which the kundalini passes, bringing increased insight and joy. When the kundalini reaches the topmost and seventh center of energy at the crown of the head, the practitioner experiences profound bliss. The topmost center of energy (*sahasrara*) appears in imagery as a lotus flower, and reaching it is compared to the opening of a lotus.

In addition to these six yogas are others. In fact, any systematic set of techniques that leads to greater spirituality can be considered a yoga.

The chakras are centers through which energy rises from the base of the spine to the crown of the head.

DEVOTIONAL HINDUISM

Indians have been primarily a rural, agricultural people. This is changing, but even today most of the population still lives outside cities. They live, as they have for centuries, in more than a half million villages. Men in the villages spend most of their waking hours working as merchants, craftsmen, and farmers, while women marry when young and spend most of their time preparing food, running their households, and caring for their children. The duties of everyday life leave little time to pursue more philosophical paths.

For the majority of Hindus, then, some of the spiritual disciplines just mentioned—study, meditation, and special physical exercises—have had limited appeal. Instead, the great majority of Hindus have followed the path of devotion (**bhakti**) to a god or gods. Hindus worship their gods in village temples and at home altars. Most worship daily, and there are special days dedicated to individual gods. **Puja,** devotional ritual commonly performed at an altar, involves the offering of flowers, food, fire, and incense to images of a god or gods, as well as the occasional singing of hymns.

The earliest layer of devotional Hinduism, probably traceable to the Harappa culture, seems to have involved the anointing of phallic stones, devotion to female divinities of fertility, and the worship of nature spirits. This type of religious devotion continues in India today.

The Vedic religion introduced its own gods as additional objects of worship. Some of these, such as Indra and Agni, were once highly popular, while others, such as Dyaüs Pitr, lost devotees and moved to the background quite early. In this devotional pattern we can see that a certain fluctuation of interest is natural; throughout history, in all religious devotion, interest in some gods rises and interest in others fades away.

Certain gods and goddesses seem to have emerged separately, not as a part of the Vedic pantheon—of these Krishna is one of the best known. Some animal forms became deified, and all deities were eventually incorporated loosely into what is today a fairly large pantheon.

Although Hinduism is often described as a religion that promotes a belief in many gods, in reality individuals tend to focus their devotion on only one of the gods. Sometimes that god is considered to be the greatest of all divine manifestations. There are also strong tendencies in Hinduism toward both monotheism and even monism, because all gods—and everything else as well—are considered, ultimately, to be expressions of a single divine reality. Devotion to an individual god or goddess is often justified by saying that although the divine is ultimately formless, human beings must worship the divine through its physical manifestations. This belief gives rise to much painting, sculpture, music, and ceremony in honor of many gods, who are described in the following sections (Table 3.1).

This Hindu temple roofline includes just a few of the many deities in the Hindu pantheon.

The Trimurti: Brahma, Vishnu, and Shiva

Three gods have been particularly important in the devotional and artistic life of Hinduism. Although of differing origins, they have sometimes been linked together—particularly in philosophy and art, where they represent the three forces of creation, preservation, and destruction. The three gods are Brahma, Vishnu, and Shiva. When linked together, they are often called the **Trimurti,** which means "triple form."

Brahma represents the creative force that made the universe. He is considered the personal aspect of Brahman and has been thought of as the special patron of the priestly class, the brahmins. Brahma is commonly

TABLE 3.1 Major Hindu Gods

Brahma	god of creation
Vishnu	god of preservation
Shiva	god of destruction and re-creation
Devi	goddess, Divine Mother
Durga	goddess of perseverance
Lakshmi	goddess of success
Kali	goddess of destruction and re-creation
Saraswati	goddess of music and culture
Krishna	loving manifestation of Vishnu
Rama	royal manifestation of Vishnu
Ganesha	elephant-headed son of Shiva, prayed to for success

depicted as an ancient, thoughtful king sitting on a throne. He has four faces, each looking in one of the four directions, and eight arms, each holding symbols of power. His companion animal is a white goose.

In India, worship of Brahma as a separate deity has declined over the past two hundred years, although he is still frequently represented in art, where he is pictured beside Vishnu or Shiva. Perhaps this decline in interest resulted from the popular view of Brahma in India as grandfatherly, distant, and less powerful than either Vishnu or Shiva. (Ironically, however, devotion to Brahma remains quite alive in Thailand, where local Buddhist practice shows many influences from Hinduism. Statues of Brahma appear frequently in outdoor "spirit houses," where food and flowers—and sometimes dance— are offered to him for good luck and protection.)

Vishnu represents the force of preservation in the universe. In the Vedas he is a god associated with the sun, although his role there appears to be small. Thought of as light and warmth that destroys darkness, Vishnu grew in stature until finally becoming a major god of Hinduism. Today Vishnu (in various forms) is the most important object of devotion in India, and about three quarters of all Hindus in India worship him or his manifestations. His followers are called Vaishnavites (or Vaishnavas).

In painting and sculpture, Vishnu is shown in many forms, though usually with a tall crown and a regal manner. Almost always he has four arms, which hold symbols of power. His companion animal is a great eaglelike bird, Garuda, on whom he flies through the universe.

Because Vishnu is associated with loving-kindness, it is believed that he can appear on earth at different times and in various physical forms to help those in need. Ten major incarnations (or **avatars**) of Vishnu are commonly listed, of which one is still to appear. Some previous incarnations were in animal form: a fish, a boar, and a tortoise. Another was Siddhartha Gautama, the Buddha—an intriguing inclusion, which helped Hinduism partially reabsorb Indian Buddhism (see Chapter 4). The incarnation yet to come will be a savior figure on horseback who will judge the human race. Two incarnations of Vishnu are wildly popular—Rama and Krishna.

Rama may have been a historical figure who later took on mythic proportions. He appears in the great epic the Ramayana, whose stories have inspired dance as well as art. Rama and his wife, Sita, who are thought of as the ideal couple, are often portrayed together. One of the most commonly told stories concerns the abduction of Sita by Ravan (or Ravana), the demon king of Sri Lanka. Rama, a king, gains the help of Hanuman, leader of the monkeys. Hanuman helps Rama in killing Ravan and in locating and returning Sita. Perhaps because of his image as a helper, Hanuman is today an immensely popular god in his own right. In northern India, Rama is so revered that the term *Ram*, or *Rama*, is really a synonym for "God."

Krishna, another incarnation of Vishnu, may have begun as an object of fertility worship. He is depicted in several forms, which might indicate that he is a coalescence of traditions. In the long epic the Mahabharata, Krishna appears as a mature and solemn god. In later devotional works, the Puranas ("legends"), he is younger; there he is friends with *gopis* (milk-maids who look after herds of cows), and he steals butter and plays the flute, expressing the playful aspect of the divine. In depictions of Krishna, his face and skin are often blue, the color of the sky and of heaven, indicating his true otherworldly nature. His closest milkmaid companion is Radha, with whom he is romantically linked in the Hindu mind.

Shiva, the third of the Trimurti and the god linked with destruction, is the most complicated of the gods, both in origin and in conception. Sitting in yogic meditation posture, the horned figure that is found on seals from the Harappa period may be an early form of Shiva, meaning that some aspects of the present-day god may extend back to pre-Vedic India. Another early form is apparently the Vedic god Rudra, a dangerous god of mountains and winds, whom worshipers probably began to call *shiva* ("lucky") in order to neutralize the fear he inspired. In later times, however, his link with destructiveness is often shown in pictures of Shiva appearing at cremation grounds above a human body that is dissolving in flames.

The power of Shiva is often symbolized by the lingam and yoni, ancient forms that represent fertility.

Shiva's connection with destruction may be hard for many non-Hindus to appreciate. In some religions, destruction is associated with divine punishment for wrongdoing. In Hinduism, however, destruction is considered to be simply another part of the divine energy at work in the world. Destruction is a type of recycling, the necessary loss of form, which occurs so that new forms may appear; and death is always thought of as leading to new life. We know that the seed disappears when the tree grows, and the flower must die to make the fruit. Thus Shiva is also associated with re-creation.

The destructive side of Shiva is portrayed in the bronze statues called *Shiva Nataraja* ("ruler of the dance"). As he dances, Shiva is surrounded by a ring of fire, which shows his ability to destroy and transform. His long yogi's hair flies in the air. He has four arms, which signify his many powers. In his upper right arm is a drum, symbolizing creation and the beginning of time; and in the upper left arm is a flame, symbolizing destruction. His lower left arm is pointing to his upraised foot, suggesting that everyone should join him in his dance and be as free as he is. His lower right arm is extended in blessing, which in a symbolic way says, Don't be afraid. He dances on a dwarf-demon, representing the ignorance

The elephant-headed god Ganesha, son of Shiva, is believed to help devotees overcome obstacles. People often pause before depictions of Ganesha to ask for success.

of all those who do not understand that death is part of the divine process. The art historian Heinrich Zimmer explains that "conquest of this demon lies in the attainment of true wisdom. Therein is release from the bondages of the world."[31]

The aspect of Shiva that brings re-creation is represented by sexually suggestive forms. (We should note here that in nonindustrial societies the bearing of children is crucial—both for the economic survival of the family and for the care of the parents in their old age. Parents pray to have many healthy children.) A frequent representation of Shiva is a columnar *lingam*—

often black, which adds to its mystery. It usually rests on a *yoni*—a circular base that is the female complement to the lingam. The lingam may be a large, natural stone worshiped outdoors; a metal object small enough to be worn around the neck; or a wooden piece of an appropriate size for worship in the home. Shaivites (devotees of Shiva) may pour various liquids, such as milk and rosewater, over the lingam in an act of devotion.

Fertility is further emphasized by Shiva's companion animal Nandi, the bull, and by Ganesha, the elephant-headed son of Shiva, who has become a symbol of strength and abundance. Both are frequently found in temples dedicated to Shiva. Worship of Shiva is most common in Kashmir and southern India. We should note, too, that Shiva is closely linked with destruction only when he is viewed as part of the Trimurti. Among Shaivites, he is the sole God and is not exclusively related to destruction.

Worship of the Divine Feminine: Devi

The three gods of the Trimurti are usually portrayed as masculine. But of all the great world religions, Hinduism, perhaps most strongly, recognizes the female aspects of divinity. This may come from a practical interest in fertility. Worship of female divinities, too, seems to have been a part of pre-Vedic religion, and elements of that early worship have lived on.

The Great Mother, also called **Devi** ("goddess"), is worshiped throughout India, but particularly in the northeast. She is portrayed in many forms and can be both loving and cruel. She is especially harsh to those who show themselves unworthy of her love. Devi is frequently worshiped with extreme human feeling. The worshiper may take on the emotions and even the clothing of a child or spouse of the Great Mother. The mystic Ramakrishna (1836–1886), priest at a temple near Kolkata (Calcutta), spoke of his special devotion to her. "I practised austerities for a long time. . . . My longing for the Divine Mother was so great that I would not eat or sleep. I would lie on the bare ground, placing my head on a lump of earth, and cry out loudly: 'Mother, Mother, why dost thou not come to me?' I did not know how the days and nights passed away. . . . When I reached the state of continuous ecstasy, I gave up all external forms of worship; I could no longer perform them. Then I prayed to my Divine Mother: 'Mother, who will now take care of me? I have no power to take care of myself.'"[33]

The Divine Feminine appears as several goddesses, of which the most popular are Durga and Kali. The goddess **Durga** ("awe-inspiring," "distant") is frequently represented with eight arms, full of implements used to destroy evil. Her face is serene, surrounded by a halo, and she wears a crown. She rides a tiger, which helps her conquer all dangerous obstacles.

Kali ("dark") is more fearsome still. She is often shown wearing a necklace of human skulls, and her fanged teeth drip with blood. Her many arms are full of weapons, which are thought to be dangerous to enemies but protective of her children. Kolkata ("Kali's stairs") is named after her temple in this city.

> Those who have riches build temples for Thee; what shall I build? I am poor. My legs are the pillars; this body of mine is the temple.
> —Basavaraja, in praise of Shiva[32]

The goddess Durga overcomes the forces of evil.

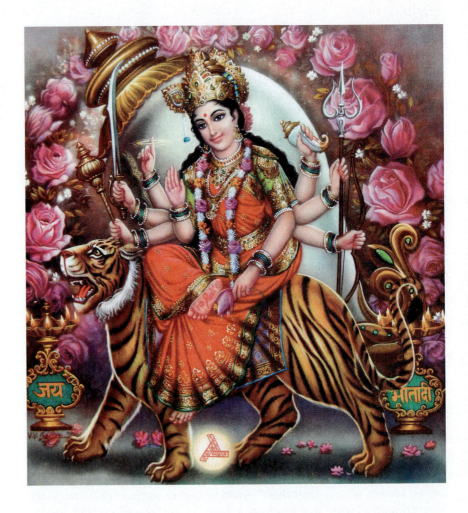

The important role of the Divine Feminine is also seen in the female consorts who accompany many male deities. They are so much a part of the male god that the god cannot be active without them, and thus they are called *shaktis* ("energies"), because they allow the male gods to be effective in the human world.

The goddess Saraswati is the consort of Brahma and is far more popular than he. She is the patron of music, the arts, and culture and is often portrayed with a musical instrument in her hand. The shakti of Vishnu is the goddess Lakshmi, who is commonly dressed as a queen and sits on a lotus. As the consort of Vishnu, she dispenses good luck and protection. Shiva is portrayed with a variety of shaktis, the best known being Parvati and Uma. Sometimes Shiva is himself portrayed as androgynous: half of his body is masculine, while the other side shows a female breast. This androgyny represents the unity that underlies all the apparent opposites of reality—a unity also spoken of in the Upanishads and the Bhagavad Gita.

Divinities of nature are frequently female. The goddess Ganga, who animates the Ganges River, is a good example. Tree spirits, too, are considered female, and frequently it is women who offer them worship.

What we see, from all these deities, is that the female element is an important part of Hindu spirituality. Many deities are female, and women frequently worship a female deity. Women are not priests, but they actually orchestrate much of the religious ritual of the home. Women may also be gurus—spiritual advisors.

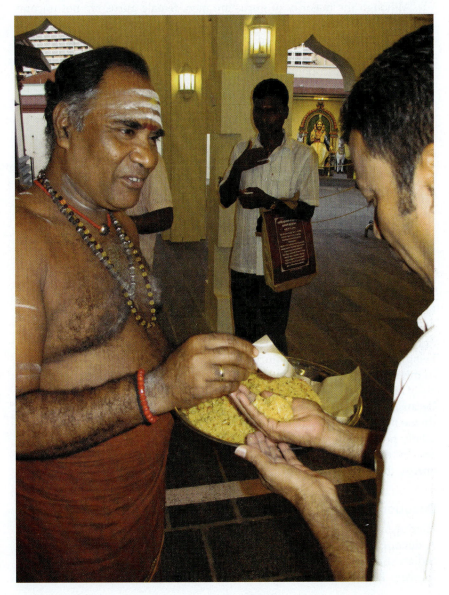

At the end of some temple services, worshipers may receive blessed food.

As a man may be blindfolded, and led away, and left in a strange place; and as, having been so dealt with, he turns in every direction and cries out for someone to remove his bandages and show him the way home; and as one thus entreated may loose his bandages and give him comfort; and as thereupon he walks from village to village, asking his way as he goes; and as he arrives home at last—just so does a man who meets with an illumined teacher obtain true knowledge.

—Chandogya Upanishad[34]

The Guru as Object of Devotion

Because Hinduism is not organized in a hierarchical fashion, devotion to a guru (spiritual teacher) is a large and ancient component of Hindu spirituality. The etymology of the word *guru* is expressive: "the one who removes darkness." Anyone who seeks spiritual growth—no matter what his or her caste or station in life—may seek a guru, whom the individual can visit regularly to seek advice. Even gurus who have taken vows of silence can offer advice and insight to their disciples by writing on tablets or simply by looking at them with love.

Although the majority of gurus are men, female gurus are not uncommon. The guru need only be recognized as a person of holiness. Because a guru expects to be surrounded by students and devotees, he or she will frequently set up an ashram. Usually an ashram is a commune of people living in a single compound, separate from ordinary society, but it may also be located in a town and consist of various buildings owned and used by the devotees. Most gurus stay within their communities, but some travel, even outside India, to set up additional ashrams elsewhere. Frequently an aging guru will designate a successor from among his or her closest disciples and those specially trained.

It is common to touch and even kiss the feet of a guru—an act of reverence that is also performed at times for parents and grandparents. To an outsider, such an act may seem excessive. However, many Hindus believe that the guru is both a saint and a living embodiment of the divine. Behind this conception is the recognition that although divine reality exists within all human beings, most people manifest their divine nature inadequately, because their ignorance and self-centeredness restrict its expression. Such people are compared to glass windows that are so dusty that only a little light shines through. However, some people, over many lifetimes of effort, have reached a stage of such achievement that their ego has disappeared and their charity has grown immense. In these rare people the innate divine light shines brilliantly. This view explains why Hindus believe that simply being in the presence of the guru allows the disciple to benefit—like a plant in the sunshine—from the guru's spirituality.

This belief also explains the intriguing practice of *darshan* ("presence"). Because people of spiritual accomplishment are thought to radiate their divine nature, disciples find opportunities to be in their presence. Sometimes a holy person will sit or stand silently, allowing devotees to come forward, one by one, to look into the teacher's eyes and to experience the divine energy that shines out.[35]

Devotion to Animals

Hinduism is distinctive among world religions for its kindness to animals. A devout Hindu does not kill or eat animals. Cows often wander along Indian streets, and cars and taxis take care to drive around them. Visitors to some Hindu temples may find monkeys and even mice well fed and

A renunciate carries water from the Ganges as part of his long pilgrimage. A sacred cow follows, perhaps hoping for food.

running free. Several extremely popular gods, such as Ganesha and Hanuman, have animal features; and gods such as Shiva and Vishnu are regularly portrayed in the company of their animal companions. A Shiva temple would often be considered incomplete without a statue of Nandi, the bull who is Shiva's vehicle.

This devotion to animals in Hinduism has several possible origins: an ancient deification of powerful animals, such as the elephant and tiger; the desire to neutralize dangerous or mischievous animals, such as the snake, rat, and monkey; and even a sense that human beings and animals have the same origin (a belief also common in native religions). Belief in reincarnation has undoubtedly also played a role. When they see animals and insects, many Hindus see prehuman beings who, in their spiritual evolution, will eventually become human themselves. This brings a feeling of closeness to nonhuman forms of animal life.

Among the animals, cows receive special veneration. This tradition may stem from pre-Vedic worship in the Indus River valley of the bull or cow, a symbol of fertility and economic value. In rural India, to have a cow is to have milk and butter, fuel (dried dung), and the warmth and comfort associated with household pets. With a cow, one is never utterly destitute. Affection for

Rituals and Celebrations

HINDU CELEBRATIONS

Religious festivals are frequent and usually joyous. Some are clearly associated with the seasons, such as a springtime fertility festival and a post-monsoon festival. Others are related to events in a god's life, such as the site of his birth or places he traveled to. Some festivals are regional, and some are national.

Although India is hot during most of the year, winters can be cold, especially in the north. The spring is therefore welcomed with the celebration *Holi*. It is traditional for boys and girls to playfully throw colored water on each other (nowadays some even use squirt guns), thus evoking images of Krishna's exploits with the milkmaids.

After the monsoons of the summer months, the land is green, the air is cool, and there is a sense of peacefulness. The season has the feeling of a second spring and a new beginning. People often spend time repairing any damages the rains may have caused. Holidays at this time reenact the power of goodness to conquer evil forces. For example, *Divali*, recalling the return of Rama and Sita, is a time when people clean their houses and illuminate them outside with candles and lights. Ganesha and Lakshmi, who are both associated with good fortune, are particularly honored at this time.

Durga Puja, held in December and particularly popular in northeast India, celebrates the goddess Durga's ability to overcome dangerous powers. People dance in front of her statues in the street, and in Kolkata the festival ends with the immersion of her statues in the river.

Every twelve years Hindus celebrate the complete *Kumbh Mela* festival. It recalls a story of Vishnu and other deities churning nectar from a primeval ocean of milk. Celebrated by dance, plays, and joyous bathing in the Ganges, it draws millions of people and is considered the largest religious gathering in the world.

the cow may also arise from the strong thread of ancient devotion to the Divine Feminine—hinted at by the commonly used term *gau mata* ("mother cow").

This affection is hard for people outside India to understand. But when one sees an Indian cow, with its gentle face, ambling peacefully along a bustling Indian street, then one experiences clearly why the cow is a powerful symbol in India of all motherliness.

Other Forms of Religious Devotion

Indian thought loves multiplicity. "As many as the sands of the Ganges" is a description applied to a variety of subjects. One example of multiplicity is the Hindu recognition of immense numbers of gods. Realizing that each god or goddess may have several forms and may be accompanied by divine consorts and animal companions, we gain a dizzying sense of the limitlessness of devotional possibilities. In everyday life, every person is expected to have a religious practice involving at least one of these deities, but the exact form generally is not dictated, and virtually no form of devotion is rejected.

Pilgrimage is a common form of religious expression in Hinduism, as it is in many religions. India is dotted with sites that are held to be sacred to the most popular gods and goddesses, and devotees of a particular deity will often try to visit all the important sites associated with that deity. Pilgrimages can also involve listening to a famous guru's sermons and meditating with the guru's followers.

P E R S O N A L   E X P E R I E N C E
A Party

Colleagues from the University moved into a house on my street not long ago. Meera and Vijay are both from India and have two daughters. I invited them all over to my house to welcome them to the neighborhood. A little later I received an invitation from them for a weekend dinner party. I accepted happily.

I planned on taking some food and a beverage to the party, but I didn't know who the other guests would be or what their food preferences or restrictions might be. Would they be vegetarian Hindus, or would they be Muslims who didn't drink alcohol? Nonetheless, I decided to take over a bottle of wine, along with some appetizers (which, here, we call *pupus*). Let the guests decide.

The house is at a bend in the road. I walked down the street and then climbed the stairs to their red front door. The house was already full of guests. The men were mainly dressed in long-sleeved shirts and long pants. Most of the women wore saris. I could see that I was something of an interloper. But soon I was talking animatedly with a woman originally from Kolkata (Calcutta). The woman, Sobharani, was a university professor.

"I came eight years ago," she said, "and I love it here. But I miss my family, and I try to go back every two years. In Kolkata most of my family—including aunts, uncles, and cousins—lives in a large compound. It's very close and friendly. My father used to live there, too, but he moved down south to stay with my eldest brother."

"Does your father like it down south?" I asked.

When Sobharani started to answer, she began to cry.

"Well, I don't know," she said. "We all thought that he liked it there. But one noon he went out. He said that he was just going to buy lunch. But he didn't return in the afternoon. That evening he still hadn't returned, and my brother called the police. They looked for my father for several weeks but were unable to find him."

"Could he be in Benares?" I asked, sounding hopeful. "Should you look there? Maybe he decided to live the last stage of his life like a recluse, praying and meditating. Perhaps he didn't tell anyone because he didn't want to bother you, and he was afraid you'd object."

"Yes," she answered, "sometimes I've thought the same. In fact, I've already gotten my plane reservation for India. I want to go back and start looking."

"Where will you search in Benares?" I asked.

"I'll look in all those old hospices beside the river. Then I'll start looking outside, along the ghats. I'll go to the police, too. But my father might have gone to the mountains alone, or he might be staying at an ashram far away. In that case, I don't know what I'll do. I'll ask and leave messages, but I might just have to accept my fate. I still don't understand. My father and I were so close. I miss him terribly. Why didn't he tell me?"

HINDUISM AND THE ARTS

Given Hinduism's tendency toward multiplicity, it is not surprising that Hindu temples, particularly in southern India, are often covered with statues, many with multiple faces and arms. The concept of multiplicity has a purpose. To appreciate this, think of a wheel that begins to turn. At first, each spoke of the wheel is visible, but as the wheel turns more quickly, the spokes disappear and dissolve into a unity. The profusion of images in Hindu art can be similarly hypnotic, with the experience of multiplicity frequently leading to an overarching sense of unity. Profusion thus fits in well with the mystical orientation common in Hinduism.

Another characteristic of Hindu artistic sensibility is symbolism. One of the clearest examples is the depiction in painting and sculpture of figures with multiple arms and faces, which are symbolic representations of power and wisdom. Specific symbols are associated with individual deities and allow them to be identified. Krishna, for example, is recognized by his flute.

Hindu painting can sometimes be disappointing, such as the rather garish devotional art sold at temple gates. Many fine paintings of the past have undoubtedly vanished because of the fragility of the paper and cloth on which they were done. The murals that remain, however, demonstrate the heights that Hindu devotional painting has sometimes attained; and some yantras—geometrical paintings used in meditation—are unforgettable.

Hindu sculpture, however, far outshines Hindu painting. Fine pieces of sturdy stone and metal are on display in India and in museums around the world. Metal sculpture advanced quite early. The finest generic example of Hindu sculpture is Shiva in his guise as "ruler of the dance" (Nataraja)—an image that was introduced in southern India more than a thousand years ago but which is still produced today. For many, this sculpture represents the perfection of Hindu art, combining visual beauty with a symbolic meaning that intensifies the visual power.

The power of stone sculpture is often quite sensuous. Given the world-denying aspect of some Hindu thought, one might expect that the great stone sculpture of Hinduism would be ascetic—perhaps elongated and otherworldly. The opposite is true, however. Some of the best-known examples of stone sculpture are the figures of sensuous men and women, enjoying life and each other, on the temples of Khajuraho in central India. This sort of sculpture was influenced by Tantrism, the antipuritanical movement that teaches that everything in the world, including sex, can be used to attain higher states of consciousness.

Popular Hinduism has made use of hymns to many gods as expressions of bhakti yoga. Their regular rhythm and repetition help produce a state of altered consciousness in the worshiper, bringing a sense of selflessness and union with the divine. Instrumental music—especially involving drums and the harmonium, a hand-pumped reed organ—has also been an integral part of religious celebrations for centuries.

Classical Indian instrumental music is less obviously religious, yet much of it has an undeniable mystical quality. It makes use of *ragas,* elements of Indian music that blend features of both scales and melodies. Frequently these ragas are played and musically developed over deep tones that are played as a drone. (The *sitar,* the best-known Indian stringed instrument, has drone strings on its side.) The drone suggests the underlying timeless world of Brahman, against which changing melodies— suggestions of the world of time—move. Musical pieces often begin quite tentatively, then gradually speed up to a very quick pace, and suddenly stop, bringing to the listener and players an experience of release and peace.

Indian classical dance is more obviously tied to religion. It interprets stories derived from the tales of the gods, such as Krishna and Rama. Much of it also originated as a part of religious ceremony, performed at religious festivals and in or near temples. Dance is meant to produce delicate states of feeling, some of which are thought to assist contact with particular gods.

Hindu worship often includes dance. Here we see a dancer in front of a small Hindu temple in Bali.

HINDUISM: MODERN CHALLENGES

India, as we have seen, is isolated from other lands by mountains and ocean. This has meant that its rural culture and ancient polytheism could develop undisturbed for centuries. But invasions did occur, inevitably bringing new beliefs and values. Many of these new elements were adopted, but others were fought.

One early invasion was only partially successful. Alexander the Great (d. 323 BCE) brought his army from Greece and reached the Indus River, where he talked with sannyasins about religion and philosophy. He had hoped to conquer India and then reach China, too; but his men, sick and discouraged, forced him to turn back, and he died in Babylon on the way home. Had Alexander been able to fulfill his plans, his influence in India would have been immense. Despite his failed plans for conquest, forms of Greek government and art, brought by the Greek invaders, profoundly influenced northwest India for centuries.

In the past millennium, two additional waves of influence washed across India: Islam and the British. Islam first came into India from Afghanistan, and a sultanate was set up in Delhi in 1206. After invasions from Turkmenistan, the sultanate was supplanted by the Mughal dynasty, beginning in 1398. The Mughal dynasty continued on into the eighteenth century, even as the British were consolidating their control over much of India.

There could hardly be two more dissimilar religions than monotheistic Islam and polytheistic Hinduism. The contrast has produced intense conflict, which continues today. The more than five centuries of Islamic rule that began in 1206 were marked by a spectrum of attitudes toward Hinduism, moving back and forth between cruel oppression and complete tolerance. The attitude of the state depended on the opinions of the ruler of the time. For example, Akbar (d. 1605) was so tolerant that he invited members of many other religions to speak at court, and he became convinced that India needed a new religion that would blend the best of all older religions. His great-grandson, Aurangzeb (d. 1707), however, was notoriously harsh in his zeal, destroying Hindu temples and sometimes demanding conversion or death.

Of course, not all conversions to Islam were forced. Islam was very attractive to many people who appreciated its monotheistic simplicity, its architecture, its literature, and its way of life. (The Mughals created many beautiful buildings; Aurangzeb's father, for example, built the Taj Mahal.) Islam was also appealing because it was the religion of the aristocratic ruling classes; and it was greatly attractive to lower-caste Hindus, who felt oppressed by the Hindu caste system. Consequently, by the end of the Mughal period, Islam was the religion of millions in north India. But this fact would later create great problems, particularly when India became an independent state, and it would remain as a major source of religious friction and violence.

European values have also, gradually, posed a major challenge to traditional Hinduism. This process began after 1500 CE, when European powers took control of parts of India. Goa, on the west coast, became a center of Portuguese culture that lasted until 1961, when Goa was taken over by Indian army forces. Similarly, Pondicherry, on the southeast coast, was at one time a center of French culture. The most significant European influence on India, however, was English. Great Britain controlled most of the subcontinent for about two centuries. Although India became independent of Britain in 1947, British influence is evident in modern India's law, education, architecture, rail transportation, and military life.

Throughout India today one can find former British churches, mostly shuttered and closed, which only hint at both the positive and negative impact of British Christianity on India. The British were not successful in making many converts, but through their schools and colleges, British Christian missionaries helped challenge and change some traditional Hindu beliefs and practices. Among those elements that were questioned were untouchability, child marriage, prohibition of remarriage for widows, polytheism, the content of education, and the role of women.

One of the earliest British-inspired Indian reformers was Ram Mohan Roy (1772–1833). He was typical of the many reformers who grew up in Calcutta (now Kolkata), which was for a long time the capital of British India and the center of westernizing thought. While remaining a Hindu and even writing articles in defense of Hinduism, his thinking was influenced by both rationalism and Christianity.[36] He began a movement, the Brahmo Samaj, that adopted Christian-inspired elements: the belief in one God, congregational worship, and an ethical urgency that sought to better the lot of the oppressed. The Brahmo Samaj later split into three branches—all of which are still active.

Possibly as a result of contact with European values, one practice that was made illegal in the early nineteenth century was that of *sati* (or *suttee*, named after the first wife of Shiva). While there is no evidence to suggest that this practice was common, in sati a woman whose husband had died could volunteer, as a sign of her wifely devotion, to be burnt alive on her husband's funeral pyre. Although the British found the notion of sati horrible, they were unwilling to intervene at first. Reform-minded Indians, however, worked with the British to make the practice illegal. Instances of sati still happen today, but they are rare.

Mohandas Gandhi

Mohandas Gandhi (1869–1948) was born in the seaside town of Porbandar in northwestern India, north of Mumbai (Bombay). At that time Britain controlled the country, and many Indians advocated violence as a response to British domination. This historic turning point became a defining time in Gandhi's life.

As a young man, Gandhi learned basic ideas of nonviolence from Hinduism and Jainism (see Chapter 5). He was a vegetarian because of his religious upbringing; yet in his day, young Indian boys believed that the British were strong because they ate meat. Young Gandhi tested this theory by eating meat for a year, but he had a dream of a goat crying in his stomach and was compelled to give up his experiment.[37] His family arranged his marriage, at the age of 13, to a girl named Kasturbai, also 13.

During his late teen years, family members recommended that Gandhi study law in London. Because his pious Hindu mother feared the bad influences he would be exposed to there, he agreed to take a vow that he would not eat meat, drink wine, or touch a woman while abroad. A Jain monk administered the vow, and Gandhi left for London in the fall of 1888 at the age of 19. Kasturbai and their young son, Harilal, remained with Gandhi's parents.

Feeling rebellious at the time, Gandhi enthusiastically adopted English clothes and manners and even took dancing lessons; but in London he also began serious study. Becoming familiar with the Christian Bible, he was particularly moved by Jesus' call to forgiveness and nonviolence, which he found in the Sermon on the Mount (Matt. 5–7) in the New Testament. It is fascinating to see the role that the New Testament played in influencing Gandhi's insistence on the importance of nonviolence.

It was in London, too, that he first read the Bhagavad Gita, discovering outside India the wisdom in Hinduism. He took to heart its ideal of the active but selfless human being. Such a person, Gandhi later wrote, is a person who is "without egotism, who is selfless, who treats alike cold and heat, happiness and misery, who is ever forgiving, who is always contented, whose resolutions are firm, who has dedicated mind and soul to God, who causes no dread, who is not afraid of others."[38]

After obtaining his law degree in 1891, Gandhi returned to India; but soon he decided to accept an offer to practice law in South Africa, where there was a large Indian population. There he experienced the inequalities of racial segregation and legal codes that favored Europeans over non-Europeans, and he began to perfect the ideologies that he would later spread in India. His thinking was influenced by writings that advocated simplicity and nonviolence, such as the essay "On Civil Disobedience," by the American author Henry David Thoreau, and the book *The Kingdom of God Is Within You*, by the Russian writer Leo Tolstoy. A farm that Gandhi bought became something of an ashram, while his law office in Johannesburg became a center for nonviolent political action. He began to employ strikes and marches to publicize his goals and to wear Indian clothing (specifically the *dhoti*, a type of loincloth) as a way of identifying with the Indian cause.

Gandhi returned to India in 1915 and dedicated his life to seeking Indian independence from Britain. Although he was repeatedly imprisoned, Gandhi insisted that all his followers remain nonviolent. For him, ahimsa (nonviolence) was fundamental. Gandhi not only believed in nonviolence for its own sake, but he felt that it gave a great moral power to its adherents and that it could sway those who were cruel, thoughtless, and violent. He called this power *satyagraha* ("reality force," or "holding onto truth"). Gandhi made use of every possible nonviolent technique: marches, hunger strikes, talks, demonstrations, and, of course, publicity. He argued that violence only begets further violence and brutalizes those who are violent, whereas nonviolence begets admiration, spiritual greatness, and ultimate freedom.[39]

One brilliant example of Gandhi's nonviolent techniques was the Salt March of 1930. At that time the British taxed all salt eaten in India and made it illegal to possess salt not bought from the government monopoly. Gandhi cleverly led a three-week march on foot from his ashram to the ocean, nearly 250 miles away. Fewer than a hundred people began the march with him, but thousands joined along the way. Reaching the sea, Gandhi collected the natural salt left on the beach by the waves—thus breaking the law. In seashore communities all around India, people came to do the same, and thousands were put into jail, along with Gandhi. This march was the turning point. Weakened both by the Indian independence movement and by World War II, the British forces at last agreed to leave India in 1947. Perceiving Gandhi's greatness following the Salt March, the writer Rabindranath Tagore had called him *Mahatma* ("great spirit"). This became his title.

Gandhi believed so much in loving tolerance that he hoped it could keep a newly independent India free of religious battles. Muslim leaders, however, fearful that the Hindu majority would oppress Muslims, worked to create the new separate Muslim state of Pakistan. Some Hindu militants wanted revenge for what they perceived as wrongs done by Muslims to Hindus in the new Pakistan, and one of these Hindu militants assassinated Gandhi early in 1948. Gandhi's last words were *Ram, Ram* ("God, God").

Gandhi's example was so powerful that the idea of satyagraha spread to other countries and was adopted in the 1960s by the Baptist minister Martin Luther King Jr. to help protest racial segregation in the United States. King insisted that activists march peacefully and sit in restaurants quietly, without responding to threats or cruelty. Their gentle persistence, magnified by publicity, brought success.

Contemporary Issues

The issues that moderate Hinduism faces, as it is evolving today, come from three sources: the conservative social teachings of traditional Hinduism, the centuries-old conflict with Islam, and the challenges of the contemporary world.

The birthday of Mohandas Gandhi, who led India to independence, is celebrated worldwide. Here we see a celebration in Waikiki.

Some Hindus find religious justification for preserving the rules of untouchability, keeping strictly the divisions of the caste system, and limiting women to traditional roles. The injustices of untouchability have long been recognized, but legal assistance for untouchables came only in the twentieth century. Untouchables, now legally allowed to enter all temples in India, have made great strides toward some social equality and opportunity. For example, there is a quota system for untouchables to ensure their inclusion in government positions and their admission to universities. The reality, however, is that in the villages untouchables still must live separately from others. They do not feel free to use wells and other water sources that are used by higher-caste persons, and they feel threatened by violence should they attempt to go beyond their traditional limits.

The caste system is weakening in large cities, but a glance at a big-city Sunday newspaper reveals its continuing hold on contemporary life. It is common, for example, for Indian parents to place ads seeking a spouse for their child, and these ads frequently detail the son's or daughter's caste, educational background, and sometimes even complexion.

The role of women has expanded in modern India, but it remains a focus of heated debate. In India's distant, pre-Vedic past, it is possible that women

Contemporary Issues

THE CHIPKO MOVEMENT

Hinduism teaches that all lives have had previous forms—thousands of them. Because of reincarnation, people were once animals and, according to many, animals were once plants. Thus there is a very strong sense of interconnection with nature in Hinduism. Gods and goddesses are shown both with guardian animals and with their favorite plants. For example, Shiva is often shown with his companion bull, and Lakshmi appears with an elephant and holds a lotus.

This connection with nature is the religious background for a conservation movement that began in earnest in India in the 1970s, when a sporting goods company announced its plans to log land in the hills of the lower Himalayas. Village women at the village of Reni saw the dangers: deforestation, inability to gather firewood, soil erosion, and flooding. They went out and surrounded the trees, literally hugging them, to protect them. Attracting a great deal of attention, the villagers were successful. They saved their trees, and out of this one act emerged hundreds of similar acts of environmental concern. The movement that arose is called the Chipko Andolan (Hindi: "sticking-together movement"). It is the Indian version of tree hugging.

The Chipko movement has had much additional influence. It has not only encouraged the protection of forests but also the planting of trees, the review of proposed dam projects, the more careful awarding of government contracts, and the growth of local decision making.

The Chipko movement began with Hindu women working to preserve trees, a form of life that deserves respect rather than exploitation.

played an important public role. The importance of female deities and the fact that there have been many female gurus may be a continuation of this early tradition. But the dominant Vedic culture was thoroughly patriarchal. Just as male domination has been canonized in other religions, so it was canonized in India by the law code of Manu (second century BCE). This code made the female subservient to the male and the wife subservient to her husband. A good wife was expected to treat her husband as a god, no matter what his character or treatment of her. Women were not trained to read and write, as this was thought to detract from their principal roles as wives and mothers.

Nowadays, Hindu women commonly learn to read and write, and many go on to higher education and important public roles. Critics, however, point out that women's education is often only basic and that women are largely limited to a few career areas—teaching, secretarial work, nursing, and medicine.

Critics also point out that in villages women are sometimes confined to traditional domestic roles under threat of violence from their husbands. A related problem involves the dowry payments made by a bride's family to the bridegroom's family. In instances when the dowry is deemed insufficient, the wives are threatened and sometimes even killed by the husband's family members, thereby freeing the husband to marry again. In recent decades a women's movement has been growing in India. It insists on the equality of women, not merely in law and theory but also in everyday life. It is working on several fronts. The first targets education; it tries to keep girls in school and thus raise the literacy rate and social capability of women. The second concentrates on the improvement of women's health through greater self-awareness and more frequent medical testing. (Testing for breast cancer is a current focus.) A third front addresses issues relating to marriage. It tries to gain acceptance for intercaste marriage and for marriages that are arranged by the couple, rather than simply by the parents. It also tries to stop child marriages and promotes the enforcement of laws regulating proper marriage age. And it opposes the persecution of wives who, even after the marriage, are considered unsuitable. A fourth emphasis is the opposition to gender testing of fetuses; male children are valued more highly than female children, and the ratio of male children to female children is unbalanced.

A second issue confronting Hinduism today is interreligious disharmony. Conflict between Hindus and Muslims has been ongoing, particularly since the partition of India and Pakistan in 1947. Gandhi had hoped that India would not have to split into parts along religious lines, but Muslim leaders insisted on separation. Ironically, the partition did not bring peace. Disagreement about the border between India and Pakistan, particularly in Kashmir, has never been resolved. Two wars have already been fought, and a third is a constant threat. Since both countries possess atomic weapons, the potential horrors of such a war are especially great.

Conflicts between the Hindus and Muslims within India itself have also continually flared up. Old wounds were reopened in 1992, when Hindu activists destroyed a mosque at Ayodhya in northern India. They argued that it was the birthplace of Rama and the site of a Hindu temple that had been destroyed by the Muslim ruler Babur and replaced with a mosque. Atrocities on each side have been the result. While India claims to be a secular state, Hindus comprise 85 percent of the population, and thus their causes carry undeniable weight; Muslims argue that the government has not adequately protected them. Similar conflicts have occurred in Kashmir at the site of a Hindu shrine to Shiva. Just as fundamentalism has risen in several other religions, it is now influential in Hinduism.

The third concern facing modern-day Hinduism is the intrusion of contemporary values, particularly individualism, women's rights, sexual freedom, modern fashion, and consumerism. Globalization has made instant some of the conflicts that once arose more slowly. There is now quick communication through e-mail and cell phones, and television is an irresistible conduit of new values. The international world of banking and finance has moved some of

Behind this Hindu temple roofline in Benares stands the minaret of a mosque. Peaceful coexistence with other religions, especially Islam, is a major challenge for Hinduism today.

its operations to India, where English-speaking graduates are plentiful and the costs of employment are favorable. American consumers making routine calls for technical help with their computers are often connected with computer specialists in Mumbai or Delhi. These jobs provide greater economic opportunities for women as well as men, inevitably raising the potential for conflict between traditional values and new freedoms.

Hindu Influence beyond India

Over the centuries, Hinduism has spread to countries near India and afar, often by way of traders and immigrants. In a few places it has remained strong, whereas in others it has surrendered to other religions. Hinduism is the dominant religion of Nepal, where about 80 percent of the population is Hindu. Hinduism was once widespread in Southeast Asia, but today only traces of it remain. In Cambodia is the great ruin Angkor Wat, originally a Hindu complex. In Thailand, vestiges of a Brahmanical priesthood are particularly active in court ceremony, and images of Brahma, Vishnu, and Ganesha are common. Some forms of ritualistic Buddhism in northern and eastern Asia have kept alive a few Hindu gods, such as Indra, in art and ceremony. Hinduism, of course, continues wherever Indians have migrated.

Hinduism was once widespread in Indonesia, where it was introduced by Indian traders. During the Muslim invasions, however, the Hindu court culture was forced to retreat from the main island of Java and settled to

Hindus around the world celebrate Krishna's birthday. Here an American temple congregation celebrates Krishna with dance.

the east on the small island of Bali, where a fascinating example of Hindu culture thrives. Here, Hinduism lives on in a complicated, beautiful form that is mixed with folk religion and Buddhism. Each village has Hindu temples, where dances based on Indian tales (especially about Rama) are performed. Shadow-puppet plays tell Hindu stories, and Balinese wood carvings reproduce images of Hindu gods, goddesses, and heroes. The central temple of Bali, a complex of buildings on the volcanic Mount Agung, is dedicated to the Trimurti. Although the rest of Indonesia is primarily Muslim, some Hindu elements remain in Indonesian dance and puppet plays.

Hinduism has had some influence on the West since the nineteenth century. The earliest impact was intellectual, when translations of the Upanishads and the Bhagavad Gita became available in Latin, French, German, and English. The translations generated great interest among philosophers, scholars, and poets. In the United States, the New England movement called Transcendentalism owes a good deal to its literary contact with Hinduism. Ralph Waldo Emerson (1803–1882), Henry David Thoreau (1817–1862), and Walt Whitman (1819–1892) all spoke in their writings of the sacredness of nature and the ultimate unity of all things, and they sometimes even used terms demonstrating Indian influence, such as *Brahma* and *Oversoul* (another name for Brahman). This literary

In the heart of Bangkok is the popular Erawan shrine, with an image of the Hindu god Brahma at its center. In much of Southeast Asia, Hinduism is alive within, or alongside of, Buddhism.

trend was expressed in another form in England, where composers such as Gustav Holst (1874–1934) and Ralph Vaughan Williams (1872–1958) put selections from the Rig Veda and Whitman's *Leaves of Grass* to music.

The next wave of influence occurred when Indian gurus began to travel to the West. The first of these gurus was Swami Vivekananda (1863–1902), who represented Hinduism at the first World Parliament of Religions, held in Chicago in 1893. He was the successor to Ramakrishna (mentioned earlier), the noted mystic and devotee of the Great Mother. Vivekananda began the Ramakrishna Mission and set up Vedanta societies and Ramakrishna centers across Europe, India, and the United States. A Vedantist center has existed in Hollywood since the 1930s, and British writers such as Christopher Isherwood (1904–1986), Aldous Huxley (1894–1963), and Gerald Heard (1889–1971) all practiced meditation there. Isherwood, under the influence of his guru, Swami Prabhavananda, became a Vedantist and translated the Bhagavad Gita into English.

The third wave of Hindu influence in the West occurred in the late 1960s. The American counterculture embraced India as the fount of wisdom. Commercial air travel made it possible for Indian teachers to come to the West and for westerners to travel to India. Some westerners, such as the Beatles, studied in India with the guru Maharishi Mahesh Yogi and became enamored of Hinduism. (George Harrison's song "My Sweet Lord" was written to honor Krishna.) The Maharishi eventually came to the United States and established the Transcendental Meditation movement, which promotes regular daily meditation to achieve health and happiness. (The North American center of the movement is at Maharishi Vedic City, near Fairfield, Iowa.) Some westerners who went to India became disciples of Indian gurus. Some took Hindu names. Western visitors to India adopted forms of yoga, Hindu vegetarian cuisine, Indian clothing, and Indian music and then took them back to Europe, Canada, and the United States, where they entered the Western mainstream.

The movement called the International Society for Krishna Consciousness (ISKCON) was founded in New York in 1967 by Swami Bhaktivedanta Prabhupada (1896–1977) to spread a form of devotional practice among westerners. Commonly known as the Hare Krishna movement, ISKCON has succeeded in attracting westerners to live a traditional form of Hindu religious life. Its practitioners worship Krishna as the highest incarnation of the divine, chant daily, eat a vegetarian diet, and, if celibate, wear the traditional orange robe. The impact of this movement in the West has been particularly strong in the area of cuisine, prompting the opening of vegetarian restaurants across Europe, the United States, and Canada.

What we have just discussed—the impact of Hinduism on Western thinkers, musicians, and poets—was in large measure achieved by non-Hindus inspired by Hindu culture. Now Hindus themselves, in and out of India, are producing internationally acclaimed works, especially novels and films. Their particular points of view result from experiences accumulated across centuries in one of the world's richest cultures. Those experiences will in time help global citizens, whatever their origins, to see themselves with an understanding that has been enriched by the Hindu worldview.

Reading **FINDING UNION WITH THE DIVINE**

An old and hallowed commentary, the Crest-Jewel of Discrimination, teaches about one's true nature, which is beyond time and is full of joy.

Calm your mind utterly and attain Samadhi. Then you will have open vision, seeing clearly the truth of the Atman. From the lips of your teacher you have learned of the truth of Brahman as it is revealed in the scriptures. Now you must realize that truth directly and immediately. Then only will your heart be free from any doubt.

How are you to know for certain that you are liberated from the bondage of ignorance and have realized the Atman, which is absolute existence, pure consciousness and abiding bliss? The words of the scriptures, your own power of reasoning and the teaching of your master should all help to convince you—but the only absolute proof is direct and immediate experience, within your own soul.

Bondage and liberation, satisfaction and anxiety, sickness and renewed health, hunger and so forth—these are matters of personal experience. You know yourself. Others can only guess at your condition.

Teachers and scriptures can stimulate spiritual awareness. But the wise disciple crosses the ocean of his ignorance by direct illumination, through the grace of God.

Gain experience directly. Realize God for yourself. Know the Atman as the one indivisible Being, and become perfect. Free your mind from all distractions and dwell in the consciousness of the Atman.

This is the final declaration of Vedanta: Brahman is all—this universe and every creature. To be liberated is to live in Brahman, the undivided reality. Brahman is one without a second, as the scriptures bear witness.[40]

TEST YOURSELF

1. The culture that flourished in the Indus River valley before 2000 BCE is named the _____ culture.
   a. Vedas
   b. Harappa
   c. Aryan
   d. Indian

2. The ancient scriptures of India are called the _____. There are four basic text collections: the Rig, the Yajur, the Sama, and the Atharva.
   a. Harappas
   b. Sanskrits
   c. Vedas
   d. "Shining Fathers"

3. Around 500 BCE, Indian civilization experienced such widespread and important changes that the period is called the _____ Age.
   a. Philosopher
   b. Prophet
   c. Axis
   d. Ascetic

4. In the Upanishads, the term _____ refers to the experience of the sacred within nature and the external universe, while _____ refers to the experience of the sacred within one-self. Both terms may be used interchangeably.
   a. karma; moksha
   b. Brahman; Atman
   c. samsara; moksha
   d. brahmins; samsara

5. The _____ is part of a very long epic poem called the Mahabharata; it recalls themes from the Upanishads.
   a. Maya
   b. Bhagavad Gita
   c. Pandavas
   d. Jainism

6. Hinduism has a(n) _____ system with five main social classes: *brahmin* (priest), *kshatriya* (warrior-noble), *vaishya* (merchant), *shudra* (peasant), and *dalit* (untouchable).
   a. work
   b. education

   c. ritual
   d. caste

7. The word *yoga* means "_____."
   a. contemplation
   b. enlightenment
   c. practice
   d. union

8. Shankara's belief that spiritual liberation was achieved when the individual personally came to understand the unity of all things is called _____.
   a. devotion
   b. Jnana
   c. monism
   d. meditation

9. When linked together, Brahma, Vishnu, and Shiva are often called the _____.
   a. Trimurti
   b. Shiva
   c. Hindu
   d. sacred text

10. Mohandas Gandhi's use of _____ techniques, including marches, hunger strikes, talks, demonstrations, and publicity, was adopted by Martin Luther King Jr. to help protest racial segregation in the United States.
    a. traditional
    b. nonviolent
    c. disruptive
    d. Mahatma

11. Imagine on an exam you are asked to express the most important ideas of the Upanishads in only two sentences. What would you write for your two sentences? How do these sentences capture what is most important in the Upanishads?

12. Choose one of the contemporary challenges facing Hinduism discussed in this chapter. According to Hindu belief, which of the following deities do you think would be especially equipped to assist Hindus in overcoming this challenge: Brahma, Vishnu, Shiva, or Devi? Why?

RESOURCES

Books

Bhagavad-Gita: The Song of God. Trans. Swami Prabha-vananda and Christopher Isherwood. New York: Signet, 2002. A justly famous translation, with a valuable introduction by Aldous Huxley.

Chapple, Christopher Key, and Mary Evelyn Tucker, eds. *Hinduism and Ecology.* Cambridge, MA: Harvard University Press/Center for the Study of World Religions, 2000. Essays on environmental concerns in Hindu literature, ritual, and culture.

Eck, Diana. *Darsan: Seeing the Divine Image in India.* 3rd. ed. New York: Columbia University Press, 1998. A description of Hindu temple worship and its effect.

Erndl, Kathleen. *Victory to the Mother.* New York: Oxford University Press, 1993. A study of devotion to the Mother, a female deity especially popular in northern India.

Gandhi, Mohandas. *The Bhagavad Gita According to Gandhi.* Edited by John Strohmeier. Berkeley, CA: Berkeley Hills Books, 2000. The first book to include Gandhi's *Gita* text and his commentary in their entirety.

———. *The Essential Gandhi.* Edited by Louis Fischer. New York: Vintage, 2002. Gandhi's writings on politics, nonviolence, spirituality, and his own life.

Hawley, John S., and Mark Juergensmeyer. *Songs of the Saints of India.* New York: Oxford University Press, 1988. Poetry of north-Indian saints with commentary.

Kinsley, David R. *Hindu Goddesses: Visions of the Divine Feminine in the Hindu Religious Tradition.* Berkeley: University of California Press, 1988. A comprehensive survey of Hindu goddesses and the role of the divine feminine within Hinduism.

Lahiri, Jhumpa. *Interpreter of Maladies.* New York: Mariner Books, 1999. An award-winning collection of short stories that chronicle the dislocation experienced by Indian migrants to the United States.

The Upanishads. Trans. Swami Prabhavananda and Frederick Manchester. New York: Signet, 2002. A readable translation of twelve basic Upanishads.

Film/TV

Aparajito (Director Satyajit Ray; Merchant-Ivory/Sony.) A depiction of a man's life in Benares and the portayal of the struggles of his father, a poor brahmin priest.

Gandhi. (Director Richard Attenborough; Columbia Tristar.) An epic rendering of the life of Mahatma Gandhi, which won several Academy Awards.

Ganges: River to Heaven. (Director Gayle Ferraro; Aerial Productions.) A documentary on a hospice in Benares, where aging Hindus come to die in the hope that death at this site will improve their karma in the next life.

Hinduism: Faith, Festivals, and Rituals. (Films Media Group.) An examination of devotional ceremonies in the southern Indian state of Kerala.

Mahabharata. (Director Peter Brook; Parabola Video.) A modern, English-language production of the great Hindu epic.

Mystic India. (Giant Screen Films.) An epic account of the late-eighteenth-century spiritual awakening of Neelkanth, an 11-year-old yogi who journeys by foot throughout India for seven years and more than seven thousand miles, seeking enlightenment.

Short Cut to Nirvana: Kumbh Mela. (Mela Films LLC.) A documentary exploring the Kumbh Mela festival.

Music/Audio

The Bhagavad Gita. (Multimedia and Culture.) An unabridged audiobook of the famed discourse between Krishna and Arjuna (translated into English by Juan Mascaró).

Darshana: Vedic Chanting for Daily Practice. (Mother Om Sounds.) A compilation of Vedic chants for daily practice, as performed by Maya Tiwari (Mother Maya).

Hymns from the Vedas and Upanishads, Vedic Chants. (Delos Records.) Traditional hymns and chants from classic religious sources.

Religious Music of Asia. (Smithsonian Folkways.) A recording of Hindu devotional music.

Sounds of India. (Columbia.) Classical devotional music of India, performed by Ravi Shankar.

World Hindu Chants. (Times Music.) A variety of religious songs.

Internet

HinduNet: http://www.hindunet.org/. A gateway site that allows users to learn about Hindu faith and ritual, visit Hindu temples online, listen to Hindu scriptures, and participate in discussion forums.

Sanatan Society: http://www.sanatansociety.org/. A useful resource for information on Hindu gods, yoga and meditation, Vedic astrology, vegetarianism, and other related topics.

Virtual Religion Index: http://virtualreligion.net/vri/hindu.html. Individual sections devoted to the Vedas, the Upanishads, the epics, theology and devotion, schools and teachers, and yoga.

KEY TERMS

ahimsa (uh-him′-sa): "Nonharm," "nonviolence."

ashram (ash′-ram): A spiritual community.

Atman (at′-mun): The spiritual essence of all individual human beings.

avatar (ah′-va-tar): An earthly embodiment of a deity.

Bhagavad Gita (bhuh′-guh-vud gee′-ta): A religious literary work about Krishna.

bhakti (bhuk′-ti): Devotion to a deity or guru.

bhakti yoga: The spiritual discipline of devotion to a deity or guru.

Brahma (bruh′-mah): God of creation.

Brahman (bruh′-mun): The spiritual essence of the universe.

brahmin (bruh′-min): Member of the priestly caste.

caste (kaast): A major social class sanctioned by Hinduism.

Devi (deh′-vee): "Goddess"; the Divine Feminine, also called the Great Mother.

dhyana (dyah′-nah): Meditation.

Durga: "Awe-inspiring," "distant"; a mother-goddess; a form of Devi.

guru (goo′-roo): A spiritual teacher.

hatha yoga (hah′-tha yoh′-ga): The spiritual discipline of postures and bodily exercises.

jnana yoga (gyah′-nuh yoh′-ga; juh-nah′-nah yoh′-ga): The spiritual discipline of knowledge and insight.

Kali (kah′-lee): "Dark," a form of Devi; a goddess associated with destruction and rebirth.

karma: The moral law of cause and effect that determines the direction of rebirth.

karma yoga: The spiritual discipline of selfless action.

Krishna: A god associated with divine playfulness; a form of Vishnu.

kundalini yoga (koon-duh-lee′-nee yoh′-ga): A form of raja yoga that envisions the individual's energy as a force that is capable of being raised from the center of the body to the head, producing a state of joy.

mantra: A short sacred phrase, often chanted or used in meditation.

maya: "Illusion"; what keeps us from seeing reality correctly; the world, viewed inadequately.

moksha (mohk′-shah): "Liberation" from personal limitation, egotism, and rebirth.

monism: The philosophical position that all apparently separate realities are ultimately one; the belief that God and the universe are the same, that the universe is divine.

puja (poo′-jah): Offerings and ritual in honor of a deity.

raja yoga: The "royal" discipline of meditation.

Rama: A god and mythical king; a form of Vishnu.

samadhi (suh-mah′-dhee): A state of complete inner peace resulting from meditation.

samsara (suhm-sah′-rah): The everyday world of change and suffering leading to rebirth.

sannyasin (san-nyas′-in): A wandering holy man.

Shiva (shee′-vah): A god associated with destruction and rebirth.

Trimurti (tree-mur′-tee): "Three forms" of the divine—the three gods Brahma, Vishnu, and Shiva.

Upanishads (oo-pahn'-i-shads): Written meditations on the spiritual essence of the universe and the self.

Vedas (vay'-duhs): Four collections of ancient prayers and rituals.

Vishnu: A god associated with preservation and love.

yoga: A spiritual discipline; a method for perfecting one's union with the divine.

RELIGION BEYOND THE CLASSROOM

Visit the Online Learning Center at www.mhhe.com/molloy6e for additional exercises and features, including "Religion beyond the Classroom" and "For Fuller Understanding."

CHAPTER 4

Buddhism

F I R S T   E N C O U N T E R

On your way to southern Thailand with a friend, you fly to Bangkok
to spend a few days there before traveling south. Your hotel is in
the old section of town, near the river, not far from the Grand
Palace. Your friend has business to do the first day, and you decide
to go by yourself to the palace and the temples nearby.

First, you tour the old palace. It is a fascinating blend of Thai
and Western architecture. The lower part of the building looks European, but the upper part is distinctly Thai. Then you walk a short
distance to visit the Emerald Buddha. Its temple, Wat Pra Kaew, is
full of visitors. The green jade Buddha sits on top of a pedestal and
is clothed in robes that change with the season. The unusual statue
holds your attention, but the crowds soon force you out.

The grounds of the temple are decorated with plants, tall statues, round stupas, and stones of intriguing shapes. As you walk
among the objects, you are reminded of a Chinese garden. Your
meandering brings you to another temple, which is not so obvious.

The sign says that it is Wat Po. You walk through a square door and at first see nothing except the base of a large square pillar on your right. As your eyes adjust to the dimmer light, the outline of a huge Buddha emerges on your left. The building is very long—maybe 100 feet (30 meters)—but the statue barely fits inside. First you see the long reclining body. Then you see the golden face high up. At the far end of the hall, you see two huge feet and ten toes. There are only a few people here. It is fairly quiet. All you hear is the sound of metal hitting metal somewhere behind the Buddha figure.

In front of the statue is an arrangement of pink water lilies. One person stands there quietly in prayer. You walk to the same spot and stop to look and absorb. The Buddha's face is happy. The Buddha is unmoving, and his square feet seem equally at peace. What is he thinking? What story in his life does this image present?

You continue on, walking to the feet of the statue. You notice that the feet are covered with designs. As you go around the statue, you see a few people in the back, dropping coins into metal bowls before they leave. Then you go out, back to the unusual garden.

You are full of questions. Who was this person? What important events happened in his life? Why is he still honored by many people around the world today?

THE BEGINNINGS OF BUDDHISM: THE LIFE OF THE BUDDHA

Buddhism is one of the world's oldest and most significant religions. It has spread through most of Asia, influencing the many cultures there, and is now gaining followers in the West. But it had its beginnings in India and arose from the experience of one person.

India in the fifth century BCE was in a state of religious ferment. Great enthusiasm for personal religious experience led people to experiment with meditation and deep breathing and to study with gurus. A growing number of schools of philosophy taught new ways of thinking, some of which opposed the growth of the priestly Vedic religion. Into this world came Siddhartha Gautama, who would come to be known as the Buddha, or the Awakened One.

Because so many devout legends have grown up around the story of the Buddha's life and teaching, it is sometimes hard to separate fact from fiction.[1] Although there is no single, authoritative biography of the Buddha, his legendary life follows these outlines. Siddhartha was born the son of a prince of the Shakya tribe in what is today Nepal, in the lower Himalaya Mountains. Legend says that his mother, Maya, dreamt that a white elephant entered her side—this was the moment of conception of the future Buddha—and that

Siddhartha was born miraculously from her side. Siddhartha's mother died a week after childbirth, and the boy was raised by his aunt.

When a sage inspected the child, he saw special marks on Siddhartha's body, indicating that he would be an illustrious person. At his naming ceremony, priests foretold that his life could go in one of two directions: either he would follow in his father's footsteps, inheriting his position and becoming a great king, a "world ruler"; or, if he were exposed to the sight of suffering, he would become a great spiritual leader, a "world teacher."

Siddhartha's father, wanting his son to succeed him, took measures to keep the boy from exposure to suffering. Kept in a large, walled palace compound, Siddhartha grew up in luxury; married, at an early age, a young woman his father had chosen; and had a son. He was educated and trained as a warrior to prepare for eventually taking over his father's role.

All was going according to his father's plan until Siddhartha disobeyed his father's command to not leave the royal grounds. Visiting a nearby town, he soon witnessed the suffering of ordinary life. He saw—and was moved by—what are called the Four Passing Sights. He came across an old man, crooked and toothless; a sick man, wasted by disease; and a corpse being taken for cremation. Then he saw a sannyasin (a wandering holy man, a renunciate), who had no possessions but seemed to be at peace.

The paintings in Buddhist temples retell dramatically Siddhartha's response to what he saw. At 29, he realized that his life up until then had been a pleasant prison, and he saw the same programmed life stretching forward into his old age. The suffering he had just encountered, however, prompted him to question the meaning of human experience, and it threw him into a depression that kept him from enjoying his luxurious and carefree life any longer.

In this joyous depiction of the Buddha's birth, we see on the left his mother, Maya, having given birth from her side, while the newly born Buddha is sprinkled with lotus petals.

125

Siddhartha, born a wealthy prince, is here portrayed as the Buddha with princely crown and raiment. This depiction is frequent in the temples of Myanmar.

Siddhartha decided to escape. Legend tells how he took a last look at his sleeping family and attendants and rode to the edge of the palace grounds, where he gave his horse to his servant, removed his jewels, and cut off his long black hair. Putting on simple clothing, he went out into the world with nothing but questions. This event is called the Great Going Forth.

It is common in Indian spirituality to seek a teacher, and Siddhartha did just that. Traveling from teacher to teacher, he learned techniques of meditation and discussed philosophy, but he was ultimately unsatisfied. Begging for food and sleeping outdoors, Siddhartha spent about six years seeking answers to his questions—particularly about the troubling facts of suffering and death. His own mother had died young, a death that was apparently without meaning. Why, he often asked, is there suffering? Why do people have to grow old and die? Is there a God or unchanging divine reality behind the surface of things? Is there a soul? Is there an afterlife? Are we reborn? Can we avoid suffering? How should we live?

Seeking answers to his questions, Siddhartha discovered that his teachers agreed on some issues but not on others. So, in the company of five other nomadic "seekers," he set out to find the answers he needed. To rid himself of distractions and to purify himself spiritually, Siddhartha also practiced great austerity. Living on as little food, drink, and sleep as possible, he hoped that he would find new insight and even gain spiritual powers.

Eventually, Siddhartha collapsed from weakness. He was found resting under a sacred tree by a kind woman, who had come from the nearby town of Gaya to worship the spirit of the great tree. (Siddhartha was so emaciated that she may have thought him to be the tree spirit.) She offered him food, which he accepted gratefully and ate under the shade of the tree, out of the hot sun. Once revived, Siddhartha realized that his austerities had not strengthened him or brought him any closer to the answers he sought. His five companions, having discovered Siddhartha's rejection of asceticism, abandoned him.

Being a practical person, Siddhartha decided to adopt a path of moderation—a middle way between self-indulgence and asceticism. He went to another

Siddhartha, as depicted here, practiced physical deprivation, hoping to achieve insight. This approach proved to be inadequate.

tree, now called the Bodhi Tree,[2] and sat facing the east, resolving to remain there in meditation until he had the understanding he needed. Various traditions give different details, but every version talks of his struggle with hunger, thirst, doubt, and weakness. Some stories describe the work of an evil spirit, Mara, and his daughters who tempted Siddhartha with sensuality and fear. But Siddhartha resisted all temptation. During one entire night, as he sat meditating under a full moon, Siddhartha entered increasingly profound states of awareness. Legend says that he saw his past lives, fathomed the laws of karma that govern everyone, and finally achieved insight into release from suffering and rebirth.

At last, at dawn, he reached a state of profound understanding, called his Awakening, or Enlightenment (**bodhi**). He saw suffering, aging, and death in a new way, recognizing them as an inevitable part of life, but also seeing the possibility of release. We might wonder about the influence of the tree and the moon on Siddhartha. The tree overhead, with its thousands of leaves and twigs, despite its appearance of permanence, would change, age, and die; and the full moon, with its brilliant light, was a promise of new understanding. Whatever the cause of his enlightenment, Siddhartha arose and said that he was now a person who had woken up. From this came his new name: the Buddha, the Awakened One, taken from a Sanskrit word meaning "to wake up."

The Buddha remained for some time at the site of his enlightenment at Gaya, savoring his new way of looking at life and continuing to meditate. Mythic stories relate that during this time, when a heavy downpour occurred, a cobra raised itself over him to protect him from the rain. (In much of Asia, the snake is not considered a symbol of evil but rather a protective animal.) At last the Buddha traveled west. He explained his awakening to his five former companions at a deer park at Sarnath, near Benares. Although they had parted with him earlier for abandoning his ascetic habits, they reconciled with him and became his first disciples.

The Buddha spent the rest of his long life traveling from village to village in northeast India, teaching his insights and his way of life. He attracted many followers, and donors gave land, groves, and buildings to the new movement. The Buddha thus began an order (*sangha*) of monks and later of nuns. The Buddha's way was a path of moderation, a middle path, not only for himself but also for his disciples. It was midway between the worldly life of the householder, which he had lived before leaving home, and the ascetic life of social withdrawal, which he had followed after his departure from home. But the specifics of monastic community life and its relation to the nonmonastic world—on whom the monks relied for food—had to be worked out over time.

A wonder of the world, this huge statue of the Reclining Buddha in Polonnaruwa, Sri Lanka, may be unsurpassed in conveying the serenity that is the core of Buddhist teaching.

Tradition tells of the warm friendship the Buddha shared with his disciples and of their way of life, wandering about begging and teaching. The monks remained in one place only during the monsoon months of summer, when the rains were so heavy that travel was impractical. Looking on the Buddha's lifestyle from a modern vantage point, we can see that it was a healthy one: moderate eating, no alcohol, daily walking, regular meditation, pure air. Probably because of this, the Buddha lived to an old age.

When he was 80, legend says, the Buddha ate food offered by a well-meaning blacksmith named Chunda, but the food was spoiled and the Buddha became terribly sick. Sensing that he was dying, he called his disciples. To those who were crying over his impending death, he reminded them that everything must die—even the Buddha himself. He then offered these final words of advice: "You must be your own lamps, be your own refuges. Take refuge in nothing outside yourselves. Hold firm to the truth as a lamp and a refuge, and do not look for refuge to anything besides yourselves."[3] In other words, the Buddha's final instruction was this: Trust your own insights, and use self-control to reach perfection and inner peace.

Following this pronouncement, the Buddha turned on his right side and died. The many sculptures and paintings of the so-called Reclining Buddha may be images of his serene moment of death.[4] In any case, Buddhists idealize the Buddha's attitude toward death as a model for everyone.

THE BASIC TEACHINGS OF BUDDHISM

It is impossible to know exactly what the Buddha taught. He did not write down his teachings, nor did his early disciples. The only written versions were recorded several hundred years after his death, following centuries of being passed on orally—and of being interpreted in multiple ways. We must rely on the basic trustworthiness of both the oral traditions and the many written texts that pass on his teachings.

The written teachings that have come down to us are in a number of languages, all of which differ from the language (apparently a variation of Magadhi) spoken by the Buddha. One of the most important languages through which Buddhist teachings have been passed down is Pali, a language related to Sanskrit; another is Sanskrit itself—often called the Latin of India because of its widespread use in earlier years for scholarly works.

At the core of what is generally regarded as basic Buddhism are the Three Jewels (Sanskrit: *Triratna;* Pali: *Tiratana*)—that is, the Buddha, the Dharma, and the Sangha. The Buddha is thought of as an ideal human being whom other human beings should imitate; the image of him, seated in meditation, is a constant model of self-control and mindfulness. He is not usually thought of as being dead but instead as existing in a timeless dimension beyond the world. The **Dharma** (Sanskrit), or Dhamma (Pali), means the sum total of Buddhist teachings about how to view the world and how to live properly. The **Sangha** is the community of monks and nuns.[5]

The Buddha's teachings are like the Buddha himself—practical. Surrounded in the India of his day by every kind of speculation about the afterlife, the nature of the divine, and other difficult questions, the Buddha concentrated on what was useful. He refused to talk about anything else—a benign neglect that has been called his noble silence. He said that a person who speculated about unanswerable questions was like a man who had been wounded by an arrow but refused to pull it out until he knew everything about the arrow and the person who shot it. The wounded man would die before he could get all the information he wanted.

The Buddha wished to concentrate on the two most important questions about existence: How can we minimize suffering—both our own and that of others? And how can we attain inner peace? The Buddha's conclusions are not just intellectual solutions; they are also recommendations for a practical way of living. Buddhist doctrines are not meant to be accepted on blind faith; rather, it is up to each individual to experience them first as truths before accepting them.

The Three Marks of Reality

Common to all forms of Buddhism is a way of looking at the world. Although this view may seem pessimistic at first, it is meant to be a realistic assessment of existence that, when understood, ultimately helps lead a person to inner peace and even joy. According to this view, reality manifests three characteristics: constant change, a lack of permanent identity, and the existence of suffering. This view is the foundation for the Four Noble Truths and the Noble Eightfold Path, which we will discuss shortly.

Change   One of the things the Buddha recommended is that we look at life as it really is. When we do, he said, the first thing we notice is life's constant change, or impermanence (Pali: **anichcha;** Sanskrit: *anitya*). We are often surprised by change—and pained by it—because we do not expect it, but the fact is that nothing we experience in life ever remains the same. We get used to things (our own face, family, friends, house, car, neighborhood), and they seem to remain basically the same every time we look at them. But that is an illusion, for they are changing daily, gradually. We usually only notice the changes over time.

Everyone knows the shock of change, such as seeing an old friend after being apart for many years, or looking at childhood photos. Even old movies on television and old songs on

In Buddhist countries, the Sangha is venerated as one of Buddhism's Three Jewels. Here, guests at a hotel make food offerings to monks who leave their temples at dawn to accept alms.

the radio—the performers now aged or even long gone—clearly convey the Buddhist sense of the inevitability of change. A family gathering can have the same effect: the death of a much-loved grandparent may be contrasted by the sight of a great-grandchild playing in a playpen in the corner.

People's viewpoints also change. Think of what the word *love* means to a five-year-old, a teenager, a new parent, or a person who has lost a spouse. Or imagine hearing the news of a divorce between two people you thought were well suited and happily married.

When we truly experience impermanence, we see that all of reality is in motion all the time, that the universe is in flux. As the kaleidoscope of reality slowly turns, its patterns change; and while old patterns disappear, new patterns are born, all of them interesting. As the Buddha taught, the wise person expects change, accepts it, and even savors it. The wise person might also reflect that just as pleasures do not last forever, neither do sorrows.

No Permanent Identity   We know that the Buddha urged people to abandon egotism and a fixation on material objects. Related to this, he denied the existence of the permanent identity of anything. Thus, the second mark of reality is that each person and each thing is not only changing but is made up of parts that are also constantly changing, a concept referred to as "no permanent identity." In the case of people, it is called "no permanent soul" or "no self." The Pali term is **anatta;** in Sanskrit it is *anatman* ("no Atman") because of the Buddha's refusal to accept the Hindu notion of timeless, unchanging reality (*Atman*) underlying everything—people, things, essences, and gods.

For the sake of logical convenience, we often talk about each person or thing as if it were a single unified reality. Let us first consider something nonhuman, say, a car. We call it *a car* as if it were one single reality, but actually it is made up of many things—glass, aluminum, rubber, paint, headlights, belts, pistons, wires, and fluids—many of which are either in need of repair right now or probably soon will be.

Then think of how each human being, though called by a single name, is actually made up of organs, body parts, instincts, memories, ideas, and hopes—all of which are constantly changing. Consider also one's self-perception. I naively think I am the same person from day to day, even if I get a haircut or lose weight or see a film. But if I recall myself at age 10 and then compare that person with who I am now, I seem now to be someone quite different.

To the Buddha, to believe that a person has some unchanging identity or soul is as mistaken as believing that a car has an unchanging essence. The car is not a car because it has a "car soul"; rather, it is a car because of a social convention that refers to its many related parts by a single word. This tendency is so strong that we sometimes think that a label (*car*) is the reality. Although the Buddhist view may seem strange at first, it is quite rational—and it helps eliminate surprise when my car won't start, when a friend becomes distant, or when a photo reveals the inevitability of aging. All these changes show the same process at work.[6]

Suffering   The third characteristic of reality, known as **dukkha** (Pali), or *duhkha* (Sanskrit), is usually translated as "suffering" or "sorrow," but it also means "dissatisfaction" or "dis-ease." It refers to the fact that life, when lived conventionally, can never be fully satisfying because of its inescapable change. Even in the midst of pleasure, we often recognize that pleasure is fleeting. Even when all the bills are paid, we know that in a few days there will be more. Try as we might to put everything in our lives in order, disorder soon reasserts itself. In the midst of happy experiences, we may worry about the people we love. And there are times when ever-changing life brings misery: the death of a parent or spouse or child, divorce, sickness, fire, flood, earthquake, war, the loss of job or home.

Dukkha encompasses the whole range, from horrible suffering to everyday frustration. Someone once compared the inevitability of dukkha to buying a new car. Your car brings the pleasures of mobility and pride of ownership, but as you go for your first ride you know what lies ahead: insurance premiums, routine maintenance, and costly repairs.

The Buddha concluded that to live means inescapably to experience sorrow and dissatisfaction. But he analyzed the nature and causes of suffering much like a doctor would diagnose an illness—in order to understand and overcome them. Those who say that Buddhism pessimistically focuses on suffering do not see the hopeful purpose behind that focus. Indeed, no one can escape suffering, but each person can decide how to respond to it, as indicated in the Four Noble Truths.

The Four Noble Truths and the Noble Eightfold Path

Perhaps to aid in their memorization, some Buddhist teachings were grouped into fours and eights. The Four Noble Truths are a linked chain of truths about life: (1) suffering exists; (2) it has a cause; (3) it has an end; and (4) there is a way to attain release from suffering—namely, by following the Noble Eightfold Path. Let's look at each concept more closely.

The eight-spoked wheel is an ancient symbol of Buddhist teachings.

The First Noble Truth: To Live Is to Suffer   To say it perhaps more descriptively, "birth is attended with pain, decay is painful, disease is painful, death is painful."[7] Having a body means that we can be tired and sick. Having a mind means that we can be troubled and discouraged. We have so many daily duties that our lives become a long list of things-to-do, and we feel like jugglers trying to keep too many balls spinning in the air. The past cannot be relived, and the future is uncertain. And every day, we have to decide what to do with the rest of our lives. (It has been remarked that adults so frequently ask children "What do you want to be when you grow up?" because the adults themselves are still trying to decide what to do with their own lives.)

To live means to experience anxiety, loss, and sometimes even anguish. In other words, "living means sorrow." Although the message sounds dark, this truth urges us to be realistic, not melancholy; it is also hopeful in the sense that if we recognize why suffering comes about, then we can lessen it.

The Second Noble Truth: Suffering Comes from Desire   When he analyzed suffering, the Buddha saw that it comes from wanting what we cannot have and from never being satisfied with what we do have. The word *trishna* (Sanskrit), or *tanha* (Pali), which is often translated as "desire," might better be translated as "thirst"; it can also be translated as "craving," suggesting both an addiction and a fear of loss. Some of our desires are obvious: food, sleep, clothing, housing, health. Some desires are more subtle: privacy, respect, friendship, quiet, stresslessness, security, variety, beauty. And some desires are simply "wants" that are cultivated by our society: alcohol, designer clothes, tobacco, entertainment, expensive food. We all have desires, and because life around us is always changing, no matter how much we acquire we cannot be permanently satisfied. Desire is insatiable, and the result is discontent, dissatisfaction, and sometimes misery. But is there a way to be free of suffering?

The Third Noble Truth: To End Suffering, End Desire   It is hard to argue with the reasonableness of this truth, yet it goes against modern Western notions. The Western tendency is to strain to achieve every imaginable desire. This tendency seems to thrive in cultures—such as many modern ones—that emphasize individual legal and moral rights, competition between individuals, and individual success in school, in one's job, and in sports. Belief in a distinct and permanent self or an immortal soul may be the origin of such individualism. This tendency is rather different from the sense of self that comes from a worldview that values the individual's membership in the group—a view of self more common, traditionally, in tribal and Asian cultures.

To our modern way of thinking, the Buddha's recommendations may seem rather stark. Nevertheless, he himself left home and family and possessions because he believed—and taught—that *any* kind of attachment will bring inevitable suffering. The shaven head and special clothing of monks and nuns symbolize their radical detachment from worldly concerns.

Buddhists themselves recognize, though, that not everyone can be a monk. Consequently, this third truth is moderated for laypeople. It is commonly interpreted as a recommendation that everyone accept peacefully whatever occurs, aiming less for happiness and more for inner peace. The individual should concentrate on the present moment, not on the past or the future or one's desires for them. Because times of happiness are always paid for by times of unhappiness (the pendulum swings in both directions), a certain emotional neutrality is the best path.

Acceptance is a step to inner peace if I recognize that what I have right now is actually enough. Ultimately, I have to accept my body, my talents,

> Look within.
> Be still.
> Free from fear and attachment,
> Know the sweet joy of the way.
> —The Dhammapada[8]

my family, and even my relatives. Of course, some adjustments can be made: I can move, have plastic surgery, change my job, or get a divorce. Ultimately, though, much of life simply has to be accepted—and appreciated when possible.

The essence of the Third Noble Truth is this: I cannot change the outside world, but I can change myself and the way I experience the world.

The Fourth Noble Truth: Release from Suffering Is Possible and Can Be Attained by Following the Noble Eightfold Path   The ultimate goal of Buddhism is **nirvana** (Sanskrit; Pali: *nibbana*). The term *nirvana* suggests many things: end of suffering, inner peace, and liberation from the limitations of the world. The word *nirvana* seems to mean "blown out," or "cool," suggesting that the fires of desire have been extinguished. Upon attaining nirvana, the individual has self-control and is no longer driven from inside by raging emotional forces or from outside by the unpredictable events of life. It may not necessarily imply the elimination of anger (stories tell of the Buddha's getting angry at disputes within the monastic community), but it does suggest a general inner quiet. Nirvana is also believed to end karma and rebirth after the present life. (More will be said about nirvana later in this chapter.) To reach nirvana, Buddhism recommends following the Noble Eightfold Path.

The Noble Eightfold Path: The Way to Inner Peace   The eight "steps" of the path actually form a program that the Buddha taught will lead us toward liberation from the impermanence and suffering of reality. Together, they describe three main goals: to face life objectively, to live kindly, and to cultivate inner peace. Although they are often called "steps," the eight recommendations are not to be practiced sequentially but rather all together. As it is usually translated, the Noble Eightfold Path sounds so old-fashioned that readers may not immediately perceive its practicality. But keep in mind that the word *right* in the following list is a translation of a word that might better be translated as "correct" or "complete."

1. *Right understanding* I recognize the impermanence of life, the mechanism of desire, and the cause of suffering.

2. *Right intention* My thoughts and motives are pure, not tainted by my emotions and selfish desires.

3. *Right speech* I speak honestly and kindly, in positive ways, avoiding lies, exaggeration, harsh words.

4. *Right action* My actions do not hurt any other being that can feel hurt, including animals; I avoid stealing and sexual conduct that would bring hurt.

5. *Right work* My job does no harm to myself or others.

6. *Right effort* With moderation, I consistently strive to improve.

7. *Right meditation* (*right mindfulness*) I use the disciplines of meditation (**dhyana**) and focused awareness to contemplate the nature of reality more deeply.

8. *Right contemplation* I cultivate states of blissful inner peace (**samadhi**).

THE INFLUENCE OF INDIAN THOUGHT ON EARLY BUDDHIST TEACHINGS

It is uncertain whether the Buddha intended to begin an entirely new religion. Early Buddhist literature rejects certain elements of the common Vedic practice of the time, particularly its ritualism, its reliance on priests, its caste system, and its belief in any permanent spiritual reality. Non-Buddhists responded argumentatively when women and slaves entered the Buddhist monastic order. Such evidence leads us to think that early Buddhists saw themselves as outside the mainstream priestly Vedic culture—a fact that may have assisted them in developing their own statements of belief and practice. Nevertheless, we do know that early Buddhist teachings accepted certain elements of Indian thought that contemporary Hinduism, Jainism, and Buddhism share to some extent.

Ahimsa: "Do No Harm"

Foremost among the elements adopted from the Indian worldview of the Buddha's day was the ideal of *ahimsa* ("nonharm"; see Chapter 3). It is not clear how old this ideal is, and it has not always been followed. We do know that Vedic sacrifice at the time of the Buddha sometimes included animal sacrifice (and animal sacrifice in Hindu practice can still be found, particularly in Nepal and Bali). But we also know that the ideal of ahimsa was already prominent in India before the time of the Buddha and may have had ancient and pre-Vedic origins.

For Buddhism, ahimsa is fundamental. The ideal holds that to cause suffering to any being is cruel and unnecessary—life is already hard enough for each of us. Ahimsa discourages causing not only physical pain but also psychological hurt or the exploitation of another. Upon reaching a real understanding that every being that feels can suffer, the individual gains wider sympathy. It is then natural and satisfying for the individual to live with gentleness.

Ahimsa is a high ideal and not always easy to achieve. Furthermore, we must recognize that there will always be a gap between the ideal and actual practice in different Buddhist cultures and among individuals. Nevertheless, however murky the definition of the "best action" may be, the ideal is fairly clear. A compassionate person does everything possible to avoid causing suffering: "ashamed of roughness, and full of mercy, he dwells compassionate and kind to all creatures that have life."[9] This empathetic ideal has been interpreted as recommending, when possible, a vegetarian or semivegetarian diet, and it warns against involvement in any jobs or sports that would hurt others, such as being a butcher, hunter, fisherman, soldier, or weapon maker. The result is a way of life that is harmonious and free of remorse.

The Soul and Karma

The Buddha rejected the notion of a soul (an unchanging spiritual reality), but he accepted some notion of rebirth. How, we might then ask, can an individual be reborn if there is no soul? Buddhism holds that while there is no individual soul, the elements of personality that make up an individual can recombine and thus continue from one lifetime to another. Buddhism offers the examples of a flame passing from one candle to another and the pattern caused by a breeze that passes over many blades of grass. The candles are separate, but only one flame passes between each candle; the blades of grass are rooted to separate places, but the pattern of the breeze travels across them and "unites" them in movement.

Closely related to the notion of rebirth is *karma*. As we discussed in Chapter 3, karma determines how one will be reborn. In Hinduism and Jainism, karma is like something that clings to the soul as it passes from life to life in reincarnation. It works automatically: good actions produce karma that brings good effects, such as intelligence, high birth, and wealth; bad actions produce karma that brings the opposite, including rebirth into animal and insect life-forms. Because the Buddha rejected the existence of a soul, explaining how karma works is more difficult in Buddhism. It is thought to accompany and affect the elements of personality that reappear in later lifetimes. Regardless

The temples of Angkor Wat, a World Heritage site in Cambodia, show the Hindu roots of Buddhism in their architecture.

of their specific manner of functioning, karma and rebirth were already such powerful ideas in the India of the Buddha's time that they continued in early Buddhism and from there have spread well beyond India. They remain highly influential concepts in Buddhist countries today.

Nirvana

In Buddhism, as in Hinduism, the everyday world of change is called **samsara**, a term that suggests decay and pain. Liberation from samsara, however, is attained in nirvana. The notion has many similarities with the Hindu goal of *moksha* ("liberation"; discussed in Chapter 3). Nirvana is thought of as existence beyond limitation. Many people in the West associate nirvana with a psychological state, because it is described as evoking joy and peace; but perhaps it is better to see nirvana as being indescribable and beyond all psychological states. Although reaching nirvana occurs rarely, it is theoretically possible to attain during one's lifetime; the Buddha is said to have "entered nirvana" at the time of his enlightenment. Once a person has reached nirvana, rebirth is finished, and in a culture that believes that individuals have already been born many times before this current life, an end to rebirth can be a welcome thought.

THE EARLY DEVELOPMENT OF BUDDHISM

Buddhism might have remained an entirely Indian religion, much as Jainism has, if it were not for an energetic king named Ashoka, who flourished about 250 BCE (see Timeline 4.1, p. 138). Ashoka's plan to expand his rule over a large part of India naturally entailed much fighting. After a particularly bloody battle in eastern India, as Ashoka was inspecting the battlefield, he saw the scene very differently than he had before. The whole experience was so horrifying that Ashoka converted to the ideal of nonviolence. Although it is uncertain whether Ashoka became a Buddhist, he did make political use of Buddhist moral values. A cynic might note that forbidding violence is a practical move for any ruler who wishes to remain on the throne. In any case, the principle of nonviolence is most effective when it is embraced widely; otherwise, the few people who are nonviolent will be preyed upon by the violent.

To bring a large number of the population around to his new nonviolent way of thinking and acting, Ashoka decided to spread the principles of nonviolence throughout India and possibly even beyond. To do this, he erected many stone columns inscribed with his principles, placing some at sites important in the Buddha's life. A number of these columns still exist today.

In the first centuries after the Buddha's death, in response to widespread and long-standing disagreements over the Buddha's teachings, many Buddhist schools and splinter groups arose. Most of these ultimately died out and are only names to us today. A few survived and crystallized into the great branches of Buddhism that we now recognize: Theravada, Mahayana, and Vajrayana.

	c. 563–483 BCE	Traditional dates of Siddhartha Gautama, the Buddha
Life of Ashoka, Indian king who spread Buddhist values	c. 273–232 BCE	
	c. 50 CE	Entry of Buddhism into China
Creation of the Lotus Sutra	c. 100 CE	
	c. 300 CE	Beginning of the spread of Buddhism in Southeast Asia
Entry of Buddhism into Korea	c. 400 CE	
	c. 520 CE	Introduction of Bodhidharma's Meditation school of Buddhism to China
Introduction of Buddhism into Japan	c. 552 CE	
	c. 630 CE	Entry of Buddhism into Tibet
Founding of Tendai and Shingon Buddhism in Japan	c. 820 CE	
	c. 845 CE	Major persecution of Buddhists in China
Revival of Theravada Buddhism in Sri Lanka and Southeast Asia	c. 1000 CE	
	c. 1100–1500	Decline of Buddhism in India
Life of Honen, founder of the Pure Land sect in Japan	1133–1212	
	1158–1210	Life of Chinul, founder of the Korean Chogye order
Beginning of the growth of Zen in Japan	c. 1200	
	1222–1282	Life of Nichiren, founder of Nichiren Buddhism in Japan
Life of Tsong Kha-pa, Tibetan Buddhist reformer	1357–1419	
	1644–1694	Life of poet Matsuo Basho
Beginning of the World Fellowship of Buddhists	c. 1952	
	1989	Award of the Nobel Peace Prize to the Dalai Lama

Timeline of significant events in Buddhism.

It was once assumed that the three branches emerged in sequence, like three waves of thought that came from India in succeeding centuries. But scholars now recognize that essential elements of all three branches frequently existed side by side, possibly even in the earliest days of Buddhism. Often, too, the boundaries between the branches have been blurred or are even non-existent. The branches are more like families that have many shared elements.

In addition, people who follow a specific Buddhist path are often not aware of other branches. The same is not true of some other religions, in which practitioners are quite aware of the division to which they belong. (For example, Muslims define themselves as Sunni or Shiite, and Christians as Protestant, Catholic, or Orthodox.) But Buddhist believers of one branch, even if they know of other forms, generally do not define themselves in contrast to those other branches. Instead, they define themselves more according to Buddhist "lineages," tracing their beliefs and practices back to the great teachers of the past who, in a long chain of masters and disciples, handed on the traditions that they follow.

Thus, before we divide Buddhism into these so-called branches, we must realize that to talk of three "branches" is to greatly oversimplify the complex reality of Buddhism. This approach is only meant to enhance the understanding of the richness of Buddhist history, belief, and practice.

FIGURE 4.1

The birthplace and traditional home of Buddhism: India, China, Japan, and Southeast Asia.

THERAVADA BUDDHISM: THE WAY OF THE ELDERS

In the early centuries of Buddhism, several schools claimed to adhere to the original, unchanged teachings of the Buddha. All of them shared the Buddha's opposition to Vedic ritual and the brahmin priesthood, and they embraced his appreciation for simplicity, meditation, and detachment. They took a conservative approach, hoping to protect the Buddha's rather stark teachings and simple practice from being altered. Of all the conservative schools, one has survived to the present day: Theravada. Its name is often used today to refer to the entire conservative movement.

The Theravada school takes its name from its goal of passing on the Buddha's teachings unchanged. It means "the way (*vada*) of the elders (*thera*)." Theravada monks originally passed on the teachings in oral form, but they eventually wrote them down. Although the school's claim to have kept its teachings relatively unchanged over time is doubtful, it is true that Theravada has a deliberately conservative orientation. Since the nineteenth century, the name *Theravada* has been commonly used to refer to the forms of Buddhism that are found mostly in Sri Lanka and Southeast Asia.

The heart of Theravada Buddhism is its community of monks. As a school, it has always stressed the ideal of reaching nirvana through detachment and desirelessness, achieved by way of meditation. (This, of course, is an ideal that some would point out has been contradicted by the Sangha's having courted wealth and temporal power.) Although Theravada does accept that laypeople can attain nirvana, the life of the monk offers a surer path. The notion is enshrined in the ideal of the **arhat** (Sanskrit; Pali: *arahat;* meaning "perfect being," "worthy"), a person who has reached nirvana.*

The Theravada monastic community had its distant origins in the wandering sannyasins and in the groups of Hindu ascetics who lived in the forests. (A sign of this connection is the orange robe; it is used by Hindu ascetics and is also worn by many orders of Theravada Buddhist monks.) But even during the Buddha's lifetime, his monks began to live a settled life during the summertime monsoon season, giving their time to discussion and

Buddhists typically visit their local temple at the New Year. They leave offerings for the temple, including money, and in return, each receives a blessing and a printed fortune from the monks.

---

*In the discussion of Theravada Buddhism, it would be more accurate to use the Pali terms *nibbana, arahat,* and *sutta,* as opposed to the Sanskrit terms *nirvana, arhat,* and *sutra;* however, for the sake of consistency, the text throughout this chapter will reflect the terminology (whether Pali or Sanskrit) that is most familiar in the West.

inhabiting caves or groves and parks donated by lay followers.

Theravada spread very early from India to Sri Lanka, where it has gone through several phases of growth and decline. By the fourth century, it had been carried—along with other elements of Indian culture—to Myanmar (Burma) and to Thailand. Theravada did not become predominant in Myanmar until the mid-eleventh century, when Bagan began to flourish as a great Buddhist city and center of Theravada under King Anawratha. Fourteenth-century Thailand, having freed itself of Khmer domination, also adopted Theravada Buddhism. The conservatism of Theravada was politically appealing to rulers for its moral rigor. Today it is the dominant religion in Sri Lanka, Myanmar, Thailand, Laos, and Cambodia.

Theravada monks must beg daily for their food, which has meant that they, like the Buddha's early followers, have to live close to laypeople. In fact, Theravada mon-

These nuns go into a shopping district of Mandalay, Myanmar, and allow shoppers and shop clerks to earn merit by making offerings.

asteries are often in the middle of towns. Many monasteries run schools, meditation centers, and medical clinics, as well as care for stray animals (which sometimes overrun the grounds). In return, monks are the beneficiaries of regular donations. When Theravada monks go out on their begging rounds in the early morning, people who wish to donate food freely offer them rice and vegetables. Donors believe they are receiving beneficial karma from their acts of generosity, and people support the monasteries much like other societies give to libraries and other social agencies. At Buddhist festivals monks are given new robes and pails of essential items, such as soap, toothpaste, razors, and canned goods. Donations are especially given at the New Year festival and at the beginning and end of the rainy season. (This period, often called Buddhist Lent, begins in late summer and lasts for three months. During this time monks stay in their monasteries for study.)

Most weddings, funerals, and other family events are considered incomplete without the presence of monks, who are expected to chant from the *sutras* (sayings of the Buddha, which we will discuss shortly) to provide merit for the family members. Monks are also an important part of festivals, many of which are organized by monasteries themselves.

Mourners and monks gather at a funeral to seek merit so that the deceased person might be reborn closer to nirvana.

In addition to the ordination performed for men who are planning to become monks for life, Theravada Buddhism commonly performs "temporary ordination." Frequently, temporary ordination lasts for an entire rainy season, but it may also be done for shorter periods. Temporary ordination is considered an effective way to "make merit" for oneself and one's family. It is thought to positively influence the formation of young men's characters, and it is sometimes undertaken by whole groups, such as policemen, for whom it is viewed as a sign of sincerity and goodwill.

Young monks gather before prayers at their temple in Luang Prabang, Laos. Temples in this area have the steep, sloping roof found in much of Cambodia, Laos, Myanmar, and Thailand.

Deeper Insights

BUDDHISM IN THAILAND

Theravada Buddhism is the state religion of Thailand, and more than 90 percent of Thais are Buddhists. Thai Buddhists, however, practice a religion that blends elements from Buddhism, Hinduism, and folk belief. Perhaps because Buddhism so emphasizes tolerance, Buddhism as it is actually practiced is rich with elements from many sources.

Buddhism's prevalence in Thailand is evident in everyday life. Thais frequently act publicly on the assumption that doing good deeds will "make merit"—bring good karma for this life and for future lives. To make merit, Thais offer coins to the needy on the street, give food and robes to monks, attend Buddhist services, and help animals. And Buddhist monks can be seen everywhere—walking in the streets and riding in the back of buses (which they ride free), in *tuk-tuks* (three-wheeled cabs), and on riverboats.

Yet equally visible are "spirit houses." These look like miniature temples, and they are erected on high posts at the corner of a piece of land, on high-rise rooftops, or under large, old trees. Spirit houses are dedicated to the guardian spirits of the property and to the spirits of former owners. Worshipers offer food and flowers to them daily.

Frequently the Hindu god Brahma is the figure inside the spirit houses, and small images of dancing girls—derived from Hindu temple worship—are left as permanent offerings. In shops a visitor might see a statue of Ganesha, the elephant-headed Hindu god associated with success. Another influence of Hinduism is readily apparent in Thai art and dance, which tell the stories of Rama, Sita, and Hanuman, whose tales are retold in the Ramakien, the Thai version of the Ramayana.

A strong magical dimension is part of Thai Buddhism as well. Thai males often wear a necklace of Buddhist amulets to defend themselves against sickness and injury (the owners will describe in happy detail the origin and power of each of the amulets). Tattoos, often with images of the Buddha, Rama, and Hanuman, are thought to have a similar effect. And taxi drivers—not to mention their often anxious passengers—hope that the multiple Buddhist images on their dashboards will offer needed protection in traffic.

Monasticism, as we can see, permeates society and everyday life in Theravada Buddhist cultures. As mentioned earlier, monasteries exist even in the centers of cities, where monks can be seen everywhere. There is a fluidity to monastic life, too, and Theravada monks often choose to leave monastic life, even after many years. But during the time that men are monks, they are considered role models and are expected to live up to strict moral standards.

The earliest Western translators and scholars of Theravada Buddhism saw Buddhism through the lens of their own culture. Key to their conception of what makes a religion was a body of written scriptures; the scholars assumed that written scriptures played a central role in believers' lives. More recent scholarship points out that Buddhist teachings have been largely passed on orally. Because the vast majority of Buddhists have been unable to read, they have learned their religious beliefs and practices not from reading books, but from hearing sermons, seeing temple paintings, and listening to older family members. And long before written material existed, certain monks were known as specialists in chanting the words of the Buddha, the rules of their order, and the precepts of right living. Eventually this oral material was indeed written down and codified. But, as we learn about the written scriptures, we must understand the primary role that oral transmission has played.

In addition to the so-called canonical scriptures, folktales have been influential. The most famous are the hundreds of Jataka Tales. They are similar to Aesop's Fables, and early forms of the stories may have influenced those tales and similar collections in other countries. The tales are about human beings and animals, and each tale teaches a moral lesson about a particular virtue, such as friendship, truthfulness, generosity, or moderation. In Theravada Buddhism the tales are often put within a Buddhist context. Typically, the tale begins with the Buddha telling the tale. The tale then ends with the Buddha saying that in a past life he was one of the animal or human figures in the story. The Jataka Tales are frequently the subject of art, plays, and dance in Southeast Asia.

Theravada Teachings and Literature

The Theravada collection of the Buddha's teachings is called the Pali Canon. As a whole, this mass of material is called *Tipitaka* (Pali), or **Tripitaka** (Sanskrit), which means "three baskets." The name comes from the fact that the writings were divided according to their subject matter into three groups.

The first collection (called *vinaya*—Pali and Sanskrit) outlines the procedural rules for monastic life. These include rules on begging, eating, relations with monks and nonmonks, and other disciplines.[10] The second collection comprises sayings of the Buddha in the form of sermons or dialogues. This type of material is called *sutta* (Pali), or **sutra** (Sanskrit). A third collection, developed later, is called *abhidhamma* (Pali), or *abhidharma* (Sanskrit), meaning "the works that go beyond the elementary teachings." It systematized the doctrine presented more or less randomly in the sutras.

Theravada Art and Architecture

Images of the Buddha did not appear in the earliest centuries of Buddhism; instead, artists used symbols to represent him and his teachings. One symbol was the eight-spoked wheel, which derived from the Noble Eightfold Path and represented all the basic Buddhist teachings, the Dharma. (The wheel may have been suggested either by the disk of the sun, symbolizing light and health, or by the wheel of a king's chariot, a symbol of royal rulership.) The umbrella, often carried to protect an important person from the hot sun, symbolized the Buddha's authority. Other common symbols included a set of footprints, a lotus flower, and an empty throne. Many types of **stupas,** which began as large mounds, arose over the remains of Buddhist monks and at important Buddhist sites. Symbols may have been used at first simply because artists were struggling with the basic challenge of depicting simultaneously the humanity of the Buddha and his great spiritual attainment, his enlightenment. By the first century of the Common Era, however, images of the Buddha began to appear. (Scholars debate the possible influence of Greek

Bangkok's Wat Arun, a temple in Hindu style, is across the Chao Phraya River from Wat Po and the Grand Palace.

sculptural traditions.[11]) In Theravada countries we now frequently see statues of the Buddha meditating, standing (with hand outstretched in blessing), walking, or reclining. Some of the most beautiful sculptures are the Reclining Buddhas of Sri Lanka and Thailand.

MAHAYANA BUDDHISM: THE "BIG VEHICLE"

The second great branch of Buddhism is called Mahayana, a word that is usually translated as "big vehicle." It suggests a large ferryboat in which all types of people can be carried across a river, and it hints at the broad scope of the Mahayana vision, which can accommodate a wide variety of people seeking enlightenment. Mahayana emphasizes that everyone, not only monks, can attain nirvana. Mahayana also stresses that enlightenment is a call to compassion, for "the Mahayana tradition maintains that a person must save himself by saving others."[12]

Some critics of Mahayana Buddhism claim that it has allowed ritual and speculation—which was deemphasized by the Buddha—to creep back in. It is possible that the Indian love of ritual and imagery remains alive in a new form in Mahayana. For example, the fire ceremony of some Mahayana sects certainly derives from Vedic practice. But this is really to say that Mahayana initially was thoroughly Indian and sought to express its truths in very Indian ways.[13]

It is possible that some practices or attitudes of early Buddhism did not always fulfill the religious needs of the many laypeople who appreciated ritual. Mahayana Buddhism, however, has abundantly met almost every religious and philosophical need.[14] It is the source of some of the most extraordinary creations of the human mind—in its art, architecture, philosophy, psychology, and ceremony.

New Ideals: Compassion and the Bodhisattva

In Mahayana Buddhism, the religious ideal broadened: from the exemplar of the monastic person, fairly detached from family life, it expanded to include nonmonks, women, and the married. Mahayana began to explore the possibilities of following a religious path that was active in the world. This difference signaled a shift in the notion of what is virtuous. It might have represented a reaction against Indian asceticism and the cult of the sannyasin, or it might have indicated a new form of devotionalism and love of ritual. It might also have come from a widening of the concept of nirvana. Nirvana was now thought to be found within samsara, the everyday world of change. In Mahayana, the human body and the material realm are viewed positively, and there is a great openness toward art and music. Mahayana grew as the senses and emotions were increasingly viewed as means of spiritual transformation.

In Mahayana, wisdom remained an important goal, but the pairing of wisdom and compassion was central to its teachings. Compassion became an essential virtue and the preeminent expression of wisdom. The term for this compassion is **karuna**, which may also be translated as "empathy," "sympathy," or "kindness." Karuna is somewhat different from the Western notion of kindness, in which one separate human being, out of an abundance of individual generosity, gives to another separate human being. Rather, karuna implies that we all are part of the same ever-changing universe. Deep down, the individual is not really different from anyone or anything else. To be kind to others is actually to be kind to oneself. Karuna in action simply means living out this awareness of the unity of the universe. With this perception of the interrelatedness of all beings, including animals, compassion comes naturally: if I am kind, my kindness must be shown toward anything that can feel pain. The great prayer of Buddhist compassion is this: May all creatures be well and happy. It is a common Mahayana practice to mentally project this wish to the world every day.

The esteem for karuna influences the human ideal in Mahayana. Instead of the Theravada ideal of the arhat, who is esteemed for detached wisdom and unworldly living, the ideal in Mahayana Buddhism is the person of deep compassion, the **bodhisattva** ("enlightenment being"). Because a bodhisattva embodies compassion, it is often said that a bodhisattva will refuse to fully enter nirvana, in order to be reborn on earth to help others. A person may even take the "bodhisattva vow" to be constantly reborn until all are enlightened.

The same kind of openness to a variety of religious paths that we saw in Hinduism is also typical of Mahayana Buddhism. Mahayana recognizes that people differ greatly and find themselves at different stages of spiritual development. For example, a person who would not benefit from study or meditation might be able to achieve a new level of understanding through the use of ritual, imagery, and religious objects. Mahayana is open to anything that can lead to greater spiritual awareness, a concept known as "skillful means" (Sanskrit: *upaya*).

Mahayana Thought and Worldview

Mahayana has encouraged a vision of reality that is imaginative, wide, and often profound. A legendary story tells of a Chinese emperor who began reading certain Mahayana sutras; he then said in astonishment that the experience was like looking out over the ocean. He sensed the vastness of the Mahayana vision, as he experienced both the quantity and the quality of the sutras that he was attempting to understand.

Several key notions must be introduced here. They show a worldview of a universe populated by holy personalities and full of the divine. These notions may seem dry when expressed in words, but they become very meaningful when expressed as art in temples and museums. These ideas underlie Mahayana sculpture, painting, and belief.

The Three-Body Doctrine (Trikaya Doctrine)   In Mahayana, the Buddha nature can express itself in three ways. This is called the **trikaya** ("three-body") doctrine. The historical Buddha who lived in India came to be considered the manifestation of a divine reality, "the cosmic Buddha nature." The Sanskrit term for this is *Dharmakaya* (often translated as "law body," "form body," or "body of reality"). According to Mahayana Buddhism, the cosmic Buddha nature, although invisible, permeates all things. (It is sometimes compared to the Hindu notion of Brahman, which may have influenced it.) In people, the cosmic Buddha nature frequently presents itself as potential. In fact, it is our true nature that we need to recognize and realize. Dharmakaya also exists in the natural world, for all things are a sacred manifestation of the cosmic Buddha nature. When we experience the mystery of the natural world, we experience the Dharmakaya.

Siddhartha Gautama's physical body, because it is considered an incarnation of this divine reality, is called Nirmanakaya ("transformation body"). In keeping with the notion of many incarnations, many Mahayana schools believe in more than one transformation body of the Buddha. We might recall that both Theravada and Mahayana schools describe the Buddha's knowledge of his past lives. Both branches of Buddhism also believe that another historical Buddha, **Maitreya** (Sanskrit; Pali: Metteya), will appear on earth in the future to inaugurate a golden age. In several Mahayana cultures, this belief has taken on great importance. In China and Vietnam, the Buddha who will come is called Mi-lo-fo and is often shown as an overweight, joyful, "laughing Buddha." In Korea, the notion of Miruk (as Maitreya is known there) has been especially influential in generating belief in a messianic future, which has prompted the creation of many beautiful statues in his honor. He is often shown seated on a stool or raised platform in the so-called Western style, with one leg down on the floor and the other crossed over it, his head resting thoughtfully on one hand as he contemplates the future.

In Mahayana philosophy, the cosmic Buddha nature has also taken bodily shape in supernatural Buddhas who live in the heavens beyond our earth. These Buddhas have radiant, invulnerable bodies and live in constant happiness. In Sanskrit, they are called Sambhogakaya Buddhas ("perfect-bliss-body" Buddhas). Mahayana Buddhism envisions many Buddhas existing simultaneously, each with his own sphere of influence (called a Buddha Land). Particularly important is the bliss-body Buddha who created a Buddha Land in the western direction of the setting sun. There he receives the dying who wish enlightenment after death. His name in India was **Amitabha Buddha** (Chinese: Amito-fo; Japanese: Amida Butsu). Many devout Buddhists hope to be reborn in his paradise. After attaining enlightenment there, they can return to the world to save other beings. Their devotion to Amitabha Buddha has inspired a great body of fine painting and sculpture that depicts a large Buddha seated on a lotus flower, surrounded by peaceful disciples in pavilions set in gardens full of flowers.

Heavenly Bodhisattvas   We have already discussed the focus of Mahayana on the earthly bodhisattva, a saintly person of great compassion. But Mahayana Buddhism also holds that many bodhisattvas who are eager to help human beings also exist in other dimensions beyond the earth. They, too, are beings of great compassion. Some once lived on earth and have been reborn beyond this world, but they retain an interest in it. They may appear miraculously on earth when needed or possibly may even be reborn to help others.

The most significant of the heavenly bodhisattvas has been Avalokiteshvara, who looks down from a location above in order to give help. In India, Avalokiteshvara was portrayed as male, but

This procession in China demonstrates the special place of Guanyin (Avalokiteshvara).

in China this bodhisattva was conceived as feminine because of her association with compassion and mercy. Her name in Chinese is **Guanyin** (Kuan-yin,* "hears cries"). She first appeared in early depictions as having both male and female characteristics, but eventually she became entirely feminine. (As an object of devotion, she plays a role in Asia similar to that of Mary in Europe.) East Asian paintings and sculpture frequently show her with a very sweet face, dressed all in white, holding the jewel of wisdom or a vase of nectar, and with the moon under her feet or in the sky behind her. Other artistic renderings of her, particularly in temple sculpture, show her with a halo of many arms (she is said to have a thousand), representing her many powers to help. In the palm of each hand is an eye, symbolizing her ability to see everyone in need. In China and Japan (where this bodhisattva became popularly known as Kannon), many temples were dedicated to her.

Shunyata   One Mahayana doctrine asserts that all reality is *shunya* ("empty"; that is, empty of permanent essence). Literally, **shunyata** may be translated as "emptiness" or "zero-ness." But what does this mean? The notion is an outgrowth of the basic Buddhist view of reality that everything is constantly shifting, changing, taking new form. If we consider an individual person, we can say the "individual" is a pattern, made of parts in continuous change. If we broaden our scope, larger patterns appear, such as the patterns of a family, a city, or a society. Similarly, nature is a combination of smaller patterns making larger patterns, like wheels within wheels. And even the parts

---

*Two systems are currently used for transcribing Chinese words into English: the *pinyin* and Wade-Giles systems. Because the Chinese government and the United Nations have adopted pinyin, it has become the most commonly used system. The older Wade-Giles was the standard transcription system until pinyin was adopted, and it is still frequently encountered (as in the spelling of *Kuan-yin*). For major Chinese terms in this book (both here and in Chapter 6), the pinyin spelling is given first and the Wade-Giles spelling second.

themselves ultimately disintegrate as new parts are born. To better understand this concept, think of clouds, which look large and substantial but are
forever appearing and disappearing, moving past each other and changing
shape and size. Because everything is in constant change, each apparently
individual person and thing is actually "empty" of any permanent individual
identity. The notion of shunyata also suggests the experience that everything
is a part of everything else, that all people and things exist together.

Tathata   Literally translated, the word **tathata** means "thatness," "thusness,"
or "suchness." This is a rich notion that invites each person's experience and
interpretation. Tathata represents a view of experience that says that reality is
revealed in each moment, as we savor patterns, relationships, and change.
Because no moment is exactly the same, and no object is exactly the same, each
can be observed and appreciated as it passes. Thus, simple, everyday events
reveal the nature of reality. We may experience "thatness" when two elements
come together in an unexpected way—for example, when a small child says
something childlike but wise. Sometimes it comes when we notice a moment
of change, such as when, after a long string of muggy summer days, we get
up to add a blanket to the bed on the first crisp autumn night. Or it might be
when we notice elements coming together somewhat unexpectedly—for
example, when a bird drinks from a water fountain or a dog joyously sticks its
nose out of the window of a passing car. It might be when we recognize the
uniqueness of a simple object or event, such as the beauty of a particular apple
in the supermarket, or the special way that the shadow of a tree falls on a
nearby building at this particular moment. The experience can also come from
something funny or sad. Although tathata involves the mundane, it is also a
poetic moment that will never return in exactly the same way.

The wonder that can be seen in everyday life is what the term *tathata*
suggests. We know we are experiencing the "thatness" of reality when we
experience something and say to ourselves, Yes, that's it; that is the way
things are. In the moment, we recognize not only that reality is wondrously
beautiful but also that its patterns are fragile and passing.

Mahayana Literature

Mahayana Buddhism in India developed versions of the Tripitaka in Sanskrit. A host of additional written works also became canonical. Many of the
new Mahayana works were called sutras because they purported to be the
words of the Buddha, but in reality they were imaginative, colorful creations
written at least several centuries after the Buddha lived, from about 100 BCE
to about 600 CE. The teachings of these sutras, however, may be seen as a
natural development of basic Buddhist insights.

Primary among these texts are the Prajnaparamita Sutras ("sutras on the
perfection of wisdom"), the earliest of which may have been written about
100 BCE. These sutras attempt to contrast ordinary understanding with the
enlightened understanding that everything in the universe is interdependent.

Worshipers are dwarfed by the Buddha image in this Mahayana temple of southern China.

The influential Vimalakirti Sutra teaches that it is possible to live a devout Buddhist life without necessarily becoming a monk. The hero of the sutra is the man Vimalakirti, who was, as one historian describes him, "a layman rich and powerful, a brilliant conversationalist, a respected house-holder who surrounded himself with the pleasures of life, but was also a faithful and wise disciple of the Buddha, a man full of wisdom and thoroughly disciplined in his conduct."[15] Because the main figure is not a monk but more like a devout gentleman, we can see why this sutra became popular with laypeople. Its purpose, though, was serious. It showed that individuals can work successfully amidst the dangers of worldly life, can avoid causing harm, and can actually help themselves and others.

Two works that would have great influence on East Asian Buddhism were the Pure Land Sutras (two versions of the Sukhavati Vyuha Sutra, "sutra of the vision of the happy land"). The sutras speak of a heavenly realm, the Pure Land, established by the merciful Amitabha Buddha, where human beings can be reborn. All that is necessary for rebirth in the Pure Land is devotion to this Buddha, as shown by repetition of his name as a sign of total trust in him. These sutras would eventually give birth to a wildly successful movement, the Pure Land movement, which is still popular today. (We will discuss the Pure Land school of Mahayana a little later in this chapter.)

One of the most widely loved works of Mahayana was the Saddharma Pundarika Sutra ("lotus sutra of the good law"), known simply as the Lotus Sutra. In this sutra, the Buddha shows his transcendent, cosmic nature. As he preaches to thousands of his disciples, his light and wisdom extend out into the universe. Using parables, the sutra insists rather democratically that all people have the Buddha nature and that all, therefore, can become Buddhas. Many of its parables talk of the "skillful means" that can lead people of differing types and mentalities to enlightenment.

The Spread of Mahayana in East Asia

Mahayana Buddhism spread out of India to central Asia and to China, which it entered in the first century of the Common Era. As Buddhism spread to China and its neighboring regions, Sanskrit writings were translated bit by bit into at least thirteen central Asian languages. In China, several Chinese versions were made of most of the major works. By the eighth century, an enormous number of Buddhist works had been translated into Chinese.[16]

The appeal of Mahayana Buddhism in ancient China is worth considering. Mahayana Buddhism had virtues that appealed to a wide spectrum of the population. It accepted local cults and continued their practice of using rituals that promised magic, healing, and fertility for the masses of ordinary people. It created great temples with beautiful art and ceremony. It promoted peace and family harmony. It answered questions about the afterlife and performed funeral and memorial services for the dead. It provided a secure way of community life for people not interested in having children or creating their own families. It offered philosophical insights not already present in Chinese culture. And it provided many rulers with prayers and rituals that would help protect the nation and the rulers themselves.

Despite occasional persecution as a dangerous, foreign import, Mahayana spread throughout China. In particular, two forms of Mahayana flourished. The school of meditation (Chan, Ch'an) became highly influential

among monks, poets, and artists. The Pure
Land movement, with its devotion to Amitabha
Buddha, became the primary form of devotion
for laypeople. Ultimately, Buddhism was
linked with Daoism and Confucianism as one
of the officially sanctioned "Three Doctrines,"
and it became an essential part of Chinese
culture.

Buddhism and its literature were carried
into Korea from central Asia and China as early
as 372 CE.[17] Buddhism was adopted widely for
its supposed powers to protect the three kingdoms then ruling the peninsula. Monasteries
were thought of as powerhouses, sending
monks' prayers to powerful Buddhas and bodhisattvas and receiving their celestial care in
return. The Silla kingdom unified Korea, producing the Unified Silla dynasty (668–918 CE),
and this unification led to a blending of religious elements from Daoism, Confucianism,
shamanism, and Buddhism. Buddhism became
the state religion and primary practitioner of
official ritual.

Buddhism in Korea reached its height during the Koryo dynasty (918–1392 CE). During

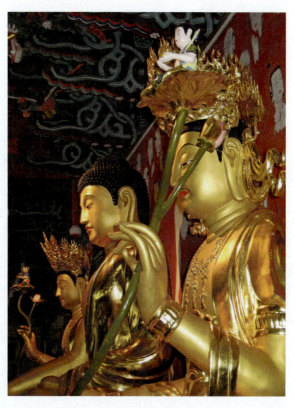

These ornate images of the Buddha allow focus both for religious services and for personal meditation at a Korean temple in the United States.

this time, 80,000 wooden blocks were carved for the printing of all Korean
and Chinese Buddhist texts of the Korean Tripitaka. After the first set of
blocks was burned during a Mongol invasion, another set, which still exists,
was finished in 1251. One of the greatest exponents of Korean Buddhism at
this time was the monk Chinul (1158–1210). Given to a monastery as a young
boy, he began meditation and textual study early. He had three great experiences of insight, all prompted by his reading of Mahayana materials. He
founded the Chogye order, which combines textual study with regular meditation. It is still influential today.

Confucianism supplanted Buddhism as the state religion during the Yi
dynasty (1392–1910). Nevertheless, although the aristocracy identified with
Confucianism, the common people remained Buddhist.

Buddhism entered Japan in the sixth century CE, where it began to grow
after some initial resistance. It became so powerful in the early capital of
Nara that in 794 the new capital city of Kyoto (then called Heian-kyo) was
founded partly in order to be free from the influence of Buddhist clergy. The
new capital was designed on a grid pattern, after Chinese models, and
Japanese culture imported many elements of the Chinese culture of the time.
Because the founding of the new capital coincided with a vibrant period of
Mahayana Buddhism in China, Japanese Buddhism also imported Chinese
Buddhist practices and teachings.

Rituals and Celebrations

BUDDHIST FESTIVALS

The most important Buddhist festivals focus on the birth of the Buddha, his enlightenment, his death, the celebration of the New Year, and sometimes the commemoration of the dead. The exact dates for these celebrations and memorials differ from culture to culture.

In Theravada Buddhist countries, one great celebration (Vesak) recalls the birth, the enlightenment, and the death of the Buddha. It is celebrated at the time of the full moon in May.

In Mahayana Buddhism, the three festivals of the Buddha's life are separate. His birth is celebrated on the eighth day of the fourth month; his enlightenment is commemorated in winter on Bodhi Day, the eighth day of the twelfth month; and his death is recalled in early spring on the fifteenth day of the second month. (Chinese and Korean Buddhists follow the lunar calendar, while Japanese Buddhists use the Western calendar.)

Celebration of the New Year often includes a visit to a temple to end the old year and the sharing of a vegetarian meal to welcome the new year. (The Japanese keep the Western New Year, while the Chinese celebrate their lunar New Year in February.)

In Japan the dead are remembered in a midsummer festival called O-Bon, derived from older Chinese practice. It has blended with Shinto elements and a belief in the Mahayana bodhisattva Jizo, who guides the dead back to the spirit world. If possible, the spirits' return is lighted with candles that drift down a stream or out into the ocean.

During summer, O-Bon is celebrated across the world at Buddhist temples of Japanese origin. Here, in early evening, the sun sets and the dancing begins at a temple in Honolulu.

The history of Buddhism in Japan shows a movement toward increasing the power of laypeople. The first period, when the capital was at Nara, was dominated by essentially monastic Buddhist schools. In the second period, after the capital moved, the dominant schools (Shingon and Tendai; Figure 4.2) were ritualistic and appealed to the aristocracy. Their prominence lasted for about four hundred years. In the thirteenth century, however, two schools (Pure Land and Zen) particularly appealed to commoners and the military. Because Zen was adopted by many in the military, which controlled Japan until 1868, it became enormously influential in Japanese culture in general. (The separate schools are described in the following section.)

Some Major Schools of Mahayana

The many ideals of Mahayana Buddhism contain the seeds for a variety of schools of intellectual interpretation and practice. One such ideal—the notion that kindness is the supreme sign of enlightened awareness—has allowed many pre-Buddhist beliefs and practices to continue within Mahayana Buddhism: old gods receive new names, making them into heavenly Buddhas and bodhisattvas; old beliefs are absorbed; and old practices persist with new meanings. As we discussed earlier, Mahayana Buddhism also recognizes that people find themselves at different stages of spiritual evolution. Thus, whatever helps a person move to the next stage of awareness may be religiously acceptable. This is the notion of "skillful means": some people need images to look at and gods to pray to; other people need a community of devout friends; and a very few need only silence and emptiness. The sects of Mahayana Buddhism thus show a wide variety of attitudes toward the use of art and ritual, toward the acceptance of pleasure, and toward worldly success. In Japan and Hawai`i, the sects have remained rather separate, and their differences may be easily experienced by interested travelers.

As part of the New Year festival at this Vietnamese temple, the head priest distributes fortunes to the congregants.

Shingon　The name of this school is Shingon (Chinese: Zhen-yan, Chen-yen) and means "true word" or "word of truth." The title refers to the use of sacred chants, called mantras. We might recall that the spread of Mahayana Buddhism in China was due in part to the magical effects that were thought to come from

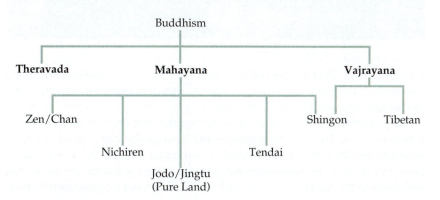

FIGURE 4.2

Branches and schools of Buddhism.

An image of the bodhisattva Jizo appears in front of a painting of the Shingon Kongo-kai mandala.

Buddhist ritual. People believed that Buddhist ritual, if carefully performed, would provide security for rulers, children for married couples, and more favorable agricultural conditions for farmers.

Behind Shingon ritual is a focus on experiencing union with the cosmic Buddha nature. This can be accomplished through the chanting of mantras, accompanied by a multitude of rituals and ritual objects. Foremost among these rituals is a fire ceremony, the *goma*, a continuation of the Vedic fire ceremony. In this ceremony, the priest builds a fire within a square sacred space

Some sects of Mahayana Buddhism use elaborate rituals. Here, at a Shingon temple, believers participate in a fire ceremony that originated in Hinduism. The ceremony is intended to burn away participants' egoistic attachments.

bounded by colored cords. The priest throws wood and leaves slowly into the fire, symbolically destroying all egotistic hindrances to mystical union.

Shingon uses two **mandalas,** which are geometrical designs, usually painted on cloth, that present reality in symbolic form. One mandala, the Kongo-kai ("diamond-world") mandala, shows the universe from the point of view of the wise person, who sees the universe as whole and perfect. It represents the universe seen as nirvana. The other mandala, the Tai-zo ("womb") mandala, shows the universe from the point of view of the compassionate person. It sees the universe as samsara, a place of suffering and growth, which needs our help.

Shingon developed from a type of magically oriented Buddhism that originated in India and was introduced to China. It was established in Japan by Kukai (774–835 CE), a Japanese monk who studied in China and returned to Japan with new knowledge of ritual and with books, mandalas, and altar implements. After his death, he received the name Kobo Daishi ("the Great Master who spreads the Dharma"), and under that name he has become a venerated cultural hero in Japan. Shingon, because of its love of ritual, has inspired many arts, particularly sculpture and painting. It has similarities with Tibetan Buddhism, and it thus contains some elements of Vajrayana Buddhism (discussed later in this chapter).

Tendai   The Tendai (Chinese: Tiantai, T'ien-t'ai) sect is named for the great Chinese monastic institution at Mount Tiantai ("heavenly terrace"), where the sect is thought to have begun in eastern China. A large complex of monasteries arose there.[18]

By the eighth century CE, there were many varied Buddhist texts, some written up to a thousand years after the time of the Buddha. When they had been translated into Chinese, the result was great confusion. How could the Buddha have uttered so many sermons, some with apparently contradictory ideas? The solution was to organize the teachings according to levels of complexity. It was taught that the Buddha had revealed his most basic insights to everybody but that he had revealed his most difficult thoughts only to those disciples who could understand them. The Tiantai (Tendai) sect attempted to categorize all the teachings and present them in a meaningful way, as a kind of ladder of steps leading to full enlightenment. Naturally, its own special teachings were at the top.

Jodo, or Pure Land   The Pure Land (Chinese: Jingtu, Ching-t'-u) school created a devotional form of Buddhism that could be practiced by laypeople as well as monks. The cult of bodhisattvas already existed in India and central Asia, but it had great appeal in China too. Pure Land Buddhism in China can be traced back to the monk Tan Luan (T'an Luan, c. 476–542). Legend says that he instituted the devotion to Amitabha Buddha as the result of a vision. Complete devotion to this Buddha, the monk thought, would result in the believer's rebirth in Amitabha's Pure Land, the Western Paradise. Devotees regularly repeated a short phrase, derived from Mahayana scriptures and praising Amitabha Buddha. At first the repetition of the Buddha's name was a monastic practice, but it then spread to the laity. In Chinese, the phrase is *Namo Amito-fo*; in Japanese, *Namu Amida Butsu*. Both mean "Praise to Amitabha Buddha." Daily repetition and recitation at the moment of death were thought to ensure the believer's rebirth in the Western Paradise.

In Japan, the Pure Land movement was spread by the monk Honen (1133–1212), who was originally a Tendai monk at Mount Hiei. His movement became a separate sect called Jodo Shu ("Pure Land sect"). Shinran (1173–1262), a disciple of Honen, continued the laicization of the *nembutsu*, as the chant is called in Japanese. He taught that human actions to attain salvation were unimportant in comparison to the saving power of the Buddha. Convinced that monastic practice was unnecessary, Shinran married. (He has often been compared with Martin Luther, who also married and emphasized simple trust as the way to salvation.) The movement that Shinran began eventually grew into the Jodo Shin Shu ("True Pure Land sect"). Pure Land sects have been extremely popular in China and Japan, and this popularity has made them the largest form of Mahayana Buddhism.

It was once common to think of the Pure Land as a real location somewhere beyond the earth. Today, however, it is often considered a metaphor for a compassionate and joyful way of living in the everyday world.

Nichiren   Unlike the other sects discussed thus far, Nichiren Buddhism began in Japan. Its founder was a Tendai monk, Nichiren (1222–1282). After being trained at Mount Hiei, Nichiren sought a simpler path than Tendai, which used many sutras and practices in the search for enlightenment. Out of the thousands of Mahayana texts, Nichiren wanted to find one that contained all the essential teachings of Buddhism. Following the lead of the Tendai tradition, which had already given much attention to the Lotus Sutra, Nichiren asserted that the Lotus Sutra was indeed the embodiment of all essential religious teaching. He thought of himself as a reincarnation of a minor Buddha in the Lotus Sutra (his monastic name Nichiren means "sun lotus"). His sect uses a chant that honors this sutra: *Namu Myoho Renge Kyo,* meaning "Praise to the mystic law of the Lotus Sutra." Devout followers repeat the mantra many times a day, especially in the morning and evening. They believe that doing so will connect them with the divine power of the universe.

Nichiren Buddhism has produced several branches. Among the most important are Nichiren Shu ("Nichiren sect"), Nichiren Sho-Shu ("True Nichiren sect"), and Soka Gakkai ("Value Creation Educational Society"). The Nichiren Shu treats its founder as a bodhisattva, or Buddhist saint. The Nichiren Sho-Shu elevates Nichiren to the role of a reincarnation of the Buddha, "the Buddha of the present age." The Soka Gakkai branch was formerly a lay arm of Nichiren Sho-Shu. However, an angry split occurred between 1991 and 1992, and Soka Gakkai became fully independent. There is in all of these branches an acceptance of the material world and an attempt to improve it. Soka Gakkai particularly works to reform society through political means, seeking peace through intercultural understanding.

Nichiren Buddhism was little known outside Japan until after World War II. It has now established itself all around the world. The goal-oriented chanting of some Nichiren groups has been very attractive to some westerners, and several celebrities (such as Tina Turner) practice a form of this faith.

Zen   Zen Buddhism, a school of Mahayana Buddhism, began in China and was carried to Japan. Its influence has been so significant that it merits discussion in some detail.

Zen takes its name from the seventh step of the Noble Eightfold Path— *dhyana* ("meditation"). In Chinese the word is *chan* (*ch' an*), and in Japanese it is *zen*. (In the discussion here, Chan refers to the sect in China, and Zen refers to the sect as it developed in Japan.) The complexity that had overtaken Chinese Buddhism helped create a counterbalancing movement toward simplification. For the Chan sect in China, simplification came from looking directly to the enlightenment experience of Siddhartha Gautama. Siddhartha had become the Buddha, the Enlightened One, through his practice of meditation. Although he did not deny the value of ritual, the Buddha did not think that it led to enlightenment. Taking after the Buddha, the members of the Chan movement, in their desire for enlightenment, favored the technique of seated meditation, just as Siddhartha Gautama had.

Chan Buddhism traditionally traces itself back to a Buddhist monk named Bodhidharma, who is said to have come to China (about 500 CE) from India or central Asia to begin his Meditation school. Bodhidharma is often shown sitting in meditation, with Western facial features, swarthy skin, a light beard, and an earring. In paintings, he faces a wall to indicate his strong desire to block out anything that would distract him from his meditation. It has been said that he meditated for so long that his legs became withered. He is the embodiment of patience and persistence.

In the long history of Buddhism, some teachers have emphasized the importance of regular meditation and the effectiveness of meditative techniques, saying that they produce enlightenment gradually but inevitably, like the coming of dawn. Others have stressed that enlightenment can occur as a sudden awakening to one's true nature, like a flash of lightning, anywhere and at any time. The enlightenment experience (called **satori,** or *kensho*) brings an awareness of the unity of oneself with the rest of the universe. The enlightened person knows that human distinctions and separations—mine, yours; this, that; one, many—are distinctions that societies and individuals' minds create and then project onto other people and things. Such distinctions are not ultimate, though, for all human beings consist of the same basic energy of the universe, appearing in many varied shapes. This experience of ultimate unity brings new insights and emotions to the art of living: less anxiety over attaining goals, less concern about death, and an appreciation for the preciousness of everyday life.

The most fundamental Zen technique for reaching enlightenment is regular "sitting meditation," called *zazen.* In Zen monasteries, zazen is normally done for several hours in the morning and evening. It involves sitting in silence with one's back straight and centered, keeping the body still, and taking deep and regular breaths. These are just simple techniques for quieting the mind and focusing on the moment. The mind becomes more peaceful, and ideally, with long practice, a state of simple awareness takes over as one's "true nature" is revealed.[19]

The **koan** is another technique for attaining awareness. Its origin is uncertain, but the name derives from the Chinese *gong-an* (*kung-an*), translated as "public discussion." The koan is a question that cannot be easily answered using logic. It demands pondering. Consider, for example, the question, Why did the monk Bodhidharma come from the West? An appropriate answer could be, "The bush in the garden"—or any response that mentions an ordinary object. The meaning of this apparently odd answer is that Bodhidharma's whole purpose was to make people wake up to the wondrous nature of even simple objects in everyday life. Sometimes a good answer to a koan need not be a verbal response but rather an appropriate action, such as lifting up a hand, taking off a shoe, holding up a flower, or even raising an eyebrow.[20]

Manual labor is also essential to Zen training. In a Zen monastery, work in the garden and kitchen and the repair and cleaning of the monastery are techniques to combat the inadequacy of words to describe reality. Zen, influenced here by Daoism, maintains that words are often barriers that keep us from immediate contact with the true nature of things. Silent meditation blended with direct experience of the physical world can take us beyond words and thoughts to experience reality itself.

As teachers, monks pass on the traditions they received from their own teachers, including knowledge of the arts. Here a monk in Vietnam teaches calligraphy.

Deeper Insights

BUDDHISM AND JAPANESE ARTS

Many people assume that Buddhism has had a role in shaping the arts of Japan. As a matter of fact, what we think of as "Japanese style" is a mixture of Shinto (see Chapter 7), Buddhist influences (especially Zen), and traditional Japanese attitudes toward nature. Over the past three hundred years, these arts have taken on a life of their own, carried on by laypeople and practitioners of several branches of Mahayana Buddhism.

HAIKU

A *haiku* is an extremely short poem. In Japan, longer Chinese poetic forms were telescoped and refined. The model haiku is a short poem written in three lines. The ideal traditional haiku should mention or suggest the season, and, like a good photograph, it should capture the essence of a moment before it passes.

Matsuo Basho (1644–1694) is considered the greatest of Japan's haiku writers. The following poem is widely quoted and considered to be his masterpiece:

> Old pond:
> A frog jumps in.
> Sound of water.

Why, we may wonder, is this poem held in such esteem? On first reading, it seems simple, insignificant. But on closer inspection, it reveals intriguing balance and contrast. There are many possible interpretations. The old pond suggests timelessness, but the splash is momentary, representing every daily event when seen against the backdrop of eternity. Or the frog could represent a human being; the pond, the mind; and the splash, the sudden breakthrough to enlightenment. Perhaps the frog signifies the Buddhist monk in meditation, while the pond suggests all of Buddhist teaching. Or maybe the frog symbolizes the poet himself and the splash the poet's insight. Thus, the imagery can be taken both literally and in several equally valid symbolic ways.

TEA CEREMONY

The making, drinking, and offering of tea to guests have developed into a fine art in Japan, called *chado* (or *sado*, "the way of tea"). Bringing guests together for a ritual tea ceremony in Japanese is called *cha no yu* ("hot water

for tea"). The drinking of tea was first used in Chinese monasteries for medicinal purposes and as an aid for staying awake during meditation. There, tea drinking also developed some ritual elements. Tea drinking was then carried to Japan and was practiced assiduously by both Zen monks and lay disciples. Under the tea master Sen no Rikyu (1522–1591), the tea ceremony took on its current highly stylized form.[21]

The essence of the Japanese tea ceremony is the gathering of a few guests, the preparation of green tea, and the offering of tea and sweets. The tea ceremony normally takes place in a tea pavilion, whose design is inspired by a rustic country hut, often mentioned in

The formal tea ceremony, which began in monasteries, has become an art.

Chinese poetry. The purpose of the ceremony is to create and enjoy together an atmosphere of harmony and beauty, where each object, action, and word contributes to the tranquil experience.

CERAMICS

Bowls used in the tea ceremony look deliberately natural, almost as if they were dug up out of the ground. They often appear rough and unfinished, with earth-colored glazes dripping down their sides. The rims sometimes are not quite even, and the colors are not always uniform. Sometimes there are even bubbles and cracks in the ceramic. All this is deliberate. The accidents resulting from firing the bowls in the kiln are appreciated, as are the subtle earth tones that are produced. The aim is, paradoxically, to create pieces that exhibit deliberate naturalness and a calculated spontaneity.

IKEBANA

The word for Japanese-style flower arrangement—*ikebana*—means "living flower." Flower arrangement can be traced back to the offerings of flowers placed on altars in the temples of China and Japan. But ikebana grew into a unique art form of its own, and examples of ikebana now are found in restaurants, offices, and homes.

Ikebana is quite different from Western flower arrangement, which tends to be dense, symmetrical, and colorful. Ikebana is the opposite. The arrangements are airy, asymmetrical, and generally of no more than two colors. Effective ikebana is temporary art, lasting but a few days and changing every day. Thus, some see ikebana as a manifestation of Buddhist insight into impermanence. Ikebana is Buddhist sculpture.

GARDEN DESIGN

In China and Japan, gardens have long been an essential part of architecture, planned along with the buildings they complement. Garden designers are ranked as highly as poets and artists. Some gardens are created for strolling, others for seated contemplation from under an eave. They are not essentially Buddhist, of course, and not all monasteries have gardens. But they are found frequently enough in Buddhist environs for us to say that gardens have been used to present Buddhist ideals.

A famous example is the rock garden at Ryoan-ji, in northwest Kyoto. Ryoan-ji garden, enclosed on two sides by a low earthen wall, consists of five clusters of large boulders set in raked white gravel. The rocks and gravel suggest mountain peaks rising through clouds or islands in a river. The fascination of the garden is the relation between the clusters of boulders. Viewed this way, the boulders seem more like ideas in a great mind. The only vegetation in the garden is the moss at the base of the stones and the trees beyond the wall. Really more like an X-ray of an ideal garden, Ryoan-ji would seem to be unchanging because of its stony nature; but it changes a great deal, depending on the season, the time of day, the weather, and the light.

CALLIGRAPHY AND PAINTING

Calligraphy (Greek: "beautiful writing") is a highly prized art form in China and Japan. Because the characters used in Japanese and Chinese writing are closer to pictures and to drawing than they are to alphabet letters, they have a great range of vitality and beauty. The Zen ideal is to produce what is spontaneous but also profound, and because writing is done with an inkbrush, great expressiveness in darkness, weight, movement, and style of characters is possible. Furthermore, the ink cannot be erased, and the result is thought to be the immediate expression of the writer's personality and level of awareness. When fine calligraphic talent is employed to write a striking phrase or poem, the result is doubly powerful. The supreme example of Zen simplicity in art is the *enso*, a black circle, almost always done in a single, quick stroke on paper or a piece of wood. The empty circle represents the emptiness of all reality.

Elements that are typical of Zen design include simple elegance, asymmetry, the use of stone and wood in their natural state, and the near emptiness that is characteristic of the rock garden. Over the past one hundred years, Zen has had a global impact as well—in architecture, art, interior design, and fashion. It is apparent, for example, in the domestic architecture of Frank Lloyd Wright and his followers, which popularized the use of large windows and natural stone. It seems even to have influenced retail chains such as The Gap and Banana Republic, where we see natural wood floors, uncluttered space, and clothing in muted earth tones.

VAJRAYANA BUDDHISM: THE "DIAMOND VEHICLE"

Mahayana Buddhism in India developed practices and beliefs that have sometimes been called esoteric (hidden, not openly taught), such as the use of special chants and rituals to gain supernormal powers. When some of these traditions entered Tibet, Indian Mahayana Buddhism blended with Tibetan shamanism to create Tibetan Buddhism, a complex system of belief, art, and ritual. Although Vajrayana actually includes other forms of esoteric Buddhism, Tibetan Buddhism is its most prominent expression.

The name *Vajrayana* means the "vehicle of the diamond" or "vehicle of the lightning bolt." The name suggests strength, clarity, wisdom, and flashes of light, all of which are associated with the enlightened awareness that this vehicle seeks to transmit. Some consider Vajrayana to be simply a special form of Mahayana. But most consider Vajrayana to be a third branch of Buddhism because of its complexity and unique elements.

Origins, Practice, and Literature of Tibetan Buddhism

The pre-Buddhist Tibetan religion worshiped the powers of nature. As was the case with many native religions, these powers were often envisioned as demons that had to be appeased. Shamanistic rituals involving animal sacrifice and the use of bones, dance, and magical incantations were intended to control the demonic powers.

This Tibetan religion was challenged by a new religion, a special type of Buddhism practiced in northeast India, named Tantric Buddhism for its scriptures, the Tantras ("spread out"). Tantric Buddhism opposed the original Buddhist detachment from the world and its negative attitude toward bodily pleasure. The Tantras taught that the body and all its energies could be used to reach enlightenment. For Tantric Buddhism, enlightenment is an experience of ultimate oneness that occurs when a practitioner unites all opposites. Sexual union is a powerful experience of unity, and Tantric Buddhism uses the imagery and (rarely) the practice of sexual union to help attain enlightenment. In its imagery and belief system, Tantric Buddhism shows influence from Hinduism—particularly its tendency to pair a male and a female deity and its love of multiple deities. Vajrayana believes the divine Buddha nature expresses itself in a multitude of male and female deities.

A form of Tantric Buddhism first entered Tibet in the seventh century and was spread by Indian missionaries. Tradition holds that a king named Song-tsen-gam-po (active c. 630) became its patron and made it the national religion. In the beginning, native priests fought against this new religion, but a legendary Buddhist monk named Padmasambhava, who

Samye monastery in Tibet, which traces its history to the eighth century, is built in the form of a three-dimensional mandala.

Long trumpets, bells, and drums often accompany chanting in Vajrayana ceremonies.

came from India in the late eighth century, reconciled the two religions and turned the native demonic gods of Tibet into guardian deities of Buddhism.

The resulting religion blended shamanistic interests, the sexual imagery of Tantric Buddhism, and traditional Buddhist elements such as the chanting of sutras, meditation, the ideal of nonviolence, and the search for enlightenment. Monks thus were called upon not only as teachers but also as doctors and shamans; they were expected to bring health, control weather, and magically protect worshipers from death. A Tibetan spiritual teacher is often called **lama** (a Tibetan translation of the word *guru*), and this title is thus frequently used as a title of honor for all monks.

Although the Indian ideals of the wandering holy man and cave-dwelling solitary did not die out in Tibetan Buddhism, they were not well suited for a climate as severe as that of the cold and barren Tibetan plateau. More compatible, it seemed, were the large monastic complexes that had grown up in late Indian Buddhism. The Tibetan version of such a complex often looked like a fortified hilltop castle and was in effect a complete city for sometimes thousands of monks, containing libraries, prayer halls, kitchens, storage areas, and large courtyards used for public performances. A written form of the Tibetan language was created for the translation of Buddhist scriptures from India. It also made possible the writing of scriptural commentaries and other treatises.

Over time, the practice of celibacy declined, and the heads of Tibetan monasteries frequently passed on their control to their sons. The consumption of meat and alcohol became common as well. A reform movement, however, emerged under the monk Tsong Kha-pa (1357–1419), demanding that monks be unmarried and that strict monastic practice be reinstituted. His sect, as a result, came to be known as Gelug-pa, meaning "party of virtue." (It is also commonly called the Yellow Hat sect because of the tall, crested yellow hats that the monks wear during religious services.) This sect grew powerful. It helped create many of the greatest monasteries, full of art and complete sets of Buddhist scriptures, and it provided Tibet with its political leadership for several centuries. The executive head of the Gelug-pa is called the Dalai Lama ("ocean superior one").

165

It became a common belief in Tibetan Buddhism that certain major lamas are reincarnations of earlier lamas, who in turn are considered emanations of Buddhas and bodhisattvas. (A belief in reincarnation thus solved the problem of transmission of leadership, which in a celibate monastic order cannot pass to a son.) The lineage of the Dalai Lama, for example, traces itself back to a nephew of Tsong Kha-pa, the first of the line of succession. Each Dalai Lama is considered to be an emanation of Avalokiteshvara, the heavenly bodhisattva of compassion. When a major lama dies, his reincarnation is sought, found, and trained. The current Dalai Lama, for example, was found in eastern Tibet. A delegation of monks, after consulting a state oracle about the place of rebirth, took objects (such as prayer beads) that had been used by the previous Dalai Lama and mixed them with similar objects. The boy who was recognized as the current Dalai Lama selected only those objects used by the previous Dalai Lama, helping to prove his identity. (The movies *Kundun*, *Seven Years in Tibet*, and *Little Buddha* vividly portray the selection of the Dalai Lama and other Vajrayana practices.) The current Dalai Lama fled from Tibet in 1959 and lives in northern India.

The literature of Tibetan Buddhism consists of two large collections of writings. The Kanjur is the core, made up of works from the Tripitaka (mostly Mahayana sutras and the vinaya) with Tantric texts. The second part, the Tenjur, comprises commentaries on scripture and treatises on a wide variety of disciplines, such as medicine, logic, and grammar. The collection exceeds four thousand works.

Ritual and the Arts

Vajrayana Buddhism is interested in the acquisition of both internal and external powers and holds that such powers may be attained through proper ritual. The ritual allows the individual to become identified with a particular Buddha or heavenly bodhisattva, thus giving the individual the power and protection of that heavenly being.

Because correctly performed ceremony brings identification with a powerful deity, ceremonial objects play significant roles. We noted earlier that some devices, such as the mantra and mandala, are used in Mahayana practice. Vajrayana adopted these devices from Mahayana, but in Vajrayana these objects and techniques take on special importance. Among the significant ritual objects is the **vajra,** a metal object somewhat like a divining rod or scepter that represents a stylized bolt of lightning. The vajra is associated with diamond-hardness, power, and insight. It is held in the right hand and suggests kind action. A bell is held in the left hand and symbolizes wisdom. When used together, one in each hand, these objects represent the union of wisdom and compassion. The vajra and bell are essential to Tibetan Vajrayana ritual in a way that other religious objects (mentioned in the following paragraphs) are not.

Another important Tibetan Buddhist object is the prayer wheel, which comes in all sizes—from the very tiny to ones as tall as a two-story building. A prayer wheel is a cylinder that revolves around a central pole. Inside the

Buddhists in Nepal do morning meditation by walking repeatedly around Boudhanath, one of the largest stupas in the world.

cylinder are pieces of paper inscribed with sacred phrases. It is believed that the turning of the written prayers creates as much good karma as if one were to recite them. The same principle applies to the wind blowing through prayer flags, which consist of square or triangular pieces of cloth containing inscriptions.

Music and dance, used by shamans to protect against demons, also play an important role in Tibetan Vajrayana. Drums, long trumpets, bells, and cymbals are used to accompany a deep, slow droning chant. The effect is hypnotic and evokes the sacredness that underlies reality.

An enormous tapestry of Guru Rimpoche, a missionary who spread Buddhism in the Himalayas, is raised once a year in front of a Bhutanese monastery. Viewers believe that seeing the image will release them from the cycle of rebirths.

In Vajrayana as well as Mahayana, a mantra is chanted or written to bring power and wisdom through repetition. The most highly revered mantra in Tibetan Vajrayana is *Om mani padme hum!* (literally translated, "Om—the jewel—oh lotus—ah!"). One translation employs Tantric sexual symbolism: "The jewel is in the lotus." The jewel and lotus represent sexual opposites, and the mantra represents sexual union—symbolic of enlightenment. In yet another symbolic translation—"The jewel *is* the lotus"—the jewel represents the divine Buddha nature, and the lotus represents the everyday world of birth and death. Hence, the mantra means that this world of suffering is the same as the Buddha nature and that the enlightened person sees that they are the same. However, it is also possible to interpret the mantra as merely a prayer to the bodhisattva Avalokiteshvara, who may be pictured holding each of the two objects. The mantra then would be "Hail to the jewel-lotus one!" No matter what the origin and meaning of the mantra, the ordinary believer simply thinks of it as a powerful prayer. In addition to this mantra, there are many others, each of which is believed to be sacred to a particular Buddha or bodhisattva or is believed to be valuable for obtaining a certain result.

Symbolic hand gestures (**mudras**) on statues of the Buddha are common throughout all forms of Buddhism. For example, the right hand extended with the palm outward and the fingers pointing up is a mudra of blessing; if the palm is open but the hand is turned downward, the mudra symbolizes generosity. In Vajrayana, a large number of mudras have evolved to convey more esoteric meanings, such as the unity of opposites.

The mandala that is used in some forms of Mahayana takes on great variety and complexity in Tibetan Buddhism. We might recall that a mandala is a sacred cosmic diagram, often used in meditation. It may represent in symbolic form the entire universe, the palace of a deity, or even the self. A common design is a circle within or enclosing a square, or a series of circles and squares that grow smaller and smaller as they come closer to the center of the design; another form looks like a checkerboard of many squares. A mandala usually appears as a painting on cloth, but it may take many forms. For some ceremonies, monks create a mandala in sand and then destroy it at the end of the ritual, expressing vividly the Buddhist teaching that everything must change.

Any painting on cloth is called a *thangka* (pronounced *tan'-ka*). In addition to mandala designs, a wide variety of subjects can appear on thangkas. Common images are Buddhas, bodhisattvas, and guardian deities, painted in both benevolent and terrifying forms (the terrifying forms both frighten away demons and chasten the believer). The female deity Tara, who represents mercy, appears in two major forms (white and green) and in several minor forms. We also find frequent representations of the monk Padmasambhava and other noted teachers. The existence of so many celestial beings and saints—with their attendants and symbolic objects—provides artists with a multitude of subjects to paint and sculpt.

P E R S O N A L   E X P E R I E N C E

The Monks and the Pond

On a trip to Southeast Asia I heard of an old and beautiful temple, entirely made of teakwood and known for its wonderful carvings. Tourists rarely visited it, I was told, because it was far off in the countryside. I would have to cross a river and then walk a good distance to the temple. It was suggested that I go with a guide.

All began according to plan. My guide was a woman who was also a teacher. We took a small bus to the river, where we waited for a ferryboat. People around us carried baskets of produce, and many had bicycles. It was a humid, brilliantly sunny day. We stood patiently under the black umbrellas we had brought for protection from the sun. At last a wooden ferryboat arrived, people wheeled their bicycles aboard, and the boat crossed.

Luckily for my guide and me, an enclosed horsecart was standing under a tree at the other side of the river. Its driver was pleased to see us. We negotiated a fare and jumped in back. The horse ambled pleasantly along the dirt road, moving in and out of the shadows of the trees at each side; but because of all the potholes, the cart bounced wildly, and we had to hold on to the sides of the cart to avoid being thrown out.

Soon I began to hear the sound of chanting over loudspeakers. (One cannot escape electronically amplified sounds these days, even in the countryside.) Coming around a bend in the road, I could see a white pagoda and white stucco temple at the base of a hill. It must be a temple fair, I thought. But as we drove closer, I saw that the temple was deserted. Instead, people were crowded together on the nearby hillside. Could it be a special ceremony?

Protected by the arms of another, this entranced woman is believed to be speaking the words of the snake.

"May we stop and look?" I asked.

The driver came to a halt near the temple. We jumped out of the cart and started walking quickly up the hill. As we came close to the top, we were astonished to see a woman lying on the ground, the people surrounding her closely. Her long black hair was in disarray, and she was in a state of great emotion. Her eyes were unseeing. She seemed to be in a trance. It was then that we saw, in the crowd behind her, four men holding a very thick and powerful-looking snake. We advanced no farther. The woman on the ground was talking excitedly. The people stood motionless but attentive, listening to her. Everyone seemed calm and unafraid. After a few minutes, monks began walking among the people.

"What's happening?" I asked my guide.

"It's a miracle," she said. "A miracle!"

"And what is the woman saying?"

"The snake is speaking through her. He is saying, 'Do not harm me. I only need for you to dig a pond for me here at the temple. I will live in the pond and protect you.'"

"And what are the monks doing?"

"They are taking up a collection to make the pond."

I was silent. We returned to the horsecart and continued on our way to the teakwood temple. Along the way I thought of the decorative snakes that adorn the handrails of so many temples in Southeast Asia. I recalled the story in the Jataka Tales of a snake whose heroic willingness to die had actually saved its life. And I recalled the story of the snake Muchalinda, king of the cobras, who had protected the Buddha at the time of his enlightenment. Even more, I thought of how varied the expressions of Buddhism are, ranging from complex philosophies to unexpected forms of popular practice. One has to be ready for everything.

At last we arrived at the famous wooden temple. After all the excitement at the first temple, this was an oasis of peace. On one side of the building, an old monk sat comfortably beside an open window, reading a local newspaper. Near him five children recited the alphabet out loud together. Passing several large statues of the Buddha, I walked to the other end of the temple. There, four monks sat on the wide wooden floor, studying scriptures in a pool of sunlight.

Three young monks study scripture with their teacher on the porch of an old teak temple not far from Mandalay.

Rituals and Celebrations

BUDDHIST MEDITATION

Because meditation is a core practice of Buddhism, many kinds of meditation have developed. Some of them have made their way to the West, where they have occasionally been modified.

In the Theravada tradition, one approach to meditation is especially significant. It is called *Vipassana* ("insight"), because it emphasizes being fully attentive to the present moment. This attentiveness, sometimes called *mindfulness*, is primarily accomplished by sitting quietly and paying attention to one's exhalation and inhalation. The same type of meditation may also be done while walking. The meditator walks extremely slowly on flat ground, being aware at each moment of the motion of the right foot, then the left foot, and so on. (In Sri Lanka and elsewhere, some monasteries have special walking tracks for this type of meditation.)

Seated meditation, particularly cultivated by Chan and Zen, is the most significant form of Mahayana meditation. Like Vipassana, it begins with a focus on breathing. It may then include reflections on a question given by a master or on the meaning of a line of poetry. It may also involve the silent repetition of a single meaningful word or phrase.

The Vajrayana tradition, with its love of art and ritual, has developed many complex meditations. Vajrayana meditation tends to make use of ritual objects (bells, candles, butter lamps), images, mandalas, Sanskrit words (mantras), hand gestures (mudras), and visualization exercises. Frequently the meditation involves forming a mental image of a favorite deity and then taking on the identity of that deity for the duration of the meditation. Other meditations involve contemplating the moon, clouds, or water.

Some meditations make use of imaginative techniques; the meditator mentally creates a lotus, a moon disc, a written Sanskrit syllable, an altar of deities, colors, or rays of light, often imagining these in a certain order.

All three traditions also have some form of what can be called a meditation of compassion. The meditator reflects on the many different kinds of sentient beings—human, animal, and insect. The next step of the meditation is to recognize that all of these beings are struggling to survive, that all are trying to avoid pain, and that many are suffering. The meditation ends when the meditator projects outward the wish that all sentient beings be well and happy. This wish is sometimes accompanied by a mental image of light and warmth radiating outward.

Beginners who are interested in Buddhist meditation can try simple seated meditation. A quiet spot is best, and the meditator should sit on a cushion or sofa, with legs drawn up. (If that is not possible, then one may sit on a chair, with the feet flat on the ground.) Some people like to face outside, looking into a garden. The back should be straight, the position comfortable, and the breathing deep, slow, and regular. The eyes may be either open or closed. The meditator should remain as still as possible and focus on each breath as it goes in and out. Thoughts need not be banished but should simply be "watched," like seeing clouds passing. One can start by meditating a short amount of time—even as little as five minutes per day. Soon it will be possible to meditate for longer periods once or twice a day. Many report that the exercise leaves them with a greater sense of inner peace and often a feeling of oneness with their surroundings.

BUDDHISM AND THE MODERN WORLD

Although Buddhism originated in India and then spread primarily through Asia, it has now become a worldwide religion. Buddhist temples and meditation centers can be found in many countries, particularly in the industrialized countries of Europe and the Americas. Buddhism is attractive in part because many of its essential teachings seem to agree with modern values. Some people appreciate what they see as its emphasis on awareness, self-reliance, and insight. Others think that Buddhism fits in well with the views of modern science. Still others are attracted to the Buddhist ideal of nonviolence as a standard for civilized behavior in a multicultural world.

Critics point out that the modern world has adopted what it likes from Buddhism and ignored the rest. The modern world, for example, has not been quick to embrace the celibacy of the Buddha or of Buddhist monks and nuns— who traditionally represent the core of the religion. The modern world believes in recycling but not in reincarnation. And the modern world turns a blind eye to the actual practice of many Buddhist believers, whose real-life Buddhist activity is performed in order to "make merit," gain health or wealth, and have good luck. Critics scorn the modern "cafeteria approach" to Buddhism. The contemporary world, they explain, has adopted only the elements it likes— meditation, Zen design, and the exoticism of Tibet—and with these it is now creating a new kind of Buddhism in its own image. Buddhism, they say, is becoming a yuppie supermarket of meditation cushions, gongs, and posters.

All of these complaints have some truth. And yet . . . Buddhism is forever changing. In its long history, as the ship of its teachings has sailed from one cultural port to the next, some of its goods have been tied to the mast while others have been tossed overboard. This fact is even truer today, and it makes studying the interrelation of Buddhism and the modern world all the more fascinating.

Buddhism's first contact with the West occurred in the late eighteenth century, when English colonials carried translations of primarily Theravada material from Sri Lanka and Myanmar to Europe. Because so many of these colonials were missionaries, they were especially impressed by Buddhist moral teachings. Thus, the view of Buddhism that they spread emphasized the religion's admirable ethical system.

The opening of Japan to foreigners in the second half of the nineteenth century created a second wave of interest in Buddhism. French, English, and American people began to read about Japanese culture and to see photographs of early Buddhist temples and examples of Buddhist-inspired art. Foreign interest dovetailed with anti-Buddhist government actions in Japan after 1868, which forced many Buddhist temples to sell some of their art. Japanese art was then collected widely in Europe and America, both by private collectors and by museums.

Just as Buddhism has influenced Japanese art, so Buddhism has influenced Western art via Japan. There is no doubt that the Japanese influence on Western art has been extraordinary since Japan opened to the West. French art of the late nineteenth century was invigorated by the discovery of Japanese prints and scrolls, which flooded into France after 1880. Asymmetry, a love of nature, and an appreciation for the passing moment—features of much Japanese art—began to appear in the work of the Impressionists and Postimpressionists, particularly Vincent van Gogh (1853–1890), Henri de Toulouse-Lautrec (1864–1901), and Claude Monet (1840–1926). (One of van Gogh's self-portraits was almost certainly influenced by pictures of Buddhist monks that he had seen.) Monet's Japanese-style water garden, with its pond of water lilies at Giverny, near Paris, is a good example of the influence Japan had at the turn of the century in France.

Haiku and other forms of Japanese poetry began to influence Western poetry at the same time. We see this particularly in the Imagist school, which

Contemporary Issues

THICH NHAT HANH

Thich Nhat Hanh (pronounced *tik'-nat-han'*) is one of the most revered teachers of nonviolence in the world. Born in Vietnam in 1926, he became a Buddhist monk at age 16. During the Vietnam War he founded a student association devoted to rebuilding devastated towns. After being forced out of Vietnam by the government, he settled in southern France. There he began a meditation center, Plum Village.

Thich Nhat Hanh calls his form of Buddhism "engaged Buddhism." He seeks to keep the meditative and devotional traditions alive, but he also seeks to promote charitable activity within the world. He wishes to present a form of universal Buddhism that can concur with Christianity or any other religion. His movement of engaged Buddhism is spreading around the world, thanks in part to the many books he has written, about forty of which have been translated into English.

Thich Nhat Hanh greets the crowds at a memorial service for those killed during the Vietnam War.

produced short poems that depended on a few strong images presented in simple language. Poets who exemplified this style include Ezra Pound (1885–1972), E. E. Cummings (1894–1962), H. D. (Hilda Doolittle, 1886–1961), and William Carlos Williams (1883–1963).

A third wave of Buddhist influence came in the decades just after World War II, when U.S. soldiers returned from the American occupation of Japan. The great interest of the time was Zen (perhaps only loosely understood), which influenced the poetry of the Beat movement and the lifestyle of the counterculture. The novels of Jack Kerouac (1922–1969) show a Zenlike love of the spontaneous. His book *On the Road,* about a cross-country trip with friends, inspired readers to make similar explorations. Zen love of the moment is also evident in the jazzlike poetry of Allen Ginsberg (1926–1997) and the ironic poetry of Lawrence Ferlinghetti (b. 1919). San Francisco, where many of the Beat writers were based, became an early headquarters of Zen thought and practice in America, as it still is today.

Zen centers, often under lay leadership, were established at this time in major cities in North and South America and Europe. These centers have allowed westerners to learn directly about Zen through both instruction and meditation. Some centers have also opened bookstores, vegetarian restaurants, and retreat centers.

A fourth wave of Buddhist influence is more recent and involves several types of Buddhism. Tibetan Buddhism has established communities of immigrant

Tibetans and converts in many places in the United States (California, Colorado, New York, Hawai`i) and in Europe (Switzerland, France, Great Britain), and Tibetan Buddhist art is now regularly acquired and exhibited by museums. Forms of Pure Land and Nichiren Buddhism have made many converts, particularly in large cities of North America. And Asian immigrants from Taiwan, Hong Kong, and Southeast Asia have all begun their own temples and celebrations where they have settled.

From the middle of the nineteenth century to the middle of the twentieth century, Buddhism outside Asia was primarily made up of ethnic Buddhists (mostly immigrants) and so-called elite Buddhists (non-Asian intellectuals and academics). These two groups have interacted and been joined by a large middle-class following. A new type of Buddhism is emerging from the interaction of the three groups: engaged Buddhism (which we discussed in the box on Thich Nhat Hanh). This movement comprises a wide variety of people who, as Buddhists, work for social betterment. A broadly based Western Buddhism—in Europe, North America, and Australia—is taking on such a life of its own that it is beginning to be called the "fourth vehicle" (*yana*) of Buddhism.

Some Buddhist traditions, particularly the Mahayana traditions in Taiwan, Korea, and Vietnam, have always ordained women. In contrast, the Theravada traditions of Sri Lanka and Southeast Asia, although they once ordained women, allowed that practice to die out, and traditional Tibetan Buddhism did not ordain women. Attitudes, though, are changing. Women are now ordained in Sri Lanka, and Thai Buddhists are being pressured to make a similar change. Tibetan Buddhism is also contemplating female ordination.

Women also play a major role in institutional Buddhism. A Taiwanese female monastic, Master Cheng Yen, began the influential Tzu Chi Foundation to help the needy. It has grown to become a worldwide social welfare agency. Western women who have become Buddhist nuns are particularly outspoken in demanding major roles for women in Buddhism. Among these women are Pema Chödrön, Tenzin Palmo, and Karma Lekshe Tsomo. Theoretical acceptance of equality is widespread, and real equality is increasingly the practice.

A Thai religious foundation provides free coffins for unidentified victims of accidents and disasters.

Ironically, even as it gains followers in the West, Buddhism has been weakened in many countries and regions that have been its traditional home. When Communist governments took over Mongolia (1921) and China (1949), Buddhism was severely repressed. This pattern continued when the Chinese government took over Tibet (1959). The Dalai Lama went into exile, and at least a million Tibetans are thought to have died in the ensuing persecution. Several thousand temples and monasteries were destroyed, particularly during the

Contemporary Issues

ENVIRONMENTAL BUDDHISM

Buddhism grew up with an inherent love of nature. Buddhism teaches human beings that they belong to a larger whole and that they should show restraint in dealing with nature.

The many branches of Buddhism are in the process of working out principles and practices of conservation. Some of the groups rely on their immediate surroundings for inspiration; for example, monks in Mongolia are creating forested zones around their monasteries. Other groups have more widespread goals. One branch of Vajrayana, the Kagyu, has created a list of principles of ideal action, including:

Planting native trees to restore forests around monasteries

Protecting existing forests from being overharvested

Protecting nearby water sources

Helping local farmers create vegetation buffers between farm fields and rivers

Promoting no-hunting zones

Prohibiting the wearing of ornamental fur from endangered animals

Discouraging traditional remedies that use illegal animal products

Using fewer things—reuse what you have, recycle what you can't reuse

Being models for composting and inspiring others to do the same

Designing energy-efficient buildings

Eating less meat and encouraging individuals to develop compassion for all living things[22]

Ogyen Drodul Trinley Dorje, a Kagyu leader, adds that the challenge of climate change "is far more complex and extensive than anything we alone can tackle. However, if we can all contribute a single drop of clean water, those drops will accumulate into a fresh pond, then a clear stream, and eventually a vast pure ocean. That is my aspiration."[23]

Cultural Revolution (1966–1976), causing both human suffering and an incalculable loss to the world of art. In recent years a modest amount of rebuilding has occurred in all these regions, with the financial support of Buddhists from abroad. While some governments fear that monasteries might become centers of antigovernment activity, they also recognize the importance of Buddhist sites both to the inhabitants and to tourists, whose goodwill (and foreign exchange) they wish to encourage.

In spite of a weakening of Buddhism in many of its traditional areas, relations with the non-Buddhist world have also brought new vigor to Buddhism. For example, we now see emerging what has been called "Green Buddhism." Although early Buddhism does not mention explicit environmental ideals, it does include principles that fit in well with environmentalism. Among these are harmony, frugality, compassion, reverence, and respect. Trees, in particular, play an important role in Buddhism. The Buddha was born, meditated, was enlightened, and died under trees. For centuries, monks in Southeast Asia have regularly set up meditation huts and small temples in wilderness forests. In Thailand, monks have played leadership roles in protecting forests. Monks use their moral authority to encourage villagers to plant new trees and to limit tree burning. Temples receive small trees from the Royal Forest Department and donations from town-bound supporters who want to earn merit by improving the natural environment. Monks have even temporarily "ordained" trees by tying orange robes around those that they hope to save from loggers.

Following his shadow, this lone monk with his eating bowl slowly places one foot in front of the other as he engages in walking meditation.

Buddhism is clearly entering a new phase in its long journey. In part, Buddhism can predict what that phase will bring: the one constant, as always, is change.

Reading **LIFE IS A JOURNEY**

The poet Basho made four trips away from his home in Edo (Tokyo). Like religious pilgrimages, his trips included visits to temples, shrines, and sites of natural beauty. He wrote about his experiences in both prose and poetry. His works are full of Buddhist sensitivity to the beauty of life and to its temporary nature. Here is a selection from his famous travel description, The Narrow Road to the Deep North.

At a certain point in the road we met an old priest—probably more than sixty years of age—carrying an enormously heavy load on his bent back, tottering along with short, breathless steps, and wearing a sullen, serious look on his face. My companions sympathized with him and, taking the heavy load from the priest's shoulders, put it together with other things they had been carrying on my horse. Consequently, I had to sit on a big pile. Above my head, mountains rose over mountains, and on my left a huge precipice dropped a thousand feet into a boiling river, leaving not a tiny square of flat land in between, so that, perched on the high saddle, I felt stricken with terror every time my horse gave a jerk.

We passed through many a dangerous place, as Kakehashi, Nezame, Saru-ga-baba, Tachitoge, the road always winding and climbing, so that we often felt we were groping our way in the clouds. I abandoned my horse and staggered on my own legs, for I was dizzy with the height and unable to maintain my mental balance from fear. The servant mounted the horse and seemed to give not even the slightest thought to the danger. He often nodded in a doze and seemed about to fall headlong over the precipice. Every time I saw him drop his head, I was terrified out of my wits. Upon second thought, however, it occurred to me that every one of us was like this servant, wading through the ever-changing reefs of this world in stormy weather, totally blind to the hidden dangers, and that the Buddha, surveying us from on high, would surely feel the same misgivings about our fortune as I did about the servant.

When dusk came, we sought a night's lodging in a humble house. After lighting a lamp, I took out my pen and ink, and closed my eyes, trying to remember the sights I had seen and the poems I had composed during the day. When the priest saw me tapping my head and bending over a small piece of paper, he must have thought I was suffering from the weariness of travelling, for he began to give me an account of his youthful pilgrimage, parables from sacred *sutras*, and the stories of the miracles he had witnessed. Alas, I was not able to compose a single poem because of this interruption. Just at this time, however, moonlight touched the corner of my room through the hanging leaves and the chinks in the wall. As I bent my ears to the noise of wooden clappers and the voices of the villagers chasing wild deer away, I felt in my heart that the loneliness of autumn was now consummated in the scene. I said to my companions, "Let us now drink under the bright beams of the moon," and the master of the house brought out some cups. The cups were too big to be called refined, and were decorated with somewhat uncouth gold-lacquer work, so that over-refined city dwellers might have hesitated to touch them. Finding them in a remote country as I did, however, I was pleased to see them, and thought that they were even more precious than jewel-inlaid, rare-blue cups.[24]

TEST YOURSELF

1. Siddhartha's encounters with an old man, a sick man, a corpse, and a wandering holy man, which prompted him to leave his luxurious and care-free life, are called the _____.
   a. temptations
   b. Four Passing Sights
   c. Enlightenment
   d. Awakening

2. After Siddhartha spent an entire night meditating under a full moon, he finally achieved insight into release from suffering and rebirth. Buddhists believe that he reached a profound understanding, called his _____.
   a. dharma
   b. stupa
   c. asceticism
   d. enlightenment

3. At the core of what is generally regarded as basic _____ are the Three Jewels: the Buddha, the Dharma, and the Sangha.
   a. suffering
   b. Enlightenment
   c. Buddhism
   d. existence

4. According to Buddhism, reality manifests three characteristics: constant change, lack of permanent identity, and the existence of _____.
   a. truth
   b. suffering
   c. death
   d. deprivation

5. According to a view common to all forms of Buddhism, reality manifests constant change. This view is the foundation for the _____ and the _____.
   a. Four Noble Truths, Noble Eightfold Path
   b. Tripitaka, Maitreya
   c. Vehicle of the Diamond, Dharmakaya
   d. Tendai, Jodo

6. In Buddhism, as in Hinduism, _____ suggest(s) decay and pain.
   a. change
   b. Four Noble Truths
   c. samsara
   d. reality

7. Liberation from decay and pain is called _____.
   a. nirvana
   b. samsara
   c. sangha
   d. Awakening

8. The key notions of _____ Buddhism are *trikaya* (the "three-body doctrine"), *shunyata* ("emptiness"), and *tathata* ("thatness").
   a. Ahimsa
   b. Theravada
   c. Mahayana
   d. Vedic

9. In _____ Buddhist countries, one great celebration (Vesak) recalls the birth, the enlightenment, and the death of Buddha. It is celebrated at the time of the full moon in May.
   a. Western
   b. O-Bon
   c. Mahayana
   d. Theravada

10. In Tibetan Buddhism, the executive head of the Gelug-pa is called the Dalai Lama, which means "_____."
    a. the Awakened
    b. ocean superior one
    c. heavenly bodhisattva
    d. compassion

11. Think of a social group you are a part of, such as a family, business, or student organization. How do you think the group dynamic would change if its members lived in accordance with the ideas of anichcha and anatta? Why?

12. Consider the following statement: Buddhism has no real deity. Using what you learned in this chapter, why might you agree or disagree with this statement? Address the different branches of Buddhism in your response.

RESOURCES

Books

Batchelor, Stephen. *Living with the Devil.* New York: Riverhead Trade/Penguin, 2005. A Buddhist's view of how human beings create illusions of permanence in their lives.

Dalai Lama. *The Universe in a Single Atom: The Convergence of Science and Spirituality.* New York: Broadway, 2005. An argument for a constructive dialogue between religion and science.

Faure, Bernard. *The Power of Denial: Buddhism, Purity, and Gender.* Princeton, NJ: Princeton University Press, 2003. An exploration of the role of gender in Buddhism and the extent to which the religion liberates or limits women.

Friedman, Lenore. *Meetings with Remarkable Women: Buddhist Teachers in America.* New York: Random House, 2000. Portraits of the author's encounters with seventeen women teachers, giving insight into the growth of roles for women in modern Buddhism.

Gross, Rita. *A Garland of Feminist Reflections.* Berkeley: University of California Press, 2009. A collection of essays by a foremost expert in both Buddhism and feminist thought.

Lopez, Donald, Jr. *Buddhism and Science.* Chicago: University of Chicago Press, 2008. A critical analysis of claims that Buddhism and science are compatible.

Nanayon, Upasika. *Pure and Simple: The Extraordinary Teachings of a Thai Buddhist Laywoman.* Boston: Wisdom Publications, 2005. A collection of the writings by the late Thai teacher of Buddhism.

Thich Nhat Hanh. *The Heart of the Buddha's Teaching.* New York: Three Rivers Press, 1999. A clear presentation of the basic teachings of Buddhism, followed by three sutras.

Music/Audio

Chants and Music from Buddhist Temples. (Arc Music.) A diverse compilation of recordings, including Buddhist chants from temples in China, India, Sri Lanka, Taiwan, and Thailand.

Japanese Traditional Music: Gagaku and Buddhist Chant. (World Arbiter.) A remastered release of an original 1941 recording of Japanese court music and Buddhist chant performed for the Imperial Household.

Mayuzumi Toshiro. *Nirvana Symphony.* (Denon Records.) Modern classical music inspired by Buddhism.

Tibetan Master Chants. (Spirit Music.) A recording of the deep-voice chanting of one of the world's foremost Tibetan chant masters, including the mantra "Om Mani Padme Hum."

Film/TV

Buddha Wild: Monk in a Hut. (Director Anna Wilding; Carpe Diem Films.) A film in which a group of Thai and Sri Lankan monks discuss their commitment to Buddhism and its way of life.

Kundun. (Director Martin Scorsese; Buena Vista.) A colorful biography of the current Dalai Lama, focusing on his escape from Tibet.

Little Buddha. (Director Bernardo Bertolucci; Miramax.) A film that interweaves two stories: the historical life of the Buddha and the modern search in Seattle for the reincarnation of a lama.

Internet

BuddhaNet: http://www.buddhanet.net/. A cornucopia of Buddhist information and resources, including a worldwide directory, e-library, online magazine, and notice board.

Virtual Religion Index: http://virtualreligion.net/vri/buddha.html. The "Buddhist Studies" page at the Virtual Religion Index site, containing individual sections devoted to general resources, the life of the Buddha, and Theravada and Mahayana Buddhism.

Wikipedia's Buddhism Portal: http://en.wikipedia.org/wiki/Portal:Buddhism. A Wikipedia compilation of links to subcategories such as culture, branches of Buddhism, deities, festivals, history, philosophical concepts, practices, temples, terms, and texts.

KEY TERMS

(Buddhist terms are often anglicized in English pronunciation. For the following terms with two pronunciations, the second is the anglicized version.)

Amitabha Buddha (ah-mee-tah'-buh bood'-huh): The Buddha of the Western Paradise, a bliss-body Buddha in Mahayana.

anatta (un-nah'-tuh): "No self"; the doctrine that there is no soul or permanent essence in people and things.

anichcha (uh-nee'-chuh): Impermanence, constant change.

arhat (ahr'-hut, ahr'-haht): In Theravada, a person who has practiced monastic disciplines and reached nirvana, the ideal.

bodhi (boh'-dee): Enlightenment.

bodhisattva (boh'-dee-suh'-tvah, boh-dee-saht'-vuh): "Enlightenment being"; in Mahayana, a person of deep compassion, especially one who does not enter nirvana but is constantly reborn to help others; a heavenly being of compassion.

Dharma (dhur'-mah, dar'-muh): The totality of Buddhist teaching.

dhyana (dee-yah'-nuh): "Meditation"; focusing of the mind; sometimes, stages of trance.

dukkha (doo'-kuh): Sorrow, misery.

Guanyin: A popular bodhisattva of compassion in Mahayana.

karuna (kuh-roo'-nuh): Compassion, empathy.

koan (koh'-ahn): In Chan and Zen Buddhism, a question that cannot be answered logically; a technique used to test consciousness and bring awakening.

lama: A Tibetan Buddhist teacher; a title of honor often given to all Tibetan monks.

Maitreya (mai-tray'-yuh): A Buddha (or bodhisattva) expected to appear on earth in the future.

mandala (mun'-duh-luh, mahn-dah'-luh): A geometrical design containing deities, circles, squares, symbols, and so on that represent totality, the self, or the universe.

mudra (moo'-druh): A symbolic hand gesture.

nirvana (nir-vah'-nuh): The release from suffering and rebirth that brings inner peace.

samadhi (suh-mah'-dee): A state of deep awareness, the result of intensive meditation.

samsara (suhm-sah'-ruh, sahm-sah'-ruh): Constant rebirth and the attendant suffering; the everyday world of change.

Sangha (suhng'-huh): The community of monks and nuns; lowercased, *sangha* refers to an individual monastic community.

satori (sah-toh'-ree): In Zen, the enlightened awareness.

shunyata (shoon'-yah-tah): The Mahayana notion of emptiness, meaning that the universe is empty of permanent reality.

stupa (stoo'-puh): A shrine, usually in the shape of a dome, used to mark Buddhist relics or sacred sites.

sutra (soo'-truh): A sacred text, especially one said to record the words of the Buddha.

tathata (taht-hah-tah'): "Thatness," "thusness," "suchness"; the uniqueness of each changing moment of reality.

trikaya (trih-kah'-yuh): The three "bodies" of the Buddha—the Dharmakaya (cosmic Buddha nature), the Nirmanakaya (historical Buddhas), and the Sambhogakaya (celestial Buddhas).

Tripitaka (trih-pih'-tuh-kuh): The three "baskets," or collections, of Buddhist texts.

vajra (vuhj'-ruh, vahj'-ruh): The "diamond" scepter used in Tibetan and other types of Buddhist ritual, symbolizing compassion.

RELIGION BEYOND THE CLASSROOM

Visit the Online Learning Center at www.mhhe.com/molloy6e for additional exercises and features, including "Religion beyond the Classroom" and "For Fuller Understanding."

CHAPTER 5

Jainism and Sikhism

F I R S T   E N C O U N T E R

On a street in Southeast Asia you ask a gentleman for directions. This leads to further conversation because your accent gives you away and he has relatives in the United States. "Maybe you know them?" he asks. "Do you live close to Tennessee?"

Even though you don't know his relatives, you are soon learning all about his family. He has two sons, already married, and a willful daughter who is of marriageable age. He is frightened that she might fall in love with a person of a different religion, and then what will he do? Soon he is taking you into his nearby *gurdwara*— the religious center for Sikhs—where he will be doing volunteer work this afternoon and having something to eat.

At the entrance, your new friend takes a piece of orange cloth and makes a turban to cover the top of your head. He does the same for himself. "We do this for respect," he says. Upstairs, you meet the resident priest, a bright-eyed man in blue, who wears an orange cap. "Our congregation brought him from India to be our priest,"

181

your Sikh friend explains as you walk to the altar area. Soon the priest is showing you copies of the Adi Granth, the sacred book of the Sikhs. They are housed in a special air-conditioned sanctuary beside the altar. Then you see the sword collection at the side of the room and discuss the *kirpan* (ritual knife) that the priest wears. "Sikhs had to learn to defend themselves," your friend explains. "These are symbols of our strength."

Afterward, you are invited downstairs to an enormous kitchen and dining room. Large vats gleam. You and your friend sit at a long table, drinking tea with milk and eating a late-afternoon snack with the kitchen workers.

At the entrance, before leaving, you give back your turban to the Sikh guide and thank him for his kindness. You commiserate about his daughter and take the names and addresses of his relatives in the United States, whom you plan to contact on your very next visit to their state. He helps you find a taxi and, as it stops, invites you to a service three days from now. "There will be wonderful Sikh music. You must come." As you are climbing into the taxi, he adds, "There will be much good food, too."

Turbans, you decide as your taxi snakes through the traffic, are fine. But swords? And priests who wear knives? Are these suitable symbols for any religion? How can religions hold such differing attitudes about violence?

SHARED ORIGINS

India is home to two religions, Jainism and Sikhism, that are now becoming better known in the West (Figure 5.1). The first is ancient, and the other is relatively young. Adherents of the two religions can be found in limited numbers around the world, but the majority of them still live in India.

Both religions have some connection with Hinduism, sharing with it certain characteristics, such as a belief in karma and rebirth. Furthermore, both of them, having developed in opposition to Hindu polytheism and ritualism, strive toward greater religious simplicity. In spite of their similarities, however, Jainism and Sikhism differ in their views of reality and in their emotional tone. It is therefore interesting to look at them side by side. Jainism rejects belief in a Creator and sees the universe simply as natural forces in motion, yet it also recognizes the spiritual potential of each person. Like early Buddhism, Jainism emphasizes the ideals of extreme nonattachment and nonharm (ahimsa). Sikhism, to the contrary, embraces a devout monotheism and accepts meat eating and military self-defense. Regardless of their differences, both religions stress the importance of the individual's struggle to purify the self, to act morally, and to do good to others.

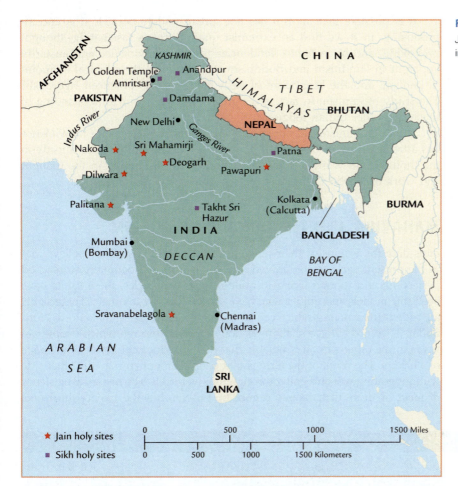

FIGURE 5.1

Jain and Sikh holy sites
in India.

Jainism

BACKGROUND

As the Vedic religion expanded eastward into the Ganges River valley, it created opposition. As we saw in Chapter 4, some people rebelled against the growing strength of the caste system, and nonbrahmins, especially the aristocrats, felt threatened by the power of the priests. Moved by compassion, some people opposed the animal sacrifices that were often a part of the Vedic ritual. Two great religious movements grew out of this opposition. One—Buddhism—is well known because it spread beyond India. The other movement—Jainism—has remained less well known because, until recently, it has not sought converts in other lands. When they arose, both Buddhism and Jainism were influenced by some early Hindu ideas, but they may have also practiced much older ascetic traditions.

It is possible that Jainism has not spread widely because it is uncompromising: in it we find an extremist quality that is fascinating, thought provoking, and often noble. Tendencies toward nonviolence and austerity apparent in Hinduism and Buddhism are carried to their logical endpoint in Jainism, and the skepticism of early Buddhism is practiced rigorously. The study of Jainism, in fact, gives greater clarity to our understanding of those two other Indian religions.

Although Jainism did not spread widely, its strong ideal of nonviolence has attracted interest throughout the world. We see its influence directly in the thought and work of Mahatma Gandhi and, indirectly, in the thought and work of Martin Luther King Jr.

MAHAVIRA AND THE ORIGINS OF JAINISM

Jains date the origins of their religion to the distant past. They believe that in the present cycle of the universe, twenty-four great people have reached perfection; and though living in quite different centuries, these saints have been role models and guides who have shown the way to others. These saints are called **tirthankaras,** which can be translated as "crossing makers" or "ford finders"—a ford being a shallow section of a river through which people can wade to the other side. It is notable that the term does not convey the image of a bridge. The point of the term is that people cannot cross to the other side without getting wet and going through the river itself. The historical existence of most of these tirthankaras cannot be proven, but the twenty-third one,

Timeline of significant events in the history of Jainism and Sikhism.

TIMELINE 5.1

	c. 850–800 BCE	Life of Parshva, the legendary twenty-third tirthankara
Life of Mahavira, the twenty-fourth and most recent tirthankara	c. 599–527 BCE	
	c. 350 BCE	Split between Digambara and Shvetambara sects
Life of Nanak	1469–1539 CE	
	1563–1606	Life of Arjan
Life of Gobind Singh	1666–1708	
	1984	Indian troops retake the Golden Temple from Sikh separatists

Jain monks leave the pilgrimage center at Belagola in India.

Parshva, may have been a real person who lived in India, possibly between 850 and 800 BCE (Timeline 5.1).

The most recent tirthankara is considered to be the greatest of them all and is often thought of by outsiders to be the founder of Jainism. His name was Nataputta Vardhamana, but he is usually referred to by an honorary title: Mahavira, meaning "great man" or "hero." When he lived is not entirely certain. An older dating, accepted by Jains, puts his life entirely in the sixth century BCE (c. 599–527 BCE), but some scholars believe he lived a bit later (540–468 BCE), possibly as a contemporary of the Buddha.

Mahavira's life story is surrounded by legend, although the basic outline—which somewhat resembles the story of the Buddha—seems clear. He was born into an aristocratic family of a noble clan. Luckily, he was the second son and thus had fewer responsibilities to care for his parents than did his older brother. One branch of Jains holds that he never married; another says that he married and had a child. But all agree that he left home at about age 30 to live the life of a wandering holy man.

After leaving home, Mahavira embraced extreme asceticism, and legend tells of his harshness toward himself and of the harshness received from others. He is said to have pulled out his hair when he renounced the world, and villagers taunted him during his meditations by hurting him with fire and with pins that they pushed into his skin. Dogs attacked him, but he did not resist. In order to avoid all attachments to people and places, he moved to a new place every day; and after losing his loincloth, he went entirely naked for the rest of his life. He lived as a wandering holy man, begging for his food along the way. He was so gentle that to avoid causing injury to any living thing, he strained whatever he drank to keep from swallowing any insect that might have fallen into his cup, and he stepped carefully as he walked down a road to avoid crushing even an ant.

After twelve years of meditation, wandering, and extreme mortification, Mahavira, at the age of 42, had an experience of great liberation. He felt completely free of all bondage to the ordinary world—no longer being troubled by pain, suffering, shame, or loss. He now felt fully in control of himself, sensing that he had won out over all the forces that bind a person to the world.

As a result of his liberating experience, Mahavira is called a **jina** ("conqueror"). It is from this title that the religion Jainism takes its name.

Mahavira spent the next thirty years of his life teaching his doctrines and organizing an order of naked monks. He died at about 72 at the village of Pava, near present-day Patna, in northeastern India.

WORLDVIEW

Jainism, like Buddhism, rather starkly rejects belief in a Creator God. The Mahapurana, a long Jain poem of the ninth century CE, states that "foolish men declare that Creator made the world. The doctrine that the world was created is ill-advised and should be rejected."[1] Jainism offers the following philosophical arguments: If God is perfect, why did God create a universe that is imperfect? If God made the universe because of love, why is the world so full of suffering beings? If the universe had to be created, did not God also need to be created? And where did God come from in the beginning?

Jains respond to these questions by denying any beginning and asserting instead that the universe is eternal. Although the universe has always existed, it must continually change, and in the process of eternal change, structure arises on its own. Jainism (like Hinduism) teaches that the universe goes through regular great cycles of rise and fall. During the periods when human beings exist, there first is moral integrity, followed by inevitable moral decay; luckily, however, in each human age, tirthankaras appear to point the way to freedom.

According to Jainism, everything is full of life and is capable of suffering. This view of reality, called **hylozoism** (Greek: "matter-alive"), may be quite ancient. In addition, Jain philosophy is dualistic, for Jains teach that all parts of the universe are composed of two types of reality, which are intermixed. There is spirit, which senses and feels, and there is matter, which is not alive and has no consciousness. Jainism calls these two principles **jiva** ("soul," "spirit," "life") and **ajiva** ("nonsoul," "nonlife"). Jains, however, see life and consciousness where others do not—even in fire, rocks, and water. Thus they extend the notion of spirit and feeling beyond human beings, animals, and insects. They are also aware of the minuscule life-forms that live in earth, water, and wood. Their way of looking at reality makes Jains cautious about injuring anything— even that which does not at first appear to have the capacity to suffer.

Jainism sees the human being as composed of two opposing parts. The material side of the human being seeks pleasure, escape from pain, and self-interest, while the spiritual side seeks freedom and escape from all bondage to the material world and from the limitation of ego. Because other forms of reality are not aware of their two opposing aspects, they can do nothing about the essential incompatibility of the two parts. Human beings, however, have the ability to understand their dual nature and to overcome their limitations. With discipline, human beings can overcome the bondage of the material world and the body, liberating their spirits through insight, austerity, and kindness.

Enriching this vision of the human situation are the Jain beliefs in karma and reincarnation. Like Hindus, Jains believe that spirits are constantly being reborn in various forms. A spirit can move up or down the scale of rebirth, as well as free itself entirely from the chain of rebirths.

What controls the direction of rebirth is karma, which is produced by every action. As discussed earlier, karma is an important notion in Hinduism and Buddhism, but for Jains, karma has a quite physical quality: it is like a powder or grime that settles on and clings to the spirit. The level of rebirth is determined automatically, according to one's state of karma at the time of death of one's current body.

Jains traditionally have believed that superhuman beings exist in realms of the universe above the earth. Often these beings are called gods or deities, but such terms can be misleading. We must recall that Jains believe that these superhuman beings are also subject to karma and change. When the karma that has brought them rebirth as gods has run out, they will be reborn in lower parts of the universe. Some Jains, however, do believe that when in their superhuman form, these celestial beings can be of help to people on earth who pray to them. Jains also believe that some beings exist in painful realms below the earth, and Jains hope to avoid being reborn there.

The Jain goal is to reach a state of total freedom. Liberated spirits, at last freed of their imprisoning material bodies, live on in the highest realm, which is thought to be at the very top of the universe. Mahavira and other tirthankaras dwell there, and although they cannot assist human beings (as deities might), they are role models whom human beings devoutly recall in order to gain strength and courage.

JAIN ETHICS

Jainism has five ethical recommendations, which monks and nuns are expected to keep quite strictly. Laypeople, however, have the flexibility to adjust their practice to their particular life situations. (We must also recall that these are ideals that are not always lived out perfectly by individuals.)

Nonviolence (ahimsa) A more accurate English translation of *ahimsa* might be "gentleness" or "harmlessness." Ahimsa is the foundation of Jain ethics, and Jains are best known for their extreme measures in this regard. Believing that Mahavira swept the ground in front of him as he walked and before he sat down, Jain monks and nuns sometimes use a small, soft brush to move ants and other insects out of the way so that no life-form—even the tiniest—will be crushed. Feeling a kinship with the animal world as well, Jains have established hospitals to care for sick animals. They have been known to buy caged animals and set them free. Jains are also strict vegetarians, and some reject the use of animal products such as leather, feathers, and fur.

Because Jain laypeople avoid occupations that would harm insects or animals, hunting and fishing are forbidden, as are slaughtering or selling animal flesh. And although some Jains are farmers, farming is often avoided because the necessary plowing could hurt small animals

> The saint, with true vision, conceives compassion for all the world. . . . The great sage becomes a refuge for injured creatures, like an island which the waters cannot overwhelm.
> —Acaranga Sutra 1:6, 5[2]

Deeper Insights

JAINS AND A HOLY DEATH

Because it so values nonattachment, Jainism defends a person's right to end his or her own life. (This is also true of Hinduism, but not so for many other religions—although most religions are indeed concerned with a good and holy death.) Jain scriptures even teach that Mahavira and his parents died by self-starvation. We must be cautious here, however, in using the word *suicide*. Jains do accept ending one's own life, but we must understand the practice from the Jain point of view and within that context. Jains see all life as a preparation for the liberation of the spirit (jiva) from the body, and when a person is sufficiently evolved spiritually, that person can make the final choice to no longer create more karma.

The Jain ideal thus allows and esteems ending one's life only after a long life of virtue and detachment, and it must be done with consideration for others. Gentle methods of ending one's life are the best, such as walking into an ocean or lake. The most highly esteemed method, however, is self-starvation, called **sallekhana,** "holy death." Jains prepare for sallekhana over the years by practicing fasting. When a person is old and growing weak, eating less and less is seen as an appropriate way to hasten the end. Self-starvation, or "the final fast," involves giving up food but continuing to drink liquids. Death comes in about a month. This kind of death by self-starvation is considered an ultimate, noble expression of nonattachment and freedom.

and insects living in the fields. Jains, instead, have gravitated to careers that ideally cause no harm, such as medicine, education, law, and business. As an indirect result, the Jains in India make up a powerful business class whose reputation for virtue earns them the trust of others.

Nonlying Jainism discourages the telling of any falsehood and avoids exaggeration, even when meant humorously. Lying and exaggeration are dangerous, Jains think, because they often cause hurt. Although these ideals are not always followed, Jains' general mindfulness of their speech and their reputation for honesty in their contractual agreements have earned them great respect.

At the same time, Jainism teaches that "absolute truth" is impossible to find or express, because everyone sees a situation from a unique point of view. A famous story illustrates the relativity of truth. In this story, several blind people touch the same elephant, but they experience it quite differently. The first person touches the ear and says it is a fan; the second person touches the leg and says it is a tree trunk; the third person touches the tail and says it is a rope; and so on. (Although this story is popular among Jains, it is doubtless older than Jainism itself.)

Nonstealing Jains may not take from others that which is not given. Stealing arises from improper desire and causes pain to others.

Chastity For the monk or nun, this means complete celibacy, and for the married individual, this means sexual fidelity to one's spouse. Mahavira saw sex as a danger, because it strongly binds a person to the physical world, strengthens desires, and can create passions that harm others. For those who are sexually active, improper sex is that which hurts others.

Nonattachment Human beings form attachments easily—to family, to home, to familiar territory, to clothes, to money, and to possessions.

A devotee anoints the feet of a Jain statue. The vines on each side (showing at the top corners of the photograph) hint at the immobility and perseverance of the tirthankara.

Jainism asserts that all attachments bring a certain bondage and that some attachments, especially to money and to possessions, can take complete control of a person. For laypeople, the ethical requirement of nonattachment suggests cultivating a spirit of generosity and detachment and limiting one's possessions to what is truly necessary. For monks and nuns, this requirement is interpreted more severely. Jainism teaches that Mahavira abandoned all attachments—family, possessions, even his clothing—and that monks and nuns must imitate him to the best of their capacity.

THE DEVELOPMENT OF JAINISM AND ITS BRANCHES

Jainism first developed in northeastern India, in the same area that gave rise to Buddhism. Both Mahavira and the Buddha rebelled against aspects of Vedic religion: they refused to accept the authority of the Vedas and the Vedic gods, and they rejected the importance of a priestly class; instead, they placed emphasis on meditation and self-purification.

Although Buddhism followed a deliberate path of moderation—a "middle way"—Jainism gloried in austerity. While the Buddha rejected both nakedness and suicide, as well as all extreme austerity, Mahavira's breakthrough experience of liberation, most Jains believe, was due to his extreme harshness toward himself. He was successful precisely because he accepted—and even sought—cold, heat, poverty, nakedness, and humiliation.

FIGURE 5.2

Branches of Jainism.

The way of extreme austerity, however, is for rare individuals only. For most people, even for monks and nuns, the harshness must be softened according to life's circumstances. Because Jainism spread to different parts of India, each with its distinct culture and climate, several branches of Jainism arose, which interpret the basic principles and teachings with some variation (Figure 5.2).

Digambaras

The name of this sect is beautiful and means "clothed in sky" or "atmosphere-clad." It is a pleasant way of referring to the monks' ideal of going completely naked, even in public. The **Digambara** branch holds that everything must be renounced, including the last scrap of clothing and the consequent shame of nakedness.

Most members of this branch live in southern India today. As tradition explains, a famine that occurred in the north drove many Jains southward. Divergences developed between those who had remained in the north and those who had moved south. Thinking that northern followers had lost an essential seriousness, the southern branch became conservative, continuing to insist on renunciation of the most literal type. Its conservatism shows itself in many ways. For example, Digambara Jainism does not accept women into monastic life, holding that they may become monks only when they have been reborn as men. Possibly because of its high regard for celibacy, it also rejects the tradition that Mahavira was ever married.

Shvetambaras

The name of this sect means "clothed in white" and comes from the fact that its monks dress in white robes. The **Shvetambara** branch allows women to enter monastic life as nuns and to dress in white as well. (Being clothed was allowed not only in deference to modesty but also because it was demanded by the colder climate of northern India.) Shvetambara Jainism teaches that Mahavira was indeed married at one time but that he left home to find liberation. Nowadays this branch has members not only in the northeast but also in western and northwestern India.

Sthanakavasis

By the standards of India, the **Sthanakavasi** branch is fairly young, having grown up within the past few hundred years. It is a reform movement that emerged from the Shvetambara branch in the early eighteenth century. Popular Jainism had increasingly developed the practice of venerating statues of

Mahavira and other tirthankaras, influenced by the Hindu practice of **puja** (devotional ritual performed in front of statues and at altars). Some Jain reformers opposed this practice because it seemed to turn the tirthankaras into deities to be prayed to for help. The Sthanakavasis, therefore, do not make use of either temples or images. (Their name comes from the simple buildings—*sthanakas*—in which they meet.) Rather than concentrate on temple ceremony, Sthanakavasis focus on meditation and individual austerities.

Terapanthis

An even newer reformist movement is the **Terapanthi** branch. It was founded by Acharya Bhikshu (1726–1803), also called Swami Bhikkanji Maharaj. The origin of the name Terapanthi, which means "thirteen," is debated. It may come from the thirteen moral principles outlined by the founder or from the number of persons comprising the earliest disciples. Like the Sthanakavasis, the Terapanthis reject the use of images. To ensure discipline, the founder instituted a hierarchical structure with a supreme guru, the *Acharya*, at the top, who oversees all operations. The Terapanthis, while being strict in their practice, have been at the forefront in spreading Jainism outside of India and in spreading basic Jain principles among non-Jains, both within India and beyond.

JAIN PRACTICES

Because they emphasize the ability of individuals to purify themselves and to perfect their own characters, Jains do not stress that devotional acts—directed toward gods or deceased leaders—bring help. Nonetheless, the practice of puja—offered to both the tirthankaras and to deities—has been adopted by most Jains. (Exceptions are the Sthanakavasis and Terapanthis.) There is a general feeling that the devotional acts have a good effect on one's state of karma and that they focus the mind on saintly behavior. Jain temples, therefore, contain statues of the tirthankaras, especially Rishaba (the first tirthankara), Nemi (the twenty-second), Parshva, and Mahavira. The temple statues often look the same. In Digambara temples, the statues are unclothed and simple; in Shvetambara temples, they may be clothed and more ornate. Puja is performed before statues regularly, both by Jains and (in some places) by brahmin Hindus employed for the task. Puja ordinarily involves the offering of food, incense, the flames of oil lamps, and flowers, and sometimes the statues are bathed and devotees circumambulate (walk around) the statues. On special occasions in some areas, large outdoor statues are bathed in milk and other liquids. Many Jains also maintain home altars where they perform puja.

Monks and nuns regularly practice fasting, particularly at the times of full and new moons. Laypeople join the monks in fasting on the last days of the Jain year in late summer, before the celebration of the New Year begins (in August or September). This period of fasting (*paryusana*) lasts fifteen days for the Digambaras and eight days for the Shvetambaras. The religious year ends with a confession of wrongdoing and a plea for pardon from anyone the devotee might have offended.

he and a Muslim friend named Mardana created a devotional association and met in the evenings to sing hymns and to discuss religious ideas.

One day Nanak had an experience so powerful that he saw it as a revelation. After bathing and performing religious ablutions in a nearby river, Nanak went into the adjacent forest, where he remained for three days. During that time he felt himself taken into the divine presence. He would later say that he had experienced God directly. This shattering experience revealed to him that there is but one God, beyond all human names and conceptions.

Nanak referred to the fundamental divine reality as the True Name—signifying that all names and terms that are applied to God are limited because the divine is beyond all human conception. Nanak now understood that Hindus and Muslims worshiped the same God and that a distinction between the two religions was mistaken. Nanak became famous for insisting that, when the True Name of God is experienced rather than just talked about, there is no "Hindu" and there is no "Muslim."

Nanak's revelation is similar to stories of the life-changing prophetic calls of Isaiah, Zarathustra, and Muhammad (as we will see in later chapters). His revelatory experience resolved his earlier doubts and was the great turning point of his life. Having decided to spread his new understanding, Nanak left his family and home, accompanied by his friend Mardana. As homeless wanderers, they visited holy sites throughout northern India. Wherever they went, Nanak preached and sought disciples, which is the meaning of the word **Sikh** (disciple). As a part of his preaching, Nanak sang devotional songs while Mardana, who was from a social class of musicians, played musical accompaniment.

Particularly startling was Nanak's style of clothing, which deliberately blended Hindu and Muslim elements. He wore the Hindu *dhoti* (a cloth drawn up between the legs to form pants), along with an orange Muslim coat and Muslim cap. He adorned his forehead with Hindu religious markings. The combination of elements was an important prophetic statement, predictably causing consternation among both Hindus and Muslims.

Nanak and Mardana continued their devotional teaching together until Mardana's death in his late 60s. Not long after, when Nanak sensed his own end approaching, he passed on his authority and work to a chosen disciple. He died in 1539 at age 70. Nanak is commonly called Guru Nanak and is recognized as the first of a line of ten Sikh gurus ("spiritual teachers").

THE WORLDVIEW AND TEACHINGS OF NANAK

Just as Nanak's clothing combined elements of Hinduism and Islam, so too did his worldview, at least on the surface. Earlier commentators spoke of Sikhism merely as a combination of Hindu and Muslim elements, yet Sikhs themselves—and more recent scholars—see Sikhism as an entirely unique religion. They speak of Nanak as having rejected both Islam and Hinduism, and they hold that Sikhism comes from a totally new revelation.

Nanak accepted—as does Hinduism—a belief in reincarnation and karma. His view of the human being was similar to that of the Sankhya school of philosophy, which views the human being as a composite of body and spirit. Because the body and physical world by nature bind and limit the spirit, the spirit must overcome physicality as it seeks freedom and absorption in the divine. This process may take many lifetimes to accomplish.

In spite of Nanak's acceptance of reincarnation and karma, there were other elements of Hinduism that he rejected. From a very early age, for example, he resisted Hindu love of ritual, criticizing it for taking human attention away from God. Similarly, he disdained Hindu polytheism, particularly Hindu devotion to images of various gods and goddesses. It is possible that Nanak's views in this regard were influenced by Islam.

According to Nanak's view of God, although God is ultimately beyond personhood, God does have personal qualities, such as knowledge, love, a sense of justice, and compassion. Because of these qualities, God can be approached personally by the individual. In Nanak's view, God is the primary guru. Although Nanak saw himself as God's mouthpiece, he preached that God dwells within each individual and can be contacted within the human heart.

Despite his emphasis on finding the divine within the individual, Nanak believed that true religion has a strong social responsibility. He criticized both Islam and Hinduism for their deficiencies in helping the poor and the oppressed. In response to his convictions, Nanak organized religious groups, called *sangats*, which were to offer both worship to God and assistance to fellow human beings.

THE DEVELOPMENT OF SIKHISM

Sikhism has gone through several stages of development. In its earliest stage, Sikhism was not defined as a distinct religion. It was simply a religious movement that sought to coexist peacefully with other religions. In the next stage, Sikhism was forced to adopt a militant, self-protective stance toward the world, and it took on some of the elements of a more formalized religion—a sacred book, a sacred city, and clearly defined religious practices. After that period of self-definition and consolidation, Sikhism, in its third and final stage, was able to move beyond its land of origin and to make converts elsewhere.

The earliest stage was that of the first four gurus—Nanak, Angad, Amar Das, and Ram Das. During this period, hymns were written, numerous communities were organized, and a village headquarters was created at Amritsar, in northern India.

The next stage—of consolidation and religious definition—began with Guru Arjan (1563–1606), a son of Ram Das. In his role as fifth guru, Arjan built the Golden Temple and its surrounding pond at Amritsar. Collecting about three thousand hymns—written by him and earlier gurus and saints— Arjan created the sacred book of the Sikhs, the **Adi Granth** ("original collection"). Because he resolutely resisted attempts by the Muslim emperor Jahangir to make him adopt Islamic practice, Arjan died of torture.

Arjan's son, Har Gobind, steered Sikhism in a more self-defensive direction. In response to his father's persecution, Har Gobind enlisted a bodyguard and an army to protect him and his followers. He adopted the practice of wearing a sword, thus abandoning the Hindu ideal of ahimsa. The growing militancy of evolving Sikhism was successful in averting persecution during the tenure of the next gurus, Har Rai and Harkishan.

The ninth guru, Tegh Bahadur, however, was imprisoned and decapitated by the Muslim emperor Aurangzeb, who saw Sikhism as a serious threat to his control. In response, the tenth guru, Gobind Rai (1666–1708) idealized the sword. Because of his military power, Gobind Rai came to be known as Gobind Singh ("Gobind the lion"). He inaugurated a special military order for men, called the *Khalsa*, and devised a ceremony of initiation, called the baptism of the sword, which involved sprinkling initiates with water that had been stirred with a sword. The Khalsa was open to all castes, for Gobind Singh had ended all caste distinctions among Sikhs. Every male within the Khalsa took the name *Singh* ("lion").

Over time, Gobind Singh suffered the deaths of his four sons and was left without a successor. Possibly foreseeing his own assassination, he declared that the Adi Granth was to be considered both his successor and the final, permanent Guru. The sacred book, both in Amritsar and in Sikh temples (**gurdwaras**), is therefore treated with the same reverence that would be shown a living guru. As such, it is called Guru Granth Sahib. At the death of Gobind Singh, Sikhism was now clearly defined as a religion, with the means to spread beyond its place of origin.

Sikh pilgrims receive and share a meal at the temple of Punja Sahib in Hasanabdal, a town near Pakistan's capital, Islamabad. Sikhs from all over the world visit this shrine every year to mark the three-day festival of Baisakhi.

Deeper Insights

THE "FIVE K'S" OF THE SIKH KHALSA

In India and in big cities of the West, Sikhs today are often associated with turbans. In fact, their characteristic dress reflects not one but five practices. These practices are not observed by all Sikhs, however, but only by those who have entered the Khalsa, the special Sikh military order. Members of the Khalsa originally adopted the five practices to promote strength and self-identity. Because the names of the practices each begin with the letter *k*, they are called the Five K's:

- *Kesh:* uncut hair and beard—in association with the lion and its power; the hair on the head is usually worn in a topknot and covered with a turban or cloth.

- *Khanga:* hair comb—to hold the long hair in place.
- *Kach:* special underwear—to indicate alertness and readiness to fight.
- *Kirpan:* sword—for defense.
- *Kara:* bracelet of steel—to symbolize strength.

In addition, members of the Khalsa are required to avoid all intoxicants. For a long time, the Khalsa was open only to men, but eventually women were also admitted.

SIKH SCRIPTURES

The primary book of Sikh scripture, the Adi Granth, is divided into three parts. The first and most important part is the **Japji,** a moderately long poem by Guru Nanak that summarizes the religion. It speaks of the indescribability of God and the joy of union with him. Its opening words declare, "There is only one God whose name is true, the Creator, devoid of fear and enmity, immortal, unborn, self-existent."[4] The second part consists of thirty-nine *rags* ("tunes") by Guru Nanak and later gurus. The third part is a collection of varied works, including poems and hymns from Hindu, Muslim, and Sikh gurus and saints.

Because the Adi Granth is believed to contain the living spirit of Nanak and his successors, it is treated with utmost reverence and given personal honors as the embodiment of the gurus. At the Golden Temple in Amritsar, it is brought out in the early morning by a gloved attendant, set on a cushion under a canopy, read from aloud by professional readers, fanned throughout the day, and then "put to bed" at night. In gurdwaras, copies of the Adi Granth are enshrined and read. It is consulted for solutions to problems by opening it freely and reading from the top of the left-hand page. (Even children are named by this method, being given names corresponding to the first letter read at the top of the left-hand page when the Adi Granth is opened randomly.) Sikh homes may have a room to enshrine the Adi Granth, and devout Sikhs daily read or recite its passages from memory.

An example of the poetic nature of the Adi Granth is the following canticle by Nanak in praise of God:

Wonderful Your word, wonderful Your knowledge;
Wonderful Your creatures, wonderful their species;

Wonderful their forms, wonderful their colors;
Wonderful the animals which wander naked;
Wonderful Your wind; wonderful Your water;
Wonderful Your fire which sports wondrously;
Wonderful the earth . . . ;
Wonderful the desert, wonderful the road;
Wonderful Your nearness, wonderful Your remoteness;
Wonderful to behold You present.[5]

A temple assistant explains the significance of the repository that houses the Adi Granth and other books sacred to Sikhs.

SIKHISM AND THE MODERN WORLD

Because of their military training, Sikhs were employed by the British as soldiers. After the British left the Indian subcontinent in 1947, however, the Sikhs experienced painful dislocation. More than two million left Pakistan to avoid conflict with the Muslim majority, and most settled in northwestern India, where today some Sikhs hope to create an independent state. Antagonism has flared up between the Sikhs and the Indian government over this matter, and although Sikh separatists have taken over the Golden Temple at Amritsar, Indian government forces have repeatedly taken it back. In retaliation for her support of Indian government troops during the first of these takeovers, Prime Minister Indira Gandhi was assassinated in 1984 by Sikhs who were among her bodyguards.

Sikhs have begun to settle widely outside India, particularly in countries open to Indian immigration, such as England and former British territories. (There is a considerable community, for example, in Vancouver, British Columbia.) They have established gurdwaras, which serve as daily prayer centers as well as charitable kitchens and social meeting places. Although Sikhs do not have a tradition of making converts, their simple and self-reliant lifestyle has attracted many new members. Their success and continued growth is likely.

Devotees and priests pay their respects to their holy book, Guru Granth Sahib, inside the Sikh shrine of the Golden Temple. They are celebrating the birthday of Guru Nanak, the founder of the Sikh faith.

P E R S O N A L   E X P E R I E N C E

A Visit to the Golden Temple

The Golden Temple of Amritsar sits in the midst of a busy Indian city on an island in an artificial lake. On the day that I visited, however, the water of the lake had been drained, and about thirty workers were moving about and chatting down below as they cleaned and made repairs. While I surveyed the scene, I overheard what sounded like American English being spoken nearby. A man with black hair and a short black beard, his blond wife, and his young daughter were taking photos and discussing the restoration work. I offered to photograph them against the backdrop of the Golden Temple, and then we fell into conversation. The man introduced himself and his family. Mr. Singh and his wife Marianne were not American, he said, but Canadian.

"I was born in Vancouver just after my parents immigrated to Canada from India. We've come here to visit my grandparents and to see the Golden Temple," he explained. "And I'm from Alberta, originally," added Mrs. Singh. "I'm not a Sikh—at least not yet. I was raised Catholic. My parents immigrated to Canada from Poland and have a farm north of Calgary. My husband and I met in college at the University of British Columbia." She turned to the girl, "This is our daughter, June." After shaking hands, we went across the walkway together into the Golden Temple.

The Golden Temple in Amritsar is serene at dawn.

The interior was hot and muggy, but a feeling of devotion overcame my discomfort. A venerable-looking man with a long white beard was reading from the Adi Granth while an attendant waved a feather fan overhead. People moved slowly in line, but the size of the crowd kept us from staying inside for very long. Outside, we decided to have lunch together. We found a restaurant not far away where we ate and talked.

Mr. Singh pointed to his short hair and neatly clipped beard. "As you can see, I do not practice all the traditions of my religion. I am proud of my religion, though, and particularly proud of the emphasis it puts on strength and endurance."

Mrs. Singh nodded. "Being in a mixed marriage, we've certainly needed strength at times, and we've found elements in both our religions that help us. I think, though, that we are typical of many Canadian couples, and our mixed marriage has been a rich experience for both of us."

"For our parents, too," Mr. Singh added, and both laughed and shook their heads knowingly. "My name means 'lion,'" he continued. "I want to use my strength to be a strong individual, not just a representative of a single religious path. Where I live, there's a large Sikh community, and it would be easy to deal exclusively with people of my own religion and ethnic background. But I want to be more universal, while keeping my religion in my heart."

As we got up to leave and were saying our good-byes, Mr. Singh lifted his arm. "Though I cut my hair and beard, I always wear this." He pulled back the cuff of his long-sleeved shirt and proudly showed me his kara—his steel Sikh bracelet.

Reading A PRAYER FOR PEACE

This modern prayer is by Satish Kumar, a Jain activist and editor of the magazine Resurgence. *Known for his autobiography, called* No Destination, *his primary goals have been international peace and environmental awareness. The prayer that follows is adapted from the Upanishads and is similar to prayers in several religions, including Hinduism and Christianity. It is framed in such a way that people of any religious tradition of belief may say it.*

Lead me from death to life, from falsehood to truth;
lead me from despair to hope, from fear to trust;
lead me from hate to love, from war to peace. Let peace fill our heart, our world, our universe.[6]

TEST YOURSELF

1. In Jainism, the greatest of all _____ was Nataputta Vardhamana, who is usually referred to by the honorary title Mahavira.
   a. buddhas
   b. mahatmas
   c. tirthankaras
   d. priests

2. As a result of his liberating experience, following twelve years of meditation, wandering, and mortification, Mahavira is called a _____. It is the title from which Jainism takes its name.
   a. jiva
   b. devi
   c. singh
   d. jina

3. The Jain goal is to reach a state of _____
   a. total freedom
   b. reincarnation
   c. physical perfection
   d. intellectual greatness

4. One of the five ethical recommendations of Jainism is _____.
   a. ahimsa
   b. dukkha
   c. nakedness
   d. yoga

5. Although Buddhism followed a deliberate path of moderation, Jainism gloried in _____.
   a. the Vedic religion
   b. austerity
   c. the middle way
   d. the priestly class

6. The founder of Sikhism, Guru _____, is recognized as the first in a line of ten Sikh gurus ("spiritual teachers").
   a. Gautama
   b. Singh
   c. Bhakti
   d. Nanak

7. Sikhism was mostly influenced by Hinduism and _____.
   a. Islam
   b. Jainism
   c. Buddhism
   d. Daoism

8. Nanak accepted, as does Hinduism, a belief in reincarnation and _____.
   a. polytheism
   b. atheism
   c. karma
   d. Trimurti

9. Sikhs wear a bracelet of steel, called _____, which symbolizes strength.
   a. kesh
   b. kach
   c. kirpan
   d. kara

10. The primary book of Sikh scripture is the _____, which is believed to contain the living spirit of the ten gurus.
    a. Qur'an
    b. Vedas
    c. Adi Granth
    d. Purvas

11. Consider the following statement: Sallekhana ("holy death") violates the Jain principle of ahimsa because it is an act of violence against oneself. Using examples from the chapter, what points might a follower of Jainism make to argue against this statement?

12. Discuss the similarities and differences between Jainism and Sikhism. What do you think is the most important similarity? What is the most important difference? Use specifics to support your answers.

RESOURCES

Books

Grewal, J. S. *The Sikhs of the Punjab.* Cambridge: Cambridge University Press, 2008. Possibly the most comprehensive and informative single-volume survey of Sikh history and religion currently available.

Long, Jeffery. *Jainism: An Introduction.* London and New York: I. B. Tauris, 2009. A philosophical treatment of the teachings of Jainism.

MacAuliffe, Max Arthur. *The Sikh Religion.* Charleston: Forgotten Books, 2008. The reprint of a classic by an early specialist.

Parikh, Vastupal. *Jainism and the New Spirituality.* Toronto: Peace Publications, 2002. An exploration of Jainism and its connection to peace movements and ecology.

Rankin, Aidan. *The Jain Path: Ancient Wisdom for the West.* Delhi: Saujanya Books, 2007. A book that uses traditional Jain belief and philosophy to call for a new global movement of compassion and interdependence.

Singh, Khushwant. *Sikhs Unlimited.* New Delhi: Rupa, 2008. Meetings with illustrious Sikhs around the world.

Tobias, Michael. *Life Force: The World of Jainism.* Fremont, CA: Jain Publishing, 2000. An introduction to Jainism, as experienced by a Western practitioner interested in ecology.

Film/TV

Around the World in 80 Faiths. (BBC.) An eight-part series that documents eighty sacred rituals across six continents in the space of a single year. Episode six includes a segment on a Sikh ritual honoring the three-hundredth anniversary of the guru Gobind Singh and another segment on Jain ritual in southern India.

Gandhi. (Director Richard Attenborough; Columbia Tristar.) The life of Mahatma Gandhi, who was strongly influenced by Jainism.

Sikhs in America. (Sikh Art and Film Foundation.) An Emmy Award–winning documentary profiling the Sikh community in the United States.

Music/Audio

Dya Singh. *Dukh Bhanjan Tera Naam.* Noble Park, Australia: Advertisingh, 2011. Contemporary versions of Sikh prayers.

Ho Shankheswarwasi. (RajAudio Music.) A compilation of ten Jain devotional chants.

Mehsopuria. *Faith.* London: Primary Records, 2008. Modern songs based on Sikh prayer and Sikh belief.

Religious Music of Asia. (Smithsonian Folkways.) A recording of Asian religious music, including a Jain puja and a Sikh Adi Granth recitation.

SikhNet Gurbani Collection–Volume 1. (SikhNet.com.) A collection of Sikh devotional recordings from around the world.

Internet

All About Sikhs: http://allaboutsikhs.com/. A comprehensive resource portal for Sikhism, including an encyclopedia, list of books, and general information on Sikh gurus, history, way of life, temples, and scriptures.

Jainism: http://www.cs.colostate.edu/~malaiya/-jainlinks.html. A resource that contains links organized by categories, such as "Songs and Prayers," "Vegetarianism and Ahimsa," "Jain Texts," "Jain Pilgrimage," "Jain Images," and "Regional Organizations."

Jainworld: http://www.jainworld.com/. Information on Jain philosophy, societies, education, literature, and temples.

KEY TERMS

Adi Granth (ah'-dee grahnt): "Original collection"; the primary scripture of the Sikhs.

ajiva (uh-jee'-va): Matter without soul or life.

Digambara (di-gam'-ba-ra): "Clothed in sky"; a member of the Jain sect in which monks ideally do not wear clothing.

gurdwara (gur-dwah'-rah): A Sikh temple.

hylozoism: The belief that all physical matter has life and feeling.

Japji (jahp'-jee): A poem by Guru Nanak that begins the Adi Granth; the poem is recited daily by pious Sikhs.

jina (jee'-nah): "Conquerer"; the Jain term for a perfected person who will not be reborn.

jiva (jee'-vah): Spirit, soul, which enlivens matter.

puja (poo'-jah): Ritual in honor of a tirthankara or deity.

sallekhana (sahl-lek-hah'-nuh): "Holy death"; death by self-starvation, valued in Jainism as a noble end to a long life of virtue and detachment.

Shvetambara (shvet-ahm'-bah-rah): "Clothed in white"; a member of the Jain sect in which monks and nuns wear white clothing.

Sikh (seek): "Disciple"; a follower of the Sikh religion.

Sthanakavasi (stun-uk-uh-vuh'-see): "Building person"; a member of a Jain sect that rejects the use of statues and temples.

Terapanthi (teh-ra-pahn'-tee): "Thirteen"; a member of the newest Jain sect.

tirthankara (tihr-tahn'-kah-ruh): "Crossing maker"; in Jainism, one of the twenty-four ideal human beings of the past, Mahavira being the most recent.

RELIGION BEYOND THE CLASSROOM

Visit the Online Learning Center at www.mhhe.com/molloy6e for additional exercises and features, including "Religion beyond the Classroom" and "For Fuller Understanding."

CHAPTER 6

Daoism and Confucianism

F I R S T   E N C O U N T E R

You are in Asia, visiting someone you met two years ago at a
college dance performance. Lin was an exchange student then,
eager to learn about other cultures, and she invited you to visit
her when you could. That time is now. You are staying with her
family.

   "I'll show you one of my favorite places," Lin says, as you climb
into a taxi. She gives the address to the driver, who knows the place
well. You pass along a street bustling with motorcycles, bicycles,
vendors' wagons, and people jaywalking between cars. After fifteen
perilous minutes, you pull up in front of a building with three wide
stairs and high pillars supporting the roof. The stone columns are
carved with writhing dragons. A large metal brazier is in front of
the temple, and from it rises a cloud of incense.

Your friend buys long sticks of incense from a nearby booth and gives some to you.

"Do the same thing I do," she says.

Lin goes to the brazier, lights the incense, lifts the sticks several times, bows, and places the sticks into the brazier. Then she helps you do the same. The people around you watch with great interest. When you are finished, you walk with Lin into the temple.

Just inside the door are two tall, furious-looking golden statues.

"They are guardian gods," Lin says. "They are keeping out bad people."

The interior is amazing. It looks like a golden opera theater. At the back of the sanctuary are several stories of windows with lighted statues inside. More altars are situated against each of the interior walls. In the center of the room are about a dozen large tables, all loaded with offerings: oranges, bananas, watermelons, water lilies, chrysanthemums, and much more.

"The main god of this temple is Mazu," Lin explains. "She was the daughter of a fisherman's family, and she helped her father and brothers when they were in danger of drowning. Mazu has been worshiped for a thousand years. She's popular in China, Taiwan, Vietnam, and other places. The Daoists claim her, but so do others, too."

Lin points out the statues of many other gods, explaining who they are. You stop in front of a circle, which appears to have two large commas inside.

"That is the symbol of the Dao, with yin and yang mixing together," Lin says.

As you walk around, you see a woman throwing what look like two crescents onto the floor.

"She is asking questions," Lin says, "and the wooden pieces that she is throwing tell her 'yes' or 'no' or 'maybe.'"

At last you emerge from the temple and sit together on the stairs in the sunlight. An old lady comes by, guiding her little grandson who is on a red tricycle. A man close to you is selling "spirit money"—paper with gold and silver printing—and three women next to him are selling water lilies from pots, for offering in the temple. Across the street are restaurants, an electronics store, and a motorcycle-repair shop. The street is noisy. Out here it is just another day.

You wonder, who is Mazu? Who are Daoists? What is the Dao? What are yin and yang? And why do the Chinese have so many gods?

BASIC ELEMENTS OF TRADITIONAL CHINESE BELIEFS

Confucianism, Daoism (Taoism*), and Buddhism have been collectively called the Three Doctrines, and together they have had a profound influence on Chinese culture and history. Buddhism, as we saw in Chapter 4, was an

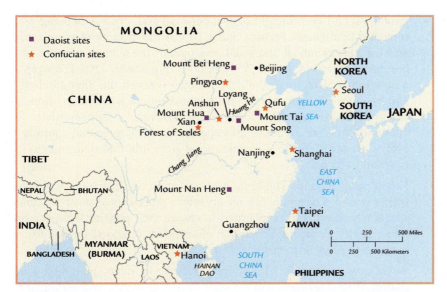

FIGURE 6.1

Daoist and Confucian
religious sites.

import to China, with roots in Indian belief. Confucianism and Daoism, on
the other hand, sprouted and grew up side by side in the soil of indigenous
Chinese belief (see Figure 6.1). We thus begin our study of these two Chinese
religious systems by considering some of the features of traditional Chinese
belief and practice.

Early Chinese belief was a blend of several elements. Some of them,
such as a belief in spirits, can be traced back more than three thousand
years. The following elements provided a basis for later developments in
Chinese religion and were especially important to the development of
Confucianism and Daoism.

> *Spirits* Early Chinese belief thought of spirits as active in every
> aspect of nature and the human world. Good spirits brought health,
> wealth, long life, and fertility. Bad spirits caused accidents and
> disease. Disturbances of nature, such as droughts and earthquakes,
> were punishments from spirits for human failings, but harmony
> could be restored through rituals and sacrifice.
>
> *Tian* During the Shang dynasty (c. 1500–c. 1100 BCE) the omnipotent
> power that was believed to rule the world was called Shang Di

---

*Note: As mentioned earlier, the pinyin system of romanizing Chinese words will be used
in this book, with the older Wade-Giles spellings of important names following their pinyin
versions in parentheses. (Pinyin pronunciation is generally similar to English usage, except
that the pronunciation of *c* is *ts*, *q* is *ch*, and *x* is *sh*.) The pinyin spelling of all Chinese
words is used by the United Nations and is becoming standard in the world of scholarship
and art. The older Wade-Giles spelling of *Taoism*, *Tao*, and *Tao Te Ching* are still common,
but they are now being supplanted by *Daoism*, *Dao*, and *Daodejing* (also spelled *Daode jing*,
Daode Jing, and *Dao De Jing*).

(Shang Ti) and was thought of as a personal god, capable of being contacted by diviners. Perhaps Shang Di was the memory of an ancestor, and the veneration of Shang Di was part of the ancient practice of honoring ancestors. In the Zhou (Chou) dynasty (c. 1100–256 BCE), a new political regime—the Zhou kings—ignored the Shang belief and began explaining life in terms of a different conception, Tian (T'ien), which is usually translated as "Heaven." It appears that Tian was envisioned both as an impersonal divine force that controls events on earth and as a cosmic moral principle that determines right and wrong.

Veneration of ancestors The same cautious reverence that was shown to spirits was also naturally felt for ancestors. Ancestors at death became spirits who needed to be placated to ensure their positive influence on living family members. Veneration of ancestors provided the soil for the growth of Confucianism.

Seeing patterns in nature China's long and mighty rivers, high mountain chains, distinct seasons, and frequent floods, droughts, and earthquakes all influenced the Chinese view of the natural world. To survive, the Chinese people had to learn that while they could not often control nature, they could learn to work with it when they understood its underlying patterns. Some of the patterns were quite easy to discern, such as the progression of the seasons, the paths of the sun and moon, and the cycle of birth and death. Others were more subtle, like the motion of waves and the ripple of mountain ranges, as well as the rhythm of the Dao (which we will discuss shortly) and the alternations of yang and yin. Daoism may be traced back to this concern for finding—and working within—natural patterns.

Yang and yin, symbolized by a circle of light and dark, represent the complementary but opposing forces of the universe that generate all forms of reality.

Yang and yin After about 1000 BCE the Chinese commonly thought that the universe expressed itself in opposite but complementary principles: light and dark, day and night, hot and cold, sky and earth, summer and winter. The list was virtually infinite: male and female, right and left, front and back, up and down, out and in, sound and silence, birth and death. It even came to include "strong foods," such as meat and ginger, and "weak foods," such as fish and rice. The names for the two complementary principles are **yang** and **yin.**

These principles are not the same as good and evil. Yang is not expected to win over the force of yin, or vice versa; rather, the ideal is a dynamic balance between the forces. In fact, the emblem of balance is the yin-yang circle, divided into what look like two intertwined commas. One half is light, representing yang; the other is dark, representing yin. Inside each division is a small dot of the contrasting color that represents the seed of the opposite. The dot suggests that everything contains its opposite and will eventually become its opposite. Both forces are dynamic and in perfect balance as they change, just as day and night are in balance as they progress. We can think of yang and

At the Temple of Heaven, in Beijing, the emperor performed ceremonies to honor Tian ("Heaven").

yin as pulsations or waves of energy, like a heartbeat or like breathing in and out.

Divination Divination is a system that is used for looking into the future. It was an integral part of early Chinese tradition. The oldest technique involved the reading of lines in bones and tortoise shells. Later, an elaborate practice was developed that involves the **Yijing (I Ching)**, the Book of Changes. It is an ancient book that interprets life through an analysis

This hexagram for "contemplation" is made from two trigrams. The lower trigram means "earth," and the upper trigram means "wind."

of hexagrams. A hexagram is a figure of six horizontal lines. There are two kinds of lines: divided (yin) and undivided (yang). A hexagram is made of two trigrams—figures of three lines each.) A hexagram is "constructed" by tossing sticks or coins and writing down the results, beginning with the bottom line. Thus sixty-four different hexagrams are possible. The hexagrams are thought to represent patterns that can develop in one's life, and the Yijing gives an interpretation of each hexagram. With the help of the Yijing, a person can interpret a hexagram as an aid in making decisions about the future.

We now turn to two great systems of Chinese religious thought, Daoism and Confucianism, which many consider to be complementary traditions. Daoism is often thought to emphasize the yin aspects of reality and Confucianism the yang. Together they form a unity of opposites. Although we'll discuss these systems separately, one before the other, separate treatment is something of a fiction. The two systems grew up together and actually, as they developed, helped generate each other. We must keep this in mind as we study them.

Daoism

Because it incorporated some of the previously mentioned elements and many others from traditional Chinese belief and practice, Daoism is really like a shopping cart filled with a variety of items: observations about nature, philosophical insights, guidelines for living, exercises for health, rituals of protection, and practices for attaining longevity and inner purity. We should note, however, that Daoism and Chinese folk religion are not exactly the same thing, although the terms are often used interchangeably, and in some cases the border between the two is not clear.

Daoism includes ideas and practices from the earliest phases, represented in the Daodejing and Zhuangzi (Daoist scriptures, which we'll discuss shortly), as well as innumerable later developments. It was once common to make a distinction between the earliest phase, which was praised for its philosophy, and later ritualistic and religious development, which was less appreciated. But scholars in recent decades have given great attention to a host of Daoist topics: liturgy, lineages of masters, religious communities, monasticism, deities, prayers, art, clothing, and even dance. Scholars see these developments as a part of the organic growth of the early insights. While continuing to value the ideas espoused in the early documents, scholars today point out that the "real" Daoism is the entire spectrum of development, from the earliest ideas to contemporary practices.

THE ORIGINS OF DAOISM

The origins of Daoism, quite appropriately, are mysterious. Its earliest documents contain many threads—shamanism, appreciation for the hermit's life, desire for unity with nature, and a fascination with health, long life, breathing, meditation, and trance. These many threads point to a multiplicity of possible sources, which seem to have coalesced to produce the movement.

Laozi (Lao Tzu)

Every movement needs a founder, and Daoists trace themselves back to a legendary figure named **Laozi (Lao Tzu),** whose name means "old master" or "old child." Whether Laozi ever existed is unknown. He may have been a real person, the blending of historical information about several figures, or a mythic creation.

In the traditional story, Laozi's birth (c. 600 BCE; Timeline 6.1, p. 212) resulted from a virginal conception. According to legend, the child was born old—hence the name "old child." Laozi became a state archivist, or librarian, in the royal city of Loyang for many years. (Legendary stories also relate how Confucius came to discuss philosophy with the old man.) Eventually tiring of his job, Laozi left his post and, carried by an ox, traveled to the far west of China. At the western border, Laozi was recognized as an esteemed scholar and prohibited from crossing until he had written down his teachings. The result was the Daodejing, a short book of about five thousand Chinese characters. After Laozi was finished, he left China, traveling westward. Later stories about Laozi continued to elaborate his myth. He was said to have taken his teachings to India, later returned to China, and ascended into the sky. He was soon treated as a deity, the human incarnation of the Dao. In this capacity he came to be called Lord Lao. Many stories were told of his apparitions. He continues to be worshiped as divine by many Daoists.

The Daodejing

The **Daodejing (Tao Te Ching)** is generally seen as one of the world's greatest books. It is also the great classic of Daoism, accepted by most Daoists as a central scripture. Its title can be translated as "the classical book about the Way and its power." Sometimes the book is also called the Laozi (Lao Tzu), after its legendary author. Possibly because of its brevity and succinctness, it has had an enormous influence on Chinese culture.

The book has been linguistically dated to about 350 BCE, but it seems to have circulated in several earlier forms. In 1972, at the tombs of Mawangdui, archeologists discovered two ancient copies of the text that differ from the arrangement commonly used. Another shorter ancient version was found in a tomb at Guodian in 1993. It contains about one-third of the standard text.[1] The version that is commonly known and used is from the third century CE.

In the eighty-one chapters of the Daodejing, we recognize passages that seem to involve early shamanistic elements, such as reaching trance states and attaining invulnerability (see chapters 1, 16, 50, and 55). The book shows

TIMELINE 6.1

Period of legendary ● Laozi (Lao Tzu)	c. 600–500 BCE	
	c. 551–479 BCE	● Life of Confucius
Life of Mozi (Mo Tzu) ●	c. 470–391 BCE	
	c. 371–289 BCE	● Life of Mencius
Life of Zhuangzi (Chuang Tzu) ●	c. 369–286 BCE	
	c. 350 BCE	● Creation of the Daodejing (Tao Te Ching)
Life of Xunzi (Hsün Tzu) ●	c. 298–238 BCE	
	c. 630 CE	● The ordering of all provinces of China to conduct regular services in honor of Confucius
Life of Zhu Xi (Chu Hsi) ●	1130–1200	
	1445	● Publication of the Daoist canon
Life of Wang Yangming ●	1472–1529	
	1949	● Communist takeover of China, repression of religion
Discovery at Mawangdui of two ancient versions of the Daodejing ● and one version of the Yijing	1972–1974	
	c. 1982	● Revival of Daoism in China
Discovery at Guodian of the oldest-known version ● of the Daodejing, written on bamboo and dated about 300 BCE	1993	
	2004	Founding of the First Confucius ● Institute

Timeline of significant events in the history of Daoism and Confucianism.

some repetition, has no clear order, and exhibits a deliberate lack of clarity. In form, each chapter is more poetry than prose. This combination of elements suggests that the book is not the work of a single author but is rather the assembled work of many people, gathered over time. It may be a collection of what were once oral proverbs and sayings.

What was the original purpose of the book? One theory holds that its overall purpose was political, that it was meant as a handbook for rulers; another sees it primarily as a religious guidebook, meant to lead adherents to spiritual insight; and still another views it as a practical guide for living in harmony with the universe. It is possible that the Daodejing fulfilled all these purposes and that its passages can have several meanings at the same time. Part of the genius of the book is its brevity and use of paradox: its meaning depends on who is interpreting it.

Throughout the Daodejing are references to the **Dao.** The book speaks of its nature and operation; it describes the manner in which people will live if they are in harmony with the Dao; and it gives suggestions for experiencing the Dao. The book also provides images to help describe all of these things. What, though, is "the Dao"?

The Daodejing begins famously by saying that the Dao is beyond any description. It states that the Dao that can be spoken of is not the eternal Dao. In other words, we cannot really put into words exactly what the Dao is—a fact that is ironic because the book itself uses words. Yet the book goes on to tell us that the Dao is "nameless"; that is, it is not any individual thing that has a name, such as a *door,* a *tree,* a *bird,* a *person.* The Dao cannot be named because it has no form. But the Dao *can* be experienced and followed by every individual thing that has a name. The Daodejing says the Dao is the origin of everything and that all individual things are "manifestations" of the Dao.

Although the Dao is the origin of nature, it is not "God," because it does not have personality. It neither cares about human beings nor dislikes them—it only produces them, along with the rest of nature. Because the Dao makes nature move the way it does, it can be called the way or the rhythm of nature.

To experience the Dao, we must leave behind our desires for individual things, a concept that runs counter to everyday concerns—how much something costs, what time it is now, whether something is big or small. In fact, the Daoist way of seeing things is so odd to some people that at first it seems like trying to see in the dark, as the end of the first chapter of the Daodejing describes:

> Darkness within darkness.
> The gate to all mystery.

The Daoist sees things differently. To illustrate, there is an intriguing example in the twentieth chapter of the Daodejing: A Daoist is observing a group of people who are in a park, celebrating a holiday. They all seem happy as they climb up to the top of a terrace where a ceremony will occur. They appear to know what they are doing and where they are going. Not the Daoist, though, who feels "formless" and "like the ocean"—adrift.[2] The Daoist is troubled by the contrast. The others seem happy and sure of themselves, but the Daoist can only watch, and feels strangely like an outsider. Then the chapter ends with a sudden,

Laozi, the "father of Daoism," is here portrayed riding on an ox.

extraordinary affirmation. The Daoist recognizes something intensely personal and difficult but willingly accepts the sense of separateness from the others and from their conventional way of seeing things. The Daoist accepts, and concludes,

> I am different.
> I am nourished by the great mother.

Thus, the Dao cannot be "known" in the same way that we see a car or hear a sound, for example. It cannot be perceived directly but rather by intuition. Perhaps it is like the difference between only hearing musical sounds and recognizing a song.

The Daodejing presents several powerful images wherein the Dao seems most active and visible. Contemplating them can help us experience the Dao, and by taking on some of the qualities of these images, we begin to live in harmony with the Dao that inhabits them. Several common images follow:

Water Water is gentle, ordinary, and lowly, but strong and necessary. It flows around every obstacle. Chapter eight of the Daodejing praises it: "The highest good is like water."[3] It assists all things "and does not compete with them."[4]

Deeper Insights

THE SEASONS OF LIFE

A famous story illustrates what it means to live in harmony with nature: Upon hearing of the death of Zhuangzi's wife, a friend, Huizi (Hui Tzu), goes to offer sympathy. Although he expects to find Zhuangzi crying and in ritual mourning, Huizi finds Zhuangzi instead singing and drumming on a bowl. Huizi is shocked—and says so. Responding in a thoughtful way, Zhuangzi says that at first his wife's death saddened him terribly, but then he reflected on the whole cycle of her existence. Before his wife was a human being, she was without shape or life, and her original self was a part of the formless substance of the universe. Then she became a human being. "Now there's been another change, and she's dead. It's just like the progression of the four seasons, spring, summer, fall, winter."[5] When winter comes, we do not mourn. That would be ungrateful. Similarly, a human being goes through seasons. Zhuangzi describes his wife as now being like someone asleep in a vast room. "If I were to follow after her bawling and sobbing, it would show that I don't know anything about fate. So I stopped."[6]

In this story, note that Zhuangzi is singing and playing on a bowl. Rather than mourn passively, he does something to counteract his sorrow. His singing is a profound human response, quite believable. And Zhuangzi does not say that as a result of his insight he no longer feels sad. Rather, he says that as far as mourning is concerned, "I stopped." In other words, despite his feelings, he deliberately behaves in a way that seems more grateful to the universe and therefore more appropriate than mourning.

This tale suggests that to live in harmony with nature means to accept all its transformations. The great Dao produces both yang and yin, which alternate perpetually. The story says that yin and yang are our parents and we must obey them. If we cannot embrace the changes, we should at least observe them with an accepting heart.

Woman The female is sensitive, receptive, yet effective and powerful.

Child The child is full of energy, wonder, and naturalness.

Valley The valley is yin, and it is mystery.

Darkness Darkness can be safe, full of silence and possibility.

Zhuangzi (Chuang Tzu)

Daoism was enriched by the work of **Zhuangzi (Chuang Tzu),** who was active about 300 BCE. What we know of him comes from the writings he left behind. His personality seems playful, independent, and in love with the fantastic. The book of his writings, called the Zhuangzi (Chuang Tzu), is composed of seven "inner chapters," which are thought to be by the author himself, and twenty-six "outer chapters," whose authorship is less certain.

The Zhuangzi, unlike the poetry of the Daodejing, contains many whimsical stories. It continues the themes of early Daoist thought, such as the need for harmony with nature, the movement of the Dao in all that happens, and the pleasure that we can gain from simplicity. It underscores the inevitability of change and the relativity of all human judgments. It also adds to Daoism an appreciation for humor—something that is quite rare in the scriptures of the world.

Perhaps the most famous of all the stories in the book tells of Zhuangzi's dream of being a butterfly. In his dream he was flying around and enjoying life, but he did not know that he was Zhuangzi. When he woke up he was struck by a question: Am I a person dreaming that I am a butterfly, or am I a butterfly dreaming that I am a person? This story hints that the boundary between reality and the imaginary is not really as clear as we might think.

Another story makes fun of people's judgments and the arbitrariness of their joy and anger. A trainer gave his monkeys three acorns in the morning and four at night. When the monkeys conveyed their dissatisfaction with receiving too few acorns in the morning, the trainer obliged, giving them four acorns in the morning and three at night. As a result, "the monkeys were all delighted."[7]

The Zhuangzi rejects every barrier, including that between the ordinary and the fantastic, between the normal and the paranormal, as hinted by the story of the butterfly dream. But the love of the marvelous really shows itself best in some stories that talk of the supernatural powers that a wise person can attain. The Zhuangzi tells of an exceptional person who could tell everything about one's past and future, another who could ride on the wind, and another who was invulnerable to heat or pain. The Zhuangzi thus elaborates the potential results of being one with the Dao.

BASIC EARLY TEACHINGS

The main teachings of the Daodejing and the Zhuangzi can be summarized as follows:

Dao This is the name for whatever mysterious reality makes nature to be what it is and to act the way it does. The Chinese character for *Dao* is commonly translated as "way," but it has also been translated as "existence," "pattern," and "process." Primarily, the Dao is the way that nature expresses itself—the natural way. Human beings can unite themselves with the Dao in the way they live.

Wu wei: the ideal of effortlessness To have stern commandments would go against the nature of Daoism; but it does offer recommendations about how to live—recommendations that do not come from a divine voice but from nature, the model of balance and harmony. The recommendation most often mentioned in the Daodejing is **wu wei,** which literally means "no action." Perhaps a better translation is "no strain" or "effortlessness." The ideal implies the avoidance of unnecessary action or action that is not spontaneous. If we look at nature, we notice that many things happen quietly, effortlessly: plants grow, birds and animals are born, and nature repairs itself after a storm. Nature works to accomplish only what is necessary, but no more. Consider the plain strength of the ordinary bird nest. Birds build homes according to their needs, and what they make is simple and beautiful; they don't require circular driveways, pillars, or marbled entryways. The ideal of "no strain" is the antithesis of all those sweat-loving mottoes such as "No pain, no gain" and "Onward and upward."

The boatman who goes with the river's flow is an example of wu wei in practice.

Simplicity Daoism has often urged its followers to eliminate whatever is unnecessary and artificial and to appreciate the simple and the apparently ordinary. In this regard, Daoists have tended to distrust any highly formal education, owing to its inherent complexity and artificiality. (This was one of their major complaints against the Confucians, who put so much trust in education.) In a passage that has delighted students for centuries, the Daodejing in the twentieth chapter states its opinion: "Give up learning, and put an end to your troubles."

Gentleness Because Daoists pursue the gentle way, they hate weapons and war. The wise person loves peace and restraint and avoids all unnecessary violence. The wise person "does not regard weapons as lovely things. For to think them lovely means to delight in them, and to delight in them means to delight in the slaughter of men."[8]

Relativity People see things from a limited point of view that is based on their own concerns. They see things in terms of divisions: I-you, good-bad, expensive-cheap, valuable-worthless, beautiful-ugly, and so forth. Daoists believe that it is necessary to attain a vision of things that goes beyond these apparent opposites.

DAOISM AND THE QUEST FOR LONGEVITY

Daoism has absorbed many practices that are thought to bring a person into union with the Dao. These practices help the person feel the flow of nature, attain spiritual purity, and live a long life.

To use the word *yoga* to describe Daoist exercises could be misleading, because *yoga* is a Sanskrit word. But this word is useful for conveying to nonspecialists the physical aspect of Daoism. The canon of Daoist literature includes recommendations for many types of arm and body movements, breathing regulation, diet, and massage. Today, several popular physical disciplines continue this interest. Most influential is *taiji* (*t'ai chi*), a series of slow arm and leg motions thought to aid balance and circulation. An astounding sight in the early morning in China is to see hundreds of people doing taiji exercises in the parks. The spectacle looks like ballet in graceful slow motion.

One "yogic" practice is called *internal alchemy.* It aims at transforming and spiritualizing the life force (**qi, ch'i**) of the practitioner. Some later forms of internal alchemy teach exercises that move the life force from its origin at the base of the spine upward to the head. From there it circles back, via the heart, to its origin. This movement is accomplished through certain postures, muscular exercises, and practices of mental imagery. Some Daoists have held that these techniques of internal alchemy can create an entity—the "immortal embryo"—that can survive the death of the body.

In ancient China, some people experimented with physical alchemy, hoping to create an elixir that could extend life and even make a person immortal. Because gold did not rust, individuals attempted to make gold either into a drinkable liquid or into a vessel from which an elixir could be drunk. Jade, pearl, mother-of-pearl, and compounds of mercury were also utilized. Some people undoubtedly died as a result of these experiments. When there seemed to be little success in this direction, the alchemical search became a metaphor for the development of the type of internal alchemy just described. In Chinese culture there remains, however, a great interest in pills, foods, and medicines that are believed to prolong life. Some of these (such as ginseng, garlic, and ginger) seem to have genuine medical benefits.

THE DEVELOPMENT OF DAOISM

Early Daoism was not an "organized religion." Many of its earliest practitioners lived alone, as some still do today. The reclusive lifestyle of the hermit dates back to ancient China, and some chapters of the Daodejing may have emerged from that way of life.

As time went on, however, the movement took on many organized forms. Elements of Daoism appealed to individuals and groups interested in achieving a variety of goals. Among their aims were longevity, supernatural abilities, control over disease, social reform, political control, and spiritual insight. Because of the wide-ranging interests within Daoism and its capacity to easily form new groups, there emerged over centuries a multitude of sects, branches, and religious communities. Their power waxed and waned, depending on their ability to maintain themselves and on the interest of current rulers. (For example, Daoism reached perhaps its lowest point of influence in 1281, when the emperor commanded that Daoist books be burned.) Among the many organizations that developed, two proved to be particularly long-lived and influential. Both still exist today.

One is an ancient organization called the Way of the Heavenly Masters (or Celestial Masters; Tianshi, T'ien-shih). The organization traces itself back to a second-century teacher, Zhang Daoling (Chang Tao-ling), who was believed to have had visions of Laozi. Zhang Daoling is thought to have developed an organization that helped Daoism survive into the present. Control of the organization is based on a hereditary model, with power usually passing from father to son to grandson. The heads of the organization have the title of Heavenly Masters. The organization set up a system of parishes. It is strong in Taiwan and has come to life again, after severe repression by the Communist government, on the mainland.

The second persistent form of organized Daoism involved monasteries and related groups of celibate monks and nuns. Although this form of Daoism was also suppressed in the early days of the Communist government, it has resumed in mainland China, though under careful governmental control. This monastic order is known as the Way of Complete Perfection (Quanshen, Ch'üan-chen). It deliberately has blended elements

At the end of a family's annual ceremony to honor its ancestors, red-robed Daoist priests conduct participants to the offering table. Venerating one's ancestors is a key element of Chinese religions.

of Daoism, Buddhism, and Confucianism. Its principal prayer book was reprinted in 2000. Morning and evening services that make use of the prayer book may be attended at many of its monasteries—most notably at the White Cloud Monastery (Baiyunguan) in Beijing.

One of the stimuli that influenced Daoism to take an organizational path was Buddhism, which entered China in the first century CE. Buddhism was brought by a monastic clergy who set up monasteries and temples that had impressive rites. Daoism followed these models in its own development. By the fifth century CE, Daoism had grown into an organization with significant political influence.

Daoism also imitated Buddhism in its production of a vast number of sacred books with wide-ranging topics: guidebooks on meditation, breathing exercises, and sexual yoga; stories of wonderworkers and of ecstatic excursions made to the stars; recipes for longevity and magical powers; manuals of alchemy; and descriptions of ritual. A small sample of titles conveys the flavor of Daoism: Scripture of Wondrous Beginning, Scripture of Great Simplicity, Like unto a Dragon, Wondrous Scripture of Inner Daily Practice,

Pillowbook Scripture, Biographies of Spirit Immortals, The Yellow Court Scripture, and Scripture on Going beyond the World. A collection of more than a thousand authoritative books was gathered and makes up the Daoist canon (Daozang, Tao Tsang). A major edition of the canon was published in 1445, but supplements continued to be added later.

Daoism developed a pantheon of hundreds of deities. Some are powers of the universe; others are people who became immortal; others are ancestral spirits. The deities include Laozi, spirits of nature, protective household gods, deified historical figures, and many others. Most important are the Three Purities (Sanjing, San Ching). These constitute a Daoist trinity (probably modeled on the Buddhist notion of the three bodies of the Buddha). The first of the Three Purities is the primordial Dao; the second, a deity responsible for transmission of Daoist insight, is called the Heavenly Worthy of Numinous Treasure; and the third is the deified Laozi, whose image may be recognized by its white hair. Several female deities are important. Among them are Mother Li, the mother of Lord Lao; Mazu (mentioned earlier), a deified girl who has become the patroness of fishermen; Doumu, a star deity called Mother of the Big Dipper; and the Queen Mother of the West, who is a mother figure responsible for all the immortals. The Jade Emperor, an ancient legendary figure, is thought of as an emperor who rules heaven and earth and who judges people's deeds at the end of each year.

Other commonly worshiped gods are household gods, such as the gods of the hearth and the doorway, and gods of the sky, earth, water, and town. Worship is also given to regional deities and to the spirits of ancestors. Daoist temples represent many of these gods with statues and paintings, and offerings of food, water, and incense are regularly placed in front of the images.

Daoism is strong in Taiwan, Hong Kong, and in overseas Chinese communities, such as in Malaysia and Singapore. After initially being repressed by the Communist Party, Daoism is experiencing a resurgence on the mainland. A large statue of Laozi was erected in 1999 in southeastern China, and pilgrims from Taiwan and elsewhere routinely travel to the mainland to honor the goddess Mazu at her pilgrimage site, Meizhou Island in southeast China.

In Chinese temples, it is not unusual to encounter entranced shamans and their followers. Some temples try to keep shamans away with warning signs.

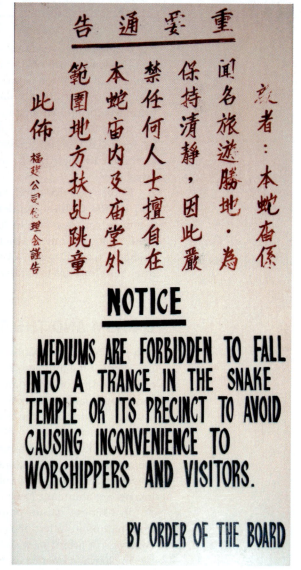

重雲通告

窓者：本蛇廟係
聞名旅遊勝地。為
保持清靜，因此嚴
禁任何人士擅自在
本蛇廟內及廟堂外
範圍地方扶乩跳童
此佈

福建公司總理仝謹告

NOTICE

MEDIUMS ARE FORBIDDEN TO FALL INTO A TRANCE IN THE SNAKE TEMPLE OR ITS PRECINCT TO AVOID CAUSING INCONVENIENCE TO WORSHIPPERS AND VISITORS.

BY ORDER OF THE BOARD

Deeper Insights

THE CHINESE GARDEN—BRIDGE TO THE INFINITE

The philosopher Wing-Tsit Chan has written of the semireligious role that a Chinese garden can play:

Nature is never looked upon by the Chinese as chaotic or disorganized. Heaven and earth co-exist in harmony, and the four seasons run their course regularly. . . . This harmony of man and nature in the flow of the great stream of rhythm makes the Chinese garden more than something merely secular. It is true that no one would look upon the Chinese garden as a religious structure. . . . But in spite of all this, we cannot deny the fact that the garden is regarded as an ideal place for meditation. Meditation may be purely moral, an effort at self-introspection. Intense and sincere meditation, however, inevitably leads to the absorption in the Infinite.[9]

Because of government support on the mainland for Complete Perfection Daoism, many of its temples and monasteries are being rebuilt, particularly in traditional mountain locations. Heavenly Master Daoism is also growing on the mainland. It was never suppressed in Taiwan and is the major form of ritualized village Daoism. Its clergy do ministerial work, attending to the needs of the public. Exorcists, who are often identified by their red hats or scarves, work to heal and restore harmony. Priests, identified by their black caps, primarily perform blessings, funerals, and other rites.

Daoist practices and beliefs are kept alive not only by Daoists but also by the Chinese tendency to blend beliefs of several systems. It is common, for example, to find Daoist images in Buddhist temples. In the mind of most Chinese, there need be no argument. In ordinary practice, elements from Daoism, Confucianism, and Buddhism are combined. The three religions are mutually supportive—as their members have generally agreed.

DAOISM AND THE ARTS

It is possible to see Daoist influences in many Chinese art forms, although the extent of the influence is impossible to determine with precision. Paintings of Laozi riding on an ox are clear examples of Daoist influence, as are references to Zhuangzi in poetry, but beyond that it is perhaps more accurate to say that poetry and the arts share many of the same concerns of Daoist thought—just as they do of Chinese Buddhist and Confucian thought.

As we know, the immensity, flow, and mystery of nature are common themes in the Daodejing, and some of the book's most important images are flowing water, the valley, and the uncarved block of stone. These themes and images are abundant in Chinese painting.

In Chinese nature painting, perspective is important. Images drawn from nature are often presented either very close up or at a great distance. Paintings of a bird or a stalk of bamboo seen close-up help the viewer see the mysterious energy at work in these nonhuman forms of life: a bird

This scroll, though painted in Hangzhou in 1953, includes many classic elements of Daoist painting—mountains, bamboo groves, streams, and waterfalls. As its inscription suggests, the scroll expresses the notion that mountains and clouds bring perfection.

Chinese gardens unite natural and constructed elements to produce a sense of harmony between human beings and nature.

The garden is more than the supplement to the house. It fulfills a higher function of life, the function that only art can fulfill.

—Wing-Tsit Chan[10]

perches in a certain way on a branch, and a stalk of bamboo emerges in its own special way into the sunshine. These paintings make us look more closely at the humbler elements of nature—cats, rabbits, birds, deer—and recognize that they, too, have their own interests and patterns of living and that our human patterns are only a small part of the much wider repertory of nature.

The great genius of Chinese nature painting is particularly evident in the paintings of landscapes seen at a distance. These paintings often depict hints of mountains far away and, beyond them, infinite space. Some portray a person gazing far into the distance, even beyond the painting itself. What we most notice in these works is the fascinating use of empty space. Some of the paintings are almost half empty, but they do not feel unfinished, as if something were missing. Ma Yuan (c. 1160–c. 1225) was a master of this effect. In his painting entitled *A Scholar and His Servant on a Terrace*, a gentleman looks out past pine branches into the distance; the upper left half of the painting, in the direction of the man's gaze, is entirely empty. In his painting *Walking on a Mountain Path in Spring*, a man strolls into an emptiness—virtually the entire right side of the painting—inhabited only by one small bird. The space of the paintings is the positive emptiness to which the Daodejing draws our attention.

Chinese poetry frequently praises themes also found in the Daodejing and the Zhuangzi: the joy of life in the countryside, away from the complications of the city; the change of seasons; simplicity; and harmony with nature. The poet who is often praised for his fine expression of

Daoist ideals was Li Bai (also spelled Li Bo and Li Po). He lived during the Tang dynasty and died about 762 CE. Little is known about his life, but his death is famous. According to tradition, he died as the result of a poetic accident. Sitting drunk in a boat one night, Li Bai reached out to embrace the moon's reflection on the water, but he fell in and disappeared beneath the surface. One of his poems is about Zhuangzi's dream of being a butterfly. Another is about Li Bai's being so absorbed in nature that he did not notice dusk coming on; when he stood up at last, flower petals fell off his clothes. His poems are so highly regarded that they have been memorized and recited by the Chinese for centuries to express their own deepest feelings.

Chinese garden design is an art form that complements and completes Chinese architecture. The house is yang, the realm of the square and the straight line; the garden is yin, the realm of the circle and the curve. Inside is family harmony; outside is harmony with nature. One realm supports the other. Chinese garden design differs from that of common Western design. Instead of straight lines and symmetry, walkways meander, and bridges may zigzag. Gates, in imitation of the moon, may be round. And water moves in its natural manner—that is, not upward, as in a fountain, but only gently down.

The serpentine form pictured here is a classical Chinese "poetry stream." Wine-sipping gentlemen challenged one another to compose a complete poem in the time it took a wine cup to float from the beginning of the stream to its end.

The rooflines of this temple in Southeast Asia reflect Chinese traditions.

DAOISM AND THE MODERN WORLD

Daoism may be expected to regain much of its earlier standing. Because it has never been suppressed in Taiwan, Hong Kong, or overseas communities of Chinese, it will remain strong there, and its only challenge will come from the secularizing forces of the contemporary world. On the Chinese mainland, as we have seen, there are many indications of a revival. In mainland China, Daoist temples are being rebuilt, often with financial aid from abroad, and Daoist temples may now be found at many traditional mountain sites, in urban locations, and in villages. Daoist pilgrimage seems to be reviving—particularly in southeastern China, probably because of its geographical proximity to travelers from Taiwan.

As scholars increasingly bring attention to Daoism, the presence of female imagery and themes is becoming more widely known. The Daodejing speaks of the value of nurturing and the role of the mother, calling the Dao "the mother of all things." Several major deities are female, as noted above. Historians have also come to realize the role that historical women have played in Daoism. Women have become Daoist nuns, teachers, and matriarchs. Women have also become Daoist priests. And many of the important symbols of Daoism are suggestive of the female, including the cave, the valley, flowing water, and the flaming pearl. These continue to influence the world of architecture and art.

In world culture, Daoist ideas such as those found in the Daodejing and the Zhuangzi continue to spread their influence. (After the Bible, the Daodejing is the world's most frequently translated book.) Daoist art and ritual are gaining increased attention as a result of recent museum exhibitions, particularly

Deeper Insights

DAOISM AND NATURE

Daoism seems to have begun as part of early Chinese attempts to understand the movements of nature. Over the many centuries of its existence, Daoism has created a body of literature, complex ritual, and a well-developed way of looking at the world. At the heart of all these lies appreciation for the forces of yin and yang, which are constantly active in the workings of seasonal change, planting and harvesting, and all forms of life.

Daoism encourages human understanding of nature's movement, so that there can be harmony between human beings and the rest of nature. Daoism encourages human beings to be simple and egoless. It promotes health through meditation, exercise, contemplation of nature, and living in a harmonious environment.

A Daoist statement of religious belief, made by the Chinese Daoist Association, summarizes these ideals.

It points out that the Daodejing states that Heaven follows the Dao and the Dao follows what is natural (chapter 25). Therefore, human beings, who must follow the way of nature, must value the earth.

We can see how Daoist ideals match well with those of the environmental movement, which also recommends human restraint, harmony, and care for the natural world. But Daoists have begun practical steps to express their ideals. At Taibaishan, for example, they have created the first temple of ecology. There they hold workshops to promote their vision. A group called the Temple Alliance on Ecology Education has helped create the Qinling Declaration. Members who sign the statement promise to use their temples for ecological education, farm their lands sustainably, protect water resources, protect species, and care for forests.

through the work of the Art Institute of Chicago and the Asian Art Museum of San Francisco. And contemporary scholars of Daoism, by shedding light on actual Daoist practice, are introducing Daoism to a wider public.

Confucianism

Daoism, as we just saw, seeks to bring human beings into union with the Dao, particularly through imitating certain qualities in nature—its harmony, lack of strain, and flowing mystery. The complex of ideals and beliefs that helped give shape to Laozi's teachings also influenced Confucius, the major teacher of the second great Chinese school of thought. Thus, it is not surprising to find Confucianism as concerned with the Dao as Daoism is; as one Confucian classic says, "He is the sage who naturally and easily embodies the right *way*."[11] This "way" is the cosmic Dao that permeates the entire universe—the Dao that we see in the everyday life of the noble person also "in its utmost reaches . . . shines brightly through heaven and earth."[12]

THE DAO IN CONFUCIANISM

There is a difference, however, between Daoist and Confucian notions of the Dao. For Confucians, the Dao of primary interest is the Dao within the *human* world, manifested in "right" relationships and in a harmonious society. It was social harmony that Confucius described when he listed his particular wishes:

The Master said, "At fifteen, I had my mind bent on learning. At thirty, I stood firm. At forty, I had no doubts. At fifty, I knew the decrees of Heaven. At sixty, my ear was an obedient organ for the reception of truth. At seventy, I could follow what my heart desired, without transgressing what was right."

—from the Confucian Analects[14]

"[In] regard to the aged, to give them rest; in regard to friends, to show them sincerity; in regard to the young, to treat them tenderly."[13]

In Daoism, everything is a part of the rhythm of nature—the Dao. In Confucianism, however, although birds and clouds and trees are what they should be, human beings do not automatically become what they should be. The sweet, spontaneous infant can quickly turn into the selfish child. The Confucian would say that training in virtue is necessary in order to enable the Dao to manifest itself clearly in the human being.

The Doctrine of the Mean, an important Confucian text (discussed later in this chapter), recommends several types of training, including training in the cultivation of personal equilibrium and harmony. We should recall that the Daoist ideal of the Daodejing warns against such "training," feeling that formal education has a potential for distorting one's originally pure state. Confucians, however, hold that the best training does not contaminate character but, by cultivating virtues, gives it definition and clarity.

THE LIFE OF CONFUCIUS

Confucius was born about 551 BCE, at a time when China was not a single empire but a group of small kingdoms. His name was Kong Qiu (K'ung Ch'iu). He later became known by the title of Kong Fuzi (K'ung Fu Tzu), meaning "Master Kong," but he is known in the West by the Latin version of his name, which was created and spread by European Catholic missionaries.

Tradition relates that Confucius was from a once-noble family that had fled at a time of political danger to the state of Lu (south of present-day Beijing). His father died when Confucius was a child, and despite their poverty, his mother raised him as an educated gentleman. He enjoyed chariot riding, archery, and playing the lute. In his teens, he became seriously interested in pursuing scholarship. He is said to have held a minor government post as tax collector, probably to support his mother and his studies. His mother died when he was in his late teens, and he entered into a state of mourning. When the period of mourning was over, he began his public life as a teacher.

Despite his eventual success as a teacher, Confucius had always wanted to play an influential part in government, and it is possible that for a time (c. 500–496 BCE)

Images of Confucius are found in many Chinese temples throughout Southeast Asia.

he became a government minister. Confucius married and is believed to have had a son and a daughter. He lived for about fifteen years outside of his home state but eventually returned to Lu to take a somewhat ceremonial post as senior advisor. He died about 479 BCE.

LIVING ACCORDING TO CONFUCIAN VALUES

The period in which Confucius was born was a time of social turmoil because of the disintegration of the feudal system. Seeing families and individuals suffering from the social disorder, Confucius concluded that society would function properly only if virtues were taught and lived.

The ideals of Confucius were two: he wanted to produce "excellent" individuals who could be social leaders, and he wanted to create a harmonious society. He believed that these ideals were complementary: excellent individuals would keep society harmonious, and a harmonious society would nurture excellent individuals.

Confucius believed that each human being is capable of being good, refined, and even great; but he differed from the Daoists because he was convinced that a human being cannot achieve those qualities in isolation. In his view, a human being becomes a full person only through the contributions of other people and through fulfilling one's obligations to them. These other people include parents, teachers, friends, aunts and uncles, grandparents, ancestors, and even government ministers.

Confucius also believed that more than social interaction (which even animals have) is needed to achieve personal excellence. For Confucius, that "more" is what makes *ordinary* human beings into *excellent* human beings,

Twice yearly during the spring and autumn equinoxes, South Korea hosts a solemn ceremony to honor the Chinese philosopher Confucius and other eminent Confucian scholars of China and Korea.

Deeper Insights

THE IDEAL HUMAN BEING

Confucianism is often thought of as a system for the regulation of social groups. Yet Confucianism is also a system for the transformation of the individual. Undergirding Confucianism is not just the ideal of an orderly society but also the ideal of a perfect human being.

This perfect person is the **junzi (chün tzu)**—a term usually translated as "superior person," although a better translation may be "noble person." The following quotations give a sense of the virtue that guides the junzi—the person who shows humanity at its best. In such a noble human being the Confucian ideals have been inculcated since childhood, and the virtues have been practiced for so long that the whole Confucian manner of relating to the world has become completely natural. The "noble person," as Alfred Bloom nicely describes, is

> distinguished by his faithfulness, diligence, and modesty. He neither overpowers with his knowledge, nor is afraid to admit error. He looks at all sides of any issue, is cautious and not concerned for personal recognition. Carrying himself with dignity, he appears imperturbable, resolute, and simple. He is exemplary in filial piety and generous with his kin. In his relations with others he looks for good points, though he is not uncritical. As a leader, he knows how to delegate responsibility and when to pardon or promote. He is sensitive to the feelings and expressions of others.[15]

A subtle portrait of such a person is given by George Kates, who describes the man who became his personal tutor in China. Kates writes about the civilized manner that manifested itself in all his tutor's actions, even in the cultivated way the tutor entered a room and sat in a chair. The tutor, Mr. Wang,

> had contrived to make his humdrum life, composed of a daily routine of monotonous teaching and domestic privation, symmetrical and reasonable indeed. . . . His eyes were kind; and his glance could at times glow when some new thought would catch and hold him. His side-face made you like him. . . . He . . . remained closed and therefore secure, if only because he knew so well by indirection how to turn aside effectively any indiscreet remark or lolloping conduct on the part of some new and immature pupil. . . . When Mr. Wang became assured that we thus had the same sense of decorum, barriers fell. Yet I remained more unwilling than ever now to press in upon his carefully guarded privacies; and upon this base we built a tranquil relation, partial it is true, but one that lasted us peaceably through many years. He became my formal teacher.[16]

"superior persons." What constitutes that "more"? What are the sources of human excellence?

According to Confucius, excellence comes partly from the cultivation of an individual's virtues and intellect. Thus, education is essential. We should recognize, though, that for Confucius education meant more than knowledge; it also involved the development of skills in poetry, music, artistic appreciation, manners, and religious ritual. Confucius valued education because it transmitted the lessons of the past into the present. He believed that much of the wisdom required to produce excellent human beings is already expressed in the teachings of the great leaders of the past. Convinced that the past provides fine models for the present, Confucius thought that education could show the way to wise and happy living.

Moreover, Confucius saw civilization as a complicated and fragile creation; because of this, he believed that civilized human beings must be full of respect and care. Care must be given to the young, who will continue human life on earth, and to the elders, who teach and pass on the traditions. There should be reverence for everything valuable that has been brought from earlier generations.

Confucius's idea of a perfect society was one in which every member of society would be cared for and protected, and no one would feel abandoned. (Contrast this with modern industrial society; in a city full of people, an individual can feel utterly alone.) Confucius believed that a perfect society could come about if people played their social roles properly. His sense of social responsibility was codified in the five great relationships.

The Five Great Relationships

In Confucianism, relationships are just as real as any visible object. Human beings are not merely individuals. They are also interwoven threads of relationships with many people. To a great extent, in Confucian thinking human beings *are* their relationships.

All relationships, however, are not equal. The level of a relationship may be determined by personal factors, such as friendship or family connection, or by more formal social factors, such as age or social status. Confucianism recognizes this inequality and actually lists relationships according to a hierarchy, beginning with the most important:

1. *Father-son* Family is the foundation of society for Confucians, with the relationship between father and son at its core. This relationship also represents all parent-child relationships. Parents must be responsible for the education and moral formation of their children. The children must be respectful and obedient to their parents, and they must care for them in their old age. Confucianism has extended this parental role in ways that some people in more individualistic societies today might not appreciate; for example, the parents are expected to help in the selection of a career and a marriage partner for each child. But the relationship of obligation is mutual: parents and children must show care for each other. The obligation of mutual care does not end upon death; even after their parents' death, children are expected to honor their parents' memory, especially by venerating photos of them at a home altar and by maintaining their graves. The parent-child relationship is considered so fundamental that it often functions as the model for all similar relationships, such as those between boss and employee and between teacher and student.

2. *Elder brother–younger brother* Languages such as English, French, and Spanish do not distinguish between an elder brother and a younger brother. But the Chinese, Korean, Vietnamese, and Japanese languages— which all have been strongly influenced by Confucian thought—have different words for the two kinds of brothers. In their cultures, the distinction is important. An elder brother must assume responsibility for raising the younger siblings, and the younger siblings must be compliant. The practicality of this arrangement becomes clear when we appreciate the possibility of an elderly father dying before all his children have been raised. The paternal responsibility then would shift to the eldest son, who has a unique status in the family.

The hierarchy of relationships governs the responsibilities between and among individuals. The responsibilities of family members, especially of children for their elders, are significant, and sometimes the duties can be problematic.

3. *Husband-wife* Each person in this relationship is responsible for the other's care. In Confucian thought, the relationship is hierarchical. The husband is an authoritative protector, and the wife is a protected homemaker and mother. The Confucian notion of marriage also implies much less romantic expectation than does the modern Western notion; in Confucian societies wives, over time, can even become quite motherly toward their husbands.

4. *Elder-younger* All older people have responsibility for younger people, because younger people need care, support, and character formation. This means, as well, that younger people must show respect to those older than they are and be open to their advice.

Important to this relationship is the role of the mentor, which is taken very seriously in Confucian cultures. The elder-younger relationship exists between a teacher and a student, between a boss and an employee, between older and younger workers, and between an expert and an apprentice. (The traditional characters for *teacher* in Chinese and Japanese literally mean "earlier-born." The term suggests the relationship of master-disciple, and it has overtones of strong mutual obligation.)

In some versions of the Five Great Relationships, the friend-friend relationship is listed fourth. The relationship between elder and younger and that between friend and friend are actually quite close, however. In friendship there is often a certain hierarchy: the friends may differ in rank, health, wealth, or knowledge. And if the difference is not evident at first, time will bring it about. In this relationship, the more powerful friend has a responsibility to assist the other friend, who is in need. In Confucian culture, a friendship entails serious commitment, and a friendship made in youth is expected to last a lifetime.

5. *Ruler-subject* It might seem that this relationship should be listed first, and sometimes it is.[17] However, more often it appears last in the lists, reflecting the Confucian perspective on the role of the ruler: above all, a ruler must act like a father, assuming responsibility and care for the subjects who are like his children. Thus, the father-son relationship is primary in that it is the model for most other relationships.

The Five Great Relationships signify that each person must live up to his or her social role and social status. This has been called the *rectification of names.* I have only to consult my social role and title to know my duty.

For example, a father must be a caring father, a manager must be a responsible manager, and a friend must be a good friend.

In Confucian societies, people see each other quite strongly in terms of their relationships and social roles. This means that proper ways of creating and maintaining relationships are crucial. Good manners are essential. The civilized person is expected to be respectful in vocabulary, tone, volume of voice, action, manner of dress, and even posture. Etiquette must especially be followed in all formal interactions—for example, between social superiors and their inferiors, between people meeting each other for the first time, and between people participating in an important social event. To follow the rules of etiquette is to show respect.

Gift-giving plays an important role in Confucian cultures. Gifts soften the anxiety of meeting new people and strengthen existing relationships. But gifts must be carefully chosen and appropriate to the situation; they must not be too personal or too impersonal, nor lavish or stingy. (When in doubt, gift boxes of food are often a safe choice.) Gift wrapping is also important; when money is given—such as in the case of a funeral offering—it must be presented in a proper envelope. At formal ceremonies, certificates and other objects are given and received carefully, with both hands extended and with a bow of the head.

The bow itself is an art form that varies according to the occasion. A small inclination of the head is used for greeting an equal; a bow from the shoulders is given to a social superior; and a deep bow is used to show profound respect, make a serious request, or offer an apology. Confucian etiquette such as this may seem artificial to an outsider, but this respectful behavior is inculcated from childhood in Confucian societies and seems perfectly natural to the participants. All of these elements are important because they are relationships made visible.

Because the family is the primary model for all groups, age determines position. We see interesting implications of the Five Great Relationships in Confucian countries today. For example, modern Japanese and Korean companies often act like large families, and management plays a fatherly role. (Bosses have a prominent place at weddings—and sometimes even oversee the matchmaking.) Similarly, an employee's identity comes largely from his or her place in the company, and job titles are significant. The exchange of business cards—on which the person's title is prominently featured—is a careful ritual. Seniors have responsibility for juniors, and one's pay and role are largely based on seniority. Privacy and individual rights are not highly emphasized, and there is far more togetherness. Harmony is all-important.

The Confucian Virtues

Just as social harmony comes from the living out of the Five Great Relationships, so personal excellence comes from the manifestation of five virtues. Although they emphasize harmony between people, the Confucian virtues do not lead to antlike conformity. Some Confucian virtues, such as love of education and the arts, help individuals develop their unique talents. But

The words of Confucius, often literally carved in stone, are teachings for those who live today. Rubbings made from inscribed surfaces are convenient reminders of his wisdom.

the virtues most prized by Confucianism are indeed largely social virtues. Individual uniqueness, although valued by Confucianism, is expected to be muted, subtle, and considerate of others.

Ren (jen) The Chinese character for **ren (jen)** illustrates the word's meaning by blending two simpler pictographs—for "person" and "two." When we look at the Chinese ideogram for the virtue of ren, we understand its meaning: to think of the other. It is translated in many ways: "sympathy," "empathy," "benevolence," "humaneness," "kindness," "consideration," "thoughtfulness," and "human-heartedness."

Some people, though, do not know how to be kind, or they have difficulty in certain situations being kind spontaneously. In Confucian thinking, to follow social conventions is an important way for such people to show ren. After all, underlying all worthy social conventions is considerateness. A motto that reflects the essence of ren is, "If you want to be kind, be polite."

Li This word is often translated as "propriety," which means "doing what is appropriate" or "doing what is proper to the situation." Originally, **li** referred to carrying out rites correctly. More generally, it means knowing and using the proper words and actions for social life. For each situation, there are appropriate words to say, proper ways to dress, and correct things to do. Sometimes propriety entails the control of one's own desires. The **Analects,** which are thought to record the sayings of Confucius and his followers, assert, "To subdue one's self and return to propriety, is perfect virtue."[18] In Western culture, which values what is different and individualistic, the notion of li may seem oppressive and suggest personal weakness. Confucianism, on the contrary, sees self-control as a sign of strength—and practicality. We all recognize that every social situation has its hidden structure. Chew gum at a job interview and you will not get the job; wear shorts to a funeral and you will probably cause hurt to the mourners. Li means good manners. It is putting ren into practice.

Shu The usual translation of **shu** is "reciprocity," but its essence addresses the question, How will my action affect the other person? It is also another version of the Golden Rule: Do unto others as you would have them do unto you. The Confucian version, interestingly, is stated in negative terms: "Do not do unto others what you would not wish done to yourself."[19] It is therefore often called the Silver Rule. It helps me consider my actions from the other person's viewpoint. This virtue also implies that obligations entailed by relationships are mutually binding.

Xiao (hsiao) The word **xiao (hsiao)** is usually translated as "filial piety" (devotion of a son or daughter to a parent). It also means the devotion that all members have to their entire family's welfare. It encompasses several notions: remembrance of ancestors, respect for parents and elders, and care for children in the family. Ideally, it means valuing the entire extended family—of past, present, and future. It is possible that later generations of Confucians emphasized this virtue more than did Confucius himself. This virtue was especially spread by the Classic of Filial Piety (Xiaojing), written at least a century or two after the time of Confucius.

Wen The term **wen** means "culture" and includes all the arts that are associated with civilization. Confucianism has a special love for poetry and literature, as well as a fondness for calligraphy, painting, and music. The educated person is expected not only to have a knowledge of these arts but also to have an amateur skill in them. Wen can also entail the general notion of art appreciation, or connoisseurship. A connoisseur has a highly developed aesthetic sense and is able to know and appreciate beauty in its many forms.

Confucianism stresses other virtues, too—particularly loyalty, consensus, hard work, thrift, honesty, uprightness, and emotional control. One virtue frequently mentioned is sincerity. The Confucian notion of sincerity, however, is not the same as the Western notion; in fact, it is virtually the opposite. The Western notion of sincerity concerns something that an individual says or does that is personal and "from the heart," free of social control. The Confucian notion of sincerity, however, means to choose naturally and automatically to do what is correct for society. It teaches that the individual should restrain selfish desires in order to fulfill job duties and social obligations properly. Through this kind of unselfish sincerity, the noble person becomes united with the force of the universe, which is already—according to Confucian thought—sincere. "Sincerity is the way of Heaven. . . . He who possesses sincerity is he who, without an effort, hits what is right. . . . He who attains to sincerity is he who chooses what is good, and firmly holds it fast."[20]

CONFUCIAN LITERATURE

Confucius considered himself primarily a transmitter of wisdom. Consequently, much of what is called the literature of Confucianism actually preceded him and was subsequently edited and added to by Confucian scholars. It is now recognized that many of the great Chinese classics, even those attributed to one person, were actually produced in layers and over many years. Books could circulate in many forms, with several generations adding their insights until a final form eventually became authoritative. We have already seen this in the case of ancient Daoist literature. Thus, it is not always possible to separate with certainty the teachings of Confucius, his predecessors, and his followers.

The most authoritative Confucian literature is made up of the **Five Classics** and the **Four Books.** It includes pre-Confucian works of poetry, history, and divination; the sayings of Confucius and his disciples; and the sayings of Mencius, a later Confucian teacher.

Early on, Confucian literature became the "core curriculum" of Chinese education. China was the first country in the world to use regular examinations as the gateway for entering the civil service, but these came to be based on the Confucian books and their commentaries. Any male could take the examinations, and success in them often guaranteed a post with the government.

Because the Confucian books were part of the established educational system, the sayings of Confucius and Mencius came to pervade Chinese culture. They have been quoted as authoritatively in China as the Bible is

Deeper Insights

THE FIVE CLASSICS AND THE FOUR BOOKS

THE FIVE CLASSICS (WUJING, WU-CHING)

The Book of History (Shujing, Shu Ching) is an anthology of supposedly historical material about kings from earliest times up until the early Zhou (Chou) period (c. 1100–256 BCE).

The Book of Poetry (Shijing, Shih Ching) is a collection of three hundred poems of the Zhou period, once believed to have been selected by Confucius.

The Book of Changes (Yijing, I Ching) speaks of the basic patterns of the universe. It is used to understand future events and to work with them properly. It is also an important Confucian document because it tells how the noble person will act in the face of life's events.

The Book of Rites (Liji, Li Chi) lists ancient ceremonies and their meaning. Another classical book, the Book of Music, is said to have once been a part of the classics but no longer exists separately. Part of it may perhaps survive, embedded in the Book of Rites.

The Spring and Autumn Annals (Chunqiu, Ch'un Ch'iu) allegedly comprises historical records of the state of Lu, where Confucius lived, and ends with a later commentary.

THE FOUR BOOKS (SISHU, SSU-SHU)

The Analects (Lunyu, Lun Yü) are presented as the sayings of Confucius and his followers. Tradition holds that his disciples collected his sayings and wrote them down, but this work may better be attributed to many later generations of followers. It is now thought that the Analects were written over a period of at least two hundred years, being created in layers and subject to regular rearrangement. The twenty sections of the Analects contain little stories and short sayings—sometimes only a sentence or two long—that often begin with the phrase "The Master said." They cover a wide variety of topics but often discuss the character of the noble person. Here are two typical sayings: "The Master said, a

gentleman takes as much trouble to discover what is right as lesser men take to discover what will pay",[21] and "A gentleman covets the reputation of being slow in word but prompt in deed."[22]

The Great Learning (Daxue, Ta Hsüeh) is a short discussion of the character and influence of the noble person. It is actually a chapter from the Book of Rites that has been printed separately since the thirteenth century CE. It was the very first book to be memorized and studied by Chinese students. This book stresses that one must begin with self-cultivation and personal virtue if one wishes to produce order in the family and state. "From the Son of Heaven [the emperor] down to the mass of the people, all must consider the cultivation of the person the root of everything besides."[23]

The Doctrine of the Mean (Zhongyong, Chung Yung), another work taken from the Book of Rites, speaks in praise of "the mean," or equilibrium. Its beginning—with its references to "heaven" and the "way"—hints at the mystical side of Confucianism. "What Heaven has conferred is called the nature [of humanity]; an accordance with this nature is called the path of duty; the regulation of this path is called instruction. The path may not be left for an instant."[24] A human being who follows "the way of Heaven" avoids extremes and remains in harmony. This balance unites the individual with the balance of the universe. "Let the states of equilibrium and harmony exist in perfection, and a happy order will prevail throughout heaven and earth, and all things will be nourished and flourish."[25]

The Mencius (Mengzi, Meng Tzu) is a long collection of the teachings of Mencius, a Confucian who lived several centuries after Confucius. Like the Analects, the sayings of the Mencius frequently begin with the phrase "Mencius said." Sometimes the tone seems quite gentle, such as in this saying: "Mencius said, The great man is he who does not lose his child's-heart."[26]

quoted in the West or the Qur'an is quoted in Muslim societies. They also have put a heavy stamp on the neighboring cultures of Korea, Japan, Singapore, and Vietnam, as well as overseas Chinese communities everywhere. Although the literature is no longer an essential part of the educational curriculum in Asia, Confucian values continue to be taught both formally in school and less formally in the family and surrounding culture.

THE DEVELOPMENT OF CONFUCIANISM

The basic nature of human beings has been one of the great topics of discussion throughout the history of China. Is human nature good or bad or somewhere in between? This is not a theoretical question at all, because how one answers this question has crucial practical results. If human nature is basically good, it should be left on its own and trusted, and moral training, laws, and punishments are of little importance. If human nature is basically evil, human beings need strict moral education, stern laws, harsh punishments, and a strong ruler. A middle position is also possible: if human nature is neutral, human beings need education that is not coercive and a ruler who governs primarily through example.

Schools of Philosophy

Before Confucianism was adopted as official state policy during the Han dynasty (206 BCE–220 CE), major schools of thought on this topic already had emerged, reflecting a full spectrum of opinion. The Confucian schools took a middle course between extremes, recognizing both the great abilities of human beings and the need for their formation.

Students pay respect to Confucius before class at a Confucian private school in Haikou, capital of south China's Hainan Province. Students here receive a different kind of education, for they read ancient Chinese classics, such as the Analects of Confucius and the Mencius.

The most liberal of the thinkers were the early Daoists, who were so optimistic about the natural goodness of human beings that they resisted formal education. The Daodejing shows clearly the Daoist rejection of artificial formation.[27] The entire book presents instead a vision of people living simple lives in small villages, governing themselves with natural good sense.[28] Laws should be few, because if life is lived simply, order will arise spontaneously. (Of course, as Daoism evolved, it became more positive about human culture and the rules needed to sustain it. Monastic Daoism, in particular, offered many regulations about correct behavior.)

Closer to the center, but still to the left, was the teaching of Mencius, a Confucian who flourished about 300 BCE. (His name is the Latin version of his Chinese name—Mengzi, Meng Tzu.) The teachings of Mencius were ultimately so acceptable to many that the book of sayings attributed to him became one of the Four Books.

Mencius did not merely repeat the thoughts and values of Confucius; it seems he was a bit more optimistic about human nature, perhaps because of his contact with Daoism. There are innumerable Daoist-sounding passages among his sayings. One of them, for example, uses an image loved by Daoists: "The people turn to a benevolent rule as water flows downward."[29]

Mencius was struck by the many virtues shown by ordinary people: mercy, kindness, conscience. "The feeling of commiseration belongs to all men; so does that of shame and dislike; and that of reverence and respect. . . ."[30] In human beings, he thought, there is an "innate goodness," and virtues exist in everyone, at least in seedling form. The sprouts need only the proper nurturing, which education can provide by helping naturally good tendencies in a child to grow properly and to flower. Education does not radically redirect human nature but helps it to become what it already potentially is.

Mencius was aware of the ideal of universal love but thought that such an ideal was impossible and unwise. According to Mencius, in society there is a hierarchy of love and responsibility: we must love our families first, then our friends and neighbors, and then the rest of society; and to reject that structure would bring about social disorder. Education is valuable in making the natural order clear and in helping individuals live with it dutifully.

Confucius's position on human nature seems to have been fairly close to the center. We have already seen this in his view on the importance of education. Confucius was also optimistic; he believed that human beings respond to kindness and good example.

Xunzi (Hsün Tzu), who was active about 250 BCE, held a darker view of human nature. He is also considered a Confucian, but because of his pessimism about human nature, his thought did not ultimately receive the official support that was eventually given to Mencius. Mencius and Confucius tended to view Heaven, the power that rules the universe, as ultimately benevolent. But for Xunzi (as for the Daoists), the universe is totally uncaring; it works according to its own nature and patterns.

Xunzi viewed human nature and human beings as functioning in a similarly mechanistic way. Human beings will veer toward self-interest unless they are taught differently. Consequently, education is not social refinement of an already good person; instead, it must be a radical moral and social reformation of human tendencies that are primarily selfish and individualistic. Education must inculcate proper ceremonies, manners, laws, and customs, for these artificial rules help transcend selfish individual interest and make civilization possible. "All propriety and righteousness are the artificial production of the sages, and are not to be considered as growing out of the nature of man. It is just as when a potter makes a vessel from the clay . . . or when another workman cuts and hews a vessel out of wood. . . ."[31]

Holding a view of human nature similar to Xunzi's was the **Mohist** school, although its exact position is not easy to categorize. Mozi (Mo Tzu, c. 470–391 BCE) was known as a self-disciplined, idealistic person who lived simply and worked actively against war and for the betterment of common people. He thought that without laws, people are predatory, and that with laws, although there is order, society is inequitable. He held that social problems arise because people's love is graded and partial. The answer, he thought, is to practice equal love for everybody. "Who is the most wise? Heaven is the most wise. And so righteousness assuredly issues from Heaven. Then the gentlemen of the world who desire to do righteousness cannot but obey the will of Heaven. What is the will of Heaven that we should all obey? It is to love all men universally."[32]

The **Legalists**, who were influential from about 400 to 200 BCE, also had a view of human nature like Xunzi's and Mozi's but possibly even starker. For the Legalists, human beings are fundamentally selfish and lazy. They will lie, cheat, steal, and kill whenever it is in their interest. "Civilization" is just a very thin veneer, easily shattered; and without stern laws and punishments, people will destroy one another. According to the Legalists, the education of children should consist mainly of warning and punishment, and society must continue these sanctions with adults, because adults are really just children in disguise.

For several centuries after the time of Confucius, the various philosophical schools strove for influence. Legalism triumphed for a time in the third century BCE. The foundation of the Han dynasty, however, provided an opportunity to find a school of thought that could make the greatest contribution to social order. Around 135 BCE, a scholar proposed to the emperor that Confucianism would help unite the country. This scholar, Dong Zhongshu (Tung Chung-shu), also recommended that the emperor set up a Confucian school for the education of government officials. The emperor followed his advice, and Confucian thought began to gain recognition as an important political philosophy.

The Development of Confucianism as a Religious System

Confucianism grew in response to many needs and interests. In its first phase, as we have just seen, it was challenged by rival philosophies. Next, it was challenged by religion.

When Buddhism entered China in the first century CE, it brought new ideas and practices (as we saw in Chapter 4). One radical idea was a general de-emphasis of worldly human concerns and duties, as exemplified by unmarried Buddhist monks. Monks did not have children to continue the family line, nor could they take care of their parents in old age—another deficiency that seemed counter to the virtue of filial piety (xiao). Buddhism appeared to focus on the topics of death, karma, nirvana, past lives, and future lives, and it built expensive temples and practiced elaborate ceremonies. It is important to not overstate the case, but to some Confucians these tendencies were socially deficient.

Of course, the aspects of Buddhism that some Confucians discounted were what made it so appealing to many people. Buddhism was colorful, imaginative, and ritualistic, and it gave people hope that there were supernatural beings who could help them. Chinese who became monks and nuns also benefited because they had a fairly secure life and paid no taxes.

Partially in response to Buddhism's success, Confucianism entered a second phase and took on explicitly religious characteristics. Members of Confucius's family had made sacrifices to the spirit of Confucius at his tomb long before Buddhism entered China. Several Han emperors did likewise. But in succeeding centuries, Confucius received posthumous titles, and in the seventh century, every province of China was expected to establish a Confucian temple and to support regular ceremonies. Statues of Confucius were set up, along with pictures of his disciples; and elaborate ceremonies, with sacrifice, music, and dance, were conducted in

This colorful night scene centers on Fuzi Miao, the Confucian temple in Nanjing, capital of China's Jiangsu Province. The temple holds an annual Lantern Fair in spring.

spring and autumn. Authorities began to place Confucianism on a par with Buddhism and Daoism, and the three traditions were viewed as a religious triad. The three systems (which, many agreed, complemented each other) were compared to the sun, the moon, and the planets—each one a necessary part of a complete religious cosmos. Pictures and statues of the three founders—Laozi, Confucius, and the Buddha—began to appear, with the three figures side by side in friendly poses. This practice continues today.

In its third phase, after 1000 CE, Confucianism was enriched by scholarship and philosophy. The movement, called Neo-Confucianism, clarified texts and codified the elements of Confucian thought. It attempted to determine which Confucian schools taught doctrine that was consistent with the views of Confucius. It also sought to provide a metaphysical vision of all reality for Confucianism, akin to that found in Daoism and Buddhism.

The greatest exponent of Neo-Confucianism was Zhu Xi (Chu Hsi, 1130–1200 CE), a scholar who gave Confucianism its mature shape as a complete system of thought and action. Zhu Xi's commentaries on the Four Books were so esteemed that the Four Books, along with his commentaries, became the basis for the civil service examinations.

Zhu Xi attempted to formulate a general vision of reality by using notions found in the teachings of Confucius and Mencius. He rejected the Mahayana Buddhist notion of ultimate emptiness and instead adopted a view of reality that was closer to the Daoist notion of the constant generation of reality. His view, though not scientific in the modern sense, was positivistic and stressed the natural order of things.[33]

Another Neo-Confucian of importance was Wang Yangming (1472–1529). Unlike Zhu Xi, he did not stress the need to look outward. Rather, he believed that truth could be discovered through intuition. Wang Yangming compared the mind to a mirror, which had the native ability to reflect but needed polishing and cleaning to keep it working properly. He saw a close connection between knowledge and virtue, holding that innate insight gives a person not only an understanding of fact but also an appreciation for virtue. Those who know about goodness, he said, will practice it.

An attempt to purify Confucian ceremony came during the Ming dynasty (1368–1644), when an imperial command dictated a simplification of Confucian temples and their ritual. Statues of Confucius and his disciples generally were replaced by tablets inscribed with their names and titles. Ritual became simpler in order to conform to what were considered ancient patterns, and the Confucian temples took on an archaic spareness that seemed truer to the spirit of Confucius. This spareness is still quite moving today.

If we look back at the 2,500-year history of Confucianism, we can see general patterns and turning points. In the first 500 years after Confucius, Confucianism began to emerge as an officially endorsed philosophy. Over the next 1,000 years, state temples and ritual were organized. In the succeeding millennium, Confucianism absorbed philosophical elements from Daoism and Buddhism but moved toward greater simplicity in its ceremonial life. About a century ago, formal Confucian education and ritual lost its governmental support in China. However, as we shall see later, official support did not entirely die out, especially beyond mainland China; and even on the mainland it is experiencing a revival. More importantly, many Confucian values live on in family, corporate, and government life.

CONFUCIANISM AND THE ARTS

Confucianism has been a great patron of the Chinese arts. The ideal human being, the junzi, does not need to be rich, but he or she must be a well-rounded lover of history, art, poetry, and music. Because of Confucianism's high esteem for education and books, the noble person must cultivate, in particular, all aspects of writing—the premier art form of Confucianism.

In keeping with Confucian values, ancestors' names are frequently inscribed on small tablets that are displayed on an altar. Here we see such a memorial altar in Malaysia.

Confucianism so values the written word that calligraphy has been the greatest influence of Confucianism on the arts. In the West, calligraphy is not valued in the same way that it is in China and the countries China has influenced. The importance of artistic writing is easily apparent to anyone visiting a country in East Asia.

(Calligraphy can appear in unexpected places. I remember a bus driver in China who was deeply pleased with a purchase he had made. We had stopped for lunch in a small, dusty town in western China. After lunch, as the passengers climbed back on board, the bus driver held a rolled-up scroll he had just bought at a tiny shop. With just the faintest urging, he unrolled the scroll carefully. The Chinese passengers were hot, tired, and ready to sleep, but everyone at the front of the bus strained to look over each other's shoulders at the scroll. The Chinese characters were solid but lively, with fine balance between the heavy black ink of the characters and the white paper. On the narrow scroll the vertical Chinese message was this: "To see the view, climb higher." I could easily envision the same scene playing out a thousand years earlier, only in an ox cart.)

The tendency to place Chinese calligraphy on the walls of homes, restaurants, and hotels is still strong wherever Chinese culture has penetrated, both in and out of China. It is sometimes even done where ordinary laypeople (such as in Korea) can no longer read many of the Chinese ideograms.

Because it combines so many elements of value, calligraphy came to be considered one of the greatest of the Chinese arts. A work of calligraphy can show physical beauty, as well as intellectual and moral beauty. It manifests the cultivated nature of the person who wrote it, shows respect for poets and thinkers of the past, and inspires the viewer to scholarship and virtue.

Just as Daoism has considerably influenced Chinese art—particularly in nature painting—so too has Confucianism, most notably in its portraiture of ancestors. It was common in the past for Chinese families to commission paintings of parents and immediate ancestors and to keep these in the home to represent the presence of the deceased person. (Nowadays a photo is used, and sometimes a wooden plaque with the ancestor's name is a suitable substitute.)

While Confucianism certainly influenced the arts, it seems the sensual nature of the arts may have softened the sharp edges of Confucianism. One cannot love the arts and hate the physical world, because the arts celebrate its beauty. But Confucianism has recognized that all artworks have a moral aspect. At the lowest level, the morality of an artwork can be judged in a way that depends on the obvious. A simple person, for example, may think that an art object is automatically moral if it has a proverb written on it. At a more sophisticated level, however, we recognize that an artwork conveys morality by its quality. Thus we say that there is "bad art" and "good art." It is interesting that we use the terms *bad* and *good* to describe both art and human behavior. Confucians would say that this usage is quite correct and that good art makes good people.

PERSONAL   EXPERIENCE
Qing Ming, a Ceremony in Spring

Manoa Valley is lush and beautiful, surrounded by green mountains and thick with large, old trees. But bring your umbrella. Since the valley reaches so far back into the mountains, sunshine is often mixed with mist and rain—especially now, in early spring. Each year on April 5, the Chinese community of Honolulu gathers at the tomb of the Grand Ancestor in the hillside cemetery at the back of the valley. Here the community celebrates the spring festival of Qing Ming (Ch'ing Ming, "Clear-Bright"). This is a time for cleaning tombs, for remembering ancestors, and for sharing a picnic. Today, the grass in the Chinese Cemetery is newly trimmed. Under the large banyan tree at the top of the hill, a pavilion has been set up. As we gather, a small orchestra plays traditional Chinese music.

I make my way up the steep road to the pavilion, the sun shining through the mist and lighting up the red ti leaves around the graves. The red contrasts with the new green of the grass, making it seem especially bright. I see little offerings on many tombstones—oranges, soda, even cans of beer. At one grave, people are burning silver and gold paper money; at others, families are lighting incense and arranging ceramic cups.

Under the red-and-white tent that is set up near the hilltop, I receive a program and find a seat. At the offering table, two women are putting the last touches on plates of rice, fish, chicken, and a whole roast pig. Two other women sit down at my left, and we talk. "We are sisters," one tells me, "and our grandmother used to bring us here every year when we were little."

"We wanted to come here again, to remember our parents and grandparents," the other sister adds. "It's been too long since our last visit here."

Resplendent in a black-and-gold coat, the master of ceremonies taps the microphone and begins the program. He thanks each of the dignitaries in the front row. In true Confucian order, he names each one according to social rank. First he thanks the mayor, then the organizers of the event, the heads of the Chinese societies, officials at the Chinese Cultural Plaza, the Narcissus Queen and her four princesses (who are in silver tiaras and blue sashes), and, finally, members of the orchestra.

The master of ceremonies reads aloud letters of congratulation from our two senators, our members of the House of Representatives, and our governor, who all wanted to be here today but could not, owing to other commitments. The master of ceremonies recalls the long history of the event and the labors of ancestors who constructed the cemetery. He thanks those involved over the past year in the maintenance of the cemetery.

The mayor is called on to speak. Dressed in a dark blue suit and black tie, he says how precious these old traditions are. "Since the time I was little, I have loved the ceremonies of the many groups who have lived

With smoke from his firecrackers still lingering behind him, a cemetery assistant, perhaps proud to have driven away evil spirits, turns back toward the main Qing Ming ceremony.

around my family. All the different traditions enrich our communities. The ceremonies also allow us to show gratitude for the work of the people who have gone before us, who loved us and made our lives possible."

The master of ceremonies then calls on the heads of Chinese societies to come forward. All of the representatives, I notice, are male and dressed in black suits and ties. They go up to light candles and sticks of incense close to the tomb of the Grand Ancestor. Next, they hold up the offering bowls of various foods—rice, pork, fruit, tea. They bow formally with each offering. There is music from the orchestra. I wonder about the memories in the minds of the silent people in the chairs around me.

It is time to drive away all evil spirits. An assistant in a yellow raincoat, who has been standing on the edge of the crowd, goes to the grass beside the terrace and lights a long string of firecrackers. Many of us rush over to the side to watch. Other people plug their ears with their fingers as the fireworks go off. Beyond all the smoke, I see marines and veterans marching up the hillside. When the fireworks are finished, the marines halt and give a salute.

I look around and wonder, What will happen next? How will the ceremony end? A few years ago, it closed with rosebuds and carnations dropping from a helicopter high in the air. But this year the final event begins closer to the ground. Several cages are opened, and out fly scores of doves. These are not ordinary doves; each one has been dyed pink, blue, red, or yellow. But quickly the rainbow doves are out of sight. One of the two sisters leans over and whispers, "Don't worry. They're trained to come back."

Just as we begin to sit down again, the master of ceremonies offers a welcome invitation: "There's lots of good food. Please come up and take a plate."

CONFUCIANISM AND THE MODERN WORLD

The modern world has been hard on government-sponsored Confucianism. In 1911 the Qing (Ch'ing) dynasty collapsed, and with it also collapsed the public system of Confucian ceremony and education. When faced with the new scientific knowledge introduced to China from Europe, Confucianism as a total educational curriculum seemed desperately inadequate. As young Chinese sought a whole new form of education, traditional Confucianism could not compete. Confucian temple ritual also came to an end in China, having always relied on support from the state.

Early attacks on Confucianism were made by the New Culture movement, beginning in 1916. While some members wished to hold on to basic Confucian ethics, others thought that all vestiges of Confucianism should be destroyed. Some of the movement's leaders had studied in the West. Among these was Hu Shih (1891–1962), who studied at Columbia University under the philosopher John Dewey (1859–1952) and returned to China to teach and write. The New Culture movement embraced the views of pragmatic thinkers, such as William James (1842–1910), John Dewey, and Bertrand Russell (1872–1970), and criticized Confucianism on many counts. Confucianism was accused of enslaving women to their fathers and husbands, of subjugating sons to tyrannical fathers, and of keeping alive a culture and literature that only looked to the past.

The Communist takeover of mainland China in 1949 further weakened Confucianism as a belief system. Continuing the earlier anti-Confucian themes, Communism has been highly critical of Confucianism for several reasons. First, Confucianism preaches elitism rather than egalitarianism. Although Confucianism maintains that anyone can become a junzi (noble person) through training, in fact Confucian education has often been limited to only those whose parents could afford it. Communism, in contrast, proposed to educate all equally.

Second, the Communists accused Confucianism of valuing males over females, reserving education and power for males, and providing no official power to wives and daughters. With only one exception in all of Chinese history (the empress Wu, who ruled from 683 to 705 CE), the official role of emperor has been confined to males. Women's roles have been traditionally concerned with childbearing, and women have derived much of their social identity from men. Communism has preached (at least in theory) that Confucianism's sexist tendencies have created oppression and a loss of talent for society.

Third, the Communists criticized Confucianism for focusing on the old rather than the new and on the humanities rather than the sciences. To Communism, this focus on the past reflects a backward vision, like driving a car by looking through the rearview mirror.

Many Communists thought that only when Confucianism was destroyed could China move forward. On the mainland, these views led to either the destruction of Confucian temples or their use for other purposes, and to the development of a Western-based curriculum for education and government jobs. Mao Zedong (Mao Tse-Tung; 1893–1976), the leader of the Communist Revolution, hated the rigidity and old-fashioned thinking that he saw in Confucianism. Mao's anti-Confucian ideals were particularly destructive during the Cultural Revolution (1966–1976), when students reviled their teachers and destroyed much that was considered to be antiquated. On the other hand, Mao also cultivated the image of himself as a benevolent Confucian ruler and father figure. He was a poet and writer; and many of the virtues he encouraged in his people are reminiscent of Confucian ideals— particularly duty, sacrifice, and self-cultivation.

The system of Confucianism has fared better in neighboring Asian countries and regions, such as South Korea and the island of Taiwan. There, Confucian temples and ritual are maintained, although in diminished form, by the government or private families. But in every country influenced by China, such as Japan and Singapore, we find the Confucian system of virtues and behaviors still very much alive. Although these countries have adopted

Reading HOLDING ONTO HARMONY

The Daoist classic the Zhuangzi cites Confucius but gives Daoist advice about overcoming the swings of life.

Confucius said, "Life, death, preservation, loss, failure, success, poverty, riches, worthiness, unworthiness, slander, fame, hunger, thirst, cold, heat—these are the alternations of the world, the workings of fate. Day and night they change place before us and wisdom cannot spy out their source. Therefore, they should not be enough to destroy your harmony; they should not be allowed to enter the Spirit Storehouse. If you can harmonize and delight in them, master them and never be at a loss for joy, if you can do this day and night without break and make it be spring with everything, mingling with all and creating the moment within your own mind—this is what I call being whole in power."[34]

TEST YOURSELF

1. Confucianism, Daoism, and Buddhism have been collectively called the Three _____.
   a. Jewels
   b. Doctrines
   c. Schools
   d. Institutions

2. The legendary founder of Daoism is _____, which means "old master" or "old child."
   a. Mencius
   b. Confucius
   c. Laozi
   d. Mozi

3. The great classic of Daoism, accepted by most Daoists as a central scripture, is the _____.
   a. Daodejing
   b. Tripitaka
   c. Three Baskets
   d. Doctrines

4. According to Daoism, the _____ is the origin of everything, and all individual things are "manifestations" of it.
   a. Yin
   b. Dao
   c. Jiva
   d. Qi

5. One of the stimuli that influenced Daoism to take an organizational path was _____.
   a. Hinduism
   b. Buddhism
   c. Jainism
   d. Christianity

6. For Confucians, the Dao of primary interest is the Dao within the human world, manifested in _____.
   a. right relationships and a harmonious society
   b. traditional mountain sites and heavenly constellations
   c. natural signs and symbols
   d. complex meditation and universal love

7. The Five Great Relationships signify that each person must live up to his or her social status. This has been called the _____.
   a. rectification of names
   b. path of righteousness
   c. way of the gods
   d. enlightenment

8. The devotion that all members have to their entire family's welfare is _____.
   a. shu
   b. wen
   c. junzi
   d. xiao

9. The most authoritative Confucian literature is made up of the Five Classics (Wujing) and the _____ Books (Sishu).
   a. Three
   b. Four
   c. Five
   d. Two

10. The Neo-Confucianist _____ attempted to formulate a general vision of reality by using notions found in the teachings of Confucius and Mencius.
    a. Zhu Xi
    b. Laozi
    c. Mao Zedong
    d. Wang Yangming

11. Explain a situation in which following the Daoist principle of wu wei might be beneficial to you or to others. In what situation might following the principle of wu wei be harmful in some way?

12. Based on what you have read about schools of philosophy in the development of Confucianism, who do you think had a more accurate view of human nature—Mencius or the Legalists? Use examples from the reading to support your answer.

RESOURCES

Books

The Analects of Confucius. Trans. Burton Watson. New York: Columbia University Press, 2009. The sayings attributed to Confucius and his disciples, in a literate translation.

Bokenkamp, Stephen. *Ancestors and Anxiety: Daoism and the Birth of Rebirth in China.* Berkeley: University of California Press, 2009. A scholarly investigation of the interaction of Daoism and Buddhism in the China of the third to the sixth centuries.

Jones, Stephen. *In Search of the Folk Daoists of North China.* Williston, VT: Ashgate, 2010. A specialist's investigation of contemporary Daoist ritual and music, based on fieldwork done in China.

Kidd, David. *Peking Story.* 2nd ed. New York: Clarkson Potter, 1988. A description by a unique individual of life in an aristocratic family at the time of the Communist Revolution.

Kohn, Livia. *Daoism and Chinese Culture.* Cambridge, MA: Three Pines Press, 2001. A summary of the history and essentials of the religion, with attention to new interpretations that have emerged in the past thirty years.

Oldstone-Moore, Jennifer. *Confucianism: Origins, Beliefs, Practices, Holy Texts, Sacred Places.* New York: Oxford University Press, 2002. A clear overview of Confucianism.

Porter, Bill. *Road to Heaven: Encounters with Chinese Hermits.* San Francisco: Mercury House, 1993. The journal of one man's search for and conversations with Daoist and Buddhist hermits in modern China.

Xinzhong Yao. *An Introduction to Confucianism.* Cambridge University Press, 2000. A comprehensive introduction to Confucianism.

Film/TV

Around the World in 80 Faiths. (BBC.) An eight-part series that documents eighty sacred rituals across six continents in the space of a single year. Episode two includes a segment on the rituals at a Chinese Confucian temple and another segment profiling Daoist devotion.

The Bride with White Hair. (Director Ronny Yu; Mandarin Films Distribution.) A martial arts film showing Daoist background.

Crouching Tiger, Hidden Dragon. (Director Ang Lee; Sony.) A popular martial arts film that illustrates both Daoist and Confucian values.

The Joy Luck Club. (Director Wayne Wang; Buena Vista.) A film in which a young Chinese American woman takes her mother's place in a social club after her mother's death. There she discovers secrets her mother kept from her. Its depiction of traditional Chinese family values reflects the values of Confucianism.

Mulan. (Disney.) An animated film based on the tale of a Chinese girl who disguises herself as a man. It depicts filial piety, gender roles, and ancestor worship consonant with traditional Confucian values.

Pushing Hands. (Director Ang Lee; Cinepix Film Properties.) A film in which a taiji master and widower moves from Beijing to New York to live with his son; the father uses a particular taiji technique called "pushing hands" to deal with the many challenges he faces.

Raise the Red Lantern. (Director Zhang Yimou; Miramax.) The story of Songlian, the fourth wife of the wealthy Chen, and the intrigues and humiliations she shares with his other three wives in a traditional Chinese household.

Tai Chi Master. (Director Yuen Woo-ping; Cine Asia.) A film about the life of Zhang Sanfeng, a great taiji teacher.

Music/Audio

Chinese Taoist Music. (Arc Music.) A collection of traditional Daoist music as performed by the Taoist Music Orchestra of the Shanghai City God Temple.

Classical Chinese Folk Music. (Arc Music.) A 24-track, two-disc compilation of the traditional folk music of China.

Dao De Jing: A Philosophical Translation. (Narrator Ralph Lowenstein; Simply Audiobooks.) An audio version of a primary Daoist text, translated by Roger T. Ames and David L. Hall.

Welcoming Guests from Heaven. (Wind Music.) Instrumental pieces on Daoist themes.

Internet

Confucian Traditions: http://www.religiousworlds.com/confucian.html. An online resource listing for the Confucian tradition at ReligiousWorlds.com, which includes categories on Confucius, the Confucian classics, and issues related to the interpretation of Confucius.

Virtual Religion Index: http://virtualreligion.net/vri/china.html. The "East Asian Studies" page at the Virtual Religion Index site, containing a list of online resources on Chinese culture and philosophy, Daoist sources, and Confucian classics.

Wikipedia's Daoism Portal: http://en.wikipedia.org/wiki/Portal:Taoism. A comprehensive reference that includes entries on scripture, deities, religious figures, texts, temples, and religious practice.

KEY TERMS

Analects: A book of the sayings attributed to Confucius and his early disciples.

Dao (Tao; dau): The mysterious origin of the universe, which is present and visible in everything.

Daodejing (Tao Te Ching; dau duh jing): The classic scripture of Daoism.

Five Classics: The classical literature of the time preceding Confucius, including poetry, history, and divination.

Four Books: The major Confucian books, which include the sayings of Confucius and Mencius.

junzi (chün tzu; joon'-dzuh): "Noble person"; the refined human ideal of Confucianism.

Laozi (Lao Tzu; lau'-dzuh): The legendary founder of Daoism.

Legalists: The strictest of the Chinese philosophical schools, which advocated strong laws and punishments.

li (lee): Appropriate action, ritual, propriety, etiquette.

Mohists: A Chinese school of philosophy that taught universal love.

qi (ch'i; chee): The life force.

ren (jen; ren): Empathy, consideration for others, humaneness; a Confucian virtue.

shu (shoo): Reciprocity; a Confucian virtue.

wen: Cultural refinement; a Confucian virtue.

wu wei (woo way): "No action," "no strain," "effortlessness"; doing only what comes spontaneously and naturally.

xiao (hsiao; shyau): Family devotion, filial piety; a Confucian virtue.

yang (yahng): The active aspect of reality that expresses itself in speech, light, and heat.

Yijing (I Ching; ee jing): An ancient Confucian book of divination, one of the Five Classics, still in use today.

yin: The receptive aspect of the universe that expresses itself in silence, darkness, coolness, and rest.

Zhuangzi (Chuang Tzu; jwang'-dzuh): Author of the Zhuangzi, a book of whimsical stories that express themes of early Daoist thought.

RELIGION BEYOND THE CLASSROOM

Visit the Online Learning Center at www.mhhe.com/molloy6e for additional exercises and features, including "Religion beyond the Classroom" and "For Fuller Understanding."

The name *Shinto* presents a problem. It is not a Japanese term but rather emerged when Buddhism came to Japan from China. Before that time, there was no need to name the religion that was already present—it was simply what everyone did. In fact, the Japanese name for Buddhism, *Butsu-do* ("the way of the Buddha"), helped give a name to the religion that Buddhism encountered. The religion that was already practiced in Japan came to be called the *shen-dao* ("the way of the gods") in Chinese, pronounced *shin'-to* in Japanese. ("The way of the gods" is also expressed in the Japanese language by the phrase *kami-no-michi*.)

Like the origin of Shinto, the origin of the Japanese people is also mysterious. Although Japanese often think of themselves as a single "race," they apparently descended from several immigrant groups that came from the northwest, possibly Siberia and Korea, and from the south, possibly from the Malay Peninsula. (We should be aware that even older peoples already lived in Japan. The Ainu, an early people who live in the north of Japan, may be their descendants.) Although the immigrant groups may have focused their primary worship on different natural forces (such as the sun and the moon), it seems their traditions eventually mixed, ultimately blending a large number of gods into a pantheon and yielding a single creation myth.

In the beginning, as the creation myth relates, there was primeval chaos, which came to be populated by several generations of deities, or spirits, called **kami** (possibly, "sacred").[1] Two of these kami—**Izanami** ("female who invites") and **Izanagi** ("male who invites")—became the cosmic parents who created the first islands of Japan. According to an ancient chronicle, the Kojiki, "Hereupon all the Heavenly Deities commanded the two Deities His Augustness the Male-Who-Invites and Her Augustness the Female-Who-Invites, ordering them to 'make, consolidate, and give birth to this drifting land.' Granting to them an heavenly jeweled spear, they deigned to charge them. So the two Deities, standing upon the Floating Bridge of Heaven, pushed down the jeweled spear and stirred [the ocean] with it . . . ; the brine that dripped down from the end of the spear was piled up and became an island."[2]

Izanagi and Izanami then gave birth to additional kami, many of them nature deities. One of the nature deities was a fire god. As a result of his birth, Izanami was horribly burned, died, and went to the underworld. In his immense grief, Izanagi traveled to the underworld to find Izanami, but she rebuffed him because of her ugliness caused by the burn and decay— maggots even crawled through her body. Horrified, Izanagi returned alone to the everyday world. Dirty from his contact with the underworld and with death, he cleansed himself in water to regain a state of purity. As he washed, from his tear-filled eyes emerged the spirit of the sun, **Amaterasu** ("shining in heaven"), and the spirit of the moon, Tsukiyomi ("moon night possessor"). From his nostrils came the spirit of the wind, Susanowo ("impetuous male").[3] Eventually, the sun goddess Amaterasu sent her grandson to bring order to the islands of Japan. From him, the myth continues, came Jimmu, the first human emperor of Japan. As a result, the imperial house mythically traces its origin back to the goddess of the sun.

This story is intriguing for a number of reasons. It puts the kami of sun, moon, and wind into a family relationship, thus harmonizing the stories of several kami who might have once been worshiped separately by different tribes. It declares the emperors of Japan to be divine in origin (which, as we shall see, has had serious ramifications throughout Japan's history). It also portrays Amaterasu as female, whereas the kami of the moon, Tsukiyomi, is male. (This is unusual in traditional belief systems; usually the deity of the moon is female and the deity of the sun is male.)

This story also expresses a concern with purity—a major focus of Shinto. Pollution (*tsumi*) comes especially from contact with death, but purity can be restored by washing and ritual expiation (*harai*).

Another significant aspect of this creation story is that the islands of Japan are believed to be the creation and the home of divine spirits. Japan is thus a sort of "this-worldly" heaven, which human beings share with divine beings. (Traditional Japanese belief maintains that the spirits live in an "upper world" but that their realm is not separate from this world and thus they can exist and appear in this world.) Such a view differs significantly from those religions that see this world not as a paradise but as a place of suffering—a prelude to a heaven that can be reached only after death. In the more optimistic Japanese view, the task of human beings is to live up to the heavenlike world into which they have been born.

THE HISTORICAL DEVELOPMENT OF SHINTO

As we have already mentioned, the entry of Buddhism into Japan in the sixth century (Timeline 7.1, p. 260) forced Shinto to define itself. It was a process that was complicated by the tendency of Mahayana Buddhism not only to tolerate but also to absorb native religious elements. Buddhist monks viewed Shinto kami simply as different forms of Mahayana buddhas, bodhisattvas, and other heavenly beings, and they preached that the Buddhist deities were already being worshiped in Japan under Shinto names. This approach made the introduction of Buddhism fairly easy. At first there was some resistance, and the new religion was viewed as dangerous and foreign. But over time, elements from both religions were drawn upon, and a certain blending of religious practice occurred.

Along with Buddhism came a torrent of cultural elements from China. Before contact with the mainland, Japan already had a culture of its own, but it was fairly simple in comparison with that of China. Contact with China introduced a system of writing, which the Japanese began to adapt for their own use. It also introduced Chinese architecture, poetry, ceramics, art, and all sorts of new ideas—from philosophy to cuisine, from clothing design to city planning. The Japanese were fascinated by all these novelties, and the importation of Chinese culture continued, with some interruptions, for a thousand years.

TIMELINE 7.1

	c. 660 BCE	● Period of the legendary Emperor Jimmu
Worship of sun ● and fertility	PRE-c. 350 BCE	
	c. 350–550 CE	● Unification of clans and of kami worship
Introduction of ● Buddhism to Japan	552 CE	
	712 CE	● Writing of the Kojiki
Writing of the Nihongi ●	720 CE	
	c. 1650–1850	● Shinto scholarly revival
Life of Nakayama Miki ●	1798–1887	
	1836–1918	● Life of Deguchi Nao
Beginning of the Meiji ● Restoration and modernization of Japan	1868	
	1882	● Beginning of State Shinto
End of State Shinto ●	1945	
	1946	Emperor Hirohito rejects ● title of divinity
Death of Emperor Hirohito and ascension of Emperor Akihito ●	1989	

Timeline of significant events in the history of Shinto.

Accommodation with Buddhism and Confucianism

Despite the enthusiasm for Buddhism and the accompanying aspects of Chinese culture, Shinto did not disappear. Instead, the two religions reached an accommodation. Although there were many exceptions, several patterns emerged: Shinto was often associated with agriculture, fertility, and birth, while Buddhism was called on for philosophy, help with serious illnesses, funerals, and the afterlife.

The accommodation was signaled in various ways. Shinto shrines frequently contained a Buddhist place of worship or had some Buddhist rites for the kami, and Buddhist temples often had a Shinto shrine on their grounds. Shinto also adopted the Buddhist practices of preaching sermons, venerating statues, and using incense. Furthermore, Shinto shrines featured Chinese architectural details, such as tile roofs and red paint. Often the mixture was so thorough that a place of worship was neither exclusively Shinto nor Buddhist. In the late nineteenth century, however, the two religions were forced to disentangle themselves. At that time, the Meiji government began to emphasize the belief that the emperor was a descendant of the founding deities, and the government appropriated Shinto for instilling patriotism. Nonetheless, one can still see many examples of their mutual influence today.

Confucianism was also introduced to Japan along with Chinese culture. It meshed nicely with Japanese practices such as the veneration of ancestors, who were thought of as kami, and the loyalty given to family and clan. As it had in China, Confucianism in Japan began to play the role of an ethical system that supported education, family, and government. The whole nation began to view itself as being joined in a family relationship, with the emperor as father and the government ministers as elder brothers. Family and school instilled the Confucian virtues of respect for the emperor, reverence for ancestors and elders, care for juniors, loyalty, discipline, and love of learning. Many of these values were subsequently reinforced by Shinto.

Shinto and Japanese National Identity

Japan tends to swing back and forth between a great enthusiasm for outside cultures and a strong desire to assert Japanese uniqueness. Chinese cultural imports that were strong in the seventh and eighth centuries weakened but then returned again in another wave in the thirteenth century. Western influence, which arrived with the Portuguese in the sixteenth century, was considered so dangerous that Japan largely sealed itself off from the outside world until the mid-1800s. After that came a great wave of Western influence that strengthened over the rest of the nineteenth century. Except for the years just before and during World War II, direct Western influence has continued through to the present.

When the West challenged Japan to modernize in the late nineteenth century, Shinto was enlisted as a cultural counterweight that would preserve the "Japanese spirit." In 1868 a young man, Mutsuhito, came to the throne and assumed real, rather than merely symbolic, power. Known to history as the Emperor Meiji, he began a deliberate process of bringing Japan into the modern world. He imported European and American experts to build up the governmental, military, and educational systems according to Western models. It was a turning point in Japanese history, known as the Meiji Restoration. Shinto was forced to separate from Buddhism, and places of worship had to decide whether to declare themselves Shinto or Buddhist. For a short time Buddhism even suffered persecution, as Japan's leaders emphasized the divine origins of the emperor and began to tie Shinto to a growing spirit of nationalism.

Conflict in Religion

KAMIKAZE PILOTS AND SHINTO

During World War II, Japanese pilots who made suicidal crash attacks achieved such notoriety in the West that a new word entered the English language: **kamikaze.** Containing the word *kami*, it means "spirit wind." Does it have a connection to Shinto?

We know that Shinto priests blessed the planes and the kamikaze pilots. The blessings were part of the larger governmental use of Shinto to further the military effort. But we might also see elements of Buddhism and Confucianism in the creation of the kamikaze pilot. Buddhism teaches the need to accept bravely the transience of life. Confucianism stresses loyalty to government leaders and superiors. Both concepts helped

generate the warrior code of loyalty, duty, and honor, called **bushido** ("warrior way"). Although bushido developed after the twelfth century as the code of the fairly small **samurai** class, it had immense influence throughout the Japanese military.

During certain periods, Shinto has been utilized to promote war, and it is possible to argue that Shinto has sometimes lent itself to nationalistic use. (The veneration of the spirits of deceased military at Yasukuni Shrine in Tokyo is a current source of debate.) In fairness, we should note that most Buddhist sects in Japan also supported Japan's role in the war effort.

Shinto was now a tool in the national buildup, and in 1882 a national religion called State Shinto was established. Thousands of shrines received a special national status, with government financial support and control by the Home Ministry. Priests at these shrines were official government employees, and in return for financial support, they were supposed to represent the imperial household and maintain traditional values. All other nongovernmental Shinto shrines and organizations were treated as independent, self-supporting institutions and together were called Sect Shinto.[4]

Unfortunately, these developments set the stage for the exploitation of Shinto during the militaristic expansion that occurred after Japan's victory (1905) in the Russo-Japanese War. The government increasingly used State Shinto to generate patriotism, both during the military buildup of the 1930s and then during World War II. The divinity of the emperor—the descendant of Amaterasu—was officially taught in schools, and schoolchildren memorized and recited daily a special statement endorsing this view, the Imperial Rescript on Education.

When World War II ended, the Occupation forces demanded that Japan become a secular country. The government abolished State Shinto; the emperor renounced his divine status; Shinto shrines were returned to private religious practice; and all religions were placed on an equal footing. In theory Shinto became a strictly private religion, but in reality Shinto retains a special place in national life.

ESSENTIALS OF SHINTO BELIEF

At the heart of Shinto is a sensitivity to the mysterious powers of nature. Kami are seen not so much as beings living in another, distant realm, but rather as powers in or near this world whose presence might be felt, for example, when we are standing in a grove of trees or looking at a waterfall or contemplating

A Shinto priest, here in red, officially greets the kami by chanting prayers handwritten on a scroll.

a distant mountain. The kami can also cause dread, such as what one might feel in the midst of a terrible storm or being lost on an ocean. The kami are the energies that animate nature: they cause rice to grow and wind to blow; they cause volcanoes to spew lava and earthquakes to split the land. The kami of nature are especially seen in places of natural power and beauty.

Kami are treated as persons and are given names—a fact that enables human beings to approach them and feel closely related to them. We have already learned the names of the major kami: Izanagi, Izanami, Amaterasu, Tsukiyomi, and Susanowo. In addition there are lesser kami. Among them are the spirit of fire, the deity of grain, ocean spirits, mountain spirits (among whom the kami of Mount Fuji is preeminent), and spirits of great trees, rivers, and waterfalls. There are also animal spirits, particularly of animals thought to have mysterious cunning, such as the badger, the fox, and the snake.

Ancestors—who have also become kami—live close by, ready to return to see how their descendants are faring.[5] Shinto is thus a way of maintaining a connection with family and clan members.

After Buddhism entered Japan, influential members of the court sought to record the early myths, both to preserve them and to defend the religious foundation of aristocratic claims. In the early eighth century, at imperial request, the myths were written down, using the new script that had come from China. The ancient myths appear in the beginnings of two core works, the **Kojiki** ("chronicle of ancient events," 712 CE) and the **Nihongi** ("chronicle of Japan," 720 CE).[6] These works also contain genuinely historical material. Ancient Shinto ritual and prayers (*norito*) were recorded in the tenth century.

Although Shinto has no clearly defined code of ethics, a type of morality does flow from the Shinto system of values and its way of looking at life. The Western notion of internal guilt is not found in Shinto. There is no moralistic God who gives commands or judges a person, nor is there a sense of original sin or of any basic sinful tendency. Instead, human beings are fundamentally good, the body is good, and this earthly life is good. Shinto worships fertility and new life, and sex is viewed positively, without guilt. Sexual imagery—particularly phallic rocks and wood carvings—can be seen at many shrines.[7]

Unlike many other religions, Shinto tends to turn its focus away from death, which is thought of as the opposite of life and growth.[8] Because Shinto worships the life force, it works to counteract whatever brings sickness or death. Just as dirt is removable, so too are all other pollutants. According to Shinto, we must keep our bodies, houses, and clothes clean and bright; and when they become dirty or contaminated, we must wash them, get rid of the dirt, and purify them with blessings. In Japan, washing, sweeping, and cleaning—seen everywhere daily—have religious implications. One's character must be unstained, too, and human relations must be kept healthy. Similarly, the human character must have "sincerity" (*makoto*)—it must be pure, without egotism, committed. (Many of Emperor Meiji's poems, available for sale at Meiji Shrine in Tokyo, are about the importance of sincerity.) Human beings conserve and restore their purity by fulfilling all obligations, repaying debts, and apologizing for misdeeds.

Because kami are everywhere, living with them demands that we show them reverence. One way is to visit them at their shrines, which are their homes. Another way is to show respect for nature, which is one reason for Japan's high esteem for farming and carpentry and for the architectural use of elements such as wood and stone in their natural state. Respect for nature also means maintaining a harmony with nature and all its processes.

SHINTO RELIGIOUS PRACTICE

Shinto practice occurs at several levels. It encompasses formal worship and blessings by priests at shrines; blessings by priests away from the shrine; Shinto observances of holidays, the seasons, and nature; everyday practice by individuals in their homes; and the ceremonial practice of Shinto by the emperor and other authorities. Active shrines have a priest—a job that is frequently hereditary.

Worship at Shrines

People visit shrines to pray for health, for success in school and career, and for the well-being of those they love. A visit begins by passing under the torii, which looks like a ceremonial entrance or gateway and is sometimes tall and magnificent.[9] Worshipers wash their hands and mouths at a water basin just inside the entrance. They proceed through an open courtyard to the building—the *haiden*—where the kami is worshiped. Behind the haiden (and often visible from it) is a small hall or cabinet where the kami is enshrined. In smaller shrines, there may be no front worship hall but only a small place where the kami is enshrined. (It is possible that the earliest shrines had no buildings at all.)[10]

Worshipers ascend the stairs to the haiden or to the space in front of the room where the kami is enshrined. They bow, donate a coin, then often ring a bell and clap several times to gain the kami's attention. They bow again and pray, either silently or by chanting. Then they bow again and leave. Sometimes they tie small wooden plaques (*ema*) or pieces of paper, with their requests written on them, to fences or to the branches of a nearby sacred tree.

When worshipers visit a shrine for a blessing, a priest says a prayer and waves over them a branch or wand adorned with paper streamers. This implement is used to purify the devotees and the surrounding area.

Each shrine has its special festival days (*matsuri*). These may be celebrated with grand processions and various types of entertainment. Sometimes, to honor the kami, celebrants parade the kami in a hand-carried litter, an *omikoshi*. On festival days, temporary booths are set up to sell food and religious souvenirs. (Large shrines, such as Meiji Shrine, have permanent booths.) Among the souvenirs are amulets of various kinds, some in brocade bags, which are thought to bring good luck. Some amulets are kept in the home, and small ones are kept in a car for protection.

Churches, temples, and shrines tend to attract people who pray for improvement in their lives. Shinto shrines often have areas where visitors leave handwritten messages for the shrine's deities and visitors.

People visit shrines for blessings at important times in their lives. Babies are brought for a blessing a month after birth. Children are brought for additional blessings when they are young, when special protection is thought to be valuable. This practice is known as "7-5-3"; girls are brought at ages 3 and 7, and boys are brought at age 5.

Shinto priests also perform ceremonies, such as weddings, away from the shrine. Once held in homes, weddings nowadays often take place in large hotels or reception rooms because they are usually followed by a banquet. Priests also bless construction sites, houses, and cars, as well as perform exorcisms at locations that have come to be associated with misfortune, in order to make people feel comfortable there again.

Shinto priests wear long robes (often white, symbolizing cleanliness and purity), which are based on old Chinese aristocratic designs that became popular in the court of the Heian period. Priests' shoes are made of carved wood (like Dutch wooden shoes) and covered with black lacquer. Priests also wear high caps of black lacquered horsehair. The hats of dignitaries have a long flexible extension, which is attached at the top or back of the hat. The extension, created in China, is believed to represent the tail of the horse. (A symbol of energy and strength, the horse came to be considered a sacred animal. A few Shinto shrines have even kept stables of horses.)

Some shrines also have female attendants (*miko*), who represent a vestige of early shamanism. They wear bright red skirts, assist in ritual, and play short, metal musical instruments covered with bells.

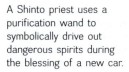

A Shinto priest uses a purification wand to symbolically drive out dangerous spirits during the blessing of a new car.

Celebration of the New Year

New Year's is a very special time in Shinto practice. In preparation for the holiday, the home must be thoroughly cleaned in order to make it attractive to the spirits, who are invited to visit. The main gate or door is decorated with a special arrangement called the *kadomatsu* ("entry pine"), which is made up of three pieces of cut green bamboo, a small branch of pine, and, if possible, a sprig of plum. The bamboo signifies persistence; the pine, freshness and life throughout the winter; and the plum, the first sign of life in early spring. Together, the branches of greenery in the kadomatsu symbolize human virtue.

During New Year's, rice is pounded into a soft dough called *mochi*, then made into round shapes that are piled on top of each other and topped with a tangerine. Rice signifies wealth and fertility, and the mochi anticipates the planting of rice in the spring. On New Year's Eve, the family gathers to eat a special soup made of vegetables and mochi, called *ozoni*, which is thought to promote health. On New Year's Day, men and women dress in kimono, take offerings to Shinto shrines, and pray there for success in the coming year. Over the following days, they make formal visits to relatives and friends and renew relationships. The themes of the whole holiday season are cleansing and the renewal of life.

Men carry shrine offerings during a cherry-blossom festival in San Francisco. Shinto shrine ceremonies are typically formal and sedate, but some nature celebrations can be raucous.

Observances of the Seasons and Nature

Traditionally, Shinto has marked the seasons with special practices, particularly for planting and harvesting rice. In the industrial nation of Japan today, however, these rituals are becoming less important.

Because respect for nature is at the heart of Shinto, reverential objects and small shrines are sometimes placed in the midst of forests, in fields, or on mountains. Among these are torii (which can even be found in the ocean), a pile of stones (possibly phallic in origin), or a sacred rope. Respect for the spirits of ancestors is shown by pouring water or tea over gravestones and by leaving offerings of food and flowers.

One noteworthy Shinto practice is purification with water, a practice that must be very ancient because it appears in several myths about the kami. As we have already mentioned, devotees always wash their hands with water at the entrance to a shrine. A related ritual, called **misogi,** involves standing under a waterfall as a ritual act of purification. Before entering the water, the devotee does calisthenics and deep-breathing exercises. The practitioner is then cleansed with a bit of salt. Backing into the water, the person stands for some time as the water falls full-force on his or her shoulders. The practitioner may shout and cut the air with a hand to enhance the experience of purification. The ritual ends with a drink of *sake* (rice wine) and possibly a meal, if it is performed with others. Misogi combines the ritual of cleansing with the ideal of self-discipline and probably began in the practices of ascetics who lived in the mountains.

Another Shinto practice is the climbing of a sacred mountain to gain union with the spirit of that mountain. The climb up Mount Fuji, for example, is something that many Japanese hope to accomplish at least once in their lifetime, and several Shinto sects specifically worship the kami of Mount Fuji.

Other Practices

Daily worship occurs in the home, where a small Shinto shrine called the **kamidana** is maintained, often on a high shelf. It may contain a mirror, and offerings are made there, especially of rice and water. It is common to offer prayers at the kamidana at the beginning of each day. Some homes also maintain an outdoor shrine in the garden.

A semiofficial form of Shinto that is practiced by the emperor and his household is also still part of the religion. The emperor has traditionally been considered the high priest of Shinto, and his reign is inaugurated with Shinto rites. In order to guarantee the fertility of the rice harvest for the entire nation, he participates every spring in a ceremonial rice-planting on the palace grounds. He and his family also visit the shrine of **Ise** annually to pray for the country. And when he dies, every emperor is buried with Shinto rites—something quite rare, because among ordinary Japanese people, funeral services are conducted by Buddhist priests.

P E R S O N A L   E X P E R I E N C E

A Temple High above Kyoto

On my first trip to Kyoto, I had planned to spend a full day walking in its beautiful eastern hills. My ambitious plan was to begin at the north end, to continue south through the eastern part of the city, and to end finally at the Buddhist "mother temple" of Kyoto, Kiyomizu-dera ("clear water temple"). I had heard that it was a wonderful spot for watching the sun disappear and the night begin.

As sunset grew near, I arrived at the stairs that lead up to the temple. To call the place a single "temple" is misleading. It is really a large complex of wooden buildings scattered across a wooded hill. The main part of the temple is built on top of an enormous deck that extends far out over the hillside, supported by wooden pillars that rise high above the treetops.

Standing on the deck, I could see across all of Kyoto. Other people were there, too, standing patiently at the railing waiting for the sunset. We all

Visitors to Kiyomizu-dera catch and drink water from a sacred stream.

watched reverently as the sun slipped beneath the horizon; then the clouds turned pink, and the city was engulfed in an orange haze. As daylight faded and the gray city turned blue, nighttime Kyoto was being born. It was easy to imagine, down below, the restaurants, noodle shops, and tiny bars all coming to life. Up here, however, the antique atmosphere of Kiyomizu-dera embraced us with its distance from the world.

On the way out was a triple stream—the "clear water" that gave the temple its name. As I walked down the high temple stairs, I could see, far below, the three thin streams of water that cascaded into a pool. Coming closer, I noticed in the twilight the bamboo ladles that lay there for visitors to use to take a drink. As I reached the bottom of the stairs, I looked again. There, at the base of the three waterfalls, obscure in the dimness and plunging water, a man in a white robe stood motionless, knee-deep in the water. I saw that his palms were held together in a gesture of prayer. I took a drink from the waterfall. I then retreated toward the path that leads out into the valley below the temple. I looked back one last time at the falling water. The man had not moved.

I'd gone to Kiyomizu-dera expecting a beautiful sunset, the scent of incense, and per-haps the sound of a Buddhist chant. What I hadn't expected to find, near the temple's base, was the practice of the Shinto ritual misogi.[11] Yet how fitting, I thought, that a religion in Japan that grew up in close contact with the native religion should today have, as the basis for its name and at the base of this grand temple's frame, waters sacred to a Shinto kami.

SHINTO AND THE ARTS

Shinto worships beauty, but the influence of Shinto on art is not immediately clear. There is no strong Shinto tradition of figurative art, in which gods are portrayed in paintings and sculpture. There are some exceptions, but kami are thought of almost universally as invisible presences, not to be portrayed. Instead, the defining features of Shinto art are openness, a use of natural elements, and a deliberate simplicity.

It can be argued that Shinto's high esteem for nature has had a profound influence on Japanese art and architecture. The Japanese screens and scrolls that portray nature that are often said to be the product of Daoism or Zen are equally the product of Shinto. The same is true of all the fine and decorative art forms, such as ceramics and kimono design, in which elements of nature are a primary inspiration. Traditional Japanese architecture, with its floor of rice matting and its unpainted wooden walls, also shows Shinto influence.

Perhaps because Shinto places such little emphasis on doctrines and ethical demands, it has focused instead on the beauty of ritual, giving Shinto an important relationship with the arts. Its love of ceremony has demanded that attention be paid to all objects and clothing used in its sacred ritual, to the places where the ritual takes place, and to the exact way the ritual is performed.

Architecture

The traditional architecture of shrines (**jinja**) is a primary expression of Shinto artistic expression. These structures seem to have begun as storehouses for grain and other foods, which were raised off the ground for protection from water and insects. These granaries functioned as the natural and comfortable homes of the gods who served as protectors of the stored foods. The original pattern of the shrine called for walls made of wood and roofs made of thatch, which would be renewed regularly. Roof beams often extended high above the roof, in a style that is also found in South Pacific island architecture. This feature of extended roof beams (*chigi*) and the fact that the construction materials seem to be appropriate for a warm climate lead many to think that the Shinto shrine originated possibly in Malaysia and islands farther south.

"Pure" Shinto style, with uncurving gabled thatch roofs, unpainted and uncarved wooden walls, and nailless construction, is most evident at Ise. Because the wood and thatch need to be replaced regularly in order to keep them bright and fresh, the maintenance of this style can be afforded at only a few sites.

The shrines of Ise, which are rebuilt every twenty years, are striking because of their extreme simplicity. They sit on a ground of white stones in

Although Tokyo's Meiji Shrine is less than a century old, its architecture is classically Shinto. Special celebrations at the shrine often feature traditional music.

the midst of tall cedar trees, and to reach the inner shrine, the visitor must cross a river. In the summer, the cicadas fill the air with cricketlike sounds, adding to the sense of primordial mystery.

The earliest torii, or ceremonial entryway, was probably made of three logs lashed together, though we don't know its exact origin. From this basic shape, many graceful variations emerged. The original torii were certainly made of unpainted wood, although today many are painted white, red, or orange. The torii usually signify sacred landmarks, but they can also be set in water. (The enormous orange torii standing in the ocean at Miyajima Island near Hiroshima is the best-known example.)

At some shrines, so many torii are set up as thanksgiving offerings that over many years they have formed a tunnel. Tied to the torii or to the front of a shrine is often a ceremonial rope (**shimenawa**), from which white paper streamers may be hung, particularly on festival days. Because kami are considered to reside in any place in nature that is awe-inspiring, shimenawa may also adorn exceptional trees and rocks.

Music and Dance

Shinto is also known for its distinctive music called **gagaku.** Originally played in the Chinese imperial court of the Tang and Song dynasties, gagaku was adapted by Shinto and so slowed down that it creates an impression of ancient solemnity. The instruments that are used make a flutelike, reedy sound that seems close yet far away, timeless yet fresh and new. Gagaku is a perfect accompaniment to Shinto ritual.

One story in the Kojiki tells of how Amaterasu was lured out of a rock cave by music and dance. Shinto shrines often include dance at festival times to entertain the resident kami. Shrine dance eventually evolved into the stately **Noh** dance dramas, which tell the stories of people and their contacts with the spirits. The making of masks and exquisite robes for Noh performers has become a fine art.

SHINTO OFFSHOOTS: THE NEW RELIGIONS

The fact that Shinto is not a strongly institutionalized religion is both a weakness and a strength. It is a weakness because Shinto generally has not had the organizational structure necessary to make converts or spread the religion beyond Japan. Shinto shrines do belong to confederations, however, which help them with staffing; and many smaller shrines are affiliated with one of the old, large national shrines.

The relative weakness of institutional structure, though, can be a great benefit. Using rituals, symbols, and values derived from Shinto, people are able to create new forms of belief and practice that are more likely to resonate with contemporary society. Thus there has been a proliferation of sects, especially over the past two hundred years. Some sects are more traditional than others. Some worship all the major kami, while others focus on just one of them. Some borrow from Confucianism, Buddhism, or Christianity and speak of a divine parent (or parents) and of the human race as a single family. Some utilize traditions derived from mountain asceticism. Some emphasize healing. Some venerate a charismatic founder who is thought to be a kami and the recipient of a divine revelation. Offshoots that consider themselves separate religions are sometimes called the New Religions.

Japan, like Korea, has had a long history of shamanism; and in both countries the shamans are often female. (As mentioned earlier, the miko—the female assistants at some shrines—are a ritual vestige of shamanism.) We might recall that the shaman acts as an intermediary between the gods and human beings. The shaman helps bring physical and emotional healing. This openness to shamanism has helped produce the offshoots of Shinto that revere an inspired leader who was the recipient of a divine revelation. These offshoots illustrate the ability of Japanese religious traditions to take on new forms.

One of the New Religions is **Tenrikyo** ("heavenly reason teaching"), founded by Nakayama Miki (1798–1887), who discovered her religious abilities by accident. When Miki called in a shaman to perform rites to improve her unhappy life and miserable marriage, she intended only to act as the shaman's assistant. Instead, she went into a trance that lasted several days. During the trance a kami spoke through her, saying, "I am the True and Original God. . . . I have descended from Heaven to save all human beings, and I want to take Miki as the Shrine of God. . . ."[12] When Miki came out of the trance, she explained that many kami had spoken to her. The greatest, she said, was the parent kami (*Oya-gami*) of all human beings. The name of the kami was Tenri-o-no-mikoto ("Lord of heavenly reason"). This kami wished her to disseminate teachings to people about how to live properly so that they might have health and long life.

The notion that physical health comes from mental health is strong in Tenrikyo, which preaches healing by faith. This religion is exceptional for its institutional structure and other traditional religious elements that allow it to spread beyond Japan. It has sacred scripture—the poetry that Nakayama Miki wrote as a result of her revelations.[13] The sect has even created a city near Nara, called Tenri City, where its ideals are put into practice. Tenri City contains a university, library, and museum; religious services are offered twice daily in the main hall.

Another New Religion is called Omoto-kyo ("great origin teaching"), or simply **Omoto.** It was founded by Deguchi Nao (1836–1918), a woman who experienced terrible poverty and misfortune. Of her eight children, three died and two suffered mental illness. Nao's husband died when she was 30, and she was reduced to selling rags. In her despair, she experienced a vision of the creation of a new, perfect world. Working with a man she adopted as her son, Deguchi Onisaburo, Nao established a religion that she hoped would begin the transformation of society.

Nao's vision grew out of the traditional Shinto view of earth as a heavenly realm of the spirits and out of its shamanistic trust in the spirits to bring healing to human life. Like many other New Religions, Omoto aims to better *this* world rather than accumulate rewards for an afterlife. It wishes to bring happiness to the individual and peace to society.

Omoto is of particular interest because it sees in the creation of art the essence of religious manifestation. For Omoto, all art is religious. To spread its belief about the connection between art and religion, Omoto began a school at its headquarters in Kameoka, near Kyoto, to teach traditional Japanese arts to non-Japanese. To encourage world peace, Omoto has promoted the study of Esperanto (a universal language) and sponsored contacts with members of other religions, such as Muslims and Christians. Omoto has even held services in New York's Cathedral of Saint John the Divine, where Shinto ritual objects remain on display.

A priest presents a symbolic offering of sake at the entrance to a haiden at Omoto headquarters in Kameoka, Japan.

Deeper Insights

SHINTO AND NATURE

Shinto is a religion that beautifully confirms the environmental movement, for it is rooted in sensitivity to the world of nature. At its heart is a feeling for natural forces, which it calls kami (spirits). These forces of nature are the great powers that make us feel awe. Among them are tall mountains, waterfalls, ocean waves, storms, lightning, the moon, and the sun. Shinto recognizes the strength of the kami of nature, and it encourages human beings to be in harmony with these powers.

Shinto is not a religion that preaches morality in a heavy-handed way. Rather, it hopes simply to inspire correct and harmonious behavior, especially through its actions. For example, Shinto shrines always include some trees, where the spirits may dwell. And Shinto shrine properties sometimes have carefully managed forests; the trees of the shrine forests are used for the repair and rebuilding of shrine buildings. Yet forests in general are also valued in their own right. As an example of this, planning is under way for a ceremony to be held soon at Ise Shrine, where representatives of major faiths will formally ascribe to an International Religious Forestry Standard. The statement will outline the ways in which forests owned by religions should be managed for environmental benefits.

A Shinto Faith Statement, prepared by the Jinja Honcho, representative of all Shinto traditions in Japan, states well the Shinto roots in the natural world:

> The ancient Japanese considered that all things of this world have their own spirituality, as they were born from the divine couple. Therefore, the relationship between the natural environment of this world and people is that of blood kin, like the bond between brother and sister. . . . But in fact, the Japanese spirituality inherited from the ancient ancestors has been gradually lost or hidden somewhere deep in our consciousness. It might not be an exaggeration if we said that not only environmental problems but also all problems of modern society have been caused by lack of the awe, reverence, and appreciation for nature that ancient people used to have and taught us.[14]

Art is the mother of religion.

—Omoto saying

Omoto has itself produced offshoots. One is the Church of World Messianity (Sekaikyusei-kyo). It was founded by Okada Mokichi (1882–1955), who was believed to be able to heal by means of a source of light within his body. He thought that he could share this healing light by writing the character for light (*hikari*) on pieces of paper, which he gave to his followers. Devotees work for the coming of a time on earth when the world will be free of war, poverty, and disease. Elements of Buddhism can be seen in this religion; for example, the supreme deity is called Miroku, the Japanese name of Maitreya, the Buddha expected to come in the future.

Other Shinto offshoots include Seicho-no-Ie ("house of growth") and P. L. Kyodan ("perfect liberty community"), which emerged from Omoto, and Honmichi ("true road"), which emerged from Tenrikyo. The goals of all these groups are similar: harmony, beauty, health, happiness, and the creation of a paradise on earth.

The New Religions are the object of some interest for what they may foretell about the direction of religions. They tend to be practical, peace-oriented, and "this-worldly." Many value the contributions of women, and many esteem the arts. Borrowing valuable elements from other religions, they are moving in new directions.

SHINTO AND THE MODERN WORLD

Shinto could have died out as a result of the successful growth of Buddhism, or it could have easily faded away when Japan adopted Western science and technology. Yet Shinto is a unique example of an early nature religion that is still vital in the modern world.

Though an ancient religion, Shinto is still relevant today. Having maintained its traditional emphasis on nature, it has much to teach the modern world about respect for the environment—for wood and stone, for flowers and fruits, and for the changing of the seasons. In its reverence for nature, Shinto is reminiscent of other indigenous religions. Many of Shinto's values also fit well with modern sensibilities. These values include low-key, nonjudgmental moral views; inclusiveness; an emphasis on healing and living contentedly in this world; a positive view of the body; and the practice of esthetically pleasing rituals.

Shinto has gone wherever Japanese people have settled: Brazil, Peru, the United States—particularly Hawai`i, California, and the state of Washington. Some devotees of Shinto see its potential as a universal religion of nature and would like to see it spread among non-Japanese people. But Shinto is not a missionary religion, nor does it generally have the institutional structure to do missionary work. It is possible, however, that some well-organized Shinto offshoot, such as Tenrikyo, will spread far beyond its country of origin.

Shinto is no longer confined to Japan. Here, the Reverend Barrish of Tsubaki America Shinto Shrine purifies a building in Seattle.

It may be that traditional Shinto derives much of its vitality from the specific terrain, climate, and geographical isolation of Japan—from its mountains, waterfalls, thick forests, and myriad islands, all in continual change from the procession of the seasons. If so, then Shinto will remain restricted to that country. Nonetheless, it is easy at least to imagine the spread of traditional Shinto, especially to areas in which its special elements might take root in a welcoming, supportive community.

Reading SHINTO PRAYER FOR PEACE

Shinto representatives used this prayerful statement at an international peace conference. It has since become widely known. It uses imagery based on natural elements to speak about human society.

Although the people living across the ocean surrounding us, I believe, are all our brothers and sisters, why are there constant troubles in this world? Why do winds and waves rise in the ocean surrounding us? I only earnestly wish that the wind will soon puff away all the clouds which are hanging over the tops of the mountains.[15]

TEST YOURSELF

1. The term *Shinto* comes from the Chinese *shen-dao*, which means "_____."
   a. the way of the gods
   b. the path of the heroes
   c. the source of knowledge
   d. the walk through a torii

2. In the Shinto creation myth, primeval chaos became populated by several generations of deities, or spirits, called _____.
   a. Meiji
   b. kami
   c. Ise
   d. kami-no-michi

3. In Shinto mythology, the sun goddess Amaterasu sent her grandson to bring order to the islands of Japan. From her grandson came Jimmu, the first _____ of Japan.
   a. guru
   b. prophet
   c. emperor
   d. god

4. The entry of _____ into Japan forced Shinto to define itself. They preached that their deities were already being worshiped in Japan under Shinto names.
   a. Hindus
   b. Chinese
   c. Sikhs
   d. Buddhists

5. A turning point in Japanese history was the _____, named after the emperor who began a deliberate process of bringing Japan into the modern world in the late nineteenth century.
   a. Motoori Age
   b. Meiji Restoration
   c. Kamo Enlightenment
   d. Shinto Scholarly Revival

6. When _____ ended, the Occupation forces demanded that Japan become a secular country, and state Shinto was abolished.
   a. the Russo-Japanese War
   b. World War I
   c. World War II
   d. the Meiji Restoration

7. A visit to a shrine begins by passing under a torii, which looks like a ceremonial entrance or gateway. After washing their hands and mouths with water, worshipers proceed to a courtyard building, called the _____, where the kami is worshiped.
    a. haiden
    b. Nihongi
    c. Kojiki
    d. ema

8. Shinto is known for its distinctive music, called _____, which uses instruments that make a flutelike, reedy sound that seems close yet far away, timeless yet fresh and new.
    a. kadomatsu
    b. ozoni
    c. gagaku
    d. Noh

9. Daily Shinto worship occurs in the home, where a small shrine called the _____ is maintained.
    a. Kyoto
    b. kamidana
    c. misogi
    d. ema

10. One of the so-called New Religions, an offshoot of Shinto, is _____ ("heavenly reason teaching"), which preaches healing by faith. A central notion of this religion is that physical health comes from mental health.
    a. Tenrikyo
    b. Kameoka
    c. Miroku
    d. Eclecticism

11. Imagine you were to give a presentation in class on the most important aspects of Shinto. Explain how you would structure your discussion. Would you place greater emphasis on Shinto beliefs or on Shinto practices? Why?

12. Review the section on the Japanese New Religions Tenrikyo and Omoto. Why do you think these New Religions would be especially attractive to some people? Why do you think some people might find these New Religions to be unappealing?

RESOURCES

Books

Blacker, Carmen. *The Catalpa Bow.* New York: Japan Library, 1999. A literate study of Japanese shamanism.

Evans, Ann Llewellyn. *Shinto Norito: A Book of Prayers.* Honolulu: University of Hawai`i Press, 2000. A collection of ancient Japanese Shinto prayers.

Kasulis, Thomas P. *Shinto: The Way Home.* Honolulu: University of Hawai`i Press, 2004. An introduction to Shinto that emphasizes lived religious experience.

Nelson, John. *Enduring Identities: The Guise of Shinto in Contemporary Japan.* Honolulu: University of Hawai`i Press, 2000. A study of Kamigamo Shrine in Kyoto—its buildings and grounds, its yearly rituals, and its people.

_____. *A Year in the Life of a Shinto Shrine.* Seattle: University of Washington Press, 1996. A firsthand account of the rituals carried on during each of the four seasons at a shrine in Nagasaki.

Picken, Stuart. *Shinto Meditations for Revering the Earth.* Berkeley: Stone Bridge Press, 2002. Reflections on the seasons and elements of nature.

Yamakage, Motohisa. *The Essence of Shinto: Japan's Spiritual Heart.* Tokyo: Kodansha International, 2007. A book that makes the case for Shinto as a living religion, stressing its nondogmatic, nondoctrinal, and decentralized character.

Film/TV

Kodo: The Drummers of Japan. (Director Jôji Ide; Image Entertainment.) A one-hour documentary of the world-famous Kodo drummers of Japan, as they perform at the Acropolis in Greece.

Princess Mononoke. (Director Hayao Miyazaki; Miramax.) Miyazaki's 1997 anime classic that chronicles the struggle between nature and civilization, drawing creative inspiration from Shinto belief in the kami of nature.

Spirits of the State: Japan's Yasukuni Shrine. (Films Media Group.) A look at Yasukuni Shrine, one of Shinto's most important and controversial shrines, dedicated to fallen soldiers.

Ugetsu Monogatari. (Director Kenji Mizoguchi; Criterion Collection.) A classic film in which two peasants follow different destinies, influenced by Shinto and Buddhist beliefs.

Woman in the Dunes. (Director Hiroshi Teshigahara; Image Entertainment.) A directorial masterpiece that examines the changing mental states of a biologist after he is imprisoned in a sandpit with a rural woman; notable for its depiction of the conflict between the modern Japanese person and traditional values tied intimately to nature.

Music/Audio

Festival of Japanese Music in Hawaii, vols. 1 and 2. (Smithsonian Folkways.) A recording of religious music accompanying Shinto festivals in Hawai`i.

Japanese Koto. (Smithsonian Folkways.) A recording of traditional Japanese koto music.

Japanese Shinto Ritual Music. (Collectables Records.) A collection of traditional Shinto ritual music for invocations, dances, festivals, and purification ceremonies.

Religious Music of Asia. (Smithsonian Folkways.) A recording of Asian religious music, including Shinto processional and congregational chants.

Shakuhachi—The Japanese Flute. (Nonesuch.) A compilation of traditional Japanese flute music, some of which is closely associated with the Japanese imperial household.

Internet

The Internet Sacred Text Archive: http://www.sacred-texts.com/shi/. The "Shinto and Japanese Religions" page of the Internet Sacred Text Archive site, containing public-domain versions of Shinto texts, including the Kojiki and the Nihongi.

Kokugakuin University Encyclopedia of Shinto: http://eos.kokugakuin.ac.jp/modules/xwords/. The most comprehensive Shinto reference database available online, including detailed information on kami, institutions, shrines, rites and festivals, belief and practice, and much more.

Yasukuni Shrine: http://www.yasukuni.or.jp/english/. The official English-language Web site of the controversial Shinto shrine in Tokyo, dedicated to the kami of those who have died fighting in the service of the Japanese emperor.

KEY TERMS

Amaterasu (ah'-mah-teh-rah'-soo): "Shining in heaven"; goddess of the sun.

bushido (boo'-shee-doh): "Warrior knight way"; military devotion to a ruler, demanding loyalty, duty, and self-sacrifice; an ideal promoted by State Shinto.

gagaku (gah'-gah-koo): The stately ceremonial music of Shinto.

Ise (ee'-say): Location in southeastern Honshu of a major shrine to Amaterasu.

Izanagi (ee-zah-nah'-gee): "Male who invites"; primordial male parent god.

Izanami (ee-zah-nah'-mee): "Female who invites"; primordial female parent god.

jinja (jin'-jah): A Shinto shrine.

kami (kah'-mee): A spirit, god, or goddess of Shinto.

kamidana (kah-mee-dah'-nah): A shelf or home altar for the veneration of kami.

kamikaze (kah'-mee-kah'-zay): "Spirit wind"; suicide fighter pilots of World War II.

Kojiki (koh'-jee-kee): The earliest chronicle of Japanese ancient myths.

misogi (mee-soh'-gee): A ritual of purification that involves standing under a waterfall.

Nihongi (nee-hohn'-gee): The second chronicle of Japanese myths and history.

Noh: Dramas performed in mask and costume, associated with Shinto.

Omoto (oh'-moh-toh): A New Religion, which stresses art and beauty.

samurai (sah'-moo-rai): Feudal soldier.

shimenawa (shee-may-nah'-wah): Twisted rope, marking a sacred spot.

Tenrikyo (ten'-ree-kyoh): A New Religion devoted to human betterment.

torii (to-ree'): A gatelike structure that marks a Shinto sacred place.

RELIGION BEYOND THE CLASSROOM

Visit the Online Learning Center at www.mhhe.com/molloy6e for additional exercises and features, including "Religion beyond the Classroom" and "For Fuller Understanding."

CHAPTER 8

Judaism

FIRST ENCOUNTER

After spending two days in Tel Aviv, you leave for Jerusalem and arrive at your hotel near the old part of the city. Once there, you can't wait to begin exploring. The Old City is a place for walking and wandering, with wonderful sights in its narrow streets.

Drawing you like a magnet is the site of the ancient temple, destroyed by Roman soldiers nearly two thousand years ago. Only its foundation stones remain. On the mount where the temple once stood is now a glittering golden dome. Built by Muslims, the Dome of the Rock covers the great stone beneath it, which is venerated by Muslims and Jews alike, who hold that their ancestor Abraham came to this spot.

You decide to walk down from the city in order to view the mount from below, after which you plan to turn back and travel, like a true pilgrim, "up to Jerusalem." You buy food for a picnic lunch at stalls as you walk inside the city. Soon you are beyond the Old City gate. Luckily, the day is sunny but not hot. You see a large stone tomb in the valley below and beyond it, in the east, Mount Scopus.

At last it is time to stop for a rest and to eat your lunch. You sit under a tree and look back, thinking to yourself about the events this site has witnessed. Your mind becomes crowded with the names of biblical kings, prophets, and priests associated with Jerusalem: David, Solomon, Melchizedek, Isaiah, Jeremiah. As the sounds of everyday traffic filter through your thoughts, you imagine the many battles over this holy city and the successive waves of conquerors—Babylonians, Greeks, Romans, Arabs, and European crusaders—who took possession of it in the past. You also think of the more recent battles and problems here. You cannot help thinking of the contrast between the violence that this place has seen and the root of the city's name—*salem*. Like *shalom* and *salaam*, words to which it is related, the word *salem* means "peace" and "wholeness."

You start back, walking uphill thoughtfully. You see the small tombstones in front of the walls, the high walls themselves, and a beautiful double stone gate, now sealed. Slowly, you make your way back through the city streets around to the western side, to what is left of the great temple. The immense foundation stones, set there during an enlargement ordered by King Herod the Great, were too solid to be knocked down and too big to be carted off. At their base is an open area in front of the **Western Wall,** now used for contemplation and prayer—on the left stand men, and on the right, women. Some hold prayer books, and many touch their hands and foreheads to the wall. You see little pieces of paper, which have prayers written on them, rolled up or folded and placed in the cracks between the stones. These have been left here by people who have come to speak with God and to remember their family members in prayer. You reflect on the historical events that led up to the building of the temple. You think of the long and great history of the Jews, who developed and flourished in spite of persecution in lands far away. It is deeply moving to be here, and you stay a long time in silent contemplation.

AN OVERVIEW OF JEWISH HISTORY

Jewish history goes back two thousand years or far longer, depending on one's point of view. This difference of opinion revolves around a major historical event—the destruction of the Second Temple of Jerusalem by the Romans in 70 CE (Timeline 8.1), which brought about the end of the temple-based ceremonial religion of that region and the widespread dispersion of its people to lands far away from Israel. Following the calamity of the temple's destruction, the earlier religion had to develop in new ways to survive. From the centralized, temple-based religion practiced in Israel, another form of religion arose that could be practiced among the Jews who lived outside of Israel. Jews anywhere in the world could now practice their religion in the home and synagogue. In recognition of this fundamental religious reorientation, a distinction is often made between **biblical Judaism** and **rabbinical Judaism.**

TIMELINE 8.1

Left events	Date	Right events
	c. 1800 BCE	Traditional date of Abraham, the legendary first patriarch
Traditional date of the exodus of the Hebrews from Egypt, led by Moses	c. 1250 BCE	
	c. 1000 BCE	Establishment of Jerusalem as the capital of the Israelite kingdom by King David
Completion of the First Temple by Solomon	c. 950 BCE	
	721 BCE	End of the northern kingdom, destroyed by Assyria
Destruction of the First Temple and exile of the Israelites in Babylonia	586–539 BCE	
	515 BCE	Dedication of the Second Temple
First public reading of the Torah	c. 430 BCE	
	c. 200 BCE	Completion of the last books of the Hebrew scriptures
Destruction of the Second Temple of Jerusalem by the Romans	70 CE	
	c. 90 CE	Completion of the canon of Hebrew scriptures
	c. 200 CE	Completion of the Mishnah
Completion of the Palestinian Talmud	c. 400 CE	
	c. 600 CE	Completion of the Babylonian Talmud
Life of the philosopher Moses Maimonides	1135–1204	
	c. 1280	Creation of the *Zohar* by the author Moses de León
Expulsion of the Jews from Spain	1492	
	c. 1700–1760	Life of the Baal Shem Tov
Beginning of the Reform movement in western Europe	c. 1800	
	1937–1945	The Holocaust (Shoah): the destruction of much of European Judaism by the Nazis
Beginning of Israel as an independent Jewish state	1948	
Recurring violence involving Israelis and Palestinians	1948–present	
	1978	Camp David Peace Agreement between Israel and Egypt

Timeline of significant events in the history of Judaism.

When we study the Judaism practiced today, what we are really studying are the forms of Jewish belief and religious practice that largely came into existence after the destruction of the Second Temple.

The two great spans of time—before and after the destruction of the Second Temple—are also commonly subdivided into two periods each. Over the first great span of time, a landless people established a homeland in Israel and made Jerusalem the capital of its kingdom. Great change occurred and another period began, however, when the Babylonians destroyed the kingdom of Judah and its First Temple (586 BCE), forcing the Israelite people into exile in Babylonia (present-day Iraq) for nearly fifty years. These events made clear to the exiled people that religious law and history had to be put in written form to guarantee their survival. As a result, the Hebrew Bible was created, and study of the scriptures and prayer in synagogues became important, even after the temple was rebuilt.

The second great time span comprises the two thousand years of the development of Judaism in the Common Era. It also can be subdivided into two periods. The first period marks the evolution of rabbinical Judaism and traditional Jewish life, from about 100 CE to approximately 1800 CE, the beginning of the modern period. The second period started about two hundred years ago, when a movement began in Judaism as a response to (1) the new thinking of the European Enlightenment, (2) the liberal thought of the American and French Revolutions, and (3) the laws of Napoleon, which were carried widely beyond France. The movement, called the **Reform,** questioned and modernized traditional Judaism and helped produce the diverse branches within Judaism that exist today. The Reform also raised the issue of Jewish identity. Who is a Jew? What is essential to Judaism? These are two questions to which we will return later.

The Hebrew Bible records that the roots of Judaism go back far into the past to a landless people sometimes called Hebrews and more commonly called Israelites, who traced themselves to an ancestor named Abraham. Because much of what we know of the first span of Hebrew history comes from the Hebrew Bible, we will examine it first. We should note, however, that the Hebrew Bible is not a history book in the modern sense; it presents instead what might better be called sacred history. It is the Israelites' view of their God's relationship with them in the midst of historical events.

We should note, too, that the Hebrew Bible is significant not only in terms of the history of the Hebrews but also in terms of its role in the development of Judaism over the past two thousand years. When the ceremonial religion of the Jerusalem Temple ended in the first century CE, it was the Hebrew scriptures that provided a foundation for the development of rabbinical Judaism. The scriptures offered a firm basis for Jewish **rabbis** (teachers) to offer their **midrash** (interpretation) of biblical laws and practices: the books outlined the Ten Commandments and other ethical teachings; they established the major yearly festivals that would guide and sanctify the lives of Jews; and they contained the psalms that became the everyday prayers of Jews everywhere.

Thus, we turn first to the Hebrew Bible, to understand its structure and to examine the laws and history of the Hebrew people. After looking at the Hebrew Bible and at Hebrew and Jewish history, we will then consider Jewish belief, practice, and influence.

THE HEBREW BIBLE

Judaism is often associated with the land of Israel, but Judaism is perhaps better associated with its most important book, the Hebrew Bible. Although nowadays the Hebrew Bible is published as a single volume, it is made up of individual "books," which were once separate written scrolls. The word *Bible,* in fact, comes from the Greek term *biblia,* which means "books." The individual books were originally oral material that was subsequently written down in some form perhaps as early as 900 BCE, although the final form was not achieved until about 200 BCE. It was once thought that Moses wrote the first five books of the Bible— the Torah—but this is no longer commonly held. Instead, scholars see the Torah as composed of four strands of material, which arose in different periods but have been skillfully intertwined by later biblical editors.[1]

The Hebrew Bible is divided into three sections: the **Torah** (the Teaching), **Nevi'im** (the Prophets), and **Ketuvim** (the Writings). Considered as a whole, it is often called **Tanakh** (or Tanak), which is an acronym made up of the first letters of the Hebrew names for the three sections: *t, n, k.*

The Torah is the sacred core of the Hebrew Bible, with its stories of the creation, Adam and Eve, Noah, and the Hebrew patriarchs and matriarchs— the early ancestors of the Hebrew people. It introduces Moses, the great liberator and lawgiver, and his brother Aaron, the founder of the priesthood.

Synagogue members take turns carrying a new handwritten Torah to their synagogue in London. The Torah is kept in the most important place within a synagogue.

Deeper Insights

BOOKS OF THE HEBREW BIBLE

TORAH

Genesis (Bereshit)

Exodus (Shemot)

Leviticus (Vayiqra)

Numbers (Bemidbar)

Deuteronomy (Devarim)

THE PROPHETS (NEVI'IM)

Joshua (Yehoshua)

Judges (Shofetim)

Samuel (Shemuel)

Kings (Melakhim)

Isaiah (Yeshayahu)

Jeremiah (Yirmeyahu)

Ezekiel (Yehezaqel)

Book of the Twelve (Tere Asar): Hosea, Joel, Amos, Obadiah, Jonah, Micah, Nahum, Habakkuk, Zephaniah, Haggai, Zechariah, Malachi

THE WRITINGS (KETUVIM)

Psalms (Tehillim)

Proverbs (Mishle)

Job (Iyyov)

Song of Songs (Shir Hashirim)

Ruth (Ruth)

Lamentations (Ekhah)

Ecclesiastes (Qohelet)

Esther (Ester)

Daniel (Daniel)

Ezra-Nehemiah (Ezra-Nehemyah)

Chronicles (Divre Hayamim)

It includes laws about daily conduct and religious ritual—material that would be of great importance to the later development of Judaism. Because the Torah comprises five books, it is sometimes called the Pentateuch (Greek: "five scrolls"). (We should recognize that the term *Torah* is also used more widely to refer to all teachings, both written and orally transmitted, that are thought to have been revealed by God.)

The second part of the Tanakh, called the Prophets, is named for those individuals who spoke in God's name to the Jewish people. The books that concentrate on the history of the Israelite kingdom are called the Former Prophets, followed by additional books, which are more strongly visionary and moral in tone, called the Latter (or Later) Prophets. In the Latter Prophets, the voices of the individual prophets tend to predominate.

The third part of the Tanakh, called the Writings, is closer to what we think of as imaginative literature. Although it includes some late historical books, it contains primarily short stories, proverbs, reflections on life, hymn (psalm) lyrics, and poetry.

We will use the term *Hebrew Bible* for all of this material. (Jews do not refer to the Hebrew scriptures as the Old Testament, as do Christians, because the title implies that the Jewish books have meaning only in relation to the Christian books, collectively called the New Testament. Also, the order of books in the Hebrew Bible, in the format that it assumed by the end of the tenth century CE, differs somewhat from the general order that is found in Christian Bibles.) The commonly used titles of some of the books are Greek, based on early Greek translations.[2]

The historical accuracy of the Hebrew Bible is not always certain, because not all biblical accounts can be verified by archeological finds or references in other historical records. Although we can presume that many of the accounts (particularly those of events after the Jewish kingdom was established) are based on historical fact, we must also recognize that they were recorded by the Jews themselves, who naturally viewed historical events from their own special perspective. Furthermore, many accounts were transmitted orally long before they were written down or assembled in final form, thus affecting the way they were recounted.

BIBLICAL HISTORY

Whatever its historical accuracy, the heroic and mythic power of the Hebrew Bible cannot be denied. It is filled with astonishing people and powerful images. Adam and Eve, for example, stand naked and suddenly aware among the trees and streams of the Garden of Eden. Noah and his wife are surrounded by animals in their big wooden boat, riding out a long flood. Moses climbs to the top of cloud-covered Mount Sinai to speak with God and receive the Ten Commandments. These images and ideas are not only unforgettable, but they are also part of Western culture and have influenced its laws, art, literature, and ways of living.

In the Beginning: Stories of Origins

The earliest stories of the Hebrew Bible, given in Genesis 1–11, have a mythic quality that is universally appealing. The story of the origin of the world presents God as an intelligent, active, masculine power who overcomes primeval chaos. To create order, God imposes separations—separating light from darkness and land from water—and completes his work of creation in stages, spread over six days. At the end of each day, God views what he has done and sees that it is good. Finally, satisfied with the result of all his labor, God rests on the seventh day.

This account (which shows parallels with the creation story in the Babylonian epic poem *Enuma Elish*) appears in the first chapter of Genesis, the first book of the Bible. This first account is cosmic and measured—possibly written that way in order to be read out solemnly by a priest at temple ceremonies. The second account (perhaps written earlier than the first) begins in the second chapter of Genesis. This account is more human, utilizes colorful dialogue, and focuses on the first human parents, Adam and Eve, and on their moral dilemma.

The Garden of Eden, which God has created for his refreshment, is based on the pattern of a walled garden, complete with fruit trees, birds, exotic animals, a central fountain, and streams to cool the air. God creates

Adam to live in the garden as its gardener and caretaker, forming his body from the dust of the earth and breathing life into Adam with his own breath. In some way, Adam is a copy of God himself, for the human being, the Bible says, is made "in the image of God" (Gen. 1:27),[3] bearing some of the dignity of God. Soon, though, because Adam is lonely, God decides to give him a companion. Taking a rib from Adam while he is in a deep sleep, God forms Eve around that rib. In the first account of creation, male and female were created simultaneously, but in the second account, the male is created first and the female afterward—leading to the interpretation that while the male is a copy of God, the female is only a copy of the male.

Interestingly, the conception of God in the creation stories is somewhat different from many later views. For one thing, although the biblical God has no apparent rivals, he does not appear to be alone, and when he declares "Let *us* make man" (Gen. 1:26),[4] he is most likely addressing his heavenly counselors, some of whom are identified in later texts (such as Psalms and Job). In addition, God is not represented as pure spirit. The account in chapter two of Genesis says that God walks and eats; and having made the garden to enjoy, he strolls in it when he wants to enjoy its cool breezes. God allows Adam and Eve to eat from almost all the trees, but he forbids them to eat fruit from one of the trees that he especially needs to nourish his supernatural life and insight. Eve, tempted to eat from the forbidden tree, does so and then urges Adam to do the same. For their disobedient act, they are exiled from God's garden. God can no longer trust them, knowing that if they were to remain they might become his rivals. Now they must live outside the garden, work, and suffer for the rest of their amazingly long lives.

To some, the portrait of Eve—a temptress who brings down punishment on Adam and herself—is distressing. But it should be pointed out that Eve is the one with ambition and personality, while Adam seems far less colorful. Whatever the interpretation—and there have been many—the story of Adam and Eve has influenced Western views of women, men, and marriage for several thousand years.

Next is the story of Adam and Eve's children, Cain and Abel (Gen. 4:1–16), whose sibling rivalry ends in Cain's murder of Abel. This tale may reflect ancient rivalries between farmers and herders.

Following this is the story of the Great Flood (Gen. 6–9), which echoes a Mesopotamian tale, the *Epic of Gilgamesh*. Disgusted with the rapidly growing, immoral human population, God sends a flood to do away with humanity—all of humanity, that is, except the righteous Noah and his family. He warns Noah to build a large wooden boat (an ark) and fill it with animals, because only those in the boat will survive the coming downpour. At the end of the flood, God makes a pact with Noah never again to destroy the earth by water. As a sign of this promise, God places his "bow" (perhaps an archer's bow) into the sky. The rainbow is a reminder of his solemn promise. Like several of the early stories, this account gives an

New Beginnings, a contemporary painting by Bruce David, is a reminder of the rainbow that signaled God's promise at the end of Noah's journey. The Hebrew inscription quotes Isaiah 11:9: "For the earth will be full of the knowledge of the Lord, as the waters cover the sea."

explanation for a natural phenomenon. This story also explains how, from the three sons of Noah, different races arise.

Chapter eleven of Genesis tells the story of the tower of Babel (or Babylonia). Wanting to reach the heavenly realm that they believe exists above the skies, people begin building a very tall tower. God, not willing to have his private world invaded, stops the construction by making the builders speak different languages. Because they can no longer understand each other, they cannot finish their tower. This story also gives a convenient answer to the question, Why are there different languages in the world?

Did Adam, Eve, Cain, Abel, Noah, and the others really exist? For centuries, Jews have thought of them as historical figures. Now, however, influenced by the views of scholars, many Jews view them instead as symbolic figures who set the stage for the events that follow. The first eleven chapters of Genesis are, in effect, a great allegorical introduction to the rest of the Hebrew Bible. There are many indications of this non-historical, symbolic purpose. For example, Adam and his immediate descendants are described as living to great ages—Adam is said to have lived to be 930 years old (Gen. 5:5) and Methuselah, the longest-lived, 969 years old (Gen. 5:7). Moreover, many names are apparently symbolic; for example, *Adam* means "humankind" and *Eve* means "life." Scholars, as pointed out earlier, believe that the stories of the creation and the flood derive from earlier Mesopotamian tales. What is important to understand, though, is that these stories were given new meanings by the Israelite scribes who adapted them.

The World of the Patriarchs and Matriarchs

Abraham is the first Hebrew patriarch (Greek: "father-source"). He is introduced in chapter twelve of Genesis, the point at which the book becomes more seemingly historical. Abraham, first known as Abram, is called by God to leave his home for another land. Originally from Ur (in present-day Iraq), Abraham migrates via Haran (in Turkey) to the land of **Canaan.** "Now the Lord said to Abram, 'Go from your father's house to the land that I will show you. I will make of you a great nation'" (Gen. 12:1–2a).[5] This passage is significant to Judaism because it is seen as establishing a claim to the region now called Israel. Abraham's migration becomes a pilgrimage of great importance, making him, his son Isaac, and his grandson Jacob the patriarchs of Judaism.

After assuring Abraham of land and many descendants, God enters into a solemn **covenant,** a contract, with Abraham. In return for God's promise to provide land, protection, and descendants, Abraham and his male descendants must be circumcised as a sign of their exclusive relationship with God (Gen. 17).

The most famous story of Abraham concerns his son Isaac. Abraham has long been unable to have a son by his wife, Sarah. At Sarah's urging, he fathers by her maid, Hagar, a son named Ishmael. But then, to the amazement of all, Sarah herself has a son (Gen. 19). Soon, though, Sarah jealously demands that Ishmael and Hagar be sent away. (This aspect of the story will be important later on in Islam.) Shockingly, God then asks (in Gen. 22) that Abraham offer Isaac, the beloved son of his old age, as a sacrifice. (Perhaps

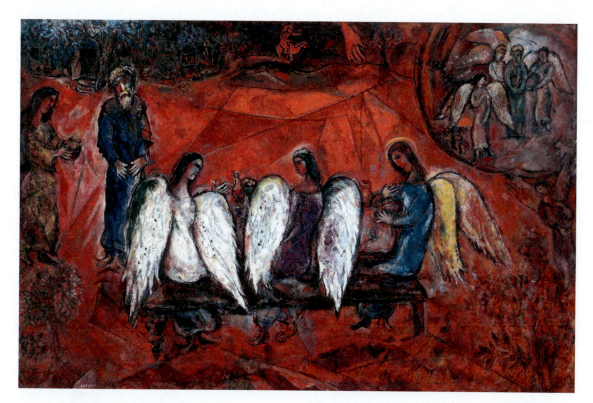

this is a vestige of an earlier practice of human sacrifice.) Abraham agrees and sets out with his son to Mount Moriah, believed by Jews to be the hill on which Jerusalem now rests. Just before the boy is to die, God stops Abraham, and a ram, whose horns had become tangled in a bush nearby, is used as the sacrifice instead. God has thus tested Abraham's devotion, and in so proving his absolute loyalty to God, Abraham has shown himself worthy of land, wealth, fame, and the joy of knowing he will have innumerable descendants. (This passage may show the replacement of human sacrifice with the sacrifice of animals.)

Marc Chagall's *Abraham and the Three Angels* includes Abraham's elderly wife Sarah, whose pregnancy is an important part of matriarchal history.

Genesis also contains stories about some extremely memorable women, the matriarchs of the Hebrew people: Sarah, Rebecca, Rachel, and Leah. Although these women are always linked with their husbands, they all have strong and carefully drawn personalities. Sarah, for example, stays modestly inside the tent when strangers arrive but laughs so loudly that they hear her and then question her about why she is laughing (Gen. 18:10–15).

The stories in Genesis also tell of mysterious contacts with God—called **theophanies**—which are sometimes friendly in nature but at other times fierce and frightening. God appears to Isaac, for example, and promises him protection and many descendants (Gen. 26:24). One of Isaac's sons, Jacob, has a vision of God in a dream (Gen. 28). He sees a stairway leading from earth into the sky. God is at the top, and angels are ascending and descending, linking heaven and earth. A more unusual theophany occurs when Jacob wrestles all night long with a mysterious stranger—God or God's angel. At dawn the fight is over, and Jacob receives from the stranger a new name: Israel ("wrestles with God"). Because Jacob and his sons would settle the land of Canaan, it came to be called Israel after his new name. Jacob, with his two wives and two concubines, has many sons, who would become the ancestors of the twelve tribes of Israel.

Joseph, Jacob's next-to-last son, is the focus of the final section of Genesis. Because Joseph's brothers sense that his father loves him best, they scheme to have him killed. Ultimately, though, they sell him as a slave, and he is taken to Egypt (Figure 8.1). There, through his special gifts, he rises in importance to become a government minister. When a famine in Israel brings his brothers down to Egypt to look for grain, Joseph is not vengeful but invites his brothers to bring their father to Egypt and to settle there permanently. They do so and settle in the land of Goshen in northeastern Egypt. The Book of Genesis ends with the death of Jacob.

FIGURE 8.1

The ancient eastern Mediterranean, with an inset of the kingdoms of Israel and Judah (c. 900 BCE).

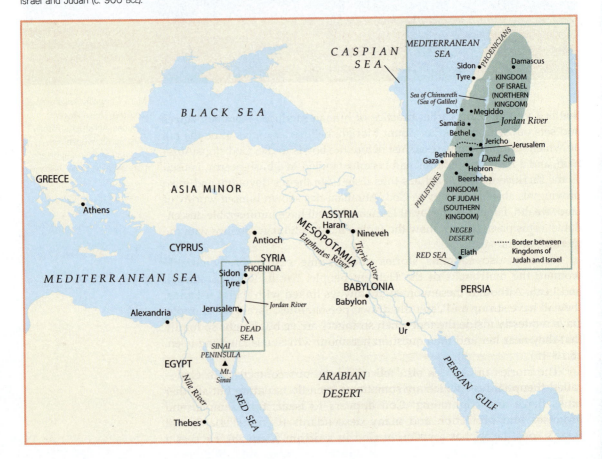

How historically true are these stories, especially that of Abraham? Traditional believers and some scholars think that the stories surrounding Abraham do express historical truth, though shaped by oral transmission. Other scholars, however, argue that the Israelites arose in Israel itself, possibly as a landless peasant class that revolted against its rulers. If that view is true, then the story of Abraham and his entry into Israel from elsewhere may not be historically accurate. In addition, no archeological evidence has yet been found to prove the existence of Abraham. The debate about the historical existence of Abraham may never be resolved.

Moses and the Law

The Book of Exodus records that the population of Hebrews in Egypt grew so large after several centuries that the Egyptians saw them as a threat. As a solution, the pharaoh commands that all Hebrew baby boys be killed at birth. However, the baby Moses (whose name is probably Egyptian) is spared by being hidden. After three months, when his Hebrew mother is afraid to keep him any longer, she and her daughter fashion a watertight basket, put him inside it, and place the basket in the Nile River. There an Egyptian princess discovers him and raises him as her own. As a young adult, Moses sees an Egyptian foreman badly mistreating an Israelite slave. In trying to stop the cruelty, Moses kills the foreman. Moses then flees from Egypt.

Our next glimpse of Moses comes when he has found a new life beyond the borders of Egypt, where he is now a herdsman for a Midianite priest named Jethro, whose daughter he has married. One day, when Moses is out with his father-in-law's herds, he sees a strange sight: a large bush appears to be burning, but it is not consumed. As Moses approaches the bush, he hears the voice of God, who commands Moses to return to Egypt to help free the Hebrews.

Living in a world that believes in many gods, Moses is curious to know the name of the divine spirit speaking to him. The deity, however, refuses to give a clear name and says mysteriously, "I will be who I will be," and then commands Moses to tell the Hebrews "that 'I will be' sent you" (Exod. 3:14).[6] In Hebrew the mysterious answer provides an etymological clue to the name for God. The name for God, usually associated with the verb *hayah* ("to be"), is Yhwh, and it is often translated as "I am." The name is usually written Yahweh, but the exact pronunciation is unknown.

As mentioned, Moses lived in an age when people believed in many gods, and he had grown up in the polytheistic culture of Egypt. People everywhere believed in multiple gods and thought of them as guardian deities of particular groups and regions. Could Moses—or the patriarchs and matriarchs before him—have really been monotheistic? We do not know. A possibility is that Moses and the Hebrew patriarchs and matriarchs believed in the existence of many gods, of whom one, possibly a major deity, declared himself the special protector of the Israelites. If this is true, monotheism was not the original belief system of the Israelites but evolved over time. Some scholars wonder whether the actions of the Egyptian pharaoh Akhenaten (Ikhnaton, reigned c. 1352–1336 BCE) influenced the development of Jewish monotheism. Akhenaten gave sole worship to the sun god Aten, and he unsuccessfully attempted to suppress the worship of all other Egyptian gods.

Ultimately, the god of the Jews would come to be proclaimed "the one true God." We see two traditions in the Torah. In one (possibly older) tradition, Yahweh is embodied and appears directly to human beings. In another (possibly later) tradition, Yahweh exists as a spirit, separate from human beings. The notion of God as being transcendent and distant grew stronger over time, and the transformation was complete when Yahweh came to be considered pure spirit and any reference to his body was considered to be metaphorical. In addition, God's name eventually was thought of as being too sacred to be pronounced; instead of speaking the name *Yahweh*, priests and lectors substituted the Hebrew word *Adonay* ("the Lord").[7] Ultimately, all other gods were considered false gods; images of anything that could be construed as a god were prohibited; and Yahweh at last was considered the one God of the entire universe.

But these changes would all occur after the time of Moses. In the Book of Exodus, Yahweh, the god of the Hebrews, simply needs to show himself to be more powerful than any of the gods of the Egyptians (Exod. 12:12). It is by his power that ten plagues strike the Egyptians and convince the pharaoh (possibly the great builder Ramses II, c. 1292–1225 BCE) to let his Israelite slaves leave.

The last and greatest of the plagues is the death of the first-born sons of the Egyptians. The Israelites' sons are spared because they have followed Yahweh's warning and have marked the doors of their homes with the blood of a substitute—a sacrificial lamb (Exod. 12:13). Because God has "passed over" Egypt, the event is thereafter called the **Passover (Pesach),** and its yearly memorial has become one of the major Jewish festivals (which we will discuss later).

The Bible tells of the Hebrews' journey out of Egypt through a large body of water, the Red Sea, on their way to the Sinai Peninsula. (The Hebrew term may be translated as either "Red Sea" or "Reed Sea." The second translation may refer to the reed-filled marshes of northeastern Egypt.) Movies have dramatized the event, showing two walls of water held back as the Hebrews marched between them. But the reality was possibly less dramatic. Although Egyptian records do not mention it, the exodus from Egypt has become a central theme of Judaism. A whole people, protected by God, leaves a land of oppression and begins the march toward freedom.

The Books of Exodus and Numbers describe in detail the migration back to Israel—a migration that lasted a full generation, about forty years. The most significant event during this period of passage is God's encounter with Moses at Mount Sinai. The Book of Exodus (chap. 19) paints a terrifying picture: the mountain is covered with cloud and smoke; lightning and thunder come from the cloud; and the sound of a trumpet splits the air. The people are warned to keep their distance, for only Moses may go to meet God at the top of the mountain. Moses enters the cloud and speaks with God.

When Moses descends, he returns to his people with rules for living—the Ten Commandments (Exod. 20). The strong moral orientation of Judaism is apparent here, for Moses does not return with an explanation of the universe, with science, or with art, but rather with ethical precepts. Parallels have been drawn to several other early codes, particularly that of the Babylonian King Hammurabi (c. 1792–1750 BCE).

Undergirding the commandments is the conviction that a covenant—a contract—exists between Yahweh and his people. He will care for them, but they must fulfill their half of the bargain by following his laws and giving him sole worship. Such an agreement had already been made between God and Noah and would later be made with Abraham. The covenant is reaffirmed with Moses and solidified by the laws and commandments, which give it legal form.

The Book of Leviticus begins with detailed laws about animal sacrifice (chaps. 1–7) and then takes up the complexities of ritual purity. In addition to laws about general honesty and humaneness, Leviticus outlines many special laws that would be important to the later development of Judaism: laws specifying which animals may and may not be eaten (chap. 11), laws prohibiting the consumption of meat with blood in it (17:10) or the cutting of one's beard (19:27), and laws governing the observance of the major religious festivals (chap. 23). The Book of Numbers returns to historical themes, recounting specifically the years of wandering before the Hebrews entered Canaan. But it also spells out laws about ritual purity and the keeping of vows. The Torah ends with the Book of Deuteronomy, which repeats the Ten Commandments and describes the death of Moses, an event that occurs just before the Hebrews enter the Promised Land of Canaan.[8]

The historicity of Moses is, like that of Abraham, another focus of debate. Virtually all Jews believe him to have been a real person. So far, however, no Egyptian archeological records have been found that mention Moses, a slave rebellion, or an exodus from Egypt. Specialists in mythology point out parallels between the story of Moses and Egyptian religious tales. Also, no archeological evidence has yet been found to give proof of the forty years of wandering in the desert. The lack of historical evidence, however, does not disprove the historicity of Moses. A common view sees the biblical account as representing basic historical truth that has been magnified and embellished over time.

The Judges and Kings

After Moses's death, the Israelites were led by men and women who had both military and legal power, called judges. To think of them as military generals is more accurate than to envision them as modern-day courtroom judges.

Deeper Insights

THE GODS OF EGYPT

Egypt, as the earliest great imperial state in history, left a significant cultural mark on the ancient Near East. Even countries that had never experienced its direct political control felt its sway through trade, which carried Egyptian goods, culture, and religion far beyond its borders. It's not surprising that Egyptian religious artifacts have been found in Greece, Israel, Lebanon, Syria, and the islands of the Mediterranean. However, not all peoples welcomed Egyptian influence, including the Hebrews, who recorded their concerns about it in their scriptures. The Ten Commandments, in particular, show a desire to escape from Egypt's influence. The first commandment, for example, implies the gods of Egypt when it orders, "you shall have no other gods before me." The next commandment reinforces this demand by forbidding the making of images that portray any creature in the sky, on the earth, or in the waters. This prohibition would especially exclude many of the animal-like gods of Egypt. In order to understand these biblical concerns more clearly, we have to consider Egyptian religious beliefs.

The culture of Egypt dates back to ancient times. Archeology reveals the existence as early as 5000 BCE of complex societies in Egypt and Nubia, a region to the south of Egypt. Egyptian life was centered on the Nile River, whose waters irrigated crops and served as a great highway on which goods, people, and ideas traveled easily. Because cultural centers were spread up and down the river, sometimes at great distances, Egyptian religion initially developed in a localized and diverse fashion, with each community having its own gods and stories of creation. Later, as a unified Egyptian state developed after 3000 BCE, so did a more unified Egyptian religion. (The same unifying process occurred in Greco-Roman religion, as we will see in the next chapter.) Some gods were blended, many were linked in myth, and a few emerged as preeminent. Here we will mention only the most important. (We will use their familiar names, some of which are Egyptian and some of which are Greco-Roman.)

THE PANTHEON

Although at least four major creation stories existed, the one that became most common told of an original watery chaos called Nun and the eventual birth of nine gods. This creation myth tells how, in the midst of the formless body of water, a mound of earth arose, and from this mound emerged the primordial sun god, called Ra (Re) or Atum. From the exertions of the sun god came an initial parent pair—a god of dry air named Shu and his consort, Tefnut, goddess of rain and mist. These two, in turn, gave birth to another pair—the sky goddess Nut and her consort, the earth god Geb. And from them came four children: one pair was Osiris and his consort, Isis; the other pair was Set (Seth) and his consort, Nephthys. (These nine interconnected deities are often called the Ennead; from a Greek word for "nine.")

The goddess Nut was especially beloved. She is frequently shown as a great female being, usually blue and covered with gold stars, who crouches protectively over

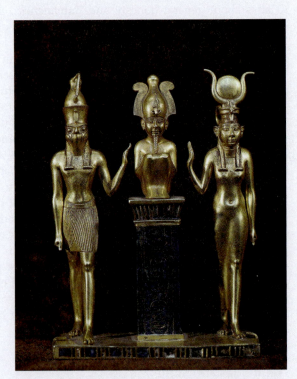

Horus and Isis stand beside Osiris in this image from between 945 and 715 BCE.

the earth. She is held up over the prostrate earth god Geb by the air god Shu, whose power keeps sky and earth separate. It was believed that the sun god Ra entered the sky goddess every night, sailed in the dark on a boat with other gods under the earth, and was reborn from Nut every morning.

Isis, Osiris, and their son Horus were also deeply revered. Their stories served as guides for generations of Egyptians. According to the primary myth, Osiris was killed by his jealous brother Set and sent down the Nile in a coffin. Isis searched for Osiris and found his body in Byblos (today in Lebanon). She brought his dead body back to Egypt, but Set found them and cut Osiris into pieces. Binding the pieces with linen, Isis put the body of Osiris back together (she fashioned one missing part—eaten by fish—from wood). Because of her love, Osiris was allowed to be reborn and to live again for one day with Isis. It was at this time that their son Horus was conceived. Osiris returned to the underworld and became the god and judge of the dead. After Horus was born, Isis hid him in the reeds of the delta so that he might escape the wrath of Set. Once Horus came of age, he conquered Set and became the ruler of Egypt. Egyptians came to believe that by imitating Osiris, they would be identified with him and could gain eternal life in his realm. Mummification, because it ritually reenacted Isis's wrapping of Osiris's body parts, was an important way of achieving that identification.

Belief in the afterlife was strong and complex. Egyptians envisioned that after death they would be led before a court of gods, where Osiris was the chief judge. The scribal god Thoth would record the testimony of the deceased, and each person's heart would be placed on a scale. On the other side of the scale was the symbolic feather of the goddess Ma'at, deity of balance and order. If the heart and the feather weighed the same, the deceased would safely enter the afterlife and would live forever with the gods.

Of the few thousand gods worshiped in Egypt, several dozen gained widespread affection throughout Egypt. Many of the most beloved deities were associated with certain animals and were shown with animal characteristics. These deities probably began as animal gods who became increasingly humanized. Among them, Hathor, shown as a cow or as a woman with cow horns, was associated with love and motherhood. Bastet, with a cat's head, was a household protector. Thoth, the god of writing, was shown with the head of an ibis (a heronlike bird); his bill suggested the scribe's reed pen. Anubis, with a jackal's head, was the god who carefully guided the dead to the courtroom of Osiris.

Gods were worshiped both at temples and in the home. Temple activity, managed by priests, involved taking daily care of the images of the gods, celebrating festivals, counseling, and producing art, medicines, and amulets. Egyptians seem to have been highly religious, organizing their lives according to the religious festivals of their area and protecting themselves with temple visits, chants, charms, and prayers.

EGYPTIAN INFLUENCES

Despite the Hebrews' desire to separate themselves from the culture of Egypt, Egyptian influences could not be entirely overcome. There are many signs of that influence in the Hebrew Bible. The name Moses, for example, is apparently Egyptian, variously translated "child," "born," or "son." (It is also found in the name Tutmose, meaning "child of Thoth," which was the name of several pharaohs.) The goddess Ma'at may have inspired the figure of the Wisdom of God in the Hebrew Book of Proverbs, where Wisdom is shown as a female figure who assists God in the work of creation (Prov. 8). Some of the psalms also may have Egyptian origins. The clearest example is Psalm 104, a hymn to the beauties of nature; it shows many parallels with an earlier hymn—found by archeologists in the ruins of the city of Aketaten (Tell el-Amarna) on the Nile—that praises Aten, the daytime sun, whose rays descend to nourish the earth.

As we've seen in previous chapters, the histories of religions show evidence of borrowings and influences, some obvious and others subtle. The history of the Hebrew religion is no exception. Archeologists and scholars will no doubt find more evidence of such connections as they continue their research and understanding of Hebrew and Egyptian history.

This small prayer room in a Bulgarian synagogue has all the elements required for the Sabbath service.

The Books of Joshua and Judges describe this period and give accounts of Israelite expansion and the eventual division of Canaan among eleven tribes. Realizing that they needed to be unified for their protection, the people of Israel soon established a king, selected a capital city, imposed a system of laws, and built a temple for centralized worship. The biblical Books of 1–2 Samuel and 1–2 Kings describe the process.

The first king, Saul (whose reign began c. 1025 BCE), became a tragic figure, suffering repeatedly from depression and then dying after a battle—one tradition says from suicide (1 Sam. 31:4). After a civil war divided the country's allegiance, a new king emerged to lead Israel. David (c. 1013–973 BCE) was a young man from Bethlehem, a town in the tribal area of Judah. As an accomplished military leader, David oversaw the buildup of the kingdom. Recognizing the need for a central city, he took over the hilltop town of Jebus, renaming it Jerusalem and establishing it as the national capital.

Recent archeological evidence seems to confirm the historical existence of David and his son Solomon, who constructed the temple envisioned by David. The Book of Chronicles records how Solomon built and dedicated the First Temple in Jerusalem. In this way he created a home for Yahweh, whose presence, it was hoped, would protect the kingdom. Services included prayers and hymns, accompanied by musical instruments such as trumpets and cymbals (see Ps. 150). Incense and grain were common offerings, and animals were ritually killed and offered as burnt sacrifices to Yahweh.[9]

Having a royal palace and the national temple in Jerusalem unified the separate Hebrew tribes for a time, but the taxes required to fund these and other extensive building projects quickly made the people rebellious. After the death of Solomon, the northern tribes broke away from the control of the king in Jerusalem and set up their own kingdom.

Division weakened the two kingdoms, and in 721 BCE Assyria, an expanding power in the northeast, took over the northern kingdom. A theological explanation for the destruction of the northern kingdom came from prophets of the time. **Prophets** (human beings who spoke in God's name) were significant figures—both as groups and as individuals. They were active from the earliest days of the kingdom; but individual prophets became especially important in the three hundred years after 800 BCE.

Deeper Insights

THE TEN COMMANDMENTS

I am the Lord your God who brought you out of Egypt, out of the land of slavery. You shall have no other god to set against me.

The Ten Commandments[10] begin with a reminder that Yahweh is the protector of the Hebrews and that because of his help they owe him their obedience. There seems to be an understanding, however, that other peoples have their own gods.

You shall not make a carved image for yourself nor the likeness of anything in the heavens above, or on the earth below, or in the waters under the earth. You shall not bow down to them or worship them; for I, the Lord your God, am a jealous god. I punish the children for the sins of their fathers to the third and fourth generations of those who hate me. But I keep faith with thousands, with those who love me and keep my commandments.

The commandment not to make images was meant to prevent worship of any deity but Yahweh, and it has been observed quite strictly over the centuries. Although a few early synagogue paintings of human figures have been found,[11] the prohibition has restrained in general the development of Jewish painting and sculpture. Only in the past hundred years have Jewish artists emerged, and many have been nonrepresentational artists.

You shall not make wrong use of the name of the Lord your God; the Lord will not leave unpunished the man who misuses his name.

The commandment against misuse of Yahweh's name opposes using God's name to bring misfortune on people, as by curses and black magic. Eventually, it was considered unacceptable to pronounce the name of Yahweh for any purpose whatsoever. Only the high priest had this privilege and did this but once a year.

Remember to keep the Sabbath day holy. You have six days to labor and do all your work. But the seventh day is a Sabbath of the Lord your God; that day you shall not do any work, you, your son or your daughter, your slave or your slave-girl, your cattle or the alien within your gates; for in six days the Lord made heaven and earth, the sea, and all that is in them, and on the seventh day He rested. Therefore the Lord blessed the Sabbath day and declared it holy.

The commandment to keep the Sabbath was a humane commandment, intended to give regular rest to servants, slaves, children, workers, and animals.

Honor your father and your mother, that you may live long in the land which the Lord your God is giving you.

The commandment to honor one's parents offers a reward: long life. We should note that Hebrews generally thought of rewards and punishments as being given on earth and in one's lifetime. The notion of rewards given in a future life or an afterlife was a later development.

You shall not commit murder.

This commandment does not prohibit all killing but prohibits murder—that is, unlawful and undeserved killing of human beings. Killing human beings in wartime and in self-defense was allowable, and execution was expected as the punishment for many types of crime.

You shall not commit adultery.

The commandment against adultery is only incidentally concerned with sex. Primarily it is a property law, because a man's wife was legally considered his property. This commandment is linked with the commandments immediately before and after it, because all three refer to property rights. To murder is to take unlawful possession of another person's body; to commit adultery is to disregard a man's right to sole possession of his wife; and to steal is to take unlawful possession of another person's goods.

You shall not steal.

You shall not give false evidence against your neighbor.

You shall not covet your neighbor's house; you shall not covet your neighbor's wife, his slave-girl, his ox, his ass, or anything that belongs to him.

In this last commandment, property rights are linked together and spelled out clearly.

Typically the prophet experienced a life-changing revelation from God and then felt commissioned by God to speak his message to the people. The prophet Isaiah, who was active in the eighth century BCE, is possibly the best known. He had a vision of God in the temple of Jerusalem, which he described as being filled with smoke—a symbol of the divine presence. In his experience there, he heard the voices of angels. They were crying out "Holy, holy, holy" in the presence of God (Isa. 6). His feeling of unworthiness dissolved when an angel touched a lighted coal to his lips, thus purifying and empowering Isaiah. From then on, he could speak his message. Isaiah and other prophets explained that political losses were punishment from Yahweh for worshiping other gods and for not having kept his laws. The losses were not a sign of God's weakness but rather of his justice and strength.

The southern kingdom, the kingdom of Judah, carried on alone for more than another century—though with constant anxiety. Unfortunately, another power had emerged—Babylonia—and at first the southern kingdom paid tribute; but when tribute was refused, Babylonia took control. In 586 BCE Nebuchadnezzar II destroyed Solomon's temple, tore down the city walls of Jerusalem, and took the aristocracy and a great part of the Jewish population off to exile in Babylonia. Their exile would last almost fifty years. Because the kingdom had ended and temple worship was no longer possible, the religion of Israel seemed to lose its heart.

Exile and Captivity

The period of exile in Babylonia (586–539 BCE) was a monumental turning point and one of the most emotional chapters in the history of Judaism. Psalm 137 is a manifestation of the sorrow felt by the Jews during their captivity. It tells of their inability to sing happy songs as long as they were in exile: "By the rivers of Babylon—there we sat down and there we wept when we remembered Zion."[12]

Without a temple, public ritual had come to an end, but in its place the written word took on new importance. During their exile in Babylonia, the Jews began to meet weekly to discuss the scriptures and to pray. What developed was the **Sabbath** service of worship, study, sermon, and psalms, performed in a meetinghouse, or *synagogue* (Greek: "lead together"). The period of exile also made it clear that the oral Hebrew religious traditions had to be written down if the Jews were to survive.

During their exile, the Jewish people began to assimilate influences from the surrounding Babylonian culture. Knowledge of the Hebrew language declined, while Aramaic, a sister language, emerged as the common tongue. (Aramaic eventually even crept into the sacred literature.[13]) Also emerging at this time was a growing sense of an active spirit of evil, often called Satan, and of a cosmic antagonism between good and evil. Although the sense of moral opposition was present in the Israelite religion from an early time, it may have been sharpened by the pain of exile.

Return to Jerusalem and the Second Temple

In 540 BCE, Cyrus came to the throne of the Persian Empire and, after taking over Babylonia, allowed the Jews to return to their homeland. The returning exiles rebuilt their temple, dedicating it in 515 BCE, and the sacrificial cult was reestablished. The Book of Psalms, containing the lyrics of 150 hymns, is often called the hymnbook of the Second Temple, and when we read in the closing psalms of all the instruments used in temple worship, we get a sense of the splendor of the ceremonies performed there.

At the same time, the work of recording oral traditions and editing written material also grew in importance. Scribes did not want the history of their people to be lost, and the result of their work was to become the Hebrew Bible. A final edition of the Torah (Pentateuch) was made, the prophetic books were compiled, and new books were written as well. Several of the last books written were literary—such as Ecclesiastes, a dark meditation on life, and the Song of Songs, a collection of love poetry. The books that would eventually be accepted into the Hebrew canon were finished by about 200 BCE.[14]

Although the Second Temple was destroyed in 70 CE, descriptions allow craftsmen to build models that show how it looked.

CULTURAL CONFLICT DURING THE SECOND TEMPLE ERA

The historical record in the canonical Hebrew scriptures ends with the building of the Second Temple. But the history of the region did not end here. Because of the geographic location of Israel, it seemed that the Jews in Israel would continually have to contend with invasions—and in some cases conquests—by foreign powers.

The Seleucid Period

When the army of Alexander the Great was on its way to conquer Egypt, it made Israel part of the Greek Empire, and after Alexander's death in 323 BCE, his generals divided up his empire. Israel at first was controlled by Egypt, which was ruled by the descendants of Alexander's general Ptolemy. Later, Israel was controlled by Syria, ruled by the descendants of Alexander's general Seleucus.

In 167 BCE a Seleucid ruler, Antiochus IV (Antiochus Epiphanes) took over the temple, apparently with the intention of introducing the worship of the Greek god Zeus to the site. He deliberately placed on the altar a dish of pork—a forbidden meat. He also forbade circumcision. His acts caused such hatred among the Jews that they rebelled. Led by a Jewish family of five brothers, the Maccabees (or Hasmoneans), the Jews took back the rule of their country, and the temple was rededicated to the worship of Israel's one God. (The winter festival of **Hanukkah,** widely kept today, joyously memorializes that rededication of the Second Temple.) The country retained its autonomy for almost a century, until the Roman general Pompey took control in 63 BCE.

Antagonism between Jewish culture and the growing Greek-speaking culture in the region was inevitable, because Jewish culture had values and practices that made absorption into Greek culture difficult, if not impossible. For example, all Jewish males were circumcised, which meant they were easily identified in the public baths or while exercising in gymnasiums. There were also Jewish dietary restrictions that forbade the eating of pork and shellfish and strict prohibitions against work on the Sabbath. These practices conflicted with the sophisticated Greek-speaking culture called Hellenism (from *Hellas,* meaning "Greece"). This culture was becoming dominant in the entire Mediterranean area, even after the Romans took control of the region. Greek plays and literature were read everywhere around the Mediterranean; Greek history, science, medicine, and mathematics were considered the most advanced of their day; and Greek architecture and city planning were becoming the norm. Because of its sophistication, Hellenistic culture was hugely attractive to educated people.

Responses to Outside Influences

Contact with Hellenistic culture led to a variety of responses. Some people welcomed it; some rejected it, clinging passionately to their own ethnic and religious roots; and the rest took a position in between. Tensions led to the rise of several religious factions among the Jews in Israel starting around 165 BCE.

The **Sadducees** were the first of the factions to emerge.[15] They were members of the priestly families, living primarily in Jerusalem, and were in charge of the temple and its activities. The fact that they derived their living from temple worship would have made them traditional—at least in their public behavior.

The **Pharisees** were the second faction that arose.[16] Their focus was on preserving Hebrew piety through careful observation of religious laws and traditions. (Later rabbinical Judaism would develop from and continue the work of the Pharisees.)

A third faction, eventually called the **Zealots,** was opposed to foreign influences and after 6 CE was bitterly opposed to Roman rule of Israel. The Romans called them "robbers." The name Zealots—from the Greek word for *zeal*—was given to them when wars began between the Jews and the Romans. The patriots sometimes used violent means to achieve their ends.

The **Essenes** were the fourth group. Not a great deal is known with certainty about them, although current interest in them is intense. Three authors of the classical world wrote about the Essenes: Philo (c. 10 BCE–50 CE), a Jewish theologian of Alexandria; Josephus (c. 37–100 CE), a Jewish general and historian; and Pliny the Elder (23–79 CE), a Roman writer. These classical writers indicate that the Essenes numbered several thousand; lived a communal, celibate life, primarily in the desert area near the Dead Sea; rejected animal sacrifice; and avoided meat and wine. We also are told that the Essenes were skilled in medicine, dressed in white, followed a solar calendar that was different from the lunar calendar used in the temple, studied the scriptures assiduously, and kept separate from the rest of society. Moreover, we now recognize that there may have been several varieties of Essenes and that a strict celibate core at Qumran (called the Covenanters) was supported by a noncelibate network of supporters and sympathizers throughout Israel.[17]

The Essenes saw themselves as an advance guard, preparing for the time when God would end the old world of injustice and bring about a new world of mercy and peace. They described themselves as "sons of light" who were fighting against the forces of "darkness." Because their center was no more than fifteen miles east of Jerusalem, they would have had some contact with the political currents of their day, and they may have shared some of the ideals of the Zealots and Pharisees.

Scrolls and scroll fragments, called the Dead Sea Scrolls, were uncovered between 1947 and 1955 in caves near Qumran, above the northwestern shore of the Dead Sea. It is possible that the scrolls constituted the library of the Essenes. It is also possible that the scrolls were a more general library of Jewish sacred books, brought from Jerusalem for safekeeping during the rebellion against the Romans that began in 66 CE. Besides containing all or part of nearly every book of the Hebrew scriptures, the cache of scrolls contained works that commented on scriptural books, gave details about the organization and practices of the Essenes, and spoke of a coming judgment and end of the world. The Dead Sea Scrolls show that during the later part

This piece of parchment from the Dead Sea Scrolls contains a selection from the Book of Isaiah.

of the Second Temple period, there was no universally accepted norm of correct religion, and the canon of scripture was still in the process of formation. Instead, there were many books and interpretations of correct practice, each competing for acceptance.

Although the Second Temple was flourishing, the older, ceremonial, temple-based religion was in fact giving way to a more decentralized religion, based on the Hebrew scriptures, on the practice of the Pharisees, and on religious practice in the synagogues.

THE DEVELOPMENT OF RABBINICAL JUDAISM

The Roman Empire assumed direct political control of much of Israel in 6 CE, and it ruled with severity. Consequently, there was much anti-Roman fervor and a widespread hope that, as in the time of the Maccabees, the foreigners could be expelled and a Jewish kingdom reestablished. A major revolt broke out in 66 CE, but Roman legions crushed it brutally in 70 CE, when they destroyed the temple and much of Jerusalem.

The end of the Second Temple was a turning point for the Jewish faith, producing two major effects. It ended the power of the priesthood, whose sacrificial rituals were no longer possible. It also forced the religion to develop in a new direction away from temple ritual, moving Judaism toward a central focus on scripture and scriptural interpretation.

The Canon of Scripture and the Talmud

Once the temple-based religion had been destroyed, it was necessary to clearly define which religious books—of the several hundred being revered and read by various groups—constituted the sacred canon. Although some scholars now question it, an old tradition holds that in about 90 CE, twenty years after the destruction of the Second Temple, Jewish rabbis gathered together in Israel at the town of Yavneh (Jamnia). There, it is said, they examined each book individually to decide which books would be included in the canon. (Some books, such as the Song of Songs and Ecclesiastes, were hotly debated and were almost excluded.) The canon of the land of Israel resulted from this process of selection. A slightly larger number of books had already been accepted by Jews in Egypt and came to be known as the Alexandrian canon.

Another revolt began in Israel in 132 CE. Some declared its leader, Bar Kokhba, to be the **Messiah,** the long-awaited savior sent by God to the Jews. In 135 CE, the Romans put down this second revolt even more cruelly than the first, with many public executions. Jewish families who had remained in Israel even after the destruction of the Second Temple now fled. They not only went to Egypt but also settled around the Mediterranean, expanding the number of Jews living in the **diaspora** (dispersion of Jews beyond Israel). The existence of a canon of scripture, which could be copied and carried anywhere, brought victory out of apparent defeat. Rabbinical Judaism, based on interpreting sacred scripture and oral tradition, could spread and flourish.

Once the Hebrew scriptures were declared complete, the next logical development was their protection and explanation. Interpretive work, called midrash ("seeking out"), became a central focus of evolving Judaism. The work of interpreting the Hebrew scriptures and applying their principles to everyday problems went on in stages. By about 200 CE there existed a philosophical discussion in six parts of specific biblical laws and their application, called the Mishnah ("repetition"). By about 400 CE, the Mishnah had received further commentary (the Gemara, "supplement"), and the result was the Palestinian **Talmud** ("study"), or Talmud of the Land of Israel.

When people use the word *Talmud,* however, they usually are referring to a second, larger collection of material. Because it was compiled by religious specialists in Babylonia, it is called the Babylonian Talmud. Complete by about 600 CE, the Babylonian Talmud consists of the earlier Mishnah and an extensive commentary. After the Hebrew Bible itself, the Babylonian Talmud became the second-most important body of Jewish literature, and it continued to be commented on over the centuries by rabbinical specialists.

The Babylonian Talmud is vast, sometimes being compared to an ocean in which a person can sail or swim. In the Babylonian Talmud, rabbis of different generations added their insights and solutions to problems. The growth of opinion is visible, because the earliest material is printed in the center of each page, and later commentary is arranged around it. The Babylonian Talmud contains legal material (*halakhah,* "direction") and nonlegal anecdotes and tales (*haggadah,* "tradition"). It is really a large encyclopedia, organized into sections, or tractates, according to subject matter. Its size and complexity, along with the difficulty of mastering it, would contribute to a strong scholarly orientation in later Judaism.

Islam and Medieval Judaism

The diaspora introduced Jewish vitality to places far from Israel, such as Spain and Iraq. After the ninth century, this Jewish presence was possible because of the tolerance with which Islam—now dominant in Spain, North Africa, and the Middle East—usually treated the Jews. Islam has held that Jews and Christians have a special status: called "people of the book," they are members with Muslims in the same extended religious family. The result was that cities such as Alexandria, Cairo, Baghdad, and Córdoba became havens for Jewish thought.

Foremost among the Jewish medieval thinkers was Moses Maimonides (called Rambam, 1135–1204). Maimonides was born in Córdoba, but he and his family fled that city when it was occupied by Muslim forces hostile to both Jews and Christians. He eventually settled in Cairo, where he practiced medicine at the court of Salah al-Din (Saladin). The work that made him famous was his book *The Guide of the Perplexed,* in which he argued that Judaism was a rational religion and that faith and reason were complementary. He wrote this work in Arabic in order to make it accessible to a wide readership. Maimonides is also known for his *Mishneh Torah,* a scholarly work written in Hebrew, which is a summary of the Talmud and other rabbinical writings. Maimonides is renowned for his list of the basic principles of Jewish belief, which we will discuss later in this chapter.

Jewish thought has consistently shown several approaches in its interpretation of the Hebrew Bible. The more conservative tendency, which produced the Talmud, has interpreted the Hebrew scriptures fairly strictly, using them as a guide for ethical living. Another trend has been speculative, using the scriptures imaginatively as a way to understand more about the nature of God and the universe. Out of this second tendency came works of Jewish mysticism, which we look at next.

The Kabbalah

The Middle Ages saw renewed interest in Jewish mysticism. The whole body of Jewish mystical literature, called **Kabbalah** ("received," "handed down"), began to emerge even before the Common Era in works that speculated on mysterious passages of the Hebrew Bible. For example, kabbalistic literature speculated about Enoch (an early descendant of Adam) and the prophet Elijah, who had not died but had simply been transported upward to God's realm (Gen. 5:24 and 2 Kings 2:11). It also speculated about Yahweh's throne (*merkebah*) and the sound of the surrounding angels (see Isa. 6:2), using the scriptures as a tool for understanding more about the reality of God and the hidden structure of the universe. A frequent mystical assumption was that the Hebrew Bible was written in coded language that could be interpreted only by those who knew the code. Much biblical language, this view held, was to be read not literally but symbolically.

New mystical speculation arose in the medieval period, sometimes as a response to the growing persecution of Jews. Common themes were the divine origin of the world, God's care for the Jews, and the eventual coming of the Messiah (spoken of in Dan. 7 and elsewhere). The human world was frequently seen as the microcosm of a greater heavenly world beyond the earth and the human being as a microcosm of the universe: "the superior and inferior worlds are bound together under the form of the Holy Body, and the worlds are associated together."[19]

The most famous book of the Kabbalah is the *Zohar* ("splendor"). It was long believed to have been written in the first centuries of the Common Era, but in actuality it was probably written about 1280 in Spain by Rabbi Moses de León. The *Zohar* sees the universe as having emerged from a pure, boundless, spiritual reality. From the divine Unity come the ten *sefiroth*—ten active, divine powers, such as wisdom, intelligence, love, and beauty. The *Zohar* compares them to colors, and sees the sefiroth as links between God and his creation. Human beings are particularly significant in creation, blending the divine and the earthly, for within their bodies is a spark of divine light that seeks liberation and a return to God. Other texts included the *Sefer Yetzirah* and the *Sefer HaHasidim*. Some Jewish circles valued the mystical texts of the Kabbalah as much as, or even more than, the Talmud.[20]

> From the innermost center of the flame sprang forth a well out of which colors issued and spread upon everything beneath, hidden in the mysterious hiddenness of the Infinite.
>
> —The *Zohar*[21]

Christianity and Medieval Judaism

The mystical movements gave comfort to European Jews as their persecution increased. Christianity had become the dominant religion in all of Europe by the late thirteenth century, but Christianity carried with it an anti-Jewish prejudice that had been present since the first century CE, when Christianity was separating—sometimes angrily—from its Jewish origins (see, for example, Matt. 27:25 and Acts 7:31–60 in the Christian New Testament).

The dominant position of Christianity in medieval Europe also had political implications, because Christians were thought of as loyal citizens, whereas Jews were treated as suspicious and even traitorous persons.

At a cemetery in Budapest, mourners shovel dirt into the grave while a rabbi chants prayers.

Because so much of Jewish religious practice was carried out in the home, superstitious stories circulated among Christians that Jews needed the blood of Christian children for their Passover meal or that they stole and misused the consecrated Christian communion bread. Because Jews were often forbidden to own farmland, they were excluded from agriculture; and because they were kept out of the guilds (the medieval craft unions), they were excluded from many types of urban work. Furthermore, because Christians in the Middle Ages were generally prohibited from lending money at interest, this role became a Jewish occupation, but it generated much ill will among those to whom money was lent. In many places, Jews were forced to wear a special cap or display some other identifying detail. They were sometimes also forced to live in a separate section of town, called a *ghetto,* which might be walled so that Jews could be locked in at night.

Jews were persecuted regularly. At the time of the First Crusade, for example, many were killed by crusaders traveling through what is now Germany to Israel. During the period of the bubonic plague, also known as the Black Death (1347–1351), Jews sometimes were blamed for the deaths. In retaliation, many Jews were killed; some were even burned alive in their synagogues.

Beginning in the late Middle Ages, European Jews were forced into exile. Often the motive was economic as much as religious, because exiling the Jews would allow the Christian rulers to confiscate their property and to be freed of debt to them. Over a period of two centuries, Jews were expelled from England, France, Spain, and Portugal. In Spain, they were forced in 1492 to become Christians or to leave. Some Spanish Jews converted to Christianity but continued Jewish practice in their homes. As a result of the Spanish Inquisition, which sought out Jews who had converted for the sole purpose of remaining in Spain, Jews fled elsewhere—to Morocco, Egypt, Greece, Turkey, Holland, central Europe, and the New World. It is at this time that two great cultural divisions of Judaism emerged—Sephardic Judaism in the Mediterranean region, North Africa, and the Middle East, and Ashkenazic Judaism in Germany, central Europe, and France. We will look at their cultural differences later, when we examine the branches of Judaism.

QUESTIONING AND REFORM

The Renaissance of the fifteenth and sixteenth centuries began a new era for Europe. As people began to travel more, they were exposed to a multitude of previously unknown religions, cultures, and regions of the world. The invention of printing with movable type quickened this process by making written material widely available. Discoveries in science and instruments such as the telescope revolutionized people's perception of the earth and its relationship to the larger universe. These changes, which presented challenges to the Christian worldview, also affected Judaism.

After the Renaissance, Judaism began to move in two directions, both of which continue today. One direction cherished traditional ways; the other saw a need for modernization. The traditionalist way, strong in eastern Europe, offered refuge from an uncertain world. In central Europe, traditionalism expressed itself both in Talmudic scholarship and in the devotional movement Hasidism ("devotion," "piety"). The Hasidic movement was founded by Israel ben Eliezer (c. 1700–1760), a mystic and faith healer known affectionately as the Baal Shem Tov (the "good master of the Holy Name"). He felt that living according to the rules of the Torah and Talmud was important, but he also felt that devout practice should be accompanied by an ecstatic sense of God who is present everywhere.[22] Hasidism emphasized the beauty of everyday life and the physical world, teaching that "only in tangible things can you see or hear God."[23] Mystical schools were sometimes considered suspicious, for they could easily supplant traditional practices with those of the school, and they could encourage disciples to proclaim their master as the long-awaited messiah. Hasidism, however, made it possible for mystical interest to be accepted in mainstream Judaism. Hasidism continued to inspire Jews for centuries and remains one of the most vital movements in Judaism today.

The other direction in which Judaism moved was toward modernization. The liberal direction, which was strongest in Germany and France, urged Jews to move out of the ghettos, gain a secular education, and enter the mainstream of their respective countries. In Germany, the modernizing movement, called the Reform, began in the late eighteenth century. With the goal of making worship more accessible, the Reform movement translated many of the Hebrew prayers into German and introduced elements such as organ and choir music. The Reform movement, however, generated many counterresponses—among them, an attempt to preserve traditional Judaism (Orthodox Judaism) and an attempt to maintain the best of tradition with some modern elements (Conservative Judaism). We will look at all these movements later in more detail.

> The creator and the object of His creation are a Unity inseparable.
> —Hasidic saying[24]

JUDAISM AND THE MODERN WORLD

The growth of freedom for European Jews over the nineteenth century did not end anti-Jewish activity. The Russian Empire, where Eastern Orthodox Christianity was the established religion, continued its restrictions on Jews, with occasional outbreaks of persecution. In response, Jews from Russia, Poland, and the Baltic area emigrated, and from 1880 to 1920 more than a million Jews came to the United States, most coming to or through New York City. Their children and grandchildren sometimes moved farther, settling in Los Angeles, Chicago, Miami, and elsewhere. Jews also emigrated to other large cities in North America and Latin America, such as Montreal, Toronto, Mexico City, and Buenos Aires—bringing a new freedom to Judaism, but at a price. Jewish identity was compromised because many Jews wished to assimilate with the surrounding culture, and intermarriage grew in frequency.

Traditional Jewish life continued in Europe until the end of the 1930s, particularly in Poland and the Baltic region, where there were still more than three million Jews. Beautiful evocations of this warm, traditional lifestyle are evident in the paintings of Marc Chagall and in the book that he and his wife Bella created together, *Burning Lights*.[25] This centuries-old culture, however, would be destroyed within ten years by Adolf Hitler.

Hitler and the Holocaust

The rise of Adolf Hitler in 1933 as German chancellor and head of the Nazi Party began a prolonged wave of anti-Jewish activity that ended in the most dreadful sufferings. Hitler was fueled by several irrational notions. One was a theory of racial classes, which imagined Jews and Gypsies to be subhuman polluters of a pure but mythical Aryan race. Another was Hitler's belief that Jewish financiers and industrialists had conspired against Germany and helped make possible the Allied victory over the Germans during World War I. Hitler sought both an imaginary racial purity and political revenge.

At first, the Nazis put pressure on Jews to emigrate by forcing them out of government and university positions, by boycotting their stores, and eventually by physically persecuting them. Many Jews did emigrate, particularly to North America—Albert Einstein is a well-known example. After the annexation of Austria and the invasion of Poland (1939), Nazi control eventually spread to Holland, Norway, northern France, and Czechoslovakia; and as Nazi domination spread to these countries, so too did the persecution of Jews. Jews who wanted to flee found it hard to find refuge, because many countries, including the United States, refused to take in large numbers of Jews. Moreover, France and England did not forcefully protest Hitler's policies against the Jews, and the Catholic leader Pope Pius XII had signed an earlier concordat of understanding with Hitler. The Jews were without defenders, and when World War II was declared, they were caught in a trap.

Hitler began plans to exterminate all European Jews. Jews in countries under Nazi control were officially identified, made to wear yellow stars in public, and eventually deported via train to concentration camps. Upon arrival at the camps, Jews were often divided into two groups: (1) those who were strong enough to work and (2) the rest—mostly women, children, the sick, and the elderly—who were to be killed immediately. (The psychologist Viktor Frankl has described the process in his book *Man's Search for Meaning.*) At first, internees were shot to death; but as their numbers increased, gas chambers and crematoria were constructed to kill them and incinerate their bodies. Those who were kept as workers lived in horrible conditions and were routinely starved, insufficiently clothed, and attacked by all kinds of vermin and disease. Few ultimately survived.

By the end of World War II in 1945, about twelve million people—Jews, homosexuals, Jehovah's Witnesses, prisoners of war, and political enemies—had died in the concentration camps. Of these, it is estimated that as many as six million were Jews, and of that number about a million and a half were Jewish children. This immense loss is called the **Holocaust** (Greek: "completely burned") or *Shoah* (Hebrew: "extermination"). It is one of the greatest crimes ever committed against humanity.

The extermination has left a shadow on civilization and a great scar on Judaism. About a third of the world's Jews were killed during the Holocaust, and of those who died, a large number had been devout traditional Jews. Their deaths, under such painful circumstances, raised haunting questions about the faith and future of Judaism.

Barbed wire and guard towers surround Auschwitz buildings, where most "guest workers" awaited death during World War II.

Creation of the State of Israel

A major result of the Holocaust was the creation of the state of Israel after more than a century of hope, thought, and work. Centuries of virulent anti-Jewish restriction and persecution had created in many Jews a desire for a Jewish nation, where they could live without fear, in the traditional historic home of their faith. The movement came to be called **Zionism,** after Mount Zion, the mountain on which Jerusalem is built.

The state of Israel emerged through several steps. The first was the notion of a separate Jewish nation, popularized by the influential book *The Jewish State,* written by the Hungarian-born Austrian writer Theodor Herzl (1860–1904) following an outbreak of anti-Semitism in France. The second step was the

Balfour Declaration, a political statement issued in 1917 by the British government, which endorsed the notion of a Jewish homeland. When World War I ended, the British received control of the area then called Palestine and authorized a limited immigration of Jews to their territory, the British Mandate of Palestine. The third step came after World War II, when the newly created United Nations voted to divide the British Mandate of Palestine into two states, one for Jews and the other for the Palestinians, the Arab residents of the mandate. The Jews accepted the U.N. plan and created the state of Israel when the mandate ended in 1948. The Palestinians, who had opposed Jewish immigration into the region under the British, rejected the U.N. plan and, along with neighboring Arab nations, resisted the creation of Israel.

The difficult relationship between Jews and Palestinians has continued to the present day. There have been repeated wars and an exchange of terrorist activities between Israelis and Palestinians, and the conflict has grown more horrifying in recent years. So far the conflict has not been resolved.

Because European Judaism was almost completely destroyed, Jewish life today has two centers: Israel and the United States. The estimated Jewish population of Israel is about five million and that of the United States is roughly six million. Judaism in the United States is largely liberal and enjoys general freedom of practice. In Israel, Judaism encompasses a wide spectrum of opinions and practices, ranging from liberal and even atheistic to highly conservative and traditionally religious. Some important control of government policy and daily life is in the hands of traditionalists, but for perhaps a majority of the population, Judaism is more a culture than a religion.

PERSONAL EXPERIENCE
A Visit to the Anne Frank House

In high school I read the diary of Anne Frank, a teenage Jewish girl of Amsterdam who had hidden with her family and others throughout most of World War II. Her sensitive diary covers her years from age 13 to 15. In August of 1944, Nazi soldiers found the family and took them away to the concentration camp of Bergen-Belsen, where Anne died in March of 1945—just months before the war ended. Her father was the only family member who survived, and when he returned to Amsterdam he was given her diary, found on the floor of the house where they had hidden.

In her diary she wrote of her discovery of the beauty of nature—something she'd never appreciated before. Hiding in the attic rooms, she began to look out an upstairs window for long periods of time. One night she wrote: "the dark, rainy evening, the gale, the scudding clouds held me entirely in their power; it was the first time in a year and a half that I'd seen the night face to face."[26] Anne described having fallen in love there and her first kiss—with her friend Peter, who was also in hiding. As she described it, "suddenly the ordinary Anne slipped away and a second Anne took her place, a second Anne who is not reckless and jocular, but one who just wants to love and be gentle."[27] She wrote as well of God, religion, and belief.

During my first trip to Europe, near the end of my college years, I sought out the narrow house beside the canal in Amsterdam where Anne and her family and others had all lived in hiding. After climbing the steep, narrow stairs, I looked out through the same window that Anne had looked out many times, and I realized that the life and young intelligence that had once lived here had been so meaninglessly destroyed. As I stood there in thought, gazing through the open window, the bells of a nearby church rang out. What complex feelings, I thought, had the sound of those bells evoked in Anne and her family. As for me, I could feel only loss and emptiness.

Afterwards, when reading her diary again, I marveled at the hopefulness she expressed there, near the end of the book, and near the end of her short life: "in spite of everything I still believe that people are really good at heart."[28]

JEWISH BELIEF

There is no official Jewish creed, but there is a set of central beliefs, first formulated by the medieval scholar Maimonides. Among them are

- Belief in God. God is one, formless, all-knowing, and eternal. God is master of the universe as its creator and judge. God is both loving and just.
- Belief in the words of the prophets.
- Belief that God gave the law to Moses.
- Belief that the Messiah, the savior to be sent by God, will come someday.
- Belief that there will be a resurrection of the good "in the world to come."

Regarding these beliefs, there is no universal agreement about the precise meaning of the Messiah, the resurrection of the good, or "the world to come." In the past, these were understood literally. The Messiah would be a heaven-sent, powerful leader who would inaugurate a new age, and at that time the deceased who had followed God's laws would come back to life. Some Jews no longer interpret these beliefs literally but see them as symbols of the ultimate triumph of goodness in the world.

Belief in personal immortality or in the resurrection of the dead has been a frequent topic of debate among Jews. Although the notions of resurrection and even of an immortal soul have been defended by many within the Jewish faith, Judaism more strongly emphasizes the kind of immortality that comes from acting virtuously in this world, living on in one's children, and leaving behind some charitable contribution to the world.

In Judaism, human beings have a special role. Because they are created in God's image, they have the ability to reason, to will, to speak, to create, and to care; and they have the responsibility to manifest these divine characteristics in the world. Jews believe that among human beings, the Jewish people have a special role—a role that some believe is to witness to the one God and to do his will in the world. Others believe that their role is to suffer for a purpose known only to God. And others have said that their role is to bring a sense of justice to a world that often has none. Although there is no agreement about *the* Jewish role, there is general consensus among Jews that they hold a unique place in this world, and there is great pride in knowing that they have contributed so much to world culture.

RELIGIOUS PRACTICE

To be a Jew, however, does not come only from holding a set of beliefs; it is even more a way of living. Scholars explain this by saying that Judaism is less interested in *orthodoxy* (correct belief) and far more interested in *orthopraxy* (correct practice). The Ten Commandments, of course, are at the heart of Jewish morality, and they direct behavior; but there are many additional laws and specific customs that dictate how time is to be used, what foods are to be eaten, and how prayer is to be conducted. And although Judaism promotes congregational worship, many Jewish celebrations are carried on in the home. Moving like wheels within wheels, the week, month, and year all have their devotional rhythms, established by religious laws and customs. The goal of all laws, however, is the recognition of God's presence and the sanctification of human life.

The Jewish Sabbath

Central to all forms of Judaism is keeping the Sabbath, the seventh day of the week, as a special day. The Sabbath, when kept properly, is felt to sanctify the entire week. Recalling the royal rest of God after the six laborious days of creation, the Sabbath is a day of special prayer and human relaxation (see Exod. 20:11 and 31:12–17).[29] In earlier times, before watches and clocks were invented, a "day" began in the evening at sundown; thus the Jewish Sabbath begins on Friday at sunset and lasts until Saturday at sunset.

The traditional purpose of the Sabbath was a compassionate one: it was to allow everyone, even slaves and animals, regular rest. The prohibition against work has been interpreted variously over the centuries. Traditionally, fires could not be built on the Sabbath because of the labor involved; this meant that food would have to be cooked beforehand or eaten uncooked (see Exod. 35:1–3). Shops, of course, would be closed. Interpreting the requirement of rest in the modern would, some Jews will not operate light switches or kitchen stoves, nor will they drive a car or use the telephone during the Sabbath. Although some restrictions might seem excessive, their purpose is to separate the everyday world of labor from the one day of the week in which everyone can enjoy leisure.

The Sabbath is meant to be joyous and is often remembered that way by adults who have grown up in traditional households. The Talmud recommends

Deeper Insights

WHAT'S IN A NAME?

Just one example of the immense cultural influence of the Hebrew Bible is evident in many commonly used names. Following are some personal names from the Hebrew Bible, along with their original meanings and places where they may be found in the Bible:

Aaron: "exalted one" (Exod. 4–6)

Abel: "breath" (Gen. 4)

Abigail: "father is rejoicing" (1 Sam. 25)

Abner: "the father is a light" (2 Sam. 2–3)

Abraham: "father of many" (Gen. 12–25)

Adam: "humankind" (Gen. 2–3)

Amos: "carried [by God]" (Amos 1–9)

Benjamin: "favorite son" (Gen. 42–44)

Caleb: "dog," meaning "faithful" (Josh. 14)

Daniel: "God is my judge" (Dan. 1–12)

David: "beloved" (2 Sam. 1–24)

Deborah: "bee" (Judg. 4–5)

Esther: "[the goddess] Ishtar" (Esther 1–9)

Ethan: "firmness" (1 Chron. 6:44)

Eve: "life" (Gen. 2–3)

Hannah: "grace" (1 Sam. 1–2)

Isaac: "laughter" (Gen. 21–35)

Isaiah: "The Lord is my salvation" (Isa. 6)

Jacob: "seizing by the heel" (Gen. 25–50)

Jared: "descent" (Gen. 5)

Jeremy: "The Lord frees" (Jer. 12–13)

Joel: "The Lord is God" (Joel 1–3)

Jonathan: "The Lord has given" (1 Sam. 20)

Joseph: "may he add" (Gen. 37–50)

Joshua: "The Lord's help" (Josh. 1–24)

Malachi: "my messenger" (Mal. 1–4)

Micah: "Who is like [God]?" (Mic. 1–7)

Michael: "Who is like God?" (Dan. 10–12)

Miriam: "rebellion" (Exod. 15)

Naomi: "my delight" (Ruth 1–4)

Nathan: "gift" (2 Sam. 12)

Noah: "rest" (Gen. 6–9)

Rachel: "ewe" (Gen. 29–35)

Rebecca: "noose" (Gen. 24)

Reuben: "behold, a son" (Gen. 37)

Ruth: "companion" (Ruth 1–4)

Samuel: "name of God" (1 Sam. 1–3)

Sarah: "princess" (Gen. 17–23)

Seth: "appointed" (Gen. 4–5)

that the mother of the household welcome the Sabbath on Friday night by lighting candles, and it recommends that the family drink wine at the Sabbath meal as a sign of happiness. During the Jewish exile in Babylonia, synagogue study and worship became a regular way to mark the Sabbath, and today it is common for religious Jews to attend a synagogue service on Friday night or Saturday morning. Friends are often invited over to share the main Sabbath meal, and on Saturday evening the Sabbath is at last bid farewell. There is an old Jewish adage: More than the Jews have kept the Sabbath, has the Sabbath kept the Jews.

Jews speak with pride of their observance of the Sabbath, pointing out that the great gift of Judaism to the world has not been the creation of a beautiful temple in physical space but rather the creation of a beautiful temple in time. Jews were once called lazy by the Romans for stopping their work one day out of every seven. But the Jewish practice has triumphed, and one day of the week is generally set aside as a day of rest throughout the world.

Holy Days

Just as the week is sanctified by the Sabbath, so the months and the entire year are sanctified by regular holy days and periods, each marked by a distinctive emotional tone—happiness, sadness, repentance, gratitude.

Before speaking of specific festivals, we must point out that the Jewish religious calendar is lunar, meaning that each month begins with the new moon. However, adjustments must be made in order to keep the lunar years in general harmony with the regular, solar calendar. Because a year of twelve lunar months lasts 354 days, one lunar year is eleven days shorter than one solar year. Therefore, in the Jewish religious calendar an extra month is added approximately every three years. The lunar months of the Jewish year thus vary somewhat, as do the holy days.

New Year's Day is **Rosh Hashanah** ("head of the year"). The Jewish religious year begins at the end of harvest season, when all debts can be paid off. Thus the religious New Year occurs in the autumn, in late September or early October. The New Year period of ten days, called the High Holy Days, ends with **Yom Kippur** ("day of covering"). Called the Day of Atonement, Yom Kippur is the most solemn day of the year. It is a day of fasting, prayer, and reflection, meant to cleanse people for the upcoming religious year.

Following soon after the High Holy Days comes the late-harvest festival of **Sukkot** ("shelters," "booths"). Temporary outdoor shelters were once used as a way of protecting crops in the fields. Devout families still construct them, eat in them, and occasionally even sleep in them. Nowadays the shelters often are constructed in backyards and on porches. The festival recalls the wandering of the early Hebrews.

An Orthodox Jewish boy practices blowing a shofar in preparation for the Jewish New Year. The shofar, made of a ram's horn, is used in conjunction with Jewish observances.

A winter festival is Hanukkah ("dedication"). It is also called the "Feast of Lights" because the festival recalls a time when the Second Temple was rededicated and oil lamps burned miraculously for eight days. To commemorate this December festival, families gather on eight evenings, light candles on a special **menorah**, and give their children presents.

In February Jews celebrate **Purim** ("lots"). The festival recalls the divine protection given to the Jews at the time of Esther and her uncle, Mordecai. Purim is marked with the giving of food and money, a reading of the Book of Esther, and a festive meal.

The springtime festival of Pesach ("pass over"), or Passover, recalls the Hebrews' departure from Egypt. It is a feast of freedom, kept with prayers and a special meal, called the **Seder** ("order"). The Seder includes several traditional foods, including breads without yeast (matzoh), wine, parsley, a hard-boiled egg (symbolizing new life), saltwater (symbolizing tears), and an animal bone (symbolizing the paschal lamb). After recalling the liberation from Egypt, the diners share a large meal and sing songs of liberation.

Jewish Dietary Practices

From its earliest biblical origins, Judaism has valued cleanliness and care regarding food. What were once basic rules of hygiene developed into rules about ritual purity. In recent centuries, some Jews have relaxed their observance of certain dietary rules, keeping them to a greater or lesser degree as they think suitable and according to the branch of Judaism to which they belong.

Amnesty International and other organizations arranged this Passover Seder in south Tel Aviv for African refugees, local Jews, and employees of nongovernmental organizations. Guests chat as they await the special meal.

One of the basic tenets of traditional Jewish dietary practice is that food consumption and food handling be done according to religious laws. The term **kosher** (Hebrew: *kasher*) means "ritually correct" and particularly applies to food preparation and consumption. In regard to meat, all blood must be drained before the meat is cooked and eaten, because blood, which gives life, is sacred to God. In temple services, blood was offered on the altar separately from the rest of the sacrificed animal, and only meat without blood could be eaten by the priests and sharers in the sacred meal (see Lev. 17). This rule also ensured that animals that had died in the field or were killed by larger animals—carcasses that might be unsafe to eat—could not be consumed (see Exod. 22:31). In practice, there are very specific methods of kosher slaughter, inspection, and preservation.

Pork and shellfish are forbidden (see Lev. 11), probably because these animals were considered scavengers and thus easily contaminated by what they ate. (Pork sometimes contains a parasite, *Trichinella spiralis*, which can be killed only by cooking at high temperatures.)[30] For traditional Jews, meat and dairy products may not be mixed or eaten together at the same meal. This also means that a household that "keeps kosher" must maintain separate sets of cooking implements, pans, dishes, and utensils—one for meat and one for dairy products. Some households even have separate sinks and refrigerators. These practices derive from a rule of uncertain origin that forbids the cooking of a baby goat or lamb in its mother's milk (Exod. 34:26). It is possible the practice was forbidden for being cruel; some fetal animals, cut from the womb before birth, were considered tender delicacies. The practice of cooking a kid in its mother's milk may also have been associated with non-Hebrew religious practice and therefore forbidden.

Marc Chagall's 1914 *Rabbi of Vitebsk* shows a Russian rabbi deep in prayer, expressing an almost shamanistic intensity.

Other Religious Practices

Devout Jews practice regular daily prayer at dawn, noon, and dusk and often at bedtime. When they pray in the morning during the week, traditionalist males use the **tefillin,** or *phylacteries*, which are two small boxes containing scriptural passages; one is attached to the forehead by leather straps tied around the head, and the other is attached to the upper left arm by straps wound down around the arm and hand. They signify quite literally that God's law is in the mind and heart of the person at prayer (see Deut. 6:8). The **talit** (a prayer shawl)—usually white, with dark stripes and fringe—covers the man's head and body during prayer and signifies humility in the sight of God. In less traditional forms of Judaism, the prayer shawl is sometimes not used, but men wear the skullcap (*kippah* in Hebrew and **yarmulke** in Yiddish, the old language of eastern European Jews). Devout males sometimes express their reverence before God during their waking hours by covering their heads continually with a skullcap.

Remembrance of God is also assisted by the presence of a *mezuzah*, which is placed on the doorpost of the entrance to a home and sometimes on the doorposts of interior rooms (see Deut. 6:9). Like the tefillin, the mezuzah is a small container that holds scriptural words; it can be touched upon entering the house or room. Unlike the tefillin, it is used even by secular Jews.

Perhaps because sexuality and the origin of life are considered especially sacred, Judaism has a number of practices relating to them. Eight days after birth, when a male receives his name, he is circumcised—the foreskin of the boy's penis is cut off by a specialist. The ceremony recalls God's covenant with the Hebrew people (see Gen. 17 and Lev. 12:3). The origin of this practice in Judaism is uncertain. It began possibly as a health measure, to prevent infection commonly brought about by hot climates; but it is also possible that circumcision began as a way of recognizing divine control over sex and generation. Males mark puberty with a coming-of-age ceremony at age 13, when a young man legally becomes an adult, or "son of the commandment" (**bar mitzvah**).

In some branches of Judaism, girls ages 12 to 18 are honored in a coming-of-age ceremony called a *bat mitzvah.* For women, menstruation and childbirth have also been considered special occasions, celebrated with a ritual bath (*mikvah*) and purification.

Although in ancient days temporary celibacy was expected of priests on duty in the temple and soldiers in the field, sex has been viewed positively in Judaism. With the exception of the Essenes, Jews have honored marriage and considered children a major goal of life (see Gen. 1:28 and 12:2).

The view of women's roles is expanding quickly, though with argument. The most liberal strands of Judaism accept complete gender equality. The most conservative traditions, however, maintain the earlier restrictions. (Actual practice can fall somewhere in between.)

Traditional groups have argued that men and women are "equal but separate." The great emphasis on family life has allowed women to be seen as the natural and best nurturers of children. Therefore, their main role has been homemaking. Men, by contrast, have been the ones who carry on study and public prayer. Men read Torah aloud in services, act as rabbis and cantors, and study Talmud and other religious texts.

This division of labor began to change in the last century. As women started to question their traditional image, barricades fell. In some traditions females can now become cantors and are ordained as rabbis.

Devout Jews place a mezuzah beside their doors and touch it reverently when they enter.

Rejection of this change, however, is particularly strong among the Orthodox. In North America, where the Orthodox constitute a small percentage of the Jewish population, their stance is not so influential. But in Israel, where the Orthodox make up a larger percentage of the Jewish population, they play a major governmental role in defining rules for Sabbath observance, food preparation, and marriage. Currently attempts are being made to include non-Orthodox leaders and female rabbis in this official machinery, but so far these efforts have had little success. The Orthodox continue to argue that the role of the woman is to be the "good wife and wise mother." They fear that women's working outside the home will damage the warmth and effectiveness of traditional family life.

DIVISIONS WITHIN CONTEMPORARY JUDAISM

We find in Judaism both cultural differences and differences in the observance of traditional rules. Some commentators, as a result, talk not of "Judaism" but of "Judaisms."

Culturally Based Divisions

The great ethnic diversity among Jews has resulted in a number of cultural divisions within Judaism. It is important to understand these divisions in order to appreciate the richness of Judaism, as well as the challenges that face Israel, where members of these groups have come to live together.

Sephardic Jews   The name *Sephardic* comes from a mythic land of Sephar (or Sepharad), once thought to exist in the distant west of Israel and often identified with Spain. After the Roman victories over the Jews in Israel (70 and 135 CE), Jews emigrated from Israel and settled in lands far away. Southern Spain particularly became a center of flourishing Jewish life, especially under Muslim rule, but this ended with the expulsion of the Muslims and Jews by the Christian rulers in 1492 CE. Sephardic Jews (**Sephardim**) carried their language and culture to Morocco, Greece, Turkey, Egypt, and elsewhere in the Mediterranean region, as well as to Holland and England. The common language of the Sephardic Jews, termed Ladino in recognition of its ultimate derivation from Latin, was a type of Spanish mixed with Hebrew words and often written in Hebrew characters. Sephardic Jews lived in significant numbers in Morocco until recent times, when most emigrated to Israel. More than half of the Jews of Israel are of Sephardic background.

Ashkenazic Jews   The name *Ashkenazic* comes from Ashkenaz, a descendant of Noah who settled in a distant northern land (see Gen. 10:3). The term **Ashkenazim** refers to those Jews who at one time lived in or came from central Europe. A very large population of Jews flourished for centuries in Poland, the Ukraine, Lithuania, Latvia, Germany, and Hungary; and before the Holocaust, three million Jews lived in Poland alone, where sometimes

This Sephardic synagogue is located in Yangon, Myanmar, far from the area ordinarily associated with the diaspora and Jewish emigration. Although the synagogue has no rabbi today, it is maintained as if a rabbi will arrive at any moment.

entire towns (called *shtetls*) were Jewish. The origin of Ashkenazic Judaism is unclear, but the most common opinion is that it arose when Jews migrated from France and other countries of western Europe to central Europe, after 1000 CE.

The common language of central European Judaism was Yiddish ("Jewish"), a medieval form of German mixed with Hebrew words and written in Hebrew characters. While it flourished, Ashkenazic Judaism produced a rich culture of books, stories, songs, and theater in Yiddish. Ashkenazic culture virtually ended in Europe with the Holocaust, but Yiddish language and culture lived on in the United States, Canada, and Israel, and although they once seemed to be rapidly declining, there are recent signs of revival.

Other Jewish Cultures   A mysterious form of Judaism exists in Africa among the Falashas of Ethiopia. The Falashas practice a religion that accepts as canonical only the five books of the Torah—a sign that Ethiopian Judaism could be quite ancient. Judaism also established itself in a small community on the western coast of India, though today it is very small. Distinctive Jewish cultures also exist in Yemen, Iraq, and elsewhere.

Observance-Based Divisions

Within Judaism today, divisions also exist based on variations in religious observance. Although some Jews have held to traditional practices, other branches have developed out of the conviction that Judaism will stay vital only if it reinterprets its traditions. Four branches have emerged. We begin with the most traditional and move to the least traditional, although the branches did not emerge in this order.

Orthodox Judaism   Traditional Judaism is often called **Orthodox** (Figure 8.2), but we might recall that until the Reform movement began, there was no need to give a special name to traditional Judaism, because all Jews were traditional in belief and practice. In a sense, Orthodox Judaism came into being only after the Reform began, and as a response to it. When we use the term *Orthodox* to refer to traditional Jews, we should also recognize the great variety among Orthodox Jews—particularly regarding social and political positions. Some, termed *integrationists,* seek to play a role in civil society, whereas others, called *separatists,* want to live their traditional lifestyle apart from society. Orthodox Jews also differ in their support for the state of Israel and the need for secular education.

With this said, we can describe Orthodoxy as a branch of Judaism committed to retaining traditional practice and belief. Some specific practices follow.

- Orthodox synagogues separate males and females, with females often sitting in an upstairs gallery.
- For a service to take place, there must be a quorum (*minyan*) of ten Jewish males.
- Services are conducted completely in Hebrew and led by male rabbis.
- Only males may celebrate the coming-of-age ceremony (bar mitzvah).
- Men at prayer use the talit and at weekday morning prayer use the tefillin.
- Males must keep their heads covered (with the skullcap, prayer shawl, or hat) as a reminder that God is above all.

FIGURE 8.2

Observance-based branches of Judaism.

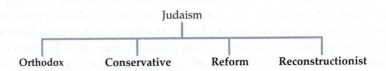

Judaism

Orthodox   Conservative   Reform   Reconstructionist

- Social roles (especially among ultra-Orthodox Jews) are strictly separate. Men are the breadwinners of the family, and women are responsible for running the household.

- The hair of the beard and in front of the ears is sometimes left uncut by males, in response to a command in the Torah (Lev. 19:27).

- Some Orthodox Jewish males (and particularly those affiliated with a specific Hasidic community) also wear a style of dress that developed in central Europe during the nineteenth century—a black hat and black coat (originally a beaver-skin hat and a black smock).

- Orthodox women who are married sometimes cover their heads with a kerchief when outside the home. The hair is covered as an expression of modesty, because a woman's hair is considered to be seductive to men.

- The Orthodox household keeps strictly the traditional laws about diet.

- Orthodox Jews closely follow rules that prohibit any manual labor on the Sabbath. Cooking is not allowed, nor is driving a car, walking long distances, using a telephone, or even turning on an electric light.

Outsiders might consider the strictness of this lifestyle burdensome. But the Orthodox themselves—particularly those who have been raised as Orthodox—say that it is not difficult. They say that it is even fulfilling, because every waking moment is consciously devoted to the worship of God.

In continental Europe, Orthodox Judaism was nearly destroyed by the Nazis. In Israel, although only a tenth of the population can be considered traditionalist or Orthodox, that segment has considerable political power. In the United States, Orthodoxy constitutes a small minority among those who practice Judaism, but it has gained recognition and visibility particularly through the efforts of Hasidic communities.

Conservative Judaism   For some Jews, the European movement for reform seemed too radical. **Conservative Judaism** traces its origins back to Germany, but it took strong root in the United States among Jews who desired moderate change that was coupled with a protection of beloved traditions, such as the use of Hebrew in services. Thus this branch of Judaism accepts change, but it uses study and discussion to guide change carefully. In the United States, almost half of all practicing Jews belong to this branch.

Reform Judaism   Reform Judaism began in Germany out of a desire of some Jews to leave ghetto life completely and enter the mainstream of European culture. An early influence on this movement was Moses Mendelssohn (1729–1786), a major thinker and writer. Mendelssohn, although he was not a Reform Jew, helped shape Reform and Orthodox Judaism. He argued for religious tolerance, held that Judaism could be combined with civil culture, and embraced many of the ideals of the European

Young women help their friend light candles at her bat mitzvah celebration.

Enlightenment of the eighteenth century—human dignity, equality, individual liberty, democracy, secular education, and the development of science. These ideals brought radical changes in the Jewish circles that espoused them, because in the name of reform, every traditional Jewish belief and practice could be questioned.

The result has been that in Reform synagogue worship, women and men do not sit separately, services are conducted in both the native language and Hebrew, choirs and organ music are common, and use of the talit and tefillin has either been dropped or made optional. Traditional ways of dressing, common among the Orthodox, have disappeared. Perhaps more important, equality is espoused for men and women. As a result, women may become rabbis, and girls have coming-of-age ceremonies in which each becomes a "daughter of the commandment" (bat mitzvah).

Reconstructionist Judaism   This newest and smallest branch of Judaism grew out of the thought of its founder, Mordecai Kaplan (1881–1983), a Lithuanian who came to the United States as a child. Kaplan was influenced by the American ideals of democracy and practicality. As a leader in the Society for the Advancement of Judaism, Kaplan promoted a secular vision that encourages Jews to become familiar with as many elements of traditional Judaism as possible but that allows them the freedom of individual interpretation. Elements of belief that traditional Jews interpret literally (such as angels, prophecy, revealed law, and the Messiah) are taken as useful symbols by **Reconstructionism;** even the notion of God is seen from a pragmatic viewpoint as "the Power which makes me follow ever higher ideals."[31] Instead of searching for a minimum number of

Contemporary Issues

ECO-JUDAISM

Because it emphasizes ethical living, Judaism has always had basic principles that address how humanity should appropriately relate to the environment. The Hebrew scriptures, however, were written long before caring for the global environment became a pressing issue. In an effort to update their faith's vision of ecological wisdom, contemporary Jews concerned with the environment have revisited traditional biblical sources.

The Hebrew scriptures offer two stories of value for environmentalists. The first is the story of Adam and Eve, designated by God to protect the Garden of Eden. The second is the story of Noah and the Great Flood. By collecting pairs of animals in his ark, Noah saved these animals (and their offspring) from extinction. As such, the modern environmentalist could regard Adam and Eve and Noah as the first defenders of plant and animal species.

The Hebrew scriptures also provide important passages that show a divine hand in creation and preach respect for nature, especially for plants and animals. The Book of Genesis ends the tale of creation by saying that God saw that the universe he created was "very good" (Gen. 1:31). Psalm 19 begins by saying, "The heavens declare the glory of God, and the earth declares his handiwork," and Psalm 104 is a hymn praising the beauties of nature. Offering specific rules, the Book of Deuteronomy says that even in wartime, fruit trees must not be destroyed (Deut. 20:19). The Bible also shows concern for the sustainable use of land and animals for agriculture. In order for land to restore its minerals and nutrients, scripture recommends that it lie fallow once every seven years (Lev. 25:3–4), and animals are to be given rest on the Sabbath (Exod. 20:10).

Contemporary Jews express an increasing concern for the environment. The Sephardic and Ashkenazic chief rabbis of Israel have issued statements calling for greater respect for the land. Israel is working to protect the Jordan River and the Dead Sea. (The Jordan River is being rapidly drained by agriculture in Syria, Jordan, and Israel, and this in turn is leading to the depletion of the Dead Sea.) Several Israeli *kibbutzim* (communes) grow organic fruits and vegetables. In England and the United States, Jewish groups are working for the preservation of wetlands, the establishment of recycling centers, and the inclusion of environmental education in Jewish schools.

Borrowing biblical language, modern Israeli environmentalist Moshe Kornfeld has reinterpreted God's commands for the modern world. According to Kornfeld, the Lord tells us today that

> You shall reduce, reuse, and recycle with all your heart, with all your soul, and with all of your resources. And concern for the planet that I command you today shall be upon your hearts. And you shall teach sustainability to your children and speak of it frequently: when you sit in your energy-star-rated home, or when you ride your bike to work, when you go to sleep and when you wake up. And you shall have a non-disposable mug as a sign on your hand and an organic cotton hat to shade your eyes.[32]

beliefs and practices that are the unchanging essence of Judaism, Reconstructionism sees Judaism as a changing cultural force, with many elements and manifestations. Judaism, in this view, is a whole civilization "which expresses itself . . . in literature, art, music, even cuisine. It never stands still but evolves."[33]

JEWISH IDENTITY AND THE FUTURE OF JUDAISM

Judaism today is particularly concerned with two great questions, which are inescapably linked. What is essential to being a Jew? Will Judaism survive?

Only a few hundred feet separate Jerusalem's Western Wall from the Dome of the Rock, one of Islam's oldest buildings. Yet they are worlds apart. Resolving the intractable conflict between Israel and the Palestinians is a key to the future of Judaism.

Appreciating the cultural and religious divisions among Jews demonstrates how difficult it is today to define what makes a Jew. Three hundred years ago, the question of identity was nonexistent, because Jews were those people who practiced traditional Judaism. Now, however, Jewish identity is no longer so easy to ascertain. Although Orthodox Judaism holds that a person is born a Jew if his or her mother is Jewish, this does not address the matter of practice, and today there are many nonobservant Jews. A person may also convert to Judaism. However, some Orthodox rabbis have refused to accept conversions to non-Orthodox branches of Judaism. Judaism is certainly a religion, but there is great disagreement about the essentials of belief and practice, and many people consider themselves Jews even though they do not practice the religion.

Furthermore, any attempt to define a Jew as a person belonging to a single culture or ethnic group is virtually impossible. Jews are as ethnically diverse as they are ideologically diverse, a fact that becomes quite clear when one visits Israel. Although there is as yet no clear answer to the question of Jewish identity, the topic becomes more important as Jews increasingly intermarry with non-Jews.

The history of Judaism has been marked by displacement and disasters. In the past century, nearly a third of the world's Jewish population was destroyed. Nevertheless, Jewish history has also been marked by the will to endure. The resilience of Judaism has in large part resided in its ability to adapt to changing circumstances and environments. This ability suggests that in the decades ahead, Judaism will again take new forms and gain new life.

Reading   **TENDING THE GARDEN**

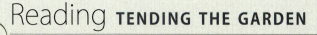

The biblical story of creation includes the making of a garden, with Adam and Eve as the first gardeners.

Then the LORD God formed man of the dust of the ground, and breathed into his nostrils the breath of life; and man became a living soul. And the LORD God planted a garden eastward, in Eden; and there He put the man whom He had formed. And out of the ground made the LORD God to grow every tree that is pleasant to the sight, and good for food; the tree of life also in the midst of the garden, and the tree of the knowledge of good and evil. And the LORD God took the man, and put him into the garden of Eden to dress it and to keep it. And the LORD God commanded the man, saying: "Of every tree of the garden thou mayest freely eat; but of the tree of the knowledge of good and evil, thou shalt not eat of it; for in the day that thou eatest thereof thou shalt surely die." And the LORD God said: "It is not good that the man should be alone; I will make him a help meet for him." And out of the ground the LORD God formed every beast of the field, and every fowl of the air; and brought them unto the man to see what he would call them; and whatsoever the man would call every living creature, that was to be the name thereof. And the man gave names to all cattle, and to the fowl of the air, and to every beast of the field; but for Adam there was not found a help meet for him. And the LORD God caused a deep sleep to fall upon the man, and he slept; and He took one of his ribs, and closed up the place with flesh instead thereof. And the rib, which the LORD God had taken from the man, made He a woman, and brought her unto the man. And the man said: "This is now bone of my bones, and flesh of my flesh; she shall be called Woman, because she was taken out of Man." Therefore shall a man leave his father and his mother, and shall cleave unto his wife, and they shall be one flesh. (Gen 2: 7–9, 15–24)

TEST YOURSELF

1. The destruction of the Second Temple of Jerusalem by the Romans in 70 CE brought about the end of the _____ ceremonial religion of Israel.
   a. temple-based
   b. polytheistic
   c. rabbinical
   d. patriarchal

2. The Hebrew Bible is divided into three sections: _____.
   a. Rig, Yajur, Atharva
   b. Adam, Eve, Noah
   c. Genesis, Exodus, Numbers
   d. Torah, Nevi'im, Ketuvim

3. _____ is the first Hebrew patriarch. God entered into a solemn covenant with him, which involved a promise of land, protection, and descendants.
   a. Abraham
   b. Noah
   c. Isaiah
   d. Genesis

4. In a story from Genesis, Jacob wrestles all night long with a mysterious stranger—God or God's Angel. At dawn, the fight is over, and Jacob receives from the stranger a new name, _____, which means "wrestles with God."
   a. Judah
   b. Israel
   c. Joseph
   d. Noah

5. In Hebrew, the name for God, usually associated with the verb *hayah* ("to be"), is commonly written _____.
   a. Baal
   b. Adonai
   c. Yahweh
   d. Adam

6. The Babylonian _____ contains legal material and nonlegal anecdotes and tales.
   a. Ketuvim
   b. Talmud
   c. Torah
   d. Testament

7. In eighteenth-century central Europe, Jewish traditionalism expressed itself in both Talmudic scholarship and the devotional movement _____ ("devotion," "piety").
   a. Hasidism
   b. Sephardim
   c. Conservative Judaism
   d. Essene

8. By the end of World War II, an estimated six million Jews had been killed. This immense loss is called the _____ (Greek:

"completely burned") or Shoah (Hebrew: "extermination").
   a. Diaspora
   b. Midrash
   c. Holocaust
   d. Purim

9. Traditional Judaism is often called _____ Judaism.
   a. Reform
   b. Orthodox
   c. Reconstructionist
   d. Sephardic

10. _____, the newest and smallest branch of Judaism, grew out of the thought of its founder, Mordecai Kaplan.
    a. Reconstructionist Judaism
    b. Reform Judaism
    c. Conservative Judaism
    d. Kabbalah

11. Consider the following statement: The concept that seems to be emphasized most strongly throughout the Hebrew Bible is that God wants his followers to devote themselves to him and him alone. Using instances from the Hebrew Bible stories discussed in this chapter, do you agree or disagree with this statement? If you disagree, what do you think is the most strongly emphasized concept in the Hebrew Bible?

12. Of the many differences between Orthodox and Reform Judaism, which two do you think would cause the strongest disagreement between these branches? Using examples from the chapter, explain why you think these differences cause so much disagreement.

RESOURCES

Books

Bellis, Alice. *Helpmates, Harlots, and Heroes: Women's Stories in the Hebrew Bible*. Westminster, MD: Westminster John Knox Press, 1994. Feminist interpretations of popular stories about women in the Hebrew Bible.

Frank, Anne. *Anne Frank: The Diary of a Young Girl; the Definitive Edition*. New York: Doubleday, 1995. The unexpurgated diary of a young Jewish girl who hid with her family in Holland during World War II.

Frankl, Viktor. *Man's Search for Meaning*. Rev. ed. New York: Washington Square Press, 1997. A two-part book that describes the author's horrifying experiences in several concentration camps and then gives his reflections on the human need for meaning.

Friedman, Richard E. *The Bible with Sources Revealed*. San Francisco: Harper, 2003. A clear explanation of the origin of the Torah.

Frymer-Kensky, Tikva. *Reading the Women of the Bible: A New Interpretation of Their Stories*. New York: Schocken, 2004. A scholarly reconsideration of the role of women in the Bible.

Grossman, David. *The Yellow Wind*. (With a new afterword by the author.) New York: Farrar, Straus and Giroux/Picador, 2002. Powerful reflections on the relationship between Israelis and Palestinians.

Grossman, Grace. *Jewish Museums of the World*. New York: Universe, 2008. Photos and information about more than one hundred museums of Judaism around the world.

Hoffman, Adina, and Peter Cole. *Sacred Trash: The Lost and Found World of the Cairo Geniza*. New York: Schocken, 2011. A description of once-unappreciated Jewish records found in Cairo.

Leegant, Joan. *An Hour in Paradise*. New York: Norton, 2003. Ten stories, rooted in Judaism, about unusual people in many places.

Film / TV

Eye of the Storm: Jerusalem's Temple Mount. (Films Media Group.) An array of perspectives on the world's most contested site—sacred ground for Judaism, Christianity, and Islam.

Heritage: Civilization and the Jews. (PBS.) A nine-part series on the history of the Jewish people from biblical times to the present.

The Jewish Americans. (Director David Grubin; PBS.) A miniseries that chronicles the lives and contributions of Jewish Americans from colonial times to the present.

Trembling Before G-d. (Director Sandi Simcha Dubowski; New Yorker Video.) An award-winning documentary examining the personal stories of gay Orthodox Jews who struggle to reconcile their sexual orientation with their faith in traditional Judaism, which forbids homosexuality.

Yentl. (Director Barbra Streisand; MGM.) The story of a girl, played by Barbra Streisand, who wished to be a rabbi.

Music / Audio

Abayudaya: Music from the Jewish People of Uganda. Washington, DC: Smithsonian Folkways, 2003. Psalms and hymns from an unexpected source.

Legendary Cantors. (Nimbus Records.) A collection of traditional Jewish liturgical music, sung by the leading cantors of the first half of the twentieth century.

Religious Music of the Falashas. (Smithsonian Folkways.) A recording of the religious music of the Jews of Ethiopia.

Rosenbaum, Chava, and Ilana Farbstein. *Lift Up Your Voice*. (Aderet.) Jewish songs sung by women a capella (without orchestration).

Sacred Chants of the Contemporary Synagogue. (Bari Productions.) A recording of mezzo-soprano Rebecca Garfein's groundbreaking performance as the first female cantor to sing in a German synagogue; it includes songs and prayers in Hebrew and Yiddish.

Taubman, Craig. *Holy Ground*. (Craig 'n Co.) Religious songs in a modern style.

Thank God It's Friday! The Music of Shabbat. (Vox.) A compilation of music for the Jewish Shabbat, including traditional music and works by Samuel Cohen, Louis Lewandowski, and Felix Mendelssohn.

Internet

The Jewish Virtual Library: http://www.jewishvirtuallibrary.org/index.html. A comprehensive online Jewish encyclopedia, with more than 13,000 articles and 6,000 photographs and maps; major subject headings include history, women, the Holocaust, travel, maps, politics, biography, Israel, and religion.

Judaism 101: http://www.jewfaq.org/index.htm. An online encyclopedia of Judaism, with sections devoted to beliefs, people, places, things, language, scripture, holidays, practices, and customs.

Navigating the Bible II: http://bible.ort.org/intro1.asp?lang=1. Intended as an online tutor for the bar mitzvah and bat mitzvah ceremony, a Web site that includes key passages from the Hebrew Bible in the original Hebrew with audio recordings, translations, and commentary.

KEY TERMS

Ashkenazim (ash-ken-ah'-zeem): Jews who lived in or came from central Europe.

bar (bat) mitzvah: "Son (daughter) of the commandment" (Aramaic); the coming-of-age ceremony that marks the time when a young person is considered a legal adult within the Jewish community.

biblical Judaism: Judaism before the destruction of the Second Temple (70 CE).

Canaan (kay'-nun): An ancient name for the land of Israel.

Conservative Judaism: A branch of Judaism that attempts to blend the best of old and new Judaism.

covenant: A contract; the contract between the Hebrews and their God, Yahweh.

diaspora (dai-as'-poh-rah): The dispersion of Jews beyond Israel, particularly to Persia, Egypt, and the Mediterranean region.

Essenes: A reclusive semimonastic Jewish group that flourished from c. 150 BCE to 68 CE.

Hanukkah (hah'-nuk-kah): An early-winter festival recalling the rededication of the Second Temple, celebrated with the lighting of candles for eight days.

Holocaust: The destruction of European Judaism by the Nazis; also known as Shoah (Hebrew: "extermination").

Kabbalah (kah-bah'-luh or kah'-bah-luh): "Received," "handed down"; the whole body of Jewish mystical literature.

Ketuvim (keh-too-veem'): "Writings"; the third section of the Hebrew scriptures, consisting primarily of poetry, proverbs, and literary works.

kosher (koh'-shur): "Ritually correct"; refers particularly to food preparation and food consumption.

menorah (meh-noh'-ruh): A candelabrum usually containing seven—and occasionally nine—branches, used for religious celebrations.

Messiah (meh-sai'-uh): A savior figure to be sent by God, awaited by the Jews (see Dan. 7:13–14).

midrash (mid'-rash): "Search"; rabbinical commentary on the scriptures and oral law.

Nevi'im (neh-vee-eem'): "Prophets"; the second section of the Hebrew scriptures, made up of historical and prophetic books.

Orthodox Judaism: The most traditional branch of Judaism.

Passover (Pesach): A joyful spring festival that recalls the Hebrews' exodus from Egypt and freedom from oppression.

Pharisees: A faction during the Second Temple period that emphasized the observance of biblical rules.

prophet: A person inspired by God to speak for him.

Purim (poo'-reem): A joyous festival in early spring that recalls the Jews' being saved from destruction, as told in the Book of Esther.

rabbi (rab'-ai): A religious teacher; a Jewish minister.

rabbinical Judaism: Judaism that developed after the destruction of the Second Temple (70 CE).

Reconstructionism: A modern liberal branch of Judaism that emphasizes the cultural aspects of Judaism.

Reform: A movement beginning in the nineteenth century that questioned and modernized Judaism; a liberal branch of Judaism.

Rosh Hashanah (rosh hah-shah'-nah): "Beginning of the year"; the celebration of the Jewish New Year, occurring in the seventh lunar month.

Sabbath: "Rest"; the seventh day of the week (Saturday), a day of prayer and rest from work.

Sadducees (sad'-dyu-sees): A priestly faction, influential during the Second Temple period.

Seder (say'-dur): "Order"; a special ritual meal at Passover, recalling the Hebrews' exodus from Egypt.

Sephardim (seh-far'-deem): Jews of Spain, Morocco, and the Mediterranean region.

Sukkot (soo-koht'): "Booths"; a festival in the late autumn that recalls the Jews' period of wandering in the desert after their exodus from Egypt.

talit (tah'-lit): A prayer shawl worn by devout males.

Talmud (tahl'-mood): An encyclopedic commentary on the Hebrew scriptures.

Tanakh (tah-nak'): The complete Hebrew scriptures, made up of the Torah, Prophets (Nevi'im), and Writings (Ketuvim).

tefillin (teh-fil'-in): Phylacteries; two small boxes containing biblical passages that are worn by Orthodox males on the head and left arm at morning prayer during the week.

theophany (thee-ah'-fuh-nee): A revelation or appearance of God.

Torah (toh'-rah): "Teaching," "instruction"; the first five books of the Hebrew scriptures; also, the additional instructions of God, believed by many to have been transmitted orally from Moses through a succession of teachers and rabbis.

Western Wall: The foundation stones of the western wall of the last temple of Jerusalem, today a place of prayer.

yarmulke (yar'-mool-kah): The skullcap worn by devout males.

Yom Kippur (yohm kip-puhr'): Day of Atonement, the most sacred day of the Jewish year.

Zealots: An anti-Roman, nationalistic Jewish faction, active during the Roman period of control over Israel.

Zionism: A movement that has encouraged the creation and support of the nation of Israel.

RELIGION BEYOND THE CLASSROOM

Visit the Online Learning Center at www.mhhe.com/molloy6e for additional exercises and features, including "Religion beyond the Classroom" and "For Fuller Understanding."

CHAPTER 9

Christianity

You have come to Egypt to see its great sights: the Nile River, the pyramids of Giza, and the temples of Luxor. In front of your hotel in Cairo, near the Egyptian Museum, you arrange with a taxi driver to take you to the pyramids late one afternoon. The traffic is slow and the horn-blowing incessant. From the window you see a donkey pulling a cart full of metal pipes, a woman carrying a tray of bread on her head, a boy carrying a tray of coffee cups, and an overloaded truck full of watermelons, all competing for space with dusty old cars and shiny black limousines.

Your taxi driver is Gurgis, a middle-aged man with a short gray beard and a kind manner. He drives with the windows open and chats with drivers in other taxis along the way. As you near the pyramids, he says, "If you wait till dusk, you can see the sound-and-light show. Tourists love the green laser lights on the pyramids. I can eat my supper at Giza and take you back afterwards." This sounds like an experience not to be missed. You agree.

You'd thought that the pyramids were far outside the city in the lonely desert, but now they are just beyond a Pizza Hut, a bridal shop, and blocks of shops and apartments. Apparently, the city of Cairo swallowed up the desert some time ago.

When the light show is over, it's hard to believe that in that huge crowd surging out you will find Gurgis. Luckily, he finds you. "Come, hurry," he says, and whisks you away. On the trip back across the river, you ask about his background.

"I'm a Copt, an Egyptian Christian" he says, "and I'm named after St. George." To verify what he's telling you, Gurgis holds up his left arm. In the dim light you see a little blue cross tattooed on the inside of his wrist. Before long, you learn about his birthplace (in Alexandria) and his relatives (in Saskatchewan). He tells you about his religion, Coptic Christianity.

"It is very old. The first bishop was St. Mark, who wrote the gospel. Our patriarchs follow him in a long line of patriarchs. We Copts are only about 10 percent of the population in Egypt, but our Church is strong." Noting your interest, he tells you about other places you might like to go. He offers to take you to the old Coptic section of Cairo. "It's along the Nile, not very far from your hotel," he says by way of encouragement. You agree to meet in front of your hotel on Friday morning.

On Friday you visit three churches. There's a lot going on because it is Good Friday, and all of the churches, already surprisingly crowded with worshipers, will be filled in a few hours for special services. Inside one church, a priest stands in front of the doors to the sanctuary, apparently explaining something to a crowd of listeners. At the last church you visit, you see a painting outside of Mary and Jesus on a donkey. Gurgis explains that the church marks the spot where the family of Jesus stayed when they visited Egypt. You are doubtful, but in the basement of the church, a large sign confirms what he tells you.

As you walk along the old street, heading out of the Coptic quarter, Gurgis tells you more about Copts. "The original Christian hermits were Copts," he says with pride. "Our pope was a monk once, and he's energizing Coptic life. Now he is even sending priests and monks to your country, too. I know there are some in New Jersey."

Back at the entrance to your hotel, Gurgis makes another offer. Sunday he will be going to a Eucharistic service at St. Mark's Cathedral. "The service will be very long, but it is beautiful. Would you like to go?"

"Wonderful," you say. "But let's sit near the door."

"Fine," he says. "There is more air there."

On Sunday you and Gurgis drive to an immense domed church behind a gate. Large men in dark-blue suits, looking like bodyguards, stand along the walkway into the church. Inside, a huge purple curtain hangs in front of the main sanctuary doors. It has a winged lion sewn onto it. "That represents

Deeper Insights

THE CHRISTIAN SYSTEM OF CHRONOLOGY: BC AND AD

The influence of Christianity is apparent in the European dating system, which has now generally been adopted worldwide. The Roman Empire dated events from the foundation of Rome (753 BCE), but a Christian monk, Dionysius Exiguus (Dennis the Little; c. 470–c. 540 CE) devised a new system that made the birth of Jesus the central event of history. Thus we have "BC," meaning "before Christ," and "AD," Latin for "in the year of the Lord," *anno Domini*. The date selected as the year of Jesus's birth may have been incorrect, and scholars now think that Jesus was born about 4 BCE. (The historical facts given in Matt. 2:1 and Luke 2:2 about the year of Jesus's birth are not compatible.) Also, the new dating system began not with the year zero but with the year one because there is no zero in Roman numerals. Because of the Christian orientation of this dating system, many books (including this one) now use a slightly altered abbreviation: "BCE," meaning "before the Common Era," and "CE," meaning "Common Era."

St. Mark," Gurgis whispers. At the left of the sanctuary is a thronelike wooden chair. "That is the pope's chair, the throne of St. Mark."

The Eucharistic service begins, with incense and singing. There is no organ, but the choir uses small drums and cymbals. It is the Lord's Supper, but in a form you've never seen before. At times you can only hear the priests, because the sanctuary doors are periodically closed and you can no longer see the altar. The service ends with communion. Through it all, the people—men on the left side, women on the right—are amazingly devout.

Back in your hotel, you think about what you have seen and heard. You know that the Lord's Supper has something to do with the last supper of Jesus with his disciples. But what about the incense and the cymbals? How did the rituals originate? And how did monks and hermits come about in

Shenouda III, the late Coptic patriarch of Alexandria, here celebrates a feast at St. Mark's Cathedral in Cairo.

Christianity? You had heard of a pope in Rome, but never one in Egypt. How did this other pope originate? What thoughts, you wonder, would Jesus have if he were with you today? And finally, what will be the future of this Egyptian Church—and, in this changing world, of Christianity itself?

THE LIFE AND TEACHINGS OF JESUS

Christianity, which grew out of Judaism, has had a major influence on the history of the world. Before we discuss its growth and influence, we must look at the life of Jesus, who is considered its originator, and at the early scriptural books that speak of his life.

Before Jesus's birth, the land of Israel had been taken over repeatedly by stronger neighbors. During Jesus's time, Israel was called Palestine by the Romans and was part of the Roman Empire—but not willingly. The region was full of unrest, a boiling pot of religious and political factions and movements. As we discussed in Chapter 8, patriots who later became known as the Zealots wanted to expel the Romans. The Sadducees, a group of priests in Jerusalem, accepted the Roman occupation as inevitable, yet they kept up the Jewish temple rituals. Members of a semimonastic movement, the Essenes, lived an austere life in the desert and provinces; for the most part, they deliberately lived away from Jerusalem, which they thought was corrupt. The Pharisees, a lay movement of devout Jews, preoccupied themselves with meticulously keeping the Jewish law.

Many Jews in Jesus's day thought that they were living in the "end times." They expected a period of turbulence and suffering and a final great battle, when God would destroy all the enemies of pious Jews. God, they believed, would then inaugurate a new age of justice and love. Some expected a new Garden of Eden, where the good people who remained after the Judgment would eat year-round from fruit trees and women would no longer suffer in childbirth. Most Jews shared the hope that the Romans would be expelled, that evildoers would be punished, and that God's envoy, the **Messiah,** would appear. The common expectation among the Jews of Jesus's day was that the Messiah would be a king or a military leader who was descended from King David. (The name *Messiah* means "anointed" and refers to the ceremony of anointing a new king with olive oil.) Many held that the Messiah had been foretold in some of their sacred books—such as Isaiah, Micah, and Daniel—and they expected him to rule the new world.

Into this complicated land Jesus was born about two thousand years ago (Timeline 9.1). Traditional teaching tells of a miraculous conception in Nazareth, a town of northern Israel, and of a birth by the virginal mother Mary in Bethlehem, a town in the south not far from Jerusalem. It tells of wise men who followed a guiding star to the baby soon after his birth. The traditional portrait of Jesus, common in art, shows him in his early years assisting his foster father, Joseph, as a carpenter in the northern province of Galilee. It is possible that the truth of some of these traditional details—as it is regarding the lives of many other religious founders—may be more symbolic than literal.

TIMELINE 9.1

	c. 4 BCE–c. 29 CE	Life of Jesus
Life of Paul	c. 4–64 CE	
	313 CE	Issuance of the Edict of Toleration by Constantine, making Christianity legal
Life of Augustine	354–430 CE	
	476 CE	Collapse of the Roman Empire of the West
Life of Benedict	c. 480–c. 547 CE	
	638 CE	Muslim conquest of Jerusalem
Split between Eastern and Western Christianity	1054 CE	
	1099	Conquest of Jerusalem during the First Crusade
Black Death	1347–1351	
	1453	Conquest of Constantinople by Muslim forces
Life of Martin Luther	1483–1546	
	1492	The expulsion of Jews and Muslims from Spain
Life of John Calvin	1509–1564	
	1517	Beginning of the Protestant Reformation
Founding of the Church of England by Henry VIII	1534	
	1565	Christianity enters the Philippines
Life of composer Johann Sebastian Bach	1685–1750	
	1805–1844	Life of Joseph Smith
Founding of the World Council of Churches	1948	
	1962–1965	Modernization of Catholicism by the Second Vatican Council
Death of Pope John Paul II and accession of Pope Benedict XVI	2005	
	2006	Evangelical Climate Initiative signed by 86 evangelical leaders

Timeline of significant events in the history of Christianity.

The birth of Jesus is celebrated throughout Christendom. This painting of the nativity is in an Orthodox church in Bulgaria.

There have been many attempts to find the "historical Jesus." Although artists have portrayed Jesus in countless ways, no portrait that we know of was ever painted of Jesus while he was alive. Of course, we can guess at his general features, but we cannot know anything definitive about the individual face or eyes or manner of Jesus.

Almost everything we know of Jesus comes from the four gospels of the New Testament. (**Testament** means "contract" or "covenant," and **gospel** means "good news.") The gospels are accounts, written by later believers, of the life of Jesus. The gospels, however, tell very little of Jesus until he began a public life of teaching and healing. He probably began this public life in his late 20s, when he gathered twelve disciples and moved from place to place, teaching about the coming of what he called the Kingdom of God. After a fairly short period of preaching—no more than three years—Jesus was arrested in Jerusalem at Passover time by the authorities, who considered him a threat to public order. From the point of view of the Sadducees, Jesus was dangerous because he might begin an anti-Roman riot. In contrast, Jewish patriots may have found him not anti-Roman enough. From the Roman point of view, however, he was at least a potential source of political unrest and enough of a threat to be arrested, whipped, nailed to a cross, and crucified—a degrading and public form of execution. Death came from shock, suffocation, and loss of blood.

Dying on a Friday, Jesus was buried quickly near the site of his crucifixion shortly before sunset, just as the Jewish Sabbath was to begin. No work could be done on Saturday, the Sabbath. On the following Sunday, the gospels report, the followers who went to care for his body found his tomb empty. Some followers reported apparitions of him, and his disciples became convinced that he had returned to life. Forty days later, the New Testament says, he ascended into the sky, promising to return again.

This bare outline does not answer many important questions: Who was Jesus? What kind of personality did he have? What were his teachings? For the answers to these questions, we must turn to the four gospels. They are the core of the Christian New Testament.

Jesus in the New Testament Gospels

The four gospels are written remembrances of Jesus's words and deeds, recorded some years after his death by people who believed in him. All the books of the New Testament are strongly colored by the viewpoints of their writers and by the culture of the period. Thus it is difficult to establish the historical accuracy of New Testament statements about Jesus or the words attributed to him. (Perhaps an analogy can clarify the problem: the gospels are like paintings of Jesus, not photographs.) In compiling our picture of Jesus, we must also recognize that the gospels are not a complete record of all essential information. There is a great deal we cannot know about Jesus. Nevertheless, a definite person does emerge from the gospels.

However obvious it may seem to point this out, Jesus believed and trusted in God, just as all contemporary Jews did. But while Jesus thought of God as creator and sustainer of the universe, he also thought of God in a very personal way, as his father. It is Jesus's extremely special relationship to God that is central to Christianity.

Raised as a Jew, Jesus accepted the sacred authority of the Law and the Prophets (the Torah and the books of history and prophecy). As a boy, he learned the scriptures in Hebrew. He kept the major Jewish holy days common to the period, and he traveled to Jerusalem and its temple for some of these events. He apparently kept the basic food laws and laws about Sabbath observance, and he attended synagogue meetings on Saturdays as part of the observance of the Jewish Sabbath (Luke 4:16). It seems he was a devout and thoughtful Jew.

Nonetheless, one striking personal characteristic of Jesus, alluded to frequently in the gospels, was his independence of thought. He considered things carefully and then arrived at his own opinions, which he was not hesitant to share. Jesus, the gospels say, taught differently: "unlike the scribes, he taught them with authority" (Mark 1:22).[1]

Perhaps Jesus's most impressive characteristic was his emphasis on universal love—not just love for the members of one's own family, ethnic group, or religion. He preached love in many forms: compassion, tolerance, forgiveness, acceptance, helpfulness, generosity, gratitude. When asked if a person should forgive up to seven times, he answered that people should forgive seventy times seven times (Matt. 18:22)—in other words, endlessly. He rejected all vengeance and even asked forgiveness for those who killed him (Luke 23:34). He recommended that we respond to violence with nonviolence. "But I tell you who hear me: Love your enemies, do good to those who hate you, bless those who curse you, and pray for those who mistreat you. If anyone

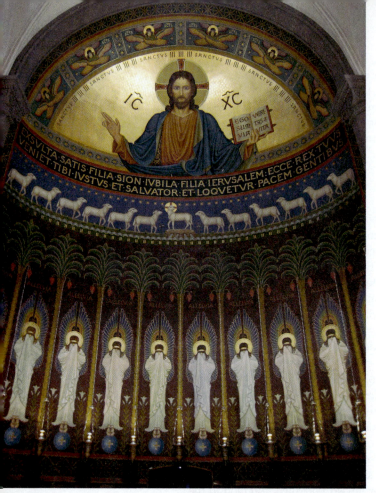

This portrayal of Jesus and his followers is influenced by the Book of Revelation. The smaller sheep represent the Apostles.

hits you on one cheek, let him hit the other one too; if someone takes your coat, let him have your shirt as well. Give to everyone who asks you for something, and when someone takes what is yours, do not ask for it back. Do for others just what you want them to do for you" (Luke 6:27–31).[2]

Although Jesus's nonviolent, loving message has often been neglected over the centuries, it is spelled out clearly in the Sermon on the Mount sections of the New Testament (Matt. 5–7, Luke 6). In the world of Jesus's day, which esteemed force and exacted vengeance, his message must have been shocking.

Jesus was wary of an overly strict observance of laws that seemed detrimental to human welfare. About keeping detailed laws regarding the Sabbath, he commented, "The sabbath was made for man, not man for the sabbath" (Mark 2:27).[3] He did not confuse pious practices, common among the Jews of his day, with the larger ideal of virtue. He disliked hypocrisy and pretense (Matt. 23:5–8).

From what we can see in the gospels, Jesus showed many human feelings. He had close friends and spent time with them (John 11:5), and he was disappointed when they were less than he had hoped for (Matt. 26:40). He wept when he heard of the death of one of his dearest friends (John 11:33–36).

Jesus urged simplicity. He recommended that people "become like little children" (Matt. 18:3). He liked directness and strived to go beyond details to the heart of things.

Much of Jesus's advice is good psychology, showing that he was a keen observer of human beings. For example, we are told that as you give, so shall you receive (Matt. 7:2) and that if you are not afraid to ask for what you want, you shall receive it (Matt. 7:7).

Jesus showed an appreciation for nature, in which he saw evidence of God's care (Matt. 6:29). But Jesus did not look at nature with the detached vision of a scientist. He knew scripture well but was not a scholar. As far as we know, he was not a writer, and he left behind no written works. He showed almost no interest in money or in business. In adulthood he probably did not travel far from his home territory, between the Sea of Galilee and Jerusalem. While he may have spoken some Greek in addition to his native Aramaic, he did not apparently have much interest in the Greco-Roman culture of his day.

Whether Jesus had a sense of humor is hard to know. The four gospels never mention that he laughed, thus giving him an image of solemnity. But some of his statements come alive when we see them as being spoken with ironic humor and even laughter (see, for example, Matt. 15:24–28). We do know that although he sometimes sought seclusion, Jesus seems to have enjoyed others' company.

Jesus had many female friends and followers. He seems to have treated women as equals, and he spoke to them in public without hesitation. In one gospel he is shown asking a woman for a drink of water at a well (John 4). In another gospel he speaks with a Canaanite woman, whose child he cures (Matt. 15:21–28). We find repeated mention of the sisters Martha and Mary of Bethany as close friends of Jesus (see John 11). The gospels also speak of other women disciples, such as Joanna and Susanna (Luke 8:3). The gospels tell how women stood by Jesus at his crucifixion, even when most of his male disciples had abandoned him. And the most prominent among the female disciples was Mary Magdalene, who was the first witness of his resurrection (John. 20:11–18).

Some people would like to see Jesus as a social activist. He cared strongly about the poor and the hungry, but he apparently was not a social activist of any specialized type. For example, the gospels do not record words of Jesus that condemn slavery or the oppression of women. Perhaps, like many others of his time, Jesus believed that God would soon judge the world, and this may have kept him from working for a specific reform. Instead, he preached basic principles of humane treatment, particularly of the needy and the oppressed (Matt. 25).

For those who would turn Jesus into a protector of the family and family values, the gospels present mixed evidence. When asked about the divorce practice of his day, Jesus opposed it strongly. He opposed easy divorce because it meant that a husband could divorce his wife for a minor reason, often leaving her unable to support herself or to remarry. He stated that the marriage bond was given by God (Mark 10:1–12). And at his death, Jesus asked a disciple to care for his mother after he was gone (John 19:26). But Jesus himself remained unmarried. If Jesus had a wife, that fact almost certainly would have survived in tradition or been mentioned somewhere in a gospel or other New Testament book. Moreover, there is no mention anywhere that Jesus ever had children.

Indeed, Jesus spoke highly of those who remained unmarried "for the sake of the kingdom of heaven" (Matt. 19:12).[5] As an intriguing confirmation of Jesus's unmarried state, it is now recognized that celibacy was valued by the Essenes, the semimonastic Jewish movement of that era, which may have had some influence on him.[6] In any case, Paul—one of the most important of the early Christians and missionaries—and generations of priests, monks, and nuns followed a celibate ideal that was based on the way Jesus was thought to have lived. In fact, the ideal of remaining unmarried for religious reasons remains influential in several branches of Christianity today.

Do not judge others, and God will not judge you; do not condemn others, and God will not condemn you; forgive others, and God will forgive you. Give to others, and God will give to you. Indeed, you will receive a full measure, a generous helping, poured into your hands—all that you can hold. The measure you use for others is the one that God will use for you.

—Luke 6:37–38[4]

The gospels mention Jesus's brothers and sisters (Mark 6:3). Some Christian traditions have held that these relatives were cousins or stepbrothers and stepsisters, hoping thereby to preserve the notion of his mother Mary's permanent virginity. But it is now widely accepted that Jesus had actual brothers and sisters who were children of his mother Mary and of Joseph. When we inspect his relationship to his family members, it seems that Jesus at times was alienated from them. They quite naturally worried about him and apparently wished he were not so unusual and difficult. But Jesus, irritated by their claims on him, said publicly that his real family consisted not of his blood relatives but of all those who hear the word of God and keep it (Mark 3:31–33). After Jesus died, however, because of their blood relationship with Jesus, his family members were influential in the early Church, and the earlier disharmony was downplayed.

The Two Great Commandments

What, then, was Jesus's main concern? His teachings, called the Two Great Commandments, combine two strong elements: a love for God and an ethical call for kindness toward others. These commandments already existed in Hebrew scripture (Deut. 6:5 and Lev. 19:18), but Jesus gave them new emphasis by reducing all laws to the law of love: Love God and love your neighbor (Matt. 22:37–40). Being fully aware of God means living with love for all God's children. Like prophets before him, Jesus had a clear vision of what human society can be at its best—a Kingdom of God in which people care about each other, the poor are looked after, violence and exploitation are abandoned, and religious rules do not overlook human needs.

It may be that Jesus's emphasis on morality was tied to the common belief in an imminent divine judgment. This belief seems to have been a particularly important part of the worldview of the Essenes, who thought of themselves as preparing for this new world. It was also essential to the thinking of John the Baptizer (also called John the Baptist), whom the Gospel of Luke calls the cousin of Jesus. John preached that the end of the world was near, when God would punish evildoers. As a sign of purification, John immersed his followers in the water of the Jordan River. Jesus allowed himself to be baptized, and when John died, Jesus had his own followers carry on John's practice by baptizing others. Whether Jesus shared John's view of the coming end of the world is debated. Some passages would seem to indicate that he did (see Mark 9:1, 13:30; Matt. 16:28). This vision of impending judgment is called **apocalypticism.** In the apocalyptic view, the Kingdom of God would soon be a social and political reality.

Whatever Jesus's views about the end times, his focus was on bringing about the Kingdom of God in each human heart. This would occur when people followed the Two Great Commandments and lived by the laws of love. Some of Jesus's closest followers were among those who seem to have expected him to be a political leader, wanting him to lead the fight against the Roman overlords to establish a political kingdom of God. But Jesus refused. The Gospel of John records him as saying, "My kingdom is not of this world" (John 18:36).[7] Instead of political violence, Jesus chose a path of nonviolence.

EARLY CHRISTIAN BELIEFS AND HISTORY

The Book of Acts records that after Jesus's ascension to heaven forty days following his resurrection, his disciples were gathered, full of fear, wondering what to do next. The Book of Acts then tells how the Spirit of God came upon them in the form of fire, giving them courage to spread their belief in Jesus as the Messiah. This first preaching of the Christian message has been called the Birthday of the Church.

The early Christian message was not complex. It is summarized in the **apostle** Peter's speech in Acts 2, which says that God is now working in a special way; Jesus was the expected Messiah, God's ambassador; and these are the "final days" before God's judgment and the coming of a new world. Early Christian practice required those who believed to be baptized as a sign of rebirth, to share their possessions, and to care for widows and orphans.

The early Christian group that remained in Jerusalem seems to have been almost entirely Jewish and was led by James, called the Just because of his careful observance of Jewish practice. Being one of Jesus's real brothers, James carried great authority. The Jewish-Christian Church, led by Jesus's relatives, was a strong influence for the first forty years. Its members kept the Jewish holy days, prayed in the Jerusalem Temple, and conducted their services in Aramaic. The Jewish-Christian Church, however, was weakened by the destruction of the temple in 70 CE, and it seems to have disappeared over the next one hundred years. Meanwhile, the non-Jewish, Greek-speaking branch of early Christianity, led by Paul and others like him, began to spread throughout the Roman Empire.

Paul and Pauline Christianity

As the Jewish Christianity of Jerusalem and Israel weakened, Christianity among non-Jews grew because of the missionary Paul. Paul's preaching in Greek, his energetic traveling, and his powerful letters spread his form of belief in Jesus far beyond the limits of Israel.

Originally named Saul, Paul was born of Jewish parentage in Tarsus, a town in the south of present-day Turkey. He was earnest about traditional Judaism and went to Jerusalem for study. At that time he was a Pharisee, and he was adamantly opposed to the new "Jesus movement," which he saw as a dangerous messianic Jewish cult that could divide Judaism.

Paul, however, came to a new understanding of Jesus. The Book of Galatians says that he pondered the meaning of Jesus for three years in "Arabia" and "Damascus" (Gal. 1:17). In a more dramatic, later account, the Book of Acts relates that while Paul was on the road from Jerusalem to root out a

In this fifteenth-century fresco, *Noli Me Tangere*, by Fra Angelico, Jesus appears to Mary Magdalene, the first person to see him after his resurrection.

cell of early Christian believers, he experienced a vision of Jesus. In it Jesus asked, "Saul, Saul, why do you persecute me?"[8] (See Acts 9, 22, 26.) After several years of study in seclusion, Paul became convinced that Jesus's life and death were the major events of a divine plan, and that Jesus was a cosmic figure who entered the world in order to renew it. Consequently, as we will soon discuss, the focus in Paul's thought is less on the historical Jesus and more on the meaning of the cosmic Christ.

Paul discovered his life's mission: to spread belief in Christ around the Mediterranean, particularly among non-Jews, whom he found more receptive to his message. His use of the Greco-Roman name Paul, instead of his Jewish name Saul, shows his orientation to the non-Jewish world.

Paul's missionary technique was the same in most towns. If the Book of Acts is correct in its portrayal of Paul's missionary work, he would begin by visiting the local synagogue. There, Paul would use Jewish scriptures, such as the Book of Isaiah, to explain his own belief that Jesus was the Messiah whom Jews had long been awaiting. He was unsuccessful with most Jews, who generally expected a royal Messiah, not a poor man who had been publicly executed. And they sometimes treated Paul as a traitor, especially when he said that it was unnecessary to impose Jewish laws about diet and circumcision on non-Jewish converts to Christian belief.

Whether all Christians had to keep Jewish religious laws was a subject of intense debate in early Christianity. Christianity had begun as a movement of Jews who believed that Jesus was the expected Messiah, but it soon attracted followers who did not come from a Jewish background. Questions about practice led early Christianity to differentiate itself from Judaism, to define itself on its own terms. Did adult males who wished to be baptized also have to be circumcised? (Needless to say, adult male converts were not always enthusiastic about the practice of circumcision.) Did new converts have to keep the Jewish laws about diet? Did they have to keep the Jewish Sabbath? Should they read the Jewish scriptures?

Some early Christian preachers decided not to impose Jewish rules on non-Jewish converts, while others insisted that all Jewish laws had to be kept. The faction that insisted on upholding all Jewish laws, however, did not prevail. Ultimately, some elements of Judaism were retained and others were abandoned. For example, circumcision was replaced by **baptism** as a sign of initiation, but Jewish scriptures and weekly services were retained.

These efforts to define what it meant to be a Christian signaled a major turning point in Christianity. Paul's conclusions, in particular, played a prominent role in shaping the movement. His views on the meaning of Jesus, on morality, and on Christian practice became the norm for most of the Christian world. This happened because of his extensive missionary activities in major cities of the Roman Empire and because he left eloquent letters stating his beliefs. Copied repeatedly, circulated, and read publicly, these letters have formed the basis for all later Christian belief.

Paul's training as a scholar of Jewish law made him acutely aware of human imperfection. He wrote that "all have sinned and fall short of the glory of God" (Rom. 3:23).[9] He came to feel, in fact, that external written laws, such as those of Judaism, hurt more than they helped; the imposition of laws that could not be fulfilled could only make human beings aware of their inadequacies. For him, Jesus came from God to bring people a radical new freedom. Believers would no longer have to rely on written laws or to feel guilty for past misdeeds. Jesus's death was a voluntary sacrifice to take on the punishment and guilt of everyone. Human beings thereby found **redemption** from punishment. Believers need only follow the lead of the Spirit of God, which dwells in them and directs them.

brothers! ³⁵Whoever does the will of God is my brother and sister and mother."

LET ANYONE WITH EARS TO HEAR LISTEN

THE SOWER SOWS THE WORD

4

The parable of the sower and the seed is an example of Jesus the teacher. This image is from the new St. John's Bible, commissioned by the monks of St. John's Abbey in Minnesota.

God's love has been poured into our hearts.
—Rom. 5:5[11]

Thus Paul preached that it is no longer by the keeping of Jewish laws that a person comes into right relationship with God (**righteousness**); rather, it is by the acceptance of Jesus, who shows us God's love and who was punished for our wrongdoing. What brings a person into good relationship with God "is not obedience to the Law, but faith in Jesus Christ" (Gal. 2:16).[10]

Despite his newfound freedom, Paul did not abandon moral rules. But his notion of morality was no longer based on laws that were imposed externally—and kept grudgingly—but rather on an interior force that inspired people to do good deeds spontaneously. The life of Jesus was for Paul a proof of God's love, because God the Father had sent Jesus into the world to tell about his love. According to Paul, our awareness of God's love will inspire us to live in a new and loving way.

Paul saw Jesus not only as teacher, prophet, and Messiah, but also as a manifestation of divinity. For Paul, Jesus was a cosmic figure—the preexistent image of God, the Wisdom of God (see Prov. 8), and the Lord of the universe. Jesus was sent into the world to begin a process of cosmic reunion between God and his human creation. **Sin** (wrongdoing) had brought to human beings the punishment of death. But Jesus's death was an atonement for human sin, and the result was that the punishment of death was no longer valid. Jesus's return to life was just the beginning of a process of eternal life for all people who have the Spirit of God within them.

The New Testament: Its Structure and Artistry

What we know of Jesus and early Christianity comes largely from the New Testament. The New Testament, which is also at the core of Christianity, is used in religious services, read regularly, and carried throughout the world.

The New Testament is divided into four parts: (1) the Gospels, (2) the Acts of the Apostles, (3) the Epistles, and (4) Revelation. The gospels describe the life and teachings of Jesus. Although we now know that the facts surrounding their authorship are complex, tradition has attributed the gospels to four early followers—Matthew, Mark, Luke, and John, who are called **evangelists** (Greek:

"good news person"). The Acts of the Apostles tells of the initial spread of Christianity, although its historical accuracy cannot be confirmed. The epistles are letters to early Christians, primarily by Paul. The New Testament ends with a visionary book, Revelation, which foretells in symbolic language the triumph of Christianity. Altogether, there are twenty-seven books in the New Testament.

All the books of the New Testament were written in Greek, the language of culture and commerce in the classical Mediterranean world of the first century of the Common Era. The quality of the Greek varies; in the Book of Revelation the language is considered rough, while in the Books of Luke and Acts it is considered particularly graceful.

The Gospels   We know of the life of Jesus primarily from the gospels, which are written in an extremely pictorial way. They are filled with powerful stories and images and have been the source of great inspiration for much later Christian art. Each of the four gospels is as unique in its artistry and style as would be four portraits of the same person painted by four different artists. The portraits would certainly be recognizably similar but also different in such details as choice of background, clothing, angle of perspective, and so on. The same is true of the "portraits" of Jesus that are painted in the gospels: each gospel writer shows Jesus in a different way.

Despite their differences, the first three gospels show a family resemblance in stories, language, and order. They are thus called the Synoptic Gospels (*synoptic* literally means "together-see" in Greek, implying a similar perspective). The synoptic writers show Jesus as a messianic teacher and healer sent by God. It is generally thought that the Gospel of Mark was written first, since it seems to be the primary source for the later Gospels of Matthew and Luke. The Gospel of John, however, is recognizably different and relies on its own separate sources. It is possible that all the gospels were originally written to be used as readings in religious services, probably in conjunction with complementary readings from the Hebrew scriptures.

The Gospel of Matthew is thought to have been written (about 75–80 CE) for an audience with a Jewish background. For example, it portrays Jesus as the "new Moses," a teacher who offers a "new Torah." In the Sermon on the Mount (Matt. 5–7), Jesus delivers his teachings on a mountain, just as Moses delivered the Ten Commandments from another mountain, Mount Sinai. The gospel also contains many quotations from the Hebrew scriptures, showing that Jesus was their fulfillment.

The Gospel of Mark is the shortest of the four gospels, which suggests that it is the oldest (written around 65–70 CE). This gospel contains no infancy stories and begins instead with the adult public life of Jesus. In the original version, it ends with an account of Jesus's empty tomb. The account of Jesus's appearances after the resurrection (Mark 16:9–19) is a later addition.

The Gospel of Luke (written about 85 CE) is filled with a sense of wonder, perhaps because it speaks repeatedly of the miraculous action of the Spirit of God at work in the world. It has been called the "women's gospel" because of its many accounts of women, including Jesus's mother Mary, her cousin Elizabeth,

Deeper Insights

THE BOOKS OF THE NEW TESTAMENT

GOSPELS

Synoptic Gospels

Matthew (75–80 CE)

Mark (65–70 CE)

Luke (c. 85 CE)

Non-Synoptic Gospel

John (90–100 CE)

HISTORY

Acts of the Apostles (c. 85 CE)

EPISTLES

Pauline Epistles (c. 50–125 CE)

Romans

1–2 Corinthians

Galatians

Ephesians

Philippians

Colossians

1–2 Thessalonians

1–2 Timothy

Titus

Philemon

Hebrews

Universal Epistles (c. 90–125 CE)

James

1–2 Peter

1–3 John

Jude

PROPHECY

Revelation (c. 100 CE)

his follower Mary Magdalene, and disciples such as Joanna and Susanna. This is a gospel of mercy and compassion, with a strong focus on the underdog.

The Gospel of John stands by itself. The time of its writing is difficult to pinpoint. Traditionally, it has been dated quite late—about 90 to 100 CE—because of its apparent elaboration of Christian doctrines. But details that might have come from an eyewitness suggest that parts may have been written earlier. Because it views human life as a struggle between the principles of light and darkness, students of the Gospel of John have wondered whether it was influenced by one or more religious movements of the period, such as the Persian religion of Zoroastrianism (see Chapter 10), Greek mystery religions, or Gnosticism (see Chapter 10)—a movement that saw human life as a stage of purification to prepare the soul to return to God.[12] The discovery of the Dead Sea Scrolls in 1947 near Qumran has shown many similarities between the language of the Gospel of John and certain phrases found in the Qumran literature (for example, "sons of light and sons of darkness"). The Jewish origins of the gospel are now clear.

In the Gospel of John, the portrayal of Jesus is full of mystery. He is the **incarnation** of God, the divine made visible in human form. He speaks in cosmic tones: "I am the light of the world" (John 9:5). "I am the bread of life" (John 6:35). "You are from below; I am from above" (John 8:23).[13] Scholars frequently question the historicity of these exact words, seeing them more as representing the author's vision of the heavenly origin and nature of Jesus.

On Christmas, Christians often display depictions of the birth of Jesus. Here, girls view such a depiction inside a Myanmar church.

The central aesthetic image of the gospel is a ray of divine light that descends like a lightning bolt into our world, passing through and lighting up the darkness but ultimately returning to its heavenly source and enabling human beings to follow. Most people, the gospel states, do not really understand the truth; only those who have an open heart can see the true nature of Jesus as divine light. Water, bread, the vine, the shepherd, and the door are additional symbols used in the Gospel of John to indicate aspects of Jesus and his meaning for the believer. These symbols later became regular features of Christian art.

The Acts of the Apostles This book (dating from about 85 CE) is really the second part of the Gospel of Luke, and scholars sometimes refer to the two books together as Luke-Acts. It is possible that the single work of Luke-Acts was divided in two in order to place the Gospel of John after the Gospel of Luke. Just as the Gospel of Luke portrays Jesus as moving inevitably toward his sacrifice in Jerusalem, so Acts portrays Paul in a parallel journey to his final sacrifice in Rome. At the heart of both books is a single beautiful image of a stone, dropped in a pond, that makes ever-widening ripples. Similarly, the life of Jesus makes ever-widening ripples as it spreads in a growing circle from its origin in Jerusalem to the ends of the earth.

The Epistles   The word *epistle* means "letter" and is an appropriate label for most of these works, which were written to instruct, to encourage, and to solve problems. Several epistles are long and formal; a few are brief and hurried. Some epistles seem to have been written to individuals; some, to individual churches; and others, for circulation among several churches. And it appears that a few of the epistles were originally treatises (for example, Hebrews) or sermons (1 Peter).

The wide category of works called the epistles can be divided into two groups. The first includes those books that traditionally have been attributed to the early missionary Paul—the Pauline Epistles. The second group includes all the other epistles—called the Universal Epistles because they seem to be addressed to all believers. The genuine Pauline letters are the earliest works in the New Testament, dating from about 50 to 60 CE. The dating of the other epistles is debated, but some may have been finished as late as about 125 CE. Of the so-called Pauline Epistles, it is now recognized that Paul did not write several of them. However, writing in the name of a famous teacher after that person's death was a common practice in the ancient world; it was meant not to deceive but to honor the teacher.

One factor that has made the epistles so much loved is their use of memorable images, many of which come from the Pauline letters. For example, life is compared to a race with a prize given at the end (1 Cor. 9:24); good deeds are like incense rising to God (2 Cor. 2:15); and the community of believers is like a solid building set on secure foundations (1 Cor. 3:9–17). Effective images also appear in the non-Pauline epistles: new Christians are compared to babies who long for milk (1 Pet. 2:2); and the devil is like a roaring lion, seeking someone to devour (1 Pet. 5:8).

The letters are also interesting in their description of roles in the early Church. Thanks are given to many women for their help. Paul, for example, in various letters mentions quite a few: Phoebe, Priscilla, Tryphaena, Tryphosa, Julia, Junia, Evodia, Syntyche, Nympha, and Apphia. Phoebe is called a helper and was quite possibly an official deacon (Rom. 16:1). Nympha owned a house at which a community of believers met (Col. 4:15). In his letter to Galatians, Paul contributed to Christianity one of its greatest passages on equality: "There is neither Jew nor Greek, slave nor free, male nor female, for you are all one in Christ Jesus" (Gal. 3:28).[14]

Occasionally, images of the Trinity include Mary, thereby bringing a female element into the representation of the divine. This depiction, with the Holy Spirit as a dove perched on the cross, stands in the middle of a Czech town square.

The themes of the epistles vary widely, but they focus generally on proper belief, morality, and church order. The topics include the nature and work of Jesus, God's plan for humanity, faith, good deeds, love, the ideal marriage, community harmony, Christian living, the conduct of the Lord's Supper, and the expected return of Jesus.

Revelation   This final book of the New Testament was originally written (around 100 CE) as a book of encouragement for Christians who were under threat of persecution. Through a series of visions, the book shows that suffering will be followed by the final triumph of goodness over evil. The last chapters show the descent of the New Jerusalem from heaven and the adoration of Jesus, who appears as a lamb.

The language of Revelation is highly symbolic, deliberately using numbers and images in a way that would make the meaning clear to early Christians but obscure to others. For example, the lamb (Rev. 14:1) is Jesus, and the dragon with seven heads (Rev. 12:3) is the empire of Rome, a city built on seven hills. The number 666, the mark of the beast (mentioned in Rev. 13:18), may be the name of Emperor Nero, given in the form of numbers. Although long attributed to the author of the Gospel of John, Revelation is plainly—because of stylistic differences—by another hand. Some of its images were seminal to the development of later Christian art—particularly the adoration of the lamb, the four horsemen of the apocalypse, the book of life, and the vision of heaven.

The Christian Canon

We should recognize that some of the books in the New Testament were not accepted universally for several centuries. Agreement on which books belonged to the sacred **canon** of the New Testament took several hundred years.[15]

Early Christians continued for the most part to accept and read the Hebrew scriptures, particularly those books—such as Genesis, Exodus, Isaiah, the Psalms, and the Song of Songs—that they saw as foreshadowing the events of Christianity. The New Testament books, therefore, were added to the Hebrew scriptures already in existence. Christians thought of the Hebrew scriptures, which they called the Old Testament, as being fulfilled by the Christian scriptures, which they called the New Testament. The Christian **Bible** thus includes both the Hebrew scriptures and the New Testament.

There is a whole spectrum of ways in which the Christian Bible is read and interpreted by Christians. One approach emphasizes the subjective aspect of the scriptures, interpreting them primarily as a record of beliefs. A contrasting approach sees the Christian Bible as a work of objective history and authoritative morality, dictated word for word by God. To illustrate, let's consider how the two approaches interpret the stories of creation in the Book of Genesis. The conservative position interprets the six days of creation and the story of Adam and Eve quite literally, as historical records, while the liberal approach interprets these stories primarily as moral tales that express God's power, love, and sense of justice. There are similar contrasts between the conservative and liberal interpretations of miracles (for example, the virgin birth) in the New Testament.

Deeper Insights

THE CHRISTIAN WORLDVIEW

The New Testament and later creeds help define the Christian way of looking at the world. Most Christians agree on the following elements.

God Behind the activity of the universe is an eternal, intelligent power who created the universe as an expression of love. Traditional Christianity holds the belief that God is made of three "Persons": Father, Son, and Holy Spirit—together called the **Trinity.** The doctrine of the Trinity is said to be a mystery beyond complete human comprehension, but it hints that the nature of God is essentially a relationship of love.

The Father The loving and caring qualities of God are especially evident in the Father, whom Jesus constantly addressed. Although without gender, God the Father is frequently depicted as an elderly man, robed and bearded.

Jesus Christ Jesus is Son of the Father, but equally divine. Because he is the visible expression of God, he is called God's Word and Image. The life and death of Jesus on earth are part of a divine plan to help humanity. Jesus willingly took on the punishment that, from the perspective of justice, should fall on all human beings who have done wrong. Some forms of Christianity also teach that Jesus's life and death redeemed a basic sinfulness in human beings called **original sin,** which is inherited by all of Adam's descendants. Jesus continues to live physically beyond the earth, but

he will someday return to judge human beings and to inaugurate a golden age.

The Holy Spirit The Spirit is a divine power that guides all believers. In art, the Spirit is usually shown as a white dove.

The Bible God's will and plan are expressed in the Bible, which was written by human beings under God's inspiration. The Bible consists of the books of the Hebrew Bible—which Christians call the Old Testament—and the twenty-seven books of the New Testament.

Human life Human beings are on earth to help others, to perfect themselves, and to prepare for the afterlife. Suffering, when accepted, allows human beings to grow in insight and compassion.

Afterlife Human beings possess an immortal soul. Both body and soul ultimately will be rewarded in heaven or punished in hell. Many Christians also believe in a temporary intermediate state called *purgatory,* where less worthy souls are prepared after death for heaven.

These basic beliefs invite a variety of interpretation. In the first five centuries of Christianity, debate was frequent until these beliefs had been clearly formulated in statements of faith. In recent centuries, however, new and diverse interpretations of all aspects of Christian belief have emerged.

Most contemporary Christians hold a position that is somewhere in between the conservative and liberal poles of the spectrum. They believe that the Bible was inspired by God in its essentials, but they see it as requiring thoughtful human interpretation. Interpretation of the Bible has been and still is a major cause of conflict and division in Christianity; however, the debate has also been—and still is—a great source of intellectual vitality.

THE EARLY SPREAD OF CHRISTIANITY

Christianity is a missionary religion. The Gospel of Mark tells how Jesus sent out his disciples in pairs to preach throughout the land of Israel (Mark 6:7). Then the Gospel of Matthew ends with Jesus's command, "Make disciples of all nations" (Matt. 28:19).[16] In the following discussion, we will see how Christianity spread in stages: from being a Jewish messianic movement in

Israel, Christianity spread around the Mediterranean; then it became the official religion of the Roman Empire; and after the end of the empire in the West, Christianity spread to the rest of Europe. (Later, we will see how it spread to the New World, Asia, and Africa.)

Paul's eagerness to spread his belief in Jesus took him to Asia Minor (Turkey), Greece, and Italy. Tradition holds that Peter, one of the original twelve apostles of Jesus, was already in Rome when Paul arrived and that both Peter and Paul died there under the Emperor Nero about 64 CE. At that point, early Christianity was only loosely organized, but it was clear even then that some kind of order was necessary. Influenced by the Roman Empire's hierarchical political organization, Christians developed a style of Church organization that has been called monarchical (Greek: "one ruler"). Population centers would have a single **bishop** (Greek: *episkopos*, "overseer"), who would be in charge of lower-ranking clergy.

In those days, before easy communication, a truly centralized Christianity was impossible. The bishops of the major cities thus played a significant role for the churches of the neighboring regions. Besides Rome, several other great cities of the Roman Empire became centers of Christian belief—particularly Antioch in Syria and Alexandria in Egypt (Figure 9.1). Because

FIGURE 9.1

Historical centers of early Christianity, with Paul's journeys.

Deeper Insights

GREEK AND ROMAN RELIGIONS AND EARLY CHRISTIANITY

If you are ever in Rome, be sure to take a walk from the Colosseum westward through the Roman Forum, along the Via Sacra ("sacred way"). Because the large stones of the ancient road are still there, you can easily imagine what it must have been like for a visitor to Rome in the first century CE. At the end of the Forum rises the steep Capitoline Hill, the ancient center of government and the location of a temple to Jupiter, the father of the Roman gods. You also will notice that just beyond the bare pillars are bell towers and crosses—signs that many of the Forum's buildings were long ago turned into Christian churches.

From its Middle Eastern roots, Christianity grew and spread within the Roman Empire, where it displaced the established religions of the Greeks and the Romans—but slowly. In fact, Christianity did not become the official state religion until the end of the fourth century. And since Rome in classical times was the largest city of the world, religions from faraway lands had also found their way there. (Rome in the imperial period was a great crossroads, much like London or Los Angeles today.) Like the temples that survive as Christian churches, elements from many of these religions were absorbed into the new religion of Christianity.

Since some of their gods came from the same source, the classical religions of the Greeks and the Romans show many similarities. But their religions were made of layers and were constantly evolving. The earliest layers, existing before recorded history, came from the veneration of local gods and nature spirits—often worshiped at sacred wells, groves, and roadside shrines. The next layer came from an array of sacred figures that were brought to Europe about 2000 BCE. The same pantheon appears in the Vedas, and some of these gods are still worshiped by Hindus today. Other layers were

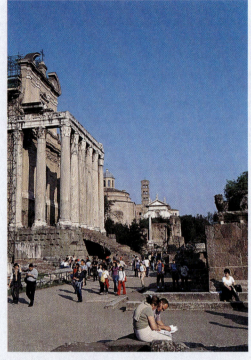

The Forum's Via Sacra today leads the visitor past remnants of temples dedicated to Roman gods, often incorporated into later Christian churches.

added when both the Greeks and the Romans absorbed gods from neighboring cultures. Great heroes of the past could be declared to be gods. Later, so could emperors. (One, when he thought that he was dying, is said to have amusingly remarked, "I think that I am becoming a god.")

---

the bishops of these important cities had more power than bishops of other, smaller cities, four early patriarchates arose: Rome, Alexandria, Antioch, and Jerusalem. The word **patriarch** (Greek: "father-source") came to apply to the important bishops who were leaders of an entire region.

However, when serious questions arose about doctrine and practice, the early Church leaders needed some way to answer them. On the one hand, they could seek a consensus from all other bishops by calling a Church council—an

There were occasional attempts at creating a complete system of deities. We find one such attempt, for example, in the works of Homer. The *Iliad* and the *Odyssey* placed the major Greek gods on Mount Olympus, living in a kind of extended family under the care of the sky god Zeus. Later, the Romans borrowed those ideas from the Greeks. There were also attempts to bring statues of major gods together for worship in the same place. The Athenians put statues of their most important gods at the Acropolis—a fact that Paul noticed and mentioned when he preached in Athens (Acts 17:19–23). The Romans placed multiple temples in the region of the Forum, and then the emperor Hadrian created the circular Pantheon (Greek: *pan*, "all"; *theos*, "god"), which had altars for the deities that he thought most important. (Today the Pantheon—perhaps the most beautiful of all classical Roman buildings—is a Catholic church.)

Despite their speculative forays, Greek and Roman religions involved practices as much as doctrine. In the days when medicine was undeveloped, charms and auspicious ceremonies were highly valued. Hence ritual, carefully performed, was essential. Ceremonies were held on festival days throughout the year. Romans had about thirty major festivals and many lesser ones—most with specific purposes, such as defense, fertility, and good harvest. These were largely acts of public religion, performed for the welfare of the nation. Thus, it is not surprising that Christianity continued such practices in developing its liturgical year, anchored in Christmas (the winter festival) and Easter (the spring rite of new birth). Saints' feast days, which were marked by special blessings and rituals, were similar to earlier veneration of the many gods.

Of great importance to the formation of Christianity were the Greek and Roman "mystery religions," so named because initiates vowed not to disclose the details of their initiations and practices. These typically involved instruction, a purification rite, a sharing of sacred food or drink, and a revelatory experience. We see clear echoes in the early training of would-be Christians (the "catechumens"), in baptism, and in eucharistic rites.

As the Roman Empire expanded during the time of Jesus and early Christianity, it imported the exotic worship of gods from Asia Minor (Turkey), Persia, and Egypt. Among the first religious imports was worship of the goddess Cybele, "the Great Mother," and Isis, a mother figure from Egypt. Such worship of goddesses undoubtedly influenced the growing Christian cult of Mary. From Persia came worship of the sun god Mithras, which practiced baptism in the blood of a bull and a ritual sacred meal. Evidence of worship involving Mithras has been found as far away from Rome as London.

As you end your walk along the Roman Forum, you may think of other parallels. Early images of a beardless Jesus, found in Christian burial chambers, resemble images of Apollo and Dionysus. The tendency to treat Zeus or Jupiter as the supreme god—as was shown by the great Temple of Jupiter that crowned the Capitoline Hill—may have helped convert the Roman Empire to monotheism. The ritual meal of Mithraism has echoes in the Christian Lord's Supper—in fact, the ancient church of San Clemente in Rome is built upon a Mithraeum, a Mithraic place of worship.

The exact amount of Greco-Roman religious influence on Christianity's evolution will never be entirely clear. But the influences we've reviewed remind us that all world religions were once new religions that were built, in many different ways, upon what came before them. At the same time, the ability of a new religion to adapt existing religions could help the new religion to be accepted and understood—as we see so well in the case of Christianity.

approach that the churches in the eastern part of the Roman Empire held to be the only correct practice. On the other hand, they could designate one bishop as the final authority. The bishop of Rome seemed to be a natural authority and judge for two reasons. First, until 330 CE Rome was the capital of the empire, so it was natural to think of the Roman bishop as a kind of spiritual ruler, like his political counterpart, the emperor. Second, according to tradition, Peter, the head of the twelve apostles, had lived his last days in Rome and had died there.

The desert monasteries at Wadi Natrun, outside of Alexandria in Egypt, date back as far as the fourth century. Some monks live in solitude as hermits in the desert, but each hermit must return to his monastery once a week.

He could thus be considered the first bishop of Rome. The special title **pope** comes from the Greek and Latin word *papa* ("father"), a title once used for many bishops but now applied almost exclusively to the bishop of Rome. (It is also, however, a term still used for the Coptic patriarch of Alexandria.)

The nature of papal authority and the biblical basis for it (Matt. 16:18–19) have been debated. Nonetheless, this hierarchical model of Christianity became common in western Europe. Although the Protestant Reformation of the sixteenth century, which we will discuss later, weakened the acceptance of papal authority, the Catholic bishops of Rome have continued to claim supremacy over all Christianity, and the Roman Catholic Church maintains this claim. Christianity in eastern Europe, however, as we will see later in the chapter, developed and has maintained a different, less centralized form of organization.

The Roman Empire made many contributions to Christianity. In the first two centuries of the Common Era, Christianity was often persecuted because it was associated with political disloyalty. But when Constantine became emperor, he saw in Christianity a glue that would cement the fragments of the entire empire. In his Edict of Toleration, Constantine decreed that Christianity could function publicly without persecution, and he supported the religion by asking its bishops to meet and define their beliefs. This they did at the first major Church council, the Council of Nicaea, held in Asia Minor in 325 CE. By the end of the fourth century, Christianity had been declared the official religion of the Roman Empire.

Thus the partnership of Christianity with the Roman Empire marked an entirely new phase and a significant turning point for the religion. Christianity formalized its institutional structure of bishops and priests, who had responsibilities within the set geographical units—based on imperial political units—of dioceses and parishes. And because it now had the prestige and financial support that came with government endorsement, Christianity could enthusiastically adopt imperial Roman architecture, art, music, clothing, ceremony, administration, and law. Most important, through church councils and creeds, Christianity clarified and defined its worldview. And just as historians had written about the history of Rome, so writers such as Eusebius (c. 260–c. 339) came to record the history of Christianity.

Because Christianity in western Europe spread from Rome, much of it was distinctively Roman in origin—especially its language (Latin). Latin was the language of church ritual and scholarship in the West. The Bible had also been translated into Latin. Indeed, scholars often say that though the Roman Empire disintegrated in the late fifth century, it actually lived on in another form in the Western Church. The pope replaced the emperor of Rome, but the language, laws, architecture, and thought patterns of Rome would continue fairly undisturbed in the West for more than a thousand years.

INFLUENCES ON CHRISTIANITY AT THE END OF THE ROMAN EMPIRE

As the Roman Empire was collapsing in the West (it would end in 476 CE), new sources of energy and direction influenced the next stage in the development of Christianity. Two individuals who had a great impact on Christianity were a bishop, Augustine, and a monk, Benedict.

Augustine

Augustine (354–430 CE) was born in North Africa in the later days of the Roman Empire of the West. Although we think of North Africa today as being quite different and separate from Europe, in Augustine's day it was still a vital part of the Roman Empire.

As a young adult, Augustine left his home in North Africa for Italy to make his name as a teacher of rhetoric. After a short time in Rome, he acquired a teaching position in Milan. He became seriously interested in Christianity as a result of his acquaintance with Ambrose, the bishop of the city. While in his garden one day, Augustine thought he heard a child's singsong voice repeating the phrase, *Tolle, lege* ("pick up, read").[17] Augustine, who had been studying the letters of Paul, picked up a copy of the epistles that lay on a nearby table. When he opened the book, what he read about the need for inner change pierced him to the heart, and he felt that he must totally reform his life. Augustine sought out Ambrose and asked to be baptized.

Augustine returned to North Africa to devote himself to church work. Ordained first as a priest and then as a bishop, he decided to live a monastic style of life in the company of other priests. Although he had a child with a mistress before his conversion, Augustine now preached an attitude toward sex and marriage that encouraged a growing Christian suspicion of the body. A reversal of those attitudes would begin only a thousand years later with the thought and work of the reformer Martin Luther, who had been a celibate member of the Augustinian order but who later married and rejected its idealization of celibacy.

In the years after his conversion, Augustine wrote books that were influential in the West for centuries. His *Confessions* was the first real autobiography in world literature, and it details Augustine's growth and conversion. *The City of God* was a defense of Christianity, which some people in his day blamed for the decline of the Roman Empire. *The Trinity* was Augustine's explanation of the relationship between God the Father, Jesus, and the Holy Spirit. He also wrote to oppose the priest Pelagius, a thinker who held a more optimistic view of human nature than Augustine did.

Augustine had incalculable influence on Western Christianity. He was *the* authority in Christian theology until the Protestant Reformation of the sixteenth century; he was an influence, as well, on Reformation thinkers such as Martin Luther and John Calvin. In short, Western Christianity was basically Augustinian Christianity for over a thousand years.

Benedict and the Monastic Ideal

As mentioned earlier, Augustine, after his conversion, chose to become a priest and live with other priests and monks in a life devoted to prayer and study. This monastic way of life became a significant part of Christianity. It is important to remember that monastic life was not just a religious choice. In the days when life was less secure, when work options were severely limited, and when marriage inevitably brought many children (of whom up to half might die young), the life of a monk offered extraordinary freedom. The monastic life provided liberation from daily cares, leisure time to read and write, a wealth of friendships with interesting people, and a strong sense of spiritual purpose. In fact, monks and nuns are found in many religious traditions today, and monasticism, far from being odd or rare, is a fairly universal expression of piety. Monasticism appears not only in Christianity but also in Hinduism, Buddhism, and Daoism; and in Judaism, the celibate monastic life was carried on among the Essenes for approximately two hundred years.

A monk is not necessarily a priest, nor need a priest be a monk. A monk is simply any male who chooses to leave society to live a celibate life of religious devotion; a priest is a person authorized to lead public worship. In the early days of Christianity, priests were often married and thus were not monks. However, under the influence of monasticism, Western priests were gradually expected to resemble monks and to be unmarried.

Christian monasticism probably sprang from a number of influences. One may have been the Essene movement and another may have been the fact that Jesus had never married. We might recall that he praised those who do not marry "for the sake of the kingdom of heaven" (Matt. 19:12).[18] Paul also was without a wife and recommended that state heartily for others (1 Cor. 7:32–35). Another influence on Christian monasticism came from Egypt, where hermits had been living in caves even before Jesus's time. Lastly, once the government stopped persecuting Christians, becoming a monk or nun was an important way for a Christian to show special religious fervor.

Benedict's *Rule for Monks* still shapes monastic life around the world. Here, twenty-first-century monks in Poland chant psalms and prayers.

The first Christian monks that we know of are called the Desert Fathers: Paul the Hermit, Antony of Egypt, Paphnutius, Pachomius, and Simon the Stylite. There were also women (of apparently shady backgrounds) among them: Saint Pelagia the Harlot and Saint Mary the Harlot. These individuals all turned away from the world to live what they thought of as a more perfect type of life. The movement may have shown a lack of interest in the needs of the world, but the movement also expressed a longing for the life of paradise—for joy, lack of conformity, individuality, and love of God. In fact, the monastic style of life was often called "the life of the angels."

The monastic movement in the West was greatly influenced and spread by a Latin translation of the *Life of Antony*, the Egyptian hermit. The movement took root in southern France and Italy. The real founder of Western monasticism was Benedict of Nursia (c. 480–c. 547 CE). Benedict was born into a wealthy family near Rome but fled to live in a cave, where he began to attract attention and followers who joined him in the monastic life. Eventually, Benedict and his followers built a permanent monastery on the top of Monte Cassino, south of Rome. From there the movement spread and became known as the Benedictine order.

Benedict's influence came from his *Rule for Monks*. Based on the earlier *Regula Magistri* ("rule of the master") and on the New Testament, the *Rule* gave advice about how monks should live together throughout the year. It stipulated that monks should pray each week the entire group of 150 psalms (biblical poems), spend time in manual labor, and remain at one monastery. It opposed excess in any way, yet it was sensible; for example, it allowed

What can be sweeter to us, dear brethren, than this voice of the Lord inviting us? Behold, in His loving kindness the Lord shows us the way of life.

—Saint Benedict's
Rule for Monks[21]

wine because, as it lamented, the monks could not be persuaded otherwise. The *Rule* became the organizing principle for all Western monasticism and is still followed today by Benedictines.[19]

Benedictine monks became the missionary force that spread Christianity—and Roman architecture and culture—throughout western Europe.[20] Among the great Benedictine missionaries were Augustine (d. 604 CE), who was sent as a missionary to England by Pope Gregory I, and Boniface (c. 675–754 CE), who spread Christianity in Germany.

THE EASTERN ORTHODOX CHURCH

Up to this point, we have focused on Christianity in western Europe. But another form of Christianity, known as the Eastern Orthodox Church, developed and spread in Russia, Bulgaria, the Ukraine, Romania, Greece, and elsewhere. These were regions that learned their Christianity from missionaries sent out from Constantinople, which Constantine had established as his imperial capital in 330 CE. **Orthodox,** meaning "correct belief," is used to designate Christianity in much of the East. The name's Greek roots—*orthos*, "straight," and *doxa*, "opinion," "thought"—reflect Eastern Christianity's desire to define its beliefs and keep them unchanged.

Early Development

In the earliest centuries of Christianity, when communication was slow and authority was rather decentralized, the bishops of Jerusalem, Antioch, Rome, and Alexandria, though often at odds in their theology, were looked to for guidance and authority. They were eclipsed, however, when Constantine made the small fishing village of Byzantion (Byzantium) the new capital of the Roman Empire. He officially named it New Rome, but it was soon called Constantinople—"Constantine's City." (Today it is Istanbul.) The large population of Constantinople, its importance as a governmental center, and its imperial support of Christianity all united to elevate the status of the bishop of Constantinople. Now called a patriarch, he became the most influential of all the bishops in the East.

Constantine had hoped to strengthen the Roman Empire by placing its capital—now Constantinople—closer to the northern frontier. From there, soldiers could be sent quickly to protect the frontier against the many barbarian tribes that lived in the north. But Constantine had in fact planted the seeds for an inevitable division of Christianity into Eastern and Western churches. For a time there were two emperors—of East and West—although this did not work well. The Latin-speaking Western empire, as we have seen, ended in the fifth century, and Western Christianity developed independently. The Greek-speaking Eastern empire, centered in Constantinople, spread its own form of Christianity and continued until its fall in the Muslim conquest of 1453.

The Orthodox Church is generally divided along ethnic and linguistic lines—Russian, Greek, Serbian, Bulgarian, and Romanian. But all these churches accept the statements of faith of the first seven Church councils, particularly those of Nicaea (325 CE) and Chalcedon (451 CE). The Orthodox Church has always held to a decentralized, consensus-based model. Although it does accept in theory that the bishop of Rome has a "primacy among equals," it holds that decisions concerning all of Christianity should be made collectively, in consultation with all patriarchs and bishops; thus, only Church councils are of ultimate authority.

Monasticism in the Eastern Church

As in the West, the monastic movement was an important aspect of the Eastern Church. It spread northward from Egypt and Syria into Asia Minor, where its greatest practitioners were the fourth-century Church leaders, Gregory of Nyssa (c. 335–394), Gregory Nazianzen (c. 329–389), and Basil of Caesarea (c. 330–379), who set the pattern for the monastic movement in **Orthodoxy.** Basil wrote recommendations for monastic living that are still followed today in Orthodox Christianity.

During this Sunday morning Orthodox service, the priest walks from the altar down the middle of the church. Devout congregants are blessed when the communion cup is placed atop their heads.

Greek-speaking monks of the eastern part of the Roman Empire carried Christianity from Constantinople into Russia and eastern Europe. The ninth-century brothers Cyril and Methodius are the most famous of these missionary monks, because they or their disciples are said to have authored the Cyrillic alphabet, based on the Greek alphabet, which is in common use in eastern Europe and Russia today.

Eastern Orthodoxy has created great monastic centers. The most famous is on Mount Athos in Greece, the current center of monasticism in that region. All Orthodox branches have sent representatives there for monastic training, and to visit or study there is considered a great honor.[22] Other monastic centers grew up in Romania, Bulgaria, the Ukraine, and Russia. Many of these monasteries still exist and may be visited today.

Eastern Orthodox Beliefs

Debate over several questions helped define and differentiate the Orthodox churches in their early development. One issue was the nature of Jesus Christ: How is Jesus related to God? Is God the Father greater than Jesus? If Jesus is divine as well as human, is he two persons or one person? And how did Jesus exist before his human life began? Some believers stressed the human nature of Jesus, while others stressed his divinity. The controversies eventually led to the creation and adoption in the fourth century of the Nicene Creed, which is accepted not only by the Eastern Orthodox but also by all traditional Western Christians. Because the creed was created to overcome several heresies, it speaks of the divine nature of Jesus in some detail:

> We believe in one God, the Father Almighty, maker of all things visible and invisible. And in one Lord Jesus Christ, the Son of God, begotten of the Father, the only-begotten; that is, of the essence of the Father, God of God, Light of Light, very God of very God, begotten, not made, being of one essence with the Father; by whom all things were made, both in heaven and on earth; who for us men, and for our salvation, came down and was incarnate and was made man.[23]

Even after the Nicene Creed, one school held that the divine and human natures of Christ were two separate persons, not one. Others argued that Jesus had only one nature, not two. The Council of Chalcedon (in 451 CE) declared that Jesus had two natures—divine and human—that were united in only one person.

After the major Church councils of the fourth and fifth centuries, certain groups of Christians, with differing views about the nature of Jesus, were labeled heretical. They continued to exist, however, though not in communion with the mainstream. Among those churches that did not accept the formulations of some early Church councils were the Church of the East, existing in Syria and the Middle East, and the Coptic Church of Egypt and Ethiopia. The variety of these early churches exemplifies the diversity of thought that existed among Christian groups in the first few centuries of the Common Era.

Another defining controversy, which has had lasting influence, occurred over the use of images for religious practice. We might recall that one of the Ten Commandments prohibits the making of images (Exod. 20:4), and Jews, as a result, have generally refrained from creating any religious images. Islam has a similar prohibition, as do some forms of Protestant Christianity today. The argument over making and using images reached a crisis when the Byzantine Emperor Leo III (680–740 CE) commanded the destruction of all images of Jesus, Mary, and the angels. It is possible that he did this for political as well as religious reasons, hoping to build bridges to Islam. But John of Damascus (c. 676–749), a monk and writer, came strongly to the defense of religious images—or **icons,** as they are often called (the Greek term *eikon* means "image"). John argued that images served the same purpose for the illiterate as the Bible did for those who could read. He also argued that God, by becoming incarnate in Jesus, did not disdain the material world. Icons, he said, were simply a continuation

Deeper Insights

INSIDE A GREEK ORTHODOX CHURCH

In his book *Eleni*, Nicholas Gage documents his childhood in Greece during World War II and the civil war that followed it. His memories include this description of the Greek Orthodox church in his native village of Lia. The church was destroyed by the Nazis.

> For seven centuries the Church of the Virgin had nourished the souls of the [villagers of Lia]. Its interior was their pride and their Bible. No one needed to be literate to know the Holy Scriptures, for they were all illustrated here in the frescoes painted by the hand of monks long vanished into anonymity. In the soaring vault of the cupola, Christ the All-Powerful, thirty times the size of a mortal man, scrutinized the congregation below, his Gospel clasped in his hand. In the spaces between the windows, the prophets and apostles, painted full-length with bristling beards and mournful eyes, made their eternal parade toward the altar.

> The villagers of Lia never tired of staring at the wonders of the Church of the Virgin: the walls glowed with every saint and martyr, the twelve feast days, the Last Supper, the life of the Virgin, and as a final warning, on the wall near the door, the Last Judgment, where bizarre dragons and devils punished every sort of evil, with the priests in the front rank of the sinners.

> The jewel of the church was the magnificent golden carved iconostasis, the shimmering screen which hid the mysteries of the sanctuary until the priest emerged from the Royal Doors carrying the blood and body of Christ. The iconostasis held four tiers of icons, splendid with gold leaf and jewels, and between the sacred pictures the native wood-carvers had allowed their imagination to create a fantasy of twining vines and mythical birds and beasts perched in the lacy fretwork.[24]

of that manifestation of divine love shown through the physical world. Church councils later affirmed the use of images, thus putting an indelible stamp on the practices of the Eastern Orthodox Church, which glories in the veneration of religious paintings.

Cracks in the unity of Christianity appeared early, but the first great division occurred in 1054, when disagreements brought the bishops of Rome and Constantinople to excommunicate each other. Despite the fact that the excommunications at last have been revoked, there remains a strong sense of separation.

Although cultural differences assisted the separation, there were small doctrinal differences, as well. The most famous concerned the doctrine of the Trinity. Did the Holy Spirit come from the Father or the Son or from both? The oldest and traditional position held that the Father generated the Spirit, but it became common in the West to attribute the generation of the Spirit to both Father and Son together. The Latin word **filioque** ("and from the Son") was added to creeds in the West from an early period. The Eastern Church rejected the notion as an improper addition to the Nicene Creed and cited it as a main reason for splitting off from the Western Church. Another dividing issue was the growing power of the pope and the claim that the bishop of Rome was the head of all Christians. Scholars today, however, point out the inevitability of separation because of many factors, such as distance, differences of language, and the political growth of northern and eastern Europe.

Relatives and friends attend a special service forty days after a death. Orthodox Christians believe that atonement for a dead person's sins can be partially achieved through the prayers and good works of the living.

Orthodox belief is, in summary, quite similar to that which emerged in the West and eventually became mainstream Christianity. The doctrinal differences are quite small, but the Orthodox Church differs in emphasis. Mainstream Western Christianity (Catholicism and Protestantism) has focused on the death of Jesus as an atonement for sin. Some scholars have said that that focus indicates a more "legal" emphasis: God is viewed as a judge, and punishment and repentance are paramount. Eastern Christianity has put more emphasis on a mystical self-transformation that human beings can experience through contact with Christ. As a consequence, Orthodox Christian art and literature focus less on the crucifixion of Jesus and more on the resurrection.

With the collapse of communism in Russia and eastern Europe, the Orthodox Church has regained some of its earlier strength. Church buildings that were banned from religious use have been transferred back to Church ownership and restored. It is notable that after the fall of communism, Russian authorities decided to rebuild the Cathedral of the Holy Savior in Moscow, which Stalin had destroyed and replaced with a swimming pool. The Russian Orthodox Church was also successful in having laws passed in 1997 that affirmed its special status, thereby giving it assistance against the missionary efforts of some other religious groups.

P E R S O N A L   E X P E R I E N C E
Inside the Monasteries on Mount Athos

Mount Athos is a finger of rocky land jutting into the Aegean Sea in the far north of Greece. The peninsula is a monastic state, where monks and hermits have lived for at least a thousand years. Although politically it is part of Greece, it is semi-independent and conducts its own affairs through a monastic council. At the center of the peninsula is a high mountain, and scattered around it, close to the shore, are twenty large monasteries. One spring, after getting proper approval from the government, I spent the week of Orthodox Easter at Athos.

From Athens I went to Thessaloníki, and from there I took a bus filled with people going back home to celebrate the festival. After staying the night in the village of Ouranopolis, I got on a ferryboat to Athos before dawn the next morning. In the small capital of Karyes, where monks run the shops, I received my passport. Over its Greek words was a picture of the peninsula and of Mary, appearing protectively over its mountain. This passport allowed me to stay overnight in any monastery I visited.

Each day I walked from one monastery to the next, a hike lasting about four hours, and was received graciously everywhere. One day I even hitched a ride on the back of one of three donkeys that were being used to carry supplies to several monasteries for the Easter celebration. The two drivers of the animals gave me brandy and Easter candy as the donkeys ambled along. Spring flowers blossomed everywhere next to innumerable streams, which were fed by water from snow melting on the mountain. At one point the drivers, no longer sober, began arguing with each other.

This view of Vatopedi Monastery gives a good sense of the design of the great monasteries of Mount Athos.

They jumped off their donkeys and began to fight, and the donkeys fled. A monk in a small rowboat came ashore, scrambled up the hill, and stopped the fighting. We recaptured the donkeys, which were feeding placidly farther up on the green hillside, and went on our way, as if nothing had happened.

The monasteries have high walls designed to protect the monks from the pirates who once roamed the coast. The lower half of each monastery is generally without windows, rising about 70 feet (21 meters) in height, and above that are as many as seven stories of wooden balconies. In the center of each monastery is a separate church building in the shape of a Greek cross, usually painted a reddish-brick color. Each arm of the church building is equal in size, and at the intersection of all the arms is the large central dome.

I can never forget the services of Easter, celebrated in those mysterious spaces. Being inside the churches felt like being in a group of caves. The floors were covered with sweet-smelling laurel leaves, an ancient symbol of victory. Chandeliers full of candles hung from the domes, illuminating the darkness like stars. For the predawn Easter service, monks used long sticks to make the chandeliers swing back and forth. As the chandeliers swayed, they lit up the murals and mosaics on the walls. I could see images of the prophet Elijah in his cave and the prophet Isaiah speaking with a six-winged angel. Jesus stood on a mountaintop, surrounded by an almond-shaped, rainbow-colored halo. Mary held her child and looked at me serenely. Above them all, an austere cosmic Christ held his hand up in blessing. Below him, each holding a lighted, orange beeswax candle that smelled like honey, monks on one side of the church began the Easter greeting. *"Christos anesti,"* they sang. "Christ is risen." Then monks on the other side answered back, *"Alithos anesti"*— "Truly, he is risen." They sang these two phrases back and forth for minutes. At last they stopped—except for one monk. He had a long white beard and was singing with his eyes closed. *"Christos anesti,"* he continued to sing loudly. *"Christos anesti."* The monks looked at each other in confusion, then smiled as a middle-aged monk came out and tapped the old monk on the shoulder. The old monk opened his eyes and there was silence.

CHRISTIANITY IN THE MIDDLE AGES

From its earliest days, when it was just another exotic "Eastern" religion in the Roman Empire, Christianity had made astonishing leaps—at first facing persecution, then becoming the official religion of the empire, and finally rising as *the* religion of all Europe. Christianity also existed on a smaller scale and in varied forms in Ethiopia, the Middle East, and India.

There were many reasons for the growth of Christianity. It preached a gospel of mercy and hope, offered divine help, promised an afterlife, treated the sick, and aided the poor. It taught skills in agriculture and architecture, introduced books, and spread use of the technology of the time. Imagine how a candlelit church at Easter—with its music, incense, candles, jeweled books, glass windows, and gorgeously robed priests—must have appeared to people who were not yet Christians. The effect must have been intoxicating. A legendary story tells of Russian ministers who attended a service at Saint Sophia's Cathedral in Constantinople about 988 CE. When they returned home to Kiev, they said that during the cathedral service they had not known whether they were on earth or in heaven.

Although many of the religious practices in both Rome and Constantinople were Roman in origin, the two centers, as we have seen, eventually split over differences. The existence of several patriarchates in the East kept any one of them from becoming a single ruling power. But the Roman Church in the West had no competitors for power in its region and thus grew in authority and strength. The pope, as the bishop of Rome, asserted his dominion over all Christians, an assertion that was not widely opposed in the West until the Protestant Reformation of the sixteenth century. The long-term effect was that the practices of the Roman Church would set the standard for language, practice, doctrine, church calendar, music, and worship throughout western Europe and then beyond, wherever European influence traveled. (To get a sense of the far-reaching impact of Roman culture, consider the fact that the book you are now reading—long after the Roman Empire has ended and probably thousands of miles from Rome—is written in the Latin alphabet: the capital letters come from the classical Latin of Rome; the lowercase letters were created by Christian monks and clerics.)

The growing size of the Christian population and the increasing cultural dominance of Christianity created a climate for a wide variety of religious expression: devotional and mystical movements, the founding of new religious communities, the Crusades and the Inquisition, reform movements, and new interpretations of the Christian ideal. Over time, traditional Church authority was questioned, giving rise to a search for new sources of authority.

Christian Mysticism

The word *mysticism* in theistic religions indicates a direct experience of the divine and a sense of oneness with God. Although not always approved of by Church authorities, this sort of transcendent experience is nevertheless an important part of Christianity. Christian mystics have spoken of their direct contact with God, sometimes describing a dissolution of all boundaries between themselves and God. Accounts of their experiences speak of intriguing states of consciousness.

The fact that Jesus felt an intimate relationship with God, whom he called Father, provided a basis for seeing Jesus as a role model for all Christian mystics. The Gospel of John, which has a strong mystical tendency, sees Jesus in this light. We also see mysticism in some letters of Paul. For example, Paul describes himself as having been taken up to "the third heaven" and having heard there things that could not be put into words (2 Cor. 12:1–13). Many monks and nuns from the earliest days of Christianity yearned to experience God, and mystical passages are common in the writings of Origen, Augustine, and Gregory of Nyssa.[25] Origen (c. 185–254) was the first of many Christians who would interpret the biblical Song of Songs mystically. He saw the young lover as Jesus and his beloved as a symbol of the mystic, "who burned with a heavenly love for her bridegroom, the Word of God."[26]

Mystical experience was especially prized in the West during the Middle Ages and early Renaissance. Francis of Assisi (1182–1226 CE) is possibly the best-known medieval mystic. Originally a playboy and son of a wealthy trader, Francis embraced a life of poverty in order to imitate the life of Jesus. He also showed a joyful love of nature, calling the sun and moon his brother and sister. One of the greatest Christian mystics was Meister Eckhart (c. 1260–1328), a German priest whose description of God as being beyond time and space, as "void," and as "neither this nor that"[27] has captured the interest of Hindus and Buddhists as well as Christians.

In this fresco, Giotto portrays Saint Francis receiving the wounds of Jesus. Some in the Middle Ages saw this as the ultimate mystical experience.

Many mystics were women. In recent years, the mystical songs of the medieval Benedictine nun Hildegard of Bingen (c. 1098–1179) have become popular through the availability of numerous recordings. An Englishwoman, known as Julian (or Juliana) of Norwich (c. 1342–1416), had a series of mystical experiences, which she later described in her book *Revelations of Divine Love*. She wrote of experiencing the feminine side of God. "God is as really our Mother as he is our Father. He showed this throughout, and particularly when he said that sweet word, 'It is I.' In other words, 'It is I who am the

Lord, make me an instrument of your peace. Where there is hatred, let me sow love; where there is injury, pardon; where there is doubt, faith; where there is despair, hope; where there is darkness, light; and where there is sadness, joy.

—Prayer attributed to Francis of Assisi[29]

strength and goodness of Fatherhood; I who am the wisdom of Mother-hood.'"[28] One of the most famous female mystics was Teresa of Avila (1515–1582), a Spanish nun who wrote in her autobiography about her intimacy with God. A dramatic statue by Bernini at the Roman church of Santa Maria della Vittoria shows Teresa lost in ecstasy.

The mystical approach to Christianity was counterbalanced by Christian attempts to offer reasoned, philosophical discussion of primary beliefs. The religious communities of Franciscans and Dominicans (discussed later in this chapter) were especially active in this work. Thomas Aquinas (1225–1274), a Dominican priest, is the best known. In two major works, the *Summa Theologica* and *Summa Contra Gentiles,* he blended the philosophical thought of Aristotle with Christian scripture and other Christian writings to present a fairly complete Christian worldview. Even he, however, was swayed by the appeal of mystical experience. At the end of his life, after a particularly profound experience of new understanding brought on by prayer, he is said to have remarked that all he had written was "like straw" in comparison to the reality that could be understood directly through mystical experience.

The Crusades, the Inquisition, and Christian Control

During the fourth and fifth centuries and thereafter, Christians all over Europe made pilgrimages to the lands where Jesus had lived and died, and the Emperors Constantine and Justinian had built churches there to encourage this practice. But Muslims took control of Jerusalem in the seventh century, and by the eleventh century, Christian pilgrimage had become severely restricted. To guarantee their own safety in pilgrimage and their access to the "Holy Land," some Europeans felt they had a right to seize control over the land of Israel and adjacent territory. Attempts to take over the Holy Land were called the Crusades—military expeditions that today might be described as religious enthusiasm gone badly astray.

The First Crusade began in 1095, and Jerusalem was taken after a bloody battle in 1099. Europeans took control of Israel and kept it for almost two hundred years, until they lost their last bit of Israel, at Acre near the port of Haifa, in 1291. The suffering inflicted on Muslims and Christians alike was appalling, and most crusaders died not of wounds but of illness. Many Eastern Christians, too, died at the hands of crusaders because they were mistaken for Muslims. The Crusades also did ideological damage, for they injured Christianity in their promotion of the ideal of a soldier who kills for religious reasons—something quite foreign to the commandments of Jesus. The romantic notion of the Christian soldier, "marching as to war," has remained in some forms of Christianity ever since.

One significant development in Christianity was the founding of nonmonastic religious communities, called *religious orders.* An order is a religious organization of men or women who live communal celibate lives, follow a set of written rules (Latin: *ordo*), and have a special purpose, such as teaching or nursing. The most famous medieval order was the Franciscan order, begun by Francis of Assisi, who idealized poverty and worked to help the poor. Other orders were the Dominicans, who became teachers and scholars, and the Knights Templar, who protected the pilgrimage sites and routes. Most orders also accepted women, who formed a separate division of the order.

In another development of the times, as western Europe became almost fully Christianized, Jews, Muslims, and heretics were considered to be religiously and politically dangerous. Jews were forced to live a life entirely separate from Christians; nontraditional Christians who had emerged in southern France were destroyed; and an effort began that would rid Spain and Sicily of Muslim influence.

The Inquisition received its name from its purpose—to "inquire" into a person's religious beliefs. Church authorities set up an organization to guarantee the purity of Christian belief, and its aim was to root out variant forms of Christianity that were considered heretical (divisive and dangerous to public order). Heretics were ferreted out, questioned, tortured, and, if found guilty, burned to death.

The Inquisition was first active in southern France in the thirteenth century, and the same inquisitorial procedures were later employed in Spain. We might recall that in the fifteenth century there was a large-scale attempt by Christian rulers to "reconquer" all of Spain. When all Spanish territory had been taken over by Christian rulers, Jews and Muslims were forced to convert to Christianity or to leave Spain, and many did leave, particularly for Morocco and Egypt. Those who stayed had to accept baptism and to publicly practice Christianity. Some of these new converts continued, however, to practice their old religions in private. The Inquisition attempted to discover who these "false Christians" were, and the religious order of Dominicans was especially active in this pursuit.

Tomás de Torquemada (c. 1420–1498), a Spanish Dominican, was appointed first inquisitor general by King Ferdinand and Queen Isabella in 1483 and grand inquisitor by Pope Innocent VIII in 1487. As he oversaw the Inquisition in Spain, he became notorious for his cruelty. The Reconquista, as the Christian movement was called, took over all Spanish territory in 1492. After this date, the Inquisition acted as a religious arm of the Spanish government both in Spain and in Spanish colonies in the New World.

The Late Middle Ages

The complete ousting of the crusaders from Israel (1291) marked the end of the Christian optimism that had been typical of the earlier Middle Ages. The loss was widely viewed as some kind of divine punishment for religious laxity. The feeling of pessimism deepened a half century later, when an epidemic of bubonic plague—called the Black Death for the black swellings that appeared on people's bodies—began to spread throughout Europe. The first major outbreak of disease occurred largely between 1347 and 1351. Beginning in France and Italy, the plague swept throughout western Europe; whole towns were emptied, with no one left to bury the corpses. Priests often fled, refusing to attend the dying—a neglect that brought the Church into great disrepute. Between a quarter and a third of the population died, and the plague continued to break out in many places for years afterward.

We now know that the disease was bacterial, caused by a bacillus found in fleas, which carried the disease to human beings. Rats that carried the fleas had arrived on ships that came from the Black Sea to ports in southern France and Italy. But the medical origin of the plague was not understood at the time, and people saw it instead as punishment from God. Some blamed the Jews, who were accused of poisoning wells or of angering God by their failure to accept Christianity. Others saw the plague as punishment for the lax behavior of Church authorities.

It is natural for a successful institution to take its authority for granted, and by the late Middle Ages it was common for bishops and abbots to be appointed to their positions purely for financial or family reasons. Some even lived away from their monasteries or dioceses. Indeed, for most of the fourteenth century, the popes lived not in Rome but in southern France. This papal dislocation led to a weakening of Church authority, until two and then finally three factions claimed the papacy.

The Middle Ages saw many changes in European society, as travelers to the Middle East and Asia returned home with new goods and ideas. New forms of trade and economy developed. Imagination and independence grew.

By far the greatest development of the late Middle Ages was the invention of printing with movable type. Before that time, all writing had to be done, laboriously, by hand, making the Bible and other works available only to scholars and clergy. Although the first book to be printed (c. 1450) was a Latin Bible, translations were soon necessary. Printing also made possible the spread in modern languages of new and revolutionary ideas. As a result, a multitude of vital new forms of Christianity would emerge.

THE PROTESTANT REFORMATION

As institutions age, they naturally lose some of their earnestness and purity, prompting attempts at reform. The Eastern Church, weakened by the Muslim invasions and its own decentralization, had less need for reform. In contrast, the Roman Church in the West had been enormously successful, spreading throughout western Europe and building a centralized power structure that had not been seriously challenged in the first thousand years of its growth.

By the late medieval period, people resented the lands and wealth of the Church and its monasteries. Thoughtful people also were troubled by what seemed to be a multitude of superstitious practices—particularly the veneration of relics of saints. Significant relics included the bones of saints and any object supposedly touched by Jesus or Mary or the saints, such as Mary's veil and the nails used at Jesus's crucifixion. Many of these items were not genuine.

Earlier attempts at reform had not been successful. John Wycliffe (c. 1320–1384), an English priest, preached against papal taxation and against the special authority of the clergy. He labeled as superstition the doctrine of transubstantiation (the notion that the sacrament of bread and wine, when blessed at the Mass, literally turned into Jesus's flesh and blood). He also oversaw the first translation of the Latin Bible into English. Accused of heresy by Pope Gregory XI in 1377, he was forbidden to teach. He died of a stroke, and after the Council of Constance (1414–1418) condemned his teachings, his body was dug up and burned and the ashes were thrown into a river.

Jan Hus (c. 1370–1415), rector of the University of Prague, kept alive many of Wycliffe's criticisms. Excommunicated in 1410 and condemned by the same council that condemned Wycliffe, Hus was burned at the stake in 1415.

Reform was inevitable. Soon another great turning point would occur in Christianity. The north and south of Europe would painfully split along religious lines, and Western Christianity would divide into Protestantism and Catholicism.

Martin Luther

Martin Luther (1483–1546), a German priest, was the first reformer to gain a large following and to survive, and his success encouraged others who also sought reforms. Their joint influence ultimately created the Protestant branch of Christianity, so called because the reformers protested some of the doctrines and practices of the Roman Church and affirmed their own biblical interpretations of Christian belief.

Luther, convinced of his own personal sinfulness, entered religious life (the Augustinian order) as a young man because of a vow made during a lightning storm. To enter religious life, he had to disobey his father, who wanted him to be a lawyer.[30] But after ordination as a priest, Luther still did not experience the inner peace he had sought.

Luther became a college professor in the university town of Wittenberg, teaching courses in the Bible with a focus on the New Testament—particularly the Pauline Epistles. At a time when he felt overwhelmed by his own sinfulness, he was struck by Paul's words at the beginning of the Epistle to the Romans: "The just shall live by faith" (Rom. 1:17).[31] Luther admitted that upon reading this epistle he felt as if he had been "born anew" and sensed that now "the gates of heaven" were open to him.

What Luther came to believe was that no matter how great the sinfulness of a human being, the sacrifice of Jesus was enough to make up for all wrongdoing. An individual's good deeds could never be enough; to become sinless in God's eyes, a person could rely on the work of Jesus.[32] Luther also recognized

Luther's writings provide a sense of his personality, here conveyed in Lucas Cranach's portraits of Luther and his wife Katharina.

the importance of his reading of the Bible as the primary inspiration for his new spiritual insight. Luther's main focuses have sometimes been summarized by the Latin phrases *sola scriptura* ("scripture alone") and *sola fides* ("faith alone").

Luther's teaching came at a time when the papacy was asking for contributions for the building of the new Saint Peter's Basilica in Rome. In return, donors were promised an **indulgence,** which would shorten the period after death that an individual would spend in purgatory, a preparatory state before the soul could attain heaven. Luther opposed the idea that anything spiritual could be sold.

To show his opposition and to stir debate, in 1517 Luther posted on the door of the castle church of Wittenberg his demands for change and reformation in the form of *Ninety-Five Theses.* Despite reprimands, Luther was unrepentant, and in 1521 Pope Leo X excommunicated him. Luther's efforts at reform might have failed—and he also might have been burned at the stake—if he had not received the support of and been hidden by the prince of his region, Frederick III of Saxony. During this period of refuge, Luther translated the New Testament into German, and he soon translated the Old Testament, as well. Luther's translation of the Christian Bible was to become for the Germans what the King James Bible became for the English-speaking world—it had an incalculable influence on German language and culture.

After his insight into the sufficiency of faith, Luther firmly rejected celibacy and the monastic style of life. He married a former nun, Katharina von Bora, had six children, and opened his home to a wide range of visitors interested in his work on church reform.

Deeper Insights

EMPHASES OF PROTESTANT CHRISTIANITY

Protestantism seeks to find—and live by—what is essential to the Christian experience. It places great emphasis on the individual's own ability to establish a personal relationship with God.

Return to simple Christianity The New Testament outlines the essentials of Christianity, both in belief and in practice. Christians should imitate the early tradition and avoid unnecessary, later alterations.

Centrality of Jesus Jesus is the one way to God the Father. Devotion to Mary and the saints has distracted believers from their faith in Jesus and should be de-emphasized or even abandoned. Trust in relics of Mary and the saints borders on superstition.

Guidance of the Bible The Bible is a divinely inspired guide for human lives. Believers should read it regularly, and ministers should explain it in sermons.

Importance of faith One's deeds alone cannot bring salvation. Faith in Jesus brings righteousness in God's eyes.

Direct relation to God Although ministers assist in religious services, they are not necessary as intermediaries between God and the individual. Every individual has a direct relationship with God.

Individual judgment The Holy Spirit helps each believer make decisions about the meaning of biblical passages and about how to apply Christian principles to everyday life. (The ability of each individual to radically question and rethink accepted interpretation is sometimes called the Protestant Principle.)

Forms of Protestantism

The right of every individual to radically question and reinterpret Christian belief and practice is at the heart of Protestant Christianity. This so-called **Protestant Principle** has been responsible for the generation of major branches of mainstream Protestantism, a multitude of smaller sects, and many thousands of independent churches, which continue to proliferate miraculously. Their styles of organization and worship run the spectrum—from ritualistic and structured to informal, emotional, and highly individualistic. Some Protestant denominations emphasize emotional conversion of individuals, while others stress broad social welfare. Some exclude people who are not in their denominations, while others are strongly inclusive, even inviting non-Christians to share in their services. Some have retained traditional ritual and an episcopal structure (that is, involving bishops and priests), while others have rejected all ritual and clergy. We must keep this variety in mind as we read about these denominations.

Lutheranism Martin Luther's version of the reform emphasized faith and the authority of the Bible. To encourage greater participation, Luther called for services to be conducted in German as well as in Latin. He also wrote hymns that were to be sung in German by the entire congregation, thus beginning a strong musical tradition in Lutheranism, which has particularly valued choral and organ music.

Luther's version of the Protestant reform spread throughout central and northern Germany and then into Scandinavia and the Baltic states. It came to the United States with German and Scandinavian immigrants, who settled primarily in the upper Midwest. Over the years, Lutheranism has retained Luther's original enthusiasm for the Bible, a trust in God, and excellent church music.

Calvinism Once the notion of reform was accepted, it was adopted and reinterpreted by others who also sought change. Among them was the French theologian John Calvin (1509–1564). Calvin's thought is sometimes said to be darker than Luther's because he saw human nature as being basically sinful and almost irresistibly drawn to evil. He also took the notion of God's power to its logical end: if God is all-powerful and all-knowing, then God has already decreed who will be saved and who will be damned (a doctrine known as **predestination**). One's deeds do not cause one's salvation or damna-

Glide Memorial Methodist Church in downtown San Francisco opened in 1931. Today the congregation works extensively with people who are sick, homeless, and socially marginalized. Its Sunday services attract supporters from a broad variety of economic and religious backgrounds.

tion; rather, they are a sign of what God has already decreed.

Calvin's view of God as judge may have been influenced by his study of law at the university. Eager for reform, when he was only 26 he published a summary of his ideas in *The Institutes of the Christian Religion*. Persecuted in France, he was forced to flee and eventually settled in Geneva, Switzerland. Because of the work of the reformer priest Huldrych Zwingli (1484–1531), the Swiss were already considering reforms. Calvin's great success in Geneva made the city a center for the expansion of the reform movement.

Where Luther had allowed much latitude in preserving elements of the Mass and other traditional Catholic practices, Calvin had a more austere view. Looking exclusively to the Bible for what might be approved, he encouraged the removal of all statues and pictures from the churches and the adoption of a style of congregational singing that had no organ accompaniment. The focus of the Calvinist service was on the sermon.

Ministers were not appointed by bishops—there were to be none in Calvinism—but were "called" by a council from each congregation. This practice, being highly democratic, threatened the political and religious leaders of the time, and believers of Calvinism were often forced into exile. Among such believers were the Puritans, who immigrated to New England, and the Huguenots (French Protestants), who were forced out of France in 1685 and settled in several areas of North America. Calvinism spread to Scotland through the efforts of John Knox (1514–1572), who had studied with Calvin in Geneva. It was in Scotland that a Church structure without bishops was refined, providing a pattern for Calvinism in other countries. Calvinism ultimately became important in Holland, Scotland, Switzerland, and the United States. Later, in the nineteenth century, it became influential in sub-Saharan Africa, Korea, China, and the Pacific. The Presbyterian Church is the best-known descendant of Calvinism. It gets its name from the Greek word *presbyter*, meaning "elder" or "leader."

The Church of England (Anglican Church)   Another form of Protestantism, which originated in England under King Henry VIII (1491–1547), unites elements of the Reformation with older traditional practices. Some see the Anglican Church as a compromise between Catholicism and Protestantism.

Henry maintained the traditional Church structure of bishops and priests. (It is called an *episcopal structure*, from the Greek word *episkopos*, meaning "bishop" or "overseer.") He also kept the basic structure of religious services much as before, initially in Latin. He even maintained priestly celibacy, although this was abolished soon after he died. As a concession to reformers, Henry had an English translation of the Bible placed in each church for all to read. The Church of England had a shaky beginning, but Henry's daughter Elizabeth, when she finally became queen, established it firmly.

The Church of England produced several works of great significance in its first century of existence. *The Book of Common Prayer,* with all major prayers in English for church use, was issued in 1559. Its rhythmic sentences set a standard by which other works in English have been measured. Throughout the sixteenth century, composers were commissioned to write choral music in English for religious services. The result was a wonderful body of music, still in use today. In 1611 the King James Bible was published, named for its sponsor, James I, who had succeeded Queen Elizabeth I. It became the single greatest influence on the English language.

The Church of England has been deliberately tolerant of a wide spectrum of interpretation and practice. Some churches have buildings and services of great simplicity (their style is called Low Church), while others use incense, statues of Mary, and stately ritual (called High Church). Furthermore, in spite of great opposition, the Church of England has generally accepted the ordination of women as priests and bishops.

Sectarianism   The powerful notion that every individual can interpret the Bible has encouraged—and still encourages—the development of an abundance of independent churches or sects. Most have been formed by a single, charismatic individual, and many have been small. Some have interpreted the Bible with literal seriousness, thus producing special emphases—among them, the rejection of the outside world and its technology, the adoption of an extremely simple lifestyle, total pacifism (rejection of war and violence), complete celibacy, and the expectation of the imminent end of the world. As a loosely defined group, this branch of Protestantism is called Sectarianism. Following are the most prominent sects:

The Anabaptists (meaning "baptize again"), a pious movement that developed during the sixteenth century, stressed the need for believers to be baptized as a sign of their inner conversion—even if they had been baptized as children. Their worship was simple. From this general movement arose several Mennonite and Amish sects, some communities of which maintain a simple, agricultural lifestyle without the use of cars or electricity. (The movie *Witness* is set against a background of Amish life.)

The Baptists, a denomination that began in England, have grown up as a major force in the United States. Baptists espouse some of the Anabaptist principles, including the need for inner conversion, baptism of adults only, simplicity in ritual, independence of personal judgment, and freedom from government control.

The Quakers were founded by George Fox (1624–1691) in England. Those who came to the United States settled primarily in Pennsylvania. Quakers are ardent pacifists; they have no clergy; and they originated a type of church service conducted largely in silence and without ritual. Their official name is Society of Friends, but the name *Quaker* came about from George Fox's belief that people should "quake" at the Word of the Lord.

The Shakers grew out of the Quaker movement. Founded by "Mother" Ann Lee (1736–1784), who came from England to New York State, the Shakers accepted both women and men but preached complete celibacy. Their religious services were unusual because they included devotional dance, from which their name derives. Settling in New York State and New England, the Shakers founded communities primarily dependent on farming. Although there are only a handful of Shakers today, their vision of Christian simplicity lives on in their architecture and furniture, which is unadorned but elegant.

The Pentecostal movement, although it has ancient roots, has been especially active in the last one hundred years. It emphasizes the legitimate place of emotion in Christian worship. At Pentecostal services one might encounter "speaking in tongues" (*glossolalia*), crying, fainting, and other forms of emotional response, which are thought of as gifts brought by the presence of the Holy Spirit.

The Methodist Church at first was simply a devotional movement within the Church of England. It was named for the methodical nature of prayer and study followed by Charles Wesley (1707–1788) and his followers at Oxford. But under the strong guidance of John Wesley (1703–1791), Charles's brother, Methodism took on an independent identity. Charles Wesley wrote more than six thousand hymns, which helped spread the movement.

THE DEVELOPMENT OF CHRISTIANITY FOLLOWING THE PROTESTANT REFORMATION

The Catholic Reformation (Counter Reformation)

Although the Protestant Reformation was a powerful movement, Roman Catholicism not only withstood its challenges but also grew and changed in response to it. That response, in the sixteenth and seventeenth centuries—called the Catholic Reformation or the Counter Reformation—strongly rejected most of the demands of the Protestant reformers. Protestants rejected the authority of the pope; Catholics stressed it. Protestants demanded the use of native languages; Catholics retained the use of Latin. Protestants emphasized simplicity in architecture and music; Catholics created churches of flamboyant drama.

Nevertheless, the Catholic Church recognized that some institutional reform was necessary. The church's first response was a long council, primarily held in the northern Italian town of Trent between 1545 and 1563. The council set up a uniform seminary system for the training of priests, who had sometimes in the past learned their skills simply by being apprenticed to older priests; it made the Roman liturgy a standard for Catholic services;

Reformers were infuriated by the sale of indulgences to pay for the building of St. Peter's Basilica in Rome. The basilica was completed during the Counter Reformation and remains a monument to Roman Catholicism.

Deeper Insights

EMPHASES OF CATHOLIC CHRISTIANITY

Catholicism accepts all traditional Christian beliefs, such as belief in the Trinity, the divine nature of Jesus, and the authority of the Bible. In addition, particularly as a result of the Protestant Reformation, it defends the following beliefs and practices.

Importance of good works The Christian must accompany faith with good works to achieve salvation.

Value of tradition Along with the Bible, Church tradition is an important guide for belief and practice.

Guided interpretation of the Bible Individual interpretation of the Bible must be guided by Church authority and tradition.

Hierarchical authority The pope, the bishop of Rome, is the ultimate authority of the Church, and bishops are the primary authorities in their dioceses (regions of authority).

Veneration of Mary and the saints Believers are encouraged to venerate not only Jesus but also Mary and the saints, who reside in heaven. As an aid to faith, believers may also honor relics (the bodies of saints and the objects that they used while alive).

Sacraments There are seven **sacraments** (essential rituals), not just two—as most Protestant reformers held. They are baptism, confirmation, the **Eucharist** (the Lord's Supper, Mass), matrimony, holy orders (the ordination of priests), reconciliation (the confession of sins to a priest), and the anointing of the sick (unction).

and it defended traditional teachings and practices (see the box "Emphases of Catholic Christianity"). This council took a defensive posture that erected symbolic walls around Catholic belief and practice.

Several new religious orders came into existence to defend and spread Catholic teaching. The most influential of these orders was the Society of Jesus, or the Jesuits. The Spanish founder of the Jesuits, Ignatius of Loyola (1491–1556), was a former soldier, and with this background he brought a military discipline to the training and life of his followers. Ultimately, Jesuits made a lasting contribution through their establishment of high schools and colleges for the training of young Catholics, and many continue this work today.

Because of the varied interpretations of the Bible and of Christian doctrine that began to emerge as a result of the Protestant Reformation, a major part of the Catholic Church's response was to stress discipline and centralized authority. The First Vatican Council (1869–1870) upheld this emphasis when it declared that the pope is infallible when he speaks officially (that is, *ex cathedra*, "from the chair" of authority) on doctrine and morals.

The International Spread of Christianity

The New Testament contains the injunction to "baptize all nations" (Matt. 28:19). As a result of this order, powerful missionary and devotional movements arose within all branches and denominations of Christianity (Figure 9.2). Over the past five hundred years, these movements have spread Christianity to every continent and turned it into a truly international religion.

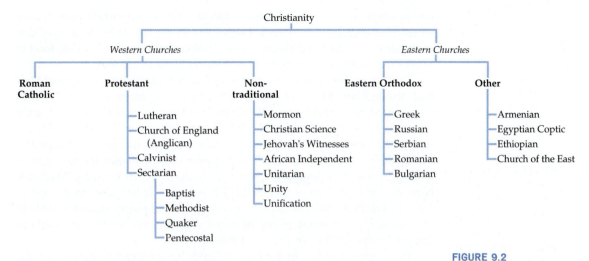

FIGURE 9.2

Branches and denominations of Christianity.

The Catholic Church conducted an early wave of missionary work. Wherever Spanish, Portuguese, and French colonists took power, their missionaries took Catholic Christianity. The Jesuit Père Jacques Marquette (1637–1675) propagated Catholicism in Canada and the Mississippi River valley, and the Franciscan Padre Junípero Serra (1713–1784) spread Catholicism by establishing missions in California. In Asia, early Catholic missionaries at first had little success. Jesuit missionaries were sent out from such missionary centers as Goa in India and from Macau, an island off of southeastern China, to convert the Chinese and Japanese. The Spanish Jesuit Francis Xavier (1506–1552) and Italian Jesuit Matteo Ricci (1552–1610) were industrious, but their attempts in China and Japan were repressed by the government authorities, who feared that conversion would bring European political control. Catholicism was, however, successful in the Philippines and Guam, where Spanish colonization contributed to the widespread acceptance of the religion. In the nineteenth century, French Catholic missionaries worked in Southeast Asia and the Pacific region. Tahiti, after being taken over by the French, became heavily Catholic; Vietnam, too, now has a sizable Catholic population. In sub-Saharan Africa, wherever France, Portugal, and Belgium established colonies, Catholicism also took hold.

Catholicism in Latin America frequently blended with native religions. In Brazil and the Caribbean, African religions (especially of the Yoruba peoples) mixed with Catholic veneration of saints to produce Santería, Voodoo, and Candomblé (see Chapter 11). In the southwestern United States, Mexico, Central America, and Spanish-speaking South America, Catholic practice incorporated cults of local deities. The cult of the Virgin of Guadalupe arose at the place where an Aztec goddess had been worshiped, and nature deities of the Mayans—gods and goddesses of the earth, maize, sun, and rain—are still venerated under the guise of Christian saints. Jesus's death on the cross was easy to appreciate in Mayan and Aztec cultures, in particular, in whose native religions offerings of human blood were an important part. Native worship of ancestors easily took a new form in the Día de los Muertos ("day of the dead"), celebrated yearly on November 2, when people bring food to graves and often stay all night in cemeteries lit with candles.

Protestant Christian missionaries and British conquests also spread their faith throughout the world. Protestant settlers who came to North America represented the earliest wave. The Church of England (the Anglican Church) traveled everywhere the English settled; although in the United States at the time of the American Revolution the name of the Church was changed to the Episcopal Church, to avoid the appearance of disloyalty to the new United States. The Anglican Church is widespread in Canada, Australia, New Zealand, and other former British colonies. It has also been a major force in South Africa—as demonstrated by its campaign against apartheid (the former government policy of racial segregation) headed by Anglican Bishop Desmond Tutu in the late 1980s.

Protestant churches in the United States have played a large role in the lives of African Americans. When slaves were brought to the English colonies of North America, the slaves were (sometimes forcibly) converted to Christianity, usually Protestantism. Most African Americans became members of the Methodist, Baptist, and smaller sectarian denominations. In the nineteenth century, Protestant denominations split over the issue of segregation and slavery, and churches were divided along racial lines. In 1816 the African Methodist Episcopal (AME) Church emerged from Methodism to serve African Americans exclusively and to save them from having to sit in segregated seating at the services of other denominations. At the same time, some New England Protestant churches became active in the abolitionist (antislavery) movement, helping runaway slaves to escape to Canada and changing public opinion about the morality of slavery. Later, southern Protestant churches played a large role in the movement that fought segregation, and their pastors (such as Martin Luther King Jr.) became its leaders.

The missionary movement gave both women and men new opportunities to spread Christianity, as well as to lead unusual lives. One example involves three women who worked together for years. Called the China Trio, they were two sisters (Eva and Francesca French) and a friend (Mildred Cable). Much of their time was spent traveling to towns of western China and to oases in the Gobi desert. They worked in China for more than thirty years, distributing Bibles and Christian literature and publishing colorful accounts of their work. They left China in 1936 but continued to write about their work for years afterward.

Methodist and Presbyterian missionaries have spread their vision of Christianity to Asia and the South Pacific. About half of South Koreans are now Christian. Protestant Chinese have been active in Taiwan, where they are politically prominent, and in mainland China, where today there are many "underground" house-churches that are not authorized by the government.

Contemporary Issues

MARTIN LUTHER KING JR.

Martin Luther King Jr. was born in Atlanta, Georgia, in 1929. The fact that both his father and grandfather were Baptist ministers led him naturally to religion. As a young man, he was troubled deeply by segregation and racism, and his studies in college and graduate school convinced him that Christian institutions had to work against racial inequality. His reading of Henry David Thoreau's essay "Civil Disobedience" and his study of the work of Mahatma Gandhi led him to believe in the power of nonviolent resistance. In Montgomery, Alabama, in 1959, King led a boycott of the city's bus system, following Rosa Parks's refusal to move from the white section to the back of a public bus.. Ultimately, the Supreme Court declared that laws imposing segregation on public buses were unconstitutional. As founder of the Southern Christian Leadership Conference, King mobilized black churches to oppose segregation. In 1964 he won the Nobel Peace Prize. He was assassinated four years later.[33]

King's powerful preaching and writing relied heavily on images taken from the Bible. His "I Have a Dream" speech is inspired by the stories of Joseph's dreams in the Book of Genesis (37:1–10). His "I Have Seen the Promised Land" speech is based on the story of Moses in the Book of Deuteronomy (34:1–4).

Martin Luther King Jr. is portrayed here with a halo, a traditional symbol of holiness and sainthood. Robert Lentz painted this contemporary icon.

Missionaries have also spread Orthodox Christianity across Russia to Siberia and even into Alaska, where 40,000 Aleuts (Eskimo) belong to the Orthodox Church. (A noted Russian Orthodox church is located in Sitka, Alaska.) The Orthodox Church also spread to North America through emigration from Russia, Greece, and eastern Europe.

Christianity has been less successful in China, Japan, Southeast Asia (except Vietnam and the Philippines), the Middle East, and North Africa. But elsewhere it is either the dominant religion or a powerful religious presence.

Nontraditional Christianity

Because Christianity is a fairly old religion and has flourished in cultures far from where it originally developed, it has produced some significant off-shoots. These denominations differ significantly from traditional Christianity, and although they are not usually considered a part of the three traditional branches of Christianity—Roman Catholic, Protestant, and Eastern Orthodox— they all sprang from Protestant origins. They differ in their beliefs, particularly regarding the Trinity, the divinity of Jesus, the timing of the end of the world, and the role of healing. Because the fastest-spreading of these religions is Mormonism, it is described in some detail. Other nontraditional groups include the Unitarians, Unification Church, and Jehovah's Witnesses (see the box "Examples of Nontraditional Christianity").

Church of Jesus Christ of Latter-day Saints   The Church of Jesus Christ of Latter-day Saints, commonly known as the Mormon Church, is one of the fastest-growing religious denominations in the world. Although Mormons consider themselves to be Christians who belong to a perfect, restored Christianity, mainstream Christian groups point out major differences between Mormonism and traditional Christianity.

Joseph Smith (1805–1844), the founder of the movement, was born in New York State. As a young man he was troubled by the differences and conflicts between Christian groups. When he was 14, he had a vision of God the Father and of Jesus Christ, who informed him that no current Christian denomination was correct, because true Christianity had died out with the death of the early apostles.

When Smith was 17, he had another vision. An angel named Moroni showed the young man to a hill and directed him to dig there. Mormonism teaches that Smith eventually unearthed several long-buried objects of great religious interest. The objects were golden tablets inscribed with foreign words, a breastplate, and mysterious stones that Smith was able to use to translate the words written on the tablets. Smith began the translation work, dictating from behind a curtain to his wife Emma and to friends Oliver Cowdery and Martin Harris. The result of his work was the Book of Mormon. Later, John the Baptist and three apostles—Peter, James, and John—appeared to Smith and Cowdery, initiating them into two forms of priesthood—the Aaronic and Melchizedek priesthoods.

Hoping to be free to practice their religion, Smith and his early followers began a series of moves—to Ohio, Missouri, and Illinois. Opposition from their neighbors resulted from the new Church's belief in the divine inspiration of the Book of Mormon and its practice of polygamy, which Smith defended as biblically justified. At each new location the believers were persecuted and forced to leave. In Illinois, Smith and his brother were imprisoned and then killed by a mob that broke into the jail.

At this point, the remaining believers nominated Brigham Young (1801–1877) as their next leader. Young organized a move to Utah, where he founded

Deeper Insights

EXAMPLES OF NONTRADITIONAL CHRISTIANITY

Christianity is capable of taking on new shapes, sometimes as a result of blending with other religions. Here are some important examples:

Unification Church Founded in South Korea, this Church blends elements of Christianity, Buddhism, and Confucianism. Reverend Sun Myung Moon (1920–2012), who called himself the Jesus of the Second Coming, founded the religion in 1954. The Church hopes to establish God's kingdom on earth. Promoting its vision of society as a harmonious family, the Unification Church arranges marriages between its followers and frequently performs joint wedding ceremonies involving hundreds of couples.

African Independent Churches (AICs) Christianity has been immensely successful in sub-Saharan Africa over the last one hundred years. Although the majority of Christians belong to mainstream traditional churches, thousands of independent churches exist. Some manifest distinctively African characteristics and interests, including a focus on faith healing, prophecy, and charismatic experience. The Harrist Church, for example, was begun in the Ivory Coast by a messianic leader who claimed to have received revelations from the angel Gabriel; and the Mai Chaza Church in Zimbabwe was founded by a woman who claimed to have died and come back to life. These churches also have often adopted elements from African culture, particularly music, dress, and ritual. The Kimbanguist Church of Central Africa, for example, uses sweet potatoes and honey, rather than bread and wine, in its services.[34]

Jehovah's Witnesses Members of this religion take biblical passages literally and expect the imminent end of the world. The religion does not allow blood transfusions because of the biblical prohibition against ingesting blood. Its members do not believe in the Trinity, the divinity of Jesus, or a permanent hell—all of which, they say, are not found in the Bible. For the same reason, they do not celebrate Christmas (or birthdays). Giving allegiance only to God, they are strongly nonpolitical, refusing to salute a flag or show allegiance to any country.

Christian Science and Unity The Christian Science Church and Unity Church began in the movement called New Thought, which emphasized the role of positive affirmations. Christian Science puts emphasis on the power of thought to bring about physical healing. In its services it uses the Bible and the book *Science and Health with Key to the Scriptures*, written by its founder Mary Baker Eddy (1821–1910). Unity Church is based in Christianity, but it also uses passages from many other religions among its readings. Its services include guided meditations, hymns, and positive affirmations.

Unitarian Church The Unitarian Church rejects the doctrine of the Trinity and prides itself on having no creed. Instead, it imitates the prophetic role of Jesus by emphasizing acts of social justice. The writers Ralph Waldo Emerson and Henry David Thoreau were Unitarians.

Salt Lake City. Prior to the move, a split had developed within the Church—in part over the matter of polygamy. Leadership of the smaller group, which did not travel to Utah, was taken over by Smith's son.

In Utah the Church faced regular opposition but grew in numbers. In 1890, the fourth president of the Church delivered a new command that disavowed polygamy. This rejection of polygamy (sometimes called the Great Accommodation) led to social acceptance of Mormonism. And in 1896, the Utah Territory won statehood.

The Mormon Church has always been a missionary Church, and it made its way very early to England and Hawai`i. The Mormon Church has spread

The Mormon Temple in Salt Lake City glitters in the Christmas season.

so far through missionary efforts that it is now found worldwide. It has been particularly successful in the South Pacific.

Mormons accept as inspired the Christian Bible, which they usually use in the King James Version. They also believe that several other works are equally inspired. Most important is the Book of Mormon. Another inspired work is the Doctrine and Covenants, a list of more than one hundred revelations that were given by God to Joseph Smith and, later, to the heads of the Church. A last inspired work is The Pearl of Great Price, containing further revelations and a compilation of the articles of faith. These three additional works are all thought of as complements to the Christian Bible. More than 100 million copies of the Book of Mormon have been distributed.

The Mormon notion of the afterlife includes a belief in hell and in several higher levels of reward: the telestial, terrestrial, and celestial realms. At the peak of the highest realm are Mormons who have performed all the special ordinances in one of the more than one hundred Mormon temples around the world. Couples who have had their marriages "sealed" in a temple service will continue as a married couple in the celestial realm and can become godlike, producing spiritual children there.

The Book of Mormon adds details to traditional biblical history. It teaches that some descendants of the people who produced the tower of Babel (Gen. 11:1–9) settled in the Americas but eventually died out. It also teaches that a group of Israelites came to North America about 600 BCE. They divided into two warring factions, the Nephites and Lamanites, and Jesus, after his resurrection, came to preach to them. The Book of Mormon tells how in the fourth century CE the Nephites were wiped out in battles with the Lamanites, who are considered to be the ancestors of Native Americans.

While Mormons follow the Christian practice of using baptism as a ritual of initiation, they are unusual in that they also practice baptism by proxy for deceased relatives, as was practiced by some early Christians (1 Cor. 15:29). This—along with a general interest in family life—is a major reason for Mormon interest in genealogy. In fact, Mormons maintain the largest source of genealogical records in the world.

Devout Mormons meet for study and worship each Sunday. Their Sunday meetings include a sacrament service (Lord's Supper), which is performed with bread and water, rather than wine. Because they view the body's health as a religious concern, devout Mormons do not smoke or use tobacco, drink alcohol, take illicit drugs, or consume several beverages, primarily coffee and tea.

Because the Mormon Church emphasizes different gender roles for men and women, its hierarchy is male. Women, however, exercise leadership roles in their own organizations, which focus on domestic work, child rearing, and social welfare. Mormons are well known for the importance they place on harmonious family life. Mormons also support the tradition of setting aside one night each week for all family members to stay at home to enjoy their life as a family.

At the top of the Church hierarchy is the church president, who is called the Prophet (as well as Seer and Revelator), because he is considered capable of receiving new revelations from God. Below him is a group of men called the Quorum of the Twelve Apostles, and below that group are the first and second Quorums of the Seventies, who act as general authorities. Below them are area authorities and stake presidents (a *stake* is the equivalent of a diocese). Pastors are called bishops, and the males in their wards (parishes), when they reach the appropriate age, are ordained in various offices of the Aaronic and Melchizedek priesthoods. Young men are expected to give two years to preaching the religion, often in foreign countries. Young women are also invited to do missionary work, but the length of their missionary work is slightly less (usually a year and a half). At any one time, about 60,000 missionaries are active. Today the Mormon Church has about fourteen million members, half of whom live outside the United States. The headquarters of the Church of Jesus Christ of Latter-day Saints is in Salt Lake City, Utah.

Mormonism has a strong choral tradition. Hymns and solo works are sung at services, and the Mormon Tabernacle Choir, which gives regular concerts in Salt Lake City, performs a traditional repertory of hymns, oratorios, and other music.

In addition to the Mormons, who form the largest branch of the movement begun by Joseph Smith, there are at least a dozen offshoots. The most important is the Community of Christ, formerly known as the Reorganized Church of Jesus Christ of Latter-day Saints (RLDS). It changed its name in 2001 in order to emphasize its closeness to mainstream Christianity. Smaller groups exist—some of them continuing the early practice of polygamy—primarily in Utah and western Canada. The Fundamentalist Church of Jesus Christ of Latter-day Saints (FLDS) is the largest of the groups practicing polygamy and has received much government scrutiny and media coverage in recent years.

CHRISTIAN PRACTICE

Christianity is very much a religion of doctrines, but it is also a religion of ritual, and after more than two thousand years, these rituals have become rich and complex.

Sacraments and Other Rituals

The most important rituals are thought of as active signs of God's grace and usually are called sacraments. The rituals that are considered essential to the practice of Christianity are the following:

Baptism This ritual cleansing with water is universally used in Christianity as an initiation rite. The ritual originally involved complete immersion of the body, but some forms of Christianity require that only the head be sprinkled with water. Baptism came to Christianity from Judaism, where ritual bathing was an ancient form of purification (see, for example, Lev. 14:8). It was also commonly used to accept converts to Judaism, and the Essenes practiced daily ritual bathing. John the Baptizer, whom the Gospel of Luke calls the cousin of Jesus, used baptism as a sign of repentance, and Jesus himself was baptized and had his followers baptize others. Early Christians continued the practice as a sign of moral purification, new life, and readiness for God's kingdom. In early Christianity, because baptism was done by immersion in water, the act helped recall vividly the death, burial, and resurrection of Jesus. Although early Christians were normally baptized as adults, the practice of infant baptism became common within the first few hundred years. Catholicism, Orthodoxy, and the more ceremonial forms of Protestantism practice infant baptism. Other forms of Protestantism, insisting that the ritual be done only as a voluntary sign of initiation, reserve baptism for adults only.

Christians see baptism as a purification that signifies one's formal entry into God's kingdom. Many denominations, including the Romanian Orthodox Church, practice infant baptism.

Eucharist Another sacrament is the Eucharist (Greek: "good gift"), or Lord's Supper. Early Christians, particularly Paul's converts, met weekly to imitate the Last Supper, which was probably a Passover meal. At this meal of bread and wine, they prayerfully recalled Jesus's death and resurrection. Sharing the Lord's Supper is a symbolic sharing of Jesus's life and death, but beliefs about it are quite varied. Some denominations see the bread and wine as quite literally the body and blood of Jesus, which the believer consumes; other groups interpret the bread and wine symbolically. All Christian denominations have some form of this meal, but they vary greatly in style and frequency. Catholic, Orthodox, and traditional Protestant churches have a Lord's Supper service every Sunday. Less ceremonial churches prefer to focus their Sunday service on preaching and Bible study, but they usually have the Lord's Supper once a month. Virtually all churches use bread, but some use grape juice or water in place of wine.

In addition to these two main sacraments, accepted by all Christians, some churches count the following rituals as full sacraments:

Confirmation The sacrament of confirmation ("strengthening") is a blessing of believers after baptism. In the Orthodox Church, confirmation is often administered with baptism, but in Catholicism and in some Protestant churches, it is commonly administered in the believer's early teen years.

Reconciliation The sacrament of reconciliation (or penance) takes place when a repentant person admits his or her sins before a priest and is absolved.

Marriage This is the sacrament in which two people publicly commit themselves to each other for life. The two individuals administer the sacrament to each other while the priest or minister simply acts as a public witness of the commitment.

Ordination This sacrament involves the official empowerment of a bishop, priest, or deacon for ministry. (Some denominations ordain ministers but do not consider the action to be sacramental.)

Anointing of the sick In this sacrament (formerly called extreme unction), a priest anoints a sick person with oil—an ancient symbol of health—and offers prayers (see James 5:14).

The Christian Year

The most important festivals are Christmas and Easter. Other festivals developed around these two focal points (see Figure 9.3 on p. 389). Traditionalist churches mark more festivals, and Orthodox churches often use the older Julian calendar to determine festival dates. The Church year begins with Advent (Latin: "approach"), which is a month of preparation for Christmas. Although the actual birth date of Jesus is unknown, Christmas is kept on

Deeper Insights

SIGNS AND SYMBOLS

In addition to the sacraments, many smaller devotional rituals have arisen over the two thousand years of Christianity. Making the sign of the cross—in which the fingers of the right hand touch the forehead, the chest, and the two shoulders—is used to begin and end prayer and to call for divine protection. Genuflection—the bending of the right knee—which originated as a sign of submission to a ruler, is a ritual performed by Catholics and some Anglicans on entering and leaving a church. Christians in general often pray on both knees as a sign of humility before God.

Devotional objects are also widely used in Christianity. Blessed water (holy water) reminds one of baptism; it is used in the blessing of objects and in conjunction with making the sign of the cross on entering a Catholic church. Oil and salt are used in blessings as symbols of health. Lighted candles symbolize new understanding. Ashes placed on the forehead at the beginning of **Lent** (a time of preparation before Easter) recall the inevitability of death. Palms are carried in a procession on the Sunday before Easter to recall Jesus's triumphal procession into Jerusalem. Incense is burned to symbolize prayer and reverence. Statues and pictures of Jesus,

Mary, angels, and saints are common in traditionalist forms of Christianity.

In addition to devotional rituals and objects, Christianity is a source of much religious symbolism. The fish is an ancient symbol of the Christian believer. It probably began as a reference to Jesus's desire that his followers go out "as fishers of men" (Luke 5:10), seeking converts. It was also used to represent the Greek word *ichthus* ("fish"), which could be read as an acronym for the Greek words that mean "Jesus Christ, God's son, savior." The cross is used to recall Jesus's death; when Jesus is pictured hanging on this cross, the cross is called a crucifix.

Letters of the Greek alphabet are frequently found in Christian art. Alpha (A) and Omega (Ω), the first and last letters of the Greek alphabet, symbolize God as the beginning and end of all things (Rev. 1:17). The logo IHS (from the Greek letters iota, eta, and sigma) represents the first three letters of the name *Jesus*. The logo XP (usually written as a single unit and called "chi-rho"—pronounced *kai-roh*) represents the first two letters of the name *Christ* in Greek. (It is also the basis for the abbreviation of *Christmas* as *Xmas*.)

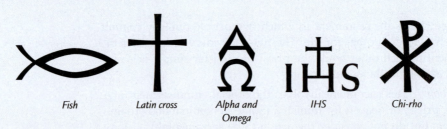

| Fish | Latin cross | Alpha and Omega | IHS | Chi-rho |

December 25, using a festival date common in classical Rome. (Some Orthodox and Eastern churches use a later date, particularly January 7.) The Christmas holiday ends with Epiphany (Greek: "showing"), which recalls the visit of the three Magi to the Christ child.

Preparation for Easter is long and solemn. Called Lent (Old English: "lengthening"), it is marked by fasting and giving up pleasures. In the Western churches, Lent begins with Ash Wednesday, when the faithful receive ashes on their foreheads to remind themselves of death. Frequently they pray or attend church regularly during Lent. A week before Easter, Palm Sunday recalls Jesus's entry into Jerusalem before his death. Holy Thursday

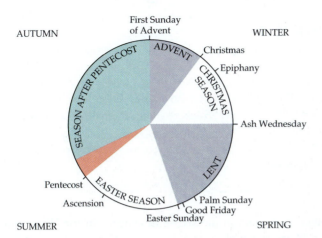

AUTUMN

First Sunday
of Advent

WINTER

Christmas

Epiphany

Ash Wednesday

Palm Sunday
Good Friday
Easter Sunday

SPRING

Pentecost

Ascension

SUMMER

SEASON AFTER PENTECOST

ADVENT

CHRISTMAS SEASON

LENT

EASTER SEASON

FIGURE 9.3

The Christian Church year.

recounts Jesus's last supper, and Good Friday remembers his death. When Easter finally arrives, it is marked by great rejoicing.

The feast of the Ascension tells of Jesus's departure from earth, and Pentecost marks the birth of the Church. Over time, festivals of Mary and the saints were added to this calendar. A few saints' days, such as Valentine's Day and St. Patrick's Day, found their way into public life.

On Thursday of Holy Week, Christians recall the last supper of Jesus and his disciples. That supper began when Jesus washed the feet of the disciples, an act today recalled in the liturgy.

Devotion to Mary

Devotion to Mary, the mother of Jesus, appeared in Christianity quite early. In the Eastern Church, its strength was evidenced in the fifth century by arguments concerning the titles that could be given to Mary. For example, although some objected, Mary was called *theotokos* ("God bearer"). In the West, Roman Catholic devotion to Mary began to flourish in the Middle Ages. Many of the new churches built after 1100 CE in the Gothic style in France were named for *notre dame* ("our lady"), and statues of Mary, often tenderly holding her child on her hip, appeared in almost every church. A large number of feasts in honor of Mary came to be celebrated in the Church year. Praying the *rosary* became common in the West after 1000 CE. A rosary is a circular chain of beads used to count prayers, with the prayer *Ave Maria* ("Hail, Mary") said on most of the beads. (The use of rosaries for counting prayers is also found in other religions, such as in Hinduism, Islam, and Buddhism.)

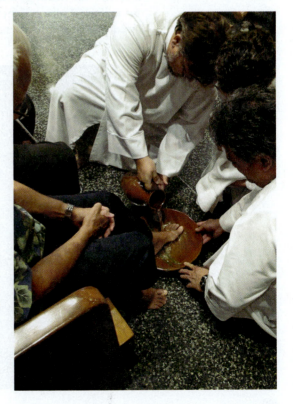

Deeper Insights

COLOR SYMBOLISM

Western Christianity has developed a symbolic system of colors, used in many churches and ministers' clothing, to mark festivals and to convey emotions:

white—joy, resurrection; Christmas and Easter
red—love, Holy Spirit, blood of martyrdom; Pentecost
green—hope, growth; Sundays after Pentecost

violet—sorrow, preparation; Advent and Lent
blue—sometimes Advent and feasts of Mary
black—death (now often replaced by white)

Although this system weakened after the Reformation, it is still apparent in weddings (white) and funerals (black).

Protestant reformers in the sixteenth century in the West criticized the devotion to Mary as a replacement for a devotion to Jesus. For this reason, devotion to Mary is less common in Protestant Christianity. But devotion to Mary remains strong in Orthodox and Catholic branches of Christianity.

Catholics believe that Mary appears in the world when her help is needed. The three most important sites where Mary is officially believed to have appeared are Lourdes (in southern France), Fatima (in Portugal), and Tepeyac (near Mexico City). Lourdes, famous for its springwater, is a center for healing, and people hoping for a cure go there to bathe in its waters. Fatima, where Mary is believed to have appeared to three children, is another center of healing. And Tepeyac is the center of the

The death of Mary, although never mentioned in the New Testament, is celebrated as a major holy day in the Orthodox churches. Here, the child in the arms of Jesus symbolizes Mary's soul being taken to heaven.

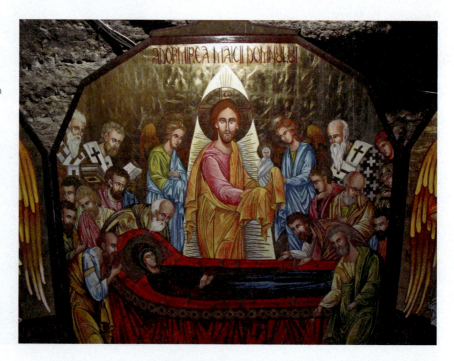

Aztec dancers perform for pilgrims at the Basilica of Guadalupe in Mexico City. The main celebration for the Virgin of Guadalupe is December 12, the date on which the image of Mary is said to have appeared on the cloak of Juan Diego in 1531.

veneration of Our Lady of Guadalupe, who is an important part of Hispanic Catholicism. Mary is believed to have appeared to a native peasant, Juan Diego, and to have left her picture on his cloak. The site is particularly crowded on December 12, the feast day of Our Lady of Guadalupe. The festival is celebrated widely with Masses and processions in many cities and towns.

CHRISTIANITY AND THE ARTS

Particularly because of its ritual needs, Christianity has contributed much to architecture, the visual arts, and music. This artistic legacy is one of the greatest gifts of Christianity to world culture—a gift that can be experienced easily by traveling, visiting the great churches and museums of major cities, and listening to Christian music.

Architecture

When Christianity began, its services were first held in private homes. As it grew in popularity, larger buildings were needed to accommodate the larger groups, particularly for rituals such as the Lord's Supper. For their public services, early Christians adapted the basilica, a rectangular building used in the Roman Empire as a court of law. In larger Roman basilicas, interior pillars and thick walls helped support the roofs. Windows could be numerous but not too large, because large windows would have weakened the walls. Rounded arches were placed at the tops of windows and doors and between the rows of pillars. This style—known as Romanesque because of its Roman origins—spread throughout Europe as a practical church design.

Eastern Orthodox Christianity used the basilica shape but also developed another shape: the model, a perfect square covered by a large dome, was based on the design of the Roman Pantheon. Mosaics with gold backgrounds help to magnify the sometimes dim light.

In the West, probably as a result of contact with Islamic architecture, a new style arose after 1140, known as Gothic style. (The designation *Gothic* was applied to this new style of architecture by a later age, which considered this style primitive and thus named it after barbarian Gothic tribes. The Gothic style, however, is neither primitive nor a product of Goths. It seems to have developed first in Persia, between 600 and 800 CE, and elements of it may have been carried to Europe by Europeans returning from Syria and Israel.) The first example of Gothic architecture appeared in France; the cathedral of Saint Denis, near Paris, is still open to visitors today.

Gothic architecture is light and airy; it leaps upward toward the sky. Typical of Gothic style are pointed arches, high ceilings, elongated towers, and delicate stone carving. The walls and roofs are held up externally by stone supports (called *flying buttresses*) that extend outward from the walls and down to the ground. Because these supports do much of the work of holding up the roof, they allow the walls to be filled with large windows, frequently of colored glass.

Gothic churches began springing up everywhere; any town of importance wanted to have a church built in the new style. This was especially true in towns that featured a cathedral. (A cathedral is a bishop's church and takes its name from the bishop's special chair, the *cathedra*, which symbolizes his teaching authority.) The great Gothic cathedrals were so impressive that Gothic style remains *the* style associated with Western Christianity.

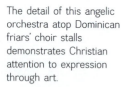

The detail of this angelic orchestra atop Dominican friars' choir stalls demonstrates Christian attention to expression through art.

The architectural style of Saint John's Abbey Church in Minnesota, completed in 1961, stands in stark contrast to Gothic and Baroque styles.

In addition to the Gothic style, other styles have been influential in the West. The Catholic Reformation popularized the theatrical Baroque style. The word *baroque* is thought to come from the Portuguese name for an irregular pearl, *barroco*. Baroque style uses contrasts of light and dark, rich colors, elegant materials (such as marble), twisting pillars, multiple domes, and other dramatic elements to create a sense of excitement and wonder.

While Catholicism was adopting the Baroque style with enthusiasm, Protestantism generally moved in a more sober direction. With the focus of worship placed on hearing the Bible read aloud and listening to a sermon, new churches were built with pews, clear-glass windows, high pulpits, and second-floor galleries to bring people closer to the preacher. In larger churches, classical Greco-Roman architecture was drawn upon to produce the Neoclassical style.

Mormon temples are architecturally interesting in that they are deliberately unlike older styles, such as Romanesque or Gothic or Byzantine. Instead, the building designs reflect an imaginative style that has been called Temple Revival. Elements of the style include large, flat building surfaces that are ornamented with elaborate grillwork and decorated with tall, narrow spires.

Art

Christianity has made immense contributions to art, despite the fact that it emerged from Judaism, which generally forbade the making of images. Mindful of the biblical prohibition against image-making (Exod. 20:4), a few Christian groups still oppose religious images as a type of idolatry. But

Benedictine monk Jerome Tupa says that all monastics are on journeys and find various means—for example, poems, letters, photos—to reflect on their journeys. He paints paths to sacred shrines.

because Christianity first began to flourish in the Greco-Roman world, it abandoned the prohibition of images and quickly embraced the use of statues, frescoes, and mosaics, which were common art forms there. By the second century, statues and pictures of Jesus had begun to appear, based on Greco-Roman models.

Orthodox Christianity has tended to avoid statues but has concentrated instead on frescoes, mosaics, and icons (paintings on wood). Icons play a special part in Orthodoxy. Churches usually have a high screen that separates the altar area from the body of the church. This screen is called an *iconostasis* ("image stand") because it is covered with icons. Individual icons also stand around the church, and during services worshipers may kiss them and place candles nearby. Many homes also display icons.

In western Europe, new directions appeared in Christian art in the later Middle Ages. Statues and paintings of Mary began to show her less like a goddess and more like a human mother, and representations of Jesus began to emphasize his bodily suffering. During the Baroque era, painting and sculpture tended toward the dramatic and showy. Paintings of saints often showed the saints' eyes lifted to the skies, the robes blown by wind, and sunlit clouds parted in the background.

Many Protestant groups rejected religious painting and sculpture as being unnecessarily sensual, wasteful, or idolatrous, and because artists in Protestant countries were not greatly patronized by churches, their subjects tended to be secular, often depicting home life, civic leaders, and landscapes. Christian art, however, has begun to flourish again, particularly because it has increasingly been influenced by non-Western traditions and cultures.

Music

From the beginning, Christianity has been a religion of music. Jesus himself is recorded as having sung a psalm hymn (Matt. 26:30; Mark 14:26). Because of its early musical involvement, Christianity has contributed much to the development of both theory and technique in music. A Benedictine monk, Guido of Arezzo (c. 991–1050), worked to help monks sing the notes of religious chants correctly; he is thought to have systematized the basic Gregorian musical notation system of lines, notes, and musical staffs, from which modern musical notation derives.

For the first thousand years, both Eastern and Western church music was chant—a single line of melody usually sung in unison without instrumental accompaniment. The origins of chant are uncertain, but it probably emerged from both Jewish devotional songs and folk music. Music in the Orthodox Church is sung without accompaniment, thus remaining closer to ancient church music and to its origins in the synagogue and the Near East.

The ancient Greeks were familiar with the principles of harmony as they related to mathematics. But the use of harmony in terms of musical composition (called *organum*) seems to have first developed in Paris, around 1100, in the cathedral of Notre Dame. In the West, initial experiments with harmonized singing eventually led to the introduction of instruments, such as the flute, violin, or organ, which could easily be used to substitute for a human voice or to accompany the chant. Even though it is now considered a primarily religious instrument, the organ at first was opposed for use in some churches because it was considered a secular instrument.

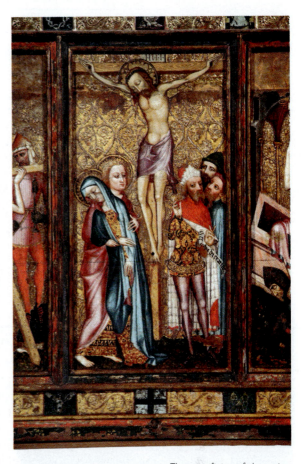

The crucifixion of Jesus is perhaps the most frequent subject of Christian art. This painting, at the center of the Despenser Reredos in England's Norwich Cathedral, dates from the late fourteenth century.

The most important early pattern for Western religious music was the Catholic Mass[35] (Lord's Supper). A variant of the regular Mass is the Requiem ("rest") Mass, the Mass for the dead. Psalms and other short biblical passages were also put to music for the services. These relatively short works, usually in Latin, are called *motets.*

The Protestant Reformation greatly expanded the variety of religious music, as each branch created its own musical traditions. Luther, we might recall, wrote hymns in German, and although he encouraged some church use of Latin, he recommended that services be conducted primarily in the language of the people. The Lutheran tradition also supported the use of the organ, both on its own and to accompany hymns. The supreme genius of the Lutheran tradition was Johann Sebastian Bach (1685–1750). A church organist and

Rituals and Celebrations

THE MASS

The Mass is a form of the Lord's Supper that evolved in the Western tradition. Five parts of the Latin Mass have been regularly put to music by composers. They are:

Kyrie (*Kyrie, eleison*—Greek: "Lord, have mercy")

Gloria (*Gloria in excelsis Deo*—Latin: "Glory to God on high")

Credo (*Credo in unum Deum*—Latin: "I believe in one God")

Sanctus (*Sanctus*—Latin: "holy")

Agnus Dei (*Agnus Dei*—Latin: "Lamb of God")

Renaissance composers, such as Giovanni da Palestrina and William Byrd, composed Masses for voice alone. Later composers (such as Franz Joseph Haydn, Wolfgang Amadeus Mozart, Franz Schubert, and Ludwig van Beethoven) all made use of organ or orchestra in their Masses. The dramatic style of church music reached an artistic peak in the luminous Masses of Mozart. Two Requiem Masses of extraordinary beauty are those by Gabriel Fauré and Maurice Duruflé. Rather than emphasizing divine judgment, they radiate joy and peace.

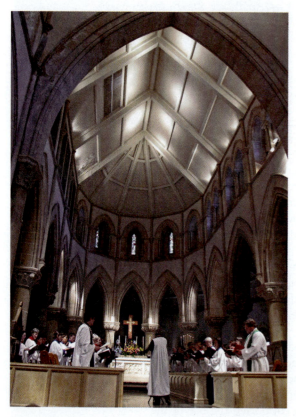

One of Christianity's greatest contributions to the arts is music. Here, a choir performs at an Episcopal church.

choirmaster for most of his career, Bach composed many beautiful musical pieces for church use, both solo organ music and choir music. His *Saint Matthew Passion,* a musical reflection on the last days of Jesus, is one of the world's most complex and moving religious compositions. Bach also wrote in forms that derived from the Roman Catholic tradition, producing a *Magnificat* in Latin and his *Mass in B-minor,* which has been compared to a voyage in a great ship across an ocean.[36]

After the Church of England decreed that services be held in English, a body of church music began to develop in England. Much of this music was written for choirs, which traditionally have been supported by Anglican cathedrals.

Other forms of Protestant Christianity have been cautious about the types of music used in church services. Wanting to keep the music popular and simple, Protestant churches have supported the writing and singing of hymns but often have avoided more complex compositions. They have allowed use of the organ and piano but until recently have generally discouraged the use of other instruments. In recent decades, however, a liberalization of practice has brought about great experimentation in both Protestant and Catholic church music.

CHRISTIANITY FACES THE MODERN WORLD

Christianity—in spite of the strength of its varied interpretations and its international influence—faces obstacles that arise from new nonreligious worldviews.

The Challenges of Science and Secularism

One of the greatest intellectual challenges to Christianity has been the growth of science, and it will remain so. Christianity speaks regularly of miracles— the virgin birth of Jesus, the healings performed by Jesus, his resurrection and ascension, and innumerable later miracles performed by apostles and saints. But critical approaches to the study of nature and modern study of the scriptures have questioned many of these miracles. Modern critical approaches view reality from a naturalistic point of view, and scientific discoveries can produce new challenges to traditional beliefs.

The theory of evolution, a prominent example of scientific criticism, emerged in the nineteenth century. It explained the multiplicity of species as the product of natural selection rather than divine plan. At first, this theory of evolution created consternation—and it still does in certain quarters. Although many denominations have accepted some form of evolution as compatible with their beliefs, certain Christians want the theory of Intelligent Design taught as a scientific alternative to evolution. This theory argues that an intelligent designer lies behind the multiplicity of species. Critics, though, say that the theory of Intelligent Design is merely religion disguised as science.

Another challenge is less theoretical. It is the rising focus on material realities—money and possessions. At one time, religion was considered the means for increasing one's personal wealth. This belief has diminished over the last century. Financial success, people increasingly believe, comes from studying business, not theology. It comes from compound interest, not prayer.

Some forms of Christianity, however, have now adjusted, teaching what they call "Prosperity Christianity." This form of Christianity teaches that God will repay in a very precise way those who contribute "love offerings." Defenders argue that this form of Christianity simply continues many of those practical features that have long distinguished Christianity, including care for the poor, attention to education, and a building up of God's kingdom in this world.

Contemporary Influences and Developments

Mainstream Christian denominations prefer to emphasize similar ideals rather than differences. On the one hand, they accept that there are denominational differences in belief and practice. On the other hand, they are influenced by the movement called **ecumenism**—from the Greek word for "household." This modern movement encourages dialogue and work between denominations. On the institutional level, the World Council of Churches includes representatives from the major Protestant denominations and Orthodox churches. It also includes non-voting representatives from the

Catholic Church. On the individual level, ecumenism encourages people from various denominations to work together, especially on social issues.

At the same time, the Christian churches have seen a growing polarization over important topics, especially gender roles, Bible interpretation, and the role of religion in political life. Two great wings have emerged—conservative and liberal.

Mainstream Protestantism has largely accepted the principles of female equality, at least in theory. Female ministers, priests, and bishops are now an accepted part of some denominations (although with disagreement from some sections). Female preachers are also common, especially on television. However, Catholicism and the Orthodox and Eastern churches do not accept the ordination of females. Whether eventually these churches will change their practice is still unknown. Right now, they remain highly resistant.

Biblical interpretation is another area of disagreement. Conservative denominations tend to retain an older literalist interpretation. They assume that the entire Bible is inerrant and presents "gospel truth." They therefore hold that biblical descriptions of creation, history, people, and miracles are literally true. Liberal denominations do not agree, but argue that the biblical accounts are a mixture of fact and devotion. Sometimes separating the two is not easy.

Because of the difficulties of correct biblical interpretation, the movement of fundamentalism has provided one practical answer. Christian fundamentalism argues that there are essential truths—fundamentals—that are central to Christianity. Among these are the virgin birth of Jesus, the physical reality of his resurrection, and the inspired nature of the Bible. Fundamentalism is also often allied with political activism, providing Christians who want to influence society with answers to difficult questions. Christianity has always

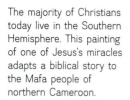

The majority of Christians today live in the Southern Hemisphere. This painting of one of Jesus's miracles adapts a biblical story to the Mafa people of northern Cameroon.

proclaimed the need to help others. But who are the others? Should they be only Christians or everyone else as well? What kind of help should be given, and what demands should be enshrined in laws? These questions have become all the more urgent as the modern world presents other, more secular views of reality.

The liberal-conservative division has resulted in coexistence among Protestants. Mainstream Protestant churches have tended to become liberal, while **evangelical** denominations have more strongly held onto conservative positions.

The Catholic Church has had more difficulty in finding central positions on which all can agree. The Second Vatican Council (1962–1965) was generally liberal, in that it permitted liturgy in native languages, endorsed ecumenism, and opened the Church to respectful contact with other religions. However, the council members rejected many other liberal possibilities, such as allowing women to become priests. They also upheld traditional positions on marriage, birth control, and divorce. This meant that the discussion of many important topics would continue after the council, with both liberal and conservative wings battling for supremacy. The papacy of John Paul II (1920–2005) was largely conservative, and this tendency has continued in his successor, Benedict XVI (b. 1927).

In the political realm, John Paul II was recognized for his pivotal role in the downfall of communism in Eastern Europe and the Soviet Union. It was during his papacy that the Berlin Wall came down. Eastern European states abandoned communism, and the Soviet Union dissolved into many separate countries. These political changes have allowed Catholic and Orthodox forms of Christianity to reassert themselves in those regions.

Congregants are overcome with emotion as they pray during an evangelical worship service in southern California. Evangelical Christianity is growing worldwide.

Contemporary Issues

CREATION CARE

Creation Care is an emerging environmental movement within Christianity that cuts across many of its denominations. Until recently, Christianity did not give much emphasis to the environment—possibly because of its orientation toward heaven as the true home of human beings. But a new, still-evolving theology has sprung up within the faith that critically examines the relationship between humanity and the environment. This theology, drawn from biblical roots, bases itself on the notion that the world is a manifestation of God's love and that, as a result, humanity has an obligation to protect the environment—to give it "care after its creation." To support its view, this theology cites the stewardship assigned to Adam and Eve over the Garden of Eden (Gen. 3), Noah's preservation of animal species in his wooden ark (Gen. 7–9), and Jesus's attention to the birds of the air and lilies of the field (Matt. 6:26–30).

Biblical stories may inform the movement's theology, but a major impetus for the development of Creation Care has been the widespread public acknowledgment in recent years that human activity is leading to climate change, including rising temperatures around the world that threaten to cause untold damage to the environment in the next century. In response to such a threat, a number of Protestant ministers have signed an Evangelical Climate Initiative, which insists on responsible human action against global warming. The Patriarch of Istanbul, Bartholomew I, has declared that acts that harm the environment are sinful. And Pope Benedict XVI has been called the Green Pope because he devotes so many sermons and speeches to the environmental cause. He has reforested thirty-seven acres of land in Hungary to offset the carbon "footprint" of the Vatican, and he even directed that solar panels be placed on top of Vatican buildings to provide electricity for the city-state. At the grassroots level, some conservative Christian leaders—not long ago associated with biblical fundamentalism—have even begun to emphasize biblical injunctions for Christian stewardship of the planet. Responses such as these suggest that the emerging Creation Care movement will do for environmentalism what Christianity has long succeeded in doing for education and in caring for the sick.

One of the great developments in contemporary Christianity is its spread in Africa. While northern Africa remains primarily Muslim, sub-Saharan Africa has adopted Christianity in many forms. Former British colonies—such as Nigeria and Zimbabwe—have large congregations of Anglicans, and former colonies of Catholic powers have large Catholic denominations. African Independent Churches also have emerged widely. Though their churches and robes are often traditional in appearance, these new churches incorporate much indigenous practice, such as faith healing and dance.

Christianity is also spreading in Asia. Although the great majority of people in Myanmar and Thailand are Buddhist, many tribal groups have taken up Christianity, especially in the north of the two countries. In China, Christianity comes in many forms. Both Protestant and Catholic churches have denominations that are approved by the State—although there is occasional dissension with state officials, especially over the approval of bishops. Parallel forms of Christianity that do not have state approval are growing, nonetheless; these groups often meet in believers' homes and are frequently called "house-churches." The population of Christians in China is unknown, but it is estimated at about 100 million. The numbers are expected to increase.

The growth of Christianity will have an impact not only on Africa and Asia but also eventually on the West, when ministers from newly Christian areas will be sent to staff European and North American churches. In the long run, these ministers will take on important roles in their denominations. Some will find their way into the World Council of Churches and other interdenominational groups. Their interests will then become a part of world Christianity.

In summary, traditionalists have much to worry about. But optimists see great vitality in Christianity. They especially appreciate its respect for the individual, its ethic of practical helpfulness, its support for the arts, and even its openness to debate.

Reading REVELATIONS OF DIVINE LOVE

In 1373, the Englishwoman known as Julian of Norwich received revelations. She first wrote them up in short form and then, much later, in long form. This passage is from chapter 32 of the long text, put into modern English. The author says that God insists that, despite the evils in the world, all will be well.

On one occasion the good Lord said, "Everything is going to be all right." On another, "You will see for yourself that every sort of thing will be all right." In these two sayings the soul discerns various meanings.

One is that he wants us to know that not only does he care for great and noble things, but equally for little and small, lowly and simple things as well. This is his meaning: "*Every* thing will be all right." We are to know that the least thing will not be forgotten.

Another is this: we see deeds done that are so evil, and injustices inflicted that are so great, that it seems to us quite impossible that any good can come of them. As we consider these, sorrowfully and mournfully, we cannot relax in the blessed contemplation of God as we ought. This is caused by the fact that our reason is now so blind, base, and ignorant that we are unable to know that supreme and marvelous wisdom, might, and goodness which belong to the blessed Trinity. This is the meaning of his word, "You will see for yourself that every *sort* of thing will be all right." It is as if he were saying, "Be careful now to believe and trust, and in the end you will see it in all its fullness and joy."[37]

TEST YOURSELF

1. Christianity grew out of _____.
   a. Hinduism
   b. Judaism
   c. Islam
   d. Buddhism

2. Almost everything we know about Jesus comes from the four gospels of the New Testament. The word *gospel* means "_____."
   a. vision
   b. good news
   c. enlightenment
   d. covenant

3. The Two Great Commandments of Jesus combine two elements: _____.
   a. love for God and an ethical call for kindness toward others
   b. missionary activity and prayer five times a day
   c. love for God and annual pilgrimage to Jerusalem
   d. refraining from immoral activities and giving to the poor

4. _____ is occasionally called the cofounder of Christianity because of the way that Jesus's teachings and his interpretation of them blended to form a viable religion with widespread appeal.
   a. Peter
   b. James
   c. Paul
   d. John

5. In the Gospel of John, the portrayal of Jesus is full of mystery. He is the _____ of God, the divine made visible in human form.
   a. inspiration
   b. transcendence
   c. incarnation
   d. spirit

6. When _____ became emperor, he saw in Christianity a glue that could cement the fragments of his entire empire.
   a. Herod
   b. Constantine
   c. Antiochus
   d. Hyrcanus

7. _____ was the dominant authority in Christian theology from the fifth century until the Protestant Reformation of the sixteenth century.
   a. Hector
   b. Herodotus
   c. John Calvin
   d. Augustine

8. _____, a Dominican priest, blended the philosophical thoughts of Aristotle with Christian scripture through writings such as the *Summa Theologica* and *Summa Contra Gentiles*.
   a. John Calvin
   b. Francis of Assisi
   c. Tertullian
   d. Thomas Aquinas

9. _____, a German priest of the late Middle Ages, was the first reformer of Western Christianity to gain a large following and to survive. The movement he founded ultimately created the Protestant branch of Christianity.
   a. John Wycliffe
   b. Martin Luther
   c. John Calvin
   d. Huldrych Zwingli

10. In 1962, Pope John XXIII convened a council of bishops that proceeded to make the first major changes in Catholicism since the Council of Trent. The _____ allowed, among other things, the use of native languages in ordinary church services.
   a. Council of Nicaea
   b. Council of Jamnia
   c. Second Vatican Council
   d. Third Council of Churches

11. Consider the following statement: Despite the tremendous importance of Jesus in Christianity, Paul played an even more important role than Jesus in shaping Christian beliefs and practices. Using the information from this chapter, explain why you agree or disagree.

12. Review the descriptions of the different forms of Protestantism. Which one do you think is most unusual? Which one do you think is most similar to Roman Catholicism? Explain your answers.

RESOURCES

Books

Beard, Steve, Chad Bonham, Jason Boyett, Scott Marshall, and Denise Washington. *Spiritual Journeys: How Faith Has Influenced Twelve Music Icons.* Orlando: Relevant Books, 2003. A study of the role of Christianity in shaping several singers and groups, including Wyclef Jean, Moby, Johnny Cash, Al Green, Bob Dylan, Lauryn Hill, and Lenny Kravitz.

Borg, Marcus. *The Heart of Christianity.* New York: HarperOne, 2004. A reevaluation of Christianity by a scholarly believer.

Hale, Robert. *Love on the Mountain.* Trabuco Canyon, CA: Source Books, 1999. An insider's account of daily life as a hermit-monk.

Ingersoll, Julie. *Evangelical Christian Women: War Stories in the Gender Battles.* New York: New York University Press, 2003. A look at conservative

Christian evangelical women who challenge the gender norms of their faith.

Jenkins, John Philip. *The Lost History of Christianity.* New York: HarperOne, 2009. A description of the little-known forms of Christianity that grew up in the Middle East, Asia, and Africa, and a reflection on their decline.

Keller, Thomas. *The Reason for God: Belief in an Age of Skepticism.* New York: Dutton, 2008. A defense of Christian belief, written by the founding pastor of New York's Redeemer Presbyterian Church, who argues that skepticism and cynicism about religion are themselves alternate forms of belief.

MacCulloch, Diarmaid. *Christianity: The First Three Thousand Years.* New York: Penguin, 2011. A thorough and well-regarded history of the strands of Christianity.

Meyer, Marvin. *The Gospels of Mary: The Secret Tradition of Mary Magdalene, the Companion of Jesus.* New York: HarperCollins, 2004. A new examination of the Gospels of Mary Magdalene, an early Christian figure who has received renewed interest.

Norris, Kathleen. *The Cloister Walk.* New York: Putnam, 1996. A personal account by a Protestant writer who describes her discovery of monastic life and its rituals.

Pagels, Elaine. *Beyond Belief: The Secret Gospel of Thomas.* New York: Random House, 2003. An exploration of the textual battles of the early Christian Church.

Tutu, Desmond. *No Future Without Forgiveness.* New York: Image, 2000. A description of participation in South Africa's Truth and Reconciliation Commission, by an Anglican archbishop and winner of the Nobel Peace Prize.

White, Michael L. *From Jesus to Christianity.* New York: HarperCollins, 2004. The story of how early Christianity developed its identity and sacred texts.

Film/TV

The Agony and the Ecstasy. (Director Carol Reed; Twentieth Century Fox.) A classic Hollywood film about Michelangelo's creation of the Sistine Chapel murals.

Brother Sun, Sister Moon. (Director Franco Zeffirelli; Paramount.) A movie about the life of Francis of Assisi.

Kingdom of Heaven. (Director Ridley Scott; Twentieth Century Fox.) A mainstream film about the Crusades.

The Mission. (Director Roland Joffe; Warner.) The tragic story of an eighteenth-century Spanish Jesuit who built a mission in the South American wilderness to convert the indigenous people.

The Robe. (Director Henry Koster; Twentieth Century Fox.) A classic film that tells the fictional story of a Roman soldier who helped kill Jesus but who was then transformed after winning Christ's robe.

Sister Rose's Passion. (Director Oren Jacoby; Docurama.) A documentary chronicling a nun's struggles against anti-Semitism within the Catholic Church.

Witness. (Director Peter Weir; Paramount.) A Hollywood film set in Amish culture.

Music/Audio

Following are religious works, listed by their composers. Especially approachable compositions are starred.

Bach: *Magnificat, Mass in B-minor,* *motets

Britten: *A Ceremony of Carols

Byrd: Masses

Distler: *Christmas Story*

Duruflé: *Requiem, Mass "Cum Jubilo,"* *motets

Fauré: *Requiem

Handel: *Messiah

Hildegard of Bingen: Hymns and antiphons

Mozart: *Coronation Mass, Requiem,* *motets

Palestrina: Masses

Pärt, Arvo: *Fratres, Te Deum,* *Magnificat

Rachmaninoff: *Evening Vigil* (other Orthodox music is available in collections)

Saint-Saens: *Christmas Oratorio*

Vaughan Williams: *Mass in G-minor,* *Fantasia on a Theme of Thomas Tallis

Vivaldi: *Gloria

Zelenka: *Missa Dei Patris, Missa Dei Filii*

Following are some specific recordings of traditional religious music performed around the world.

Beautiful Beyond: Christian Songs in Native Languages. (Smithsonian Folkways.) Christian hymns and songs sung by Native Americans and Hawaiians.

Chant. (Angel Records.) A best-selling compilation of Gregorian chant by the Benedictine Monks of Santo Domingo de Silos.

Christmas Vespers. (Smithsonian Folkways.) A performance by a Russian Orthodox cathedral choir of evening prayers.

Gospels, Spirituals, and Hymns. (Sony.) An annotated set of Christian gospel songs, sung by Mahalia Jackson.

Praise to the Lord: Favourite Hymns From St. Paul's Cathedral. (Hyperion UK.) A collection of hymns sung at St. Paul's Cathedral in London.

Wade in the Water: African American Spirituals. (Smithsonian Folkways.) A two-volume collection of African American spirituals.

Internet

King James Bible Online: http://www.kingjamesbible-online.org/. An unabridged, annotated online version of the classic English translation of the Bible.

Religions—Christianity: http://www.bbc.co.uk/religion/religions/christianity/index.shtml. The BBC's online encyclopedic Web site on Christianity, with sections on beliefs, history, holy days, rituals, ethics, texts, women, and more.

The Vatican: http://www.vatican.va/. The official Web site of the Vatican, the headquarters of the Roman Catholic Church.

KEY TERMS

apocalypticism: The belief that the world will soon come to an end; this belief usually includes the notion of a great battle, final judgment, and reward of the good.

apostle (ah-paw'-sul): One of Jesus's twelve disciples; also, any early preacher of Christianity.

baptism: The Christian rite of initiation, involving immersion in water or sprinkling with water.

Bible (Christian): The scriptures sacred to Christians, consisting of the books of the Hebrew Bible and the New Testament.

bishop: "Overseer" (Greek); a priest and church leader who is in charge of a large geographical area called a *diocese.*

canon (kaa'-nun): "Measure," "rule" (Greek); a list of authoritative books or documents.

ecumenism (eh-kyoo'-men-ism): Dialogue between Christian denominations.

Eucharist (yoo'-kah-rist): "Good gift" (Greek); the Lord's Supper.

evangelical: Emphasizing the authority of scripture; an adjective used to identify certain Protestant groups.

evangelist (ee-van'-jeh-list): "Good news person" (Greek); one of the four "authors" of the Gospels—Matthew, Mark, Luke, and John.

filioque (fee-lee-oh'-kway): "And from the Son"; a Latin word added to the creeds in the Western Church to state that the Holy Spirit arises from both Father and Son. The notion, which was not accepted by Orthodox Christianity, contributed to the separation between the Western and Eastern churches.

gospel: "Good news" (Middle English); an account of the life of Jesus.

icon (ai'-kahn): "Image" (Greek); religious painting on wood, as used in the Orthodox Church; also spelled *ikon.*

incarnation: "In flesh" (Latin); a belief that God became visible in Jesus.

indulgence: "Kindness-toward" (Latin); remission of the period spent in purgatory (a state of temporary punishment in the afterlife); an aspect of Catholic belief and practice.

Lent: "Lengthening day," "spring" (Old English); the preparatory period before Easter, lasting forty days.

Messiah: "Anointed" (Hebrew); a special messenger sent by God, foretold in the Hebrew scriptures and believed by Christians to be Jesus.

original sin: An inclination toward evil, inherited by human beings as a result of Adam's disobedience.

orthodox: "Straight opinion" (Greek); correct belief.

Orthodoxy: The major Eastern branch of Christianity.

patriarch: "Father source" (Greek); the bishop of one of the major ancient sites of Christianity (Jerusalem, Rome, Alexandria, Antioch, Constantinople, and Moscow).

pope: "Father" (Latin and Greek); the bishop of Rome and head of the Roman Catholic Church; the term is also used for the Coptic patriarch of Alexandria.

predestination: The belief that because God is all-powerful and all-knowing, a human being's ultimate reward or punishment is already decreed by God; a notion emphasized in Calvinism.

Protestant Principle: The right of each believer to radically rethink and interpret the ideas and values of Christianity, apart from any church authority.

redemption: "Buy again," "buy back" (Latin); the belief that the death of Jesus has paid the price of justice for all human wrongdoing.

righteousness: Being sinless in the sight of God; also called *justification*.

sacrament: "Sacred action" (Latin); one of the essential rituals of Christianity.

sin: Wrongdoing, seen as disobedience to God.

Testament: "Contract"; the Old Testament and New Testament constitute the Christian scriptures.

Trinity: The three "Persons" in God: Father, Son, and Holy Spirit.

RELIGION BEYOND THE CLASSROOM

Visit the Online Learning Center at www.mhhe.com/molloy6e for additional exercises and features, including "Religion beyond the Classroom" and "For Fuller Understanding."

CHAPTER 10

Islam

F I R S T   E N C O U N T E R

You are in Malaysia, on your way south to Singapore. A friend has recommended that you visit the modern national mosque in Kuala Lumpur. Your first try is unsuccessful because the mosque is closed for midday prayer. After two hours at a nearby museum of Islamic art, you return to the mosque. You leave your shoes at the bottom of the stairs and walk up into the building.

The mosque is extraordinary. You are amazed at how well the traditional Islamic love of geometrical design has been adapted to modern architecture. The marble floors reflect the colors of the stained glass above and the movement of the many visitors walking toward the main prayer area.

As you approach the core of the mosque, you notice a sign on a rope indicating that only Muslims are allowed to enter. You overhear some Chinese visitors explain to a woman at the rope that they are Muslims. She directs them in. You come up behind them, just to get a better look. The large space is carpeted, and people are prostrating themselves in prayer. You and the woman begin to talk.

"My name is Aminah," she says. "I'm an elementary-school teacher. Right now school is not in session, so I volunteer my time here."

Aminah is dressed in a floor-length blue robe with a full head covering. Only her face and hands are visible. "Do you have any questions?" she asks.

From what you have seen on the streets of Kuala Lumpur, you know that Aminah is conservatively dressed. So you ask the obvious question: "Why do you dress as you do?"

"I expected that," she says with a smile. "So many westerners want to talk about clothes." You look down, slightly embarrassed to be just another westerner with an obvious question.

"The way I dress makes me feel safe," she says. "For me it's comfortable. It reminds me that within Islam, women are protected."

You look a bit doubtful.

"Yes, I know," she continues. "It is possible to be too protected. Fathers and uncles and brothers sometimes make it their career to watch out for you, and that's not always welcome." You both laugh. "And sports can be difficult if one is all covered up. But we're working on it."

Aminah has finished her duty and is replaced by a man standing nearby.

"What about arranged marriages, especially of very young women?" you ask her. "And what about women being kept from education in some Muslim countries?" You ask these things just for the sake of argument, as you both begin to walk toward the exit.

"Things like that are cultural," she says. "There are many old traditions that are not a part of true Islam, and they can be changed. A whole new kind of modern Islam is developing, especially here in Malaysia, and the roles of women are widening. You know the saying, 'Do not judge a book by its cover.' What you see of women like me may look traditional, but it's a disguise. Inside, we're modern. Come back again in ten years and you will see it even more clearly."

Together you go down the steps in front of the mosque to a little kiosk. Aminah reaches into a drawer there.

"I want you to have this," she says, as she hands you a blue book with gold writing on the front. "You can find all you need to know here. After you read it, maybe you can give us fresh ideas for a new, modern type of Islam."

You look down at the book. Printed in both Arabic and English, it is a copy of the Qur'an.

As you wait for a taxi, you wonder about the Qur'an. Who wrote it? What does it say about Muhammad? And does it say anything about other religions? What does it say about women? As you climb into your taxi, you decide to start reading your new book that evening.

THE LIFE AND TEACHINGS OF MUHAMMAD

Muhammad[1] (570–632 CE) was born in Mecca, in what is today Saudi Arabia (see Timeline 10.1, p. 410). Much of what we know about him comes from his sermons and revelations in the Muslim sacred book, the **Qur'an** ("recitation"), and from the **hadiths** (also spelled *ahadith;* "recollections," "narratives"), the remembrances of him by his early followers.

In the days before Islam arose, the religions of the Arabian Peninsula were Judaism, Christianity, Zoroastrianism (which we'll discuss later), and traditional local religious practices. These local practices included worshiping tree spirits, mountain spirits, tribal gods, and *jinni* (the origin of the English word *genie*)—capricious spirits that were thought to inhabit the desert and even to enter people. The supreme god Allah was an object of faith but not of worship. Allah "was the creator and sustainer of life but remote from everyday concerns and thus not the object of cult or ritual. Associated with Allah were three goddesses, his daughters: al-Lat, Manat, and al-Uzza,"[2] goddesses related to nature, the moon, and fertility.

At the time of Muhammad's birth, Mecca was already a center of religious pilgrimage. Located in Mecca was a black meteorite that had fallen to earth long before Muhammad's time. It was venerated because it was believed to have been sent from heaven. A squarish shrine had been constructed to contain it, called the **Kabah** ("cube").[3] By Muhammad's day, as many as 360 religious images of tribal gods and goddesses had been placed within the Kabah, and tradition tells that twenty-four statues, perhaps associated with the zodiac, stood around the central square of Mecca. By Muhammad's time, yearly pilgrimages to Mecca were already common, and a four-month period of regular truce among the many Arabian tribes was kept in order to allow this.

Muhammad's grandfather, Abd al-Muttalib, played an important role among the Quraysh, the dominant tribe of Mecca, and is even thought to have been custodian of the Kabah. Muhammad's father died not long before Muhammad's birth, and his mother seems to have died when he was just a child. Muhammad then went to live with his grandfather, and after his grandfather's death two years later, he lived with his uncle, Abu Talib.[4]

As an adult, Muhammad worked as a caravan driver for a widow named **Khadijah**,[5] who had inherited a caravan company from her deceased husband. The friendship between Khadijah and Muhammad grew over time. They married in about 595 CE, when Muhammad was 25 and she (tradition says) was about 40.[6] This marriage brought financial, spiritual, and emotional support to Muhammad; Khadijah proved to be his mainstay until her death. Together they had about six children. But sadly no boy survived into adulthood to become Muhammad's hereditary successor. After Khadijah's death, Muhammad remarried a number of times. It is possible he married several of his wives out of compassion, because in his society widows of soldiers often needed a husband for financial support and legal protection.

TIMELINE 10.1

	570–632 CE	● Life of Muhammad
Muhammad's first revelation ●	**610 CE**	
	622 CE	● Hijra: Muhammad's flight from Mecca to Yathrib (Medina); Muslim year 1
Muhammad's gain of control over Mecca ●	**630 CE**	
	680 CE	● Death of Hussein, grandson of Muhammad
Battle of Tours; Muslim incursion into France is halted ●	**732 CE**	
	922 CE	● Execution of the mystic al-Hallaj
Life of the Sufi scholar al-Ghazali ●	**1058–1111 CE**	
	1099	● Conquest of Jerusalem by Crusaders
Life of the Sufi poet Jalal-ud-Din Rumi ●	**1207–1273**	
	1291	● Muslim expulsion of the Crusaders from Israel
Muslim capture of Constantinople ●	**1453**	
	1492	● Expulsion of Muslims from Spain
Period of the Mughal Empire in India ●	**1526–1857**	
	1947	● Independence of Pakistan as a Muslim nation
Islamic Revolution in Iran, led by Ayatollah Khomeini ●	**1979**	
	2011	● "Arab Spring" begins to bring changes to Egyptian and other Arab governments

Timeline of significant events in the history of Islam.

From his travels as a caravan worker, Muhammad undoubtedly learned a great deal about several religions, including the differences within and among them. Although the monotheistic religions of his region shared a belief in one High God and emphasized the need for morality, there was much disagreement as well. Jews and Christians disagreed about the role of Jesus and the nature of God. Christians disagreed with each other about the nature of Jesus. Jews and some Christians forbade image-making, although most Christians allowed it. And another major influence, the Persian religion of Zoroastrianism, so emphasized the moral struggle in human life that many people saw the world as being subject to two cosmic forces—good and evil.

As a religious person, Muhammad spent time pondering and meditating. To do this, he frequently went to caves in the hills surrounding Mecca that had long been used for prayer. When he was 40, during a religious retreat in a cave at Mount Hira, he received his first revelation, as recorded in the Qur'an. A bright presence came to him and held before his eyes a cloth covered with writing. It commanded three times that he recite what was written there:

> Recite in the name of the Lord who created—created man from clots of blood.
> Recite! Your Lord is the Most Bountiful One, who by the pen taught man what he did not know.
> Indeed, man transgresses in thinking himself his own master; for to your Lord all things return. . . .
> Prostrate yourself and come nearer.[7]

At first, Muhammad doubted the nature of this revelation. Could it be madness or hallucination or some kind of demonic apparition? He confided in his wife Khadijah, who knew him well and encouraged him to accept his experience as a true communication from God. He became convinced that the bright presence was the angel Gabriel, and when further revelations came to him, Muhammad began to share them with his closest friends and family members—particularly his wife, his cousin Ali (600–661), and his friend, Abu Bakr (573–634). These were the first **Muslims,** meaning "people who submit" to God (Allah).

When Muhammad began to proclaim his revelations more openly, he was not well received. Much of Muhammad's message was unthreatening—he urged kindness and taking care of the poor and weak. But Muhammad also insisted that there was only one God to worship. The revelations forbade the worship of other gods and demanded the destruction of statues and images. Muhammad also denounced usury (lending money at exorbitant rates) and the failure to make and keep fair contracts. These messages threatened businesspeople, particularly those involved in the pilgrimage trade, because the revelations denounced both common business practices and the multiple tribal gods whose images were kept in the Kabah. In 615 CE, some of Muhammad's followers fled for safety to what is today Ethiopia. In 619 CE, Khadijah died. When Abu Talib, Muhammad's protective uncle, died soon after, Muhammad became concerned for his own safety. He and the rest of his followers considered eventually leaving Mecca.

During this stressful time, Muhammad, in 620 CE, experienced himself being carried to Jerusalem and ascending from there into paradise. In this experience, called his Night Journey or Night of Ascent, the angel Gabriel guided him upward. As Muhammad ascended toward the highest heaven, he encountered angels and the great prophets of the past, including Abraham and Jesus, and at last entered into the presence of God. Muslims disagree about whether this event constituted a personal vision or an actual physical ascension from Jerusalem. Regardless, artistic tradition treats Muhammad's experience as a physical and bodily ascent from the city of Jerusalem.[8] He is pictured being carried on the back of the celestial steed Buraq, surrounded by flames and flying through the sky. This experience confirmed for Muhammad his vocation as a prophet and messenger of God.

Persecution of Muhammad and his followers in Mecca intensified. At the invitation of leaders of Yathrib, a city about three hundred miles to the north, Muhammad and his followers finally left Mecca in 622 CE. Muhammad's migration is called in Arabic the **Hijra.** The word means "flight" or migration," and the occurrence is a central event in Islam. It marks (1) the point at which Muhammad's message was favorably received and (2) the start of the Islamic community (*umma*). For these reasons, the Muslim calendar dates the year of the Hijra as year 1. (In the West, dates according to the Muslim calendar are given as AH—*anno Hegirae,* Latin for "in the year of the Hijra.")

Muhammad's initial success in Yathrib was not complete. Jews there allied with his political enemies and rejected his beliefs because he accepted Jesus as a prophet and disputed the completeness and correctness of the Hebrew scriptures. Muhammad eventually banished or executed these enemies, and over time he gained control of the city. In Yathrib he set up the first Islamic **mosque** (*masjid*), where many early rules about worship and social regulation were worked out. Yathrib is now called Medina (*madinat an-nabi,* "city of the prophet"). Along with Mecca and Jerusalem, Medina has become one of the three most sacred cities of Islam.

In spite of his success in Yathrib, Muhammad's goal was always to return to Mecca, the religious center of Arabia. In a battle in 624 CE at Badr between citizens of Mecca and Yathrib, Muslim soldiers triumphed against great odds. There were skirmishes and threats and a tentative treaty over the following few years until, finally, Muhammad returned as the victor in 630 CE to Mecca, where he then took control of the city, destroyed all images in the Kabah and marketplace, and began to institutionalize his religious ideals.

Muhammad extended his control over further territory in Arabia; at the time of his death, he was planning to spread his religion into Syria. In his final sermon, he opposed merely tribal loyalties and preached the brotherhood of all believers. Muhammad died in Yathrib in 632 CE.

Muhammad viewed himself, as did his followers, as the last of the long line of prophets who transmitted God's word to humanity. He did not consider himself to be divine but simply an instrument in the hands of God, a

Muhammad, accompanied by angels, is portrayed during the Night of Ascent on the back of the steed Buraq. Following Islamic tradition, the face of Muhammad is not depicted.

messenger transmitting God's will to the human world. Muslims view Muhammad as a man who showed perfection in his life, and they revere him as an ideal human being, a model for all believers.

ESSENTIALS OF ISLAM

Islam literally means "surrender" or "submission," indicating wholehearted surrender to God, and a Muslim is one who submits to God (Allah). The words *Islam* and *Muslim* are related to several words for peace, such as the Arabic *salam* and the Hebrew *shalom.* They suggest the inner peace that is gained by surrendering to the divine. The word *Islam* also connotes the community of all believers, suggesting inclusion in a large family. As the Qur'an states, "the believers are a band of brothers."[9]

At the heart of Islam is a belief in an all-powerful, transcendent God who has created the universe and who controls it down to the smallest detail. Islam is thus a cousin to the other monotheistic religions of Judaism and Christianity, and all three religions worship the same God. It is possible, however, that the notion of God's power and transcendence receives the greatest emphasis in Islam. Some observers have commented that in Islam, prostration of the entire body during prayer fittingly indicates a belief in divine power and the believer's submission to it. Prostration is compared to other characteristic prayer postures, such as kneeling (common in Christianity) and standing (common in Judaism). The physical posture of prostration illustrates well the Muslim attitude of total surrender to God.

Muslims refer to God as Allah. The word is a contraction of *al* ("the") and *ilah* ("God") and simply means "the God" or "God." (The Arabic word *Allah* is related to *El*, the general Hebrew word for "God.") Muslims explain that the word *Allah* is not the name of God—it simply means "God." It is said that Allah has ninety-nine names, among which are "the Merciful," "the Just," and "the Compassionate." These names demonstrate that Allah is not abstract—not just an impersonal force—but has characteristics of a personal being. In the Qur'an, Allah describes himself as personal and caring, as well as all-knowing, all-seeing, and all-powerful. Allah, because of this personal nature and the attribute of power, is referred to in Islam in "male" terms, although, strictly speaking, Allah has no gender.

It is sometimes hard for non-Muslims to understand the Muslim notion that God is omnipresent and controls every detail of life. The name of God is invoked in daily conversation, particularly in the frequently used phrase, "if God wills." People are called to prayer several times a day by a **muezzin,** a chanter who announces that Allah is great, greater than anything else. The chanted voice suggests that God is as active in the world as sound is active in the air, unseen but present. Some visitors to Muslim countries have remarked that people there live in a shared belief in God as easily as fish live in water or birds fly in air. God's active, present reality is taken for granted.

In Islamic belief, God has spoken repeatedly through human beings—prophets—revealing his mind and will. Muslims believe that divine revelation began just after the creation of the human race, when God spoke to Adam and Eve. It continued to occur, as when God spoke to patriarchs and prophets such as Abraham (Ibrahim) and Moses (Musa). Islamic belief also thinks of Jesus (Isa) as a prophet of God, although Muslims reject both the notion of Jesus's divinity and the Christian doctrine of the Trinity. Muslims believe that both Judaism and Christianity express true revelation from God but that in various ways those religions have contaminated God's word with human misunderstanding. It was Muhammad, Muslims believe, who freed the divine message from human error and offered it, purified, to all people. Because he is considered the last and greatest figure in the long line of prophets, Muhammad is called the "seal of the prophets."

Muslims trace their ancestry back to Abraham, the same patriarchal ancestor of the Jews, and to his son Ishmael (Ismail). Ishmael (as discussed in Chapter 8) was conceived by Abraham and Hagar, who was a maid to Sarah, Abraham's wife. When Sarah, at an advanced age, became pregnant and gave birth to her son Isaac, Hagar and Ishmael were forced to leave Abraham's care, purportedly because of Sarah's jealousy. They survived in the desert only because an angel revealed to them a source of water, which Muslims believe was found near Mecca.

Muhammad learned about Judaism from the Jews who lived in Arabia. He also absorbed and considered religious elements from Christianity and Zoroastrianism—religions that share with Islam a belief in the soul, bodily resurrection, a final judgment (the Day of Doom), and an afterlife of hell for the wicked and paradise for the good.[10] All three religions also share with Islam a belief in angels and devils, who can have influence on human beings. Indeed, there are numerous similarities between Islam and other religions, and non-Muslims might speculate that Muhammad was influenced by these religions. However, Muslims hold that Muhammad's religious ideas came directly from God.

The overall worldview of Islam (as with the other three religions) is highly dramatic. Muslims believe that good and evil forces are in constant battle and that life on earth is filled with choices that lead to the most serious consequences. This conception goes hand in hand with the overall emphasis of all Western prophetic religions on morality. Religion is viewed as a strongly ethical enterprise; one of its most important purposes is to regulate human life. This moral emphasis appears clearly in the essential Five Pillars of Islam, which we will now consider.

The Five Pillars of Islam

All Muslims must accept and practice the following Five Pillars, so called because they support one's faith. The Five Pillars are mentioned in the Qur'an.

Creed (Shahadah) "There is no God but Allah, and Muhammad is his messenger." This single sentence, when recited with belief, makes a person a

Muslims are called to prayers five times each day. At this Cairo mosque, men pray on the left, in front of an arched niche called the *mihrab*, which points to Mecca. Women here stand to the right of the *minbar*, a pulpit from which an imam may preach.

Muslim. It is the first sentence whispered into the ears of a newborn infant; it is recited daily in prayer; and it is written in Arabic inside the domes of mosques and over people's doors everywhere in the Islamic world.

The most noticeable quality of the Muslim creed is its simplicity, for it emphasizes that there is only one God and that God is a unity. As the Qur'an says, "Your God is one God. There is no God but him."[11] The simplicity of the creed is in deliberate contrast to the rather long and complicated creeds of Christianity, and within it is a rejection of several Christian notions. It rejects the Christian doctrine of the Trinity, which Muslims see as a belief in three gods. It also rejects the idea that Jesus was divine or that any human being can be divine. It emphatically does not see Muhammad as a divine or supernatural figure but specifies his role as God's prophet and messenger.[12]

Prayer (Salat) Devout Muslims are called on to pray five times a day: before dawn and at midday, midafternoon, sunset, and nighttime.[13] Times for prayer are announced by a muezzin, who calls out from the top of a tower called a **minaret.** (Nowadays, recordings of the call to prayer are often played over loudspeakers.) The muezzin's call to prayer begins with *Allahu akbar* ("God is supreme"),[14] and it continues, "I witness that there is no God but Allah; I witness that Muhammad is the messenger of Allah; hasten to prayer." In towns and cities with many mosques, the call to prayer comes from the most prestigious mosque first and is then followed up by other mosques.

Muslims may stop by mosques at any time to worship privately. Here, a man in his pharmacist's smock prays at a mosque in Istanbul.

Before prayer, the individual is normally expected to perform a ritual purification with water, washing the hands, arms, face, neck, and feet. If water is unavailable, purification may be done with sand.

Those who pray face toward Mecca—inside a mosque the direction (**qiblah**) is indicated by a special arched niche (**mihrab**). In the earliest days of Islam, Muslims faced Jerusalem for prayer, but later revelations received by Muhammad in Yathrib changed this direction to Mecca. The Qur'an directs: "Turn your face toward the holy mosque; wherever you be, turn your faces toward it."[15] When several people are praying together, one person acts as the leader, standing at the head of the group in front of the mihrab. Passages from the Qur'an and other prayer formulas are recited from memory in Arabic, accompanied by several basic bodily postures: standing, bowing, prostrating, and sitting. Each time of prayer demands a certain number of sets (*rakas*) of prayers: two at morning prayer, three at dusk, and four at the other times of prayer.

Friday is the day of public prayer. On other days, people may pray privately, at home or at work or in a mosque. Originally, the day of public prayer was Saturday, following the Jewish practice; but Muhammad received a revelation that public prayer on Friday was God's will. In most Muslim countries, public prayer is performed at midday on Friday. Usually only men perform public prayer at a mosque, while women ordinarily pray at home; but where women are allowed to pray with men at a mosque, they are assigned their own area, separated by a curtain or screen or located in an upstairs gallery. The Friday service usually includes a sermon by a religious leader. Although Friday is a day of public prayer, it is not necessarily a public day of rest. In many Muslim countries, offices are open on Fridays, and because of European colonial influence, the public day of rest is Sunday. Some Muslim countries, however, recognize Friday as the weekly day of public rest.

Charity to the Poor (Zakat)   Muhammad was troubled by injustice, inequality, and poverty, and the demand that people give to the poor was a part of his overall vision of a more just society. Islamic practice demands that believers donate certain percentages of their total income, herds, and produce from fields and orchards each year to the poor. This is not a tax on yearly income but rather a tax on all that one owns. The percentages vary, depending on what is taxed, but are commonly about 2.5 percent. Nowadays, government involvement in this taxation varies among Muslim countries. (In industrialized countries, government taxes commonly pay for systems of welfare, disability, social security, and other forms of assistance. This is a fairly recent phenomenon, however, that is practical only in money-based economies. Nonindustrial societies, which often use barter instead of money, depend much more on voluntary care for the poor.) In addition to established yearly donations, a good Muslim is expected to perform isolated acts of generosity and charity for the poor when such acts are called for in everyday life.

Fasting during Ramadan (Sawm)   To fast means to abstain from food for a specified period of time. The purpose of fasting is to discipline oneself, to develop sympathy for the poor and hungry, and to give to others what one would have eaten. Fasting is thought to be good for individual spiritual growth, and it is also an important bond that unites Muslims during the period of shared fasting known as **Ramadan.**

Ramadan, the ninth month of the Muslim calendar, is the period during which Muhammad first received his revelations. Fasting during this month, followed by a feast of celebration at the month's end, is considered a fitting way to remember this special event. During the month of Ramadan, devout Muslims avoid all food, liquid, tobacco, and sex from dawn until dusk. Exceptions are made with regard to food and drink for travelers, pregnant women, and the sick, but these people are expected to make up the days of fasting at a later time.

Because Islam follows a strictly lunar calendar, Ramadan occurs at a slightly different time each year, as measured by a solar calendar of 365 days. Twelve lunar months equal only 354 days; thus, Ramadan begins 11 days earlier each year than in the previous year. As a result, Ramadan can fall in any season. When Ramadan falls in winter, when the days are cool and short, it involves the least discomfort. But when the month of Ramadan falls in the summer, fasting can be a great hardship; when evening finally comes and the day's fast is ended, water and food seem miraculous.

We should note that periods of abstinence are common in many religions. The Christian observance of Lent, for about a month before Easter, is

Minarets that are used to call Istanbul's Muslims to prayer stand alongside an Egyptian obelisk that is covered with hieroglyphics. Istanbul has played important roles in almost two thousand years of history.

a well-known example, as is the Jewish practice of fasting on Yom Kippur, the Day of Atonement, in autumn.

Pilgrimage to Mecca (Hajj)   Pilgrimage—a religious journey by a believer to a sacred city or site—is a common practice in many religions. Besides fulfilling religious demands, pilgrimage offers other, less obvious rewards. It allows people to travel and experience new sights, brings people of different backgrounds together, and engenders a sense of unity. Best of all, it becomes a powerful symbol of an interior journey to the spiritual goals of new understanding and personal transformation. All Muslims, both men and women, unless prevented by poverty or sickness, are expected to visit Mecca at least once in their lifetime. Because Islam is central to the nature of Mecca, only Muslims may visit the city.

Pilgrimage to Mecca, or **Hajj,** was already a practice before Muhammad was born, possibly because worshipers wanted to visit the mysterious black meteorite that had fallen in the area. Muhammad, following divine revelation, continued the practice of pilgrimage to Mecca. He also continued many earlier aspects of that pilgrimage—including veneration of the black meteorite. Although this veneration might seem to contradict Muhammad's call for pure, nonidolatrous worship of the One God, the meteorite was thought of as a special gift from God. It was also connected with Abraham and even with Adam, who are said to have venerated it, and with the angel Gabriel, who was thought to have carried it to earth.

Because the present-day form of pilgrimage offers many deeply emotional experiences for believers, it deserves special description.[16] Contemporary pilgrims generally arrive by plane at Jiddah, the port city on the west coast of Saudi Arabia. In earlier times, people came by more romantic (and dangerous) methods—by boat or camel caravan. Air travel, however, has enabled people to come in great numbers. In the past, about thirty thousand people visited Mecca each year; now more than two million people make the journey. In earlier days, the pilgrimage took months or even years. Some pilgrims died along the way, particularly when the special month of pilgrimage fell in the summer. Often it was the only long trip a person might ever take from a home village. Despite the enormous number of pilgrims, returning home as a *hajji* (male pilgrim) or *hajjiyah* (female pilgrim) still confers much prestige.

Muslims distinguish between the "greater pilgrimage," which is made only during the special month of pilgrimage (*dhu'l-Hijjah*), and the "lesser pilgrimage," which can be made at other times of the year as well. The lesser pilgrimage consists simply of a visit to Mecca and nearby holy sites. The greater pilgrimage, which is described in the following paragraphs, adds several days of arduous travel and ritual in the plains beyond Mecca. A trip to the city of Medina is often included.

Pilgrims first come to Mecca and are expected to arrive by the seventh of the month for the Hajj. For men there is special clothing, called the robe of Abraham, consisting of two pieces of white, seamless cloth. One piece is worn around the waist and lower body; the other covers the upper body and the left arm. (Women have no special clothing, but many dress in white. They do not veil their faces when they are participating in the pilgrimage.) The uniformity of clothing for males emphasizes their basic equality before God. In addition to the robe of Abraham and special prayers, all pilgrims are expected to refrain from sex, violence, and hunting. (It is easy to see how these pilgrimages and the associated practices drastically reduced intertribal warfare on the Arabian Peninsula.)

After settling into their hotels or hostels, pilgrims proceed to the Grand Mosque. Inside the huge rectangle of the mosque area is a large courtyard, open to the sky. The four sides of the courtyard consist of pillared colonnades, which open out onto the central area and offer shade. At the center of the courtyard is the Kabah shrine. It is a building approximately 50 feet high and 40 feet wide and deep. (Its metric dimensions are approximately 15 meters high and 12 meters wide and deep.) The building is covered with a black cloth,

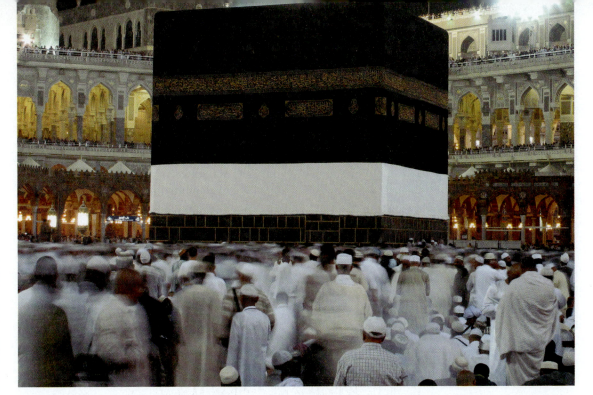

Tens of thousands of Muslim pilgrims move around the Kabah, the great cube in the center of Mecca's Grand Mosque.

remade every year, whose edges are embroidered in gold with words from the Qur'an. The interior of the Kabah is empty and is entered only by caretakers and dignitaries, who ritually cleanse the interior with rosewater. The black meteorite, known as the Black Stone, is embedded in one external wall of the building and is visible on the outside from the courtyard.

After ceremonially purifying themselves with water, pilgrims immediately walk counterclockwise around the Kabah seven times. As they pass the eastern corner, they kiss or salute the Black Stone, which extends from the shrine about 5 feet above the ground. Today the Black Stone is surrounded by silver and has become concave from being touched and kissed over the years by so many millions of people.

Pilgrims reenact important events in the life of Abraham, their forefather. Islam holds that Hagar and Abraham's son, Ishmael, lived in the region of Mecca and that Abraham visited them here. Muslims believe that Abraham was asked by God to sacrifice his son Ishmael—not Isaac, as Judaism and Christianity teach—and that the near-sacrifice took place in Mecca. In their actions, they relive Abraham's spiritual submission as a means of emulating his close relationship to God.

After walking around the Kabah, pilgrims ritually recall Hagar. A long covered corridor nearby connects the two sacred hills of Safa and Marwah, which the Qur'an calls "signs appointed by Allah."[17] Between these two hills Hagar is believed to have searched desperately for water for her son Ishmael. Pilgrims walk speedily seven times along the corridor (the *Masa*), reenacting Hagar's thirsty search. They drink from the well of Zamzam in the mosque area, which is believed to be the well shown to Hagar by an angel.

Muslim children have a special perspective on Hajj pilgrims.

On the eighth day of the month, after another visit to the Kabah, pilgrims go to Mina, a few miles outside Mecca, where they pray through the night. The next morning, the ninth day, they travel to the plain of Arafat, about twelve miles from Mecca, where Muhammad preached his final sermon. At noon they hear a sermon and stand all afternoon in prayer, exposed to the sun. The day of prayer at Arafat is often crucial to the experience of exaltation that the pilgrimage experience can bestow. That night is spent outdoors at Muzdalifa, halfway between Arafat and Mina.

The following day, the tenth of the month, is called the Day of Sacrifice (**Id al-Adha**). Pilgrims return to Mina, where they throw small stones at three walls, a ritual that recalls how Abraham responded to a temptation: when a demon tempted him to disobey God's command to sacrifice his son, Abraham threw stones at the demon and drove it away.

Pilgrims then select for themselves and their families one animal (sheep, goat, cow, or camel) to be sacrificed to reenact another important event in Abraham's life: after showing his willingness to sacrifice his son Ishmael to God, Abraham was divinely directed to substitute a ram for his son. The slaughtered animal is then cooked and eaten. Any meat that is left over is processed and given to charity. (This act of animal sacrifice is carried out throughout the Muslim world at the same time during the month of pilgrimage.) After the sacrifice, the men's heads are shaven, the women's hair is cut, and all fingernails and toenails are trimmed to signify a new, purified life and a return to ordinary activities. Pilgrims then return to Mecca to again walk around the Kabah. Although this concludes the essential ritual of the Hajj, many pilgrims go on to visit Medina to honor the memory of Muhammad, who is buried there.

Additional Islamic Religious Practices

Islam aims at providing patterns for ideal living. Controls and prohibitions are imposed not to signify a love of suffering but to increase social order and happiness. Where outsiders might see only limitations, Muslims see instead the benefits that sensible regulations bring to individuals and societies. People who visit Muslim cultures often comment on the rarity of crime and the sense of security that people regularly feel on city streets.

Although it is strict, Islamic practice also values pleasure and happiness in this world. Believers must fast during the daylight hours of Ramadan; but

Rituals and Celebrations

THE ISLAMIC RELIGIOUS CALENDAR: FESTIVALS AND HOLY DAYS

Like other religions, Islam has developed a sequence of religious festivals and holy days. The main observances follow.

- The Day of Sacrifice, or Id al-Adha, is celebrated during the month of the Hajj (the twelfth lunar month). The head of every Muslim household is expected to sacrifice (or to pay someone to sacrifice) a sheep, goat, cow, or camel to recall Abraham's sacrifice of a ram in place of his son. The meat is cooked, eaten by the family, and shared with the poor.

- The Day of Breaking the Fast, or **Id al-Fitr,** is observed just after the month of Ramadan (the ninth lunar month) has ended. People have parties and often visit the graves of ancestors. Sometimes the festival goes on for three days.

- During Muharram (the first month of the Muslim year), believers remember the migration of Muhammad and his followers to Yathrib (Medina). For the Shiite branch of Islam, found primarily in Iran, Iraq, and Pakistan, the month has additional significance because it is associated with the death of Hussein, the son of Muhammad's son-in-law Ali. The first nine days of the month are solemn, and on the tenth day the devout reenact publicly the assassination of Hussein. Plays and processions vividly recall his death, sometimes with devotees cutting themselves and crying aloud during processions in the street.

- Muhammad's birthday occurs on the twelfth day of the third month of the year. In some countries it is a public holiday, and in some regions the whole month is given to celebrating and reading religious texts.

- Birthdays of other holy men and women are variously marked by devotees in different regions and groups. Shiites observe the birthday of Ali; religious communities honor the birthdays of their founders; and the birthdays of regional saints are celebrated locally.

when night comes, families gather to enjoy a good meal together. The same general attitude applies toward sexuality. Although sex is regulated, Muslims do not value celibacy. Muhammad was no celibate and opposed celibacy as being unnatural. In this regard, Muslims are puzzled by Jesus's never having married and by the religious ideal of monasticism. It is within this framework of an ideal society that we should view some of the prohibitions of Islam.

Dietary Restrictions   The Qur'an forbids the consumption of pork and wine. Both Judaism and Islam view the pig as a scavenger animal, whose meat can transmit disease. Wine is forbidden because of its association with violence and addiction. Although only wine is forbidden in the Qur'an, Islam has interpreted that prohibition to include all alcohol.[18]

Prohibition against Usury and Gambling   Charging interest on loans is not allowed. We might recall that in Muhammad's day money was lent at very high rates of interest, which impoverished and exploited the borrower. (Some Muslims today get around this prohibition by charging a "commission" for making a loan, although the loan itself is officially without interest.) Gambling is forbidden because it is considered a dangerous waste of time and money, as well as a potential financial risk for gamblers and their families.

Circumcision   Male circumcision is a religious requirement in Islam, although it is not actually demanded by the Qur'an. Circumcision at about age 7 or 8 is common. In circumcision, a small amount of loose skin (called the foreskin) is cut off from the end of a boy's penis. (We might recall that Jews circumcise boys on the eighth day after birth. Circumcision is also common among many Christians, although for them it is not a religious commandment; and it occurs frequently in native religions.) Explanations for the practice of circumcision vary. One is that the practice shows submission to the role of God in human procreation. Another relates to reasons of hygiene; in a hot climate, where daily bathing is not always possible, circumcision might have served as a preventive measure against infection. Perhaps both are true. In Islam, however, it is also done in imitation of Muhammad, who was circumcised.

In some primarily Muslim countries, particularly those in eastern Africa, Muslim girls are also circumcised at puberty. The act involves the removal of part or all of a girl's external sexual organs. A common explanation is that it decreases sexual desire in the circumcised young woman, helping her to remain a virgin before her marriage and to be faithful to her husband afterward. Non-Muslims in the West commonly criticize the practice as being repressive and dangerous; but some traditionalists see it as a valuable initiation rite and a preparation for marriage. In any case, we should recognize that it is not a Qur'anic command, nor does it have the same religious authority as does male circumcision.[19]

Marriage   In Islam, marriage is basically a civil contract, although a certain amount of ritual has grown up around it. In traditional Muslim societies, marriage is arranged by the parents and formalized by a written contract. Usually the bridegroom's family makes an offer of money or property to the family of the bride as a part of the contract. The marriage ceremony, which often is held at home, is essentially the witnessing and signing of the contract. A passage from the Qur'an might be read, and there is usually a feast following the signing of the contract. Marriages can be annulled for serious reasons, and divorce is possible and can be initiated by a wife as well as by a husband. Neither annulment nor divorce, however, is frequent. After marriage, a woman takes on a new, more responsible role. As a wife she has left the protection of her father and is now the legal responsibility of her husband.

Death Rituals   The general simplicity of marriage ceremonies is also characteristic of death and funerals. Prayers from the Qur'an are recited for the dying person, and after death the body is buried in a plain white shroud. Ideally, for a male who has made the pilgrimage, the shroud is the white robe of Abraham that he wore in Mecca. The face of the deceased is turned toward Mecca at the burial, and the headstone is usually an undecorated stone marker, which signifies equality of all people in death.[20]

Two women view a weaving with verses from the Qur'an during an exhibition at the Imam Khomeini Grand Mosque in Tehran, Iran.

Scripture: The Qur'an

The name *Qur'an* (*Koran*) means "recitation" and recalls the origins of these sacred writings in the sermons of Muhammad. The name also suggests the way in which the Qur'an is best communicated—by being recited. Although the Qur'an has been translated into many languages, only the Arabic version is considered to be fully authoritative. The beautiful sounds of the original are considered a part of its nature and are essential to its spiritual power.

The Qur'an is believed to be of divine origin, for it is God's Word, which was revealed to Muhammad during the approximately twenty years from his first revelation in 610 CE until the end of his life. Disciples memorized and wrote down the words of Muhammad's revelations, but after his death, when people became concerned that variations would arise and spread, it was thought necessary to establish a single authorized version. Tradition holds that this work was begun by Abu Bakr, Muhammad's first successor, or **caliph** (*khalifa,* "successor"), and that the work was finished in the caliphate of Uthman, which ended in 656 CE. However, recent scholars question this tradition, and the emergence of the authorized edition is now seen as more complex than was formerly thought. The authorized edition that did emerge became the basis for all later copies.[21]

There is a repetitive quality about the Qur'an—common to memorized material—due largely to the fact that the Qur'an is not a carefully constructed argument divided into segments, nor is it a series of stories. Rather, it is a body of sermons and utterances that repeats images and themes in a natural way.

The Qur'an covers a wide variety of topics and discusses figures who are also found in the Jewish and Christian Bibles: Adam, Eve, Noah, Abraham, Isaac, Jacob, Joseph, Moses, David, Solomon, Jesus, Mary, and others. It also gives practical admonitions about everyday life—about property rights, money, inheritance, marriage, and divorce. It refers to events in the life of Muhammad and to specifically religious beliefs and

Islamic graves vary from country to country. In some places, graves have simple markers in the desert sand; in others (such as this cemetery in Turkey), graves may have individualized tombstones with flowers.

regulations—angels, divine judgment, fasting, and the pilgrimage. The topics and types of material are often blended together.

The Qur'an has 114 chapters, or **suras.** Each sura has a traditional name, derived from an image or topic mentioned in it, and many of these names are evocative: "The Elephant," "Light," "Dawn," "Thunder," "The Cave," "Smoke," "The Mountain," "The Moon," "The High One." The order of the suras does not reflect the exact order in which they were revealed. Except for the first sura, which is a brief invocation, the suras are arranged by length, from the longest to the shortest. The last chapters are extremely short—and the easiest for beginners. In general, the placement of the suras is, in fact, in reverse chronological order, with some intermixture of periods. The short suras are probably the earliest teachings of Muhammad, while the long ones are the products of his final years, when the details of Islamic life were being revealed to him. The suras of the Qur'an have been compared to leaves that have fallen from a tree: the first-fallen leaves are on the bottom.

The Qur'an has profoundly affected Islamic art. Indeed, some handwritten copies of the Qur'an are great artworks in themselves, often filled with gold letters and colorful geometrical designs. Because Islam generally prohibits the making of images, artists have developed the most wonderful calligraphy to record the sacred words of the Qur'an.

Frequently the words of a phrase from the Qur'an are also cunningly interlaced to make integrated designs, which are used to beautify mosques and religious schools (*madrasas, medersas*). On buildings, passages from the Qur'an are carved in stone or wood or set in mosaic. Of the many writing systems in the world, cursive Arabic, with its wondrous curves, is possibly the most visually beautiful of all. The fluid form of this writing is suggested nicely by the French word *arabesque,* which has entered the English language to describe a pattern of interlacing lines that are curving and graceful.

The repetition of phrases and images from the Qur'an is comforting to Muslims, who have heard them recited aloud in daily prayers and in sermons since childhood. Passages are recited regularly on the radio, particularly during Ramadan, and in some countries are also broadcast on television. Present everywhere, every day, such phrases have a hypnotic resonance. Because Arabic is an especially beautiful language, chanting the Qur'an in Arabic is an art form, and some chanters have become famous for the beauty of their voices and their interpretation of Qur'anic material.

At this Qur'anic school in Sudan, students copy and recite Qur'anic verses until they are memorized. The writing boards are then cleaned, and the process is repeated with new verses.

THE HISTORICAL DEVELOPMENT OF ISLAM

Because his sons had died in infancy, Muhammad died without a clear hereditary male successor.[22] He apparently had not appointed anyone to succeed him,[23] and the result was confusion and an unclear line of succession—a fact that ultimately created significant divisions in Islam, whose effects remain today.

Muhammad had asked Abu Bakr, his friend and the father of his youngest wife, to be the principal leader of prayer. Because of this position, Abu Bakr was recognized as the first caliph. When Abu Bakr died two years later, he was succeeded by Umar, the second caliph, and followed by Uthman, both of whom were assassinated. The fourth caliph was Muhammad's cousin and son-in-law, Ali, the husband of his daughter Fatima. Ali was also assassinated, and his opponents, who ruled from Damascus, assumed control of Islam in 661 CE. This period marks the first and most significant division of Islam, which broke into two factions, Shiite and Sunni (which we will discuss shortly).

The earliest stage of growth of Islam came during the time of the first four rulers, called the orthodox caliphs. These men had been close to Muhammad, and their home was Arabia. A major change occurred, however, as Islam spread outside Arabia. From an early, deliberate simplicity, Islam would now become more urbane and complex.

In the name of God
The Compassionate
The Merciful.
Praise be to God, Lord
  of the Universe,
The Compassionate,
  the Merciful,
Sovereign of the Day of
  Judgment!
You alone we worship,
  and to You alone we
  turn for help.
  —Opening (Al-Fatihah)
    of the Qur'an[24]

Expansion and Consolidation

Islam arose at a time that was congenial to the growth of a new political and religious power. The Byzantine Empire, ruling from Constantinople, had fought repeatedly with the Persian Empire, and both were weakened by the effort. Areas theoretically controlled by the Byzantine emperor, such as regions of northern Africa, were far away from the capital.

The weakness of the Byzantine and Persian Empires—and what Muslims believe was divine purpose—helped Islam quickly expand into their territories. Islamic armies took Syria in 635 CE and Persia in 636 CE. They

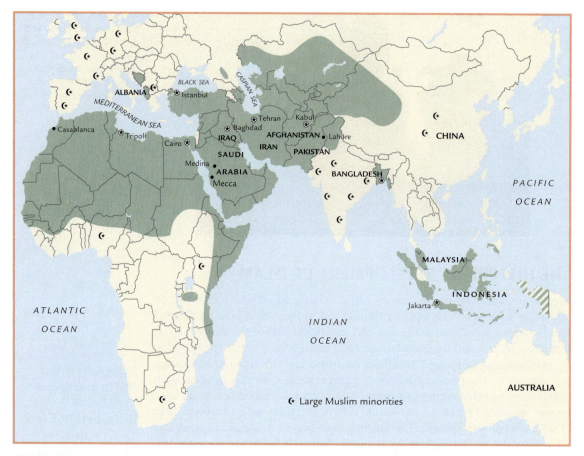

FIGURE 10.1

Map of the Islamic world today.

began to move westward, taking control of Egypt in about 640 CE. The success was intoxicating. Islam spread across most of northern Africa over the next seventy years, and it spread across the Red Sea and Indian Ocean from Arabia to eastern Africa (Figure 10.1).

Islamic forces entered Spain in 711 CE, when a Muslim general named Tariq landed in the south—the name of Gibraltar ("mountain of Tariq") recalls this event. In fact, Muslim forces might have spread Islam through much of western Europe if they had not been stopped in southern France by the Christian forces of Charles Martel, the grandfather of Charlemagne, in 732 CE at the Battle of Tours.[25] This battle—just a hundred years after the death of Muhammad—was one of the defining battles of world history.

Although Islam was stopped from expanding northward, Islamic rulers remained in Spain for nearly eight hundred years, with capitals in Córdoba and Granada. Many remember the Islamic period in Spain with nostalgia and longing, for it is universally thought to have been a paradise-like time, when the arts flourished and Muslims, Jews, and Christians generally lived together in harmony. The only other significant incursion into the West in these early centuries was into Sicily, where Islam was a force for about two hundred years.

At the mosque of Al-Azhar in Cairo, students can ask questions of tutors in order to learn some of the complicated concepts in Qur'anic theology.

From 661 CE to 750 CE, Islam was controlled by the Umayyad dynasty—a period called the Damascus caliphate (the caliphate was now hereditary). During this period Islam adopted elements—from architecture to cuisine—that were introduced to Syria by the Roman Empire. It also adopted and refined the administrative and military apparatus of a political state. This fruitful contact with Roman-influenced Syria is just one example of the genius that Islam has shown in absorbing elements from other cultures and giving them new life.

Control of Islam shifted to Baghdad in 750 CE under the Abbasid dynasty—a hereditary line that claimed connection to Muhammad. It is often thought that this period, also known as the Baghdad caliphate, which did not end until 1258, was the golden age of Islam—its cultural peak. Just as the Umayyads had adopted Roman-inspired elements from Syria, so the Abbasids adopted much that was Persian—music, poetry, architecture, and garden design. Classical Greek texts on philosophy, science, and the arts were translated into Arabic. Under the influence of Indian artists, Islam relaxed the prohibition of images in court art, and miniature paintings and drawings of dazzling images were created. Baghdad became a world center of civilization and taste.

Islam continued to spread eastward into non-Arab cultures, and Arab domination of Islam waned as Islam spread to present-day Azerbaijan, Kazakhstan, Afghanistan, Pakistan, northern India, and Bangladesh. Islam also spread into western China, where millions of Muslims still live today.

After the Mongols invaded and sacked Baghdad in 1258, the political center of Islam shifted to Egypt. Then in 1453, Muslims captured the ancient Christian capital of Constantinople, making it the center of the Ottoman Empire as well as of the Muslim world until 1921, when the Ottoman Empire ended. During

FIGURE 10.2

Branches of Islam.

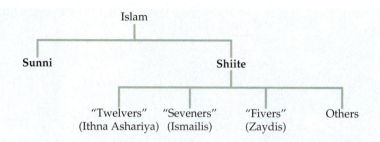

this long period Islam spread, primarily through trade, to Southeast Asia—to what is today Malaysia, southern Thailand, and Indonesia, which presently has the largest Muslim population of any country in the world. Islam also spread to Mindanao, the southernmost island of the Philippines.

Because of the great size of Islamic territory—a span from Morocco and Spain to Indonesia and the Philippines—completely centralized control was impossible. Thus, secondary centers, which were sometimes totally independent caliphates, were established. In Spain, the cities of Córdoba and, later, Granada became local political capitals, until Muslims were expelled from Spain in 1492. In India, Delhi became the center of the Muslim Mughal (Mogul) Empire until the British took control of the subcontinent. The fiction of a single caliph ruling all of Islam, however, was kept alive until the Ottoman caliphate in Turkey was dissolved in 1924. (Some contemporary Muslims would like to see the caliphate revived.)

The Shiite and Sunni Division within Islam

Over the centuries of its growth, Islam has experienced several divisions. The most significant division is between the Shiites and Sunnis. Today about 10 to 15 percent of Islam is Shiite, and the remaining majority is Sunni (Figure 10.2). The division began as a political argument over who should succeed Muhammad, but it has widened over the centuries into a division over belief, practice, and general religious approach.

The real argument over succession centered on different conceptions of the caliphate. Some thought that it should be held by a man of Muhammad's tribe (the Quraysh), someone chosen by his peers as being the person who was strongest and most capable of governing. This was a fairly practical notion of leadership. Others, however, saw the caliph as a spiritual leader, and they believed that God gave the spiritual power of the caliph only to those males who were descended directly from Muhammad's immediate family.

Shiite Islam   **Shiites** derive their name from the word *shia,* which means "faction"—namely, the group who followed Ali, the son-in-law and cousin of Muhammad. We might recall that most early Muslims accepted the legitimacy of the first four successors of Muhammad (Abu Bakr, Umar, Uthman, and Ali). Some early Muslims, however, held that Muhammad had assigned Ali to be his first successor, but that a series of political and religious intrigues

Shiite pilgrims gather in Karbala, Iraq, on the fortieth day after the anniversary of the killing of Imam Hussein, grandson of Muhammad. His death occurred in 680 CE.

had initially kept Ali from the caliphate. These disagreements led to further arguments during the period of Uthman and continued even into Ali's eventual caliphate. Muawiya, leader of the Umayyad clan, rejected Ali's leadership, but when arbitration declared Ali to be the legitimate leader, Ali was assassinated. Following Ali's death, some believers held that succession rightfully belonged to his two sons, Hassan and Hussein. Ali's first son, Hassan (625–669), renounced his rights to succession; he was poisoned nonetheless by enemies. Ali's second son, Hussein (626–680), fought against Umayyad control but was killed and beheaded after being defeated in 680 CE at the Battle of Karbala, in Iraq. Hussein's death allowed the Umayyad dynasty to maintain control for a hundred years, but it also created strong opposition, which became the Shiite movement. Shiites, who trace Muhammad's line of succession from Ali to Hussein, see Hussein as a martyr whose heroic death is a redeeming sacrifice that invites imitation. His burial site at the main mosque of Karbala in Iraq is considered a major holy place and, for Shiites, a center of pilgrimage.

Shiite Islam believes that the legitimate succession was hereditary, descending from the immediate family of Muhammad. Most Shiites believe that a God-given, hereditary spiritual power, called the Light of Muhammad, has been passed to a total of twelve successors, or **Imams.** For them, the first legitimate Imam was Ali. The line ended with the disappearance of the last Imam, Muhammad al-Mahdi, about 900 CE. According to tradition, he did not die but entered a hidden realm from which he works by guiding Shiite scholars and leaders. Some Shiites believe that he will emerge from this state in the future to help restore Shiite Islam and that his reappearance in the world will usher in a messianic age, heralding the end of the world.

There are several divisions within Shiite Islam that differ on how many Imams there were and on the exact line of succession. Most Shiites believe in twelve Imams, as previously mentioned, and thus are sometimes called Twelvers—Ithna Ashariya. But members of one group, the Ismailis, are often called the Seveners because they disagree with the Twelvers about the identity of the seventh Imam; they trace descent from Ismail, whom they consider to be the seventh Imam. Disagreement over the fifth Imam produced a division called the Zaydis (named after Hussein's grandson, Zayd ibn Ali). They are commonly known as the Fivers and live predominantly in Yemen. The Alawites in Syria are an unusual group, whose practice has apparently been influenced by other religions. They believe in reincarnation and, in addition to Muslim holidays, they celebrate Christmas and Epiphany. Smaller groups also exist, some of which (such as the Druze of Lebanon) are not considered orthodox Muslims.

Shiite Islam has been attractive to non-Arab Muslims, who have sometimes felt that they were relegated to an inferior role in a religion whose origins were in Arabia. Iran is the center of Shiite Islam because of its large Shiite population. But Iraq is the spiritual home because of the connection with Hussein.

Sunni Islam **Sunni** (or Sunnite) Islam, the other great division of Islam, takes its name from the word *sunna* ("tradition," "example"). The name refers to the entire body of traditional teachings that are based on the life and teachings of Muhammad, as given in the Qur'an and the authoritative hadiths.

Sunni Islam developed to some degree in response to the claims of Shiite Islam. Because Sunnis accepted the legitimacy of the orthodox caliphates, they were compelled to develop a religious, political, legal, and cultural system that was consistent with their beliefs. The system included the caliphs, who were thought to rule in God's name; the Qur'an and hadiths, seen as expressing God's will; the schools and scholarly debate that interpreted the Qur'an and hadiths to apply to everyday life; and the scholars who carried on this debate. Traditional Islam does not separate political life from religious life; it aims to create a public life that is shaped by the Qur'an. Although scholarly debate has been a tradition of Shiite Islam, it is central to the ideology of Sunni Islam, which has often been distinctive in its openness to reason and practicality.

Sunni Islam does not have the clear divisions that we see in Shiite Islam. However, it does have its own divisions. Like any large-scale human development, Sunni Islam has generated interpretations of Islam that run the spectrum from ultraconservative to very liberal. We will speak briefly of the most important ones here and then return to them at the end of the chapter, when we discuss Islam in the modern world.

The interiors of major mosques are often designed to lift the spirit of worshipers. Occasionally, a mosque's impact extends beyond its interior to include the entire neighborhood, as we see in this photo from outside Cairo's Ibn Tulun Mosque.

One division that is frequently spoken of today is the Wahhabi sect, a conservative movement. It is named after its founder, Muhammad Ibn Abd al-Wahhab (c. 1703–1791), who was born in Medina. The movement began in Arabia in the eighteenth century, experienced several declines, and underwent a revival in the past century. Its influence is now spreading throughout the Sunni world.

The Wahhabi movement arose from a desire to return to an ideal purity that was thought to have existed in early Islam. The Wahhabi movement emphasizes doctrinal orthodoxy, and the name that Wahhabis themselves use for their movement may be translated as "monotheism." Muhammad, as we know, opposed polytheism and emphasized that worship be reserved for God alone. A continual struggle, therefore, goes on in Islam over the veneration of deceased teachers, leaders, and holy persons. Should they have shrines or special tombs? Should memorial days be celebrated for them? Should they be prayed to or referred to in prayer? The Wahhabis have opposed veneration of deceased people, no matter how saintly, saying that such veneration takes away from the unique worship of the One God. Thus Wahhabis do not even celebrate the birthday of Muhammad, and some oppose visiting his burial place in Medina. (Wahhabis earlier destroyed the shrines built to honor Muhammad and his companions.) The Wahhabi movement also has a strongly moral dimension. Among its goals are simplicity, modesty, separation in public of males and females, and strict prohibition of alcohol.

Another reform movement began in India in 1867. The Deobandi movement is named after the town of Deoband, about ninety miles north of Delhi, where the first school was established. This sect resembles the Wahhabis in its emphasis on a simplified Islam: veneration given solely to God, rejection of devotion to saints, and strong differences between male and female social roles. But it gives great attention to the importance of Muhammad and his early companions, who are thought of as role models for Muslims. It argues that education should be entirely religious—it should be based only on the Qur'an and hadiths. Thus it opposes education in business and modern science.

These fairly stern movements have come into existence because Sunni Islam encompasses so many countries and millions of individuals with varied degrees of commitment. Within the immense numbers of Sunnis—who make up almost 90 percent of all Muslims—many are simply "cultural Muslims." They have been born into the faith but pick and choose the customs that they wish to follow. The most devout visit a mosque daily and follow all requirements about prayer, charity, and fasting. Others would call themselves moderate Muslims, attending the Friday prayer and doing some daily prayer, but not being otherwise involved. Some limit their practice to prayer at a mosque only on major festivals. Most observe the fast of Ramadan strictly, but some do not. Hence, the appeal of reformers. (We see something similar among Christians who attend church only at Christmas and Easter, or among Buddhists whose religious practice is confined to attending funerals.)

Another common pattern in some Sunni regions is the blending of Islam with older, local elements. One striking example is the traditional form of Islam in Indonesia, which is blended with Indonesian Hinduism and includes ceremonies to honor spirits of nature. A news article described one typical service on the island of Java.

> "In the name of God, the compassionate, the merciful," the turbaned priest begins in the orthodox Muslim style. . . . As the annual labuhan ceremony unfolds, he blesses the various offerings the Sultan of Yogyakarta has prepared for Loro Kidul, the goddess of the surrounding seas: silk, curry, bananas, hair and toenail clippings. The goddess, apparently, will be pleased with these items when they are carried in procession to the sea and thrown in, as will another local deity, who receives similar gifts tossed into a nearby volcano.[26]

Clearly, this service—which resembles ceremonies that one might also see in Hindu Bali—owes much to the nature worship and Hinduism that preceded the coming of Islam.

Similar blendings can be found in many countries—particularly those that are away from the centers of orthodoxy, such as in western Africa and Southeast Asia. For many people, Islam is a veneer over much older practices. All mixed forms of Islam, however, can be—and often are—the object of reformers' criticism.

Liberal movements have also regularly emerged, although they have not yet coalesced into a clearly defined sect. Perhaps this is because they have spread largely from books espousing their ideas. These movements argue that Muhammad was a humanitarian reformer and that he himself would reinterpret his insights in light of modern needs. The liberal movements urge, in addition to religious studies, the study of science and business. They point out the early achievements of Islam in medicine, astronomy, and other sciences, and they encourage the continuation of this type of achievement. Perhaps the most influential of these liberal developments has been the Aligarh movement. Its founder, Sayyid Ahmad Khan (1817–1898), began a college at Aligarh, in India, which he devoted to principles of modern education. His ideas, promoted widely by his books and disciples, remain influential. Such ideas inspire like-minded groups in many countries.

Because Mecca is located in Saudi Arabia, it is one center of power in modern Sunni Islam. This (and the influence of a reformist movement) has meant that the government of Saudi Arabia expects its country to be a model of proper Muslim belief and behavior—as tourists and foreign workers who have been forbidden from importing alcohol have sometimes been shocked to discover. This has also led to occasional friction, particularly with Iran, which reflects the long-standing differences between Sunni and Shiite points of view.

Another center of power in the Sunni world is Egypt. Its universities, particularly Al-Azhar in Cairo, give it prestige as an interpreter of Islam; and its large Muslim population makes it politically important in the Muslim world.

SUFISM: ISLAMIC MYSTICISM

Islam began as a rather austere religion. But as it moved beyond Arabia, Islam came into contact with the luxurious lifestyle of the settled old cities in the Near East and northern Africa. The Umayyad dynasty, we recall, ruled Islam for one hundred years from Damascus, which even then was an ancient city. Damascus had become one of the most important cities in the eastern part of the Roman Empire, and it had retained its prominent role under the Byzantine Empire. The caliphate of Damascus simply carried on the aristocratic lifestyle already present.

Islam had contact not only with sophisticated city dwellers there, but also with the Christian monks and hermits who lived elsewhere in Syria and in Israel and Egypt. The monks' simple lives made a great impression on Muslims, who seemed to desire something similar for Islam. Because Islam rejected celibacy as a religious ideal, the Christian model of monasticism could not be imitated exactly. What emerged, however, were lay individuals who cultivated the spiritual life on their own and groups of devotees loosely organized around charismatic spiritual leaders.

Sufism is the name of an old and widespread devotional movement—or group of movements—in Islam. The name *Sufism* is thought to derive from the Arabic word *suf* ("wool"), because early Sufis wore a simple robe made of common wool. It is possible that this type of ordinary cloth was not only practical but also a visual statement opposing needless luxury. Sufism has been a religious movement that values deliberate simplicity.

But Sufism was not only a reaction against superficial luxury. The movement also grew out of a natural desire to do more than the merely formalistic. As Islam defined itself further, establishing religious practice in even the smallest areas of life, it was possible for some people to think that "keeping the rules" was all there was to being a good Muslim. Sufism, however, recognized that it is possible to "go through the motions" but to leave the heart uninvolved. As a result, Sufism sought the involvement of emotions. Because of this it has been called "the heart of Islam."

Sufi Beliefs

The core of the Sufi movement is its mysticism—its belief that the highest experience a person can have is a direct experience of God. Sufism holds that an individual can, on earth, experience God "face to face." Moreover, it teaches that experiencing God is the whole purpose of life, not something that has to wait until after death.

Sufi mysticism was encouraged by several religious movements that had been active in Egypt and Syria long before Sufism arose in the seventh and eighth centuries CE. One was Neoplatonism, a mystical philosophical school that began in Alexandria in Egypt with Plotinus (c. 205–270 CE). Plotinus's work *The Enneads* spoke of the emergence of the entire cosmos from the One and the journey of the soul as it returns to its divine origin. Another movement that influenced Sufism was Gnosticism, which similarly saw life as a spiritual journey. Gnosticism produced its own literature and interpreted other religious literature symbolically. Christian forms of Neoplatonism and Gnosticism flourished in Syria not long before the Umayyad period and produced such books as *The Divine Names* and *The Mystical Theology* by Pseudo-Dionysius, who is thought to have been a Syrian Christian monk of the sixth century. It is also possible that influences from Hindu mysticism, coming from India into Persia, were behind a great flowering of mystical poetry.

Sufis saw in the Qur'an a number of passages that invited mystical interpretation. These became their favorites. A beloved passage says that Allah is so near to every human being that he is even "closer than the jugular vein."[27] Another favorite passage says, "Whether you hide what is in your hearts or manifest it, Allah knows it."[28]

> To God belongs the east and the west. Whichever way you turn, there is the face of God.
>
> —Qur'an[29]

The image of Muhammad also took on new meaning. To the Sufis, Muhammad was himself a mystic. He lived a life of deliberate simplicity, sought God, and had profound revelations. Because he submitted himself so fully to God's will, in his Night Journey he was carried up to the highest heaven, where he spoke with God as one friend speaking to another friend. This event, the scholar A. J. Arberry remarks, "for the Sufis constitutes the Prophet's supreme mystical experience and an example which they may aspire to follow."[30]

One of the great early Sufi saints was Rabia (c. 717–801 CE), who left behind ecstatic writings that speak of God as her divine lover. She is famous for her statement that she sought God not because of fear of hell or desire for heaven but simply for himself alone. In other words, she sought God not for her sake but for his.

Sufis have commonly spoken about the sense of loss of self (**fana,** "extinction") that occurs in mystical experience: when the self is gone, all that remains is God. Some Sufis have spoken about this experience in language that has been shocking to the orthodox—their mystical descriptions seeming to weaken the distinction between God and his created world, which is strong in orthodox Islam, and even seeming to embrace pantheism, the belief that everything is God. The Persian mystic Abu Yazid (d. 875 CE), when he was in ecstasy, is reputed to have said, "Glory be to me—how great is my majesty."[31] Al-Hallaj (d. 922 CE) was one of the most alarming Sufi figures; he publicly and repeatedly applied a name for God to himself, calling himself al-Haqq ("the Truth," "the Real," or "Reality Itself"). His comments were so shocking to his contemporaries that they executed him.

Sufis continued to come into conflict with religious authorities who feared that Sufi meeting places would supplant the mosques and that a vague command simply to love would replace the clearer, specific commands of traditional Islam. The veneration of both living and dead Sufi masters also seemed to the orthodox to be opposed to the traditional demand to worship God alone.

Deeper Insights

ZOROASTRIANISM

Zoroastrianism is a monotheistic religion that was once widespread in the Near East and Middle East. Although today it is a small religion, it was once a religion of millions, and its influence spread far beyond its home in Persia. Because other religions that originated in the same region share many distinctive elements with Zoroastrianism, there is lively debate about its role in their development and spread. Some see possible influence on the worldview of the Essenes (a semimonastic faction of Judaism), early Christianity, and Islam. New Year's customs still practiced today in Iran certainly reflect Zoroastrian origins.

The prophet Zarathustra (or Zoroaster), the founder of the religion, was born about 650 BCE in what is now Iran. Zarathustra was surrounded by the worship of nature gods, common to the Aryan religion, which was also practiced in India. As in Indian Vedic religion, the religion of Zarathustra's culture involved the worship of gods at fire altars, the use of a ritual drink (*haoma*, like the Vedic *soma*), and a hereditary priesthood. Like the Buddha after him, Zarathustra was distressed by the sacrifice of animals at the fire altars and by the power of the priests.

At about the age of 30, Zarathustra experienced a vision that changed his life. He felt himself transported heavenward by a spirit he called Vohu Manah ("good mind") into the presence of the High God Ahura Mazda ("wise lord"), a god associated in Zarathustra's mind with cosmic justice. Like the calls of Isaiah and Muhammad, this revelation led Zarathustra to preach his new message. At first, Zarathustra was met with strong rejection, which he blamed on demons (*daevas*) and the satanic head of evil forces, Angra Mainyu ("wicked spirit"). Zarathustra's bitter experiences deepened his sense that evil forces constantly oppose the forces of goodness. He was undaunted, however, and his preaching eventually converted an Iranian king, Vishtaspa, who used his power to spread Zarathustra's new religion. Zarathustra condemned animal sacrifices, but he maintained the ceremonial use of the Aryan fire altar. Although fire was not to be worshiped, Zarathustra considered it to be symbolic of divine goodness. Tradition relates that Zarathustra died in his 70s, killed by invaders while praying at his fire altar.

What we know of Zarathustra comes from the most ancient part of the Avesta, the Zoroastrian scriptures. They teach of a High God, Ahura Mazda, who expresses himself through good spirits whose names are virtues. Whether these spirits are simply aspects of Ahura Mazda or independent beings is unclear. The most important is called Spenta Mainyu ("holy spirit"). Others, for example, have names that mean "power," "devotion," "immortality," and "obedience." (We find some tantalizing similarities in the Jewish mystical literature of the Kabbalah, in Gnosticism, and in some New Testament letters. See Chapters 8 and 9.)

Although Zoroastrianism is ultimately monotheistic, it sees the universe in morally dualistic terms. Forces of good are in perpetual conflict with forces of evil—a conflict that mysteriously began at the start of time. Each person is involved in this cosmic struggle and thus must make moral choices between good and evil. Good actions include telling the truth and dealing honestly with others—in the Avesta, good actions include cultivating farmland and treating animals kindly. There is a belief in divine judgment and in an afterlife of reward or punishment, which begins at death, when each individual's soul must cross a bridge that can lead to paradise. If the individual has been good, the bridge is wide and the journey to paradise is easy; but if the individual has been evil, the bridge becomes so narrow that the soul falls into the depths of hell.

Zoroastrianism also presents an apocalyptic vision of the end of time: when the world comes to an end, there will be a resurrection of all bodies and a great general judgment; at this time the world will be purified by fire, which will punish the evil but leave the good untouched.

Zoroastrianism has long been a highly ritualistic religion. At the center of its worship is the fire altar, where priests dressed in white attend an eternal flame. To keep the flame from impurity, an attendant must wear a white cloth (*padan*) that covers his nose and mouth. Believers who come to pray take off their shoes and touch the door frame reverently.

The central festival is NoRuz, a New Year's festival that is held at the time of the spring equinox, on or near March 21. It is celebrated not only by Zoroastrians but also by Iranians of many faiths, who do spring

Iranian Zoroastrians celebrate the midwinter "feast of fire," Jashn-eh-Sadeh.

cleaning, wear new clothing, and eat festive meals. Jumping over outdoor fires is a unique practice—it is thought to bring health during the coming year. Because seven is a sacred number, people create side tables at home with seven ritual items, many of which are symbolic of new life. These may include new green shoots of wheat, colored hardboiled eggs, garlic, wine or vinegar, candles, a mirror, and a bowl of goldfish. Meals made of seven other foods, such as apples, pudding, dried fruit, and pastries, are also eaten. These groups of seven originally recalled Ahura Mazda and the six Holy Immortals, the spirits through whom Ahura Mazda expresses himself.

Contemporary Zoroastrianism is threatened by its dwindling numbers. Although Zoroastrianism was once the widespread state religion of Persia, only about fifty thousand Zoroastrians live in Iran today. Large numbers moved to India more than a thousand years ago, where they settled in Mumbai (Bombay) and created their own distinctive culture. In India they are called Parsees ("Persians") and number about a hundred thousand. Because of their regard for education and hard work, their contributions to science, industry, and music in India have been extraordinary. As a result of recent emigration, perhaps another fifty thousand Zoroastrians live in large cities in North America, England, and Australia.

Kashmiri Muslims in Srinagar, India, pray at the shrine of Sufi saint Sheikh Dawood, who preached Islam to the region over three hundred years ago.

Al-Ghazali and Sufi Brotherhoods

The conflict was softened by the life and work of the scholar al-Ghazali (or al-Ghazzali, 1058–1111). Al-Ghazali was a renowned professor in Baghdad who adopted Sufism. In his autobiography he says that despite the respect his job gave him, he was deeply unhappy. What he was doing did not seem important to his own spiritual life. He was torn between leaving his post and staying on in comfort. At last, he followed an inner voice that demanded that he go "on the road." He did this for more than ten years, traveling in Syria and Arabia and living simply. He eventually returned to Baghdad and formed a brotherhood of Sufis, but he insisted on keeping orthodox law and practice as well. His blend of Sufism with traditional practice, his later books on Sufism, and his scholarly reputation made an indelible mark on Islam. He explained that the Sufi language of "extinction" (fana) is metaphorical, which he compared to "the words of lovers passionate in their intoxication,"[32] or to a diver lost in the sea.[33] His explanations of Sufism and his prestige gave a legitimacy to Sufism that it had not had before. Sufism and orthodoxy no longer needed to run like parallel lines, never meeting. Now they could enrich each other.

After al-Ghazali, more Sufi brotherhoods were founded and their techniques became slightly more institutionalized. Disciples gathered around a master. The disciple—in Arabic called *faqir* and in Persian *darwish*, meaning "poor"—would learn a distinctive spiritual discipline (*tariqa*) from the *shaykh*, a Sufi expert. Often a master and his disciples lived in a compound of many buildings, and the life was semimonastic. Laypersons could also be associated with the religious order, even while living an outwardly secular life.[34]

Many Sufi orders emerged and spread widely. One of the most famous was the Maulawiya (in Turkish, Mevlevi), founded by Jalal-ud-Din Rumi

Whirling dervishes dance near the thirteenth-century Mevlana mausoleum, the burial place of Sufi poet Rumi.

(1207–1273). Born in Persia, Rumi eventually settled in what is today Turkey. Rumi's exquisite poetry is now well known beyond the Muslim world. His great work is called *Mesnevi* (or *Mathnawi*). The Maulawiya order became famous for its type of circular dance, which Rumi asserted could assist mystical experience. (The English phrase *whirling dervish* refers to a member of this order, and the Mevlevi dance is still performed in Konya, where Rumi lived, and in other places.) Among other orders to emerge, with different emphases, were the Qadiri, Suhrawardi, and Naqshbandi.

Sufi Practice and Poetry

Sufism has incorporated many techniques to encourage spiritual insight, some possibly derived from Hindu yoga or from Christian monastic practice in the Near East. One technique involved jerking the head to encourage an upward flow of blood during prayer. Two other techniques were deep, regular breathing during meditation and the repetition of the ninety-nine names of Allah (**dhikr**), sometimes counted on a rosary, to enable a constant remembrance of God. Some groups used music and others used spinning or dancing in circles or occasionally ingesting wine and psychedelic plants to alter consciousness.

Sufism has also used poetry in the same allegorical and symbolic ways. When read one way, a poem might resemble the lyrics of a romantic song. Read another way, the same poem might suggest a longing of the spirit for God, a search for God, or the ecstasy of final union with God. Sufism has inspired some of the world's greatest poets, as famous in the Muslim world as are Shakespeare and Goethe in Western countries.

Until recent decades, only one Muslim poet was well known in English-speaking countries. Omar Khayyám (c. 1048–1122), who was also an astronomer and mathematician, gained fame in the West from a late Victorian translation (by Edward FitzGerald) of the long poem *The Rubaiyat*. Many people are familiar with "a loaf of bread, a jug of wine, and thou," which is paraphrased from the poem and brings to mind a romantic picnic. But a Sufi could interpret a loaf of bread symbolically as the depth of ordinary reality, the jug of wine (intoxicating but suspect) as ecstasy, and "thou" as the divine Thou—God. Through modern translations, many great Sufi poets, such as Rumi, Hafiz (c. 1325–1390), and Jami (1414–1492), are gaining recognition.

There is a warmth about Sufism that appeals to the ordinary layperson, and some Sufi groups have served as fraternal societies, providing comfort to those in distress, helping the poor, and even burying the dead. Sufism's characteristic warmth and practicality helped Islam spread to countries far from its place of origin, such as Malaysia and Indonesia.

The Sufi connection with common people, however, has sometimes made the orthodox think of Sufism as a superstitious folk religion. Although mosques are plentiful and visible in the Islamic world, Sufi meeting places are hard to find, as are individuals who will actually admit to being Sufis. Luckily, however, Sufism has been buoyed in recent years by a growing appreciation for Sufi poetry and practice.

P E R S O N A L   E X P E R I E N C E

Ramadan in Morocco

During my first trip to Europe as a college student, I found myself spending a very cold February in "sunny" Spain. No one had told me that snow falls in Madrid. But there it was, pure, white, everywhere. As I trudged through Plaza Mayor one night, looking at my breath and feeling ice in my veins, I realized that if I were to survive, I had to go south—quickly.

I took a train from Madrid, then a ferryboat across to Morocco, and finally a bus inland. At first the land was sandy, dry, and flat, but soon the country-side grew greener, with small hills and low trees. I saw children watching over flocks of sheep, and donkeys pulling carts and carrying food on their backs. Animals seemed to be as much a part of everyday life there as cars are in Los Angeles. As I traveled south, Morocco appeared to be much like Spain, except that many of the men were dressed in long, hooded robes, and I could hear the call to prayer regularly during the day and early evening.

I reached Fez at the beginning of Ramadan. Old Fez is a traditional, Islamic-style city on a hill, brimming with mosques, shrines, and medersas (religious schools). Its streets, just wide enough for two people to pass, twisted and curved. Mules laden with saddlebags rushed past, their drivers yelling,

"*Balek!*"—"Watch out!" On each side of the narrow streets, tiny shops sold fruit, vegetables, sweets, spices, perfumes, robes, brass, and leather. All kinds of fruit were piled high; spices were arranged in neat pyramids of red, yellow, and orange; and sweet desserts made of honey and almonds were heaped in thick stacks. People were buying for the evening meal that would end the day's fasting, but I never saw anyone eat or drink during the daytime. In the evening, the recitation of the Qur'an could be heard loudly, coming from radios placed in shops and on windowsills.

Many shops sold spiral candles with paper decorations on them, meant as offerings at shrines. At a shop where I stopped to buy a candle, the old owner was reading a copy of the Qur'an. I was hesitant to disturb him, but then two young customers came and helped. They each bought a candle, too, then introduced themselves. Moulay and Noureddine were students in Casablanca and were in Fez on vacation. Moulay was Berber, a member of the native tribal people of Morocco, and his parents lived in the north, near Oujda. Noureddine was Arab, from Ouarzazate in the south. He told me proudly that his name (which he pronounced *nur-deen'*) means "light of religion." The two friends were making a pilgrimage together to the main religious sites of Fez, Meknes, and

The owner of this shop reads from the Qur'an as he awaits pilgrims who might buy his spiral candles. Note the black mark on his forehead, the result of repeatedly touching his forehead to the ground during prayer.

places in central Morocco. Soon their pilgrimage would end with a visit to the shrine of the saint after whom Moulay was named, in the hilltop town of Moulay-Idriss. They invited me to join them, and I accepted gladly.

All along the way we talked about religion—about my beliefs and theirs. They explained that their way of practicing Islam was not strict. They did not pray at all the times of daily prayer, and they did not keep all the customs. But, they told me, they prayed at the public prayer on Fridays, and they kept Ramadan. I could see that: they rose before dawn to eat and would not eat or drink again till after sunset. They kindly encouraged me to eat whenever I was hungry, thinking I must be weaker than they were. "You have no practice in fasting," Noureddine explained. They recommended, however, that during the day I not let others see me eat the bread and oranges or drink the water that I carried in my shoulder bag.

From our conversations, I discovered that Moulay and Noureddine were both interested in Sufism. Commenting on its teachings, Moulay said, "Allah is not something always clear and certain, like a tree or a mountain, that you only have to look at to see. Allah is a reality that you have to look for and

Deeper Insights

THE MEANING OF MUSLIM NAMES

Muslim names, mostly from Arabic, can sound exotic to some Western ears. But their meanings frequently involve everyday virtue and beauty. Many refer to religion, particularly by making reference to Allah or by recalling the names of Muhammad or of his wives, children, and companions. Some names are used for females, others for males, and some have both male and female forms (whose spellings may vary). Among the most common names are these:

Abdul: "servant [of God]"
Abdullah: "servant of Allah"
Afaf: "modesty"
A'ida: "returning"
A'isha: "generous" (name of a wife of Muhammad)
Amal: "hope"
Amin (m.), Aminah (f.): "faithful"
Barak (Barack): "blessing"
Hassan: "lovely"
Hussein (Husayn): "lovely"
Iman: "belief"

Jamal: "beauty"
Jamila: "beautiful"
Kareem (m.), Kareema (f.): "generous, noble"
Khalid: "eternal"
Latifah: "gentle"
Leena: "tender"
Mahmoud: "praised"
Mustafa: "chosen"
Noor: "light"
Nurdeen: "light of religion"
Rasheed (m.), Rasheeda (f.): "wise"
Saleem (m.), Saleema (f.): "safe, whole"
Shafiq: "compassionate"
Shakira: "grateful"
Shareef: "noble"
Tareef: "rare"
Waheed: "unequaled"
Zahir (m.), Zahira (f.): "shining"

discover for yourself. The word *Allah* is an invitation, like an invitation to a meeting or a party. You don't quite know what will happen until you go there yourself. I practice my religion to see what will happen. I think you have to do it in order to know it."

Noureddine pointed to some boys on the road who were riding bicycles. "Maybe it's like that," he said. "You don't know how to ride a bicycle until you do it. In fact, it looks a little crazy. It even looks impossible. But when you do it, it works, and you get where you need to go."

Our first vision of Moulay-Idriss was from a distance: a white town at the top of two steep hills. "They say it's shaped like a camel's back," said Noureddine. When we arrived, the town was mobbed with people. Luckily, we found a small place to stay and left our things there. We then walked down to the entrance to the shrine, the burial site of Moulay Idriss I (d. 791 CE), a descendant of Muhammad and an early Muslim ruler of Morocco. My friends bought colorful green candles, decorated with cut paper, and asked me to wait for them. They went up a long corridor and disappeared; a small sign high up on the wall said, "No entry for non-Mussulmans." I passed the time observing people's faces and their clothing. One thing that struck me was how differently some of the women were dressed: their faces were modestly veiled, almost to the point of being entirely covered, yet their gowns attracted one's attention because of their bright colors—purple, red, yellow, chartreuse.

When my friends returned, they took me up a seemingly endless flight of stairs to the top of the town. We looked down on square towers with roofs of green tile and across to the beautiful green mountains beyond. "That is the shrine down there," Moulay said, "but I'm sorry you cannot go inside." Noureddine smiled but looked serious. Then he had an idea. He asked me, "Wouldn't you like to become a Muslim, too?"

ISLAMIC LAW AND PHILOSOPHY

Islamic thought focuses on both practice and belief. It asks, How should I live my life according to God's will, and how am I to understand and relate to God? Over the first five hundred years of Islam, these questions were debated intensely, and some basic principles were acknowledged. Islam also recognized that there could be reasonable disagreement. Thus, various schools of opinion emerged.

Because the Qur'an does not give specific laws for every possible human situation, Muslims have found it necessary to discuss how to interpret the Qur'an. Muslims believe that the Qur'an offers principles for correct guidance in all of human life; but rules for specific instances have to be worked out by considering parallels and utilizing those basic principles.

The Qur'an is, of course, the primary authority. Also authoritative are the hadiths—remembrances of Muhammad's words and actions. The most important collection is that of al-Bukhari (died c. 870), which contains almost three thousand hadiths. The use of hadiths enlarged the body of material that could be drawn on for guidance, but it also created problems of its own. Disagreement about which hadiths were genuine prevented their universal acceptance. Also, even apparently worthy hadiths showed inconsistencies. Islam has a long history of scholarly debate. Over the centuries (from the eighth century on), four major schools of Islamic law have emerged in Sunni Islam and three schools in Shiite Islam, each school differing on what it has looked to as an authoritative guide for making judgments on particular cases: On what grounds may a wife request a divorce? Can a village without a mosque be taxed and forced to build one? How many witnesses are necessary to legitimize a marriage? and so on. In arriving at decisions, scholars have relied on a variety of things: the Qur'an (which has been interpreted both literally and symbolically), the hadiths, logic, precedents, analogy (*qiyas*), the consensus of early jurists, and the decisions of religious scholars.

Islamic Law and Legal Institutions

Islamic law, called **Sharia** (also spelled Shariah), is the entire body of laws that guides the believer in this life. The legal ideal of Islam is different from what is now considered the norm in many countries. Most modern industrialized countries expect laws to reflect a kind of civilized minimum, something that all citizens, of any background or belief, can be expected to accept and obey in their public life. Often these laws have a distant religious background or origin, but they are framed for very diverse populations and are deliberately secular in nature. In everyday life, we often hear a distinction made between church and state. In industrialized countries, the two realms—secular and religious—generally exist somewhat apart.

The traditional Islamic ideal, however, does not separate religious and secular spheres, and this ideal is the subject of intense argument in strongly Muslim countries today. In the traditional Islamic ideal, laws bring everyday life into ever-closer harmony with the regulations of the Qur'an and traditional teaching.

Traditional Islam is theocratic, seeking the "rule of God" in all aspects of everyday life, for in its view there is one God and one correct religion. Nature is orderly because it follows the laws of God spontaneously—for example, gravitation governs the movement of the planets and the change of tides. Similarly, in Islamic thought God presents human beings with laws of human order. There cannot be different sets of laws for different human beings; otherwise, chaos would ensue. The laws of God must be obeyed not only because they are his commands but also because they lead to human fulfillment.

Of course, this ideal of a single religion guiding an entire society has rarely been attained. Muhammad himself recognized that there must be exceptions. Although he demanded that people who followed tribal folk religion convert to Islam, he was more lenient toward Jews and Christians. In fact, he allowed Jews and Christians to continue their own laws and practices (although they were charged a special tax for this right). In Muhammad's eyes, Jews and Christians were "people of the book" and were thus considered as followers of the same general "religion of Abraham" as were Muslims—although living at a less perfect level.

Some governments, such as that of Iran since 1979, have imposed a theocratic rule. There and in a few other strongly Muslim countries, the rules of the Qur'an and the rulings of religious scholars have had great political power. Although Islam does not have an official clergy, it does have religious specialists and scholars (*ulama, mullahs*) who have various levels of influence, both religious and political.

Islamic Philosophy and Theology

Many profound questions emerged quite naturally as early thinkers began to consider the basic beliefs of Muhammad and of Islam. One of the first questions regarded intellectual investigation itself. Is a good Muslim allowed to question religious topics? Does the philosophical study of religion (*kalam*, "theology") hurt a person's spiritual life, or can it deepen it? Do faith and reason contradict each other, or can they coexist happily?

In theory, there is a distinction between philosophy and theology. Philosophy considers all questions by the light of reason alone, without making use of religious revelation. Theology, however, mixes philosophy and religion, for it uses philosophy to investigate religious doctrines. In reality, pure philosophy is rather difficult to find, for the religion of a surrounding culture will inevitably color both the questions and the methods of its philosophers. This happened frequently, as we will see, from the beginning of Islam.

Early thinkers posed important questions that had to be addressed. Some questions were simply intriguing, but others presented serious philosophical problems. For example, the Qur'an calls God both just and merciful. But how is it possible to be strictly just and also to be really merciful? Doesn't one virtue exclude the other? Or a second question: If God is truly all-powerful, how can a human being really be free to make a choice? Doesn't God make everything happen? And even when human beings think they are acting by their own choice, isn't God really doing the choosing? Or another question: If God is all-loving, why does he allow bad things to happen? Wouldn't an all-loving God prevent evil things from happening in the world? The list of many similar questions goes on.

Some philosophical questions arose early as a result of studying the Qur'an. Others, however, emerged as Islam encountered the philosophies and religions of its neighbors, such as when Greek philosophical works were first translated into Arabic and were then taught in the great schools of Baghdad, Córdoba, and Cairo. Aristotle, for example, taught that the universe was eternal. But didn't this conflict with the Qur'an's vision of God as creator of the universe? Further questions arose when Islam moved into India and had contact with a monistic Hindu spirituality. Certain schools of Hindu thought taught that everything, ultimately, was God. But didn't this conflict with the Muslim notion that Allah, as creator, is different from his creation?

In general, there have been two philosophical poles within Islam. The more liberal view values reason and maintains that everything can be examined intellectually. It argues that human beings are basically free and that reason is a God-given gift that illuminates and complements faith. The other, more conservative view is suspicious of reason, which it sometimes sees as an expression of false human pride. It therefore values intellectual submission, believing that ultimately neither God nor anything else can be explained fully by reason. It tends to see the entire universe, including human lives, as being strongly determined by God. Like a pendulum, the history of Islamic thought has swung back and forth between these two poles.

The value that Islam has placed on philosophical reasoning appears in the works of two Muslim thinkers who are considered prominent figures of world philosophy. They are Ibn-Sina (980–1037) and Ibn-Rushd (1126–1198), known in medieval European philosophy by their Latin names Avicenna and Averroës, respectively. Because of their interest in medicine and the natural sciences, as well as philosophy, they thought that using reason to explore nature would give insight into nature's Creator.

Perhaps the most influential philosophical formulations, however, were more conservative. They came from al-Ghazali (mentioned earlier) and his intellectual disciple al-Arabi (d. 1240). Both rejected rationalism. Defending the conservative approach, al-Ghazali wrote two influential books: *The Incoherence of the Philosophers* and *The Revival of the Religious Sciences*. In these books he showed the inconsistency of several philosophers who had based their thought on Aristotle's. He criticized philosophy for generating arguments and false pride, and he distanced himself from both rational theology and legalism. The elements that he considered to be the core of religion, instead, were direct religious experience and submission of the heart to God—ideals attainable by anyone, not just by philosophers.

Al-Arabi continued this line of thought, but, influenced also by Sufism, he moved even further in a mystical, monistic direction. For him, all apparently separate realities were images of God, and all activity was ultimately the activity of God.[35] Submission to God meant a lived awareness of God's active presence in all things.

This mosque displays the genius of Islamic architecture, which attempts to hint at heaven, even here on earth.

ISLAM AND THE ARTS

Islam has had a unique influence on the arts. Its prohibition of much figural art, its love of the chanted word, its weekly public worship, and its focus on the Qur'an have channeled the inspiration of its artists in intriguing directions and helped create works of great imagination.

Architecture

Perhaps the greatest art form of Islam is its architecture. When we think of Islam, we envision tall towers and immense domes. It takes only a few visits to Islamic destinations to sense the architectural genius of Islam, whose uniquely shaped spaces express beauty in what is vast and empty.

Islamic architecture expresses itself most importantly in the place of public prayer, the mosque (*masjid*, meaning a space for prostration). Because a mosque can be any building or room where Islamic prayer is offered, its design can be quite simple, as it is in villages or in cities where the Muslim population is small. Grand mosques, however, provide greater opportunity for artistic attention. Some of the finest examples are the Umayyad Mosque in Damascus, the Sultan Ahmet "Blue Mosque" in Istanbul, the former grand mosque of Córdoba, and the Hassan II Mosque of Casablanca.

Cairo's skyline provides multiple examples of Islamic architecture.

A mosque has at least one formal entry to the compound, where shoes are to be taken off and left outside. Because purification is necessary before prayer, there is at least one fountain inside the compound for washing one's hands, face, neck, and feet. There is a high pulpit indoors or outdoors for sermons—although as an act of humility the speaker does not stand at the very top. Worshipers stand and prostrate themselves in rows, facing the mihrab (the special marker that indicates the direction of Mecca). The floor is usually covered with rugs or mats. Frequently, there are covered porches for protection from the sun and rain. Other wings or buildings—used for schoolrooms and libraries—are often a part of the complex. Outdoors there is also usually a minaret—a tall tower, either round or square, from which people are called to prayer. Although only one minaret is needed, there are frequently two; in grand mosques there might be four or even six. Inside the minaret is a staircase, which leads up to a balcony near the top, from which the muezzin can chant his call.

Most styles of religious architecture in the world emphasize ornamentation, but the aesthetic principles of Islamic religious architecture are more austere. This simplicity enhances one's appreciation of space and balance, particularly in the mosque and its attendant structures.

The value of empty space is one of an art student's first lessons; the blank spaces in some paintings and drawings may at first seem to have no function, but the student learns that the empty space actually acts in harmony with whatever is depicted. The space gives rest to the eye and directs the viewer's focus. In art this necessary emptiness is called *negative space*. In architecture, negative space is the space above or beside or around a building. The building shapes the space within and without, and both the space and the building work together to balance each other. Large mosques especially

449

This Cairo dome was constructed of stone inlay and wood. Some art historians see Islam's fascination with complex designs as an outgrowth of the prohibition against the portrayal of persons in religious art.

demonstrate a skillful use of negative space, such as in the shaped space between a dome and a minaret.

Because many mosques, particularly in dry climates, have extensive open courtyards, the negative space of most importance is the sky. It is beautifully balanced and complemented by the columns, arches, and walkways below. Other types of mosques, particularly in wetter climates, are almost entirely enclosed, frequently covered with one or more domes. But even inside, a person can experience the beauty of negative space—especially in the large mosques of Turkey, which are primarily domed buildings. A vast dome, although it shelters one from the sky, is itself like the sky in its feeling of expansiveness. The internal and external shaping of space also helps one experience the divine, for in Islam space is an important symbol of God, invisible but present everywhere.

In Islamic architecture, balance is another important feature, especially as it relates to the use of color. Perhaps because Islam spread throughout hot, sunny regions, most of its architecture is white, to reflect the sunlight. White is balanced by black, particularly in the dark shadows that are created by windows and doors, covered porches, and colonnades. Sometimes, too, alternating lines of black and white are painted on walls for decorative effect.[36] This white-black contrast is a fundamental theme of much Islamic architecture. A second color scheme contrasts blue with gold, often in the form of ceramic tiles on domes, where the dome is covered in one color and its base in another. (Good examples are the golden Dome of the Rock in Jerusalem and the blue domes of Isfahan in Iran.) The blue can vary in shade from sea-blue to blue-green. The Islamic tendency toward a blue-green palette is suggested by the original meaning of the word *turquoise*, which in French means "Turkish."

Fine Art

To talk of "Islamic art" might seem a contradiction in terms, owing to the Muslim prohibition against making images of human beings or animals. Nonetheless, Islam has a rich tradition of pictorial art.

Paradise as a Theme in Art   One theme that seems to have inspired much Islamic art—in addition to architecture and garden design—is the theme of paradise. In the Qur'an and the Muslim imagination, paradise is quite concrete and sensuous. It is not just a heaven of diaphanous angels, singing hymns and resting on wispy clouds. Paradise is more like a fertile oasis or an enclosed garden. The Qur'an repeatedly says that paradise is "watered by running streams."[37] Wildflowers are at our feet, and we sit under date palms and other fruit trees, whose fruit is ready to be eaten.[38] In the afternoon, we feel cooling breezes. Paradise is safe, too. (Literally, the word *paradise*, from Middle Iranian, means "build around.") We can stay outdoors in this garden, enjoying nature without fear.

This image of paradise in Islamic art often appears in symbolic form in the prayer carpet. Although the prayer carpet is not usually recognized as religious art, it is to Islam what stained-glass windows are to Christianity. Both are objects of contemplation for people at prayer. Interestingly, both manifest the same fundamental color scheme—every shade of red and blue. A major difference between the stained-glass window and the prayer carpet is that the latter does not depict human images. Instead of portraying figures of saintly persons, prayer carpets often contain a symbolic image of the garden of paradise. At the center of the carpet might be a stylized fountain that sends water in straight lines to each of the four directions and then around the entire border, the four sides of the border representing the walls of the garden. The rest of the carpet might be filled with stylized flowers. To walk into a large mosque where immense carpets are laid out side by side, such as the Umayyad Mosque in Damascus, gives the feeling of entering a magical garden.

The paradise theme is carried over in Muslim architecture as well: slender pillars resemble the trunks of trees, and arches that come to a point suggest adjoining tree branches. Ceilings often suggest a night sky full of stars: blue ceramic tiles may form a backdrop for golden six-pointed stars, clustered in complex patterns. Or delicate wood and plaster stalactites hang from the ceiling, suggesting light coming from heaven. The paradise theme is sometimes evident in and around mosque buildings, shrines, palaces, and even homes. It may express itself in fountains and narrow canals, in a grove of orange trees, in a garden full of fragrant plants (such as rose and jasmine), or in a decorated porch from which one can enjoy the sights and sounds of the garden.

The Islamic love of the Qur'an often continues the theme of paradise. The words of the Qur'an are symbolically the sounds of heaven: they are the voice of God, heard not only by human beings but also by angels. In spoken and chanted form, they fill the air and remind us of God and paradise. In written form, they decorate the domes, doors, walls, and windows

The reflected window in the Hassan II Mosque of Casablanca shows how Islamic artists can create a paradise in the worshiper's imagination.

The Generalife gardens, constructed when Granada was the center of Islamic power in Spain, illustrate the Muslim ideal of paradise.

to remind us of the divine presence. The care and beauty that are lavished on handwritten copies of the Qur'an extend the sense of paradise: because the Qur'an is the book of God's speech, to open the Qur'an is to psychologically enter God's presence. Thus, beautiful writing has become an integral part of the Islamic art of creating paradise on earth.

Despite what has been said about the Islamic love of simplicity, Islamic art, particularly in manuscript writing and illustration, demonstrates an appreciation for ornamentation. Extremely fine, handwritten copies of the Qur'an feature pages surrounded by filigree. Similarly, geometrical designs on doors and walls create an effect of hallucinatory complication. Although Islamic ornamentation is complex, it is usually also subtle, allowing the eye to wander and inviting the mind to lose itself in the experience. Because many geometrical designs have no visual center, experiencing them can be like looking at stars or waves, inducing a gentle ecstasy.

Exceptions to the Prohibition against Image Making   The prohibition against image making has been widely observed in Islam, but there have been three important exceptions. One is the imagery surrounding Muhammad's Night Journey—his ascent to the highest heaven. As shown by many Muslim artists, Muhammad rises through the air on his human-headed horse Buraq. Both are surrounded by golden flames and by hovering angels. As a bow to the Muslim prohibition against image making, however, Muhammad's face often appears as a rather ghostly blank space.

The second exception to image making is a whole category of art—Persian miniatures. (This tradition was continued in Turkish and Indian Mughal art as well.) Influenced by artistic traditions from nearby India, the Persian court commissioned innumerable small paintings of its personages and its activities—rulers on horseback, picnicking courtiers, and lovers enjoying the afternoon in a garden pavilion. The topics are usually secular, but the treatment has that same hallucinatory quality—evoked by complex designs—that we see in Islamic mosaic, stucco, and woodwork. Thousands of tiny flowers seem to carpet the meadows, and tens of thousands of leaves cover the trees. The eye becomes lost in infinity.

The third exception to image making belongs to the realm of folk art. Pilgrims who return successfully from Mecca have a natural pride in their accomplishment, as have their families. Often they will make or commission a picture of their pilgrimage on the way to or from Mecca—nowadays looking happily out of an airplane. Sometimes this picture is even placed outside the house near the front door, where it cannot be missed.

Over the past century, the prohibition against making images has begun to break down. Statues are still not made, but photographs are common, often of religious leaders and family members. It is even possible nowadays to see carpets and wall hangings woven with recognizable human figures.

ISLAM AND THE MODERN WORLD

Modern life presents great challenges to traditional Islam. Industrial work schedules make daily prayer and other religious practices difficult; women are demanding total equality with men and complete independence; and individualism is weakening family ties and social responsibility. Islam is being pulled in many directions.

Islam and Contemporary Life

Soon after its beginnings, Islam became and remained a world power for about eight hundred years. During that period, Islamic universities—in Baghdad, Córdoba, and Cairo—were among the great centers of learning and scientific investigation in the world. Islamic cities were centers of civilized living. Islamic strength contrasted with the general weakness of western Europe: the Roman Empire had ceased to exist in the West by the late fifth century, not long before Muhammad was born. Ruling from Constantinople, the Byzantine emperors continued the Eastern Roman Empire in weakened form. Islam's last great military victory was the conquest of Constantinople, and thus of the Eastern Roman Empire, in 1453. Islam continued to spread and consolidate eastward, as far as Indonesia and the Philippines, but after that its expansion slowed.

Toward the end of the fifteenth century the pendulum of power swung in the opposite direction. While Islam became fairly settled in its territory, western Europe began to expand its control. Significant turning points were Columbus's journeys to the New World, beginning in 1492, and Vasco da Gama's journey around Africa and his arrival in India in 1498. These explorations changed the patterns of trade. Before then, trade was conducted primarily by land routes, which were frequently controlled by Muslim rulers. Now journeys could be made by ship, a form of travel that greatly enlarged the opportunity for travelers to influence others. These journeys were just the beginning of powerful waves of expansion by European traders, soldiers, political figures, and Christian missionaries. Coupled with circumnavigation were the growth of scientific understanding during the European Renaissance of the fifteenth and sixteenth centuries, the Enlightenment of the seventeenth and eighteenth centuries, and the development of technology during the Industrial Revolution of the eighteenth and nineteenth centuries. As Islamic and European cultures came into more frequent contact with each other, their differing values and social ideals led to conflict. Beginning in the twentieth century, the industrial world's growing dependence on oil—much of it from predominantly Islamic nations—has created a new shift in economic and cultural balance.

In the twenty-first century, Islamic women's attire—often assumed to be mainly dark robes—sometimes includes colorful headscarves. These women pause during a Sunday stroll in Istanbul.

Islam and the Roles of Women

Recent decades have seen increased focus on the roles of women in Islam. There are different ways to view women's roles in Islamic society. On one hand, traditional Islam protects women and emphasizes their important place in caring for home and family. On the other hand, women's work has been restricted to domestic settings, thus keeping them from reaching their full human potential. We should begin by trying to understand Muhammad's views, and then we can go on to examine the situation today.

Before the time of Muhammad, restrictions on females in Arabia were severe. Unwanted female babies could be buried alive or left to die. Women were often treated as property, being bought and sold, and men could take as many wives as they wished. Women often could not initiate divorce, and sometimes they had little right to own land or money. Seen against this background, some of Muhammad's views can seem quite liberal. For example, the Qur'an forbids infanticide. It gives women the right to initiate divorce. Women may own money and property. And religious duties are demanded of women and men alike. Thus it has been argued that Muhammad did a great deal to improve women's individual rights.

Today, however, what some see in Islam as protection of women, others see as repression. Women's attire is a good example. In Muhammad's day, women were required to dress modestly and in a way that protected them from any possible scrutiny from male visitors. But since that time, extreme forms of veiling have emerged in some countries, where women must be entirely covered when they are outside the home; even their hands are to be covered with gloves and their eyes with cloth mesh.

The meaning of the veil, however, is not always a conservative one. Although the wearing of a headscarf has long been imposed in Iran, head covering is not required in all Muslim countries. In fact, in some societies with more lenient dress customs, women are now adopting the veil, such as in Turkey, Egypt, and Malaysia; these women claim that covering one's head can be a liberal assertion of female power and personality. In western Europe, the optional wearing of the veil is strongly debated by legislators, who see secular-religious neutrality being questioned.

Related to clothing requirements, in some cultures women are not allowed to go outside their homes without a companion, and they may not travel abroad without male permission. Critics point out how limiting these and other restrictions are for women, making it difficult for some to go to school, participate in certain sports, or even seek various kinds of employment.

Women are rebelling, however. Some examples are quite newsworthy. In Saudi Arabia, where women generally have not been allowed to drive cars, some women have begun to drive in public demonstrations, demanding changes in the law—which will certainly come. Women have also been denied the right to vote in Saudi Arabia, but this has been challenged and will soon change.

Another potential area of reform is the mosque. Traditionally, women have been limited to praying at home or in the mosque in a special area reserved for women. Only men have led public prayer. But these restrictive practices are now being questioned. In several countries, women have joined men in the main prayer area of mosques, and a few have led public prayers.

Some of the influences behind women's questioning of Islam are images and ideas presented via film, television, travel, international education, and the Internet. Most popular films and television programs, for example, are not produced in predominantly Muslim countries. Instead, they come from North America, South America, Europe, and China, and they depict cultures in which women drive, dress according to their own personal preference, exercise political power, and have control over money and property.

In addition, tourism and employment opportunities bring non-Muslims, along with their non-Muslim practices and values, into traditionally Muslim societies. For example, the demand that women not drive in Saudi Arabia has fueled the need for personal drivers. There are now more than seven million foreigners living in Saudi Arabia, many of them working as drivers and domestics. Dubai and Abu Dhabi also have attracted large populations of foreigners for business employment.

Although the Internet, entertainment industry, tourism, education, and migrant employment serve as challenges to traditional Muslim societies, they also provide sources for new ideas and a means of global communication. While some Muslim people seem to be presenting an assertive, conservative face, others appear to be open to absorbing ideas from other cultures. Both non-Muslims and Muslims will be affected by this intercultural exchange.

The Challenge of Secularism

The most difficult of the Western models for Islam to accept is secularism. The word *secularism* comes from a Latin word for "world" (*saeculum*) and implies a focus on this world, without reference to values or entities beyond this world. Secularism seeks to create political institutions that are independent of any established religion.

Secularism is not necessarily antireligious. In its political form, it actually developed in part for religious reasons—to avoid religious fights and to enable all religions to flourish. The point of the secular model was not to destroy religion but to allow all religions to exist without hindrance from any one religion or from government. But secularism is based on a governmental system of laws, courts, and legislatures that operate independently from any religion. That ideal of independence from religion has caused dismay in many Islamic countries.

Science has also promoted secularism. Although investigators such as Isaac Newton (1642–1727) once looked into the properties of light in order to better understand the nature of God, scientists nowadays rarely carry on their work in this spirit. Science pursued for its own sake has led to a view of the universe that does not include God, as either its creator or its moral guide. In this worldview, God is not necessarily excluded but is simply not mentioned. (To appreciate this fact, look for the word *God* in a textbook on biology, chemistry, or physics.) But Islamic tradition holds that to view the universe apart from God is to live without God.

A Range of Solutions

One of the great challenges for Islam, therefore, has been to adopt from the West what is obviously useful, to avoid what is dangerous, and to continue holding on to what it thinks valuable. There are a variety of intriguing solutions to this challenge—a few are extreme responses, but the majority are attempts at compromise. Yet change can happen quickly.

Turkey arrived at the most clearly secular solution. For centuries, Islam had a caliph, God's representative on earth, who united in himself religious and political power. As we discussed earlier in the chapter, the last caliphate existed for centuries in Istanbul. But in 1924, trying to build a modern country, Kemal Atatürk (1881–1938) dissolved the caliphate and created a new secular nation, modeled after the European pattern. He replaced the Arabic alphabet with the Roman alphabet for writing Turkish; he created a legal system independent of Muslim religious authorities; and he set up a democratic form of government that allowed women to vote. In his desire to Europeanize, he even outlawed men's wearing the fez (a traditional round hat) and women's wearing the veil, and he encouraged European styles of clothing. Turkey has generally held onto its secular vision, which has especially been promoted by the military. But this secular approach is now being questioned and changed as conservative politicians come into power.

At the other end of the spectrum is Saudi Arabia. When Saudi Arabia was declared an independent nation in 1932, the Qur'an was named the constitution of the country and the strict Wahhabi interpretation of Islam became dominant. There are no movie theaters, and alcohol is forbidden. Women must be covered by the cloaklike *abaya* in public, and they go to their own schools, separated from men. Religious police (*mutawa*) ensure conformity to these rules. Because of Saudi Arabia's influence and wealth, the Wahhabi interpretation of Islam is spreading in many countries, particularly in those where Saudi citizens and government agencies finance religious schools.

Iran, because it no longer has a king (shah), is even more clearly a theocracy. It has been influential in the Muslim world as a modern attempt to create an Islamic state. The situation was once quite different. For decades, Iran seemed to be moving inexorably toward westernization. All this ended when an exiled mullah, the Ayatollah Khomeini, returned to Iran in 1979 and Shah Mohammad Reza Pahlavi, in turn, went into exile. Iran rapidly became a Muslim theocracy. A new constitution was written by the religious authorities, who also held a majority of the seats in the legislature. Khomeini had a new post created for himself as "legal guide," from which he could oversee and validate all legal and political developments. Mosques became centers of civil as well as religious activity; women were forced to veil themselves in public; and alcohol was strictly forbidden. Iran thus became a fully Muslim state.

Most countries that are primarily Muslim, however, lie uncomfortably between the two poles of secular government and theocracy. Increasingly, conservative Islamic groups nudge them in the direction of becoming Islamic states. Liberal movements in Islam are accused of giving in too much to modern secular thought and abandoning Islam. Consequently, countermovements, sometimes violent, have arisen; they attempt to create a path that makes Islam relevant and active in the modern world.

Egypt is typical of those countries that have to work out a compromise, partly out of necessity. At least 10 percent of its population is Coptic Christian, and Jews and Greeks living primarily in Alexandria play an important role in Egyptian shipping and business. Moreover, because Egypt is dependent on foreign tourism for its economic survival, it has at least a limited acceptance of alcohol in tourist hotels. The Egyptian government has generally recognized that solely Islamic laws would not work well for everyone. However, fundamentalist groups (such as the Muslim Brotherhood) offer a different vision—of an Egyptian Islamic state, governed by Sharia. Because they believe that tourism brings influences that are considered corrupting, these groups tolerate or even sponsor attacks of the sort that have sometimes been made on tourist groups.

In many countries the debate is becoming broader and the volume is rising. In India, conflict between Muslims and Hindus has broken out frequently, particularly over the status of Kashmir (which is predominantly Muslim but ruled by India) and about mistreatment of each group by the other. The destruction of a mosque at Ayodhya by Hindus in 1992 became a flashpoint. Mob violence at the time caused the death of about two thousand people, and another thousand people were killed in 2002.

In Pakistan, the government tries to find a balance between official tolerance of all religious groups and support for Qur'anic schools, some of which preach extreme fundamentalism. The population of Pakistan is both Sunni (77 percent) and Shiite (20 percent), and there is a small but important minority of Christians, Hindus, and Parsees (Zoroastrians). Unfortunately, attacks on mosques and churches are increasing.

In Indonesia the fundamentalist view is in conflict with the Western influence that comes from tourism and business. (Bombings at a bar in Bali in 2002 and a hotel in Jakarta in 2003 were violent responses.) It is also in conflict with the traditional Indonesian form of Islam that blends Islam with Hinduism and native religions. Reformers (sometimes called *santri*) oppose the traditional practitioners (*abangan*), and they criticize traditional Indonesian practice as impure. Some of this reformism is also caused by the fact that great masses of people can now make the pilgrimage to Mecca; they learn there that their own form of Islam is considered to be imperfect.

The conflict between two visions—of a fairly secular government and of an Islamic state—has been clearest in Afghanistan. The country was taken over in 1996 by the puritanical Taliban. The core of their movement was made up of students from Deobandi schools in Pakistan. (*Taliban* literally means "seekers of truth"—religious students—but we should note that the Taliban's views are even stricter than those of the founders of the Deobandi school itself.) The goal of the Taliban is to create the world's purest Islamic state, and they follow their own strict interpretation of the Qur'an. Taliban regulations about gender forbid men to cut their beards; women are restricted solely to domestic roles. When the Taliban took control in Afghanistan in 1996, women were no longer allowed to work outside the home, they had to be totally covered when in public, and when away from home they were to be accompanied by a male relative.[39] The Taliban forbade all non-religious music. Films, television, e-mail, and the Internet were banned. Public executions and amputations were performed in soccer stadiums. The Taliban were subsequently ousted from power by Western forces in 2001, but the movement eventually regrouped and remains active in many parts of the country.

Other countries that are being pressed by mostly conservative Muslim groups are the Philippines, China, and Malaysia. In the Philippines, Muslim groups are fighting for the independence of Mindanao, the large southern island, which is home to almost five million Muslims. In China, the majority of its twenty million Muslims live in the western province of Xinjiang; and of the more than thirty thousand mosques of China, more than two-thirds are in that province. On one hand, Islam has gained official respect as a legal religion of China, and Muslims have been granted legal rights to practice their religion. (For example, time off to make the pilgrimage to Mecca is coordinated with work schedules.) On the other hand, the Chinese government is vigilant against Islamic independence movements—particularly after protests and bombings in Urumqi between 1996 and 1997. There are also claims that non-Muslim Han Chinese are being encouraged to relocate in the western part of the country in order to dilute the power of the Muslim population there. At one time constituting only 4 percent of the population in Xinjiang, non-Muslim Han Chinese now make up 50 to 60 percent of its people. Elsewhere throughout the country, the Chinese government tightly controls mosques and Islamic religious training.

Malaysia is perhaps the most successful of all predominantly Muslim countries in integrating Islam with the modern industrial world. Malaysia is now the tenth-largest trading nation in the world, and its national income has gone up every year for the past thirty years.[40] Its educational system is excellent, corruption has been controlled, private property is protected by law, and the courts are generally trusted. About a quarter of the population is Chinese and 8 percent is Indian, and the government works actively to minimize racial and religious conflict. Emphasis is placed on passages from the Qur'an that support private property, women's rights, and tolerance. There is also a system of affirmative action in place for Malays. However, religious groups are gaining success in promoting the wearing of the headscarf by Muslim women, the keeping of the fast during Ramadan, and other Islamic practices.

Conflict in Religion

SUNNI VERSUS SHIITE: WHY THE CONFLICT?

Sunnis and Shiites, the two dominant branches of Islam, share the Qur'an, the Five Pillars of Islam, and many articles of faith. Yet, as we know from contemporary news reports, conflict between the two groups is common.

The division arose when Sunni forces killed Hussein, Muhammad's grandson. Shiites viewed Hussein's assassination as the denial of his rightful place as successor to Muhammad, and they saw his death as the heroic death of a martyr. As a result, veneration of Hussein and of his father Ali has become a major characteristic of Shiite practice.

Although Shiites and Sunnis share many essential elements of faith, over the centuries some of their beliefs and practices have diverged. For example, Shiites and Sunnis differ not only in their interpretation of many passages of the Qur'an but also over which sayings of Muhammad (hadiths) are authoritative. There are also major differences in ritual. Shiites normally combine some of the daily prayers, praying three times a day rather than the five times a day typical of Sunni Muslims. When engaged in ritual prayer, Shiites lower their foreheads to a small prayer stone on the floor and hold their arms at their sides, rather than crossing them in front of the body, as do Sunnis. More significantly, Shiite prayer explicitly invokes the figure of Ali. Also, Sunni and Shiite periods of prayer and fasting may begin and end at different times. The many differences have led the two groups to worship at different mosques. (Shiite places of prayer are often called *husseiniyahs* rather than mosques.)

The two branches differ over important religious laws, particularly those regarding marriage and inheritance. Smaller differences abound as well. Shiites often have pictures of Hussein in their cars and homes, and they regularly name their children after Ali, Hassan, and Hussein.

Distinctive Shiite rites appear at New Year's, when Shiites ritually mourn for Hussein, whose death occurred during the first lunar month of the Muslim calendar (Muharram). This mourning period (Ashura) reaches its peak on the tenth day of the new year, when men perform public reenactments of the Battle of Karbala. Dressed in black, with red and green headbands, devotees walk in procession, beating their chests. Others go shirtless, flogging themselves with chains and metal whips and cutting themselves with swords and knives to draw blood. In this way, they recall and imitate Hussein's tragic death.

Veneration of Ali and his sons, Hassan and Hussein, thus marks Shiite Islam. (A common Shiite saying, for example, is "God, Muhammad, Ali.") Some Shiites even hold that Ali was sinless. Sunnis, however, see this veneration as being too close to worship of a mere human being. Thus Sunnis prohibit veneration of Ali or of his sons. Because Sunnis so emphasize the absolute uniqueness of God (*tawhid*) alone, they see Shiites as dangerous heretics. By opposing them, Sunnis seek to assert pure Islamic belief in the one God.

Islam in the West and Beyond

Islam has begun to spread to the West through immigration and conversion. It has spread to England, Canada, and Australia through emigration from some former British colonies, particularly Pakistan and India; and many French cities have large populations of emigrants from Algeria. Large cities in North America have also attracted Muslim emigrants, particularly from Iran, Lebanon, and Africa; for example, there are now more than 300,000 Muslim émigrés from Iran living in Los Angeles. Islam is also spreading in Chicago and Detroit, cities with special appeal to minorities.

Because of its simplicity and strong moral guidance, Islam has been successful in attracting converts in places far away from traditionally Muslim

461

Wherever there were trade routes in Africa and Asia, Islam has left its mark. This mosque in Xi'an, China, is still in use today.

regions. For example, Koreans who worked in the oil fields of Saudi Arabia have taken Islam back to South Korea. It is also growing strongly in sub-Saharan Africa, where it is attractive to some converts because it is a way of expressing a deliberate rejection of Christianity, which many people associate with European exploitation. Islam is also attractive in sub-Saharan Africa because of its acceptance of the traditional practice of polygamy.

Some relatively new forms of Islam have emerged that are not as inclusive as orthodox Islam, and their relation to mainstream Islam has occasionally been questioned. The movement known at first as the Nation of Islam, for example, was begun as an Islamic religious movement meant exclusively for African Americans. Its founders were Wali Farrad Muhammad (W. D. Fard, born c. 1877; he mysteriously disappeared in 1934) and his successor Elijah Muhammad (Elijah Poole, 1897–1975), who set up the first centers of worship in Detroit and Chicago. The Nation of Islam, whose members are known as Black Muslims, attempted to bring pride to African Americans by instilling the virtues of thrift, hard work, education, and self-defense. It created an organization for young men, called the Fruit of Islam, and one for young women, called Muslim Girls Training.

The Nation of Islam's original vision was anti-white, but this emphasis has softened due to the preaching of one of its most important members, Malcolm X. Under Wallace Deen Muhammad (1933–2008), the son of Elijah Muhammad, the Nation of Islam renounced its purely racial basis, changed its name to the American Muslim Mission, and worked to integrate itself into mainstream Sunni Islam.

A follower of the early views of Malcolm X, Louis Farrakhan (b. 1933) has attempted a revival of the Nation of Islam, particularly through preaching the values of hard work and social responsibility. Marches organized by him and his followers in Washington have been successful ways to generate self-pride and political activism among African Americans.

It is hard to predict the development of Islam in the future. One possibility, encouraged by liberals, involves the gradual emergence of modern democratic states, with elections, written constitutions, and a guarantee of individual rights.

At the other end of the spectrum are those who would like to spread a very conservative vision of Islam. Some of these voices seek to install a single caliph once again all over Islam. Best known for its conservatism is al-Qaida (also spelled al-Qaeda, meaning "base" or "foundation" in Arabic.) Begun in the late

Contemporary Issues

ISLAMIC ECOLOGY

Islam began in a desert region, where water is highly prized. We see the high value given to water in the Qur'an. Paradise, which is frequently spoken of, is described as a garden full of flowing water. Islamic religious practice also uses water in several ways. A ritual washing is necessary before daily prayer. And when pilgrims visit Mecca, they expect to drink from the Well of Zamzam in the Grand Mosque area.

Traditional teachings say that people should share water and not waste it, and that people have a right to the water they need.[41] The Qur'an contains many principles that fit in well with this notion. One of the most important is the rejection of waste: "Allah loves not the wasters."[42] This Qur'anic statement applies not just to water but also to food, trees, and animals.

With the assistance of several secular organizations, Islamic leaders have begun to identify twenty-first-century goals. Some goals are quite visionary, including the ideal of publishing the Qur'an only on recyclable paper—creating so-called green Qur'ans. Additional goals are the establishment of a television channel dedicated to teaching conservation; the creation of model environmental cities, Medinah being the first; and the establishment of an international prize for environmental work. And there is one last goal: making the pilgrimage to Mecca truly an environmental model.

1980s, it grew into an international movement that encouraged anti-Western activity in many regions. Whether it is carefully structured or loosely organized is a matter of debate. The death of its founder, Osama bin Laden (1957–2011), weakened it, but its adaptability allows it to take new shape in many countries.

Conservative Islamic groups are becoming increasingly influential in the policy making of their governments. Because the Qur'an contains a great many specific laws about such things as property rights, marriage, divorce, and sanctions for crimes, some Islamic groups wish to replace the laws of their country with Qur'anic laws (Sharia). Saudi Arabia has followed Sharia since its beginnings in 1932, and the establishment of a Muslim theocracy in Iran in 1979 has encouraged people to seek the introduction of Sharia elsewhere—particularly in Algeria, Egypt, Sudan, Nigeria, and Pakistan. Increasingly we will see a struggle between those who wish to have a secular system of laws, modeled at least to some extent on Western practice, and those who wish to follow Sharia instead.

This struggle is actually part of a larger struggle between fairly different cultures, and conflict perhaps will be inevitable. As we have already seen, Islam has several important areas in which it differs strongly from mainstream European and American culture. Public prayer must be performed on Friday, which is a workday in Western countries. Interest on loans is forbidden—a demand that opposes a cornerstone of Western business practice. Wine (as well as other alcohol) is forbidden; whereas in traditional Western cuisines wine or beer plays an important role. Meat eaten by Muslims must be *halal* (slaughtered according to religious rules). Gambling is forbidden.

An intractable problem that adds fuel to the conflict is resentment within the Muslim world over the Palestinian issue. Muslims are distressed by the ever-increasing number of Palestinians living in poverty, the land that Palestinians lost when Israel was created in 1948, Israeli control of the West Bank, and the lack of a Palestinian state. There can probably be no peace until the Palestinian issue is resolved. Resentment has led to regular clashes

A worshiper prays in the mosque of the Islamic Center in Washington, DC.

and bombings, both in Israel and beyond, and those countries that are perceived as supporting Israel have become targets.

The religious and cultural conflict is further exacerbated by the fact that Islam is often embraced for political reasons. We must recall that virtually all Muslim regions were once colonized by European powers. Colonization began when the British began to take over India in the eighteenth century and Napoleon invaded Egypt (1798). During the nineteenth and twentieth centuries, France colonized Morocco, Algeria, Tunisia, Lebanon, and Syria. At the same time, England colonized Libya, Egypt, Jordan, India, and Malaysia; and the Dutch took Indonesia. Muslims in once-colonized countries will quite naturally utilize Islam to emphasize their own national identity.

Yet this conflict is no longer a matter of enemies looking at each other from opposite, distant trenches. Islam is already a major religion in Europe and North America. At least five million Muslims now live in France, making up one-tenth of the population, and France has at least 1,500 mosques. It is estimated that by the end of this century, Muslims will make up one-third of the French population. In England there are perhaps two million Muslims today, with about 600 mosques. A large minority of Germans, whose parents came from Turkey, are Muslim. In the United States, the size of the Muslim population is uncertain but is estimated to be at least five million. That population will be increasingly influential.

Approaches to reducing conflict vary. In England, the emphasis is on accepting differences as legitimate forms of multiculturalism. In France, the official approach has been to maintain a secular ideal and force people to assimilate to that (one topic of debate concerns the wearing of the headscarf by girls in public schools). The approach in North America, though less clearly formulated, seems to be closer to the British model.

Conflict in Religion

JIHAD AND THE MODERN WORLD

The word **jihad** in Arabic means "strive" or "struggle." Two types of jihad are called for in Islam. The first is individual; it involves the personal daily struggle to live virtuously. The second is public; it is the attempt to establish in all of society the Islamic ideals of truth, justice, and morality. When the word *jihad* is used, the second meaning is the more common, but we should also be aware of the first meaning. Jihad, because of its importance, has sometimes been called "the sixth pillar of Islam."

Believers in Islam generally agree about their obligation to spread the Muslim view of justice and truth. However, Muslims disagree on exactly which elements to emphasize and where and how to spread their faith. Disagreement particularly exists around the use of force. Muhammad was a fighter and at times played the role of a military general. He endorsed the use of force when he thought it necessary. We do not have to read far in the Qur'an to realize that it urges believers to fight for their beliefs. "Fighting is obligatory for you, much as you dislike it"[43] and "Fight for the cause of God and bear in mind that God hears all and knows all."[44] Yet we also find passages in the Qur'an that command tolerance of other religions, such as this famous passage: "There shall be no compulsion in religion."[45]

Clearly, the general principles that guide Islamic life already present a way of living (Sharia) that is quite different from the ordinary secular life of non-Muslim societies. A further difficulty arises because the Qur'an presents a rather detailed system of punishment and legal practice (*hudud*) that differs from much contemporary legal practice. For example, adultery is considered a serious public offense, to be punished by public whipping; and robbers are to be punished by the amputation of limbs. Of course, many devout Muslims do not want the laws of Sharia and hudud to be imposed on their societies; however, conservative Muslim groups in some countries, as mentioned earlier, are working toward just such a goal. Some believers even approve violent means to achieve their traditionalist agendas. (For example, there have been explosions in Indonesian markets where pork was being sold; barbers have been killed in Pakistan for removing men's beards; and some teachers in Afghanistan who have taught female students have been killed. These are, however, exceptional cases.)

Of the world's more than one billion Muslims, most are moderate. They recognize that in a multicultural world, tolerance of all religions is necessary. Many Islamic rulers are now trying to create policies that retain Muslim ideals and at the same time teach tolerance. Saudi Arabia has begun to sponsor conferences that explore ways to encourage moderation and to discourage extremism. But can the devout Muslim accept the moral and religious differences in the modern world yet still be faithful to the ideals of Sharia and jihad? This is the challenge that Islam, one of the world's largest religions and social forces, is facing today.

Adding to the complexity is an uncertainty: the role that popular culture will play in the cultural and religious mix. Popular culture is spreading everywhere. There have been attempts to shut it out, of course. Countries that have tried hardest include Saudi Arabia, Iran, and Afghanistan. Muslims in Europe and North America, of course, are inundated with popular culture. It is already changing the way young people act, dress, and entertain themselves. Those in the entertainment industry may ultimately have the greatest influence on the future of Islam.

The most recent case of conflict is perplexing. The Arab Spring, so named because it flowered in the early part of 2011, would seem to be a liberal upsurge, because it has ended the control of dictators in several countries, including Libya and Egypt. At the same time, it has brought conservative elements to the fore—groups, for example, that seek to overturn laws that have empowered women to vote, own property, institute divorce, and have custody of their children. The Arab Spring is raising many questions—about democracy, political control, women's rights, and the treatment of religious minorities. How it will end is unclear.

Some people focus on the differences between traditional Islamic culture and the dominant cultures of Europe and North America. They fear the conflicts that will necessarily arise. Yet religions show a strong tendency not only to change over time, but also to change radically when they enter new cultures. Those who are fearful about the ability of Islamic and Western cultures to mix should reflect on the religious blending that has already occurred since the Middle Ages. Scholastic philosophy owes its spread to the fact that many of Aristotle's great works were first translated into Arabic and then later into Latin. Gothic architectural style is thought to have originated in the Muslim world, and Western mathematics, chemistry, and astronomy were all enriched by Muslim thinkers. We get a sense of the contributions of the Islamic world to many areas of our Western world when we consider some of the words that have come into English from or through Arabic. A good number of English words that begin with *al* come from Arabic (*al* means "the"): *alcove*, *alchemy*, and (ironically) *alcohol*. We might also note the number of words used in science. For example, the words *algebra*, *algorithm*, *nadir*, and *zenith* all have their origins in Arabic. But we also find Arabic origins in many names for foods: *orange*, *lemon*, *lime*, *sugar*, *sherbet*, *syrup*, and *coffee*. Other words with Arabic origins refer to objects that have added, in their own way, to human life: *lute*, *lacquer*, *mattress*, and *magazine*. The West has been greatly enriched by Muslim cultures.

These examples illustrate how enriching the exchange of cultural ideas can be. Yet there are elements of Western culture that orthodox Islamic societies will wish to avoid: alcohol abuse, gambling, high divorce rates, and urban violence. There will be regular debate about the roles and dress of women. And Muslim nations will continue to grapple with how much traditional Islamic law can be imposed on modern society. Particularly under pressure from conservative movements, Islamic countries will do what they can to oppose what they see as dangerous elements. In the long run, however, we should expect them to maintain long-standing practices—regular prayer, charity, the Ramadan fast, pilgrimage to Mecca, and the ideals of generosity and justice.

Reading BEAUTY LEADS TO GOD

The Turkish writer Fazil bin Tahir Enderuni (1759–1811) became famous for his poetry. Everything that is beautiful, he taught, brings an experience of the divine.

Beauty, wherever it is to be seen, whether in humanity or in the vegetable or mineral world, is God's revelation of Himself; He is the all-beautiful, those objects in which we perceive beauty being, as it were, so many mirrors in each of which some fraction of His essential self is revealed. By virtue of its Divine origin, the beauty thus perceived exercises a subtle influence over the beholder, waking in him the sense of love, whereby he is at last enabled to enter into communion with God himself. Thus God is the ultimate object of every lover's passion. . . .

So Love is the guide to the World Above, the stair leading up to the portal of Heaven; through the fire of Love iron is transmuted into gold, and the dark clay into a shining gem. Love it is that makes the heedless wise, and changes the ignorant into an adept of the Divine mysteries; Love is the unveiler of the Truth, the hidden way into the Sanctuary of God.[46]

TEST YOURSELF

1. *Islam* literally means "_____."
   a. sacred
   b. holy
   c. enlightened
   d. submission

2. Muslims refer to God as _____. The word is a contraction of two Arabic words that mean "the" and "God."
   a. Elohim
   b. Salam
   c. Allah
   d. El Shaddai

3. The _____ is the single sentence, when recited with belief, that makes a person a Muslim.
   a. Salat
   b. Shahadah
   c. Ramadan
   d. Hajj

4. Fasting is thought to be an important bond that unites Muslims during the period of shared fasting known as _____.
   a. Salat
   b. Shahadah
   c. Ramadan
   d. Hajj

5. All Muslims, unless prevented by poverty or sickness, are expected to visit Mecca at least once in their lifetime in the religious journey (pilgrimage) known as _____.
   a. Salat
   b. Shahadah
   c. Ramadan
   d. Hajj

6. The name *Qur'an* means "_____."
   a. successor
   b. recitation
   c. the book
   d. the writings

7. _____ was the father of Muhammad's youngest wife and was recognized as the first Caliph.
   a. Abu Bakr
   b. Umar
   c. Ali
   d. Uthman

8. _____ derive their name from an Arabic word that means "faction" and are the group that followed Ali.
   a. Sunnis
   b. Shiites
   c. Sufis
   d. Zaydis

9. _____ take their name from the Arabic word for "tradition," referring back to the entire body of traditional teachings that are based on the life and teachings of Muhammad, as given in the Qur'an and the authoritative hadiths.
   a. Sunnis
   b. Shiites
   c. Sufis
   d. Zaydis

10. Islamic law, called _____, is the entire body of laws that guides the believer in this life.
    a. Sharia
    b. Decalogue
    c. Faqir
    d. Dhikr

11. "Although Islam is similar in many ways to Judaism and Christianity, its greatest difference from these religions is _____." What word or phrase would you use to fill in the blank? Explain your answer using information from the text.

12. Imagine you are writing a research paper about the relationship between Islamic architecture and Islamic understandings of God. Choose a one-sentence thesis statement that you might use to express your paper's main argument about this relationship. Why would you choose this statement?

RESOURCES

Books

al-Arabi, Ibn. *101 Diamonds from the Oral Tradition of the Glorious Messenger Muhammad*. New York: Pir Press, 2002. A modern version of Ibn al-Arabi's collection of oral traditions (hadiths), which illuminate the wisdom of Islam.

Armstrong, Karen. *Islam: A Short History*. Rev. ed. New York: Modern Library, 2001. A popular historical survey of the growth and spread of Islam.

Aslan, Reza. *No God but God: The Origins, Evolution, and Future of Islam*. New York: Random House, 2006. A chronicle of the growth of Islam, from its origins in Muhammad's community up to the present conflict between modernizers and fundamentalists.

Dirks, Debra L., and Stephanie Parlove, eds. *Islam Our Choice: Portraits of Modern American Muslim Women*. Brattleboro, VT: Amana, 2003. The personal accounts of six American women who converted to Islam.

Esposito, John. *Who Speaks for Islam?* New York: Gallup Press, 2008. An exploration of the thought of Muslims throughout the world, based on interviews made in thirty-five countries.

Idliby, Ranya, Suzanne Oliver, and Priscilla Warner. *The Faith Club: A Muslim, a Christian, a Jew—Three Women Search for Understanding*. New York: Free Press, 2007. Three American women of different faiths explore the meaning of their beliefs.

Lewis, Bernard. *The Crisis of Islam*. New York: Modern Library, 2003. A review of Islamic history, with the conclusion that Islamic countries need to embrace the future.

Nasr, Seyyed Hossein. *The Garden of Truth: The Vision and Promise of Sufism, Islam's Mystical Tradition*. New York: HarperOne, 2008. A concise overview of Sufism, the mystical branch of Islam, including a detailed history of the movement and an examination of its various orders.

Ramadan, Tariq. *Western Muslims and the Future of Islam*. New York: Oxford University Press, 2003. An argument that Islam and Western values are compatible.

Film/TV

Expressing the Inexpressible: Shirin Neshat. (Films Media Group.) A documentary about the many dimensions of Islamic women's experiences.

Hajj: The Pilgrimage. (Films Media Group.) A documentary about the events performed during the pilgrimage to Mecca.

Inside Mecca. (Director Anisa Mehdi; National Geographic.) A documentary that follows the stories of three different people—a Muslim American professor, a South African journalist, and an Indonesian businessman—as they make a pilgrimage to Mecca.

Islam: Empire of Faith. (PBS.) A three-part documentary that explores a thousand years of Islamic history, from the prophet Muhammad to the height of the Ottoman Empire under Suleyman the Magnificent.

Islam in America. (Films Media Group.) Interviews with Muslims living in a post-9/11 America.

Looking for Comedy in the Muslim World. (Director Albert Brooks; Warner.) A film that explores Albert Brooks's attempts to determine what makes Indian and Pakistani Muslims laugh.

Malcom X. (Director Spike Lee; Warner Brothers.) A film about the life of Malcolm X, including his pilgrimage to Mecca.

The Message. (Director Moustapha Akkad; Anchor Bay.) An epic film about the time of Muhammad.

Muhammad: Legacy of a Prophet. (Directors Omar al-Qattan and Michael Schwarz; Unity Productions Foundation.) A documentary that recounts the story of Muhammad and explores the significance of the prophet's life and teachings.

The White Balloon. (Director Jafar Panahi; Evergreen Entertainment.) The adventures of a Muslim girl in Tehran on Iranian New Year's Day.

Music/Audio

Islamic Liturgy. (Smithsonian Folkways.) The Islamic call to prayer and Qur'anic odes and litany.

The Last Prophet. (Real World.) Devotional hymns, sung by the world-renowned Pakistani qawwali singer Nusrat Fateh Ali Khan.

The Music of Islam. (Celestial Harmonies.) A comprehensive seventeen-disc set of Islamic music from around the world, including Qur'anic recitations, Sufi qawwali, the music of whirling dervishes, and songs from many Muslim countries.

Sufi Ceremony. (Smithsonian Folkways.) A recording of the Sufi Rifai ceremony honoring the Sufi saint Abdul Hadir Beker.

Sufi Chants From Cairo. (Institute du Monde Afrique.) A collection of Egyptian Sufi prayers.

Zain, Maher. *Thank You Allah.* (London: Awakening Records, 2010.) Modern songs by a Swedish Muslim.

Internet

Compendium of Muslim Texts: http://www.msawest. net/islam/. An online database of Islamic texts in English, maintained by MSA West, an organization of Muslim Student Associations representing campuses across the West Coast.

Islamic Arts and Architecture: http://www.islamicart. com/. A Web site whose mission is to promote the awareness of Islamic arts as a discipline of humanistic study.

IslamiCity.com: http://www.islamicity.com/. A leading online source of Islamic information.

KEY TERMS

caliph (kay'-lif): (Arabic: *khalifa*) "successor"; a religious and political leader.

dhikr (tik'-ur): A devotional remembrance of Allah through the recitation of his ninety-nine names and other devotional practices.

fana (fah-nah'): "Extinction"; the sense of loss of self in mystical experience.

hadith (huh-deeth'): "Recollection"; a remembrance of an act or saying of Muhammad. (The plural is spelled *hadiths* or *ahadith*.)

Hajj (hahj): Pilgrimage to Mecca.

Hijra (hij'-rah): "Flight"; Muhammad's escape from Mecca to Yathrib (Medina).

Id al-Adha (eed' ahl-ahd'-hah): The Day of Sacrifice during the month of the Hajj when an animal is sacrificed to recall the submission of Abraham.

Id al-Fitr (eed' ahl-fee'-tur): The festival at the end of the month of Ramadan during which people feast and visit friends and often the graves of ancestors.

imam (ee-mahm'): A religious leader; specifically, one of the hereditary successors of Muhammad, venerated in Shiite Islam.

Islam: "Submission"; the Muslim religion and the community of believers who have submitted themselves to Allah.

jihad (jee-hahd'): "Struggle"; the ideals of (1) spreading Islamic belief and (2) heroic self-sacrifice.

Kabah (kah'-bah): "Cube"; the square shrine at the center of the Grand Mosque of Mecca.

Khadijah (kah-dee'-juh): First wife of Muhammad.

mihrab (meeh'-rahb): The decorated niche inside a mosque that indicates the direction of Mecca.

minaret (min-ah-ret'): A tower used by a chanter to call people to prayer.

mosque (Arabic: masjid): a Muslim place of worship.

muezzin (moo-edz'-in): A chanter who calls people to prayer.

Muslim: A person who submits to Allah.

qiblah (kib'-lah): The direction toward Mecca; the direction toward which Muslims pray.

Qur'an (koor-ahn'): "Recitation"; God's words as revealed to and recited by Muhammad; an authorized edition of the written words that appeared after Muhammad's death.

Ramadan (rah'-mah-dahn): The month of fasting; the ninth month of the Muslim calendar.

Sharia (shah-ree'-uh): "Path"; the whole body of Islamic laws that guides a Muslim's life. (Also spelled *Shariah*.)

Shiite (shee'-ait): A minority branch of Islam, which holds that Muhammad's genuine successors descended from his son-in-law Ali.

Sufism (soof'-ism): A group of devotional movements in Islam.

Sunni (soon'-ee): The majority branch of Islam, which holds that genuine succession from Muhammad did not depend on hereditary descent from his son-in-law Ali.

sura (soo'-rah): A chapter of the Qur'an.

RELIGION BEYOND THE CLASSROOM

Visit the Online Learning Center at www.mhhe.com/molloy6e for additional exercises and features, including "Religion beyond the Classroom" and "For Fuller Understanding."

CHAPTER 11

Alternative Paths

FIRST ENCOUNTER

After years of thinking about traveling to Asia, you finally take the plunge. Following a tour of the major cities of China, you are now in Vietnam on your own. During your first days there, you explore Hanoi, a beautiful city of two-story pink and yellow buildings, red-pillared temples, lakes, and large old trees. You visit its Confucian Temple of Literature, where a genial statue of Confucius seems to focus its glass eyes directly on you. Afterward, you fly south to Hué, a former royal city that sits beside the Song Huong River, whose slow-moving water is so thick with brown silt that it looks like chocolate pudding. When you visit Hué's square of old palaces, you are amazed by the extent to which its royal enclosure was patterned after the Forbidden City of Beijing. Clearly, you think, China has had a profound influence on Vietnam.

Eventually you arrive in Ho Chi Minh City, formerly Saigon. In your hotel lobby, you see a poster advertising tours to the underground tunnels at Cu Chi that were used by the North Vietnamese soldiers during the Vietnam War. You walk over to talk with the agent at the tour desk, and she tries to interest you in additional tours. "Have you heard of Cao Dai?" she asks. You hadn't till now. "It is a big religion here in Vietnam," she explains. "Its cathedral is not far from the tunnels, and there is a Mass every day at noon. Why don't you go there, too?"

At 11:30 the next morning, you arrive at Tay Ninh, a quiet town of yellow stucco buildings, gravel roads, and people dressed in white. You can't miss the cathedral; it is an immense yellow building with two tall towers that face the main road. Upon entering the building, you are directed up a long flight of stairs to a narrow visitors' gallery that runs along three sides of the interior. Looking down from the observation gallery to the front of the church's interior, you see a huge eye painted on a large blue globe that seems to hover in the sanctuary. Around you, decorative green dragons climb tall pillars to the sky-blue ceiling. Just before noon, people dressed in robes of red, blue, yellow, and white take their places in groups on the shining marble floor below. Chanting starts. The service begins.

What, you wonder, does the large eye represent? What are the people chanting, and what is the significance of the variously colored robes? Why are there Chinese dragons on the pillars inside a building that looks like a Christian cathedral? Why do they call their service a "Mass"?

ORIGINS OF NEW RELIGIONS

One of the most fascinating things about religions is that, like all forms of life and culture, they are constantly changing. Change occurs for many reasons. Sometimes followers of one religion move to another culture, and their religion mixes with a locally established religion, thereby producing a hybrid faith. Sometimes social problems lead to the emergence of a new religion, one that helps people cope with the new social issues they face. Sometimes followers of an older religion argue with each other and then separate, creating a new branch or, occasionally, an entirely new religion. And sometimes individuals have life-changing insights, attract followers, and create a new religion around themselves. We should recognize that many of the major religions and denominations began in similar ways—as new, small, and sometimes persecuted religious movements. In this chapter, we will look at some of the vital new religious movements that are currently small but that might someday become venerable old religions, after growing and changing for one or two thousand years. (The vitality of these new religious movements is apparent from their many Web sites.)

In the religions that we examined in previous chapters, we sometimes saw the emergence of a religious variant that was close enough to its origin to be considered a modern interpretation of an older religion. As we learned, from Shinto emerged the New Religions of Tenrikyo and Omoto; from Christianity, Mormonism and Christian Science; and from Buddhism, Soka Gakkai.

Contemporary Issues

"CULTS," "SECTS," AND "NEW RELIGIOUS MOVEMENTS"

Because they are small and unfamiliar, new religious movements are often looked at suspiciously. Critics may accuse them of hurting society or endangering their followers. The words *sect* and *cult* are sometimes applied to these movements. The word *sect* (Latin: "to cut") usually has no negative meaning. But the word *cult* (Latin: "to cultivate") brings to mind a charismatic, overly powerful leader, docile followers, and separation from society.

We might recall that early Christianity was once viewed as a dangerous import into Roman society and that Buddhism was once viewed as a dangerous import from India into China. Because of the emotional overtones of some words that are used to describe small and new religious groups, scholars now try to use emotionally neutral terms. One of the most common is "new religious movement," often referred to by its abbreviation NRM.

There are, however, some movements that emerge from one religion and take on such independent forms that they ultimately constitute new, even if small, religions: Baha'i, which in the nineteenth century grew out of Shiite Islam, is a good example. And then there are other movements that emerge independently of established religions and eventually are recognized as distinct religions; Scientology is an example of such a religion.

Quite often, a new religious movement is *syncretic*—a blend of religions. The Vietnamese religion of Cao Dai, for example, blends Christianity with Buddhism, Daoism, and Confucianism. Santería and other related religions, prominent in the Caribbean, mix Christianity with elements from West African religions. We also see syncretism in religious movements that have grown out of Shinto, Buddhism, and Hinduism.

In this chapter we will consider some of the most significant new religious movements, along with a few older alternatives that are generating new interest. We will begin with religious movements that share features with indigenous religions (Contemporary Paganism and the Yoruba-tradition religions) and then proceed to religions that appear to have elements of Indian spirituality (such as Theosophy and Scientology). Next, we will take a look at religions that are close to traditional Chinese religions (Falun Gong and Cao Dai) and then end with religions that have some roots in Christianity and Islam (Rastafarianism and Baha'i).

CONTEMPORARY PAGANISM: WICCA AND DRUIDISM

The past hundred years have seen both a great growth in world population and a depletion of natural resources. As a result, many people sense an urgent need to reestablish harmonious relationships with the global environment. At the same time, developments in genetics, anthropology, and psychology have brought human beings to a clearer understanding of their closeness to the animal world. Perhaps for these reasons, new religious movements that reclaim ancient nature-based religions or that promote new environmental sensitivity are attracting many followers. Some of these followers are reacting against the insensitivity to native cultures and values that some mainstream religions exhibit. Others find the philosophies of these old-yet-new religious movements to be more compatible with their views on various social issues, including gender equality and environmentalism.

Contemporary Paganism is a general name for religious movements that attempt to return to earlier, nature-based religions, primarily religions associated with early cultures of Europe. Followers point out that the term *pagan,* although often used in a demeaning way to mean "uncivilized" and "debased," more properly refers to early, nature-based religions; they note that the term *pagan* actually comes from a Latin term for "countryside" (*pagus*) and that the term was used simply because nature religions lived on longer in rural areas than they did in cities. Followers of Contemporary Paganism claim that when Christianity spread throughout western Europe, older pagan practices did not entirely die out. At least some of the practices went underground or took on a Christian appearance in order to survive.

Although small movements exist that attempt to re-create early Scandinavian and Germanic religions, the most common forms of Contemporary Paganism look back to Celtic mythology as their foundation. The best-known manifestation of the Contemporary Pagan movement is **Wicca.** *Wicca* is an Old English word that suggests association with magic, separation, and holiness. Its modern practitioners focus on Wicca's practical uses by calling it the Craft. Sometimes they also call their path simply the Old Religion.

Several strands or traditions of Wicca exist, but they agree on many points. Like many of the world's religions, Wiccans worship both goddesses and gods whose sacred imagery is rooted in nature. Some Wiccans speak of multiple deities, while others prefer to speak of a single divine reality that has male and female aspects and images. Some groups personify the female aspect of the divine as "the Goddess" and the male aspect as "the God." Wicca teaches that the divine manifests itself in opposites that are reminiscent of yin and yang—dark and light, female and male, and so on. Yet, as in Daoism, some traditions of Wicca give special emphasis to the female aspect of the cosmos—perhaps because it has been underemphasized by some other religious traditions. In Wicca, women play a prominent role as bearers of knowledge and as leaders of ritual.

For Wiccans both the moon and the sun are sacred symbols, and the Wiccan yearly calendar receives its structure from their movement. Each year Wiccans celebrate the solar cycle by keeping as many as eight seasonal turning points, called **Sabbats,** which include the **solstices** and **equinoxes.** Wiccans celebrate the lunar cycle at the new and full moons. The times of the full moon, called **Esbats,** are often marked by gatherings and ceremony. The seasonal festivals and holidays indicate both turning points in the world of nature and changes in the inner world of the practitioners. Regarding initiation and entry into higher levels of knowledge, Wiccan groups tend to recognize three stages. The first stage is initiation, and at the second or third stage the practitioner is considered competent to start an independent coven (worship group). Contemporary Wiccans call themselves *Witches,* and they use this term for both females and males.

Rituals and Celebrations

THE CONTEMPORARY PAGAN YEAR

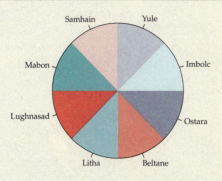

Yule (December 21)–midwinter solstice, when sunlight begins to grow stronger

Imbolc (about February 1)–beginning of spring

Ostara (about March 21)–spring equinox, named after the goddess of dawn

Beltane (May 1)–festival of fertility, probably named after the Celtic sun-god Bel

Litha (June 21)–summer solstice and beginning of harvest

Lughnasad (about August 1)–celebration of the grain harvest, named "the games of Lugh" after the Celtic god of music and play

Mabon (about September 22)–final harvest festival at the time of the autumn equinox

Samhain (about October 31)–end of old year, temporary return of the spirits of ancestors

The contemporary pagan year is a cycle of eight celebrations.

Wicca has an ethical dimension. The primary commandment, called the Wiccan **Rede** (Middle English: "advice," "counsel"), is a gentle form of the Golden Rule. The Wiccan Rede is a rule of tolerance: "An [if] it harm none, do what you will." In other words, the individual is free to do anything except what harms others. This command, though, includes not harming animals, and many Wiccans are therefore vegetarians. It also prohibits harming the earth; thus Wicca has a strong moral interest in protecting the natural environment. Another Wiccan moral belief is expressed as the Law of the Triple Return. It states, "Whatever you do, good or bad, will return to you threefold." Wiccans believe that the energy that an individual sends out will return triply to the sender—that deeds bring their own punishment or reward.

It is possible that some of the beliefs and practices of contemporary Wicca are genuinely old, such as the rituals of Halloween and May Day. The anthropologist Margaret Murray (1863–1963) provided strong evidence for the view that earlier forms of Witchcraft existed in Europe up to modern times. Her book *The Witch-Cult in Western Europe* quotes extensively from early sources in Latin, French, and English, written during the Middle Ages and Renaissance, that testify to the presence of earlier forms of a nature religion akin to Wicca. Her later book, *The God of the Witches,* establishes the same points in more approachable style. In the United States, the Wiccan writer and political activist Leo Martello (1931–2000), whose work helped open the way for the practice of Wicca in North America, traced his own knowledge back to ancient practices of his Sicilian ancestors.[1]

The midsummer sunrise at Stonehenge attracts Druids, Wiccans, and other followers of pagan beliefs.

Some scholars, however, argue that Wicca is an artificial, quite new creation, a "mythic reconstruction." They point to the work of three people who did a great deal to establish contemporary Wicca: Gerald Gardner (1884–1964), Alex Sanders (1926–1988), and Doreen Valiente (1922–1999; see Timeline 11.1). In writings and practice, these three recommended—and often created—rituals, phrases, and other elements that are now part of modern Wicca. Yet other commentators see these people as adapters of an older religious tradition who attempted to bridge the gap between a rural culture and a modern, urban one.

Although Wicca is the best-known form of Contemporary Paganism, there are others. Particularly popular in England is the **Druid** movement, which began in the eighteenth century as an attempt to reintroduce the religion practiced in France and England by the Celts about two thousand years ago. Early information on Druidic practice came from classical Roman literature, mainly from the writings of the emperor-general Julius Caesar and the historian Tacitus. Although Roman description of the Druids was undoubtedly colored by prejudice, its details certainly portray some actual practices and events. In fact, archeological finds have confirmed the truth of much early description.

Druids were an elite group of professionals who acted as judges, teachers, counselors, doctors, and priests. Their preparation lasted up to twenty years before full initiation. They were polytheists who worshiped about thirty major deities of nature and many lesser deities (about three hundred names of deities are found in the remaining literature). The sun and fire were important symbols of the divine. Druids conducted their services in groves of sacred oak trees; in fact, although the exact origin of their name is uncertain, *Druid* is commonly thought to mean "oak-tree wisdom."

Because so little is known of the ancient Druids, the modern Druid movement has not only had to borrow from the data of literature and archeology,

Left Event	Date	Right Event
	1503	Slaves from West Africa first arrive in Haiti
Development of religions of the Yoruba tradition	c. 1550–1850	
	1817–1892	Life of Baha'u'llah, founder of Baha'i
Life of Madame Helena Blavatsky	1831–1891	
	1844	Beginning of the Babist movement, precursor to Baha'i
Founding of the Theosophical Society	1875	
	1884–1964	Life of Gerald Gardner, major influence on modern Wicca
Life of Marcus Garvey, Jamaican activist	1887–1940	
	1891–1975	Life of Ras Tafari (Haile Selassie)
Life of Jiddu Krishnamurti	1895–1986	
	1911–1986	Life of L. Ron Hubbard, founder of Scientology
Founding by Marcus Garvey of the UNIA (Universal Negro Improvement Association)	1914	
	1922–1999	Life of Doreen Valiente, writer who helped establish modern Wicca
Life of Alex Sanders, founder of modern Wicca	1926–1988	
	1928	Beginning of Cao Dai in Vietnam
Life of Bob Marley, reggae musician	1945–1981	
	1954	Founding of Scientology by L. Ron Hubbard
Visit of Emperor Haile Selassie to Jamaica	1966	
	1992	Beginning of Falun Gong
Repression of Falun Gong in mainland China	1999	

Timeline of significant events of alternative paths.

it has also had to rely on imaginative re-creations of organization and ritual. The Druids recognize three paths of practice, which may also be seen by some as stages of knowledge: **bards, ovates,** and druids. Modern Druids generally follow the same eight-part seasonal calendar as the Wiccans; they also celebrate the period of the full moon. Although Stonehenge in England predates the Druids, it is commonly associated with the modern Druids, who use the ancient circular stone complex for celebrations of the summer solstice.[2]

RELIGIONS OF THE YORUBA TRADITION: SANTERÍA, VOODOO, AND CANDOMBLÉ

When people from one culture enter another culture, they bring their religion with them. It sustains them and provides a bridge into their new lives. Sometimes elements of the two cultures mix in interesting ways. This is the case with the new religions that have their roots in the indigenous Yoruba tradition of Africa.

As the Americas were being colonized, a large slave trade arose. Enslaved Africans, largely from West Africa, were subsequently carried to South America, the Caribbean, and North America. Among the descendants of these slaves, new syncretic religions emerged that blended elements from indigenous African religions and the colonizers' Christianity.

Of the West African religions that were brought to the New World, those of the Yoruba people, who live in what is today Nigeria and Benin, were the most influential. (Other peoples whose religions were influential during the colonization of the Americas included the Fon, Nago, Kongo, and Igbo.) While **Santería** is perhaps the best-known religious movement to result from the mixture of Yoruba religions and Christianity, **Voodoo (Voudun)** and **Candomblé** are also prominent. These three related religions are sometimes referred to as religions of the Yoruba tradition.

These Yoruba-based religions are now several hundred years old, but for a variety of reasons they are today the focus of renewed interest. One reason is that an influx of Cuban and Haitian immigrants over the past thirty years has introduced these religious traditions to the United States. Another reason is that many African Americans today are interested in exploring their cultural and religious heritage. We should note, however, that there are significant historical differences among the three religions. Santería was influenced by Spanish colonial Catholicism and grew up in Cuba; Voodoo, influenced by French Catholicism, developed in Haiti; and Candomblé, influenced by Portuguese Catholicism, developed in Brazil.

There is some disagreement about the names given to two of these religions. Although the term *Santería* ("saint-thing" or "saint-way") was originally a negative way of identifying the movement, it is used here because most of the religion's practitioners accept it and use it themselves. However, the alternate name *Lukumí* or *Lucumí* (from the Yoruba language) is gaining some acceptance. The word *Voodoo* comes from the Fon word *vodun* ("mysterious

A Cuban worshiper weeps over an image of Babalú-Ayé on the feast of Saint Lazarus.

power"), but because the word *voodoo* has taken on so many negative connotations, some authorities prefer to use the word *Voudun* instead. In all three religions we find variations in spellings of terms and of the names of gods.

Although the three religions are a mixture of native African religions with Roman Catholicism, describing how elements have mingled is far from easy. Sometimes the terms *syncretism, synthesis,* and *symbiosis* are used to describe the mixture, suggesting a happy blend of complements; the environment within which these religions emerged, however, was one of coercion and fear. Slaves were often forcibly baptized into Roman Catholic Christianity, and African religious practice was suppressed—sometimes harshly.

Among the slaves, however, were many committed practitioners and even priests of the Yoruba religions; as a consequence, their religious beliefs did not die out. In order to survive, the African religions took on an appearance of conformity to Catholic belief and practice. On the surface, devotees were venerating Catholic saints, but in reality they were using the images of the saints as representations of their native gods. Raúl Canizares, a priest of Santería, describes the result not as syncretism but rather as *dissimulation,* a term he uses to emphasize that the practitioners often deliberately hid their beliefs and practices behind "masks"—especially behind the veneration of saints.[3]

We should not, however, overstress the aspect of dissimulation. It is possible that apparent similarities in belief and approach between the Yoruba religion and Roman Catholicism permitted syncretism. Both systems believed in a single High God, in supernatural beings who mediate between God and

Women close their eyes and pray during a ceremony on Fet Ghédé, a Voodoo holiday commemorating dead ancestors. Fet Ghédé is a national holiday in Haiti, where Voodoo, or Voudun, has been actively practiced since French colonial rule.

human beings, and in the existence of spirits of the dead. Both systems trusted in the power of ritual and made frequent use of ritual elements. Moreover, it was easy to adapt the Catholic calendar of saints' days to the worship of native African deities.

Although the new religions of the Yoruba tradition do believe in a single High God, they differ from Catholicism in that the Yoruba God (as in many African religions) is in essence a neutral energy that does not show personal interest in individual human affairs. Human beings must approach the High God and can gain power only by contacting invisible supernatural beings, called **orishas.** (In Santería, they are often called **ochas;** in Voodoo, they are called **loa** or **lwa;** and in Candomblé they are called *orixas.*)

The orishas are sometimes called gods. They are appropriately likened to the gods of the Greeks and the Romans because the orishas have individual humanlike characteristics. They may be gentle, capricious, playful, or wise, and they like particular foods and colors. They are in charge of certain aspects of nature (for example, oceans, plants, lightning), and they know specialized crafts (such as metalworking). In order to make the orishas strong, to keep them happy, and to extract favors from them, human beings have to keep them fed—and the orishas are not vegetarian. When the orishas are interested in human contact, they may temporarily "mount" a believer, who goes into a trance and magically "becomes" the god, often displaying his or her personal characteristics. While there are hundreds of these gods in the Yoruba religion of Africa, only about twenty are prominent in the Caribbean religions of the Yoruba tradition, and about a dozen are particularly popular. We should also note the difference between orishas and Catholic saints. Although both orishas and saints are prayed to in order to receive

Deeper Insights

MAJOR ORISHAS OF SANTERÍA

Santería worships deities called *orishas* (*orixás, ochas*). The most important orishas and the dates on which they are celebrated follow:

Elegguá (Elegbara, Eshu)—god of beginnings, a messenger god; his colors are black and red; his parallel saint is Saint Anthony (June 13).

Oshún—goddess of love and marriage; her colors are yellow and white; her parallel saint is Our Lady of Charity (September 8).

Shangó (Changó)—god of lightning and storms; his colors are red and white; his parallel saint is Saint Barbara (December 4).

Babalú-Ayé—compassionate god of healing; his colors are white and blue; his parallel saint is Saint Lazarus (December 17).

Obatalá—god of intelligence; his color is white; his parallel saint is Our Lady of Mercy (September 24).

Ochosí—god of the forest, who knows plants and animals; his color is purple; his parallel saint is Saint Norbert (June 6).

Oggún—god of metalworking, patron of barbers and butchers, associated with war and accidents; his colors are black and green; his parallel saint is Saint Peter (June 29).

Yemayá—goddess of the sea and protector of women, associated with coral and seashells; her colors are blue and white; her parallel saint is Our Lady of Regla (September 7).

Oyá—goddess associated with high winds, who gives help to the dying; her colors are burgundy and white; her parallel saint is Our Lady of Candelaria (February 2).

assistance with the problems of life, it is clear that orishas are considered divine, whereas saints in traditional Catholic piety are not.

An individual is initiated under the protection of one of the orishas, who becomes the person's guardian deity. Priests perform initiations (a male priest is called a **santero** and a female priest a **santera**). Above them are the high priests (in Santería called *babalawos*). Only men may become high priests, although this tradition may be changing.

Services involve prayer, drumming, dance, offering of foods, and the descent of orishas. The sacrifice of animals—mainly chickens, doves, and goats—is a part of some rituals. Although many groups oppose Santería's sacrificial practice, its legality has been upheld by the United States Supreme Court (1993). In deference to the controversy, some Santería practitioners have begun using alternative offerings (such as drink and dishes of food) as substitutes for animals.

In Brazil, Candomblé has been recognized as an official religion, with its headquarters in Bahía, in northeastern Brazil. And because of widespread emigration from the Caribbean, Santería and Voodoo are becoming known in some large cities of the United States, including Miami, New York, and Los Angeles. Voodoo has long been a part of the history of New Orleans, and several Voodoo museums exist in Louisiana. In addition to these three religions, related movements have developed in Jamaica (Obeayisne) and in Trinidad (the cult of Shangó).

THEOSOPHY

We turn now from movements rooted in indigenous religions to movements that draw upon the traditions of Hinduism and Buddhism. The first new religious movement of this type that we will consider is **Theosophy.** The term *Theosophy* means "divine wisdom" in Greek. In general, Theosophy refers to mystical movements of all types, but it also refers specifically to a movement, beginning in the nineteenth century, that attempts a synthesis of esoteric (hidden) religious knowledge. The movement of Theosophy is eclectic. It shows particularly strong interest in mystically oriented teachings from all sources—among them, Hindu Vedanta, the Jewish Kabbalah, and Gnosticism.

The principal founder of Theosophy was the Russian writer Madame Helena Blavatsky (1831–1891), who with several associates began the Theosophical Society in 1875. Two of her books, *Isis Unveiled* (1877) and *The Secret Doctrine* (1888), were among the first works to popularize among westerners significant elements from Indian thought, such as karma, reincarnation, yoga, and meditation.

Blavatsky learned of these topics from her reading and travel, but she also claimed that she was taught by "ascended masters"—highly evolved teachers. After time spent in the United States, Blavatsky moved to southern India in 1878, where at Adyar, on the outskirts of Madras (Chennai), she established her world center of Theosophy. She was ably assisted by Colonel Henry Steel Olcott (1832–1907). Olcott was one of the earliest westerners to formally adopt Buddhism, which he did in 1880. He wrote a *Buddhist Catechism* and worked

Madame Helena Blavatsky was assisted in her work by Colonel Henry Steel Olcott. Together they established the Theosophical Society in India.

in Sri Lanka to revive and purify Buddhism there. Olcott stayed on in India while Blavatsky guided European Theosophy from her center in London. After Blavatsky's death in 1891, her work was continued by Annie Besant (1847–1933) and Charles Leadbeater (1854–1934).

Theosophists have a wide range of interests but generally share a similar view of reality. One premise, similar to Vedantist thought, is that all reality is basically spiritual in nature—that visible matter is "condensed spirit." Theosophists hold that the spiritual nature of reality can be experienced and that training—especially in meditation techniques and in achieving trance states—can make possible and can deepen that experience. Sometimes Theosophists say that there are several increasingly spiritual levels of the human being (such as the *astral body*) and spiritual aspects of all physical realities (such as *auras*) that can be seen at times. Theosophists are interested in exploring what they believe are the little-known powers that lie hidden both in the nonhuman world and in human beings, such as levitation and clairvoyance.

Blavatsky had prophesied that a "world teacher" would arise to lead the world to a new stage of evolution. Leadbeater and Besant identified this person as a young man, Jiddu Krishnamurti (1895–1986), whom they discovered in Madras. At first Krishnamurti accepted the role imposed on him by the Theosophical Society and was trained to take over as its leader. However, he eventually abandoned that role and began to teach that each person must be his or her own guru.

Despite his disavowals of spiritual leadership, Krishnamurti attracted a large following of disciples. He created a center on a hilltop in Ojai, California, north of Los Angeles, where he wrote and taught for many years. Today, the Krishnamurti Foundation runs a retreat center there and continues his teachings through videos, books, and seminars.

Theosophy has undergone a series of splits. There has long been a rift between American groups and the international society headquartered in India. Consequently, there are several branches of Theosophy. The type of Theosophy that has been centered in India is naturally closer to Hindu and Buddhist sources and interests. In contrast, Western Theosophy has a greater interest in European and American thinkers and in scientific experimentation into claims of telepathy, clairvoyance, and similar special powers.

One influential branch of Theosophy is **Anthroposophy** ("human wisdom"). Its founder, Rudolf Steiner (1861–1925), was a thinker who was born and trained in central Europe. Steiner began as a Theosophist but broke away in 1909 and founded Anthroposophy in 1913. Influenced by the works of German writer Johann Wolfgang von

In a photo from early in his career, philosopher Jiddu Krishnamurti lectures to a crowd.

Contemporary Issues

ECOLOGY AND THE NEW RELIGIOUS MOVEMENTS

Principles of ecology include restraint, recycling, respect for nature, ending pollution, protection of species, and forestation. We find many of the same principles in some religious movements that have emerged in modern times.

- Among the most obviously connected with nature are Wicca and Druidism. They envision the divine as the energy of the universe and see that everything has a right to existence. These religions follow a calendar that respects the seasons. Primary to them are the seasonal turning points that include Yule, May Day, and Samhain.
- Theosophy emphasizes the interdependence of everything in the universe and holds that all things share a divine nature.

- The religions that came from Africa pray to gods of nature, such as Shangó, who is associated with storms and lightning, Ochosí, god of the forest, and Yemayá, goddess of the sea.
- Baha'i (discussed later in this chapter) teaches ideals that fit well with environmentalism. Among them are a love of biodiversity; the belief that science and technology should bring harmony between human beings and nature; a sense of nature as an expression of God; sustainability; and a recognition that all is interconnected.

Shades of blue appear during moments of devotion.
—Rudolf Steiner, speaking about human auras[4]

Goethe, English naturalist Charles Darwin, and German philosopher Friedrich Nietzsche, Steiner developed his own theories of spiritual evolution. Desiring to focus on practical means to achieve human wholeness and spirituality, he began the first Waldorf school for the training of young people. Its curriculum encompassed not only traditional academic matters but also agriculture, art, and interpretive dance, called **eurhythmy.** Waldorf schools around the world still promote Steiner's interest in the complete development of the individual. Among Steiner's many books are *Philosophy of Spiritual Activity, The Course of My Life,* and *The New Art of Education.*[5]

A more recent offshoot of Theosophy is the **Church Universal and Triumphant,** begun by Elizabeth Clare Prophet (1939–2009). Followers believe that the Church gains assistance from the spirits of great people who help human beings from a realm beyond the earth. The Church Universal and Triumphant blends elements from Catholic Christianity with Asian beliefs. For example, it encourages the use of the Bible and the rosary, as well as devotion to the saints. But it also teaches reincarnation and includes the Buddha, Jesus, and his mother Mary among its saints.

Theosophy has had much greater influence than its small numbers might attest. Blavatsky's books have influenced other movements, such as New Thought, the Unity Church, and Christian Science. Blavatsky's openness to phenomena of many types has led to reputable investigations by others into automatic writing (writing done in trance states), hypnotism, and the paranormal. Modern Western interest in Hinduism and the whole New Age movement can be traced back, at least to some extent, to the influence of Blavatsky and Theosophy.

SCIENTOLOGY

Like Theosophy, **Scientology** has roots in Indian spirituality. L. Ron Hubbard (1911–1986), who had initially made his name as an author of science-fiction books, founded Scientology as a religion in 1954. Beginning as a human-potential movement in the early 1950s, Scientology evolved quickly into the religion that is now called the Church of Scientology.

Hubbard created a system that he thought would help people clarify their understanding of the human process of knowing. He created a hybrid name for this system, from *scientia* (Latin: "knowledge") and *logos* (Greek: "reason," "understanding"). Scientologists think that if we can come to understand the human process of perceiving and reacting to the world, we will be able to see reality more clearly and respond to the world more rationally.

The underlying belief system of Scientology has parallels with many religions, but particularly with Gnosticism and some schools of Hinduism. The Church believes that there is a spiritual purpose to life, and it holds that the core of the human being is a soul or spiritual reality, which it calls the **thetan.** According to Scientology, the thetan is in a state of imprisonment in the material world, which is called **MEST**—an acronym for matter, energy, space, and time. (MEST recalls the notion of samsara, found in both Hinduism and Buddhism.) The thetan, the immortal spiritual being that is the core of each human being, longs for liberation.

Although belief in rebirth was at first a minor teaching of Scientology, it soon began to assert itself. People undergoing Scientology training spoke repeatedly of their need to overcome difficulties that had harmed them in previous lives and whose injurious results continued on into their present lives.

> Scientology has accomplished the goal of religion expressed in all man's written history, the freeing of the soul by wisdom.
> —L. Ron Hubbard[6]

Scientology has made an effort to attract celebrities, as is evident in the name of the Scientology Celebrity Centre in Los Angeles.

This notion is clearly similar to Indian teachings about karma and reincarnation. As mentioned earlier, another similarity with Hindu and Buddhist worldviews is the notion that the goal of each individual human being is some type of psychological liberation that can be brought about by insight. Although Scientologists do not use the terms *moksha, nirvana,* or *enlightenment,* those ideas are strongly suggested.

Scientology presents a grand scheme of stages toward which the individual can aspire, each representing a step upward toward increased understanding and liberation. The steps are shown on an illustrated chart called the Bridge to Total Freedom—or simply, the **Bridge.** Scientology offers techniques and books (such as Hubbard's text *Dianetics*) to lead the individual upward. The person at the beginning of the Bridge is called a **pre-clear,** and the person who has reached a state of mental liberation (called **clear**) is known as an **operating thetan** (or OT).

Individuals may proceed along the path of mental liberation by themselves, using the books provided by Scientology. Individuals are encouraged, however, to undertake the path of mental liberation with the help of another person, a spiritual counselor called an **auditor.** The auditor guides the less-experienced person by means of exercises, called *processes,* which make use of a series of questions and mental images. The processes help the pre-clear learn new ways of mental focusing. Together the auditor and pre-clear work to find blockages to the individual's growth. (These blockages, caused by earlier painful experiences, are called **engrams.**) Sometimes the auditor makes use of an **e-meter,** an electronic machine that reads the galvanic skin response of the pre-clear. The responses of the e-meter help detect blockages that can then be resolved. Fees are charged for the auditing sessions and for advancing through the stages of the processes, although service to the organization is sometimes accepted as a substitute for payment. Processing can also be done for groups.

Scientologists insist that their religion can be practiced along with other religions and that it does not displace them. Scientology centers, in fact, do not look like churches or temples; they are usually office buildings located in urban areas. Nonetheless, the amount of time that followers must devote to Scientology makes it difficult for them to practice another religion simultaneously.

Scientologists meet on Sundays for a service that includes a reading from Hubbard's writings (or watching a videotape of one of his speeches), a sermon by a minister on some point of Scientology, a sharing of viewpoints, announcements, and a closing prayer written by Hubbard. Ministers conduct naming ceremonies, weddings, and funerals. Scientologists keep some religious festivals (such as Christmas) that appear in their surrounding society. They also keep March 13 as a festival in honor of Hubbard's birthday.

FALUN GONG

We now move to new religious movements closely related to traditional Chinese religions. One of the youngest new religious movements was founded by Li Hongzhi (b. 1951), who was born in China but currently lives

Sydney's Bondi Beach is the site for this dawn Falun Gong ritual.

in the United States. As a young man he began to practice and then teach **Qigong** ("energy force"). Qigong (pronounced *chee'-gong*) is a system of exercises based on Chinese martial arts that are thought to bring about increased health and strength. The movement called **Falun Gong** grew out of Li's interests in Qigong and in meditative practices; and although it was not publicly initiated in China until 1992, it has begun to grow into a worldwide movement. It is reminiscent of several strands of Chinese religious practice that we have already studied, such as Buddhist meditation, Daoist physical exercise, and Confucian self-cultivation.

The name *Falun Gong* literally means "law-wheel energy." (We might recall that the eight-spoked wheel is a Buddhist symbol and note that *law* is a synonym for Buddhist teaching.) The **falun** is believed to be an invisible spiritual wheel located in the lower abdomen that can be activated by a master. The falun, once it has begun to turn in one direction, is believed to draw energy from the universe. Then, when the wheel turns in the opposite direction, it sends that energy out in purified form through the body of the practitioner, bringing benefits to the practitioner and to others.

Followers practice five series of physical exercises, done while standing and sitting. The exercises are closely related to Daoist exercises and exercises associated with Chinese Buddhist monasticism, and the names of the exercises borrow from Daoist and Buddhist terminology. (Readers interested in knowing the names and details of these exercises can check Web sites for Falun Gong or Falun Dafa, another name for the movement.) People who perform the Falun Gong exercises believe that they gain not only health and strength but also paranormal powers, such as physical invulnerability and the power to see and hear things at a great distance.

The practice of Falun Gong is currently banned in China (though not in Hong Kong). Some see behind this prohibition a fear of repeating history, since Chinese history offers several examples of religious groups that have destabilized governments. In response to the ban on their religion, Falun Gong followers have attempted to bring attention to their religious position through a variety of public demonstrations. Many of these demonstrators in China have been jailed.

It is hard to gauge the number of Falun Gong followers. Leaders of the movement claim that there are as many as thirty million practitioners in China and in Chinese-immigrant communities throughout the world. Critics, however, argue that the numbers are far lower.

CAO DAI

Cao Dai (pronounced *kao'-dai*), another strongly Chinese religious movement, is one of the world's most unusual religions. It blends elements of Daoism, Confucianism, Buddhism, and Chinese belief in spirits with Christian monotheism; it has a pope and an organizational structure that is reminiscent of Catholicism; and it venerates among its many saints the English statesman Winston Churchill, the Chinese leader Sun Yat-sen, and the French novelist Victor Hugo.

The name *Cao Dai* is a title for God. Literally, it means "high palace" and is used as a title of respect. According to followers of the religion, God revealed himself, beginning in 1921, to Ngo Van Chieu (1878–1926?), who was the government prefect of a rural Vietnamese island. This revelation occurred while Chieu was practicing spiritism (a ritualistic calling on spirits). After praying for the ability to worship God in some visible form, Chieu repeatedly saw in the air the image of a large eye. Chieu realized that this was God's way of presenting an appropriate visual symbol to represent himself. (This symbol is very common in European Catholic churches, particularly in France. The eye is often enclosed in a triangle, a symbol of the Trinity. The same symbol is also used by the Masons, a fraternal organization; through their influence it found its way onto the back of the United States dollar bill.)

In 1924 Chieu went to Saigon, where followers who also practiced spiritism gathered around him. Some of his followers repeatedly contacted what they believed to be the spirits of their parents and ancestors. Increasingly, one spirit continued to manifest itself. That spirit revealed itself as the Supreme Being. Chieu and the others, convinced that they were all the recipients of some new divine revelation, joined forces and developed an organizational structure. In 1928 Chieu's followers announced the new religion.

A primary teaching of Cao Dai is that all religions are based on revelations of God but that earlier revelations have suffered from human misunderstanding. Cao Dai holds that God inspired all the great religious founders and teachers and that God's revelation, which has gotten progressively clearer, has occurred in three great phases, or **alliances.**

The first period of revelation, called the First Alliance, came in the distant past, when mythic figures (such as an early incarnation of Laozi and a legendary early Buddha called Dipankara) brought divine revelation to the world. The Second Alliance occurred in that thousand-year period of religious ferment that gave birth to Laozi, Confucius, Siddhartha Gautama, Jesus, and Muhammad. The Third Alliance began in the nineteenth century, with the works of Victor Hugo, Sun Yat-sen, and the Vietnamese scholar Trang Trinh Nguyen Binh Khiem, all of whom pursued the ideals of justice and human liberation. The Third Alliance continued in the revelations to Ngo Van Chieu and his followers, to whom God seemed to be speaking in the clearest way possible. In Cao Dai belief, however, revelation has not ended. Cao Dai followers believe that the divine realm continues to contact human beings through revelations both from God and from heavenly spirits.

Cao Dai tenets include belief in God the Father (Cao Dai), a celestial Universal Mother, heavenly spirits, and souls of the living and the dead. Buddhist influence is apparent in a belief in karma, reincarnation, and a state of liberation called nirvana. Buddhist influence is also evident in much Cao Dai practice. For example, Cao Dai promotes the avoidance of alcohol and drugs, of luxury, and of lies and hurtful speech. It also prohibits the killing of living beings, which is expressed in the Cao Dai practice of a vegetarian ideal: regular believers are expected to abstain from eating meat for ten days a month, and higher spiritual authorities are expected to maintain a completely vegetarian diet. The influence of Confucianism is also apparent in many Cao Dai virtues: self-cultivation, family responsibility, social harmony, and attention to duty. The deliberate blend of religions is symbolized by the four colors of robes used at major services: yellow for Buddhism (the original color of monks' robes, symbolizing renunciation), red for Confucianism (the color represents yang), and blue for Daoism (the color represents yin). The pope, legislators, and ordinary laypeople dress in white.

Adherents of Cao Dai may follow a communal path of practice by attending services at Cao Dai churches (services are held four times a day, every six hours, beginning at dawn), or they may pray at individual home altars. Special services are held during a new moon and a full moon. Believers of Cao Dai may also follow an individual path of self-perfection, which involves meditation and breathing exercises.

Cao Dai is governed by a hierarchical structure reminiscent of Catholicism: it is led by a pope and cardinals, and its headquarters, like the Vatican, is called the Holy See (the word comes from the Latin *sedes,* "seat"). The center of the religion, along with its large cathedral, is located in southern

Believers offer incense before the all-seeing Eye in the Cao Dai Cathedral of Tay Ninh, Vietnam.

Vietnam in the town of Tay Ninh, just outside Ho Chi Minh City (Saigon). A center of the Cao Dai religion outside Vietnam is in Garden Grove, California, in the Los Angeles area. A new temple also exists in Sydney, Australia. There are about five million followers worldwide, although most live in Vietnam or abroad in Vietnamese-immigrant communities.

RASTAFARIANISM

Rastafarianism, a religion strongly influenced by Christianity, arose in Jamaica in the 1930s. The history of the island—held by the Spanish until 1655 and then by the British until 1962—is a history of antagonism toward colonial power. Anticolonial feeling expressed itself in the development of a distinctly local culture and a deliberately antiestablishment form of Jamaican English; it also prompted the formation of communities of runaway slaves (and their descendants), who left urban society to lead communal lives in Jamaica's mountains. Ironically, Protestant revivalism and Bible reading, derived from British Christianity, contributed to the anticolonial feelings. Out of this milieu Rastafarianism emerged.

The most important early figure of Rastafarianism was Marcus Garvey (1887–1940). Garvey was born in Jamaica and in 1914 organized there the Universal Negro Improvement Association (UNIA), which taught a pioneering form of black pride. After a brief stay in the United States, Garvey returned to Jamaica in the early 1920s to preach in Kingston, Jamaica's capital.

Garvey taught that people of African descent were in a state of psychological and political servitude in Jamaica; he preached that his followers in Jamaica—and others like them elsewhere—should take pride in their African origins, rid themselves of their oppression, and unite in a world federation. He longed for the day when African culture would be taught in schools. To illustrate his ideas he wrote several plays, of which one was especially influential, *The Coronation of the King and Queen of Africa.*

According to the accounts of followers, Garvey taught them to look to Africa for the crowning of a native king who would be their redeemer. In a fateful twist of history, in 1930 a nobleman named **Ras Tafari** (1891–1975) was crowned emperor of Ethiopia. (The name *Ras* is a title akin to *duke*, and Tafari means "worthy of respect.") The coronation ceremony in Addis Ababa was a major event, attended by diplomats from many countries and widely covered in newsreels. Ras Tafari took a new name when he became ruler of Ethiopia: Emperor Haile Selassie ("Power of the Trinity").

Ethiopia was already widely esteemed by Jamaicans as a great example of an ancient black African kingdom that had remained independent. Many Jamaicans also accepted the belief of Ethiopians that their emperor was descended from the biblical King Solomon and Queen of Sheba. In addition, some Jamaicans began to believe that Haile Selassie was a new appearance of Jesus—and that he was therefore divine (Haile Selassie, a devout Coptic Christian, did not share these last beliefs).

> Princes shall come out of Egypt; Ethiopia shall soon stretch out her hands unto God.
> —Psalm 68:31[7]

Hope began to build in Jamaica that Haile Selassie would send ships to return black Jamaicans to Africa. This hope grew stronger after 1938, when Haile Selassie founded the Ethiopian World Federation and granted it five hundred acres of land in Ethiopia, intended for any people of African descent who wished to resettle there. The great symbolic importance of Haile Selassie was obvious when the emperor came to visit Jamaica in 1966: he had trouble leaving his plane because of the enormous crowds that came to greet him.

Haile Selassie died in 1975, yet Rastafarians believe that he is still alive in his spiritual body. Prayed to under the name *Ras Tafari,* he remains a symbol of liberation. His importance for many Jamaicans both explains the name of the Rastafarians and makes understandable their focus on him as a center of their religious belief.

Rastafarianism is not a single, organized church; rather, it is a diffuse movement that continues to produce new branches. Among its many offshoots are the Rastafarian Movement Association, the Ethiopian National Congress, and a more recent branch called the Twelve Tribes of Israel. Despite differences among the various groups, several beliefs and practices have emerged that are shared by most Rastafarians. The first shared belief

Dry up your tears and come to meet Ras Tafari.

—Rastafarian hymn[8]

Some Rastafarians have made connections with Ethiopian Christianity, as in this baptism at an Ethiopian Orthodox church in Kingston, Jamaica.

is that there is one God, who is referred to by the biblical name *Jah* (the name is related to *Yahweh* and *Jehovah*). A second common belief is that Haile Selassie, called King of Kings and Lion of Judah, was (and is) divine. Third, all Rastafarians believe that the Bible not only is the word of God but that it also has hidden meanings that are important for people of African descent. These passages can particularly be found in the Psalms and the prophetic Books of Daniel and Revelation, which speak of a Messiah and a "golden age" in the future. Fourth, Rastafarians hold that people of African descent—like the Israelites who were held in captivity for fifty years in Babylon—must seek liberation from any society that oppresses them.

Rastafarianism at first was sharply racial, condemning white society (called Babylon) and seeking emancipation from it. These sharp edges, however, have been softened over recent decades as Rastafarians have sought to change society by entering government in Jamaica and elsewhere; moreover, many whites have converted to Rastafarianism. Increasingly, Rastafarians have begun to focus on the ideals of human unity and on harmony with the environment.

Representative practices have grown up over time, although their origins are debated. One of

Although no longer living, reggae singer Bob Marley remains something of a Rastafarian missionary.

these is the sacramental use of *ganja* (marijuana). The practice may have come from its use by immigrants from India to the Caribbean. Rastafarians call ganja the "holy herb," and they point to several passages in the Christian Bible that they say refer to it. One favorite passage is taken from the story of creation: "And God said, 'Let the earth bring forth grass, the herb yielding seed'" (Gen. 1:11).[9] Another describes a future "golden age," when a river flows from the New Jerusalem. On each side of the river God has planted trees with medicinal leaves, for "the leaves of the tree were for the healing of nations" (Rev. 22:2).[10]

Another Rastafarian practice involves allowing one's hair to grow into long coils, called **dreadlocks.** (In Jamaican English, *dread* has often been used as an adjective to mean "strict," "upright," "righteous.") Although this custom probably began as a symbolic rejection of oppressive social norms, it has also been interpreted as adherence to scripture. The Torah prohibits males from cutting their beards and side-whiskers (see Lev. 19:27), and it prescribes a special vow that keeps a male from drinking wine and cutting any hair of the head whatsoever (Num. 6:5). Biblical examples of people subject to this vow were Samson (Judg. 13:5), known for his bodily strength, and John the Baptist (Luke 1:15), known for his strength of character.

Rastafarians, partially influenced by the dietary laws of the Hebrew scriptures, usually avoid pork and shellfish (Lev. 11:7–12). They prefer food with no preservatives, additives, pesticides, or herbicides. For health reasons, many Rastafarians are vegetarian—such as Ziggy Marley, Bob Marley's son, who has demonstrated on television how to make his recipe for "Rasta Pasta."

Rastafarians have adopted the symbolic use of four colors: black, to represent people of African origin; green, to represent the hills of Jamaica and hope for the future; red, to represent the blood that was shed by martyrs for the cause; and gold, to represent Ethiopia, a focus of African pride. This color scheme can often be seen in hats, shirts, and flags.

Elements of Rastafarianism have entered mainstream culture, particularly through music. Following African practice, Rastafarians from the beginning used drumming for religious purposes, but it was the development of reggae music and songs after 1960 that particularly spread Rasta ideas and vocabulary. Jimmy Cliff, Bob Marley, and Bob's son Ziggy Marley are perhaps the best-known reggae musicians. (Bob Marley's house, since his death in 1981, has become a shrine.) The influence of this music has created a "reggae culture" (for example, in the world of surfing) that is far wider than Rastafarianism itself. Rastafarianism and its influence have spread throughout the Caribbean and to England, Canada, and the United States.

BAHA'I

We end our examination of specific new religious movements with a look at a movement descended from Islam. The origins of the **Baha'i** faith, another monotheistic religion, can be traced to the Shiite Islam of Persia (Iran). We might recall that Shiite Islam sees divine authority as residing in the line of Imams, the hereditary successors of Ali, who was the son-in-law of Muhammad. Many Shiite Muslims believe that the last Imam did not die, but lives in another realm beyond the earth, and that he will return. Many also expect that a messianic figure (sometimes identified with Jesus) will appear on earth in the future.

This Shiite sense of expectation was the context for a nineteenth-century religious movement in Persia. It grew up around a man named Siyyid Ali Muhammad (1819–1850), who declared in 1844 that he was the long-awaited Mahdi—the last Imam, returned to earth. He took a religious name, **Bab,** meaning "gate" or "door," and preached that there would soon arrive another divinely sent messenger who would be of even greater stature and would bring full revelation from Allah. That figure, he prophesied, would begin a golden age of unity and peace. Because of conflict with orthodox Muslims, the Bab was thrown into prison and executed in 1850.

One of the Bab's followers and a leader of the Babist movement was a young Persian aristocrat, Mirza Husayn Ali (1817–1892), who later became known as **Baha'u'llah** ("glory of Allah"). After the death of the Bab, Baha'u'llah was himself nearly killed by government authorities. Instead of being executed, however, he was jailed in Tehran, in the notorious "Black Pit"—an underground reservoir used as a prison. There he experienced several months of divine revelations. After release, he was banished from Iran and began a life of exile, wandering in many places, including Baghdad and cities in Turkey, Egypt, and Palestine. He continued to be the focus of the Babist movement, and in 1863 he at last declared that he was indeed the messianic figure whom the Bab had prophesied. He lived the last years of his life in Acre, near Haifa, in what is today the west coast of Israel.

Baha'u'llah wrote innumerable letters to his followers and public letters to world leaders, such as Pope Pius IX and Queen Victoria, outlining his practical ideas for a future of human harmony. In his books, such as the *Kitab-i-Iqan* ("book of certainty") and the *Kitab-i-Aqdas* ("book of holiness"), he proposed the establishment of a world government. His ethical teachings are summarized in a short work called *The Hidden Words*.

After the death of Baha'u'llah in 1892, his son, Abdul Baha (1844–1921), carried his message to Europe and North America. His grandson, Shoghi Effendi (1897–1957), continued to lead the religion and translated its scriptures into English.

The term *Baha'i*, which means "follower of Baha'u'llah," was widely used during the lifetime of Baha'u'llah. Muslims consider the Baha'i faith to be a heretical sect. Orthodox Muslims call Muhammad the "seal of the prophets," meaning that Muhammad was not only the greatest of the prophets but also the last. They therefore do not accept that Baha'u'llah was a prophet, and followers of the Baha'i faith in Iran—of whom about 350,000 still remain—have been severely persecuted. The Baha'i movement, however, is now a separate religion, fully independent of Islam, and has followers all around the world.

The Baha'i faith is among the most universalistic of religions. While it retains its monotheistic origins, the religion defines God and other religious realities in broad terms that are appealing to a wide range of people. A major expression of Baha'i universalism is that Baha'is see all religions as partially true, but also as separate elements of a great mosaic of divine revelation that is still being shaped by God. Baha'is argue that all religious founders have offered some revelation from God, but that earlier revelations have been tempered by the cultures and times in which they appeared. For Baha'is, revelation is necessarily progressive, because human beings continue to evolve in understanding. Baha'is believe that the revelations of Baha'u'llah, while being the most advanced, nonetheless continue the revelations given to earlier prophets, including Abraham, Moses, Zarathustra (Zoroaster), Krishna, the Buddha, Jesus, Muhammad, and the Bab.

Baha'is teach that all religions, in some fundamental sense, are one, and Baha'is therefore look forward to the day when divisions between religions will disappear. Although the writings of Baha'u'llah are considered scriptural, Baha'is also read selections from the scriptures of many world religions at their services. Baha'is not only strive for harmony among

World unity is the goal towards which a harassed humanity is striving. Nation building has come to an end. The anarchy inherent in state sovereignty is moving towards a climax. A world, growing to maturity, must abandon this fetish, recognize the oneness and wholeness of human relationships, and establish once for all the machinery that can best incarnate this fundamental principle of its life.

—Shoghi Effendi[11]

Visitors line up to enter the Baha'i Mashriqu'l-Adhkar, the "Lotus Temple" in New Delhi.

people of different religious faiths, they also try to overcome the differences between religious and scientific endeavors, which often seem to be at odds with each other.

Baha'i belief about the afterlife is reminiscent of other monotheistic religions, yet it is deliberately left somewhat undefined—a fact that gives Baha'i wide appeal. Baha'is believe that each individual has an immortal soul and that after death the soul can go on developing in realms beyond the earth. They also speak of places of reward and punishment in an afterlife. When Baha'is speak of "heaven" and "hell," however, they explain that these are metaphors for closeness to or distance from God.

Rather than focusing on an afterlife, Baha'is emphasize improving human life in this world. Baha'is seek complete equality between men and women, an end to poverty, and education for all. They work to end prejudice, and to accomplish this they not only allow intermarriage but also encourage it.

Baha'is have a strongly international focus. They want to see the establishment of an auxiliary world language—to augment rather than replace regional languages—for use in international communication. On a very practical level, Baha'is are active supporters of the United Nations and other organizations that, in their opinion, foster world harmony. Their ultimate hope is that a single world government will supersede independent nations and thus make war impossible. And although Baha'is do not become politicians themselves, they work in many other practical ways to achieve their goals.

One unusual aspect of the Baha'i faith is its religious calendar, created by the Bab. It is made up of nineteen months, each being nineteen days long (with four extra days added before the final month). The last month of the

Contemporary Issues

HUMANISM: A NEW RELIGION?

During the Renaissance (c. 1350–1600) an important movement emerged. Because it was inspired by classical scholarship, contemporary science, and the quest for human betterment, it came to be called *humanism*. The movement represented a sharp departure from the other philosophical movements of its time, because it focused exclusively on the earthly concerns of human beings and disregarded the supernatural. Drawing upon this earlier Renaissance tradition, the modern movement of Humanism (also called Ethical Humanism) has been developing over the last hundred years.

The main principles of modern Humanism are simple. The most recent Humanist Manifesto describes the movement as a philosophy of life that, while rejecting supernaturalism, insists on the ability of human beings to lead lives that are moral, personally fulfilling, and helpful to others. Because Humanism gives special emphasis to social welfare, it has similarities with socialism and secularism. Yet it is not a political ideology, and it openly considers various means to achieve its objectives.

Because of its focus on practical issues and its disregard for the supernatural, some people debate whether the movement should be called a religion. Humanism, however, does share certain characteristics with religion. For example, some of its chapters perform weddings, funerals, and other rituals common to religions. Also, like many religions, Humanism places great emphasis on ethical standards, particularly those associated with the pursuit of social welfare.

year is a period of fasting, reminiscent of Ramadan in Islam, when no food or drink may be consumed during the daytime. This period of purification lasts from March 2 through March 20; the new year begins on March 21. The first day of each Baha'i month is a time of meeting, prayer, and celebration.

Baha'is are not allowed to drink alcohol, and they are discouraged from smoking. In conjunction with a belief in gender equality, Baha'i does not allow polygamy, but it does allow divorce.

Baha'i has no priesthood; it is governed by assemblies that operate on the local, national, and international level. Followers often meet in each other's homes. Each continent, however, has one large templelike house of prayer, open to all, and more are planned. (The exotic, filigreed North American house of prayer is in Wilmette, Illinois, in the suburbs of Chicago. It has fine gardens and ponds. The Baha'i house of prayer in New Delhi, a totally unique building, is shaped like a water lily.) All houses of prayer have nine sides; for Baha'is the number nine, being the highest single-digit number, symbolizes completeness and perfection. The Baha'i world headquarters and its governing body, the Universal House of Justice, are in Haifa, Israel. There are about six million Baha'is worldwide.

NEW RELIGIOUS MOVEMENTS: A SPECIAL ROLE

In reflecting on the new religious movements that we have studied, questions naturally come to mind. What traits make these movements attractive to people? What do they say about where religion is heading in the twenty-first century?

One notable trait of these new religious movements is that they are still relatively small and their members usually meet in small groups. Thus there is a strong sense of intimacy among members, giving them a feeling that they have a function, that "everyone counts." Members are also attracted to belonging to a group with a unique identity and purpose.

A second notable trait is the role that women play in several of the new religious movements—a role that many mainstream religions have blocked. Theosophy was cofounded by Madame Helena Blavatsky, a self-confident, well-traveled woman who was a writer as well as an organizer, and it was continued by Annie Besant, also a writer and organizer. Moreover, women are the main practitioners of Wicca, and through it they worship the divine that is manifested as the female and mother. In the Yoruba-based religions, female deities play a major role, and worship of them is a significant part of the ceremonial life. Women play an important role, too, in the organizations of several other new religious movements.

A third trait is the importance of an active devotional life. We especially find an emphasis on the mystical element—the sense of union with something greater than oneself. This mystical element is often assisted by music and dance that lead to trance states, or by meditations on a divine spirit that everyone shares. The mystical orientation is strong in Wicca, in the Yoruba-based religions, in Theosophy, and in Rastafarianism, and it is a significant part of Baha'i and Cao Dai.

Lastly, many of the religions present clear programs for self-development, which often involve the body as well as the mind. In Cao Dai, self-cultivation is a major goal, and virtues are clearly described. Anthroposophy has worked out a system of self-development that is meant to complete the entire human person—physical, intellectual, and artistic. Followers of Falun Gong use exercises in meditation and bodily motion to increase inner harmony and strength. And Wicca encourages participants to imagine and work for practical goals that will enrich their lives.

The new religious movements fulfill human needs that may be unmet in the older mainstream religions. They also tell us about larger trends in the future of world religions. They are, consequently, a bridge to our discussion, in the final chapter, of the modern religious search.

PERSONAL EXPERIENCE
Celebrating the Goddess

"Do you want to talk about your future?" a young woman asked me from the roots of a large banyan tree. I hadn't seen her sitting there at a small table at the base of the tree. It was about two weeks before Christmas, and I was walking quickly through one of the few leafy places left in Waikiki, looking for some last-minute presents at the nearby booths that sold coral jewelry, sarongs, aloha shirts, and carvings. "Would you like me to do a reading for you?"

A Tarot card reader in New Orleans helps a client understand his future.

I sat down, and she quoted me a price for my reading. She also told me her name—Diana—and then asked me my name and the date and time of my birth. She laid down her bright Tarot cards—first in intersecting lines, then a straight line on the side—and told me what she saw. She interpreted the colorful images on the cards: a tower with a bolt of lightning, a knight on horseback, an angel with two chalices, a hermit, two lovers, and a wheel of fortune.[12]

"Now you might like to ask some questions," she said. As I asked specific questions about my work and my future, she turned over one additional card for each question and gave me her interpretation of the cards. I liked her careful choice of words and her feeling for the symbolic nature of the images on the cards. She clearly believed in what she was doing.

One of my last questions was about an aging relative who was terminally ill. "He is beginning to feel terribly sick," I said. "How long will he live?"

Diana looked at her cards. "Actually," she answered after a long pause, "he is very strong inside. He will die when he wants to." It was an ambiguous answer, but a good one. Diana made me think of a priestess at the oracle of Delphi, who was known to be equally adept at such answers.

At last we had gone through all my questions and all her cards. "Now I have a question myself," she said. "Would you like to come to a Yuletide celebration here in Waikiki next week?" I answered that I would and asked if there was anything I could bring. "Oh, just some food," she replied, "but wear red or green for the celebration."

A week later I was taking my shoes off (as we do in Hawai`i) outside the door of a ground-floor apartment in a small building from the 1930s. Somehow the low-rise building had survived in the middle of bustling, high-rise

Waikiki. I'd brought sushi, wine, and a piece of mistletoe that I'd seen for sale at the grocery store. As I lined my shoes up next to twenty other pairs of shoes and sandals, I noticed that only a few were men's.

Lady Diana welcomed me. (She had told me that this was her name as a high priestess of Wicca. Her given name was Lorraine.) She wore a floor-length gold dress with long sleeves. She held a child in her arms. Diana introduced me to her friends Isis, Aurora, Bridget, and at least a dozen others. Most of them wore elaborate necklaces and dangling earrings. A few even wore tiaras. The men, except for one named Thor, had less exotic names, but all wore red shirts.

I looked around. A five-pointed star, made of Christmas lights, hung on the wall near the Christmas tree. A low square altar, covered in gold cloth, stood in the middle of the room, and on it were a statue of a woman with a deer and another of a horned Pan figure, a small cauldron, tall candles, and what looked like a fancy letter opener. A smaller round table next to the larger altar was covered with about twenty vigil candles.

About two dozen silver goblets stood on a side table, and I added my bottle of wine to the other bottles, some already open. People were eating and talking. Diana handed me a goblet of wine. "Circulate," she said.

After half an hour of socializing, Diana asked us to stand in a circle around the altars. The women began a slow chant, which they repeated in a hypnotic way: "We all come from the Goddess/and to her we shall return/ Like drops of rain/flow into the ocean." Carrying her child, Diana went to each wall of the room, praying to the spirits of the four directions. She then circled the room to enclose the group. We sat while Bridget and Isis enacted a short playlet about the myth of Demeter and Persephone, Greek goddesses who went into the darkness of the underworld.

When the two women had finished, Diana spoke. "We are celebrating the winter solstice and unite ourselves with this cosmic turning of time. The Christmas tree, the candles, and the greenery represent the return of life and light. Like the sun, we also will grow in strength as the year progresses."

She passed around a large goblet of wine, and each person put into it a bit of bread, as an offering to the Goddess. Diana put it on the altar. Each person lit a candle on the smaller altar and talked about hopes for the coming year. Then everyone joined hands and moved in a slow circular dance around the altars. "Peace on earth, good will to all," Diana sang during the dance. At last Diana stopped the dance and asked everyone to sit again in a circle on the floor.

Diana now went to each of the four sides of the room to address the spirits of the four directions. She spoke finally to the Goddess, ended the ceremony, and officially "opened the circle." She gave each of us a small cloth bag with instructions to write down our wishes for the coming year on a piece of paper, to put the written wishes inside the bag, and to place the bag on our home altar. Then, just before we left, Diana said a blessing: "May the circle be open but unbroken. May the peace of the Goddess be forever in your heart. Merry meet, and merry part, till we merry meet again."

Isis, Bridget, and I left together. In the dim light just outside, my attention was devoutly focused on my feet: I was afraid that I might trip. I looked down carefully at each crooked, mossy stone of the uneven pathway, which was lined with ferns. When at last we reached the street, Bridget said, "Look!" She pointed up. Isis and I looked upward, but I saw only streetlights, bright shop signs, and the lighted upper floors of a condominium building. Then I saw what had caught her eye. Overwhelmed by all the lights below, but still visible in the sky, shone a crescent moon.

READING BAHA'I PRAYER

Baha'u'llah, the founder of Baha'i, wrote this prayer, full of ardent devotion. It is reminiscent of the mystical poetry of several religions.

O Thou Whose face is the object of my adoration, Whose beauty is my sanctuary, Whose habitation is my goal, Whose praise is my hope, Whose providence is my companion, Whose love is the cause of my being, Whose mention is my solace, Whose nearness is my desire, Whose presence is my dearest wish and highest aspiration, I entreat Thee not to withhold from me the things Thou didst ordain for the chosen ones among Thy servants. Supply me, then, with the good of this world and of the next. Thou, truly, art the King of all men. There is no God but Thee, the Ever-Forgiving, the Most Generous.[13]

TEST YOURSELF

1. The term _____ is used to describe the mixture of various elements from different religions.
   a. polytheism
   b. imminent
   c. transcendent
   d. syncretic

2. _____ is the best-known manifestation of the Contemporary Pagan movement. It is an Old English word that suggests associations with magic, separation, and holiness.
   a. Druid
   b. Wicca
   c. Voodoo
   d. Santería

3. _____ were an elite group of ancient Celtic professionals who acted as judges, teachers, counselors, doctors, and priests.
   a. Druids
   b. Wiccans
   c. Thetans
   d. Orishas

4. _____, a religion that grew up in Spanish colonial Cuba, is a mixture of Yoruba religions and Catholicism.
   a. Santería
   b. Theosophy
   c. Scientology
   d. Voodoo

5. _____, a religion that developed in French colonial Haiti, is a mixture of Yoruba religions and Catholicism.
   a. Santería
   b. Theosophy
   c. Scientology
   d. Voodoo

6. _____ shows a strong interest in mystically oriented teachings from all sources—among them, Hindu Vedanta, the Jewish Kabbalah, and Gnosticism.
   a. Santería
   b. Theosophy
   c. Scientology
   d. Voodoo

7. _____ was founded by L. Ron Hubbard. It holds that the core of the human being is a spiritual reality, which it calls the thetan.
   a. Santería
   b. Theosophy
   c. Scientology
   d. Voodoo

8. In Falun Gong, the _____ is believed to be an invisible spiritual wheel located in the lower abdomen that can be activated by a master.
   a. falun
   b. gong
   c. cao
   d. dai

9. _____ is the most important early figure of Rastafarianism.
   a. W. E. B. DuBois
   b. Martin Luther King Jr.
   c. Marcus Garvey
   d. Zaydis

10. The term *Baha'i* means follower of _____. The Baha'i faith is among the most universalistic of religions.
    a. the Bab
    b. Baha'u'llah
    c. Baal
    d. Babal

11. Review the new religions described in this chapter. Do you think there is greater emphasis overall on a transcendent or an immanent understanding of sacred reality? (You may want to review the definitions of "transcendent" and "immanent" in Chapter 1 to help explain your answer.)

12. Imagine you have the opportunity to interview a member of any new religion described in this chapter. Which new religion would you choose? What are two questions you would especially like to ask?

RESOURCES

Books

Berry, Thomas. *The Sacred Universe: Earth, Spirituality, and Religion in the Twenty-First Century.* New York: Columbia University Press, 2009. Essays on the need for a new religious responsibility to the earth.

Bowers, Kenneth E. *God Speaks Again: An Introduction to the Bahá'í Faith.* Chicago: Bahá'í Publishing, 2004. The story of Baha'u'llah and the Baha'i faith.

Bui, Hum Dac, and Ngasha Beck. *Cao Dai: Faith of Unity.* Fayetteville, AR: Emerald Wave, 2000. A thorough introduction to the religion.

Cowan, Douglas, and David Bromley. *Cults and New Religions: A Brief History.* Oxford: Blackwell, 2008. A survey of eight new religions, including Scientology, Wicca, and the Unification Church.

Cunningham, Scott. *Wicca: A Guide for the Solitary Practitioner.* Minneapolis: Llewellyn, 1993. A how-to guide for the practice of Wicca, with information on holy days, ceremonies, altars, and rituals.

Horsley, Kate. *Confessions of a Pagan Nun: A Novel.* Boston: Shambhala, 2002. A novel that describes the life of a woman in Ireland circa 500 CE, who trains as a Druid priestess before converting to Christianity and becoming a nun.

Ownby, David. *Falun Gong and the Future of China.* New York: Oxford University Press, 2008. A description of Falun Gong as a continuation of Chinese practices for health, with an explanation of governmental opposition.

Film/TV

The Believers. (Director John Schlesinger; Orion.) A Hollywood film set against a background of Santería practice in New York City.

Beyond the Red Wall: The Persecution of Falun Gong. (Director Peter Rowe; CBC.) A documentary about Kunlun Zhang, an artist and professor at McGill University, who was jailed for nearly three years in a Chinese labor camp because of his participation in the Falun Gong movement.

I Married a Witch. (Director René Clair; Warner.) An elegant classic, one of the first Hollywood films to mention witchcraft.

The "Kitchen Goddess": The Reemergence of the Village Psychic (Films Media Group.) A look at modern divination and healing as practiced by members of Wicca and the users of Tarot, astrology, and palmistry.

Rebel Music: The Bob Marley Story. (Director Jeremy Marre; Palm Pictures.) A documentary profile of the legendary reggae singer and Rastafarian.

The Spiritual Quest of Generation X. (Films Media Group.) An exploration of the role of spirituality in the lives of young people and their movement toward New Age religions.

The Truth Within: Towards a New Spiritual Utopia. (Films Media Group.) An examination of New Age religious movements, including interviews with Huston Smith, Marilyn Ferguson, Thich Nhat Hanh, and Sheikh Abd al-Wahid Pallavicini.

Voodoo and the Church in Haiti. (Director Bob Richards; CustomFlix.) A documentary that examines the religious fusion of Voodoo and Christianity in Haiti.

Music/Audio

The Best of Pagan Song. (Serpentine Music Productions.) A compilation of devotional songs from the Contemporary Pagan movement.

Falun Dafa Practice Music. Music to be played while performing Falun Dafa meditation and exercise (available at Falun Dafa Web site: www.falun-dafa.org).

Goddess Chant. (Ladyslipper.) Ritual chants to the Goddess by the Wiccan priestess Shawna Carol.

Rhythms of Rapture: Sacred Music of Haitian Vodou. (Smithsonian Folkways.) A recording of ceremonies contrasted against performances by Haitian artists whose music is influenced by Voodoo.

Sacred Rhythms of Cuban Santería. (Smithsonian Folkways.) A recording of Santería drumming and singing recorded in several Cuban provinces.

The Spiritual Roots of Reggae. (Deja vu Italy.) The music of Count Ossie, the legendary Jamaican drummer and bandleader, who first introduced Rastafarian elements into Jamaican popular music.

State of Mind Music. A collection of songs and poems set to music written by L. Ron Hubbard (available at Scientology bookstores and on its Web site: www.scientology.org).

Internet

Covenant of the Goddess: http://www.cog.org/. The official Web site for an international organization of Wiccan congregations and individual practitioners, offering information about religious beliefs and practices.

Rastafarianism: http://www.bbc.co.uk/religion/religions/rastafari/. An easy-to-understand source of information about Rastafarian history, beliefs, practices, and holy days.

The Witches' Voice: http://www.witchvox.com/. An educational networking Web site that provides news, information services, and resources for Pagans and Wiccans.

KEY TERMS

alliance: In Cao Dai, one of three periods of special divine revelation.

Anthroposophy (an-thro-pah′-so-fee): "Human wisdom" (Greek); a movement that grew out of Theosophy and emphasizes education and other practical means for spiritual development.

auditor: In Scientology, a counselor who, through a series of questions, works to guide a person to greater self-understanding.

Bab (bahb): "Door," "gate"; a prophet who was the forerunner of Baha'u'llah, the founder of Baha'i.

Baha'i (bah-hai′ or bah-hah′-ee): A modern monotheistic religion that grew out of Islam and emphasizes unity and equality of individuals, cultures, and religions; a follower of the Baha'i religion.

Baha'u'llah (bah-hah′-oo-lah′): "Glory of Allah" (Arabic); the founder of Baha'i.

bard: A first-level initiate in Druidism; also, a follower of a path in Druidism.

Bridge: In Scientology, a diagram of the stages toward personal liberation.

Candomblé (cahn-dohm-blay'): The syncretic religion of Brazil that blends elements of Portuguese Catholicism and African religions.

Cao Dai (kao'-dai): "High palace"; a syncretic religion that began in Vietnam and that blends Confucianism, Daoism, Buddhism, and Catholic Christianity.

Church Universal and Triumphant: A religion that unites elements from Theosophy and Christianity; also referred to as CUT.

clear: In Scientology, the state of mental liberation; the person who has achieved mental liberation; also referred to as *operating thetan,* or *OT.*

Contemporary Paganism: A general name for several movements that attempt to reestablish a pre-Christian European nature religion; also called Neo-Paganism.

dreadlocks: The long coiled hair worn by some Rastafarians.

Druid (droo'-id): "Oak-tree wisdom"; a Celtic priest of two thousand years ago; a follower of the modern re-creation of Druidism.

e-meter: In Scientology, an electronic machine that reads galvanic skin response; sometimes used to assist the auditing process.

engram: In Scientology, an experience of earlier suffering (even from a past life) that keeps a person from relating healthily to the present.

equinox: "Equal night" (Latin); the two days of the year, in the spring and autumn, when the hours of daylight and nighttime are equal.

Esbat (es'-baht): In Wicca, the time of the full moon, often marked by a meeting or ceremony.

eurhythmy (yoo-rith'-mee): "Good rhythm" (Greek); a type of interpretive dance utilized in Anthroposophy as a technique for spiritual growth.

falun (fah'-loon): "Law wheel" (Chinese); an invisible spiritual wheel, believed by followers of Falun Gong to spin in the abdominal region, distilling and spreading energy from the universe.

Falun Gong: "Law-wheel energy" (Chinese); a modern Chinese religion that uses meditation and physical exercises in its practice.

loa (lwa) (lwah): A deity in Voodoo.

MEST: In Scientology, an acronym for matter, energy, space, and time; the world of time and space, the world in which spirits must live.

ocha (oh'-shah): In Santería, any deity.

operating thetan: In Scientology, a fully liberated person; also referred to as *OT* or *clear.*

orisha (oh-ree'-shah): A general name for a deity in the Yoruba-tradition religions.

Oshún (oh-shoon'): A female deity in Santería who is associated with love and marriage.

ovate: A second-level initiate in Druidism; also, a follower of a path of Druidism.

pre-clear: In Scientology, a person who is not yet spiritually liberated and who is just beginning to undergo the auditing process.

Qigong (chee'-gong): "Energy force" (Chinese); a type of martial art that is thought to increase health and strength.

Ras Tafari (rahs tah-fah'-ree): The original name of Emperor Haile Selassie, often used by Rastafarians to emphasize his religious significance.

Rastafarianism: A religion that began in Jamaica in the 1920s to emphasize African pride; it considers Haile Selassie (Ras Tafari) to be divine.

Rede (reed): "Advice," "counsel"; a term used in Wicca to describe its maxim that an act is allowable if it does no harm: "An [if] it harm none, do what you will."

Sabbat (sah-baht'): One of eight seasonal turning points marked by Wiccans and Druids.

santera (san-tay'-rah): a priestess of Santería.

Santería (sahn-tay-ree'-ah): "Saint-thing" or "saint-way" (Spanish); a Yoruba-based religion that developed in Cuba and was influenced by Spanish Catholicism.

santero (sahn-tay'-roh): A priest of Santería.

Scientology: "Knowledge-study" (Latin and Greek); a modern religion that promotes a process of focusing thought and clarifying life goals.

Shangó (Changó) (shahn-goh'): In Santería, a popular god associated with lightning and powerful storms.

solstice: "Sun-stands" (Latin); the two days of the year, at midwinter and midsummer, when the season begins to reverse itself.

Theosophy (thee-ah'-soh-fee): "Divine wisdom" (Greek); an eclectic movement, particularly influenced by Hinduism, that focuses on the mystical elements of all religions.

thetan (thay'-tun): In Scientology, the human soul.

Voodoo (Voudun): A religion that developed in Haiti that blends elements from French Catholicism and African religions.

Wicca (wik'-ah): A Contemporary Pagan movement that seeks harmony with the forces of nature and worships both the female and male aspects of the divine.

RELIGION BEYOND THE CLASSROOM

Visit the Online Learning Center at www.mhhe.com/molloy6e for additional exercises and features, including "Religion beyond the Classroom" and "For Fuller Understanding."

The Modern Search

F I R S T   E N C O U N T E R

You learn from your university's newspaper that your campus will be hosting a large gathering of religious leaders for three days. There will be large and small meetings, some of them open to students and the general public. At the end of each day there will be a nondenominational service in a nearby church or temple, and at the end of the conference there will be a large meeting that everyone may attend. You decide to go to the final conference meeting.

The gathering is in a modern auditorium, which is usually used by the theater department. Upon entering, you see a stage full of people in bright-colored clothes. Among them you notice Sikh representatives in white, Hindus in orange, Buddhists in gray and orange, Muslims in brown, Christians in black and purple, and Native Americans in various-colored tribal dress. To open the session, a cantor sings a Jewish festival song and a Native American chants a song in praise of the sun.

After the music, the president of the university thanks everyone for attending. Next, the keynote speaker sums up the ideas discussed at the various meetings held over the three days. After his remarks, he opens the floor to questions and asks the audience members to please use the microphones standing in the aisles, so that everyone can hear. People line up quickly. The first question is a bit startling and provokes laughter.

"Why are most of you men?" a faculty member asks the keynote speaker. "I see only a few women among you. Where are all the female religious leaders?"

Before answering, one of the representatives pauses to collect his thoughts. The silence is uncomfortable.

"Women ministers and religious leaders do exist," he says at last. "In fact, some religious groups, like Christian Science, were begun by women. But I admit that most religious traditions are only beginning to appreciate gender as an issue, and many religions are still closed to the idea of female clergy. Fortunately, some religious schools are now training female candidates. Although leaders in most religions are still male, we can expect in the future that more leaders will be women."

Nice try, you think. The people around you do not seem convinced either.

A man on the far left of the auditorium comments, "Religious leaders have been getting together to engage in dialogue for years. But has it really led to anything substantial? For example, have any religions come together to help survivors of catastrophes, such as the people of Haiti and Japan whose lives were devastated by earthquakes?"

A Buddhist monk answers. He speaks about the relief-work groups from Asia, like the Tzu Chi Foundation in Taiwan and the Ruamkatanyu Foundation in Thailand. But he concedes that their work has been done primarily in coordination with other organizations of the same religion. "It is hard to get religions to work together on global matters. I wish I knew why." A Christian bishop adds information about Christian welfare groups, such as Catholic Relief Services and World Vision, but he admits the same problem of getting different religions to work together. "And there's always the issue of sensitivity to the local religions of the countries needing assistance. Sometimes they don't want our help."

Another audience member asks about the future of religions. "Will the future just bring more of the same—the same religions, the same rituals, the same beliefs? Or is it possible that religions will influence each other and even blend? Can new beliefs emerge from the old religions? Could there be entirely new religions?"

A Shinto leader from the West Coast answers. "Some religions and denominations are very open to new ideas. My own religion of Shinto has many modern offshoots, like Tenrikyo and Omoto, which try to address the problems of the modern world. And there are branches of old religions that deliberately reject prescribed beliefs—among them are the Unity Church, the Unitarians, and some forms of Judaism. They want to be open to new ideas.

For example, they seek new understandings of what God might be and of what revelation means."

Another representative adds that interfaith meetings like this really are having an effect on belief and practice. "Some Christian groups now practice meditation and silent prayer. These new practices have been influenced by Hinduism and Buddhism. And, in turn, Hinduism and Buddhism have taken ideas from other religions, such as the need for social involvement and welfare work. Maybe we are only at the beginning of our dialogue. I wish I could be here a hundred years from now to see what comes about."

The questions and discussion go on for another half hour. At last, the keynote speaker makes his closing comments from the stage. Many of the leaders say a final prayer, and the conference is adjourned.

You walk out with Marianne, a friend from one of your classes. "What do you think?" you ask.

"I'm not quite sure," she says. "I'm thinking about it, though, because I have to write a paper about the conference. What about you?"

"I think it was 'same old same old.' My parents are regular churchgoers, and they hear the same teachings as they did when they were children. I stopped following their religion, but I did try several others for a while. Right now I'm still looking. Maybe I'll have to invent my own! What about you? What are you going to write?"

"I think I'm going to write about where religions could be headed in the future. Bringing women into leadership positions is inevitable, and it will change religions. I think it could make them more tolerant. And I also think that new religions will emerge. Maybe they already have—but we don't see them as religions yet. People will always need a moral code. But maybe morality needs rethinking."

Marianne and I make plans to meet again and to talk more about what we've learned. As I walk away after saying good-bye, I wonder, What new religions will emerge? What will the future bring?

MODERN INFLUENCES ON THE FUTURE OF RELIGION

It is obvious that religions in the modern world face both challenge and inevitable change. Numerous social and technological developments are responsible for bringing about change. Women are demanding roles in arenas traditionally dominated by males—including institutional religions. Scientific advances in such areas as reproduction, genetics, and organ transplantation pose ethical questions that people in earlier times never had to answer. Many Western cities are homes to religions, such as Hinduism and Islam, that not too long ago were considered exotic and foreign. Finally, television, the Internet, cell phones, immigration, and travel expose human beings worldwide to new cultures and religions.

Change is happening so quickly that we must wonder about the future of religion. What if we could return to earth a few hundred years from now?

In ways that weren't even imagined a few decades ago, today's political, religious, and economic movements are spread by technology—and involve people who were previously overlooked.

Would the religions that we know now have changed a great deal? What religions would even still exist? Would there be new great religions?

We cannot know exactly how the religious landscape will look in another several hundred years, but we can make a guess based on the influences at work today—influences that are pulling religions in different directions. As we've seen throughout this book, religions in general tend to be conservative and often change more slowly than their surrounding societies. But, indeed, they do change. They change as a result of forces both from within themselves and from their surrounding cultures.

In this chapter we will first look at a few of the modern developments that are shaping our future in general and the future of religions in particular. We will consider the recurrent theme of change in religion. And we will look at two alternatives to organized religion. The first is the environmental movement and its almost religious view of nature. The second is what has come to be called eclectic spirituality, a union of various sources of inspiration, often expressed through art and music, which are frequently associated with spirituality.

The New World Order

A century ago the great majority of people lived rural lives, and many people were ruled by monarchs. Now the majority of people live in cities, and monarchs are in short supply. The economic and political landscape has changed rapidly. The Berlin Wall fell, uniting Germany, and Communism ended in the Soviet Union. Although China remains Communistic in name, it is now a major force in world capitalism. International companies are becoming as powerful as nations.

Once people had to travel far to experience different cultures. Now people in large cities have their pick of international cuisines—Thai, Japanese, Chinese, Italian, French, Vietnamese. And contact with people of different cultures is a daily occurrence. In large cities one can watch television programs in many languages, attend religious services of different cultures, and visit community centers of varied ethnic backgrounds.

We cannot help but wonder how this rich cultural change will affect religion. So far, most of the world's religions have remained fairly separate traditions—even those that have spread to different countries and cultures. But globalism may make it impossible for individual religions to remain separate.

Modern capitalism will also challenge religion, primarily by exposing relatively broad segments of populations to its promotion of financial success as a means to attaining personal satisfaction. In the past, many religions preached the values of poverty, simplicity, and detachment—values that at one time were consistent with life as experienced by the vast majority. Now, many religions are influenced by capitalist ideals, which esteem individual and group betterment; but it is a betterment that can be measured in material terms and can be paid for with money. As Robert Ellwood, a noted scholar of religions, has commented, the "idea that poverty could be a state of blessedness in itself, a favorite of preachers as recently as a century ago, is now hopelessly discredited. . . . Even the most conservative pulpiteers nowadays exhort their poor to get ahead, but to do it by nonviolent means."[1] We know that money can be used just as selfishly in the modern world as it was in the past. But money is not always used for selfish and useless reasons; take, for example, scholarships, contributions to disaster-relief projects, endowments to the arts. The modern culture of money-based betterment will increasingly challenge religions to produce what material cultures value. It will challenge the religious idealization of poverty and will question religions carefully about how much they contribute to measurable human betterment.[2]

The global economic crisis that began in 2008 will be a further challenge to religious thought and action. Religions may be influenced by the crisis to develop a new approach to the financial world, and religions could conceivably offer help by providing both theoretical and practical solutions.

Globalism will also challenge any incomplete visions of reality offered by traditional religions. Finally, urbanism will challenge traditional religions to confront the tribulations of large-scale city life and to take advantage of urban opportunities, such as a wide choice of educational and career opportunities.

Multiculturalism and Interfaith Dialogue

The new world order makes cross-cultural contact practically unavoidable, as television, radio, film, travel, books, and the Internet all work to narrow the gulfs that once separated people, nations, and even religions. It will thus be very difficult in the future for any religion to belong to a single culture or to be unaware of the teachings and practices of other religions. With awareness often comes adaptation, a phenomenon we have already seen with current religions. For example, certain forms of Pure Land Buddhism outside Japan have adopted the use of hymns and the Christian tradition of Sunday school. In Western forms of Zen and Tibetan Buddhism, married laypersons sometimes take leadership roles that have traditionally been performed by monks. African and Native American forms of Christianity now deliberately make use of native art, music, and dance. Roman Catholicism, which only a generation ago celebrated its rituals in Latin with uniform prayers and music, is today often as much a reflection of its specific community as it is of Rome. Some Christian monasteries and other religious groups have adopted Zen meditation. Moreover, entirely new religions may frequently blend elements from several religions. We see this, for example, in the Unification Church, which began in Korea and blends Christianity and Confucianism, and in some new Shinto religious offshoots, which blend elements of Shinto, Buddhism, and Christianity.

Another response to the growing awareness of cultural multiplicity can be seen in the increasingly frequent meetings held by representatives of different religions. The fact that these interreligious meetings are now being held is really a hopeful new direction. (It was not typical in the past.) Although religions have too often battled each other, they all preach human harmony and offer visions of peace. They have much to gain from and share with each other.

One of the earliest examples of modern religious dialogue was the first World Parliament of Religions, held in Chicago in 1893. Swami Vivekananda (1863–1902), a disciple of Ramakrishna, brought the inclusivist Hindu approach to the attention of the world through his insistence at that conference that all religions value holiness and love. And in 1993, Chicago hosted a second World Parliament of Religions, with simultaneous meetings of religious leaders at many places around the world. Yasumi Hirose, an interfaith representative of Omoto, has used the language of several religions to speak of his hope. "Unless we awake to the love and compassion of the God who created the heavens and earth, and realize that all creatures are filled with Divine Spirit and live by the grace of Amida Buddha, it will be impossible to change history to bring about a new century of co-existence."[3] There is ongoing dialogue as well in less spotlighted circles, such as the Ecumenical Institute at Saint John's Abbey in Minnesota, where scholars of different faiths spend months in conversation, study, and reflection. These dialogues may well chart a new path for religion in the future.

Women's Rights Movements

Some of the most significant movements of the past hundred years have sought to liberate women from oppression and inequality. Just as the nineteenth century is seen as the century in which slavery was abolished worldwide, the present century may well be seen by future generations as the century in which women worldwide achieved real equality and political freedom.

In many societies, women have been restricted by tradition in multiple ways. They have been kept from acquiring an education, owning land, having

Young monks share school desks with female students, an uncommon occurrence in Buddhist cultures even today.

professional careers, traveling, marrying and divorcing as they wish, voting, and holding office. But education and women's political movements—along with scientific advances that produced contraceptives and minimized the complications of pregnancy and childbirth—have slowly changed attitudes toward women's roles and rights. As a result, women are now indispensable in the workplaces of many cultures; they are earning their own incomes and making use of their new economic power. This new independence has led women closer to equality in government, business, and the arts.

Many religions, following traditional patterns, have been slow to allow women to assume leadership roles. But there have been notable exceptions; this has been especially true of smaller, more charismatic groups, such as some of the New Religions derived from Shinto and those Christian churches (such as the Christian Science Church and the Foursquare Gospel Church) whose founders were female. Christian churches in the Lutheran and in the Episcopal and Anglican traditions now ordain women priests and bishops. And in 2006, the American Episcopal Church elected a female bishop, Katharine Jefferts Schori, as its presiding bishop.

Resistance to allowing women in key roles is, however, still strong. In Christianity, the Catholic and Orthodox Churches so far have staved off pressures to ordain women or otherwise allow them full participation in decision making. In Judaism, females have been ordained in the Reform and Conservative branches; the Orthodox, however, still will not accept the notion of a female rabbi. Buddhism is seeing stirrings in its communities of nuns, who traditionally have played only a small role in leadership.

Women's gains have been broader in areas that don't affect a religion's basic power structure. Thus we find new translations of sacred literature and prayer forms that attempt to be more gender-neutral. For example, words such as *Ruler, Creator,* and *Parent* are used in place of the exclusively male terms *Lord* and *Father* in some translations of the Bible. Unity Church congregations address God as Father-Mother—a term used as early as 1875 by Mary Baker Eddy (see Chapter 9), the founder of Christian Science, in her explanation of the Lord's Prayer.

There is also heightened interest in religions that envision the divine as being female or that value its feminine aspect. This explains the renewed attention paid to early nature religions that worshiped a major female deity (such as Astarte) or in which women have had an important role. As discussed in Chapter 11, Wicca worships the Goddess in nature and in all women. In Judaism and Christianity, research into the contributions of women is common and even encouraged. Bible studies now talk of the great matriarchs, as well as the patriarchs, of Hebrew history. In Christianity, there is growing interest in medieval female mystics such as Hildegard of Bingen (see Chapter 9), Margery Kempe (c. 1373–1438), and Mechtild of Magdeburg (c. 1210–1285). Likewise, Hinduism is being appreciated not only for its female divinities but also for the many female gurus it has produced; Shinto and shamanistic religions are being studied for the important roles women have played in them; and Daoism is receiving attention for its female imagery.

Much of this new insight still remains theoretical. Whether male-dominated religions will be able to stand firm against the momentum of women's movements is anyone's guess. But many observers assume that women's liberation efforts, at least in industrialized countries, will eventually succeed.

Reassessment of Human Sexuality

Scientific developments and the economic and ideological developments that we have already discussed in this chapter have all broadened our understanding of human sexuality to include more than procreation as its purpose. Psychology has contributed an understanding of sexuality as being essential to the makeup of human beings. Biology has demonstrated the human connection with the animal world and its great variety of sexual expression. Anthropology has raised awareness of the variety in attitudes toward sex among different cultures and across historical periods. At the same time, through its development of artificial insemination and in vitro fertilization, science has expanded the possibilities for reproduction and, as a result, transformed reproduction into a more intentional event—and even forced the rethinking of the purpose of marriage. The growing availability of medicine, clean water, and public sanitation has led to an explosion of the world population.

These advances and findings have all contributed to our new understanding of sexuality. Many people now grant that sex has key functions in human existence beyond the creation of children; among these functions are intimacy, pleasure, self-expression, and even self-understanding. The acknowledgment of these functions has led many to question traditional sexual ethics and to rethink the appropriateness of sexual prohibitions in religious traditions.

The ongoing clash between traditional views of sexuality—views often codified in religions—and modern outlooks on sexuality probably will not be resolved anytime soon. What we are likely to see, however, is greater tolerance for beliefs and practices that are somewhat contradictory—as is evident in teachings about the indissolubility of marriage as compared to the actual toleration of divorce or annulment.

Another area of controversy exists regarding same-gender sexual expression and relationships. Some religions hold that all homosexuality runs counter to divine or natural laws. Although some religions and denominations accept homosexuality as an orientation that occurs naturally in some people, they say that acting out that orientation in sexual behavior is wrong; still others value compassion and privacy more than any traditional judgment of sexual acts and thus accept gay men and lesbians as full members. Of course, for heterosexual men and women, with full membership come the rights to a religious marriage and ordination. Few religions, however, have yet to extend the same benefits to gays and lesbians. Nonetheless, as the contradictions in a partial acceptance of gay members become more obvious and even painful, religions are beginning to reconsider past practice. Same-gender commitment ceremonies are celebrated in increasing numbers of religious congregations—examples are to be found among Jewish congregations, Unitarians, Quakers, the Metropolitan Community Church, Unity Church, Episcopalians, and Lutherans. In 2003 the Episcopal Church in the United States consecrated as bishop a man who is in a gay relationship, but this has caused conflict with other branches of the Anglican Church, particularly in Africa.

Although debate over what constitutes legitimate sexual expression will continue, there is no denying the impact that the sexual revolution has had

Some countries, some states, and some religions recognize and perform same-gender marriage ceremonies.

The orbiting Hubble telescope captured this image of the Carina Nebula.

on religion. Traditions that emphasize conservative principles will be most challenged by the changing views on sexuality.

Science and Technology

One of the engines that powers to some degree all of the movements that we are analyzing has been science. Modern science made great early progress in the sixteenth and seventeenth centuries, with the work of Copernicus (1473–1543), Galileo (1564–1642), Kepler (1571–1630), and Newton (1642–1727). At first, the developments were theoretical, without much practical application. While theoretical science continued to advance, applied science in the eighteenth and nineteenth centuries led to many practical benefits, including the invention of machinery that could do the work that human beings had formerly done by hand. Scientists investigated the mysteries of lightning and electricity; inventors made engines powered by steam and coal; researchers made advances in understanding and preventing diseases; engineers designed train tracks that linked large cities to each other; and the telephone and electric light became commonplace. In the next century came the airplane, radio, television, and computers. Over these same centuries, scientific theory advanced, resulting in the theory of evolution, molecular theory, the theory of relativity, and theories regarding astronomy and quantum physics. These accomplishments have transformed both our physical world and our view of the universe.

Some religions have tried to reject or even ignore the contributions of science, arguing that science displaces God, questions religious belief, and undermines morality. Scientists, however, argue that science gives us a valuable view of the universe that should be appreciated. It represents, they say, the collective work of thousands of people over many centuries. If we think about how long it took for human beings to draw a map of the whole earth, we can admire the efforts of science to give us an even grander "map"—a general view of reality.

The current scientific view of reality can be summarized quickly. Scientific theory and research state that our universe emerged in a great explosion approximately fourteen billion years ago. (What came before the explosion is not and possibly cannot be known by science.) In fact, the universe is still expanding from that explosion. As the universe cooled, galaxies formed; there are at least a hundred billion galaxies, each containing about a hundred billion stars. Our planet, earth, is about six billion years old, belongs to a galaxy we call the Milky Way, and travels around a sun whose energy will be exhausted in another six billion years. All physical things are made of smaller units, called molecules, which in turn consist of even smaller units, called atoms; and, ultimately, the physical world can be seen as various forms of energy. Phenomena such as lightning and earthquakes have natural causes. Carbon-based life-forms—possibly assisted by lightning, volcanic eruptions, and matter from comets—began to emerge on earth in one-celled form several billion years ago and, growing more complex, evolved in many directions on land and sea, finally producing the plants and animals we know today. The human being, which appeared in early form several million years ago, is part of the same evolutionary process but is the most complex life-form known so far.

Just as science has advanced our understanding of reality, so it has replaced earlier worldviews. For example, we now see the earth not as a flat surface but as a sphere, in orbit around the sun; and we know that earthquakes are generally caused by the movement of tectonic plates. Just as surely as electricity, television, and basic literacy are penetrating to the far corners of the world, so also will the scientific model of reality. Prescientific religions may continue to exist in the remotest cultures, but major religions will have to accommodate the scientific view of reality. It is the anvil on which all religions will be hammered and tested.

Science and Ethical Issues

Science and technology have broadened our knowledge and enriched our lives. In addition, they have given people new choices. In some cultures and religious traditions, having choices can pose ethical dilemmas that force people to examine their most basic philosophical positions.

Following are some areas that may raise ethical questions in some of the religious traditions we have considered in this text:

Fertility assistance   Through fertility drugs and in vitro fertilization, medical science has made conception possible for some women who in earlier times could not have conceived. But fertility drugs often produce multiple births and the potential for some of the babies to die. Is the survival of one or a few babies worth the potential loss of the others?

Birth control   The number of contraception options for women and men is growing all the time, including a contraceptive pill for men that will be available in the future. However, in some religious traditions, divine will, not contraception, determines the number of children born.

Ethical termination of pregnancy   At what point in its development is an embryo or a fetus to be considered a human being and thus accorded basic human rights? Is there a moral difference between early abortion and late-term abortion?

Ethical termination of adult life   Do individuals have the right to end their own lives? Do they have the right to end the lives of others, such as spouses, relatives, or friends?

Organ transplantation   Human body parts that have failed can sometimes be replaced by organs from another human being. Among the organs that are commonly transplanted are hearts, kidneys, livers, and corneas. Do we have an obligation to donate our body parts for transplantation? Is it ethical for people to sell parts of their bodies before or after death?

Genetic manipulation and stem-cell research   Scientists are hopeful that research on the human genetic code will result in heightened intelligence, extended life spans, and new treatments for disease. What kinds of experiments are ethically acceptable and on whom should the experiments be performed?

Species rights   Most laws derive from an assumption that human beings have basic rights. But some thinkers assert that animals, trees, and other elements of nature have rights of their own. Some argue, for example, that all animals and sentient beings have the right to not suffer from human infliction of unnecessary pain.

The founders of the major religious traditions never had to address these issues specifically. That does not mean, however, that their followers today should not concern themselves with these issues. At the same time, some would argue that these issues should be decided not in churches and temples by religious authorities but rather in secular courts by representatives of civilian governments. Deciding who should determine what is ethical and how ethics should be expressed in law are themselves important issues for this century.

The scientific approach to reality generally has helped—at least potentially—to make the earth a more interesting and pleasant place for human beings to inhabit than it was in past centuries. Granted, applied science has done a great deal to alter the landscape for the worse. Applied science has damaged non-industrial cultures and polluted the environment. But science has also done much to help. Through advances in sanitation and medicine, in particular, it has reduced infant mortality, extended human life spans, and made human life generally more secure. Today, life spans in industrialized countries are double what they were two hundred years ago. People now routinely expect to live 80 years or more. Scientists are working on life extension, and someday it may be common for people to live 100, 110, or even 120 years. (We know that this is at least possible, because Jeanne Calment, a Frenchwoman who died in 1997, lived to be 122.) And scientists will attempt to extend human life even further. When this happens, death and the afterlife will seem increasingly distant, and the earth will seem more like our permanent home. The resultant feeling of security that has grown up among people of industrialized countries may have helped them place a new value on the earth and on earthly life. It has helped foster an approach to living that is secular, rather than traditionally religious.

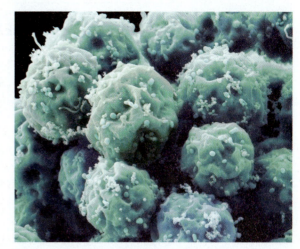

Secularism

The word *secular* is often used as the opposite of *sacred.* As mentioned in earlier chapters, *secularism* refers to the modern tendency to separate religion (which deals with the sacred) from everyday life (the secular). In earlier centuries, as we have seen throughout much of this book, religion and everyday life were quite commonly intertwined. Today, they remain intertwined mostly in societies that have one predominant religion.

Embryonic stem cells can potentially be used to repair damaged tissue in diseases such as Parkinson's and insulin-dependent diabetes. However, most research using stem cells is controversial because it requires the destruction of a human embryo.

The impetus to separate religion from public life found its greatest support in Europe. Primarily because of the horrific religious wars of the sixteenth and seventeenth centuries, influential thinkers there began to envision a type of nation in which there would be no state religion. They wanted individuals to be free to practice their religions as they chose. This model was drawn on in the creation of the new United States and was detailed in the Bill of Rights, which was appended to the Constitution. Because the model is based on a general separation of church and state, it has led to a secular type of government.[4]

Furthermore, the model of no established religion has encouraged a secular style of life. After all, if people are free to practice any religion, they are equally free to practice no religion at all. *Secularism* thus has come to refer to a way of looking at life in which human values and rules for living are taken from experience in *this world,* not from divine revelation, from a world beyond this one, or from religious authorities or religious traditions.

As science finds ways to extend human life and make it more secure, secularism seems to be gaining ground. For many people, traditional religious worldviews have lessened in influence. Religions of the future will continue to be challenged by the secular vision, particularly when they have to work within secular political entities. To survive on a large scale, they will have to add to and give greater meaning to the modern secular world. This may not be impossible, however. After all, science seeks to describe reality, but religions seek to describe and create meaning. As the philosopher K. N. Upadhyaya has explained, "Religion is not antagonistic to science. . . . The antagonism comes only through a misunderstanding. It has to be understood that science deals with the physical. Religion, on the other hand, deals with something that is beyond the physical.

Conflict in Religion

RELIGIONS, SACRED TEXTS, AND VIOLENCE

Religions almost universally preach peace. But they also face questions about the use of violence. Are there situations in which violence is justified?

Most religions accept that violence is justified if it is needed for the protection of oneself or one's family—a position that many people hold as reasonable. There are exceptions, though. Jainism and early Buddhist teachings reject using violence for any purpose whatsoever. The Dhammapada, an early Buddhist document, says this: "All beings tremble before violence. All fear death. All love life. See yourself in others. Then whom can you hurt? What harm can you do? He who seeks happiness by hurting those who seek happiness will never find happiness. For your brother is like you. He wants to be happy. Never harm him."[5] Nonetheless, in later Buddhism, particularly in China and Japan, Buddhist teachings about detachment and transience were sometimes employed to idealize the skillful soldier and the warrior-monk. And Buddhist sculpture shows many figures holding symbolic swords and other weapons.

Hinduism values nonviolence highly, as we see in Gandhi's teachings about non-harm (ahimsa). But we also know that the Bhagavad Gita, perhaps the most influential book in Hinduism, endorses fighting to overcome serious injustice. In the popular epic the Ramayana, Rama and his brother Lakshman engage in warfare in order to rescue Rama's wife, Sita. And some of the Hindu deities, such as Durga and Kali, are known for their love of blood. Animal sacrifice is still used in Hindu worship, and human sacrifice has not been unknown.

The Daodejing says that the person of the Dao opposes force. "Whenever you advise a ruler in the way of [Dao], counsel him not to use force to conquer the universe," for "thorn bushes spring up wherever the army has passed."[6] It says that the person of the Dao hates weapons. But then the text adds that "he uses them only when he has no choice."[7] This opens a very wide door for fighting, as anyone who has seen a Chinese martial arts film can attest.

We see a fairly militant approach in some religions, possibly as a result of the tribal nature of their original societies. Perhaps because biblical Judaism grew up in a land without strong natural borders, it viewed Yahweh as "Lord of hosts" (Isa. 6:3)—a commander of angelic armies that could protect his people. Psalm 135 makes clear this notion of Yahweh as a national protector: "He struck down all the first-born in Egypt, both man and beast. . . . He struck down mighty nations and slew great kings" (Ps. 135:8, 10).[8]

Psalm 18 also sees him as a personal protector: "Thou settest my foot on my enemies' necks" (Ps. 18:40). Psalm 137 is even more graphic about the treatment of the enemy: "Happy is he who will seize your children and dash them against the rock" (v. 9). Since God "sets the time for war and the time for peace" (Eccles. 3:8), warfare seems at times to be approved and even

But the methodology of the two is—or should be—exactly the same: observation, experimentation, and verification."[12] We might note, too, the many contemporary scientists, such as physicists Russell Stannard (b. 1931) and Paul Davies (b. 1946), who have shown considerable interest in religion.

Agnosticism is a concept often associated with a secular worldview. The English biologist T. H. Huxley (1825–1895), who coined the term, was of the opinion that the existence of God could be neither proven nor disproven from a scientific point of view. He argued that agnosticism—a middle ground between theism and atheism—was the most reasonable theoretical position to hold. It is a view that is commonly held today by scientifically minded people, because it accommodates the study and teaching of science without reference to God or gods. Some people have found that everyday life can be carried on, too, without reference to God or gods. Agnosticism may begin to replace commanded by God. The Books of Joshua and Judges, for example, offer much justified warfare (Josh. 8:1–29). Yet we should also recognize that the Hebrew Bible balances this harshness with a vision of a God of compassion, concerned for the good of the lowly and poor (1 Sam. 2:8).

Christianity began with strongly nonviolent principles, evident in the Sermon on the Mount (Matt. 5–7). We know that Jesus refused to lead an armed revolt against the Romans. Early Christianity continued this pacifism, and Christians at first did not become soldiers. Yet change came quickly, both in society and in sacred texts. The Book of Revelation—one of the last biblical books written—portrays Jesus on a white horse, dressed in a robe that is covered with the blood of battle. Out of his mouth comes a sword; he rules with an iron rod; and he tramples on sinners like a harvester crushing grapes under his feet (Rev. 19:13–15). (This passage inspired the rhyming words of the "Battle Hymn of the Republic": "the Lord," who holds "a terrible swift sword," tramples out "the vintage where the grapes of wrath are stored.") After Constantine became emperor, Christians were no longer prohibited from becoming soldiers—perhaps because Constantine was a soldier himself. A century later, Augustine elaborated principles that justified warfare. He also approved of using political force to compel "heretics" (nonmainstream Christians) to conform to orthodoxy. By the time of the Crusades, the cult of the Christian soldier was complete, and it had

military patrons such as Saint George, Saint Barbara, and Saint Michael, who are often portrayed holding swords. (Saint George is the patron saint of England, and his red cross is in its flag.)

We find a similar mixture of responses in Islam. The name of the religion itself is related to the Arabic word for peace, and Muhammad worked tirelessly for harmony among the many tribes of Arabia. Yet Muhammad thought that violence was sometimes justified, and he led his followers into battle. As the Qur'an records, God commanded him, "Prophet, rouse the faithful to arms."[9] Muhammad spoke of a final day of divine reward and punishment, just as Zoroastrianism, Judaism, and Christianity also teach, and he described vivid punishments prepared by God for sinners: "Garments of fire have been prepared for the unbelievers. . . . They shall be lashed with rods of iron."[10] Yet the Qur'an equally counsels fairness and patience, such as in this passage: "If you punish, let your punishment be commensurate with the wrong that has been done you. But it shall be best for you to endure your wrongs with patience."[11]

What we see in the scriptures of many religions are words of peace and compassion, side by side with warnings of violence and punishment. Unfortunately, most texts offer possibilities for individual believers to choose passages that give authority to their cruelty and anger. Only scriptures (like those of the Jains) that allow no harm whatsoever can avoid being used to justify the use of violence.

traditional theistic religious belief and practice. This tendency may also generate attempts to redefine the conceptions of God; it may inspire a turn toward the nontheistic religions (such as Jainism or Theravada Buddhism); and it may promote the development of nontheistic expressions of values and beliefs.

Communism, even where it has now been abandoned as an official ideology, succeeded in creating a fairly secular milieu. In Russia and many parts of eastern Europe, new generations of people have been raised without religion. Schools in the Communist era often spoke of religion as an outdated method for providing solutions to life's problems—as outdated as horse-drawn carriages and whale-oil lamps. The same antireligious stance has also been true of China, particularly since the Communist Revolution of 1949. The resultant secularism among many mainland Chinese may have a significant influence on the world as China, with its population of more than a billion, gains power in the international arena.

Some people welcome secularism—possibly with the same relief felt by many in the early confederation of the United States—because they seek lives free of religiously inspired hatreds. Machines, such as computers, cars, and telephones, are secular in that they do not ask the religion of the person who operates them. In secular cultures, some wish that human beings could be similarly accommodating.

Science offers explanations of reality that once came only from religion. Secular governments often promote values that were once primarily espoused by religion. And secular governments run hospitals, schools, and welfare programs, which at one time were under the exclusive control of religion. What, then, does this leave for religion? Will current religions move in the direction of secularism? Will religions survive as pockets of belief and practice in a basically secular environment?[13] Could completely secular "religions" emerge? Or will religious instincts be expressed in increasingly nontraditional forms?

Environmental Challenges

Four centuries ago, the total human population was about 500 million. Now, the world's population is about 7 billion. This growing population has migrated to cities to find jobs, and cities with a million people—once extremely rare—are now sprouting like mushrooms. Megacities—such as Mexico City, São Paulo, Shanghai, Tokyo, New York, and Cairo—are becoming more common, even though most of them find it difficult to cope with their unchecked growth. Some cities have become bleak, inhospitable urban environments.

At the same time, the natural environment is being ravaged to provide resources for the increasing world population. The rain forests of Malaysia, Thailand, Indonesia, and Brazil are disappearing to provide wood and farmland; and the habitats of many animals, including those of the great apes, are being threatened. Nuclear energy is used to make electricity, but no one knows where to safely store the spent fuel. (The dangers of radioactivity were underscored by the 2011 earthquake and tsunami in Japan.) Pesticides are used for growing and storing many foods, despite their related health dangers.

The great religions of the past grew up in a quite different world and did not have to deal with the moral issues raised by population growth, urban life, corporate business policies, nuclear waste, and environmental pollution. Old religions today must try to discover within themselves the wisdom to handle these entirely new challenges. They will have to fundamentally rethink morality. Doing so will not be easy or straightforward, as we will see in a moment.

THE RECURRING CHALLENGES OF CHANGE

If our textbook pilgrimage of world religions has revealed a common denominator among religions, it is this: all religions that survive must ultimately adapt to changing circumstances, whether they acknowledge the adaptations or not. If there is a second common denominator, it is probably the fact that adaptation is seldom achieved without confusion and pain. Indeed, debate, struggle, and the formation of new divisions are necessary means for religions seeking to remain relevant in a changing world.

The view from the moon . . . gave new meaning to the word "religion." The English word for religion came from the Latin word *religare*. It means to connect. Religion is about how we are all connected to each other and to every creature and to the earth. Religion is about including, about every part belonging to the whole. "Religion" is the old word and "ecology" is the new word. The view from the moon shows that religion and ecology share the same meaning of connectedness.

—James Parks Morton, Dean Emeritus of the Cathedral of Saint John the Divine in New York, speaking of the photo of the earth taken from the moon[14]

This NASA photo of earth has sometimes been called a religious icon that makes viewers realize the beauty of the earth and the interrelatedness of all its parts.

The recent history of Roman Catholicism is a good case study of a religion's process of adaptation. Catholicism, because its adherents are spread across the globe, is always being challenged somewhere by changing circumstances. At the beginning of the twentieth century, Catholicism was challenged by new "scientific" understanding, particularly Darwinism and modern biblical criticism. Its response was initially a set of proclamations against the evils of modernism and secularism. Nonetheless, despite its apparent conservatism, it was also adapting to the changing world order. This was particularly true in its development of new Catholic social doctrine, spelled out in papal encyclicals, concerning social justice and workers' rights. The two world wars increased the pace of social change and the need for religious adjustment. The movement of social and religious "tectonic plates" eventually produced a Catholic earthquake in the person of Pope John XXIII (1881–1963). This elderly, mild-mannered pope stated his desire to open the Church to the modern world, and he initiated meetings of the world's Catholic bishops that were intended to help Catholicism remain relevant. By the end of the Second Vatican Council in 1965, Roman Catholicism had a different face, marked by an emphasis on human equality, a new tolerance for the secular world, an acceptance of separation between church and state, and an openness to diversity. This was the face of an old religion taking major steps to adapt itself to the modern world.

But the case study does not end with the liberalization initiated by John XXIII. As history would have predicted, the pendulum swung back, particularly at the urging of Pope John Paul II, the first pope from a Communist country, and from his successor, Benedict XVI. Pope John Paul II insisted that only males could be priests and bishops. He also appointed bishops who reflected his own conservative beliefs; he reasserted the primacy of Rome; and he condemned the thought of some liberal Catholic theologians. Nonetheless, he also furthered his church's defense of human social rights, condemned the excesses of capitalism, and fought capital punishment. He is often credited with being a major force behind the downfall of Communism in Russia and eastern Europe. His death in 2005 ended one of the most influential papacies in history. Although Benedict XVI, the first pope chosen during this century, attempts to strike a balance between the conservative and liberal factions of his church, his general approach has been conservative. At some point in the future, however, the pendulum will undoubtedly swing in the other direction.

This case study, with its tensions and vacillations, is typical of many religions. As we saw in preceding chapters, religions must adapt and change. Often they fight the forces of change, but such conservatism can be a stage of adaptive development that eventually evolves into flexible forms of belief and practice.

The inevitability of conservative reaction to the onslaught of change is one way to understand a phenomenon that is sometimes called fundamentalism. Fundamentalist movements—occurring in many parts of the world—are often fueled by calls for a "return to the values of our founders" and to an earlier, more traditional vision.

Fundamentalist movements reflect an effort to simplify a religion. They emphasize what followers see as the basics, the essential elements, of a religion. The personal rewards of fundamentalism are multiple: a sense of bettering society, of uniting with like-minded people, and of repairing a religion to make it useful once again as a clear guide to what is right and wrong. Although fundamentalist movements are motivated by many reasons, they represent primarily a response to the threat of change.

The best-known example of fundamentalism is possibly the Islamic Revolution in Iran, initiated by the late Ayatollah Khomeini (see Chapter 10); but Islamic fundamentalist movements are also occurring in many other countries, such as Egypt, Turkey, Pakistan, Indonesia, Malaysia, and Algeria. As mentioned in earlier chapters, we see fundamentalism active in other religions as well—in Christianity, especially in the United States and Africa; in Hinduism in India; and in Judaism, particularly in Israel. Some people see religious fundamentalism, especially if it takes control of nations' armies and weapons, as one of the greatest dangers currently facing the human race. Others believe that the attraction of fundamentalism will either be eroded by the secular values (including democracy) that they see spreading throughout the world, or it will be replaced with new religious ideals.

The image of a swinging pendulum is a recurrent metaphor in this chapter. We return to it one last time, as we imagine the pendulum swinging away from fundamentalism toward another phenomenon, which may well be at the other end of the arc: a kind of neopantheism expressed through a semi-deification of nature. Just as Muslim and Christian leaders have articulated the aspirations of traditional monotheistic movements, so other thinkers have articulated the "doctrines" of the "nature movement." Among the many important writers have been Julian Huxley (1887–1975), Rachel Carson (1907–1964), David Brower (1912–2000), and E. O. Wilson (b. 1929).

Major religions are now taking note of the inescapable ethical attention that the natural world demands. Buddhism in both Asia and the West is quickly developing environmental awareness, and so is Christianity. These developments in traditional religions are an entirely new and important extension of religious morality. The potential of the environmental movement to grow—and to influence existing religions—suggests that it is a possible new scaffolding for the cathedral of humanity's future religious expressions.

ENVIRONMENTALISM: A RELIGIOUS PHENOMENON?

The Green Movement, as we have seen, is flourishing. It now extends to a host of practical areas, including architecture, waste disposal, car design, clothing materials, energy sources, agriculture, and much more. The threat of global warming and related environmental damage has moved it to the forefront of our consciousness. So significant is the need to care for nature that the major religions have made environmentalism an important ethical commandment.

Sensitivity to nature, however, did not begin with the Green Movement. Because nature can be viewed contemplatively, it has long been a source of religious inspiration. In Asia, we can see great sensitivity to nature in the origins of Daoism, and the beauties of nature appear as a major theme in the poetry of China and Japan as early as the seventh century. In the West, we find awareness of the spiritual aspect of nature in the medieval thought of Francis of Assisi and the Cistercian monks. A profound feeling for nature reasserted itself in the Romantic movement of the eighteenth and nineteenth centuries, which taught that nature was the most important manifestation of the sublime.

In the late nineteenth and early twentieth centuries, the movement toward nature was strikingly evident in the painting of the Impressionists, among whom Claude Monet (1840–1926) was a significant example. Monet not only painted occasional scenes of nature in the countryside, but he left Paris to create a country home with a garden featuring a large water lily pond, which he painted regularly for the last forty-three years of his life. The garden he created at Giverny is virtually a place of pilgrimage today; his paintings of nature hang in many major museums; and reproductions of his paintings of water lilies have made his work well known and loved throughout the world.

The great open spaces of North America also inspired a feeling for the spirituality of nature—as depicted in the works of European and American painters of the nineteenth century. Travelers who visited the western part of North America wrote of its extravagant beauty. One of these was the Scottish-born naturalist John Muir (1838–1914). In several books, Muir demanded that beautiful regions that are important to the whole nation be protected. Because of his efforts, Yosemite was made a national park; in fact, his work helped ignite the establishment of the national park system and local nature preserves. Muir Woods, a fine grove of redwoods just north of San Francisco, is named after him.

This photo, showing both what's above and below the waterline, focuses on a piece of an Alaskan glacier that's in the process of melting. This phenomenon raises concern over the effects of human behavior on planet earth.

Today, signs of this new approach to the natural world—an approach that is both practical and spiritual—are evident everywhere. Earth Day was established a few decades ago as a celebration of nature. Television is crowded with wonderfully photographed programs on animals and insects, forests and lakes, coral reefs, fish, and oceans; these nature films have become an art form in their own right. Many specialty stores now sell nature-themed items—from semiprecious stones and interesting mineral formations to posters of dolphins and whales. A whole new type of environmentally sensitive travel is becoming popular; ecotourism takes people to places like the Amazon and the Galápagos Islands. Zoos, which used to be little more than prisons for animals, are undergoing a revolution in design; they now try to provide a familiar, comfortable, and spacious environment for their animals. Legal protections are being created for endangered species. Art and music—discussed in more detail later in this chapter—have actually pointed the way to environmentalism through over a century of works that have been strongly inspired by the natural world.

As environmental consciousness has spread, the issue of sustainability has moved from the fringes into the mainstream. As we have seen in earlier chapters, it has been embraced by leaders of several religions. It has also become part of political-party platforms across the world. What remains is the hard work of transforming sustainability from a goal into a set of actions that produce real results, and those results might be achieved more quickly if politicians and religious leaders worked together rather than separately. Chapter 2 suggested that the Green Movement can be seen as a sort of twenty-first-century indigenous religion. Indeed, the entire environmental movement has interesting parallels with traditional religions. For example, it has a strongly prophetic aspect because of its moral rules. Like many religions, it dictates what a person should or should not eat, wear, and do. (Some bumper stickers illustrate this: "If it's got a face, don't eat it," "Fur looks good on animals," and "Think globally, act locally.") Environmentalism also has a mystical aspect in its emphasis on the fundamental unity of human beings and the universe. In fact, it offers as its supreme experience the sense of oneness with animals and the rest of nature.

So far, this movement is deficient in the sacramental, ritualistic element that usually characterizes religions—although this aspect has great potential for development in the next centuries—and may even have already begun. The religion of Wicca, for example, re-creates pre-Christian nature rituals. And we might also be seeing the beginnings of additional nature-based rituals for the major seasons: Earth Day marks spring; summer and winter solstice celebrations mark the turning points (measured by daylight hours) of summer and winter; and Thanksgiving meals and rituals mark autumn.

Like religion, environmentalism also has its "sacred places." Destinations of ecopilgrimage include Yosemite, the Rocky Mountains, wildlife preserves in eastern Africa and Costa Rica, Mount Everest, the whale sanctuary at Maui, Glacier Bay and Denali National Parks in Alaska, and

Watching a sunset in silence can be a form of meditation.

many others. (The word *sanctuary,* used in reference to animal preserves, is religiously significant.) Environmentalism is also developing its role models, many of whom, interestingly, are women: Dian Fossey (1932–1985), Jane Goodall (b. 1934), Brigitte Bardot (b. 1934), Pamela Anderson (b. 1967), and Ellen DeGeneres (b. 1958). There is a growing body of environmentalist "scripture"—for example, *Walden* by Henry David Thoreau (1817–1862) and *Animal Liberation* by Peter Singer (b. 1946). And sacred iconography extends from the nature photographs of Yosemite by Ansel Adams (1902–1984) to popular paintings of whales and porpoises by Christian Lassen (b. 1956), Robert Wyland (b. 1956), and others. Equally important are environmental films, such as *An Inconvenient Truth,* by Al Gore (b. 1948), who received the Nobel Peace Prize in 2007 for his work on climate change.

ECLECTIC SPIRITUALITY

It is quite common now to hear people say that while they are not particularly interested in any one religion, they are interested in spirituality. It is not always clear what they mean by *spirituality*, but the fact that people use this word to describe their religious stance does reveal an important contemporary phenomenon. Individuals now assemble elements of different belief systems to create their own spiritual system. Highly valued are practices that promote inner peace and a feeling of harmony between oneself and the outer world. The key belief of those who embrace eclectic spirituality is the interrelatedness of all elements in the universe. That belief is often expressed in an attitude of respect and reverence for all people and creatures. Respect and reverence are often cultivated through contemplative acts that dissolve separateness and promote ways of seeing beyond the superficial to the essential relatedness, even oneness, of all beings.

Traditional religions often engender spirituality, and eclectic spirituality is marked by borrowings from traditional religions. These borrowings range from meditative practices inspired by Buddhism to dancing inspired by Sufism. But there are other means to attain spirituality, and many find it outside traditional religion. We have all had the experience, for example, of going to a movie theater, sitting down in the darkness, and gradually being drawn into a film that does far more than merely entertain. At a certain point, we recognize that the film is evoking in us a response that is somehow fundamental to the human experience and at the same time transcendent—an experience of the "spiritual." Often we sense that others in the audience are sharing in that experience. At the end of such films, there is a silence that may prevail even in the lobby as people leave the theater. Musical concerts can also induce a similar experience.

Psychologists such as Carl Gustav Jung (1875–1961) and Abraham Maslow (1908–1970) wrote extensively about the necessary spiritual development of the human being. Maslow became preoccupied with it, first describing what he called "peak experiences," which are rare and transient, and then describing what he called "plateau experiences," which are contemplative experiences in everyday life that may be frequent and long-lasting.

A heightened interest in spirituality may also have influenced the changing attitude toward the home. People increasingly think of their home as their "sanctuary." They want to include elements in their apartment or house that will promote tranquility in everyday life. (This may in part explain the popularity of home makeover programs on television!) Some homes feature intriguing elements of religious design: a small home altar, a meditation area, or a garden room for reflection. Plants and gardens are taking on a new importance, reminding us of their significance in several Asian religious traditions. Indoor and outdoor fountains, of all shapes and sizes, have become popular. They recall the use of water in so many religions, such as Shinto, Hinduism, Christianity, and Islam. Sometimes larger houses even have "cathedral" ceilings. The home—as well as the church and temple—is now being conceived of as a sacred space.

Contemporary Issues

RELIGION AND POP CULTURE

Popular culture often presents religious themes. Comic strips and animated cartoon films, for example, look uncomplicated but sometimes have a depth that belies their appearance. (Pablo Picasso and other artists have highly valued comics for their economy of line—a great deal can be said with minimal drawing.) Some comic strips indict society in a prophetic way (such as *Doonesbury and Dilbert*); other comic strips often are explicitly religious (such as *Peanuts*). In many of Disney's animated films (*Bambi, Cinderella, Little Mermaid, Lion King, Dinosaur, Finding Nemo*), a host of loving animals have been created with such personality and charm that their portrayal as conscious, feeling beings on a par with human beings may have contributed to the growing animal liberation movement.

The creation of Superman and other heroic comic-book figures may be a popular form of biblical messianism. Like the messianic agent given authority by the Ancient of Days in the seventh chapter of the Book of Daniel, Superman comes to earth from another world to bring justice and truth. Biblical influence may have inspired the semibiblical "Krypton names" of Superman and of his father: Kal-El and Jor-El. (We might recall that *El* means "God" in Hebrew and occurs in names such as *Israel, Samuel,* and *Michael*). Superman and other similar heroes help reinforce the human desire for justice and compassion.

The cult of Elvis Presley ("Presleyanity"), while perhaps not what one would call "spiritual," has multiple religious parallels: the death of Elvis at an early age, his later "apparitions" to the faithful, the supposed healing power of his photos, the common image of him dressed in white, the commemoration of his birth and death, the pilgrimage to Graceland and other sites where Elvis lived and worked, and the marketing of his gospel music. Followings centered on other musicians—Jim Morrison, John Lennon, Bob Marley, Kurt Cobain, and the Grateful Dead—show similar religious parallels. These followings suggest that the religious urge remains, though its forms of expression change.

Because eclectic spirituality is difficult to define, we will try now to understand it through examples. We will look at three aspects that most frequently characterize modern spirituality: the sense of interrelatedness, an attitude of respect and reverence, and a contemplative approach to experiencing reality.

Interrelatedness

As we saw in earlier chapters, many religions have emphasized a relatedness among all beings, expressed perhaps most strongly in Buddhist and Hindu thought but also in the mystical teachings of many other religions. Science has also shown great interest in interrelatedness, sometimes linking the worlds of religion and science. The scientific exploration of the subatomic world has helped us understand that the connections that we observe in the visible world mirror the structures in the very building blocks of the universe. This same interest in interrelatedness helps account for the popularity of such abstruse topics as chaos theory, cosmology, and the meteorological relations between ocean temperature and distant weather patterns; it also explains the popularity of such books as *The Whole Shebang* by Timothy Ferris (b. 1944) and *A Short History of Nearly Everything* by Bill Bryson (b. 1951).

Popular interest in interrelatedness is also evident in the reinterpretation of some artworks, particularly the paintings of Georgia O'Keeffe (1887–1986). O'Keeffe's paintings of flowers and close-to-the-earth architectural forms have

This painting by Georgia O'Keeffe is based on a red canna lily. Her paintings often take our everyday eyes into that which is usually unseen.

always been regarded as technically excellent. Her paintings have become so popular that one was reproduced on a commemorative U.S. postage stamp. Their recent popularity, however, may hinge more on their expression of inter-relatedness and interchangeableness: because many of her paintings depict objects at very close range, the viewer may be unable at first glance to tell if the painting represents a flower, an adobe church, a hillside, or even a seashell. This ambiguity is surprising because, in fact, O'Keeffe's work is often closer to realism than abstraction. However, even that distinction is broken down by O'Keeffe's highlighting of the abstract within the specific. Overall, her paint-ings express interrelatedness on several levels; they invite the viewer to contemplate patterns and underlying similarities. Some reproductions of O'Keeffe's paintings have become almost icons of spirituality.

Abstraction has been used repeatedly to suggest both the state of interre-latedness and the human experience of oneness. Georgia O'Keeffe's nonrepre-sentational works frequently use curves of color with this intent, as in her paintings *Music: Pink and Blue* and *Blue #1*.[15] Mark Rothko (1903–1970), one of the greatest painters of pure spiritual experience, achieved a similar effect by superimposing squares of subtle color, which seem to float luminously above their backgrounds. Jackson Pollock (1912–1956) created spontaneous but very

The later paintings of Mark Rothko are like windows into eternity.

complicated worlds of relationship in color by spattering paint on canvases that he had placed on the ground. Other spiritually oriented painters include Mark Tobey (1890–1976) and Rufino Tamayo (1899–1991). These artists' works can evoke a feeling of being either out in space, surrounded by stars and blackness, or within an atom, amid the active particles and surrounding emptiness.

Reverence and Respect

As we've already discussed, nature is coming to be seen not as something only to use, but rather as a part of ourselves that must be nurtured for the well-being of all. Beyond this reconceptualization of nature, best expressed in environmental movements, is a turn to nature as revelation—as an expression of the spirit that permeates all reality and as a phenomenon to be revered. This attitude is perhaps best expressed in the art of photography.

In an article that compares the qualities of some creative photographers with the virtues of the Daoist sage as espoused in the Zhuangzi, writers Philippe Gross and S. I. Shapiro describe Daoistic ideals, often using both the words of the Zhuangzi and of modern photographers themselves, placed side by side. The authors conclude that the vision of the Daoist sage and of many great photographers is the same: "Both . . . have the capacity for seeing with unconstricted awareness and are therefore capable of seeing the miraculous in the ordinary."[16] According to Gross and Shapiro, the virtues shared by the Daoist sage and the contemplative photographer include freedom from the sense of self, receptivity, spontaneity, acceptance, and nonattachment—attributes that promote a general attitude of respect and reverence.

Contemplative photography reached a peak of sorts in the nature photography of Ansel Adams (mentioned earlier). His black-and-white photographs of Yosemite National Park, whose mountains and waterfalls recall the subject matter of traditional Chinese landscape painting, evoke a feeling of respect for the power and the beauty of nature. Another devotee of nature, Eliot Porter (1901–1990), photographed in brilliant color to let nature speak fully of its beauty. He became well known for his photographs of trees turning yellow in autumn, of reflections in ponds, and of river canyons. These photographs often elicit the same reverence in the viewer as a Daoist sage might have experienced in contemplating a waterfall or a distant mountain.

Photography has been particularly effective in recording the most minute details of the human face and of human life, once again inviting insight, respect, and reverence. Photography of the American Civil War by Matthew Brady (c. 1823–1896) includes portraits of people in terrible circumstances. Not long after, Edward Curtis (1868–1952) sensitively documented the vanishing indigenous life of Native Americans. Dorothea Lange (1895–1965) and Walker Evans (1903–1975) produced moving studies of people during the Great Depression. More recent masters have been Edward Steichen (1879–1973) and Diane Arbus (1923–1971). Steichen's influential anthology of photographs, called *The Family of Man,* includes studies of the spiritual expressed in human faces and actions from around the world. Arbus drew our respectful attention to marginalized people in our urban societies.

The ability to evoke an attitude of respect and reverence is by no means limited to the art of photography. The details of ordinary human life can be treated with reverence in painting as well. Vincent van Gogh (1853–1890) did this repeatedly in his works—from his earlier portrayal of peasants in *The Potato Eaters,* to his later paintings of the neighborhood postman, of sunflowers arranged in a vase, and of a neighborhood cafe at night. The same attitude of respectful attention can even be found in cartoons (consider the role of Lisa in *The Simpsons*). In fact, this attitude can be expressed by any art form or technique that promotes contemplation—the method for revealing spirituality—to which we now turn.

Contemplative Practices

Although eclectic spirituality emphasizes the interrelatedness of all creation, it does not maintain that each person is automatically able to see interrelatedness. However, one can develop this ability, as well as acquire an attitude of respect and reverence, through a variety of contemplative practices.

> I'm not responsible for my photographs. Photography is not documentary, but intuition, a poetic experience. It's drowning yourself, dissolving yourself. . . . First you must lose your self. Then it happens.
> —Henri Cartier-Bresson, photographer[17]

During the meal Peggy asked me, "What have you been thinking about?"

"I've been thinking about the good and bad effects of religions, and I've been wondering about their future."

"Why that topic?" John asked. "Aren't all religions good?" (John was laughing.)

"It's complicated," I said. "Some people see religions as mostly bad—as institutions of persecution and mental oppression. Others are more moderate. They see good aspects in religions, too." Then I asked him: "Do *you* think that all religions are good?"

"You know me," John said. "I'm an engineer. I think that religions are anti-science and give people a lot of wrong answers."

Peggy threw out some general questions. "Are some religions good and others bad? And how can we identify which is which?"

"When I look at religions," Robert said, "I don't see any one of them as being entirely bad or entirely good. There can be good and bad elements in the same religion. So maybe what we need to think about is where religions *should* be going. And what an ideal religion would be."

"The problem is that many religions focus on life *after* this one," Peggy said. "They should focus more on *this* life, don't you think? They should teach us how to open our eyes and appreciate every moment."

"If you identify with just one religion," John said, "you tend to dismiss the others. Maybe the best religion would move beyond religion. Maybe we need a religion of no-religion."

"So how are you going to get religions to move in *that* direction?" I asked.

A gray-and-white bird flew down onto the grass. It looked up hopefully, and John tossed out a small piece of bread. More birds followed, John tossed out more bits of bread, and we began to talk about birds instead of religions and people.

Reading **A STARRY NIGHT**

The author Audrey Sutherland has helped popularize kayaking, camping, and trekking. She has written books about her travels in Hawai'i and Alaska. The following reading, from Paddling My Own Canoe, *describes an experience at a hiker's cabin in Hawai'i, where she was camping for the night.*

A full moon is rising over the mountain's left shoulder. What have I been doing, cowering in the corner bunk each night with all of Van Gogh's *Starry Night* out here? I bring the air mattress and the down bag out onto the grass. So it was not just the glory that the thin, bearded painter saw, but the vast wheeling across the sky, the movement through the night of the stars and planets spinning on their axes, whirling through their orbits. I watch and sleep, until the rain on my face sends me back inside. But as I step through the door, I look back across the bay. The setting moon has created an unearthly miracle. Arched above the mountain is a moonbow—a lunar rainbow—of pale colors arched on a dark cloud.[18]

TEST YOURSELF

1. The modern culture of _____ betterment will increasingly challenge religions to
   produce what material cultures value.
   a. nature-based
   b. money-based
   c. spirit-based
   d. peace-based

2. Entirely new religions may frequently blend
   elements from several religions. For example,
   the _____ Church, which began in
   Korea, blends Christianity and Confucianism.
   a. Unitarian
   b. Unification
   c. Trinity
   d. Trimurti

3. One of the earliest examples of modern religious
   dialogue was the first _____, held in
   Chicago in 1893.
   a. Council of World Religions
   b. World Religion Convention
   c. Religious Ecumenical Council
   d. World Parliament of Religions

4. In Christianity, there is growing interest in
   medieval female mystics such as _____.
   a. Mary Baker Eddy
   b. Catherine the Great
   c. Elizabeth I
   d. Hildegard of Bingen

5. In 2003, the _____ Church in the
   United States consecrated as bishop a man
   who is in a gay relationship; this has caused
   conflict with other branches of the Church of
   England.
   a. Episcopal
   b. Baptist
   c. Catholic
   d. Presbyterian

6. The term _____ has come to refer to a
   way of looking at life in which human values
   and rules for living are taken from experience in
   this world, not from divine revelation.
   a. agnosticism
   b. secularism
   c. tritheism
   d. monism

7. _____, even where it has been abandoned as an official ideology, succeeded in
   creating a fairly secular milieu.
   a. Communism
   b. Theocracy
   c. Nazism
   d. Democracy

8. Scottish-born naturalist _____ helped
   ignite the establishment of the national park
   system and local nature preserves.
   a. E. O. Wilson
   b. Jane Goodall
   c. Christian Lassen
   d. John Muir

9. In Europe, a contemplative interest in nature
   can be traced back many centuries to the nature
   mysticism of some medieval monks and friars,
   beginning with Saint _____.
   a. Augustine
   b. Anne Jahouvey
   c. Francis of Assisi
   d. Anselm of Lucca

10. The key belief of those who embrace
    _____ is the interrelatedness of all
    elements in the universe—a belief that is ex-
    pressed in an attitude of respect and reverence
    for all people and creatures.
    a. the new world order
    b. structuralism
    c. eclectic spirituality
    d. secularism

11. Based on what you have read in this chapter,
    what do you think twenty-first-century religious
    leaders view as the greatest threat to religion?
    Using information from the media and this
    chapter, explain your answer.

12. Why do you think eclectic spirituality has become
    very popular in the contemporary world? Do
    you think the majority of twenty-first-century
    Americans find eclectic spirituality more
    appealing than traditional religions? Explain
    your answer.

RESOURCES

Books

Allison, Jay, and Dan Gediman, eds. *This I Believe: The Personal Philosophies of Remarkable Men and Women.* New York: Holt, 2007. A collection of essays, from the weekly NPR segment begun in 2005`, that portray the personal credos of Americans.

Ammerman, Nancy, ed. *Everyday Religion: Observing Modern Religious Lives.* New York: Oxford University Press, 2006. Essays on unusual aspects of lived religion.

Azara, Nancy. *Spirit Taking Form: Making a Spiritual Practice of Making Art.* York Beach, ME: Red Wheel/Weiser, 2002. An encouragement of inner growth through the creation of art.

Byock, Ira. *Dying Well: Peace and Possibilities at the End of Life.* New York: Riverhead/Penguin Putnam, 1997. A book for both patients and caregivers about the spiritual possibilities of dying, written by a compassionate specialist in hospice care.

Gottlieb, Roger S. *A Greener Faith: Religious Environmentalism and Our Planet's Future.* New York: Oxford University Press, 2006. A hopeful, ecumenically oriented book that argues that religion can be a powerful force for environmental activism.

Hoffstaedter, Gerhard. *Modern Muslim Identities: Negotiating Religion and Ethnicity in Malaysia.* Denmark: Nordic Institute of Asian Studies, 2011. A study of how the modern Malaysian government has influenced Islamic identity in Malaysia.

Ruether, Rosemary Radford. *Integrating Ecofeminism, Globalization, and World Religions.* Lanham, MD: Rowman and Littlefield, 2005. A discussion of the links between feminism, ecology, and religious thought.

Smith, Huston. *Why Religion Matters: The Fate of the Human Spirit in an Age of Disbelief.* New York: HarperOne, 2001. A defense of the religious impulse and its way of looking at the universe.

Sutherland, Audrey. *Paddling My Own Canoe.* Honolulu: University of Hawai`i Press, 1978. On the surface, a lyrical description of paddling along the shore of Moloka`i; underneath, a charming classic by a legendary canoer and kayaker that presents a spirituality akin to Zen.

Wirzba, Norman. *The Paradise of God: Renewing Religion in an Ecological Age.* New York: Oxford University Press, 2003. An argument for a new religiously based environmentalism.

Film/TV

Gifts from God: Women in Ministry. (Films Media Group.) A CBS News special in which Jewish and Christian women who are in the ministry discuss their experiences.

God Is Green. (Directors Mark Dowd and Bruno Sorrentino; 3BM Television.) A documentary profiling the rise of the evangelical environmental movement.

An Inconvenient Truth. (Director Davis Guggenheim; Paramount.) An award-winning documentary that speaks of the perils of global warming.

Journeys of the Spirit: A Pilgrimage to New Mexico. (Films Media Group.) A CBS News special on an ecumenical gathering at the Sanctuary of Chimayó, New Mexico.

The Land and the Sacred: Nature's Role in Myth and Religion. (Films Media Group.) A three-part series exploring the spiritual relevance of the environment in Africa, Asia, Europe, and South America.

Music/Audio

Music has pointed the way for modern spirituality and contemplation. Here are important musical selections. Especially approachable pieces are starred:

Debussy: *Prelude to the Afternoon of a Faun,*Nocturnes, La Mer, Syrinx*

Delius: *On Hearing the First Cuckoo in Spring, Summer Night on the River, Brigg Fair*

Fauré: *Berceuse*

Hovhaness: *Mysterious Mountain*

Ravel: *Mother Goose Suite, Le Tombeau de Couperin, Daphnis and Chloe* (concert version), *String Quartet in F, Piano Concerto in G*

Satie: *Gymnopedies nos. 1–3*

Vaughan Williams: *The Lark Ascending, *Fantasia on Greensleeves, *Fantasia on a Theme of Thomas Tallis, Serenade to Music* (orchestral version), *String Quartets nos. 1 and 2*

Internet

Center for Religious Tolerance: http://centerforreligioustolerance.org/. The Web site of a nonprofit organization whose mission is to promote peace and harmony through interfaith activities and dialogue.

Marvel, Believe, Care: http://www.marvelbelievecare.org/. An online Christian environmental resource, devoted to raising awareness about the importance of caring for God's creation.

RELIGION BEYOND THE CLASSROOM

Visit the Online Learning Center at www.mhhe.com/molloy6e for additional exercises and features, including "Religion beyond the Classroom" and "For Fuller Understanding."

Answer Key

Chapter 1
1. b., 2. c., 3. a., 4. b., 5. c., 6. d., 7. a., 8. d., 9. a., 10. c.

Chapter 2
1. c., 2. a., 3. d., 4. a., 5. b., 6. d., 7. b., 8. a., 9. c., 10. d.

Chapter 3
1. b., 2. c., 3. c., 4. b., 5. b., 6. d., 7. d., 8. c., 9. a., 10. b.

Chapter 4
1. b., 2. d., 3. c., 4. b., 5. a., 6. c., 7. a., 8. c., 9. d., 10. b.

Chapter 5
1. c., 2. d., 3. a., 4. a., 5. b., 6. d., 7. a., 8. c., 9. d., 10. c.

Chapter 6
1. b., 2. c., 3. a., 4. b., 5. b., 6. a., 7. a., 8. d., 9. b., 10. a.

Chapter 7
1. a., 2. b., 3. c., 4. d., 5. b., 6. c., 7. a., 8. c., 9. b., 10. a.

Chapter 8
1. a., 2. d., 3. a., 4. b., 5. c., 6. b., 7. a., 8. c., 9. b., 10. a.

Chapter 9
1. b., 2. b., 3. a., 4. c., 5. c., 6. b., 7. d., 8. d., 9. b., 10. c.

Chapter 10
1. d., 2. c., 3. b., 4. c., 5. d., 6. b., 7. a., 8. b., 9. a., 10. a.

Chapter 11
1. d., 2. b., 3. a., 4. a., 5. d., 6. b., 7. c., 8. a., 9. c., 10. b.

Chapter 12
1. b., 2. b., 3. d., 4. d., 5. a., 6. b., 7. a., 8. d., 9. c., 10. c.

Notes

Chapter 1

1. *Webster's New World Dictionary,* 2nd ed. (New York: William Collins, 1972). Other Latin roots are also possible.
2. *Cassell's New Latin Dictionary* (New York: Funk & Wagnalls, 1960).
3. Julian Huxley, *Religion Without Revelation* (New York: Mentor, 1957), p. 33.
4. Similar lists can be found, for example, in William Alston, "Religion," in *The Encyclopedia of Philosophy,* vol. 7 (New York: Macmillan, 1972), pp. 141–42; and Ninian Smart, *The Religious Experience,* 4th ed. (New York: Macmillan, 1991), pp. 6–10.
5. William James, *The Varieties of Religious Experience* (New York: Collier, 1961), p. 377.
6. Rudolf Otto, *The Idea of the Holy* (New York: Oxford University Press, 1963), p. 62.
7. Some have criticized Otto's notion of the *mysterium tremendum,* arguing that his theorizing was overly influenced by Protestant Christianity, in which he was raised.
8. Carl Jung, *Memories, Dreams, Reflections* (London: Collins, 1972), p. 222.
9. "Between Mountain and Plain," *Time,* October 20, 1952, p. 33.
10. Alston, "Religion," pp. 143–44.
11. Catholics touch the left shoulder first; Orthodox Christians touch the right shoulder first.
12. Kusan Sunim, *The Way of Korean Zen* (New York: Weatherhill, 1985), p. 168.
13. *New Oxford Annotated Bible* (New York: Oxford University Press, 1991).
14. *Good News Bible* (New York: American Bible Society, 1976). This version is a paraphrase.
15. For example, the Shrimaladevisimhanada Sutra speaks of the enlightenment of a female lay ruler.
16. See Daniel Pals, *Eight Theories of Religion* (New York: Oxford University Press, 2007).
17. Martin Luther King Jr., *Strength to Love* (New York: Harper & Row, 1963), p. 3.
18. Joseph Campbell, *The Power of Myth* at http://www.jcf.org/new/index.php?categoryid=31&s=a9f928db362de56d58171766ec22b06c.

Chapter 2

1. Nancy Parezo, "The Southwest," in *The Native Americans,* ed. Colin Taylor (New York: Salamander, 1991), p. 58.
2. Geoffrey Parrinder, *Religion in Africa* (New York: Praeger, 1969), pp. 18, 21.
3. Foreword to Peter Knudtson and David Suzuki, *Wisdom of the Elders* (Toronto: Stoddart, 1993), p. xxiv.
4. Gladys Reichard, *Navaho Religion* (Princeton: Bollingen, 1963), p. 286.
5. Frank Willett, *African Art* (London: Thames and Hudson, 1993), p. 35.
6. One entire room at the Gauguin Museum in Tahiti illustrates Gauguin's interest in discovering a "primary religion." It also shows the religious origin of much imagery in his paintings. A significant collection of Gauguin's paintings and carvings can be seen at the Musée d'Orsay in Paris.
7. Florence Drake, *Civilization* (Norman: University of Oklahoma Press, 1936), quoted in John Collier, *Indians of the Americas* (New York: New American Library, 1947), p. 107.
8. Sword, Finger, One Star, and Tyon, recorded by J. R. Walker, in "Oglala Metaphysics," in *Teachings from the American Earth: Indian Religion and Philosophy,* ed. Dennis Tedlock and Barbara Tedlock (New York: Liveright, 1992), p. 206.
9. For more detail, see Parrinder, *Religion in Africa,* pp. 47–59.
10. Åke Hultkrantz, *Native Religions of North America* (San Francisco: Harper, 1987), p. 20, cited in *Ways of Being Religious,* ed. Gary Kessler (Mountain View, CA: Mayfield, 2000), p. 71.
11. Quoted in T. C. McLuhan, ed., *Touch the Earth* (New York: Promontory Press, 1971), p. 42.
12. McLuhan, *Touch the Earth,* p. 56.
13. Knudtson and Suzuki, *Wisdom of the Elders,* p. xxv.
14. Colin Turnbull, *The Forest People* (New York: Simon & Schuster, 1968), p. 14.
15. Knudtson and Suzuki, *Wisdom of the Elders,* p. 29.
16. Ibid., p. 27.
17. Parrinder, *Religion in Africa,* p. 43.
18. Ibid., p. 32.
19. Joseph Campbell, *The Power of Myth* (New York: Doubleday, 1988), p. 6.
20. Parrinder, *Religion in Africa,* pp. 80–81.
21. Ibid., p. 81.
22. Collier, *Indians of the Americas,* p. 105.
23. For details, see William Sturtevant, "The Southeast," in Taylor, *The Native Americans,* pp. 17–21.
24. Sam Gill, *Native American Religions* (Belmont, CA: Wadsworth, 1982), p. 98.
25. Ibid.
26. From Drake, *Civilization,* quoted in Collier, *Indians of the Americas,* p. 107.
27. See John Mbiti, *Introduction to African Religion* (London: Heinemann, 1986), pp. 143–44.
28. Isabella Abbott, *La`au Hawai`i: Traditional Hawaiian Uses of Plants* (Honolulu: Bishop Museum Press, 1992), p 37.

29. Ibid., p. 18. Four days were sacred to Ku, three to Kanaloa, two to Kane, and one day at the end of the month to Lono.

30. This is not unprecedented. In Samoa, universal claims were made for the god Tangaroa, possibly as early as 800 CE. See John Charlot, *Chanting the Universe* (Hong Kong: Emphasis, 1983), p. 144.

31. John Charlot remarks that the first public Hawaiian temple service since 1819 was carried out by Samuel H. Lono on October 11, 1980. See ibid., p. 148.

32. Joan Halifax, *Shaman: The Wounded Healer* (London: Thames and Hudson, 1994), p. 5.

33. Quoted in Knudtson and Suzuki, *Wisdom of the Elders*, p. 70.

34. Isaac Tens, recorded by Marius Barbeau, in *Medicine Men of the North Pacific Coast*, Bulletin 152 (Ottawa: National Museum of Man of the National Museum of Canada, 1958), found in Tedlock and Tedlock, *Teachings from the American Earth*, pp. 3–4.

35. Ibid.

36. For a detailed study of the religious use of peyote by Native Americans, see Omer C. Stewart, *Peyote Religion: A History* (Norman: University of Oklahoma Press, 1987).

37. John Fire/Lame Deer and Richard Erdoes, *Lame Deer, Seeker of Visions* (New York: Simon and Schuster, 1972), p. 220.

38. Mbiti, *Introduction to African Religion*, p. 165.

39. Ibid., p. 166.

40. These are the commonly used names; nomenclature is in a process of change for some Northwest tribes.

41. Pat Kramer, *Totem Poles* (Vancouver: Altitude, 1995), pp. 48–49.

42. Richard W. Hill Sr., "The Symbolism of Feathers," in *Creation's Journey*, ed. Tom Hill and Richard W. Hill Sr. (Washington, DC: Smithsonian Institution Press, 1994), p. 88.

43. *The Kumulipo*, Martha Warren Beckwith (Chicago: University of Chicago Press, 1951). The original is printed with few diacritical marks; interlinearization by David Stampe. http://www.ling.hawaii.edu/faculty/stampe/Oral-Lit/Hawaiian/Kumulipo/_kumulipo-comb.html.

Chapter 3

1. Arthur Basham, *The Wonder That Was India* (New York: Grove, 1959), p. 16. Chapter 2 of Basham's book contains a detailed description of the Harappa culture.

2. Ibid., p. 23.

3. Also spelled *Rg Veda*. For representative prayers, see William T. de Bary, ed., *Sources of Indian Tradition*, vol. 1 (New York: Columbia University Press, 1958), pp. 7–16.

4. Rig Veda 10:129, quoted in Basham, *The Wonder That Was India*, p. 16.

5. The same tendency toward philosophy existed in Greece at the time and a few centuries later in the Roman Empire.

6. The philosopher Shankara offered another interpretation—"to wear away completely."

7. These six notions are not fixed concepts in the Upanishads. They are more like centers around which speculation revolves, and there may be differences in how they are described, even within the same Upanishad. The notion of Brahman, for example, sometimes varies from that of a divine reality quite beyond the world to that of a spiritual reality that exists within the world.

8. Chandogya Upanishad 6:13, in *The Upanishads*, trans. Juan Mascaró (New York: Penguin, 1979), p. 118.

9. Shvetasvatara Upanishad, end of part 3, *The Upanishads*, pp. 90–91; emphasis added.

10. Ibid., part 4, p. 91.

11. Ibid.

12. See, for example, ibid., p. 92.

13. Ibid.

14. Brihadaranyaka Upanishad 2:4, *The Upanishads*, p. 132.

15. *Bhagavad-Gita: The Song of God*, trans. Swami Prabhavananda and Christopher Isherwood (New York: Mentor, 1972), chap. 5, p. 57.

16. Ibid., chap. 1, p. 34.

17. Ibid., chap. 18, p. 127.

18. Ibid., chap. 2, p. 38.

19. Rig Veda 10:90, as quoted in de Bary, *Sources of Indian Tradition*, vol. 1, p. 14.

20. See chap. 2 of the *Bhagavad Gita*.

21. Sometimes the term *caste* is reserved for what I call here subcastes—the hundreds of occupation-based social divisions (*jati*).

22. I follow the common practice of using the word *brahmin* (priest)—rather than the Sanskrit term *brahman*—to avoid confusion with the term *Brahman* (spiritual essence of the world) with a capital B.

23. See, for example, the description of Gandhi's "fast unto death" for untouchables in Louis Fischer, *Gandhi* (New York: New American Library, 1954), pp. 116–19.

24. The six orthodox schools of Hindu philosophy all developed as systems of personal liberation but disagreed about the views and methods that would bring liberation. The six schools are Nyaya, Vaisheshika, Sankhya, Yoga, Mimamsa, and Vedanta. (The terms *Yoga* and *Vedanta*, when used to denote schools of philosophy, have a precise and different meaning than when used more generally.) Nyaya ("analysis") valued the insight that comes from clarity, reason, and logic. Vaisheshika ("individual characteristics") taught what it considered to be the correct way of understanding reality—seeing reality as essentially being composed of atoms. Sankhya ("count") was originally an atheistic philosophy that considered the universe to be made of two essential principles—soul and matter. Yoga ("union," "spiritual discipline") emphasized meditation and physical disciplines. Mimamsa ("investigation") defended the authority of the Vedas as a guide to salvation. Vedanta developed several subschools but tended to see a unifying principle—Brahman—at work behind the changing phenomena of everyday life; the individual can find salvation by attaining union with this principle.

25. Shankara's conception of Brahman is debated. For him, Brahman may have been a positive spiritual reality, or it may have been closer to the notion of emptiness found in Buddhism.

26. Shankara (attrib.), *Shankara's Crest-Jewel of Discrimination* (New York: Mentor, 1970), p. 72.

27. *Bhagavad-Gita*, chap. 2, p. 40.

28. Although these sutras are attributed to an ancient grammarian named Patanjali, who lived before the Common Era, they may have been written later, from about 200 CE.

29. Basham, *The Wonder That Was India,* p. 326.

30. Ibid., chap. 18, p. 128.

31. Heinrich Zimmer, *Myths and Symbols in Indian Art and Civilization* (Princeton: Princeton University Press, 1972), p. 153.

32. Basavaraja, quoted in de Bary, *Sources of Indian Tradition,* vol. 1, p. 352. Basavaraja was a twelfth-century Indian government official who founded a religious order devoted to Shiva.

33. *The Gospel of Ramakrishna,* quoted in de Bary, *Sources of Indian Tradition,* vol. 2, p. 86.

34. *The Upanishads,* trans. Swami Prabhavananda and Frederick Manchester (New York: Mentor, 1970), pp. 70–71.

35. The term *darshan* also extends to viewing images of deities in order to experience the divine presence that they mediate.

36. See Ainslie T. Embree, ed., *The Hindu Tradition* (New York: Vintage, 1972), p. 279.

37. Fischer, *Gandhi,* p. 11.

38. Quoted in Fischer, *Gandhi,* p. 18.

39. Gandhi compromised his position on nonviolence somewhat during World War I, when he urged Indians to join the war effort on the side of the British. Later, he said that this position had been a mistake.

40. Shankara (attrib.), *Shankara's Crest-Jewel of Discrimination,* pp. 102–103.

Chapter 4

1. Arthur Basham put it nicely: "Much doubt now exists as to the real doctrines of the historical Buddha, as distinct from those of Buddhism." *The Wonder That Was India* (New York: Grove, 1959), p. 256.

2. The tree might have been a form of banyan, which today is called the *Ficus religiosa* ("religious fig") because of its supposed connection with the Buddha.

3. As quoted in William T. de Bary, ed., *Sources of Indian Tradition,* vol. 1 (New York: Columbia University Press, 1958), p. 110. The same word that is usually translated as "lamp" may also be translated as "island." The meaning remains that the disciple must make judgments that are independent of those of the ordinary world.

4. Some scholars think that the Reclining Buddha images may also depict the Buddha sleeping, sometimes with his cousin Ananda looking on protectively. It is often explained that those statues in which the Buddha's feet are joined represent him at the moment of death, while those that show his feet separated and relaxed represent the Buddha at rest.

5. Sometimes the term *Sangha* is used more widely to include devout laypersons.

6. See David Kalupahana, *Buddhist Philosophy: A Historical Analysis* (Honolulu: University of Hawaii Press, 1976), pp. 38–41.

7. *Buddhist Suttas,* trans. T. W. Rhys Davids (New York: Dover, 1969), p. 148.

8. *The Dhammapada: The Sayings of the Buddha,* trans. Thomas Byrom (New York: Vintage, 1976), chap. 15, p. 76.

9. From the Sammanaphala Suttanta, in *The Teachings of the Compassionate Buddha,* ed. E. A. Burtt (New York: New American Library, 1955), p. 104.

10. Sometimes the order is reversed, and the sutra is designated as the first basket, with the vinaya listed second.

11. The commonly accepted view about the introduction of form into Buddhist imagery has been questioned. See Stanley Abe, "Inside the Wonder House: Buddhist Art and the West," in *Curators of the Buddha: The Study of Buddhism under Colonialism,* ed. Donald S. Lopez Jr. (Chicago: University of Chicago Press, 1995), pp. 63–106.

12. Hirakawa Akira, *A History of Indian Buddhism* (Honolulu: University of Hawaii Press, 1990), p. 258.

13. For details about the origins of Mahayana, see John Koller, *The Indian Way* (New York: Macmillan, 1983), p. 163.

14. For information about Buddhist schools of philosophy, see "The Nature of Reality," in John Koller, *Oriental Philosophies* (New York: Scribner's, 1970), pp. 146–79.

15. Kenneth Ch'en, *Buddhism in China* (Princeton, NJ: Princeton University Press, 1972), p. 385.

16. For more information see Richard Robinson and Willard Johnson, *The Buddhist Religion,* 4th ed. (Belmont, CA: Wadsworth, 1997), pp. 181ff.

17. Robert Buswell, *Tracing Back the Radiance: Chinul's Korean Way of Zen* (Honolulu: University of Hawaii Press, 1991), p. 5. See the introduction for a description of Korea's early Buddhist contacts with China and central Asia.

18. For a traveler's description of the monastery complex in the seventeenth century, see Li Chi, *The Travel Diaries of Hsü Hsia-k'o* (Hong Kong: The Chinese University of Hong Kong, 1974), pp. 29–42.

19. Shohaku, Okumura, *Shikantaza: An Introduction to Zazen* (Kyoto: Kyoto Zen Center, 1990) is a meditation guidebook that contains instructions for zazen and a good selection of passages by Zen masters on the practice and effects of zazen.

20. See the story of Rinzai, who received a beating from his master Obaku as a koan-like response to his simple-minded questioning, in D. T. Suzuki, *Studies in Zen* (New York: Delta, 1955), pp. 68–70. Suzuki gives many examples of koan, with commentary. The actual use of the koan in Japanese monasteries over the last three centuries has become more

formalized. Instead of working through a koan, a person in training (who hopes to take over his father's temple) now often refers to books for the appropriate answers.

21. For connections between Christianity and the tea ceremony, see Heinrich Dumoulin, *A History of Zen Buddhism* (Boston: Beacon, 1963), pp. 214–24.

22. http://www.arcworld.org/news.asp?pageID=308, edited.

23. Ibid.

24. Basho, *The Narrow Road to the Deep North and Other Travel Sketches* (Harmondsworth, UK: Penguin, 1974), pp. 131–33.

Chapter 5

1. Mahapurana 4:16, cited in William T. de Bary, ed., *Sources of Indian Tradition,* vol. 1. (New York: Columbia University Press, 1958), p. 76.

2. Acaranga Sutra 1:6, 5, cited in de Bary, *Sources of Indian Tradition,* vol. 1, p. 65.

3. See John Koller, *The Indian Way* (New York: Macmillan, 1982), pp. 114–15.

4. Selection from the Mul Mantra, cited in M. A. Macauliffe, *The Sikh Religion,* vol. 1 (Oxford: Oxford University Press, 1901), p. 195.

5. From Asa Ki Var, Mahala I, cited in Macauliffe, *The Sikh Religion,* vol. 1, p. 221.

6. From http://www.liturgy.co.nz/reflection/peace.html.

Chapter 6

1. See Livia Kohn, *God of the Dao* (Ann Arbor: Center for Chinese Studies, University of Michigan, 1998), p. 9, n. 6.

2. *Lao-Tzu: Te-Tao Ching,* trans. Robert Henricks (New York: Ballantine, 1989), p. 72.

3. *Tao Te Ching,* trans. Gia-fu Feng and Jane English (New York: Random House, 1972), chap. 8. This translation is used unless stated otherwise.

4. *The Wisdom of Laotse,* trans. Lin Yutang (New York: Modern Library, 1948), p. 76.

5. *Chuang Tzu: Basic Writings,* trans. Burton Watson (New York: Columbia University Press, 1964),p. 113 (sec. 18).

6. Ibid.

7. Ibid., p. 36 (sec. 2).

8. Cited in *The Way and Its Power,* ed. and trans. Arthur Waley (New York: Grove, 1958), p. 181.

9. Wing-Tsit Chan, "Man and Nature in the Chinese Garden" in *Chinese Houses and Gardens,* ed. Henry Inn and Shao Chang Lee (Honolulu: Fong Inn's Limited, 1940), pp. 35–36.

10. Ibid., p. 33.

11. *The Doctrine of the Mean* 20:18; in *Confucius: Confucian Analects, The Great Learning, and The Doctrine of the Mean,* trans. James Legge (New York: Dover, 1971), p. 413. In the original translation, the word *right* is italicized and the word *way* is not. I have changed this to make my point clearer. Legge's translation of the Four Books—the major Confucian

books, which include the sayings of Confucius and Mencius—is used unless otherwise noted.

12. Ibid., 12:4.

13. *Analects* 5:25, 4.

14. Ibid., 2:4, 1–6.

15. Robert D. Baird and Alfred Bloom, *Indian and Far Eastern Religious Traditions* (New York: Harper & Row, 1972), p. 169.

16. George Kates, *The Years That Were Fat* (Cambridge, MA: MIT Press, 1976), pp. 28–29.

17. See *The Doctrine of the Mean* 20:8 for a different order.

18. *Analects* 12:1, 1.

19. See *Analects* 12:1, 2; and *The Doctrine of the Mean* 13:3.

20. *The Doctrine of the Mean* 20:18; adapted.

21. *Analects* 4:16, in *The Analects of Confucius,* trans. Arthur Waley (New York: Vintage, 1938), p. 105.

22. Ibid. 4:24.

23. *The Great Learning,* "Text of Confucius," verse 6.

24. *The Doctrine of the Mean* 1:1–2; adapted.

25. Ibid. 1:5.

26. *Mencius* 4:2, 12; adapted; in *The Works of Mencius,* trans. James Legge (New York: Dover, 1970).

27. See chapters 18–20 of the *Daodejing* (*Tao Te Ching*).

28. See chapter 80 of the *Daodejing* (*Tao Te Ching*).

29. *Mencius* 4:1,9.2.

30. Ibid., 6:1.6.7.

31. Given in an introductory chapter of ibid., p. 81.

32. Cited in William T. de Bary, ed., *Sources of Chinese Tradition,* vol. 1 (New York: Columbia University Press, 1960), pp. 45–46.

33. Ibid., p. 436.

34. *Chuang Tzu: Basic Writings,* chap. 5 ("The Sign of Virtue Complete"), p. 70, or http://www.terebess.hu/english/chuangtzu.html#5.

Chapter 7

1. This myth begins the Kojiki ("chronicle of ancient events"); see *Translation of Ko-ji-ki,* trans. Basil Hall Chamberlain, 2nd ed. (Kobe: J. L. Thompson, 1932), pp. 17–23. The etymology of *kami* is debated.

2. Ibid., pp. 21–22. The same story, with many variants, appears at the beginning of another ancient work, the Nihongi.

3. Ibid., pp. 50–51.

4. Also called Shrine Shinto. For details, see H. Byron Earhart, *Religions of Japan* (New York: Harper & Row, 1984), pp. 43–45 and 93–100.

5. Sometimes a distinction is made between the spirits of nature and the spirits of the deceased. It is debated whether a belief in one type of spirit was the origin of a belief in the other. See, for example, Carmen Blacker, *The Catalpa Bow* (London: Allen & Unwin, 1975), pp. 45–46.

6. For a translation, see *Nihongi,* trans. W. G. Aston (London: Allen & Unwin, 1956).

7. Such imagery was apparently much more common before Western influence—and its sense of decorum—entered Japan in the nineteenth century.

8. The sense that death is polluting and dangerous explains the regular rebuilding of some Shinto shrines and the destruction of the clothing and personal effects of a deceased person.

9. The torii is used as a gateway, but it can be placed anywhere to indicate the presence of kami.

10. See H. Byron Earhart, *Japanese Religion: Unity and Diversity*, 2nd ed. (Encino, CA: Dickenson, 1974), p. 21.

11. Later, on a return journey to the temple, I discovered a Shinto shrine on a path just above the temple—another sign of the intermingling of Shinto and Buddhism. Dedicated to fertility and childbirth, Jishu Jinja is a place for worship of the protective kami that guards the temple.

12. Keiichi Nakayama, *Tenrikyo Kyoten Kowa* (Tenri, Japan: Tenrikyo, 1951), p. 3; cited in Harry Thomsen, *The New Religions of Japan* (Rutland, VT: Tuttle, 1963), p. 34.

13. A translation of Miki's poetic work, *Mikagura Uta*, can be found in Thomsen, *The New Religions of Japan*, pp. 41–48.

14. http://www.sapphyr.net/peace/prayersforpeace.htm.

Chapter 8

1. This theory is called the "documentary hypothesis." For details, see Stephen Harris, *Understanding the Bible*, 3rd ed. (London: Mayfield, 1992), pp. 53–59.

2. The Greek translation of the Hebrew Bible is commonly called the Septuagint. For details about the Septuagint translation, see Henry Jackson Flanders, Robert Wilson Crapps, and David Anthony Smith, *People of the Covenant*, 4th ed. (New York: Oxford University Press, 1996), p. 21.

3. Translation from *Tanakh—The Holy Scriptures* (Philadelphia: The Jewish Publication Society, 1985).

4. Emphasis added.

5. The New Oxford Annotated Bible (New York: Oxford University Press, 1991).

6. The translation in *Tanakh—The Holy Scriptures* simply gives the Hebrew phrase "Ehyeh-Asher-Ehyeh"; it adds a footnote, saying that the exact meaning of the Hebrew is uncertain but that a common translation is "I am who I am" (p. 88).

7. The words *Yahweh* and *Adonay* (also spelled *Adonai*) were ultimately blended to create the name *Jehovah*, used in English Bibles.

8. It is possible that the Book of Deuteronomy constitutes the first volume of a history about the Hebrews' entry into Canaan, which is continued in the Books of Joshua and Judges.

9. Although today we might recoil at the thought of animal sacrifice, we must realize that it was common throughout the world of the time, even in India and China. It fulfilled several functions. Worshipers often thought the ritual of sharing a sacred meal would unite them with their deity. Punishment that might have fallen on human beings was thought to be transferred to the sacrificial animal. It was also a sign that the deity was in charge of all life.

10. Exodus 20:2–17, from *Tanakh—the Holy Scriptures*.

11. The most famous is at Dura-Europos, in southern Syria.

12. The New Oxford Annotated Bible.

13. There are two long passages in Aramaic: Daniel 2:4–7:28 and Ezra 4:8–6:18. Short Aramaic passages also appear in Genesis (31:47) and Jeremiah (10:11).

14. Many other religious books were popular but were not finally accepted as canonical by Jews in Israel. A few additional books, however, were accepted as canonical by Jews living in Egypt, such as Sirach, the Wisdom of Solomon, and Maccabees. (Later, they were also accepted as canonical by Catholic and Eastern Orthodox Christians.)

15. The name *Sadducee* may derive from the name *Zadok* (or *Sadoc*), a priest at the time of King David.

16. The name *Pharisee* may derive from a Hebrew word meaning "separate"—referring to a ritual purity associated with the careful practice of religious laws.

17. It is possible that the dualistic worldview of the Essenes was influenced by the Persian religion of Zoroastrianism and that their semimonastic lifestyle was influenced by monastic ideals that had come from India to Egypt.

18. *Union Prayer Book* (New York: Central Conference of American Rabbis, 1959), part 1, pp. 166–67.

19. A passage from the *Zohar*, quoted in *The Wisdom of the Kabbalah*, ed. Dagobert Runes (New York: Citadel, 1967), p. 172.

20. The beginning of the movie *Yentl* illustrates the value put on the mystical interpretation of the Book of Genesis.

21. Quoted in Gershom Scholem, *On the Kabbalah and Its Symbolism* (New York: Schocken, 1969), p. 103.

22. Martin Buber, the great Jewish writer, collected and published two volumes of Hasidic sayings. Many tales of the Baal Shem Tov appear in the first volume, *Tales of the Hasidim: Early Masters* (orig. pub. 1947; New York: Schocken, 1973).

23. Louis Newman, *Hasidic Anthology* (New York: Schocken, 1975), p. 148.

24. Ibid., p. 149.

25. Bella Chagall, *Burning Lights* (New York: Schocken, 1972). This book contains thirty-six drawings by Marc Chagall.

26. Anne Frank, *The Diary of a Young Girl* (New York: Pocket Books, 1959), p. 222.

27. Ibid., pp. 192–93.

28. Ibid., p. 233.

29. The origin of the Sabbath is uncertain. It may have been inspired by Babylonian culture, or perhaps it was unique to the Hebrews. It is logical, however, to divide a lunar month into four seven-day periods.

30. It is also possible that pigs and shellfish were considered "imperfect" animals. Perfect land animals (such as sheep and goats) chewed a cud and had divided hooves; perfect sea animals had scales. All others were considered "less perfect."

31. Leo Trepp, *Judaism: Development and Life* (Belmont, CA: Dickenson Publishing, 1966), p. 75.

32. http://www.zeek.net/708environment/.

33. Trepp, *Judaism: Development and Life*, p. 75.

34. See http://www.mechon-mamre.org/p/pt/pt0102.htm.

Chapter 9

1. Jerusalem Bible (Garden City, NY: Doubleday, 1966).
2. American Bible Society translation, in *Good News Bible* (Nashville: Nelson, 1986).
3. Jerusalem Bible translation.
4. American Bible Society translation.
5. Jerusalem Bible translation.
6. See James Charlesworth, *Jesus and the Dead Sea Scrolls* (New York: Doubleday, 1992).
7. King James Version (Cambridge: Cambridge University Press, n.d.).
8. Acts 9:4, Revised Standard Version (RSV) (New York: New American Library, 1974).
9. RSV translation.
10. Jerusalem Bible translation.
11. RSV translation.
12. For more information on Christian Gnosticism, see Elaine Pagels's *The Gnostic Gospels* (New York: Random House, 1979) and *Adam, Eve, and the Serpent* (New York: Vintage, 1989).
13. Jerusalem Bible translation.
14. New International Version (Grand Rapids, MI: Zondervan Bible Publishers, 1984).
15. Earlier lists, such as the Muratorian Canon, differ from the present-day canonical list of New Testament books. The list, as we now have it, is mentioned in the *Festal Letter* of Athanasius of Alexandria, circulated in 367 CE, and is the same list of books translated by Jerome into Latin. For further details, see Dennis Duling and Norman Perrin, *The New Testament: Proclamation and Pareness, Myth and History*, 3rd ed. (New York: Harcourt Brace, 1994), p. 134.
16. Jerusalem Bible translation.
17. *The Confessions of Saint Augustine*, trans. Rex Warner (New York: New American Library, 1963), pp. 182–83.
18. Jerusalem Bible translation.
19. See David Knowles, *Christian Monasticism* (New York: McGraw-Hill, 1972), which emphasizes the development of Benedictine monasticism.
20. See Christopher Brooke, *Monasteries of the World* (New York: Crescent, 1982), for excellent maps, diagrams, and photographs.
21. *St. Benedict's Rule for Monasteries* (Collegeville, MN: Liturgical Press, 1948), chap. 1, pp. 2–3.
22. Nikos Kazantzakis, author of *Zorba the Greek* and *Saint Francis*, lived for a time on Mount Athos and considered becoming a monk.
23. *The Disciplinary Decrees of the General Councils*, trans. H. J. Schroeder (St. Louis: B. Herder, 1937), p. 19; quoted in Colman Barry, ed., *Readings in Church History*, vol. 1 (Westminster, MD: Newman Press, 1960), p. 85.
24. Nicholas Gage, *Eleni* (New York: Ballantine Books, 1983), pp. 122–23.
25. For the mysticism of Gregory of Nyssa, see *From Glory to Glory: Texts from Gregory of Nyssa's Mystical Writings* (New York: Scribners, 1961), particularly the introduction by Jean Daniélou. For Augustine's mysticism, see *The Essential Augustine* (New York: Mentor, 1964), pp. 127 and 148.
26. Origen, prologue to the "Commentary on the Song of Songs," in *Origen*, trans. Rowan Greer (New York: Paulist Press, 1979), p. 217.
27. From Sermon 6, in *Meister Eckhart*, trans. Raymond Blakney (New York: Harper, 1941), p. 131.
28. Julian of Norwich, *Revelations of Divine Love*, trans. Clifton Wolters (New York: Penguin, 1982), Chap. 59, p. 167.
29. Pamphlet, *Prayer of Saint Francis* (Columbus, OH: Christopher House, 1996), p. 4, adapted.
30. See Erik Erikson, *Young Man Luther: A Study in Psychoanalysis and History* (New York: Norton, 1962).
31. King James Version.
32. A similar development occurred in the Buddhist Pure Land movement. In Japan, Shinran concluded that only trust in Amida Buddha's grace was enough for the devotee.
33. J. Raboteau, "Afro-American Religions," in *World Religions* (New York: Simon and Schuster Macmillan, 1998), p. 18.
34. Bennetta Jules-Rosette, "African Religions," ibid., pp. 7–10.
35. The term *Mass* comes from the dismissal at the conclusion of this ceremony, when the priest said in Latin, *Ite missa est* ("Go, it is the dismissal").
36. Albert Schweitzer's classic study *J. S. Bach* (orig. pub. 1905; Neptune, NJ: Paganiniana, 1980) emphasizes the religious character of all of Bach's work.
37. Julian of Norwich, in *Revelations of Divine Love*, pp. 109–110.

Chapter 10

1. Also spelled *Mohammed*, although this spelling is now considered less accurate than *Muhammad*. We might also note that there is some disagreement about the details of Muhammad's life, particularly those regarding his early years.
2. John Esposito, *Islam: The Straight Path*, 3rd ed. (New York: Oxford University Press, 1998), p. 3.
3. Also spelled *Kaaba, Ka'bah,* and *Kaba.*
4. For further details see Thomas Lippman, *Understanding Islam* (New York: New American Library, 1982), pp. 34–38.
5. Also commonly spelled *Khadija.*
6. It is possible that Khadijah was younger than this, given the fact that she gave birth to at least six children.
7. 96:1–19 passim; from *The Koran*, trans. N. J. Dawood (London: Penguin, 1993).
8. Lippman, *Understanding Islam*, p. 44. Guides in Jerusalem sometimes point to marks in stone, which they say are footprints left by Muhammad. The account of Muhammad's journey may have influenced Dante's vision of paradise in the *Divine Comedy*.
9. 49:10 (Dawood translation).
10. In Islamic belief, punishment in hell is not necessarily eternal for all.

11.   2:163; from *Holy Qur'an*, trans. M. H. Shakir (Milton Keynes, England: Mihrab Publishers, 1986).

12.   In Islam, a messenger is a prophet with a special call from God.

13.   Some Shiite Muslims combine these into three periods of prayer.

14.   Another translation is, "Allah is greater (than anything else)."

15.   2:144 (Dawood translation).

16.   Although only Muslims may make the pilgrimage to Mecca, many films document the practice. See, for example, the classic film *Mecca, The Forbidden City,* by Iranfilms.

17.   2:158 (Shakir translation).

18.   Muslims were originally permitted to drink wine, but later revelations to Muhammad prohibited it. There is, however, some variation in the keeping of this regulation. Countries that have experienced strong European influence (such as several in northern Africa—Morocco, Algeria, and Tunisia) often produce wine, and countries that depend heavily on tourism usually allow the serving of alcohol in tourist hotels.

19.   Female circumcision is sometimes said to be based on a hadith (a remembrance of Muhammad's early followers); see Annemarie Schimmel, *Islam: An Introduction* (Albany: State University of New York Press, 1992), p. 55.

20.   An exception is made in some cases, such as the tombs of rulers and publicly recognized holy persons.

21.   Although the early versions did not contain vowels or diacritical marks, later versions do; consequently, some differences exist between versions.

22.   Esposito, *Islam: The Straight Path,* p. 6.

23.   There is some disagreement over this matter among Sunni and Shiite Muslims.

24.   1:1–5 (Dawood translation).

25.   Also called the Battle of Poitiers.

26.   "Islam in South-East Asia: Incense, Silk and Jihad," *The Economist,* May 31, 2003, p. 37.

27.   50:16 (Dawood translation). See also John Williams, ed., *Islam* (New York: Washington Square, 1963), pp. 122–58.

28.   3:29 (Shakir translation). See A. J. Arberry, *Sufism* (New York: Harper, 1970), pp. 17–22.

29.   2:115 (Dawood translation).

30.   Arberry, *Sufism,* p. 28.

31.   Ibid., p. 228.

32.   Afkham Darbandi and Dick Davis, introduction to *The Conference of the Birds,* by Farid Ud-Din Attar (Harmondsworth, England: Penguin, 1984), p. 10.

33.   Quoted in F. C. Happold, *Mysticism* (Baltimore: Penguin, 1963), p. 229.

34.   Esposito, *Islam: The Straight Path,* pp. 105–106.

35.   Williams, *Islam,* pp. 138–41. Williams claims that al-Arabi influenced the Spanish mystics and poets John of the Cross and Ramón Llull, and possibly the Dutch philosopher Benedict de Spinoza.

36.   Islamic influence on Christian architecture is almost certainly demonstrated by the use of these alternating lines of color, such as in the cathedrals of Siena, Pisa, and Florence.

37.   See 2:25, 3:136, and 10:9.

38.   See 2:25.

39.   http://www.bbc.co.uk/news/world-south-asia-11451718.

40.   Jon Basil Utley, http://mises.org/daily/1313.

41.   http://www.greenprophet.com/2010/10/islam-water-scarcity/.

42.   7:31; *The Meaning of the Holy Qur'an,* trans. Abdullah Yusuf Ali (Butterworth, Malaysia: Sekretariat Dakwah Pulau Pinang, 2005).

43.   2:216 (Dawood translation).

44.   2:244 (Dawood translation).

45.   2:256 (Dawood translation).

46.   Happold, *Mysticism,* pp. 222–23.

Chapter 11

1.   See Leo Martello, *Witchcraft: The Old Religion* (New York: Citadel Press, 1991), chap. 5.

2.   For further information, see Philip Shallcrass, "Druidry Today," in *Paganism Today,* ed. Graham Harvey and Charlotte Hardman (London: Thorsons/HarperCollins, 1995), pp. 65–80.

3.   See Raúl Canizares, *Cuban Santería* (Rochester, VT: Destiny Books), pp. 38–48.

4.   Rudolf Steiner, *Theosophy* (Hudson, NY: Anthroposophic Press, 1989), p. 164.

5.   "Rudolf Steiner," in *The Encyclopedia of Philosophy,* vol. 8 (New York: Macmillan, 1967), pp. 13–14.

6.   *The Church of Scientology: An Introduction to Church Services* (n.p.: L. Ron Hubbard Library, 1999), p. 32.

7.   King James Version (Cambridge: Cambridge University Press, n.d.).

8.   Quoted in Leonard Barrett Sr., *The Rastafarians* (Boston: Beacon, 1997), p. 123.

9.   King James Version.

10.   Ibid.

11.   *The Baha'is* (Oakham, UK: Baha'i Publishing Trust of the United Kingdom, 1994), p. 54.

12.   For a good sampling of illustrations and interpretations, see Leo Martello, *Reading the Tarot* (New York: Avery Publishing, 1990).

13.   http://reference.bahai.org/en/t/c/BP/bp-7.html.

Chapter 12

1.   Robert Ellwood, *The History and Future of Faith* (New York: Crossroad, 1988), p. 137.

2.   Ibid., p. 141.

3.   "Which Humanism for the Third Millennium?" *Aizen* 16 (July–August 1997): 3.

4.   Government in the United States, however, is not fully secular. We might note, for example, the use of prayer and chaplains in legislative houses, the mention of God in the

Declaration of Independence, the use of the word *God* in court and on currency, and tax benefits given to churches and church property. See Ronald Thiemann, *Religion in Public Life* (Washington: Georgetown University Press, 1996), in which the author argues against the complete separation of church and state.

5. *Dhammapada,* trans. Thomas Byrom (New York: Vintage, 1976), chap. 10, p. 49. The translation presents the material divided into stanzas.

6. *Tao Te Ching,* trans. Gia-Fu Feng and Jane English (New York: Random House, 1972), chap. 30.

7. Ibid., chap. 31.

8. All biblical quotations here are taken from the New English Bible.

9. 8:65; all Qur'anic quotations here are taken from *The Koran,* trans. N. J. Dawood (London: Penguin, 1993).

10. 22:19 (Dawood translation).

11. 16:126 (Dawood translation).

12. *Honolulu Advertiser,* 26 July 1997, sec. B, p. 3, adapted.

13. For a good discussion of secularism in the modern world and its relation to religion, see Ellwood, *The History and Future of Faith,* chap. 5, pp. 96–117. Ellwood sees religions surviving in the future within a secular milieu but existing rather separately from it.

14. "Speech of the Very Rev. James Parks Morton at the Esperanto Conference, 1996, July 22, Prague," *Aizen* 16 (July–August 1997): 6.

15. For many examples, see Maurice Tuchman, ed., *The Spiritual in Art: Abstract Painting 1890–1985* (New York: Abbeville Press, 1986).

16. Philippe Gross and S. I. Shapiro, "Characteristics of the Taoist Sage in the *Chuang-tzu* and the Creative Photographer," *Journal of Transpersonal Psychology* 28:2 (1996), p. 181.

17. *Modern Photography* (October 1988), p. 94; quoted in ibid., p. 177.

18. Audrey Sutherland, *Paddling My Own Canoe* (Honolulu: University of Hawaii Press, 1987), p. 122.

Credits

Photo Credits

Photo/Hadi Mizban; **p. 433**: © Thomas Hilgers; **p. 439**: © AP Photo/Hasan Sarbakhshian; **p. 440**: © Fayaz Kabli/Reuters/Corbis; **p. 441**: © Kerim Okten/epa/Corbis; **p. 443, p. 448, p. 449, p. 450, p. 452**: © Thomas Hilgers; **p. 453**: © Paul Almasy/Corbis; **p. 455, p. 462**: © Thomas Hilgers; **p. 464**: © Ocean/Corbis. **Chapter 11 p. 470**: © Thomas Hilgers; **p. 476**: © Gideon Mendel/Corbis; **p. 479**: © Reuters/Corbis; **p. 480**: © Les Stone/Sygma/Corbis; **p. 482**: Theosophical Library Center; **p. 483**: © Corbis; **p. 485**: © Marianna Massey/Corbis; **p. 487**: © Reuters/Corbis; **p. 490**: © Thomas Hilgers; **p. 492**: © Daniel Laine/Corbis; **p. 493**: © Pictorial Press Ltd/Alamy; **p. 496**: © Dallas and John Heaton/Free Agents Limited/Corbis; **p. 499**: © Ricardo Azoury/Corbis. **Chapter 12 p. 506**: © Phil Nijhuis/EPA/Newscom; **p. 510**: © Monique Jaques/Corbis; **p. 513**: © Thomas Hilgers; **p. 515**: © Rick Friedman/Corbis; **p. 516**: NASA, ESA, and M. Livio and the Hubble 20th Anniversary Team (STScI); **p. 519**: © Steve Gschmeissner/Science Photo Library/Getty Images; **p. 523**: NASA; **p. 526**: © Paul Souders/Digital Vision/Getty Images; **p. 528**: © Thomas Hilgers; **p. 531**: Collection of The University of Arizona Museum of Art & Archive of Visual Arts, Tucson. © 2012 Georgia O'Keeffe Museum/Artists Rights Society (ARS), New York; **p. 532, p. 535**: © Thomas Hilgers.

Text Credits

Chapter 1, p. 29: From THE POWER OF MYTH by Joseph Campbell, & Bill Moyers, copyright © 1988 by Apostrophe S Productions, Inc. and Bill Moyers and Alfred Van der Marck Editions, Inc. for itself and the estate of Joseph Campbell. Used by permission of Doubleday, a division of Random House, Inc. **Chapter 2, p. 68**: from *The Kumulipo*. Martha Warren Beckwith, editor and translator. Copyright 1951, University of Chicago Press. Used with permission. **Chapter 3, p. 117**: *Shankara's Crest-Jewel of Discrimination*. New York: Signet, 1970, pp. 102–103. Copyright © 1970 Vedanta Society of Southern California. Used with permission. **Chapter 4, p. 176**: Excerpt from Matsuo Basho, *The Narrow Road to the Deep North and Other Travel Sketches*, translated with an introduction by Nobuyuki Yuasa. Copyright © Nobuyuki Yuasa, 1966. (Hammondsworth: Penguin, 1974), pp. 131–133. **Chapter 5, p. 201**: Copyright © Satish Kumar. Used with permission. **Chapter 6, p. 250**: The Zhuangzi (Chuang Tzu). *Chuang Tzu: Basic Writings*. Tr. Burton Watson. Copyright © 1964 Columbia University Press. Reprinted with permission from the publisher. **Chapter 7, p. 276**: Provided courtesy of www.sapphyr.net. **Chapter 8, p. 327**: From Jewish Publication Society, 1917 edition. Translation copyright © Lawrence Nelson. Used with permission. **Chapter 9, p. 401**: From REVELATIONS OF DIVINE LOVE by Julian of Norwich, translated by Elizabeth Spearing, introduction and notes by A. C. Spearing (Penguin Classics, 1998). Translation copyright © Elizabeth Spearing, 1998. Introduction and Notes © A. C. Spearing, 1998. Used with permission. **Chapter 10, p. 466**: Written by Fazil Iskander, translation by E.J.W. Gibb. **Chapter 11, p. 501**: General prayers, Aid and Assistance, p. 18, © Bahá'í International Community. Reproduced with permission. **Chapter 12, p. 536**: Excerpt from Audrey Sutherland, *Paddling My Own Canoe*. Copyright © 1987 University of Hawaii Press. Used with permission.

Index

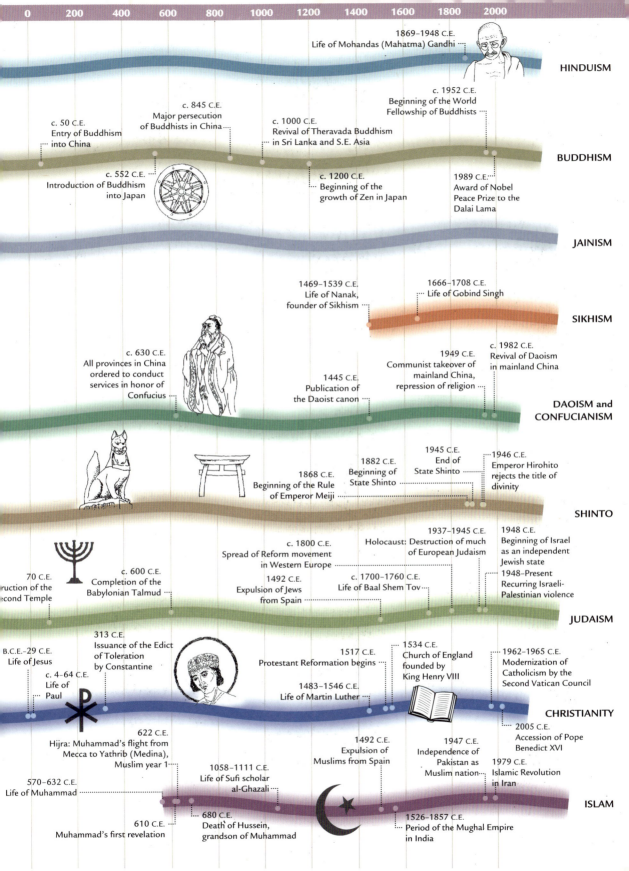

Timeline scale (C.E.): 0, 200, 400, 600, 800, 1000, 1200, 1400, 1600, 1800, 2000

HINDUISM

1869–1948 C.E.
Life of Mohandas (Mahatma) Gandhi

BUDDHISM

c. 50 C.E.
Entry of Buddhism into China

c. 845 C.E.
Major persecution of Buddhists in China

c. 1000 C.E.
Revival of Theravada Buddhism in Sri Lanka and S.E. Asia

c. 1952 C.E.
Beginning of the World Fellowship of Buddhists

c. 552 C.E.
Introduction of Buddhism into Japan

c. 1200 C.E.
Beginning of the growth of Zen in Japan

1989 C.E.
Award of Nobel Peace Prize to the Dalai Lama

JAINISM

SIKHISM

1469–1539 C.E.
Life of Nanak, founder of Sikhism

1666–1708 C.E.
Life of Gobind Singh

DAOISM and CONFUCIANISM

c. 630 C.E.
All provinces in China ordered to conduct services in honor of Confucius

1445 C.E.
Publication of the Daoist canon

1949 C.E.
Communist takeover of mainland China, repression of religion

c. 1982 C.E.
Revival of Daoism in mainland China

SHINTO

1868 C.E.
Beginning of the Rule of Emperor Meiji

1882 C.E.
Beginning of State Shinto

1945 C.E.
End of State Shinto

1946 C.E.
Emperor Hirohito rejects the title of divinity

JUDAISM

70 C.E.
Destruction of the Second Temple

c. 600 C.E.
Completion of the Babylonian Talmud

c. 1800 C.E.
Spread of Reform movement in Western Europe

1492 C.E.
Expulsion of Jews from Spain

c. 1700–1760 C.E.
Life of Baal Shem Tov

1937–1945 C.E.
Holocaust: Destruction of much of European Judaism

1948 C.E.
Beginning of Israel as an independent Jewish state

1948–Present
Recurring Israeli-Palestinian violence

CHRISTIANITY

B.C.E.–29 C.E.
Life of Jesus

c. 4–64 C.E.
Life of Paul

313 C.E.
Issuance of the Edict of Toleration by Constantine

1517 C.E.
Protestant Reformation begins

1483–1546 C.E.
Life of Martin Luther

1534 C.E.
Church of England founded by King Henry VIII

1962–1965 C.E.
Modernization of Catholicism by the Second Vatican Council

2005 C.E.
Accession of Pope Benedict XVI

ISLAM

570–632 C.E.
Life of Muhammad

610 C.E.
Muhammad's first revelation

622 C.E.
Hijra: Muhammad's flight from Mecca to Yathrib (Medina), Muslim year 1

680 C.E.
Death of Hussein, grandson of Muhammad

1058–1111 C.E.
Life of Sufi scholar al-Ghazali

1492 C.E.
Expulsion of Muslims from Spain

1526–1857 C.E.
Period of the Mughal Empire in India

1947 C.E.
Independence of Pakistan as Muslim nation

1979 C.E.
Islamic Revolution in Iran

TURN KNOWLEDGE INTO MEANING AND UNDERSTANDING

Experiencing the World's Religions, 6th edition, immerses students in the practices and beliefs of the world's major religions.

Michael Molloy's vivid narrative, coupled with integrated primary sources and digital assessment in **CONNECT** Religion, helps students understand the origins of the world's religions and explore their common themes.

In turn, students will begin to think critically about religion as a framework for interpreting how the world's major religious traditions shape individuals and whole cultures.

The results are greater engagement and greater course success.

The 6th edition program ultimately helps students turn knowledge into meaning and understanding, while developing skills that will benefit them beyond this course, into their chosen careers.

www.mcgrawhillconnect.com

The **McGraw·Hill** Companies

Mc Graw Hill

Connect
Learn
Succeed™